A HISTORY OF THE
WEIMAR REPUBLIC

VOLUME II

From the Locarno Conference to
Hitler's Seizure of Power

originally published by Harvard University Press

A HISTORY OF THE
WEIMAR REPUBLIC

By

Erich Eyck

Translated by

Harlan P. Hanson and Robert G. L. Waite

ATHENEUM

New York

1970

Published by Atheneum
Reprinted by arrangement with Harvard University Press
Copyright © 1963 by the President and Fellows of Harvard College
All rights reserved
Library of Congress catalog card number 62-17219
Manufactured in the United States of America by
The Murray Printing Company,
Forge Village, Massachusetts
Published in Canada by McClelland and Stewart Ltd.
First Atheneum Edition

TRANSLATORS' FOREWORD

In this second volume of his *History of the Weimar Republic,*
Erich Eyck shows his remarkable ability to describe with judicious
balance a period of history which saw the destruction of so much
that he valued. The book also sets the capstone to the author's distinguished career as a historian, a career which began only in his
sixtieth year when, having been driven from his homeland by the
Nazis, he published his biography of Gladstone (Zurich, 1938).
Important volumes on Bismarck (Zurich, 1941–1944), and his study
of William II and the Empire (Zurich, 1948), soon followed. He
then turned his attention back to English history and published his
study of the Pitts and the Foxes (Zurich, 1948). The concluding
volume of his history of Weimar, first published in Zurich in 1956,
marks the completion of Dr. Eyck's long ambition to record Germany's political development from the birth of Bismarck in 1815,
through the Wilhelminian Empire, to the end of the Republic in
1933.

Dr. Eyck's lifelong interest in the classics and in history was first
awakened in a Berlin Gymnasium. He took degrees in law and
history at the universities of Freiburg and Berlin, practiced law and
journalism, and served both as a leader of the Democratic Party and
as a member of the City Council of Berlin. Thus in each stage of his
professional career he joined contemplation with action, reflection
with involvement. This striking combination is clearly reflected in
the style of the book, alternating as it does between the passions of a
man intimately involved and the reflective calm of a detached
observer. And throughout one feels both the roll of classical cadence
and the bite of bitter wit.

In translating this second volume, we have continued our efforts
to carry over into English the style which is such a distinctive and
compelling feature of the original. We have sometimes altered the
structure of a sentence, expanded a phrase slightly, or broken a
paragraph. The reader may be assured, however, that we have
constantly sought to convey both the flavor and the fact of Dr. Eyck's
words and to record what he actually said. All translations, except
for specific quotations that originally appeared in English sources,
are our own.

In preparing this text we remain greatly indebted to John F.
Naylor, who edited the endnotes and supplied the necessary biblio-

graphic data, referring wherever possible to American and British editions of the German books cited by Dr. Eyck. We wish to thank the President and Trustees of Williams College for their generous assistance in the preparation of the manuscripts. We are also glad to have this opportunity to acknowledge the wise and painstaking help we received from Mrs. Anna Leonard and Professor Kurt P. Tauber, among many others. Dr. Eyck kindly read our manuscript, making many useful suggestions. While fully accepting responsibility for the shortcomings of our translation, we wish especially to thank Margaretta Fulton of the Harvard University Press, that gentle but firm critic who brought to our work something of the usefulness and grace that Horace requires of art.

H. P. H.
R. G. L. W.

Williamstown, Massachusetts
February 18, 1963

AUTHOR'S PREFACE

It is with gratitude to fate that I have concluded the final chapter of this book. The task has taken longer than I had hoped; but as one approaches eighty one can unfortunately not work as fast nor as steadily as in one's younger years. Yet any man who, at such advanced age, is given an opportunity for scholarly work has good reason to be grateful.

In all likelihood these will be my last published words as a German historian. Perhaps, therefore, I may allow myself to address a word or two to my German readers. For in this book many of them will find arguments to which they will wish to object. I should like only to beg such readers not to avoid a careful consideration of my interpretations by dismissing them lightly with the easy epithet, "expatriate's resentments." In no way do I desire to give the impression that I have forgotten the injustice done to me and to others like me in the name of "the German *Volk*." But I am much too conscious of my debt to German education and, in broader terms, to German intellectual life, and I have too many fine German friends who are inspired by a true appreciation of humanity, to let myself be dominated by sentiments conjured up by the term "expatriate." Nor would I, especially in a scholarly work like this, permit such sentiments to warp my historical judgment. If I have expressed my criticism rather sharply at times, I have done so for a quite different set of reasons: The peaceful reconstruction and survival of Western civilization is impossible without the wholehearted collaboration of the German people. But this collaboration will yield full value only if in addition to their many, marked talents — which the whole world recognizes — the Germans develop further the arts of self-knowledge and self-criticism, and if greater numbers of them lose the habit of blaming someone else for every misfortune while only pitying themselves. It is for this reason, indeed, that a historian sins against the future if he obscures the errors of the past in ambiguities.

"Drawing implies leaving out" (*Zeichnen heisst Weglassen!*) were the words of the great painter Max Liebermann. These words are also true for the work of any historian who, not content with merely pasting a chronicle together, wishes rather to compose a readable, organized account. To be sure, the determination of what is to be omitted remains subjective. But it seems to me that one has to be prepared to grant the author this degree of freedom so long as the details he does report comprise a whole.

AUTHOR'S PREFACE

In writing Chapters I through VII, I was able to make use of Gustav Stresemann's papers, photographic copies of which were made available to me at the Public Record Office here in London. My dear friend the former state secretary Hans Schäffer placed a voluminous and valuable store of notes and reports at my disposal; I learned much from these, even though I could not always share their point of view. Otto Gessler, whom I was still able to thank in the preface to my first volume, has since died — before I could profit from the thorough discussion we had planned of this second volume. I consider myself, however, obligated to record here Gessler's objection to my interpretation of Seeckt's reply to Ebert as reported by Rabenau and quoted by me on page 240 of the first volume: "The Reichswehr stands behind me." Gessler wrote to me, "Seeckt did not talk that way." I am indebted, further, to conversations with my old friends, the former Reichstag delegates August Weber and Oskar Meyer, and with such other gentlemen as the former minister Hans von Raumer and the former consul Henry Bernhard. To all who helped me, one way or another, I wish to express my sincere thanks.

ERICH EYCK

London
July 1956

CONTENTS

I

LOCARNO

Oɴ May 12, 1925, in a strikingly perfunctory ceremony which lasted barely fifteen minutes, Field Marshal Paul von Hindenburg was inaugurated President of the German Republic. A few days later Foreign Minister Gustav Stresemann presented himself to report his plans for conducting foreign policy, plans which must have astonished and alarmed the old gentleman. For what Stresemann proposed — and, indeed, had already undertaken — was nothing less than a German campaign for international agreements which might give France her sorely needed sense of security against German attack.

This policy had been set in Friedrich Ebert's time: on February 9, 1925, after the formation of Luther's cabinet, Stresemann had sent the French government a memorandum proposing discussion of a pact that would guarantee the status quo along the Rhine with respect to both French and German interests. The earlier history of this memorandum can be traced to two sources. One, to which the note explicitly referred, was the abortive attempt by Cuno in December 1922. The other was the Geneva Protocol concerning the peaceful settlement of international disputes, which had been adopted in October 1924 by the fifth session of the League of Nations. The Geneva Protocol contained a grandly conceived attempt to amend the League's Covenant so that all nations might enjoy complete security against unjustified military attack. To this end it not only proposed a broad extension of courts of arbitration, but also sought to establish the principle that "the signatory States assume the obligation, individually and collectively, of coming to the assistance of the attacked or threatened State" (Article XI, Paragraph 3).

The prospects of the Protocol depended on the favor of the great powers. France immediately agreed, and Briand, her representative at the League's fifth session, eulogized the Protocol in an impassioned speech as a benefit to all mankind.[1] Poland and Czechoslovakia, allies of France, followed her example without hesitation. This was not surprising, for all three lived in fear of future German invasion and wished for nothing more than an international guarantee of security on this score.

The attitude of Great Britain was of crucial importance, for, though this power would probably not be the object of aggression, her help in launching a counterattack against an aggressor would be indispensable. Now the Labour government of that time contained men who supported the Protocol enthusiastically, as did their representatives in Geneva, Arthur Henderson and Lord Parmoor. But we shall never know what the cabinet's decision would finally have been, for that same October of 1924 saw the Labour government's defeat in an election which it had unwisely called. It was clear from the beginning, however, that the overseas dominions, to which every English government had to pay careful attention, had not the slightest desire to guarantee European boundaries, which lay completely outside their range of interest. Canada's representative at the League pointed out a critical facet of the problem involved when he argued that in the case of this sort of mutual fire insurance the risks are not equitably apportioned among the individual states. Canadians, he said, live in a fireproof house widely separated from any incendiary material. However magnanimous and moving the concept of collective security might be, even it must be reconciled with the fact that nations, like men, are prepared to make sacrifices only when their vital interests are clearly at stake.

After the elections of October 1924 Baldwin formed a Conservative cabinet, entrusting the Foreign Office to Austen Chamberlain. This eldest son of the controversial Joseph Chamberlain had already headed several ministries in his more than thirty years of public life; but not till now had he been foreign secretary. He had, of course, concerned himself continually with matters of foreign policy, regarding Lord Curzon's way of doing things with a jaundiced eye. "Curzon," he once observed, "is convinced that all is well if he delivers an oration or pens a 'superior' dispatch." [2] Baldwin had had enough of Curzon, too, and preferred to seize this chance to effect reconciliation with Chamberlain, who had been one of Lloyd George's most loyal supporters, rather than to satisfy Curzon, who wanted very much to return to his former post.

The basis of all Chamberlain's thoughts on foreign affairs was the maintenance of the grand alliance with France, a nation toward which he had felt a special sympathy and concern ever since his youth. But this affection did not make him feel inclined to sign the Geneva Protocol. For to do so would have pledged England to the defense not only of France, but of Poland as well, against German attack; and the English public had no taste for that. Poland, after all, lay well outside the ordinary Englishman's field of vision, and whenever he did think of that creature of the Versailles treaty, he recalled its borders — especially those of the Polish Corridor — with something less than ecstasy.[3] Chamberlain expressed this point of view in a letter to the British ambassador in Paris. Paraphrasing Bismarck, he concluded that "no British government ever will or ever can risk the bones of one British grenadier [in defense of the Polish Corridor]."[4] These words sound rather strange if one thinks of the events of 1939 and the policies of Austen's half brother, Neville. But the statement undoubtedly reflected general British opinion at the time.

Final rites for the Geneva Protocol were not held until March 12, 1925, when Chamberlain explained to the League Council that his government found the Protocol unacceptable. By then, of course, the decision of the British cabinet had long been known in European capitals. In particular, it was no secret to the British ambassador in Berlin, who had gone to London in late November 1924 for detailed conferences with his superior.[5] At that time Lord d'Abernon had successfully advocated the conclusion of a commercial treaty between Great Britain and Germany — a treaty which he regarded as a step toward his principal goal: the political reconciliation of the two nations. He was delighted to find Chamberlain so sympathetic with his hopes. He realized, however, that his francophilic superior would not rest content with a simple rejection of the Geneva Protocol but would instead seek some other means to satisfy France's need for security. Now it seemed reasonable to assume that an Anglo-French treaty of alliance would strike Chamberlain as the most appropriate instrument for the purpose. But d'Abernon was certain that such a treaty would, in the nature of things, be directed against Germany and thus would represent a fundamental threat to the goal he had set himself upon going to Berlin. Concerning the necessity of meeting France's need for security, he was in complete agreement with Chamberlain and such other English experts on foreign affairs as, for example, Lord Grey. But he wondered if there were no other way, one which might also lead to a Franco-German rapprochement.

In Stresemann's posthumous papers there is a report — apparently written by State Secretary von Schubert — dated February 28, 1925, and describing the background of the German memorandum of February 9, 1925, which formed the basis of the entire Locarno policy.[6] The report begins with a note on a conversation Schubert held with d'Abernon on December 29, 1924: the English ambassador had "quite casually" touched upon the question of French security, expressing warm approval of the proposal Chancellor Cuno had made on December 9, 1922. D'Abernon had then proceeded, logically enough, to the thought of a mutual nonaggression pact among powers with interests on the Rhine. Schubert, according to his note, did not make any "significant" response to the ambassador's allusions, but he doubtlessly made prompt report of them to his superior.

Now at that time Stresemann was in difficult straits, for Marx's cabinet had just resigned. Furthermore, German public opinion had just been stirred up against the West by the Entente's declaration that, because of German failures to fulfill the provisions of disarmament, occupation forces would not be removed from the Cologne Zone on January 10, 1925, after all. Nevertheless Stresemann immediately recognized the scope and real nature of the problem. He realized that the question of French security would have to be settled sooner or later; indeed, he believed that the Allied refusal to evacuate the Cologne Zone was a symptom of these Gallic fears.

Stresemann gave detailed expression to this belief in a message he had his ambassador, Count Brockdorff-Rantzau, deliver to the Russian Commissar Litvinov on April 7, 1925:

From the start the German government has presumed that the French government will not be persuaded to withdraw its forces unless France's so-called need for security is satisfied in some manner. The approach of the deadline of January 10 has confronted France with the problem of deciding whether to accommodate itself to the Allied Rhineland policy enunciated by the British and Americans at Versailles over the opposition of French military interests, or to preserve the possibility of pursuing further, even if unilaterally, the plans of that military group. The present government of France [Herriot's] seems rather inclined toward the first alternative. It is, however, unwilling — or, at any rate, unable — to make and execute this decision without first assuring France some substitute for the formal Anglo-American guarantees which had been planned at Versailles in 1919 but which had subsequently failed to materialize; for these guarantees had been promised by Wilson and Lloyd George as a logical complement to the Rhineland provisions of the Treaty of Versailles. France, of course, would be happiest if . . . a Franco-Anglo-Belgian treaty could be concluded, strengthened by explicit military obligations on England's part . . . Entirely apart from the fact that such a pact between the three Allies would have been directed at Germany, thus perpetuating the Entente, the possibility of such a move cannot be considered real because England is categorically opposed to such a three-party alliance.[7]

We now know that the final clause in this memorandum was not quite accurate. But whatever may have been Stresemann's shortcomings as a prophet, he was on firm ground when he argued that active German participation in the solution of France's problem was of utmost necessity at the time because the liberation of the Rhineland depended upon it. If no solution were found, France would see to it that her disarmament demands on Germany were "increased and intensified to the point that in the foreseeable future . . . there would be neither an abolition of the Inter-Allied Control Commission nor an evacuation of the Cologne Zone." The extensive efforts which Stresemann made to solve the problem of France's security show how dedicated he was to the task of freeing Germany from the Allies' military control.

It is clear from the evidence that Stresemann realized how important it would be for his international political relations if Germany were to seize the initiative in this matter of French security. But he could not fail to observe that German public opinion was not yet ripe for such a step and that his truly dangerous opposition would come from the Right. This was one of the reasons he had wanted Rightists to participate in the new government. For he was confident of his ability to win the German Nationalist ministers over to his plans once they had joined the cabinet — particularly if their admission were conditional upon their pledge to support and continue its former foreign policies.[8] Indeed he had good reason to have faith in his ascendancy over these gentlemen. But he thought that, having won the party's leaders, he would win the party too. And this was the point at which he erred. For he overestimated the German Nationalists' sense of political responsibility and underestimated the power of their cant. Thus he tried to follow two lines of policy at the same time, lines which, as this book will show, did not intersect but rather diverged ever further.

And so it was that as early as January 20, 1925, Lord d'Abernon was able to send Chamberlain a short but extraordinarily pregnant memorandum from Stresemann expressing Germany's desire for an amicable reconciliation with France and recognizing the legitimacy of French desires for assured security. The memorandum went on to suggest, as one of the ways to meet this demand, the discussion of a treaty among powers with interests on the Rhine — a treaty which would guarantee not only present boundaries but also the continued demilitarization of the Rhineland.

Austen Chamberlain did not receive this proposal in the manner which Stresemann and d'Abernon had expected. He had been asked to maintain the strictest secrecy. This request had aroused in him, quite mistakenly, the suspicion that he was being asked to negotiate with Germany behind the backs of his allies. Being a candid and honest man, he felt especially repelled by the imputation. As a matter of fact this thought had not entered Stresemann's mind at all; he was only following the British ambassador's advice. What Stresemann feared — and with good reason — was that a premature statement of his proposal would leak into the public press. For if this were to happen, there was every reason to fear that, not only in Germany, but in France as well, the nationalists would raise cries so vehement as to blow out the "Baby's" — as d'Abernon and Schubert called their plan — candle of life. In England, on the other hand, they feared opposition from those circles which supported a general assurance of peace, as outlined in the Geneva Protocol, and which therefore rejected bilateral agreements between individual governments.[9]

On the ninth of February a second ill-considered step was taken: the transmission of a similar memorandum to the French Premier. Herriot contented himself with the simple reply that he would have to discuss the proposal first with his allies. He closed with the promise to keep the memorandum secret. And he succeeded; indiscreet uses of the Parisian press, otherwise so frequent, were carefully avoided.*

The practical difficulties which the French Premier had to face were closely related to those which had ruined the Geneva Protocol. The guarantee treaty which Germany was prepared to sign dealt with Germany's western boundary. But what about the East? Herriot knew very well that in Germany people not only regarded their new eastern border as an insult and a grave injustice, but also regarded the Poles with almost universal disdain. Was there not good reason to fear the outbreak of hostilities there, in the East, especially if Germany felt protected from another war on two fronts by a treaty guaranteeing the status quo along the Rhine? What sort

---

* Herriot's discretion also had its amusing side, as is shown by a conversation Stresemann had with the French ambassador, de Margerie, in June 1926, in which de Margerie complained that Stresemann's memorandum had caused him, de Margerie, severe embarrassment. For Herriot had kept it secret even from him, while rumors concerning its transmission ran rampant in Berlin. The French ambassador investigated the matter for his superior and, on the strength of what information he could gather, had reported to Paris that the rumors must be false, that Germany could not possibly have sent such a memorandum. To this Herriot had replied with thanks for his attentiveness and best wishes for his sources — and with word that the memorandum was already in his hands. (Stresemann Papers, 7328H.)

of security was Germany prepared to offer against this danger? Was one not obliged to demand of the Germans the same guarantees in the East as in the West? Yet under no circumstances would Stresemann deliver these. They lay beyond his power; for German public opinion would have rejected such an Eastern guarantee almost unanimously. Stresemann offered instead to sign treaties of arbitration with all interested governments. The eastern border was not explicitly mentioned in this offer, but one had every reason to conclude from it that Germany would seek changes in her eastern border in peaceful ways alone, not with the sword.

It was in this sense that the English foreign secretary understood the proposal. On March 24, 1925, in the House of Commons, Chamberlain discussed the German memorandum in considerable detail, thus giving the European public its first reasonably clear notion of the negotiations being held behind their governments' closed doors.[10] He helped create a favorable atmosphere for these negotiations by expressing his conviction that the German government was making an "honest and honorable" effort to improve the international situation and by saying that the English government was seriously investigating the German proposal in the hope of helping it yield fruitful results. Concerning the contents of the German note he spoke as follows: On her western border Germany wishes to guarantee voluntarily and for the future what she formerly had merely accepted under the compulsion of the peace treaty. And even along her eastern borders Germany wishes to forswear war as an instrument of policy. "Thus not only in the West but in the East she is prepared absolutely to abandon any idea of recourse to war for the purposes of changing the treaty boundaries of Europe." To be sure, Germany did reserve the hope of altering her eastern border some day "by friendly negotiation, by diplomatic procedure or . . . by recourse to the good offices of the League of Nations." And Chamberlain expressed the hope that the very fact that peace had been assured in the West would serve as an additional guarantee in the East.

This optimistic interpretation of the German proposal was clearly directed principally at French ears. The French government and Frenchmen in general were thus to be assured that Poland was not being abandoned, even though England declined to guarantee its boundaries. But Chamberlain was to learn quite quickly that whatever was meant to relieve French suspicions brought with it the danger of stirring up German distrust. The German ambassador to St. James, Dr. Stahmer, having listened to Chamberlain from the gallery of the House, asked him immediately for an appointment.

Stahmer protested that the English foreign secretary had gone too far in what he said about the East. To this Chamberlain reacted immediately and with great sharpness: "Do you mean you reserve the right to wage war in Eastern Europe in furtherance of your political aims? If so I will go back into the House and revoke what I have said about going through with the German proposals." [11] At this Stahmer understandably retreated, and Chamberlain's interpretation remained undisputed by the Germans. He later said that he would have immediately resigned if obliged to retract his declaration. In these difficult negotiations he said that he was playing the role of "honest broker" between France and Germany. "Perhaps," as he put it in a letter to Lord Crewe,[12] the British ambassador in Paris, "even a little more honestly than the author of that well-known phrase!" *

And in fact it proved quite difficult to phrase the Allies' reply to the German government in a way as acceptable in Paris as in London. Negotiations on this point lasted into June. Hindenburg's election as President of the German Republic hardly simplified the talks, and before they were completed there had been a change of government in France. Herriot's fall, on April 10, 1925, was occasioned by the ever worsening French finances. His place was taken by Painlevé, the Radical President of the Chamber of Deputies, who entrusted the foreign portfolio to Aristide Briand, the man whom Poincaré had felled in January 1922 during the conference at Cannes.

And so onto the stage of international affairs strode once more the man who, for the rest of Stresemann's life, was to play his opposite in France and finally to become his friend. Like his predecessor, Briand was naturally intent upon maintaining for France the advantages which victory had brought and, thus, upon defending the inviolable integrity of the Treaty of Versailles. No French statesman dared speak or even think otherwise. Now it is certainly simpler for the victor than for the vanquished to be content with peace. But one would misconstrue Briand's entire being if one were to explain in this way alone his earnest efforts to establish a reign of peace on earth and to ensure its permanence through international organization. However clever and at times cunning a practical politician he may have been, he was at the same time an idealist who hated war from the depths of his soul and who sought to bring the blessings of peace and of good will among men not just to his fatherland but to the entire world. In one of his grand

* Bismarck used the term on February 19, 1878. In accepting the chairmanship of the Congress of Berlin after the Russo-Turkish War of 1877, he promised that he would serve all the nations "as an honest broker looking out for the interests of all my clients." TRANSLATORS.

addresses to the French Chamber he told how, in the days of the fighting at Verdun, when he had borne the heavy responsibilities of French Premier, he had promised himself in the face of that frightful human slaughter that, should victory finally be won, "he would dedicate his whole heart, his whole mind, his whole being to the cause of peace in order to help prevent a recurrence of such horror." [13]

This alone was enough to make him sympathetic to a proposal which was designed to satisfy France's need for security — which Briand naturally affirmed — through peaceful reconciliation with a neighbor who for centuries had been a foe. As a practical politician, however, he knew very well how carefully a statesman seeking such goals must treat national sensitivities, which so easily can bring public opinion into confusion; and he knew equally well that the facts of political life were not otherwise across the Rhine. In a Reichstag speech of May 18, 1925, for instance, Stresemann had complained that the Allied governments had not yet explained in detail just which violations of the disarmament regulations they were holding against Germany and he went on to accuse them of violating their own treaty by failing to evacuate Cologne. Briand was well aware that the detailed note concerning violations of the disarmament requirements was being withheld in hopes of avoiding further popular agitation in Germany during the negotiations for a mutual security treaty, and he suspected the German foreign minister knew it, too. Consequently, Briand used the following words when addressing the French Senate a few days later: "M. Stresemann had to direct his speech not only to the delegates whom he was addressing, but also to the broader German public, without whose consent no government can act. One should therefore seek the reality of fact behind his words. One must ignore those elements of his speech which betray the character of popular polemics and seek in the words of a statesman only those thoughts which point toward his real goal." [14] Alluding to Hindenburg's election he went on to say: "I have not found, in Stresemann's words, that brutal *non possumus* which, after certain elections, one might have expected to meet." This was spoken like a statesman and, at the same time, with the skill of an experienced tactician who knows how to take the wind out of his own critics' sails.

It was June 16, 1925, before the French government was able to transmit to the Germans its reply to Stresemann's memorandum of February 9. The reply contained the express statement that France's allies — which naturally meant England — were in full accord. Briand had, of course, been able to purchase this British agreement only at the price of accepting the British basic point of view. The note therefore contained no hint of an English guarantee of Germany's eastern border. Briand had had to be satisfied with a demand for treaties of arbitration between Germany and her neighbors to the east. Now the German February memorandum had already expressed a basic willingness to conclude such treaties, but fears began to be voiced in Germany that the treaties of arbitration which Briand had in mind were considerably broader in scope than those to which Stresemann had alluded.[15] Even more important, Briand emphasized that the conclusion of a mutual security treaty in the West would be possible only if Germany were to join the League of Nations — and under the conditions which the Council of the League had already set.[16]

There was clearly much to be discussed between Germany and the Allies before the security pact could be signed. But these foreign problems were as nothing compared with the domestic difficulties with which Stresemann found himself surrounded. For now the German memorandum and the French reply had to be published simultaneously. Their publication gave the signal for lively discussions in the newspapers — and the comments were anything but congratulatory. On June 26 Stresemann himself noted in his diary: "We had a perfectly miserable press." It immediately became apparent what troubles he had made for himself by taking the German Nationalists into the government. To be sure, upon entering the cabinet they had declared their willingness to see Stresemann's foreign policy continued. But now they were "crouched on the running board, ready to jump off at any time."[17]

Even the first statements in the cabinet meeting made it painfully clear to Stresemann that he was not among friends. Only one colleague stood firmly by his side, and that was Rudolf Krohne, minister of transport, the only other representative of the People's Party in the cabinet. On the other hand the whole concept of reconciliation was emphatically opposed by Joseph Frenken, minister of justice, who was considered influential in the Catholic Center. Stresemann wrote: "He regarded the entire affair from the standpoint of a father who cannot get over the loss of his sons in the war and who thinks therefore only of revenge."[18] Frenken, however, was only a former chief justice of a provincial supreme court who had never played a significant political role. But General von Seeckt took the floor after him and, with brutal candor, expressed "the thought that we must acquire power, and that *as soon as we have power, we will naturally retake all that we have lost*."[19]

Here was a bald expression of the demand for a war of revenge and, with it, the exact opposite of the standpoint represented by the German government and its proposal for a security treaty. While this government was trying to convince the world that Germany was considering no further call to arms but hoped to join, as a "believing" fellow member, the world organization designed to preserve the peace, that Germany would seek improvements in her lot and in her boundaries only through peaceful means, Seeckt was proclaiming the unaltered power policy of the Prussian militarists, who saw in defeat only an invitation to rearm for new campaigns and who never doubted for one moment that in the final battle the preponderant power, and thus victory, would be theirs.

One must admit that the feelings which Seeckt expressed with the apodictic certainty of a general were shared by many, many Germans. What was it that the German Nationalists held against Stresemann's proposal and that Nationalist newspapers drummed into their readers' brains with indignation and pathos? Germany prepared to renounce Alsace-Lorraine! That is a national disgrace! Now in any real sense this so-called renunciation was merely a repetition of what Germany had already formally acknowledged in signing the Treaty of Versailles. For there, in the fifth section of the third part, stood the clear and unmistakable words:

ALSACE-LORRAINE

The High Contracting Parties, recognizing the moral obligation to redress the wrong done by Germany in 1871 both to the rights of France and to the wishes of the population of Alsace and Lorraine . . .

Agree upon the following Articles:

Article 51.

The territories which were ceded to Germany in accordance with . . . the Treaty of Frankfort of May 10, 1871, are restored to French sovereignty as from the date of the Armistice of November 11, 1918.

Was that not as solemn a renunciation as anyone can make? When in all history had the victors in a great war regarded the voluntary repetition of such a renunciation as a favor on the part of the vanquished which had to be purchased with counterfavors? Naturally, victorious France would always be afraid lest a restrengthened Germany begin a new war to wrest the disputed provinces away. And, indeed, this fear never ceased to disturb the French. But was not such a war exactly what the whole world — Germany excepted — was determined to prevent? And was not Germany at that time completely unable to reach for the sword? Could any German Nationalist or Racist doubt these facts? Indeed, could he believe that the population of Alsace-Lorraine harbored the slightest wish to be rejoined to the Reich? The position of the German Nationalist press amounted to this: Germany reserved the right to start a new war of conquest — at whatever time seemed favorable — seeking the annexation of a reluctant population and thus blatantly denying that right of self-determination which Germany had otherwise been constantly citing in her own behalf. Thus the German Nationalists announced to all nations that they would have to cope with a German war of revenge once the Rightists came to power. The single logical conclusion which the former victors could draw from all this was that it would be necessary to enforce to the letter all the provisions of the Versailles treaty which might prevent Germany from becoming powerful again.

The effectiveness of this Rightist agitation can be judged not only from the fact that the German Nationalist ministers stepped, as Stresemann put it, "out on the running board," but also from the Chancellor's new uncertainties. To be sure, Chancellor Luther supported his foreign minister in the cabinet meeting — after a fashion — by objecting that the policy proposed by the Nationalists amounted simply to waiting for the day when Germany would again have a big army while, in the meantime, folding their hands in their laps and hoping that the Lord would send Germany some miracle weapon with which to fend off her foes. But he went on to try to slough off all responsibility for foreign policy, heaping it on Stresemann alone.

The main question involved here is the time at which Luther first learned about the German memorandum (of February 9, 1925) to the French. Stresemann's published papers are full of references — many of them quite pointed — to this question. The issue was really rather unimportant, for as early as January 30, in an extensive speech to the press, Luther had spoken in favor of a mutual security pact. Moreover, he would have been an odd chancellor if he had learned only in June of the foreign policy his government had been pursuing since January. But at the moment the differences between the two men seemed so great that, in a private conversation on July 1, Stresemann asked him point blank, "whether Luther wished to resolve the crisis for himself and the German Nationalists by having me leave the cabinet." That was not at all what Luther wanted — if only because such a step would have severely endangered his government. But from the tenor of the conversation Stresemann gathered the distinct impression that the Chancellor would have been happiest to send Stresemann off to London as ambassador.

But here Luther had misjudged his man. Stresemann made it perfectly clear to his Chancellor that he had no intention of leaving political life in such a way. If he were to resign as minister, "he would naturally return to political activity as leader of his party." [20] This was obviously the only position Stresemann could take that did justice both to his personal dignity and the spirit of parliamentary government. But it was equally evident that such a step would not help Luther one whit. As a political opponent Stresemann would have been extremely formidable — especially to a man as unsure of his parliamentary footing as was Luther. Moreover, the Chancellor could foresee that Stresemann would eventually gather the entire Left including the Social Democrats about himself, leaving Luther only German Nationalists — strengthened perhaps by Communists and Racists — for support.

The Communists had their own peculiar reason for opposing the security pact: they fought it in the interests of Russia. For in such an agreement with England and France they saw Germany inclining to the West at the cost of the East. And they regarded the projected admission of Germany to the League of Nations in the same light. This attitude became apparent even before the publication, in June, of the German memorandum and the French reply. On May 18, in the Reichstag debate on the Foreign Office budget, Stresemann made the statements quoted above. The speaker for the Communists, Mrs. Golke (Ruth Fischer), answered him with furious words: "Herr Stresemann, you are not deceiving anyone. Everybody knows that you have offered German soil and German workers for a future war against Russia as the price of reconciliation with England and France. Your foreign policy is attempting to turn Germany into a village of timorous vassals who seek union with the great British robber baron in order to share in further spoils." She called Stresemann a "betrayed betrayer" and the League of Nations a "consortium of bandits for the purpose of sugar-coating war with idealism." [21]

Whether she really believed all this nonsense is beside the point. What is important is that her words strictly adhered to the line dictated from Moscow. For in the light of Article 16 of the Covenant of the League,* the Soviets feared that if Germany were admitted to

---

* Article 16 of the Covenant stipulated that if any member of the League should resort to war, all other members would immediately prevent "all financial, commercial, or personal intercourse between the nationals of the covenant-breaking State and the nationals of any other State, whether a Member of the League or not." It further stated that all members would mutually support one another against a covenant-breaker and that "they will take the necessary steps to afford passage through their territory to the forces of any of the Members of the League which are co-operating to protect the covenants of the League." The Soviet Union was disturbed by the prospects of two eventualities which might occur if Germany became a member of the League: First, if Germany started a war against France, all other members of the

the League Russia might lose the single contact which, since the Treaty of Rapallo, it had enjoyed with the capitalistic world. Grigorii Chicherin, the Soviet foreign commissar and the victor at Rapallo, was particularly eloquent on this point.[22] And he won over a quite non-Communist German to his side: Count Ulrich Brockdorff-Rantzau, the German ambassador to Moscow.

One would probably be doing Brockdorff-Rantzau an injustice if one were to attribute his attitude to personal motivation alone. But it played a strong role. For he could never forget the personal defeat he had suffered at Versailles and yearned with all his heart for an opportunity to strike back.[23] His biographer tells us that Brockdorff was basically in favor of Germany's joining the League, but that he did not believe the proper time had come.[24] Now this qualification was certainly a very narrow and precarious foundation upon which to base his strident opposition to Stresemann's policy — an opposition which even led Brockdorff to tender his resignation.[25] Brockdorff returned to Berlin in mid-April 1925 and stayed there through June. Stresemann can hardly have enjoyed this visit, but he clearly did not consider himself strong enough politically to send his ambassador back to Moscow to represent the German government there.

Stresemann was having troubles enough calming down the Russian ambassador, Nicolai Krestinski. He tried to explain that neither the projected security pact nor Germany's entry into the League implied any threat to Russo-German relations and that under no circumstances would Germany let herself be made an ally of Poland. He went on to say that in the West Germany was trying to assure peace where she felt threatened, "while in the East Germany planned to watch developments, defend her interests, and maintain freedom of action." As for Article 16 of the Covenant, for which the Russians had such fears, the German government intended to strip it of all dangerous implications.[26]

In the Reichstag, too, there were strong forces in favor of sticking to the course which had been set at Rapallo. As early as January 1925, Ernst Scholz, the leader of the People's Party delegation, had declared that the situation in the East should make the German government extremely cautious with respect to the League of Nations. And in May Count Bernstorff, a Democrat, had stated that his party still stood on the platform of Rapallo. Stresemann made

---

League might completely boycott Russia, even though she were not a member of the League of Nations. Second, if a new Russo-Polish War were to break out, Germany might be obligated "to afford passage" to French troops coming to the aid of France's Polish ally. TRANSLATORS.

good use of this argument, especially in conversations with Lord d'Abernon, in his attempts to win compromises from the Allies.[27]

On one important point Stresemann differed sharply from Brockdorff-Rantzau: he did not ignore the fact that the Russian regime was not just one more government but rather was the headquarters of the Comintern, which was still plotting world revolution and the destruction of the German state. He had learned this all too well as Chancellor, and even now disturbing incidents ensued that he did not forget. He treated this matter in his diary on the occasion of a talk by a People's Party Reichstag delegate, Siegfried von Kardorff, on Bismarck's Reinsurance Treaty. Kardorff had praised the treaty in the then customary manner as a masterstroke on Bismarck's part, but Stresemann noted: "If the Russia of today were the Russia of the past, the problem would be simple. But to marry Communist Russia is to go to bed with the murderer of one's own people. In the long run the artificial distinction cannot be maintained between a Russian government friendly toward Germany and the Third International which seeks to undermine the German state." [28] Stresemann made it quite clear to Litvinov, who visited Berlin in June as deputy foreign minister of Russia, that the fiction was untenable.[29]

In addition to all these difficulties Stresemann had to contend with the President's attitude. And he discussed this problem, as he had all the others, candidly with d'Abernon. One could, of course, hardly expect the old field marshal to engage himself deeply in matters so foreign to his mind. On June 6, at a council of ministers chaired by Hindenburg to consider the demilitarization note from the Allies, Stresemann noted that the President "did not take part in the conversation," making only "a rather tired and tormented impression." [30] And yet German disarmament was certainly an issue that concerned the old general more intimately than did security treaties and the League of Nations. In an intimate conversation with the British ambassador, Stresemann could not suppress the complaint that he was having considerable difficulties with his President on the matter of Germany's joining the League. "Hindenburg," he said, "is not opposed to the League of Nations, but, like most military men, he is skeptical about the efficacy of any alternative to war. I do not meet with deliberate opposition from him, but he is unversed in political affairs." [31] What else could one expect of a man who really was still living in the days of William I? But of course the people who elected him had not worried about that.

When one considers all the obstacles that littered Stresemann's path one cannot help but be amazed at his continued progress toward his goals. His greatest danger remained, of course, the Nationalists. But these were tangled in their own snare. Had they responded to the French note of June 16 by leaving the cabinet, no one can tell what the consequences may have been. But they could not bring themselves to take that step. It is hard to leave a post of power which took years of difficult struggle to attain. Then too, the economic interests of agriculture were at stake. For, spurred by the German Nationalists, the government had proposed a supplemental revision to the tariff laws of 1902 which involved a considerable increase in duties on foodstuffs. Naturally this change was sharply opposed by the Social Democrats, who were by no means alone in this fight, and who were most likely to be heirs to the Nationalists should the latter leave the cabinet. The Nationalists preferred, of course, that Stresemann leave instead. Professor von Freytagh-Loringhoven, a German Nationalist member of the Reichstag, went so far as to demand Stresemann's resignation in the press. The leaders of his party were embarrassed by his act, but the sort of measures they were using became apparent to Stresemann from a party circular letter which a friend showed to him. Here the Nationalist leaders explained that they were staying in the cabinet solely in order to knock Stresemann's foreign policy "stone dead." [32]

Even worse were the intrigues into which the Nationalists sought to entice the Social Democrats. In mid-July, just before the Germans were to reply to Briand, Stresemann was paid a highly secret visit by Dr. Breitscheid, the chairman of the Social Democratic delegation in the Reichstag.[33] Breitscheid was politically opposed to Stresemann but well-disposed toward international conciliation and deeply revolted at the imputation of readiness to engage in foul play which the Nationalists had made to his delegation. Having first begged the minister never to mention him as his source, Breitscheid revealed that, through middlemen, the German Nationalists in the Reichstag had approached the Social Democrats with the question whether the latter were prepared to consult with the Nationalists in search of a successor to Stresemann who might be acceptable to both parties. The Social Democrats rejected the compromising imputation with the constitutionally correct observation that the choice of foreign minister was the responsibility of the governing coalition, and they added that, in foreign affairs, they were concerned with policies rather than with personalities. In other words, the Nationalist plotters had received a clear rebuff. Breitscheid went on to say that the German Nationalists hoped to block any prospective conference between Germany and the Allied Powers, and, if unsuccessful in this, to make certain at least that Stresemann would not be there.

They intended to use such a conference as a means to force him to resign and had sought the Social Democrats' aid for their plan. The Nationalists had no love for parliamentary government, denouncing it before the nation as un-German and harmful. But they were ruthlessly prepared to make every possible use of the system's back doors when it served their ends to do so.

The Nationalists were equally ruthless, moreover, in matters of patronage. Stresemann's papers include notes of a conversation in early August with Martin Schiele, the German Nationalist minister of interior, in which Schiele proposed a massive shuffle of personnel among the most important federal posts, the sole purpose of which seemed to be the awarding of a position as undersecretary in the Foreign Office to a German Nationalist Reichstag delegate. "The interesting thing . . . about this proposal," Stresemann observed, "is the unscrupulous and wholesale manner in which Schiele deals with matters of personnel. The Nationalists do not even object to this sort of democratic leveling so long as it helps their cause." [34]

Among the German Nationalists Alfred Hugenberg was particularly active in his opposition to Stresemann.[35] This is in no way astonishing. As early as 1923, when Stresemann became Chancellor, Hugenberg had warned Hugo Stinnes that Stresemann would turn out to be "the misfortune of the German middle class." Hugenberg reported this himself in an article of January 1926 in the *Lokalanzeiger*. Hugenberg, formerly the general manager of Krupp, had, like Stinnes, prospered during the inflation. But, unlike Stinnes, he had tended his fortune successfully through the days of deflation and stabilization. He had done so not out of any personal interest in wealth: he regarded his fortune simply as a powerful means to serve those ends to which he had dedicated his life. Even men who stood in sharp political opposition to Hugenberg testified that in his way he was a passionate patriot, always thinking of Germany's glory first — as he understood it.[36]

When Hugenberg decided to devote his large fortune to influencing popular opinion, his impact was by no means inconsiderable. He had already acquired the Berlin *Lokalanzeiger* and, with it, a channel to the middle and lower-middle classes. Through the Telegraph-Union wire service and other organs he exercised large influence over the provincial press. And he owned the great German film corporation Ufa. Stresemann was granted a glimpse into Hugenberg's operations when an editor of the *Lokalanzeiger* came to his office to inform him confidentially that the Hugenberg empire, formerly neutral with respect to Stresemann, was about to engage in a sharp attack upon the foreign minister and his policies. And in a

subsequent conversation the editor reported that his superior —
doubtlessly speaking for Hugenberg — had called Stresemann "a
national pest [Rightist circles had formerly used this same term for
Rathenau] which must be rendered politically harmless" and had
gone on to explain that prospects for the security pact must be
ruined and, with them, Stresemann's political future.[37] Evidently
Hugenberg's theory was that the German People's Party would
shatter on this issue, leaving Stresemann only a minority of his
former forces while their greater number joined the German Nationalists. This was Hugenberg's way of thanking Stresemann for having
admitted German Nationalists to the cabinet.

Fortunately Stresemann had his party almost unanimously
behind him this time. On July 19, 1925, during a short vacation in
Bansin, Stresemann recorded his pleasure in his diary: "I was delighted . . . by the attitude of my party's Reichstag delegates. As
Chancellor I suffered more from them than from any others, and
their readiness to sacrifice me in the summer of 1924, after I alone
had saved them in the campaign, was indeed the nadir of our mutual
relationship. In the debate on the Dawes measures they came into
line after a bit of struggle. But with respect to the security issue
there has been no trouble at all." [38]

The difficulties within the German National People's Party, the
differences between that party and Stresemann's, and the differences
between the Chancellor and his foreign minister had become so
generally known that the Leftist opposition decided to exacerbate
them by means of a general discussion in the Reichstag which was
calculated to pull the coalition apart. And so on July 3, 1925, the
Social Democrats and the Communists requested a debate on foreign
policy. Discussion at that time was hardly to the interest of the
government parties, and Stresemann personally preferred to discuss
his intended reply to the French behind closed doors — with the
cabinet, the Reichstag committee on foreign affairs, and representatives of the land governments — and to publish it only after it had
been delivered. A majority of the Reichstag rejected the Leftists'
request. In the course of this debate former Chancellor Wirth differed with the rest of his Centrist colleagues and called for an open
discussion on the matter. Seeckt, however, wrote at this time to his
wife: "It is not desirable to induce a crisis at this time — one
doesn't change jockeys in the middle of the race — but the question
does remain whether it is not even more important to get that man
[Stresemann of course] out of the way in order to open a path for
a different foreign policy." [39] But this was precisely the case in
which Seeckt was to learn that neither he nor the Reichswehr was

strong enough to cause the fall of a minister who had a majority of the Reichstag behind him. Not until the parliament had fallen into utter disorder could the generals' political harvest be reaped.

Consequently, on July 20 Stresemann did succeed in having Leopold von Hoesch, the German ambassador in Paris, transmit the German answer to the French. The contents of the note were, of course, largely determined by considerations of domestic politics. Thus it was, for instance, that whatever objections Stresemann had made to the French note were painted as large as possible and placed in the foreground. It was in this spirit that Stresemann had deliberately made an unwarrantedly extreme interpretation of the French proposals concerning treaties of arbitration, as though he understood the Allied governments to be planning, under certain circumstances, to intervene with force against Germany even in the absence of any specific transgression on her part. Similarly he tried to connect the security pact which was under consideration with the demand that the Allies evacuate their zones of occupation earlier than had been planned even though he acknowledged at the same time that the conclusion of such a treaty "would imply no alteration of existing treaties."

Such shadings improved the note's reception in Germany, but they had the opposite effect in England and, especially, France.[40] Stresemann's skill at judging the German public's mood became evident in the Reichstag debate of July 22 and 23, which ended with the adoption of a resolution in support of Stresemann's reply by a vote of 235 against 158. Even Count Westarp, speaker for the German Nationalists, approved the note, taking pains to explain that it represented "the policy of the entire cabinet" — that is, the German Nationalists, too. In truth, Stresemann's policies enjoyed even greater support in the Reichstag than the vote had shown, for the official spokesmen for the Democrats and Social Democrats — parties which were formally opposed to the cabinet — had supported the note. The Communists and the Racists, among them the National Socialists, closed ranks in a common bloc of opposition.

The French and English governments were able to overcome their misgivings at the general tone of the note because in the final paragraph they could observe a transition to a different, more positive mood. Here Stresemann had spoken of "significant prospects of agreement on essential points" and had expressed his confidence that remaining differences could be overcome. Briand and Chamberlain, supported by d'Abernon in this conciliatory spirit, responded quickly to the note. On August 10 Briand went to London, where the two ministers quickly discovered that they agreed on all important points. Chamberlain was particularly pleased to learn that Briand joined him in his desire to substitute direct, personal negotiations for written notes as soon as possible. Thus Briand's reply of August 24, sent to the Germans in the name of the Allied governments, ended with the suggestion that representatives of the governments concerned meet in the near future. By way of preparation for this conference he proposed that legal advisers to the three governments meet first in London to prepare a draft of the security pact complete enough to serve as the basis for negotiations at the ministers' conference. On this point, too, the two Allied ministers had found themselves in perfect, spontaneous agreement.[41]

The proposal was received warmly by the Germans, who had become much more cooperative after they had watched the French unhesitatingly fulfill the promises that Herriot had made to Stresemann in London about giving up the occupation of the Ruhr and of the so-called sanction cities. The last French left the Ruhr on July 31 and evacuated Duisburg and Düsseldorf on August 25. And so the nationalistic journalists and politicians, who had stubbornly maintained that Stresemann was letting himself be hoodwinked by empty French promises, were refuted by events.

On August 3, 1925, when Lord d'Abernon explained to Stresemann the idea of a conference of legal advisers, the German foreign minister at first had grave doubts. He clearly feared that such conversations could lead to political concessions which might later tie his hands. But Stresemann had sufficient insight to repress his hesitations; and the results of the conference, which took place in London during the first week in September, completely justified his decision.

Both the French legal adviser, Fromageot, and his English counterpart, Sir Cecil Hurst, were dispassionate, professional men who had not the slightest intention of taking any political advantage of their German colleague, Undersecretary Gaus, head of the legal division on the Wilhelmstrasse. On the contrary, their secret negotiations were marked by an astonishing degree of candor. A note in Stresemann's papers that seems to have come from Gaus affords a typical illustration of this cordiality.[42]

While they were discussing the French intent to guarantee the treaties of arbitration in the East, Sir Cecil said that, as long as they were speaking in strictest confidence, he wished to set forth the attitude of Chamberlain and the English government with complete frankness. Now, the Franco-Polish alliance was a given fact. It seemed to the British that one of the chief tasks of European diplomacy would be to render as *harmless* as possible this alliance, which Poland's attitude and situation made so dangerous. One could — indeed, would — direct this entire Franco-Polish relationship in a different direction if at this time, upon the occasion of a Rhenish agreement, a firm German-Polish treaty of arbitration were to be concluded under the guarantee of France. The fact that the guarantee would be promised both parties would, in turn, give France an effective way to restrain Polish aggressive tendencies. To this Fromageot replied that his English colleague had just described the diplomatic intentions of France — or, at least, of the present French government — with great precision. Naturally, words like these could never have been exchanged in public.

The most important technical result of the jurists' conference was their agreement on an answer, conceived by Hurst and Fromageot and accepted by Gaus, to the difficult question: In what manner and under what conditions should the guarantor of the treaty, that is, Great Britain, be permitted to intervene if a violation occurred? Here the distinction was made between dubious and "flagrant" violations. In doubtful cases the question of guilt was to be put to the League of Nations. In the event of a flagrant violation of the security treaty or of Articles 42 and 43 of the Treaty of Versailles (concerning the demilitarization of the Rhineland), all parties to the pact would immediately come to the aid of the offended state. These provisions solved the problem as well as any treaty clauses can. But such clauses, if they are to be effective, require the determined willingness of peoples and their governments to assume the responsibilities and the dangers of such guarantees when the critical moment is come. And no treaty, however well thought out, could promise that.

After the legal conference had arrived at conclusions which could be used as the base for further, personal negotiations, the French government invited Germany to a ministers' conference in Switzerland, where Great Britain, France, Italy, Belgium, Poland, Czechoslovakia, and Germany were to be represented. Now the moment had arrived when the German people — and the German Nationalist ministers in particular — had to answer yes or no to the question of participating in such a conference. The fact that the Rightist press had been thundering against the security pact day after day for weeks on end hardly made it easy for those ministers to say yes. Indeed, there were such strong feelings at work within the party that its leaders, Hergt and Westarp, told Stresemann that they would probably have to bow to extremist opinion in their ranks.[43] The director of the German Nationalists' press demanded, among other things, that German representatives be permitted to go to the conference only if the evacuation of the Cologne Zone had been completed before the meeting or, at the very least, was being carried out simultaneously with the *start* of the conference.[44] The German Nationalist delegation in the Reichstag further declared that they approved of Stresemann's participation — but only if it "were clearly understood that no formal commitments would be involved." [45]

It was as if these gentlemen wished to give Poincaré and his friends explicit proof that the only way to deal with Germany was by dictation. Stresemann obtained insight into the Nationalists' tactics in the course of a conference with the German Nationalist Schiele, the Centrist Braun, and Chancellor Luther. Schiele argued that Stresemann should be Germany's sole representative at the meeting, whereupon Luther made quite clear the importance he placed upon also being there. He was ready, he explained, to help Stresemann shoulder the responsibility, and if their efforts came to naught, he was prepared to suffer the consequences. To this Schiele exclaimed: "But that is precisely what we do not want!" He went on to argue that the Chancellor must be spared at all costs. From this incident Stresemann correctly concluded that the German Nationalists intended "to load the foreign minister with so many demands and reservations that his mission would predictably collapse, and then to dispatch him to the wasteland, keeping, however, the rest of Luther's cabinet." [46]

Their hope was dashed on the Chancellor's firm stand. His firmness showed, too, how sincerely Luther supported the plan for a security pact. If the German Nationalists, as their public statements forced one to conclude, wished to block the pact and to hinder Germany's admission to the League, then they would have to resign from Luther's cabinet at this moment. Ah, but no! They chose to stay, contenting themselves with raising obstacles in the form of demands designed to embarrass their country's representatives at the conference.

First on the German Nationalists' list was, of course, their eternal campaign against the "war-guilt lie." This always worked, for in truth a majority of the German people had gradually convinced themselves that Germany had had absolutely nothing to do with starting the war. As a result of this popular feeling, Stresemann, in his note of September 26 accepting Germany's invitation to the conference, felt obliged to include a statement which the German ambassadors were to deliver at the same time. Here he expressly agreed that the conclusion of a security pact and Germany's admission to the League of Nations were closely related; but he also repeated, with explicit reference to Germany's earlier statement of

August 29, 1924, that Germany did not acknowledge the statement of her war guilt which was included in the Versailles treaty. He then went on to demand the immediate evacuation of the Cologne Zone and "the final settlement of questions concerning German disarmament."

Stresemann can hardly have been astonished to learn that his declaration aroused bad feeling in Paris and London. Pessimists were quick to conclude that prospects for the conference had been ruined by the note. Chamberlain was indignant, likening the German government to a nagging woman who insists on having the last word.[47] But in the end he contented himself with a simple, clear refutation of the German statement. With respect to the war-guilt question the English reply merely said: "His Majesty's Government is at a loss to know why the German Government have thought proper to raise it at this moment . . . the negotiation of a Security Pact cannot modify the Treaty of Versailles or modify their judgement of the past." And in regard to the evacuation of the Cologne Zone Chamberlain explained that this depended on the Germans themselves: as soon as they had fulfilled their treaty obligations, the Allies would be glad to leave Cologne. The French replied in the same vein, and Stresemann could do nothing but retreat, asking Briand, through Ambassador von Hoesch, to ignore whatever reservations his statement of September 26 may have expressed concerning the coming negotiations.[48] Thus on October 5 in Locarno the conference could finally begin.

But before Stresemann could depart for Locarno, he had to receive a caller whom happenchance alone had certainly not brought to Berlin just at this moment. This was Comrade Chicherin, the Russian minister of foreign affairs. The men in Moscow were evidently convinced that the German Communists were neither strong nor clever enough to lay successful obstacles in Stresemann's way. And so it was that Chicherin chose this time for a "vacation trip" to the West, with Warsaw his first stop. Here he was the complete personification of friendliness and benevolence, proclaiming to the press that Russo-Polish relations had been steadily improving in recent years. He went on to praise the "natural and irresistible development of friendship between Russia and other nations of Eastern Europe, a friendship based upon Russia's recognition of the principle that all people have a right to self-determination, and one which can in no way offend the interests of the Polish state." [49]

The Wilhelmstrasse did not find it hard to read between the lines of Chicherin's remarks: the Soviet Union was threatening Germany with a Russo-Polish rapprochement if Germany persisted in following the path which led to the West and the League of Nations. The Germans were quite prepared to accept this Soviet gambit, for they knew that real animosities existed between Moscow and Warsaw, and they were well aware of the degree to which the Russians honored self-determination. But the sudden arrival of Chicherin in Berlin on September 20, with the obvious intention of applying direct pressure on Germany, forced Stresemann to deal with him immediately and personally.[50]

Chicherin's fundamental argument was that the English Tories, represented by Austen Chamberlain, were engaged in a massive attempt to create a united European front against the Soviet Union. In an interview which he granted on October 3 to the editor of the *Deutsche Allgemeine Zeitung*, a conservative, nationalistic Berlin paper, he declared: "The English quest for a security pact represents the chief campaign in British strategy, the final aim of which is world war against Russia." He hoped to block this British "maneuver" by persuading the German government to conclude certain agreements with Russia before going to Locarno. He had two kinds of treaties in mind: a commercial agreement, to which Stresemann could raise no objection and which, in fact, was approved by the Germans on October 2 and signed in Moscow on October 12; and a political pact designed to renew and extend the Treaty of Rapallo.

Stresemann had already told the Russians, through their ambassador Krestinski in June, that he was not going to sign any secret treaty with Russia so long as the political situation in the West remained unclear, that is, until the prospective security pact was either definitely signed or finally repudiated.[51] Stresemann gave the Russian an illuminating reason for rejecting the offer of a covert agreement: "If I am asked whether we have a secret treaty with Russia, I wish to be able to say no." He wished, in other words, to avoid that appearance of duplicity which had been the error at Rapallo.

Moreover, since Rapallo events had occurred which had served only to strengthen his fundamental conviction that the Soviet republic differed from other states in the observation of the traditional considerations and manners of international polity. Thus, for instance, two German citizens, Kindermann and Woltsch, studying in Russia, had been arrested in Moscow in July 1925, charged with planning the assassination of Stalin and Trotsky, and sentenced to death. In the course of their trial the Russian legal authorities had made the fantastic accusation that an official of the German embassy in Moscow was party to this German "plot." Naturally, no one in Germany believed this nonsense, and the German press gave a unanimous expression of national indignation. Stresemann, too, explained to the Russian chargé d'affaires that such incidents would mean that "in the German Foreign Office and in the cabinet men would despair of the possibility of Russo-German agreement." [52] The outcome of the whole affair was the exchange of the two condemned Germans for a Russian Communist who had been sentenced to death by the German Supreme Court. This probably had been the Russians' purpose from the start — as Stresemann quite quickly surmised. This incident did not remain the only sample of their technique.

When Chicherin finally got around to seeking Stresemann out — at night, as was the Russian's habit — the German foreign minister took this opportunity to chide his visitor about the continued Russian machinations in Germany. After this introductory skirmish Stresemann went to the point: the security pact, Germany's entry into the League, and the possible effects of these two steps upon Russo-German relations. It was easy for him to refute the Russian notion of a British plot. If Germany were to enter the League of Nations she would be in an even better position to make sure that the League "would not be transformed into an instrument of aggression with 'Fight Russia' written on its flag." Furthermore, Stresemann pointed out, he was fighting against Article 16 of the Covenant precisely because he wanted to make it clear that Germany did not wish "to be forced into an aggressive action against Russia." And he insisted that Germany would continue to maintain this position as a member of the League. War against Russia was therefore, he concluded, quite out of the question.

Stresemann also assumed a clear and definite position with regard to Poland: Germany would offer neither direct nor indirect guarantees of Polish boundaries. "Naturally we refuse to see any justification for the continued existence of the present Polish state; we shall therefore never recognize the Polish borders of our own free will." Chicherin's reply was even more interesting.[53] He said in effect: I do not understand you German diplomats. In February 1925 you proposed a security pact with the Western powers, thus attempting reconciliation with them. Yet, just two months before, in December of 1924, your ambassador, Count Brockdorff-Rantzau, appeared in my office with the proposal of Russo-German collaboration against Poland. The purpose of this collaboration, Brockdorff explained to me, was to enable the two powers "to push Poland back to its ethnic borders." Now, the words "to push Poland back" can be understood only to imply "joint military action against Poland, with the aim of destroying the present Polish state." Chicherin then went on to explain that he had considered this German invitation so important that he had immediately called a meeting of the Russian cabinet, and that same December the Russians had presented their German would-be collaborators with the draft of a mutual nonaggression pact. And what had been the German answer? An empty formula, fit perhaps for banquet toasts but not for papers of state; one which might better be called a rough quotation from Goethe's "Confessions of a Beautiful Soul."

Stresemann was so "distressed and disturbed" by Chicherin's argument that in spite of the lateness of the hour — midnight was already past — he called State Secretary von Schubert in order to learn how much truth there was in what the Russian said. The subsequent discussion with Chicherin lasted so long that Ambassador Krestinski, who had accompanied his superior on this visit to Stresemann, fell asleep, thus giving the German an excuse to terminate the talk. The conversation was, however, renewed on October 2, the day of Stresemann's departure for Locarno. In the meantime the German had had an opportunity to consult the relevant documents and thus was able to show Chicherin that the Russo-German negotiations concerning possible joint action against Poland had stemmed not from the Germans, but rather from a Russian, more exactly, a colleague of Chicherin's named Kopp. But the Wilhelmstrasse had taken active part in these negotiations, and the Russian minister was able to refer to a telegram from Berlin (evidently composed by Maltzan), sentences of which had been read to him by the German ambassador.

But, Stresemann objected, Brockdorff's own report stated that in his first conversation with Kopp he had said that the use of force against Poland would be madness. Chicherin, however, stuck to his version of the affair and went on to tell Stresemann that Count Brockdorff had hesitated some time until, "evidently after making a difficult decision," he had read Chicherin a sentence from this Berlin telegram — number 568 according to Stresemann's notes — about "pushing Poland back to its ethnic borders." "I was able to explain," Stresemann's notes continue, "that this sentence was indeed in the telegram from Berlin, but not as the burden of our message — not as the purpose of a proffered alliance — but rather, according to copy before me, as a topic of possible consideration, which Count Brockdorff-Rantzau was completely free to mention or keep secret, as he thought best." In his subsequent report, the notes go on, Rantzau "described the sentence upon which Rantzau [*sic*, probably an error for Chicherin] laid such critical importance as a mere allusion, although he did add that Chicherin had greeted the allusion most warmly." [54]

From all this it appears certain that the German ambassador had indeed spoken of Russo-German collaboration with the aim of "pushing back" Poland and that, in doing so, he was carrying out instructions from Berlin. This same expression occurs again in a précis of remarks made by Count Brockdorff-Rantzau in the name of his government to the Russian Deputy Foreign Minister Litvinov on April 7, 1925 — that is, well after the beginning of German negotiations with France and England. The expression must be regarded as an official statement of the German government because it occurs in a formal note delivered to the Russian ambassador, Krestinski, on April 25. This note, in discussing the effects on Russia of Germany's entrance into the League of Nations, states: "If events should occur which would make it feasible to push Poland back to its ethnic borders [*eine Zurückdrängung Polens in seine ethnographischen Grenzen*], Germany's active participation in such an operation would, to say the least, be seriously hindered by her membership in the League of Nations. This is indubitably a consideration of great importance. But, on the other hand, its significance is limited by the fact that, in such an event, a Germany that was not a member of the League would still have to reckon with the certain opposition of the Entente — at least of France, Belgium, and Czechoslovakia — and thus would find herself in practice unable to participate in any active operations against Poland." [55]

The Germans' *Realpolitik* had been much more evident in these words than in Brockdorff's conversation with Chicherin the preceding December, and one cannot wonder that the Russians took them to imply the possibility of military cooperation. Perhaps this change in tone was connected with Ago von Maltzan's departure from the German Foreign Office in the interim. For, as Lord d'Abernon observed, Maltzan had been ready "to sacrifice everything for the sake of relations with Russia."

Yet, even if one is prepared to accept Stresemann's milder exegesis of the official statement of April 1925, one still is perplexed by a confidential letter of Stresemann's which has been the ground of more dispute than any other document of his career. Stresemann wrote this letter to the former German crown prince on September 9, just before Germany's formal invitation to Locarno. [56] (Fearful lest the letter might fall into improper hands, Stresemann had not signed it.) The letter is concerned with Germany's prospective admission into the League of Nations and relates this step to three grand goals of German foreign policy. Of these, the first two are hardly astonishing: a solution of the reparations problem and the protection of extraterritorial Germans. The third goal Stresemann describes as "the correction of the eastern boundary: regaining Danzig and the Polish Corridor and revising the border in Upper Silesia. A German-Austrian union stands in the further future, although I am quite certain that such a union [*Anschluss*] will not bring only advantages to Germany," a point which he goes on to develop by referring to the danger of a Catholic preponderance in Germany and of the Bavarian inclination toward Austria.

If we wish to recognize the full significance of these expectations, we must first note that Stresemann and the German government not only had categorically refused to include the eastern border in the security pact, thus gaining England's support, but also had vigorously opposed French guarantees of the arbitration treaties Germany was about to sign with her eastern neighbors. Now to the extent that Stresemann's goals were to be realized through peaceful means, there was nothing illicit about them. For the treaty of arbitration that the Germans were about to conclude with the Poles solemnly announced Germany's determination to keep peace with Poland by ensuring, through this instrument, the amicable settlement of whatever differences might arise between the two nations. But could Stresemann really believe that Poland would ever be brought by peaceful ways to the "correction of the eastern border" that he sought? The rest of the letter provides an indirect answer to this question, for Stresemann goes on to defend the inclusion of the western German border in the security pact with the argument that, although the treaty involves a German renunciation of the forceful retaking of Alsace-Lorraine, such renunciation has "only a theoretic character" because "no possibility of war against France exists." Is one not obliged to conclude from this that the Germans' refusal to make similar renunciations with respect to their eastern borders was based upon the hope that some day in the future Germany would be ready for a war against Poland?

One's misgivings about this letter can only be strengthened by the following sentences from its penultimate paragraph: "The most important task with respect to question Number One (that is, reparations) is the liberation of German soil from foreign occupation. First we must get the throttler from our throat. Therefore, as Metternich might well have said after the events of 1809, our policy in this respect will have to consist principally of being artful [*finassieren*] and avoiding major decisions."

The objectionable word here is *finassieren.* One American translates it as "to maneuver"; [57] but his translation is certainly too innocuous. The *Grosse Meyer* of 1908, an unimpeachable source, defines *finassieren* as "to use tricks, to employ artifice." This is in full accord with the meaning given in Heyse's dictionary of foreign terms (*Fremdwörterbuch*) and with the translation Sachs-Villatte gives for the French *finasser*. Stresemann may well have taken the word from Heinrich von Srbik's definitive biography of Metternich. It had just been published and, given Stresemann's lively interest in Napoleonic history, in all probability had been read immediately by the German foreign minister. Srbik uses the word several times (for example, I, 114, 122, 144) to typify Metternich's unheroic but successful diplomacy after Austria's defeat in 1809 and suggests that it might have been from Talleyrand and Fouché, when he was Austrian ambassador in Paris, that Metternich had learned "how to be artful [*die Kunst des Finassierens*], how to dupe others slyly while seeming their friend, the art of the double tongue and the double path." If Stresemann really used the word in this sense, then he certainly merits the darkest suspicions. Yet this identification of Stresemann with Srbik is not compelling, for one cannot arrive at so exact an interpretation on the tenuous assumption that a writer might possibly have read a certain book. [58]

One can safely assume, however, that the recipient of the letter, the son of William II, took the expression in Srbik's sense, understanding Stresemann to mean that neither the security pact with the West nor membership in the League would keep Germany from using military force — once she was strong enough again — to force Poland to retract its western border. And the former crown prince probably expanded on the letter in this sense when discussing it with German political friends. For one can almost certainly assume that Stresemann regarded his letter as a means of reaching the minds of German Nationalists and other Rightists who were close to the former crown prince and from whom Stresemann feared opposition. Whether he also hoped thus to assure Hindenburg, who resisted Stresemann's policies more for emotional than for rational reasons, is beside the point.

Did Stresemann really desire this military encounter? Was he, as many of his critics assume, merely a hypocrite when, at Locarno and elsewhere, he spoke of peace? He never pressed for a Polish war with unambiguous words, and so anyone who differs with the critics — as do almost all who knew him well — will let him enjoy the benefit of the doubt. After learning of this letter, Sir Austen Chamberlain explicitly refused to regard Stresemann as the "betrayer" and Briand as the "betrayed." Perhaps one can best judge

Stresemann's words by considering them a document of the period of his transition from the nationalist that he certainly had been for many years to a European statesman. Like all German nationalists he had a disdain for the Poles that was derived from hatred and from scorn. It seemed to him proper and just that Germans should rule over Poles; but that Poles should rule Germans struck him as a perversion of nature. The abolition of this perverted state of affairs struck him as a most desirable goal, and if military force were to prove necessary toward this end — well, he was prepared to stomach that. Only gradually and slowly was Stresemann able to bring himself to the realization that European peace was indivisible, and that each nation had to accommodate itself to those less pleasant aspects of the general settlement which could not be changed through peaceful means. To recognize and act upon this truth is also patriotism; sometimes not only a wiser but also a purer patriotism than that of the sharp sword.

If our interpretation is correct, then to Stresemann's honor one can add that he worked his way quite quickly from the obscure and ambiguous standpoint of his letter to the crown prince to the clear realization that German hopes in the East could be realized — if at all — only in peaceful ways. On April 16, 1926, after the conclusion of the Treaty of Locarno but before Germany's admission to the League of Nations, he sent Stahmer, the ambassador in London, a "top secret" message concerning Poland and Danzig. Here, with all the clarity one can wish, Stresemann wrote: "English collaboration is an absolute prerequisite to a *peaceful* solution of our eastern problem, and *only a peaceful* solution can be considered." [59] He evidently expected that financial and economic difficulties would force Poland to come to terms.

After his second conversation with Chicherin Stresemann stepped aboard the train that was to take him to Locarno. Chicherin, however, not only remained in Berlin, but also continued to give interviews to the press; interviews in which — according to the Russian custom which has since become well known — he kept repeating the same old arguments over and over again. His statements were, of course, immediately forwarded to Stresemann at Locarno, where the German foreign minister was forced to comment on them at his first press conference. "We see no necessity to choose between East and West," he explained. "We wish to enjoy good relations with both sides."

However much Chicherin's behavior may have contradicted the rules of diplomatic etiquette, one need by no means assume that Stresemann was very angry at the Russian's extraordinarily lengthy visit to Berlin. For in Berlin Chicherin served as a constant reminder to the Western powers that Germany could also reach her hand out to the East. This thought could serve only to make them more receptive to German requests, thus simplifying Stresemann's task. During the conference the American ambassador to Berlin cabled the State Department that Chicherin was the Germans' highest trump card.[60] The Russian minister, who liked to quote Goethe so much, should have remembered Alba's words about William of Orange in *Egmont*: "He is not coming! I see the clever man was clever enough not to try to be clever."

On October 5, 1925, in the town hall of Locarno on the shore of Lake Maggiore, the German Chancellor, Hans Luther, and his foreign minister, Gustav Stresemann, met the foreign ministers of France and England, Aristide Briand and Austen Chamberlain. Among the other Western powers, Belgium was represented by its Socialist Premier Vandervelde and Italy by its Senator Scialoia. (The Italian Duce, Benito Mussolini, also appeared for a few days, but not so much to take part in the deliberations as to prove to himself and the world that he embodied a European great power in his very person.) The foreign ministers of Poland and of Czechoslovakia, Skrzyński and Beneš, were also in Locarno. But they were invited to join the negotiations only when the treaties of arbitration were being considered. During the truly decisive deliberations they were obliged, so to speak, to wait in the antechamber. So long as the security pact in the West was on the agenda, representatives of Great Britain, France, Belgium, Italy, and Germany — and, with emphasized care, these alone — were admitted to the square table in Locarno's town hall. The equal rights of all these powers were demonstrated with similar care by the fact that no chairman was empowered to recognize individual speakers.

Chamberlain had come to Locarno with certain misgivings about Stresemann. But these quickly disappeared after he had observed him a few times in debate. The German minister's features — his bull neck, his almost completely bald head, and his frequently overpowering, strident voice — were hardly such as to excite immediate sympathy in either Chamberlain or Briand. He looked too much like a caricature of the "Hun." But they both were trained, experienced parliamentarians and had appreciation for the skill with which Stresemann was playing his piece: fingering the keys gently when he felt that the situation was delicate, then again emphatic — even rhetorical — when he sensed the need to make a certain point of view perfectly clear to the other side. Gradually the leaders of the West became convinced that however stubbornly Stresemann might fight for his demands, he was seeking rapprochement in all good faith, never letting this goal out of sight.

Luther enjoyed an advantage over Stresemann in that he spoke French — as a youth he had studied in Lausanne — while Stresemann was constantly dependent on an interpreter. Thus Luther was able to join Briand in Ascona for a confidential conversation in which together, and with some success, they sought to clear the conference's path as best they could.[61] Chamberlain also spoke excellent French and knew enough German to be able to follow the Germans' remarks with careful attention, at times correcting or completing an incorrect translation by the interpreter. Sir Austen was firmly determined to lead these negotiations to a positive conclusion and even went so far, now and then, as to cut off a remark that threatened to endanger the progress of the talks with an impatient gesture, a monocled stare, and a curt comment.

While Chamberlain always remained the self-controlled, outwardly stiff English gentleman, Briand's unselfconscious informality, his warm humanity, and his never failing wit also helped to keep the talks from foundering. Once, when Luther was dwelling unnecessarily long and emotionally on the sufferings of the German people, Briand interrupted him with the interjection: "Stop or we shall all begin to weep!" Luther started as though insulted; Briand affected embarrassment; Stresemann exploded in a loud laugh that quickly infected the entire meeting.

Chief among Briand's many gifts was his ability to tell when the German delegates were stating their own, professional views and when they were simply mouthing the opinions of the nationalists, with whom they thought they had to reckon at home. Stresemann tells us how Briand once said to him that he truly believed a majority of the Germans really desired peace.

But in your politics you Germans have a force which I can only call the cult of the German mystique — those Germans, namely, who are unwilling to join in a mutual guarantee of peace at this time because they hope for some miracle in the future. If one asks them just what this miracle is going to be, they are unable to say. But the fond hope that a miracle could happen keeps them peering into the misty future — even building their home there — and, at the same time, keeps them from casting their bright eyes upon the present.[62]

Briand comprehended why Stresemann raised the war-guilt question once again, although this was quite contrary to the earlier agreement; he realized that the German foreign minister needed to have it on the record to show the folks back home. To him and to

Chamberlain the important thing was that the intrusion of this awkward matter should have no visible effects. They therefore cut off discussion of the issue immediately in the correct assumption that even the Germans would be glad to see the issue successfully skirted.

In spite of all these gifts and good intentions, there remained, of course, a whole set of real issues on which the two sides were initially quite far apart. In order to facilitate a meeting of minds, the discussions had been held in strictest privacy from the very beginning. The journalists who had gathered in Locarno from all the countries of the earth had to be content with the extremely laconic official statements which were released after every session. Under these circumstances it was inevitable that the reporters began to base their stories on rumor and guess. From time to time Stresemann and Luther gave confidential information to representatives of the German press, only to see their words distorted in Rightist papers.

Yet the official meetings of the conference were not its most important part. Many issues were raised only to be referred immediately to legal experts for solution, while the delegation heads discussed the great political questions in intimate conversations behind closed doors. The most important of these confidential talks took place in a setting peculiarly appropriate to the locale. On October 10, the delegates took a lake cruise on the little steamboat *Fiori d'Arancis.* This was, however, not the sort of pleasure trip that the newspapers portrayed. For five hours Luther, Stresemann, Briand, and Chamberlain sat in the cabin discussing the two issues of greatest political significance: Article 16 of the Covenant of the League and guarantees of arbitration treaties in Eastern Europe.

Article 16 required that every member of the League of Nations cooperate — even militarily — in the application of sanctions by the League. This article had been the subject of discussion and debate from the first moment that Germany's admission to the League had been seriously considered. The article was of special relevance with respect to German relations with Russia, for it required members of the League to permit the passage of League forces, and it was easy to conceive of a Russo-Polish war in which the League might wish to send reinforcements to the Poles through German territory. The question had to be decided at this time, for the Western powers regarded Germany's entry into the League as a prerequisite to the security pact, while Germany kept pointing out that the demilitarization forced on her by the Treaty of Versailles required her release from Article 16 or at least from its major provisions.

Briand tried first to assure Stresemann that Germany would have a permanent seat in the Council of the League and thus would be able to veto any sanction it opposed. But Stresemann offered immediate rebuttal in a very emphatic address that clearly did not miss its mark: "If, in the event of a Russian attack, we should join in labeling Russia as aggressor, thus ensuring the League's unanimity, we should therewith place our entire moral influence and prestige on the side of the League . . . This act alone could have great political repercussions in Germany. We are ready to face these risks, but we must also ask that our willingness be given its full due." [63]

The solution to these difficulties was finally found in a formula taken from the draft for the ill-fated Geneva Protocol (Article 11, Paragraph 2). The six members of the League then at Locarno committed themselves, in a common note directed to the German delegation, to an interpretation of Article 16 according to which every member of the League would be obliged to cooperate loyally and effectively in support of the Covenant and in opposing aggression "to an extent which is compatible with its military situation and takes its geographical position into account." [64] Although the signers of this note, as they explicitly stated, could not speak for the League, they were able to cite other negotiations as precedent for their interpretation. And the Germans could not doubt that such an interpretation, supported as it was by France and especially England, was as good as a formal rule. Nor could one doubt that, with this written assurance in its pocket, every subsequent German cabinet would be able to escape participation in whatever League sanctions it might find inconvenient. And if, at this point, Stresemann recalled his last conversation with Comrade Chicherin, he could now be assured that the Russian's most dangerous weapon had been wrested from his hand.

Although the German delegation had to be satisfied with a compromise on Article 16, it won a complete victory with respect to the eastern treaties of arbitration. For France decided not to offer guarantees. Thus Stresemann was able to face his critics with the fact that the German Republic had allowed no foreign power to guarantee its eastern boundary — a boundary which it still refused to recognize, although it had expressly forsworn any attempt to change the border by forceful means. He was, of course, unable to keep Briand from concluding with Poland and Czechoslovakia mutual security treaties against the danger that one of them should fall "victim to a breach of the common obligations, agreed upon with Germany, for the maintenance of general peace."

The importance which the German delegation placed upon the

fruits of the confidential conversations aboard the *Fiori d'Arancis*
was demonstrated by their sending the state secretary of the Chancellery, Dr. Franz Kempner, to Berlin immediately to brief those
members of the cabinet who had stayed behind. But here his
reception was cool, for the German Nationalist ministers were still
intent on avoiding any final settlement.[65]

In addition to those items which were official topics of discussion,
Luther and Stresemann raised other issues of special concern to
them in their intimate talks with Briand and Chamberlain. Chief
among these was the matter of the so-called "subsequent effects"
(*Rückwirkungen*) which the conclusion of the security pact was
bound to have upon the Allies' treatment of Germany. Stresemann
catalogued his hopes in a note he made on a conversation with
Briand: "I began with the question of the Cologne Zone and then
went on to the government of the Rhineland, emphasizing the
matter of decrees, delegates, a lessening of the occupation forces, a
shortening of the occupation time, the effects of the security pact
upon conditions in the Saar, the return of the last prisoners of war,
a general pardon for those convicted *in absentia*, also changes in
the regulations for military investigation and for German air transport as well."

One can well understand Briand's retort that these representatives were distinguished by a temerity which bordered on rashness
and that, if the Germans wished to raise all these questions, they
would in all likelihood need a conference that would take longer
than that of Locarno. Both Briand and Chamberlain declined to
discuss Stresemann's items further, pointing out that they did not
have such authority from their cabinets. And Briand added, with
perfect justice, that in military matters such as a decrease in the
occupation forces he could not act alone, but rather would have to
consult the French minister of war, Painlevé, who was also his
Premier. (Briand knew, of course, that the French generals would
insist on having their word, too.) But both the Frenchman and his
English colleague gave Stresemann to understand that they would
use all their influence to effect the satisfaction of these German
wishes. Briand openly called it only "natural" that the impending
pact would have major consequences for Germany's problems. And
the Germans had to be content with that general assurance.[66]

Finally, on October 16, negotiations had proceeded to the point
where the several, interrelated treaties could be provisionally signed.
Formal signatures were attached only to a final protocol that
referred to all the separate treaties which were to go into effect the
day Germany became a member of the League of Nations. These

various treaties were simply signed *ne varietur*, that is, initialed by the responsible ministers. The final protocol was signed for Germany not only by Stresemann but also by Chancellor Luther, while the separate treaties bore Stresemann's initials alone. Through his signature Luther assumed, with Stresemann, full responsibility for the whole structure of treaties, including Germany's entry into the League of Nations, to the consternation of his German Nationalist colleagues, who would gladly have separated his political fortunes from those of his foreign minister. The final protocol went on to set December 1, 1925, for the final, formal signing of the treaties, on which day representatives of the nations concerned were to gather in London.

October 16 was also Chamberlain's birthday. The delegates took delight in honoring the man whose assuring, conciliating presence had proved so fruitful. Among the addresses given at this final meeting, those of the German and French foreign ministers made the greatest and most lasting impressions. Luther had left it up to Stresemann to speak the Germans' final word, and his minister knew how to achieve a full effect through understatement. Chamberlain — whom no one would call hyperemotional — testified to the effectiveness of Stresemann's closing speech in a letter sent to Tyrrell, the British ambassador to Paris, two days after the Locarno Conference.

And then the closing scene and last words. None of us who were there will ever forget them . . . First, Stresemann in a few simply spoken sentences told how the representatives of Germany initialed with a full sense of their responsibility and made the Pact their own, and then in a few words of great restraint, with no direct mention of those things which lay nearest to their heart, added that they initialed in the sure confidence that these accords would have their natural consequences "in the political and economic sphere."

My dear Tyrrell, there are silences that say more than words and make a greater appeal than any rhetoric!

And then Briand, large-hearted, generous Briand, spoke and I was proud for my friend and proud for his country. There spoke the true heart of chivalrous France. There shone the spirit of a Bayard, *sans peur et sans reproche*, of all that is best and noblest in her people and her history . . . he pledged himself immediately on his return to set to work to give the largest measure of satisfaction to the hopes which the German representatives had left unuttered but which he understood so well and found so natural and so sympathetic.[67]

Even today, when all the hopes awakened at Locarno lie buried under blood and ruins, one cannot read the conclusion of Briand's speech without being stirred:

If we have done nothing more here than negotiate and exchange treaties, each then returning to his native land, leaving it up to good luck to
see that promises are kept, then we shall have merely executed an empty
gesture. If *a new spirit* does not accompany this gesture, if our act does
not mark the beginning of an *era of mutual trust*, then our deeds will not
have the effects for which we hope. Between our two nations there are
still areas of friction and points of pain. May the pact which we have
just signed serve as balsam to these wounds. For the problems which still
remain must be resolved. I am certain that France will comprehend the
full significance of this document and that a sense of satisfaction will be
its result. Then we shall be able to work together toward the realization
in every area of life of the ideal we all bear in our hearts: a Europe that
will fulfill its destiny by remaining true to its tradition of civilized and
generous spirits.[68]

When the session was concluded, Briand rushed to Stresemann
with both hands outstretched. "I seized his right hand," Stresemann
reports, "and told him I was sincerely grateful for the words which
he had spoken, whereupon he replied: 'No, do not speak of words.
I shall give you proof that those were not just words, but rather
deeds.'"

And outside, from all the churches of Locarno and even from
the little chapel of the Madonna del Sasso, bells were ringing a
welcome to the new era of peace that was about to spread across
Europe. In the square in front of the town hall the citizens of
Locarno were gathered in applauding, jubilant approval. Paul
Schmidt recalls: "As we descended the few steps of the little stairway
with Stresemann and Luther, the crowd exploded in another roar
of acclaim. Then suddenly everyone was still. All the men in the
crowd removed their hats and formed a silent, immobile double row
through which we, deeply moved, proceeded to our carriage." [69]

But when the train in which the German delegates were returning
arrived at the Anhalt Station in Berlin, they found it surrounded by
cordons of police — not because the authorities feared lest Berliners
turn out by the thousands to greet their representatives, who were
bringing back "peace with honor," with an overwhelming ovation,
but rather because they had good reason to believe that the returning
delegates would be met with a disgusting and hateful reception, one
which might well include criminal acts. For it was just three years
since Stresemann's predecessor, Rathenau, had been murdered.
Only a few ministers and the diplomatic corps were present to
welcome the delegates. Lord d'Abernon stepped forward to tell
them: "I have been expressly requested by Mr. Chamberlain to
congratulate you upon the success of the conference and to say that

he will always recall with pleasure the first meeting at Locarno and the spirit of candor and good faith which the German delegation lent to the discussions. The German government will always enjoy the honor of having seized the initiative which led to the Treaty of Locarno."

What was that? Great Britain's foreign minister is happy about the treaty? Then Germany has reason to be sad. This sounds like madness, but it was the argument of the chief editorial, entitled "Warning," in the *Deutsche Allgemeine Zeitung* of October 21: "If our enemies are rejoicing — and, despite Locarno and the League of Nations, they are our enemies so long as they stand on German soil — it is a bad sign for Germany." The author of this article was the editor-in-chief of the paper, Dr. Paul Lensch, a former Social Democrat who, in his *Leipziger Volkszeitung*, had, with real virtuosity, waged a filthy attack on all those less radical than himself.[70]

In its reports from Locarno the Rightist press had maintained a deep pessimism concerning the conference's prospects so long as possible. But when, in spite of these dour predictions, the conference proved a success, a storm of indignation broke forth to the effect that the German delegation had lightly offered up massive sacrifices, receiving nothing but empty promises in return. Readers of these papers and all those who listened to German nationalists were pumped full of this nationalistic hatred for the "traitors." Naturally, the Democratic and Social Democratic newspapers were employing a completely different tone, and in all likelihood they had a majority of Berliners on their side. For one has no reason to assume that most Germans thought otherwise than did the other inhabitants of Europe, whose dearest hope was to be able to enjoy the fruits of their labor in peace. But the voices of these Germans were overpowered at this time by a loud and passionate minority.

Stresemann had left Locarno with the feeling that he had achieved everything that was in any sense a practical possibility. But not so Luther! In a private memorandum of December 1925 Stresemann observed: "Luther returned from Locarno a beaten man. Even at sessions of the conference we had to keep reminding him not to make such a sour, discontented face." This sour face had not escaped Briand, who some years later told Stresemann in fun that Luther had sulked in Locarno like a black cloud over Lake Maggiore.[71] What disturbed Luther was most certainly the thought of his cabinet in Berlin — more precisely, his German Nationalist colleagues. Would they not demand the impossible of him and then desert him when he failed to bring it home?

At first it seemed as though his fears had been exaggerated. On

Monday, October 19, the day after the delegates' return, the first
cabinet meeting was held. Schiele, to be sure, made a few difficulties, demanding that they wait to see the actual wording of the
treaties. But he also said that, if it were a question of acknowledging
the good work of the German delegation to Locarno, he would gladly
answer with a happy yes.[72] At any rate, Hindenburg, who presided,
couched the sense of the meeting in words to the effect that the
cabinet was unanimous in approving the initialed treaties and in
thanking both its delegates for what they had achieved.

But the German Nationalist ministers' restraint had been due
only to their ignorance of the position their party would assume
toward the fait accompli of Locarno. The German National People's
Party had been tagging along, step by step, reluctant and suspicious,
on a path it by no means enjoyed, enticed by the hope of staying in
power after Stresemann's policies had foundered on foreign
obstacles. Now this hope was dashed, and the moment had come
when the party had to give a final yes or no. In the case of the
Dawes Plan the party had found a way to say a loud no and yet,
at the same time, by the ill-famed splitting of its votes, to let
Germany say yes. This trick had won it a place in the government.
But its very reward had made a repetition impossible now. The
party was consequently confronted with the question whether to
sacrifice the earlier gain by a clear, unambiguous no.

The German Nationalist ministers clearly had no taste for such
a stand. On October 16, the day when the treaties were being
initialed at Locarno, Schiele, minister of interior, had invited Lord
d'Abernon to lunch with the German Nationalist ministers with the
obvious intent of affording his colleagues an opportunity to learn
from an expert the true significance of the treaties. The ambassador
was little impressed by the men; they struck him as essentially
"country gentlemen" whose conversation dwelt principally on the
deer they had shot and the wines they had drunk. But in the final
analysis these men were not the determining factors. For they were
obliged to take their political directions from the party, the provincial chairmen of which were hastily summoned to a meeting in
Berlin.

An intransigent, completely negative mood filled the air at this
meeting, To be sure, no one could say just what else the German
Nationalists had expected when they agreed to Germany's participation in the international conference. But it was simplicity itself
for them to declare now that the results of the conference did not
meet the requirements "for the German nation's necessities of life."
This irresponsible, political playing with words, which was literally

sacrificing the true interests of the German people to the partisan need for agitation, finally infuriated even the conspicuously tolerant Chancellor.

Luther knew that he had done more to meet the German Nationalists' wishes than had any chancellor before him, and he was beside himself with rage at the thanks he was now receiving for his pains. Count Westarp, who tried to present and justify his party's point of view, was treated to an extraordinarily violent scene during which Chancellor Luther — otherwise such a calm and patient man — "quivered all over" while Westarp, as Stresemann notes in his diary, "became very pale and seemed much abashed." [73] For what could Westarp say when the Chancellor reminded him that the German delegation to Locarno had gained every single one of their goals and that the German nation, recently a downtrodden people, had once again attained world-wide prominence? It is true that Luther overestimated the German people when he prophesied that a hurricane of their wrath would blow the German National People's Party to shreds. But he was not wrong at all when he objected to Westarp that the Nationalists' tactics might well lead not simply to a cabinet crisis, but to one endangering the entire German state. At any rate, Luther succeeded in keeping Hindenburg in line, despite the old general's sentimental sympathy for the Rightists. "I am sorry for the German Nationalists," the President told Stresemann. "They will hurt themselves badly." In this instance at least the old gentleman's military forms of thought served his country's interests: from his point of view the German Nationalists were displaying "a lack of discipline," and that he could not abide.

Thus, in the end, the German Nationalist ministers were the only victims of their party's intransigence. They received the order to resign their posts, and they obeyed. But with what feelings of regret! On October 26, as they took their leave from the cabinet, Schiele wanted to make a farewell speech. But he was unable to utter more than the first few sentences and only with difficulty repressed his tears. Stresemann noted in his diary: "For several minutes he could not speak for sobbing. When he recovered himself he said that he and his friends had been overwhelmed by a flood. There was no question of any sense of real opposition or triumph and indeed there was a feeling of grief and profound disappointment over the foolish attitude of [his] Party." [74]

The German Nationalists' desertion had no effect on subsequent events. The government was not dissolved. The responsibilities of the ministers who had resigned — including the "nonpartisan" minister of justice, Frenken — were temporarily assumed by those who had remained. On November 23 the cabinet presented the Reichstag with the issues of the Locarno treaties and Germany's entry into the League of Nations. On November 27, after several days' debate, the treaties were ratified by a vote of 300 to 174 and entry into the League was approved 275 to 183. The opposition consisted of German Nationalists, Racists, the Economic Party, and Communists. The majority was composed not only of the coalition parties, but also of Democrats and Social Democrats — parties which ordinarily had little use for Luther. But at the beginning of the debate, the Chancellor had announced that, with the approval of his cabinet, he firmly intended to tender his resignation to the President immediately after the final conclusion of the Treaty of Locarno, that is, after the signing scheduled for December 1, 1925. His resignation, he said, would permit the formation of a new government.

For the most part the Reichstag debate turned about the so-called subsequent effects (*Rückwirkungen*) of Locarno, that is, less about the treaty itself than about the concessions *beyond the treaty* which the Entente powers would grant Germany in return for her signature. Luther and Stresemann were able to point out that such effects could already be perceived in considerable number. The issue of the Cologne Zone in particular, which had excited so much passion among the Germans, had been settled on November 14 by a declaration of the Allied Conference of Ambassadors which set December 1 as the beginning for the evacuation of the zone. Furthermore, the Conference of Ambassadors had offered the prospect of a meaningful reduction in the impact of the occupation on the second and third zones: a reduction in occupation forces, the granting of freer action to German authorities, the recall of the occupation powers' delegates, the limitation of the jurisdiction of their military courts, and the recognition of a special National Commissioner (*Reichskommissar*) who would be charged with the defense of German interests vis-à-vis the occupation authorities.

Naturally the German Nationalists and their Rightist friends labeled all these concessions totally unsatisfactory — one can always cloak oneself in the robe of patriotism and voice this cant. Luther answered their charges courageously by insisting "in clear language that these measures — taken together — promised important relief to the occupied areas and that some of them were of extreme significance." The address by Count Westarp, speaker for the German National People's Party, was especially remarkable, for he had completely adopted Chicherin's argument that England was trying to impress Germany into the Allies' service in a common war against Bolshevism. But since his party was the loudest voice in the fight against Bolshevism and Marxism, he had nothing but the lame disclaimer that Bolshevism and Russia might not always be identical. There is no use today in wasting words to discuss that observation.

Since authoritative legal opinion did not find the Locarno treaties tantamount to a constitutional amendment, the German Nationalists were spared the dilemma this time which they had escaped by their well-known maneuver at the time of the Dawes Plan. They could therefore vote en bloc against ratification, secure in the knowledge that the treaties would be accepted anyway. But Westarp over-reached himself when he declared that his party would not consider the ratification binding unless it were passed by the two-thirds major-ity required by Article 76 of the Weimar constitution. This statement furnished weapons to French nationalists and, indeed, to all foreign enemies of Germany. For if one took Westarp's declaration seriously it meant that if the German Nationalists ever came to power they would not feel themselves bound by treaties negotiated by preceding German governments.

Was not such a statement bound to excite the most violent suspicions of Germany abroad, bringing the value of her national word in doubt? But was it a statement that one was obliged to take seriously? In January 1927, when the German Nationalists joined Marx's cabinet, thus becoming Stresemann's colleagues once again, they signed a protocol by which they attested that "the legal validity of the Treaties of Locarno can be questioned under neither interna-tional nor constitutional law." And the same Count Westarp who in November 1925 had proclaimed the Locarno Laws null and void declared to the Reichstag in February 1927: "The treaty structure of Locarno and the closely related entrance of Germany into the League of Nations have become the legal and political bases of German foreign policy. Today we assure the world again that we have adopted the goal of peaceful conciliation and that we continue to cherish it." [75] Does that not remind one of Gustav Freytag's Schmock,* who could write in any direction? But one dare not forget that in the Bavarian Landtag a National Socialist delegate yelled, "I could understand it if a refugee from Alsace-Lorraine shot Stresemann dead," nor that the German Nationalist provincial press was explaining that the sister of Stresemann's wife was married to Poincaré even as Rathenau's murderers had whispered that his sister was Radek's wife.

On November 28, 1925, Hindenburg signed the Locarno Laws

---

* In Freytag's play *Die Journalisten*, Schmock, a hack journalist, tells Bolz: "I have learned . . . to write in all directions. I have written both for the Left and the Right. I can write in any direction." TRANSLATORS.

and the next day saw Luther and Stresemann leave for the ceremonies at London. The reception which awaited them there showed
how great was the hope of the English — from the king to the man
in the street — that a new era of international relations was being
ushered in; an era in which there no longer would be conquerors
and the conquered, but one in which all men would work together
in the common cause of peace and understanding. The speeches
which Briand and Stresemann delivered at the signing ceremony
echoed this sentiment in an especially moving manner.

Whoever reads their speeches today cannot escape the feelings
expressed by the lamenting chorus in Schiller's *Bride of Messina*:

> What are the hopes and what are the projects
> Which a man, impermanent son of his time,
> Builds up on the treacherous slime?

Stresemann and Briand did not live to see their work ruined by a
criminal act of force, and by that time Austen Chamberlain — who
had been honored with the Order of the Garter for his share in this
work — was an old man who could warn but was no longer heard.[76]
Those who had come to power in Paris and London contented
themselves with paper resolutions, letting fate decide what should
occur. But does this mean that one must call the whole structure of
Locarno worthless nonsense? Was it an infantile illusion to think
that two nations which had been enemies for centuries could be
reconciled and united in the common work of peace?[77] Did the
illusion not lie, rather, in placing too great a faith in the binding
power of international treaties and organizations? For such arrangements are no more able to support themselves than the laws of any
state would be with neither police nor courts.

In an address at Cambridge at a later time, Sir Austen Chamberlain argued that if one wishes to replace the rule of force with the
rule of law, then one may not act according to one principle today
and another one tomorrow; one must assume a constant attitude and
steer a steady course. But in 1936 neither the French nor British
cabinet was able to face this truth, and — what was still worse — the
great majority of Western Europeans were happy in this cowardice,
not least of all those who were forever mouthing the motto of
"Collective Security." It is therefore no wonder — indeed, given
this state of collective opinion, it was inevitable — that the structure
built at Locarno with such great care and so much creative idealism
collapsed like a house of cards. This was, however, not the fault of
the treaties, but rather that of the men whose holy task it was to
guard those treaties well.

One question does force itself upon us: was the underlying assumption on which Locarno was based valid? This assumption was that an international treaty freely arrived at by both sides would prove more lasting and more reliable than a treaty dictated by one side to another. Hitler, in castigating the "Versailler Diktat," repeatedly and publicly proclaimed that he favored the theory of negotiated treaties — but he endorsed this principle only up to the moment when he felt strong enough to smash it with his fist. And Germans applauded when the Wehrmacht marched into the Rhineland. One must, regrettably, record that the Treaty of Locarno did not stand the test of time. But one must also say that in so far as Germans rejected the principle of this negotiated peace, they have few moral grounds for complaining about "the dictated Treaty of Versailles."

Critics have frequently accused the Locarno treaty of creating two different kinds of international boundaries: the guaranteed borders in the West and the nonguaranteed borders in the East. They argue further that in time of crisis this differential could be construed as an indirect encouragement to attack the nonguaranteed borders. There is something to this line of thought. But, in fact, things worked out quite the other way. The first provision of the treaties to be broken was England's guarantee to preserve the demilitarization of the Rhineland. Only after Hitler had seen that he could carry out this flagrant international crime with utter impunity did he decide to ignore the treaties which prohibited the use of force against his eastern neighbors.

But all this has nothing to do with the criticism which the German Nationalists and the National Socialists hurled at the treaty. Their thesis was that it favored France exclusively and granted Germany nothing in return. Now it is true that the principal purpose of the treaty was to assure French security. But would the Germans have preferred to see this need satisfied by an Anglo-French alliance, the blade of which, as Stresemann quite correctly foresaw, would have been directed at Germany by the very nature of things? And did not Germany receive her full return in England's simultaneous promise to defend her against French aggression? Every German, and the Nationalists most of all, had burned with rage when the French occupied the Ruhr in 1923. Had they forgotten these events so completely by 1925 that they could regard as unimportant a British guarantee which would make a recurrence of this invasion impossible?

There was still another way of looking at the treaties, as Briand sought to explain to his Chamber of Deputies on February 25, 1926, when ratification of Locarno was under debate:

To me the great merit of this document is that it imposes no injury on any of the signatory powers. It has not been drafted and concluded to give any one nation advantages over another. To judge the treaty correctly one must comprehend its true, pervading spirit, and this is not the spirit of narrow, egoistic nationalism. The treaty was drafted and concluded in a European spirit and for the purposes of peace . . . The best thing about it is that it has given the people of Europe confidence once more at a time when everything seemed dark; in an atmosphere beclouded with threats it affords a small glimmer of light to which the people of all nations point their hopes.

The German Nationalists took such words to be mere sentimental declamations. Their thoughts were those of Seeckt, who observed during the conference at Locarno that "reconciliation can mean only victory for our enemies." [78] And yet even General von Rabenau, Seeckt's biographer, was forced to admit that Locarno marked the beginning of a perceptible relaxation: "One cannot deny that Locarno had some immediate beneficial consequences." [79] In Germany, as in the West, people breathed more freely now and dared to hope that peace would be preserved and that in place of mutual, hostile baiting an inclination toward compromise, toward reconciliation, toward cooperation, would gradually fill the European scene. Germany certainly profited economically from Locarno. Her spiritual benefits depended, of course, primarily on the extent to which interparty strife would let her catch her breath and attain domestic tranquillity.

It was typical of the nationalistic opposition that it concentrated its criticism of the treaties on their "subsequent effects." In other words, the advantages that accrued to Germany were treated as unimportant or nonexistent so long as other favors, to which the treaties has given her no legal claim, were denied her. Now these efforts to shorten the period of occupation specified at Versailles, to lighten the costs borne by the German people for their own occupation, and the like were completely legitimate. The Western powers indicated as much in making many, quite significant concessions. But German nationalists called each of these insufficient and, having acknowledged their receipt, demanded further concessions which they knew perfectly well the Allies would not grant because of nationalistic pressures in the West. No wonder, then, that the French said if one gives the Germans one artichoke leaf, they regard that more as an appetizer than a treat and immediately demand another.

The dissident public opinion that German Rightists were provoking embarrassed Luther's government, which was further weakened by the very measures it took to counteract this agitation. For instance, when the Allied concessions were announced, the government informed the German press that it was disappointed in these subsequent effects, while, in truth, as Stresemann noted, "they had exceeded our fondest expectations." On this point there was clearly a difference between the Chancellor and his foreign minister, a difference which, as late as London, had provoked "a violent argument" between the two because Luther wished, in his address, to make a "reference to the [continued] occupation of the Rhineland" while omitting any reference to the spirit of Locarno.[80]

Most important of the Allies' concessions was the evacuation of the Cologne Zone. The Germans regarded this move as the fulfillment — the tardy fulfillment — of a right granted them by the Versailles treaty. The Allies, however, had countered this thesis with the invincible argument that Germany, by failing to meet her requirements for disarmament, had postponed the time at which the periods of occupation specified at Versailles had, de jure, begun. Regardless of one's personal views on this legal debate, it was clearly a concession on the Allies' part to evacuate the zone in spite of their knowledge that German disarmament had *not* been carried out.

That Germany was not disarming, but rather rearming, at the time, is so generally realized today that it may suffice here simply to offer a few quotations from Rabenau's biography of General Seeckt. The reader is told, for instance, that in 1924 Seeckt accepted "as a point of general knowledge . . . the fact that the Reichswehr's forces-in-being were slowly exceeding their legal limits." In June 1924, when the German government was obliged to permit another control inspection, Seeckt was enraged because, again according to Rabenau, "it was not at all easy for Seeckt to conceal from the Allies the increasingly evident signs of the Army's illegal growth." And we are told that Seeckt's opposition to the entire "spirit of Locarno" was based on his realization "that it would gravely jeopardize the whole undercover reconstruction of the Reichswehr." But as early as 1926, Rabenau assures us, "Seeckt made the first moves to free himself from [the constrictions of] the Treaty of Versailles in preparation for the time when the Inter-Allied Commission of Military Control would be gone." And in triumph Rabenau reports that the enemy constantly tried "to lift the veil that obscured the training of our general staff — but always in vain."[81]

On the other hand, there can be no doubt that the governments of the Western powers knew that Germany had no intention to disarm. The last general control inspection had made that point perfectly clear. Only an extract of the commission's report was published, but in November 1933, the first year of Hitler's regime, the British General Morgan, who had read the original, addressed the following words to the London *Times*:

I am not going to be drawn into a disclosure of what the Commission did in fact report unless and until I am officially requested to do so. I will content myself with stating that if and when the British and French Governments decide to publish the Final Report, and particularly the earlier reports of the Effectives Sub-Commission, the whole world will be convinced that Germany *never was disarmed, never intended to disarm*, and for seven years did everything in her power to obstruct, deceive, and "counter-control" the Commission whose duty it was to disarm her.[82]

In other words, the governments of the former Entente powers had been operating with open eyes when they reduced and finally abolished the military controls designed to ensure the execution of the disarmament provisions of Versailles. [83]

At any event the evacuation of the Cologne Zone was preceded by an exchange, between the Allied Conference of Ambassadors and the German government, of voluminous notes concerning previous shortcomings in German disarmament and their redress. On some points the ambassadors gave way; on others they required a strict fulfillment of treaty obligations. In particular they insisted that the direct authority (*Befehlsgewalt*) of the Army chief of staff over military forces be abolished.[84] Seeckt had opposed this plan with all his energy, and he was extremely angry at Stresemann for having yielded the point. But in reality the Allies achieved little more than verbal satisfaction through this move. Rabenau tells us as much with the words: "But this abolition of direct command was a formal matter only. For Seeckt's powers of administrative authority [*Kommandogewalt*] — in contrast to those of direct command — had not been abolished . . . In effect everything was still the same. The Army hardly noticed the change in Seeckt's official position . . . And Seeckt's behavior did not change one bit." [85] One did not have to be a prophet to be able to predict that.

Nevertheless the Allies declined to press for a military control of German disarmament. They wished instead to make a visible display of the "spirit of Locarno." On November 8, 1925, Briand informed Stresemann through the French chargé d'affairs in Berlin that he intended not only to evacuate Cologne but also to exclude the control commission from any further role in negotiations. The commission, he explained, had the simple task of overseeing the execution of measures already decided upon; with them its activities would end. And indeed, after a few more months of twilight existence, the commission was disbanded by the Conference of Ambassadors on December 12, 1926.[86]

Thus in the realm of military affairs, where the Germans were so sensitive, the Allies were prepared to give them a clear and visible sign of how much their policies had changed since the days of Versailles, of ultimata, and of the occupation of the Ruhr. This was indeed a gesture of magnanimous statesmanship. But did it have to be accomplished through the complete abolition of military controls? Would it not have been wiser to raise — and continue to police — the legal limit of 100,000 men, a number which every reasonable French and British statesman of the time knew to be insufficient and hence untenable in practice?

By abandoning their control over German rearmament, the Allies set the creators of the new Reichswehr free to experiment in all the forms of armament which filled the next few years. And for this they bear before the tribunal of history a share of the responsibility for those subsequent developments which brought to the peoples of the West fully as much suffering as they did to the Germans.

II

ADMISSION TO THE LEAGUE OF NATIONS, THE TREATY WITH RUSSIA, AND A CONVERSATION AT THOIRY

LUTHER and Stresemann were scarcely back from London when, on December 5, 1925, the Chancellor kept his promise and handed Hindenburg his and his entire cabinet's resignations. The President charged him with the maintenance of an interim government until a new one could be formed.

But what was this new government to look like? Only one thing was certain and that was purely negative: the German Nationalists would have to be excluded. But then a majority government would be possible only if the moderate parties — the People's Party, the Center, and the Democrats — were to unite with the Social Democrats, thus re-establishing the Great Coalition as it had existed before the Social Democratic ministers left Stresemann's cabinet in 1923. Such a government would enjoy the same strong majority with which the Reichstag had ratified the Locarno treaty. But was it a possibility now? Were not too many domestic issues in the way? Hindenburg proceeded in a strictly constitutional manner, conferring first with party leaders and then asking Fehrenbach and, after he declined, Koch-Weser to try to form a government on the base of the Great Coalition.

Koch, as leader of the Democratic Party, considered it wise to construct a platform which he thought all other potential parties to the coalition would approve. But here he was only partly successful, for his welfare plank proved an object of partisan dispute. The legal limitation of the working day, for instance, provoked sharp differences between the Social Democrats, who demanded a restoration of the eight-hour day, and the German People's Party. Another bone of contention was the matter of settlements for the former German princes, of which more will be said below. Actually it was the Social Democrats who ruined Koch-Weser's efforts to form a government. The leaders of the People's Party, at a meeting held on December 17, announced that in spite of some misgivings they were prepared to accept Koch-Weser's platform. The Social Democrats, however, declared that they considered it no proper base for the establishment of a new government. Thereupon Koch reported his failure to Hindenburg and the hope of another Great Coalition — indeed, of a cabinet representing a majority in the Reichstag — was temporarily dashed. There remained nothing else to do but fashion another minority government.

Thus, the Social Democrats' decision was of enormous significance. It had been preceded by vigorous intraparty struggles, in which Carl Severing and Dr. Eduard David, among others, had pressed hard in favor of joining the coalition.[1] One must agree that the party's decision was a difficult one to make. To the German worker the eight-hour day was more than a clause in the welfare plank: it was an article of faith. Then too, the level of national economic activity had begun to sink, while in December the number of unemployed — quite low in the summer of 1925 — exceeded one million for the first time in German history.[2] It was apparent that the Communists, who were trying to win labor votes from the Social Democrats, would employ the most vicious tactics against the latter if they were to join a government that did not swear by the eight-hour day. But, as Severing and his friends saw all too well, the real question was not one of welfare policy, however important that may have been: the survival of German parliamentary government and, with it, of the Republic was at stake.

Until the German Nationalists resigned, Luther's former government had enjoyed a majority in the Reichstag. And even after the Nationalists jumped ship, the Social Democrats had ensured continued parliamentary support of Stresemann's foreign policies. For his policies were still hotly contested, and the Social Democrats, who strongly supported his goals — especially Germany's admission to the League, on which all the Locarno treaties depended — found themselves forced to assume a share of the legislative responsibility for them. Now a small party can perhaps afford the luxury of remaining outside a government, lending it support only in critical emergencies, but not one with millions of voters and more than one hundred Reichstag seats. Minority cabinets deny the very essence of parliamentary government.

When Article 54 of the Weimar constitution required that the national government enjoy the confidence of the Reichstag, it was only stating a corollary of parliamentary rule. And since, under the political circumstances prevailing in Germany at that time, only coalition governments were possible, no party could reasonably expect to see its program put into action without compromise and change. *Each* party to a coalition government had to make sacrifices when it entered. And any party that was unready to make its sacrifice at the critical hour helped ruin the prestige of the Reichstag and, thus, of the entire political system. Such fear of responsibility is the mortal sin in a parliamentary state. In the end it leads not only to an exclusion of the dissenting party from the councils of state, but also to an improper redistribution of responsibility and power among the organs of constitutional government. For the power which the Reichstag found itself unable to wield passed by necessity into the hands of the *President*, who was empowered by the constitution to select the Chancellor and his ministers (Article 53).

The solution of the crisis at hand quickly made this clear. After Koch returned his commission, Hindenburg waited until after Christmas before trying again. Then, on January 11, 1926, he summoned both Fehrenbach and Koch and gave them three days to bring the question of another Great Coalition to a final decision. On January 13, when they reported that the continued refusal of the Social Democrats made further efforts useless, Hindenburg on his own responsibility charged the former Chancellor, Hans Luther, with the formation of another cabinet. This meant another so-called "bourgeois" government. Yet difficulties arose even here, and so on January 19 the President had to summon the leaders of the four relevant parties — the German People's Party, the Center, the Bavarian People's Party, and the Democratic Party — and give them, through Luther, their ultimatum. This time they had until ten o'clock that same evening. "I beseech the parties represented here," he said, "to place their private, partisan interests behind those of the fatherland and to make whatever sacrifices prove necessary to bring an end to this saddening spectacle of eternal governmental crisis and to bring about, instead, the possibility of that fruitful cooperation which is more critically necessary now than ever before."

And, indeed, a government was formed, but not before another significant episode had occurred. For his minister of interior Luther had had in mind Erich Koch-Weser, leader of the Democrats in the Reichstag. Koch had filled this post before, in 1920. But the Bavarian People's Party protested the appointment, saying that Koch was too much in favor of a strong central government. So Luther, who

wished to have — indeed had to have — the Bavarians in his government, yielded. The Democrats, not without good reason, took this
as an offense and their delegation came within *one* vote of leaving
the government. Koch himself cast the determining ballot, having
enough self-control and insight to place the common interest above
his personal pride.

Thus, on January 19, 1926, after a crisis of six weeks, Luther's
second cabinet was formed. Stresemann naturally kept the Foreign
Ministry; Gessler, who at first had declined, retained the Defense
Ministry; and Brauns, that of Labor. From the People's Party Curtius assumed control of the Ministry of Economics; from the Center
Marx was given the Ministry of Justice. The Democrats also received
the two important Ministries of Interior and of Finance: the
Reichstag delegate Wilhelm Külz, previously mayor of Dresden,
became minister of interior while the former Saxon minister of finance, Peter Reinhold, now assumed the national portfolio.

It was inevitable that the course and denouement of this crisis
should strengthen the authority of the President at the expense of
the Reichstag. Political parties had never enjoyed a very high reputation in the minds of the German populace. But now they had fallen
even lower. People said that the politicians could not even agree
upon a government. But Hindenburg — he got things done! And
with this observation the Germans took the first step toward their
doom. The Social Democrats were directly responsible for this development, yet they could only suffer from it. The basic reason
for their failure to contribute more effectively to German parliamentary government lay in their inability to free themselves from the
old notions of class struggle, although their own development had
long since opened their eyes to broader, more advanced political
goals. Then too, their fusion with the Independents had increased
the importance of those delegates who were always looking anxiously to the Left.

So far as the Social Democrats' prospects were concerned, it
was certainly no improvement to have Luther, whom they dis-
trusted, as their Chancellor, in place of Koch-Weser, in whom they
had personal confidence. To be sure, they had reason to believe that
they could always chase Luther from office if he should wander too
far to the Right. But that would only mean another governmental
crisis, and with every crisis the people's respect for their Reichstag
and their parties melted further. In short, Severing was quite right
when he wrote: "In the course of such a lengthy absence from governmental affairs the Social Democrats were bound finally to lose
close touch with national problems and all influence upon the na-

tional administration. Yet administering laws is often fully as important as writing them." [3] Insight into this simple truth was made obscure to many Social Democrats by the fact that they had considerable influence upon the government and administration of Germany's largest state, Prussia, and many of her larger cities. But they were to learn how terribly wrong they were in thinking that these posts outweighed the national power which they were yielding by default.

Luther presented his cabinet to the Reichstag on January 27, at which time the Chancellor found himself obliged to use rather sharp language, especially with Count Westarp. When, in the course of this exchange, Luther remarked that "after all, Germany must be governed somehow," he was answered with "great merriment" from the distinguished chamber. But his words were as true as they were banal. For essentially he was only repeating the words that Wellington had spoken some hundred years before: "The King's government must be carried on." And it might well have been better for Germany if many a German politician had been constantly reminded of the wisdom of this commonplace. The political confusion of the time can be seen in the vote of confidence which Luther and his entire cabinet had demanded. It was passed by all of ten votes — 160 to 150 — while 130 Social Democrats abstained. The opposition consisted of German Nationalists, Racists, and Communists. Luther had come within a hair of being voted down. And how would things have looked for Social Democracy then?

It was only natural that foreign policy should play a large role in the debate. In this discussion the delegate Major Henning, formerly an officer on the General Staff and more recently a deserter from the German Nationalists to the Racists, called the cabinet "assassins of their own people," whereupon Luther sprang to his feet and "quite vehemently" protested such an insult. Even the German Nationalists dissociated themselves clearly from Henning's attack, but the incident does show the extremes to which demagogic agitation against Locarno and Stresemann had led. With such insults reechoing in the Reichstag, it is no wonder that some verbal tinkerer came out with the rhyme, "Stresemann, verwese man" (Stresemann, drop dead), and sought to enlist assistance for his assassination with the slogan: "The pig must be slaughtered" (*Das Schwein muss gekillt werden*)! [4] More significant, however, was Hugenberg's article in his *Lokalanzeiger* of January 9, 1926, about the "alleged" plans to assassinate Stresemann. He argued that one should not make martyrs out of people, least of all those who had not earned such a distinguished fate and "whose political star was fading anyway." For

"Stresemann was an example of the errors of the post-Bismarck, ante-bellum generation, which had ripened from its prewar blossoms to its present harvest and therefore — one had reason to hope — would soon fade away." [5] I repeat this nonsense here solely because its author was subsequently to exert a critical influence on the fate of Germany.

Stresemann did not lose his way along the path that he had taken at Locarno. The next step had to be Germany's entrance into the League of Nations. The Reichstag Committee on Foreign Affairs approved the step February 3, 1926, by a vote of 18 to 8, just two days after the evacuation of the Cologne Zone had been completed. Throughout Germany people were stirred by the realization that "great and holy Cologne with its great and mighty minster," the object of so many sentiments and memories, had once again become a free and German city. Even the Nationalists had to admit that this was a visible result of Locarno. But for the most part de Margerie unfortunately was right when he told Stresemann on February 4 that he had often heard the Germans say that this concession or that one would make a great impression on their nation, yet often the impression disappeared as soon as the concession was granted.[6]

And even so pacific a man as Briand found it necessary to inform the German foreign minister that he found it most unpleasant to see that all the concessions made by the Allies counted for naught, while all the German demands which had not yet been met were considered of critical importance.[7] He could justly claim to comprehend the difficulties in which the German government found itself; indeed this comprehension served as the very basis of his request that Stresemann give some consideration to the difficulties which he, Briand, had to face in France. It is true that many relaxations of the occupation did not occur as swiftly as the Germans desired — and perhaps had good reason to desire. This was true, for example, of the reduction of troops in the second and third zones of occupation. But this was precisely one of those issues on which Briand had to proceed with special care — not only with respect to French public opinion but especially with regard to the French officer corps. For the generals of France were convinced that, whatever their colleagues across the Rhine were up to, it was anything but disarmament.

On February 10, 1926, the Secretary-General of the League of Nations, Sir Eric Drummond (later Lord Perth), received Stresemann's note requesting in the name of his government that Germany be admitted to the League. The note made reference to previous exchanges concerning the Germans' request for a permanent seat in

the Council of the League. Their claim had encountered no objection
in the past nor was there any opposition at this time. But several
other powers did seize this opportunity to make their own demands
for permanent Council seats.

According to the original Covenant (Article 4), the Council
consisted of representatives of the principal Allies and Associated
Powers, that is, Great Britain, France, Italy, and Japan, together
with representatives of four other members of the League.[8] In 1922
the number of this latter group was raised to six. While the places
of the first group were, by their very nature, permanent, the other
members of the Council were to be chosen by election at regular
intervals. But in fact no such election had been held for quite some
time. And three powers, Belgium, Brazil, and Spain, had kept their
technically temporary seats since 1920.

It was generally understood that the seat Germany was requesting on the Council belonged to the first, or explicitly permanent,
group. The acquisition of such a seat would have made Germany a
peer among four of her former foes. And, indeed, a commentary on
the Covenant that was published by the British government in 1919
made clear the Allies' intent to grant both Germany and Russia such
permanent seats if and when they should become members of the
League. There was, therefore, no dispute upon this point.

But now a number of other members of the League declared
that if Germany was going to get a permanent seat in the Council
they should get theirs too. And since an enlargement of the Council
required a unanimous vote in the League Assembly, any country
which felt its claims were not being satisfied could block Germany's
admission.

The Germans were especially shocked to learn that Poland demanded a permanent Council seat and that her claim was being
vigorously supported by the French press. Indeed, many people
maintained that the Poles' request had been initiated by nationalistic newspapers in France. [9] On the other hand, it was significant
that British public opinion reacted very critically to the growing
feeling that Chamberlain had promised his country's support to a
Spanish quest for a permanent seat.[10]

From the French and Polish point of view the Polish candidacy
was easy to understand. There were many areas of German-Polish
dispute, and both the Poles and the French assumed that Germany
would use her new Council seat to press her claims with special emphasis. This had, indeed, been Stresemann's firm intent, and he
cannot have been surprised by his neighbors' conclusion that Poland
should be enabled to defend her interests from the same vantage

point if the duel were to be fought with equal weapons. Further-more, the French wished to be freed from the constant duty of tend-ing Poland's interests in her absence, for this task was forever em-broiling them in quarrels with the Germans.

The German position was equally understandable: the Reich had been promised one of five permanent seats, and that was more valuable than one of six or perhaps eight temporary places. For it meant that Germany was once more recognized as a great power. No German was prepared to see the Poles granted such a status. Yet the Germans went too far when they began to accuse the signers of Locarno, Briand and Chamberlain in particular, of playing false with them. For it was clear that the Allies had not foreseen this com-plication any better than had the Wilhelmstrasse. On the other hand, it is certainly true that the question of enlarging the Council had been discussed within the League for several years, and it was both astonishing and disturbing to have it brought to a head in such close connection with Germany's admission, an event which the en-tire League had hoped to see.

A special meeting of the Assembly had been scheduled in Geneva for March 8, at which time Germany was to be formally admitted to the League. Luther and Stresemann attended as German representa-tives. Again, as the British ambassador observed, their moods were entirely different: "Luther rather troubled and anxious about the outlook; Stresemann in high spirits, preparing for a long sleep in the train, with a bottle of good wine under his arm." [11]

But this time, unfortunately, Luther's pessimism was more justi-fied than Stresemann's optimism. The first bad omen was the aston-ishing news they learned upon arriving in Geneva: Briand had just been voted out of office — on a financial issue — by the French as-sembly. He was, nevertheless, on the scene Sunday afternoon, March 7, in order to take part in a preliminary conference among the Locarno powers. For both Briand and Chamberlain had come to Geneva firmly resolved to maintain the bonds between the signers of Locarno no matter what might happen at the meeting of the League.

The meeting that Sunday afternoon showed that the statesmen's task was not as simple as had seemed. Briand, Chamberlain, Luther, and Stresemann presented their separate views on the question of increasing the number of Council seats, and they found that their opinions differed sharply. Stresemann introduced still another ele-ment of tension when he stated with emphasis: "I wish to make it clear that, if Germany's admission is made conditional upon an in-crease in permanent Council seats, Germany might well retract her request for admission." [12] He probably felt obliged to make this statement because on February 18 the Reichstag's Committee on Foreign Affairs had resolved to approve Germany's entering the League only if the Council were to remain as it was. But at this particular moment at this particular place Stresemann's declaration could have only an extremely negative effect. Fortunately he quickly noticed what he had done and sought to correct the impression he had made by assuming a more tactful attitude, contenting himself with the formal observation that Germany could have no opinions on questions of the League's constitution so long as she was not a member. Later, of course, she would be ready to make concessions concerning even the enlargement of the Council. Thus, while Stresemann gave the Western powers reason for some hope, he offered them no base for immediate action. That same evening Briand returned to Paris to form his eighth cabinet; he could tell himself that at least things had not been completely ruined yet.

At the same time the issue was becoming increasingly complex within the League itself. Along with Poland, Brazil and Spain now demanded permanent seats in the Council, while Sweden's Minister Undén declared that his country opposed any enlargement of the Council beyond the addition of Germany. To this the representative from Brazil announced that he would oppose Germany's admission unless his country's claim to a permanent seat were satisfied.

During these discussions, in which, of course, Germany did not take part, Chamberlain and Briand — who had returned on March 11 — were engaged in constant negotiations with Luther and Stresemann in search of a compromise. But the Germans were not to be moved. At first they were supported in this stand by many of the neutral nations. And as a result, in all likelihood, of the efforts of Chamberlain and Briand, Sweden and Czechoslovakia declared their willingness to yield their seats on the Council in order that Poland and, as a counterweight, Holland might be elected in their — temporary — places. Finally the Germans were offered a compromise which asked of them only that after their admission to the League they not oppose an increase in the number of temporary seats within the Council. This agreement would have left them free to vote against whichever candidates — such as Poland — they pleased.[13] But the German delegates continued to insist that their country be admitted unconditionally and without any assurances for the future just as they thought they had been promised at Locarno.

Their reply was in complete accord with the legal position which Germany had assumed from the beginning. But there is a point where the legalistic defense of one's rights becomes pedantic bickering. This point, according to neutral observers, had now been reached. That the delegates' attitude toward Germany had now shifted completely was evident in the Bavaria Bar, where representatives of the world press regularly met with the diplomats. As it turned out, the Germans could have accepted the compromise with no harm to their position; for Brazil — or rather its dictator, Bernardes — assumed an utterly intransigent position with respect to a permanent Council seat. In his vanity he was even willing to incur the odium of threatening the whole structure of peace on which the hopes of the entire world hung.

But in this moment of danger it became apparent that the foundations for peace were too firmly established to be shaken by the winds of legalistic argumentation. The open meeting of the Assembly at which the issue was to be decided had been called for March 17, and scarcely a hope remained that Germany would be admitted. It was under these circumstances that Briand and Chamberlain called a meeting on March 16 of the Locarno powers in the hope of finding a way to salvage at least the kernel of their plans. "Unfortunately," Briand explained, "we shall have to postpone Germany's admission until the September meeting, but we dare not let this delay endanger the fruits of Locarno." And at his suggestion the Locarno powers passed a resolution stating that they were on the verge of reaching agreement on the question of Germany's admission to the League; that they regretted being unable to reach their goal at this time; but that "they are happy to recognize that the work for peace which they had realized at Locarno . . . remains intact. They remain attached to it today as yesterday and are firmly resolved to work together to maintain and develop it." [14] Thus spoke the representatives of Germany, Great Britain, France, Belgium, and Italy.

Even the negative results of the League Assembly meeting the following day could not shake the Locarno powers' resolve. [15] After the Brazilian representative had cast his veto, Chamberlain, speaking for the appropriate committee, declared that Germany had fulfilled all the conditions for her admission but that a formal vote on her request to join the League would have to be postponed until September. [16] And once again it was Briand who showed his unique ability to find warm words with which to praise the Germans' recent conduct and to express his firm expectation that a final solution to the impasse could be found. His motion to this effect was accepted unanimously.

But neither glowing words nor fine gestures could obscure the fact that the Germans had suffered at least a temporary setback, for which, however, they could not be entirely blamed. The only positive result of this Assembly meeting was the establishment of a study commission charged with the task of finding a solution to the question of the Council seats. Germany was invited to become a member of this group.

On March 22 the Reichstag opened an extended debate on foreign policy. The German Nationalists painted the scene in deepest black and demanded the retraction of Germany's request for admission to the League. One of their speakers was Admiral von Tirpitz, a typical representative of "the errors of the post-Bismarck, antebellum generation," to use Hugenberg's phrase. He was particularly angry about the Locarno powers' communiqué of March 17, seeing in it the danger that the German foreign policy would decline "into complete dependence on France." The German Nationalists' resolution of no confidence failed by a vote of 200 to 141, and the government won the Reichstag's formal consent to keep to the same course in foreign affairs. On April 15, therefore, the cabinet accepted the League's invitation that a German serve on the study commission.

But a few days earlier de Margerie, the French ambassador in Berlin, had sought out his British colleague, Lord d'Abernon, opening their conversation with the excited query: "What do you think of the German-Russian agreement?" In response to the Englishman's doubting interjection, de Margerie told him that the German ambassador in Paris, von Hoesch, had officially informed Briand that the German government intended to sign a pact with Russia before the month was out. Now d'Abernon had been informed that such negotiations were in the air, but he did not realize they had taken such firm shape. He guessed — correctly — that Stresemann himself had not expected such quick results.

Russian pressures on Stresemann had not let up even after the conclusion of the Locarno treaties. In December 1925 Chicherin was in Berlin again, where he had another conversation with the German foreign minister. Again Stresemann tried to convince him, this time with respect to negotiations at Locarno, that his fears of an English conspiracy against Russia were ill-founded.[17] Of course these efforts were in vain, for it was a basic rule of Russian diplomacy never to abandon a position once it had been assumed. And that same December Stalin, who had begun to come to the fore, termed Locarno simply a repetition and reinforcement of Versailles in an address to the Communist Party Congress in Moscow.[18] To all these blandishments Stresemann had steadily replied that he intended —

indeed, desired — to come to an agreement with Russia, but only *after* Germany's admission to the League, which it had promised at Locarno, had been accomplished.

Then came the great debacle of Geneva. It was, of course, greeted with jubilation in Moscow. In early April Chicherin published a triumphant statement in *Izvestia*, taunting the Germans with the observation that now they saw what came from sacrificing the advancement of friendly relations with Russia in favor of a so-called westward orientation which really meant union with the victors of Versailles. "In place of the firm international structure in which Germany had hoped to find a corner for herself, nothing is left but a heap of ruins." If the Locarno powers had not even been able to push through the simple formality of a country's admission to the League of Nations, what help could Germany expect of them when more serious matters were at stake? [19]

Stresemann had wished to wait until September, at which time he hoped Germany's admission to the League would be effected. But the Russians in Berlin made it clear that, if agreement were not reached immediately, they would regard former assurances as void and resume their full freedom of action.[20] And all this time politicians of various persuasions, from the Right all the way in to the People's Party, were calling for a treaty with Russia. On March 11, 1926, that is, while negotiations were under way in Geneva, *Izvestia* was able to publish an interview with several German party leaders who unanimously declared themselves in favor of an agreement with the Russians.[21] Among these was Dr. Ernst Scholz, the People's Party leader in the Reichstag — another sign of the way Stresemann's own party created problems for him.

In this situation Stresemann did not believe it prudent to resist further. Every statesman finds it necessary to balance a defeat in one area with a victory in another, and he had no doubt that a pact with Russia would be regarded as a success in Germany. But he took careful pains to keep the treaty free of anything which could be taken as a blow at the Locarno treaties or as a hindrance to Germany's admission to the League. Furthermore, as we have seen, he exercised the caution of notifying the French and British governments before the treaty had finally been concluded.

The London *Times* made a special point of Stresemann's discretion when, on April 14, the day before Germany announced her acceptance of the League's invitation to serve on the study commission, it broke the news of the forthcoming treaty. Briand and Chamberlain considered it best not to take too tragically something they could not forfend, hoping thus to keep it from appearing a defeat for the Western powers. Of course their discretion did not keep the Russians from celebrating the treaty as a triumph of Soviet foreign policy. On April 24, 1926, the day the pact was signed, Litvinov delivered a speech before the Executive Committee of his party, expressing his supreme satisfaction with the outcome of the negotiations. He explained that the Russians did not care whether the treaty accorded with the so-called "Spirit of Locarno." But if, as they had always believed, one of the aims of Locarno had been the creation of a united front against Russia and the country's isolation, then the new treaty most certainly did contradict the Spirit of Locarno, and the Russians could congratulate themselves for having robbed Locarno of its anti-Soviet sting.[22]

This new treaty consisted of only four articles. The first stated that the Treaty of Rapallo remained the basis of Russo-German relations. To this, however, was added the statement that the two governments would remain "in friendly relations" with each other "in order to promote the solution of all questions, both political and economic, which concerned their countries." By way of expansion on this point Stresemann made clear in a note which he directed to Krestinski, and to which Krestinski acknowledged his agreement, that the main purpose of Soviet-German reconciliation was to help maintain the general peace. The second article of the treaty pledged either party to neutrality in the event that the other, "despite its peaceful behavior," should be attacked by one or more powers. According to the third article, neither party was to join in any coalition for the purpose of an economic or financial boycott of the other. Stresemann's note to Krestinski took pains to explain that these pledges conflicted neither with Germany's joining the League of Nations nor with Articles 16 and 17 of the League's Covenant. Krestinski limited his reply to a simple acknowledgement that he had noted the German explanations. The fourth article set the treaty's duration at five years.

This could all mean very much or very little, depending on the policies pursued by the two contracting parties and the use they made of the treaty in this pursuit. In Germany the treaty was received with almost universal acclamation. On April 27 the Reichstag Committee on Foreign Affairs, generally the scene of sharp clashes of opinion, gave it unanimous approval. Some members voted for it because it conflicted with neither Locarno nor Germany's admission to the League; others, because they regarded it as a counterbalance to Locarno. (See, for example, the speech of delegate Hoetzsch in the Reichstag meeting of June 10.)

And so Stresemann's position was restrengthened and he could look forward with confidence to the September meeting of the League. But before that meeting was held, domestic troubles shook the Reich again.

Chief among German domestic issues in the first half of 1926 was the disposition of the fortunes of the former ruling princes. In the winter of 1918–19, when the federated German principalities turned themselves into republics, the people and their elected representatives in the several Landtags had, as a rule, not the slightest disposition to invade the private rights of their deposed rulers. Only a few especially radical Landtags and land governments, such as the Communist-Socialist regime in Gotha, engaged in confiscation without compensation. The Weimar constitution put an end to such practices by ensuring the rights of private property in Article 153, permitting the exercise of the lands' rights of eminent domain only when accompanied by payment of proper damages. The Gotha measures were therefore found unconstitutional by the German Supreme Court and annulled.

But in the final analysis the issue of the princes' claims could not be left to the courts for decisions under the rules of private property. In this matter political and legal elements were all too intertwined. Much that the princes claimed as private property belonged by its very nature to the lands and had come to be considered a part of princely fortunes as a result of purely fortuitous circumstances. The smaller lands especially, like those in Thuringia, were simply not in a position to compensate their former princes to the full measure required by civil law. Furthermore, it must have seemed to make little political sense for the new lands to outfit the princes — who, after all, were the born enemies of the Republic — with astronomic fortunes which they could then put to use against the new Germany.

In some individual instances, especially in the South, the question was settled in a friendly manner. In others, particularly in Prussia, all efforts failed. In consequence of these difficulties the national government sought to achieve order through a national law. But these efforts also were denied success, yielding only a Law of Suspension (*Sperrgesetz*) in February 1926, according to which any suit concerning such a claim could be postponed until the enactment of a relevant national law.

But within the German nation there was another movement afoot, one which wished to cut this Gordian knot in the simplest way; namely, through the uncompensated expropriation of the former princes and their families. The Communists proposed this first, in November 1925. Their petition was rejected by the Reichstag, but the petitioners' store of weapons was by no means exhausted. For the Weimar constitution had, after all, opened the way to direct legislation by the people (Article 73 and the Referendum Law of June 27, 1921). The operation consisted of several steps. First the petitioners had to present, in final form, the measure they were proposing. Then those voters who supported this "popular demand" had to sign official petitions. If more than one-tenth the total qualified electorate supported the popular demand in this way, then the national government was obliged to present the proposed measure to the Reichstag, making clear at the same time its attitude toward the bill. If the Reichstag rejected the proposal, it would become the subject of a referendum. According to Article 75 of the constitution a referendum was effective only if a majority of qualified voters took part. Since the electorate at this time numbered some forty million, the Communists had to bring over twenty million Germans to the polls if they were to push their petition through to law. For their opponents would express their point of view most simply — and most effectively — by staying home.

Now in the Reichstag elections of December 1924 the Communists had received somewhat more than 2,700,000 votes. In the presidential election of 1925 Thälmann had not even won 2,000,000 votes. From the very beginning, therefore, it was clearly impossible for the Communists to get some twenty million voters to support a referendum they were proposing. But this fact was in no wise important to them. The expropriation of the princes was a delightfully inflammatory issue. Furthermore, it could be used to embarrass the Social Democrats. In fact, the Social Democratic leaders, who would really have preferred to pursue a less radical path, found themselves obliged to initiate an identical referendum which in the end was simply joined to the Communists' petition.[23]

In the first stage (March 4–17), the petitioners enjoyed a great success: more than 12,500,000 signatures were obtained; that is, over two million more than the sum of Social Democratic and Communist votes in the last Reichstag election. Many voters must have crossed former party lines to join them now. It is easy, for instance, to conceive of victims of the inflation who saw no reason why the princes should get off better than they. Among them were probably many who had voted for Hindenburg just one year before.

And so the proposed measure came before the Reichstag. Here its demagogic nature was emphasized by the fact that the Racists submitted a supplementary petition calling for the expropriation of the "banking and brokering princes and other national parasites."

On May 6 the Reichstag denied the Socialist-Communist petition by a vote of 236 to 142. The popular vote necessitated by this legislative defeat was then set for June 20.

The referendum was, of course, preceded by an extremely vehement campaign. The National Citizens Council, directed by Friedrich von Loebell, a Prussian minister under William II, became especially prominent. Von Loebell and his associates succeeded in persuading the President to compose a letter in which he called the Leftists' proposal "a most serious threat to the structure of our constitutional state" and "contrary to the axioms of morality and law." Hindenburg went on to point out the future danger "of a deliberate excitement of the baser instincts of the masses and an exploitation of popular distress through such referenda with the aim of depriving the German nation of the necessary bases for cultural, economic, and civil life." [24] Both Hindenburg and the German nation lived to witness the realization of his prophecy. But in 1926 the directors of this later demagogic plundering opposed the expropriation of the princes, and the man who was to put them in positions of power composed this letter of protest.

Von Loebell managed to publish Hindenburg's letter immediately (June 7, 1926) in order to give momentum to his campaign. By this step the President became involved in the partisan skirmishing that attends any impending legislative issue. And so his letter must have raised second thoughts in the minds of even those men who might have agreed with its actual contents. For the Weimar constitution was clear in its intent to keep the President above political parties and untouched by partisan strife. To the extent that this determination could be put into legal terms, it was expressed in Article 50, which required that the Chancellor countersign all presidential orders and decrees. The Democrats made this point well in a statement which Koch-Weser read to the Reichstag on June 10 in the course of the very vigorous debate which had developed on the issue. "The Democratic Party holds firm to Bismarck's axiom that the chief of the German state may appear before the public only in ministerial dress — a rule from which William II departed only on false, irresponsible advice. This limitation on the public utterances of the chief of state is not a demand of democracy, nor of parliamentary government, nor of liberalism; it is a simple requirement of German constitutionalism." [25]

Herr von Loebell was certainly supposed to take this reference to "false and irresponsible advice" personally. But one may well doubt that the admonition was heeded. For once again Hindenburg showed that he preferred to listen to his old friends and the representatives of the defunct Empire — people who spoke his language — rather than to the parliamentarians and politicians whose thought processes he could follow only with the greatest exertion, if at all. One has no reason to doubt Hindenburg's desire to observe the constitution loyally; yet, on the other hand, one dare not close one's eyes to the dangers which his sympathies necessarily entailed.

Loebell's action was particularly objectionable because the referendum had never had any prospect of success. On June 20, 15,500,-000 votes were cast in its favor; and therewith it failed. But to record this defeat is not to say that this number of votes did not constitute a really significant success. These were more votes than Hindenburg had received for president in April 1925; two million more, indeed, than Hitler was to receive in the run-off election for president in 1932, and only four million less than Hindenburg gathered at that time as the choice of all the moderates and the Left (save for the Communists). If one keeps these figures in mind, one can observe not only the often noted inconstancy of the masses, but also — and much more clearly — the fact that in Germany at that time the truly popular mood was one of sheer negation.

There is only one point to be added to the discussion of the princes' fortunes: the national government's proposed law was blocked by resistance from both Right and Left. Since the German Nationalists as well as the Social Democrats opposed the measure, the cabinet withdrew it from debate. This retreat left the separate lands with no choice but to make whatever settlements they could with their former princes. (See, for instance, the Prussian Settlement of October 6, 1926, adopted by the Landtag October 12.) Naturally it was not the lands that profited from this duress. The German Nationalists, of course, were content with this outcome. But what about the Social Democrats?

It is worthy of note that Otto Braun reports how he had to threaten the Social Democrats in the Prussian Landtag with his resignation in order to get them to accept the settlement their government had concluded with the House of Hohenzollern.[26] It is understandable that the Social Democrats found this acceptance hard. But had they not blocked every alternate path themselves when they kept a national law from being passed? And would not that national law have conformed more to the Social Democrats' desires if they had *joined the government*? But instead of this, they had participated in a demagogic scene under the direction of the Communists, in whose success they had never believed and for whose radical excesses at least the reasonable men among them had no sympathy. The Social Democrats' behavior in the matter of settling with the princes serves as a prize example of the tension between their sense of responsibility and their thirst for agitation, between their desire to help secure the Republic and their fear of losing voters in so doing. Their anxiety was strengthened even more by the system of party lists (*Listenwahl-System*),* which had severed the connection between the electorate and their elected representatives, leaving ample room for demagogues between.

While this issue was still the object of the nation's attention, a new crisis was occasioned by the government itself. For on May 5, 1926, a presidential order concerning the use of flags at official German offices abroad appeared over Chancellor Dr. Luther's countersignature.

Now, in addition to the official national colors of black, red, and gold, the Weimar constitution had provided for a merchant ensign of black, white, and red with the national colors in the upper, inner corner (Article 3, Paragraph 2). This was the compromise with which the supporters of the old, imperial colors were supposed to have been reconciled. But they were not reconciled. President Ebert had already issued one order, on September 27, 1919, in execution of this constitutional provision. Hindenburg's order of May 5, 1926, amended and expanded Ebert's.[27] The only part of Hindenburg's order that was of real and political significance was the requirement that German legations and consulates outside of Europe and in European seaports display the merchant ensign, that is, the black, white, and red, alongside the national service flag of black, red, and gold.

Whether this was constitutionally correct was certainly dubious at best. When the Weimar constitution spoke of a "merchant ensign," it meant what the words say: the flag for merchant ships.[28] And the flag which an ambassador flies over his embassy is not and never has been a merchant ensign, whether or not the place of his residence has a harbor.

But whatever one's opinion of the legality of Hindenburg's decree, one is obliged to find it an almost incomprehensible piece of political folly. Anybody even slightly acquainted with the political mood of the time knew that the issue of the flag was a sore spot which no reasonable man would think of touching. Millions of Germans

---

* One of the results of the Republic's proportional representation system was that political parties, in their efforts to gain seats in the Reichstag, drew up long lists of candidates. Many of these political aspirants were totally unknown to the electors, yet the voter had no choice but to vote for the party list in its entirety. Personal contact between candidates and voters was thus rendered virtually impossible. TRANSLATORS.

were gathered under the *Reichsbanner* † of black, red, and gold, while other millions attacked the national colors with the extremists among them engaging in vituperations which centered around objectionable alternatives to the "gold." Supporters of the Republic and of its colors could see in the new decree nothing but an appeasement of those who were promoting the black, white, and red. These were principally the German Nationalists, who had deserted Chancellor Luther over Locarno and were now opposing him most sharply. The decree could only serve to irritate Luther's more faithful supporters, especially the Social Democrats, upon whose votes he was particularly dependent in pursuing his foreign policy. Under these circumstances what possible results could Luther expect of his decree? And yet a part of the responsibility must be borne by the Democrats and Centrists in his cabinet, for they should have warned him against taking such a step.

Many people assumed that Luther had meant to do Hindenburg a favor. The President's sympathy for the black, white, and red was widely known and in no wise held against him so long as he did not let this private loyalty affect his public acts. But this is exactly what his "old comrades" most likely wanted when they filled the Old Gentleman's ears with their complaints and vicious remarks about the Republic. Severing, who became officially involved in these affairs as minister of interior, tells of several official ceremonies at which Hindenburg expressed his distaste for the Republic's colors in a manner at times so coarse that Severing found himself obliged to tell him firmly that the national colors were black, red, and *gold* and not black, red, and *yellow*. The general impression that the President had been the real author of the decree was strengthened further by a letter he sent the Chancellor for publication on May 9, 1926. In it Hindenburg insisted that he had not the slightest intention of altering the national colors as determined by the constitution; on the other hand, he implied that the public arguments concerning his decree had shown "how threatening and dangerous to our people the unresolved question of the colors has become."

If Luther had thought to quiet his critics by publishing this letter, he was mistaken. The storm exploded in the Reichstag on May 11, when Dr. Breitscheid accompanied a Social Democratic inter-

---

† The *Reichsbanner Schwarz-Rot-Gold* was a paramilitary volunteer formation loyal to the Weimar Republic. It had been formed as a counterweight both to the volunteer formations of the Left, such as the Red Front Fighters' League, and to the dozens of Rightist-sponsored groups such as the *Stahlhelm*, the *Schutz und Trutzbund*, Ernst Röhm's *Reichskriegsflagge*, Hermann Ehrhardt's *Viking Bund,* and Adolf Hitler's Storm Troops. TRANSLATORS.

pellation with an impassioned speech which bespoke the nationalistic student he once had been as well as the party leader he had
become. Luther, in his reply, failed completely to find the right tone
to calm his opponents. One can do full justice to Luther's many material achievements in government finance and economics and still
report that he seemed almost completely indifferent to the Republic
and its symbols. And, at least at that time, the Germans did not wish
to put up with such indifference on the part of the Chancellor of
the Reich, of all people. Koch-Weser, leader of the Democrats in the
Reichstag, finished Luther off with a motion which, to be sure, approved the intention the President had expressed of settling the flag
question in a conciliatory fashion, but which also went on to condemn the attitude of the Chancellor, "who through his behavior in
the matter of the flag . . . made any final solution . . . more difficult and who, in these troubled times, gratuitously kindled a new
conflict." This motion of no confidence was adopted by 176 votes to
146. The German Nationalists abstained.

Of course Luther had no choice but to resign (May 12). His political career was finished, although the Republic would later make
use of his talents in other ways. After his fall he remarked to a party
leader: "I do not understand how they could put a government out
of office on account of such a bagatelle." To which he received the
apt retort: "That's exactly why." [29]

And so once more the President had to find a new chancellor.
He turned first to Gessler, who now was the senior minister and in
whose political expertise Hindenburg had special confidence. But
after two days Gessler declared himself unable to form a cabinet.
Evidently on his advice, Konrad Adenauer, mayor of Cologne and
close to the Center, was summoned to Berlin.[30] Adenauer hoped to
establish another government of the Great Coalition, but he too
returned his commission after a conversation with Scholz had convinced him that the People's Party would not participate.

Then the President charged the leader of the Center, Wilhelm
Marx, Luther's former minister of justice, with the task of forming a
government. After overcoming initial difficulties with the People's
Party, Marx accepted the post. The People's Party joined the Center
in a joint declaration calling for the quickest possible formation of a
government which might be supported by a majority of the Reichstag. But, the declaration went on to say, in the search for this majority only those parties would be considered "which recognize the
legal validity of existing international agreements and which offer
assurance that Germany's recent foreign policies will be continued."
This message had obviously been meant for the Nationalists' ears,

and they suddenly realized that they had no prospect of regaining ministers' chairs unless they retracted Westarp's foolish statement and that, at any rate, they would have to wait until Germany's admission to the League had been completed.

Thus, for the third time, Wilhelm Marx became Chancellor of Germany. He brought the crisis to a quick end by the simple method of retaining all the other ministers in their offices. And what became of Hindenburg's flag decree? It stayed in effect! Not even the Social Democrats took the liberty of suggesting to the President that it be revoked.[31]

At about this same time, while the cabinet crisis was taking place, the Prussian police had undertaken an action which quickly led to vigorous partisan strife. The authorities had learned of plans to overthrow the constitutional regime and to establish a dictatorship. Severing, whose health had broken under the pressures of his duties and the fullness of events, was in Switzerland on vacation at the time. The Prussian premier, Otto Braun, mindful of what he had been told about the prelude to the Kapp Putsch, ordered a general search, in the execution of which, however, the police failed to observe necessary caution.

In the houses of such magnates of industry as Albert Vögler, a former People's Party member of the Reichstag and director of many corporations, they made investigations which understandably provoked loud protests from the Right and for which there evidently had been no real justification. But the activities of the police had brought a good deal of suspicious material to light of day. Most severely implicated was Counselor of Justice Heinrich Class, chairman of the Pan-German League. His scheme had been the usual one: a Communist uprising was to be used as an excuse for carrying out the plans for a dictatorship. The Prussian government forwarded the evidence to the solicitor general in Berlin, in order that he might bring the culprits to trial for high treason.

A former division head in the Ministry of Justice, Karl Werner, was at that time solicitor general. Otto Braun reports in his memoirs that he had had grave doubts about Werner because of his reactionary views, but that he had ignored them when his party colleague, Gustav Radbruch, formerly a minister of justice, had warmly recommended Werner for the post.[32] But Braun seems to have judged Werner better than did Radbruch. For Werner declined to prosecute. Nor was this the last time that Werner failed to devote the same energy to policing the Right that he devoted to suspicious persons on the Left. Today one would be inclined to assume a connection between this behavior on Werner's part and his political tendency toward National Socialism. Indeed, after Hitler's seizure of power the National Socialists declared quite openly that Werner had been one of their supporters even while still in the service of the Weimar Republic.[33]

A few months later the Prussian government suffered a severe loss when Severing retired. He did this exclusively for reasons of his health. Severing himself blamed the decline of his formerly sturdy constitution primarily on the unjustified attacks which had struck not only at his political character but even at his personal honor. How easy, in contrast to this, the lives of imperial ministers had been! At all times they could rest assured that the state's attorney would lay hands on the first person to mutter even one word against their honor. But now? If the state's attorney did not fail them, the courts would. Severing's successor was Albert Grzesinski, the Berlin police commissioner.

That autumn the political spotlight shone on Stresemann's foreign policy. For September was to determine whether Germany would become a member of the League of Nations under conditions of its own choice. Stresemann knew that in this a majority of the Reichstag would support him, but President Hindenburg's attitude is described in Lord d'Abernon's diary entry for August 20, 1926:

> The President, Hindenburg — essentially a soldier — instinctively distrusts everything but force, and is skeptical about the efficacy of the mild idealism of the League of Nations. He is supported in his skepticism by his old comrades in arms as well as by friends on the Right. These circles have an instinctive fear that Germany's claws will be drawn when she enters the League. Any such procedure they regard as an infidelity to Mars.[34]

In spite of his skepticism, however, no further resistance was to be feared from Hindenburg.

The study commission had carried out its work with considerable success. Most important, it had adopted Germany's thesis that she alone should be given a new permanent seat on the Council, thus becoming a political peer of the Allied powers. The other issues resolved themselves into mere technical points, for which solutions satisfactory to at least the great majority of members had been found: the number of temporary Council seats was raised from six to nine; of these, one third could be re-elected by a two-thirds vote of the Assembly. In effect, this meant that three Council seats could become permanent de facto if not de jure. These seats became known as "semipermanent."

Among the powers that had been pressing for permanent seats,

Poland declared its satisfaction with the plan. Both Spain and Brazil, however, threatened to withdraw from the League if their demands for truly permanent seats were not granted. The other nations made it clear that they would prefer to see these two states leave than to have Germany kept out. This reply cannot have pleased Spain and Brazil, for the two countries immediately declared their withdrawal from the League. The Assembly, refusing to yield to this pressure, accepted the study commission's report on September 8. Later that day the secretary-general of the League was able to telegraph the German foreign minister that Germany had been admitted to the League of Nations with a permanent seat on its Council. That same evening the German delegation left for Geneva.

Stresemann was the only German minister who went. Chancellor Marx had taken the position that he would go to Geneva only if the premiers of the other great powers would also be there. But Great Britain was to be represented by Sir Austen Chamberlain alone; France by Briand. And Briand was no longer Premier but only foreign minister under Poincaré. France, in desperate financial straits, had stumbled from one government crisis to the next until finally, on July 23, President Doumergue had offered the reins of government to the man who, more than any other Frenchman, enjoyed the nation's confidence in his ability to solve the difficult problems of the country's finances and currency. But this had meant no change in French foreign policy, no return to the views of 1923. For Briand remained on the Quai d'Orsay and was encouraged by Poincaré to continue along his former path. Indeed, he had already assured Berlin that such would be the case.

Stresemann had every reason to be pleased at the reception he was granted by the League. Not only did the members of the Assembly greet the German delegates as they entered the hall, but the crowds in the streets also applauded. And the applause broke out most vigorously again when Stresemann arose to address the League Assembly for the first time. Indeed, the significance of the moment stirred him so deeply that he had to struggle to keep his feelings from interfering with his opening sentences.[35] But he quickly found words which preserved Germany's dignity while making clear the nation's desire to take part in candid, practical international cooperation: "Only on the basis of a fellowship which includes, without distinction, all countries in full equality can charity and justice become the true guiding stars of man's destiny . . . On this basis alone can be set that principle of freedom towards which every nation strives, as does each human being."

When the applause which greeted this speech had died away,

Briand welcomed Stresemann in the name of the entire Assembly. His address, delivered with all the magic of his incomparable rhetoric, not only stirred the audience deeply, but spread with full effect around the earth. Briand declared that day a day of peace for Germany and for France, the ending of all the bloody, painful conflicts which had defiled every page of human history. When he declared "Away with the rifles, away with machine guns, away with the cannons! Make room for reconciliation, for courts of arbitration, for peace!" the applause grew into a storm.

The really important thing here was that Briand had demonstrated his confidence in Stresemann in a clear manner before the entire world, declaring that he was counting "on the insight, the peaceful intentions, and the noble sentiments of the German delegation" who, like himself, would do anything in their power to keep the spirit of battle and the lust for prestige away from the conference table.

Throughout the world Briand's speech evoked a wave of enthusiasm in the hearts of millions who had been haunted by nightmares ever since August 1, 1914. Perhaps this speech and its effect marked the highpoint of the common tendency to seek a better world order after such a frightful war. For it was to become apparent all too soon that hard, conflicting issues still remained, and that even the best-intended efforts to drive history too fast can lead to disillusion and, hence, to reaction. On either side of the Rhine there were not only far too many skeptics who, with "the prudence of the dust, revile inspiration, the flower of heaven," but also too many short-sighted nationalists who did not wish to be cheated of either the fruits of victory or the sweetness of revenge. Could there be a grander project than that of settling at one time all the issues that separated Germany and France? Yet if it failed, the venturers would not find themselves more or less where they had begun; they would have wandered farther from their goal.

Briand wanted to follow the expression of confidence which he had given the German delegation in his speech with a speedy demonstration in the form of deeds. He therefore engaged the German foreign minister in an intimate conversation which sought to solve all their common problems. This was the thought behind their celebrated luncheon at Thoiry on September 17, 1926 — a lunch which produced first a sensation, then hope, and finally disillusionment.

The idea of such a private conversation was quite typical of Briand's unconventional nature and had been on his mind for several weeks. In Geneva, he had assured himself of Chamberlain's approval, and so, on the evening of the day that Germany was formally admitted to the League, the foreign ministers of France and Germany agreed to meet upon the morrow someplace where no unauthorized third party could observe or overhear them. Only Professor Hesnard, who had already served as intermediary between the two, was to be present as interpreter.

The men realized that they would have to take extremely careful pains to escape from the representatives of the world press, who, of course, were watching the ministers with eager eyes. They decided, therefore, to put the French border — so conveniently close to Geneva — between their pursuers and themselves, and to hold their conversation over a good wine and an excellent luncheon in the little French village of Thoiry, at the inn that Briand knew quite well. Their flight from the bloodhounds of the press was almost a complete success, but the excitement which it stirred up only increased the sensational way the world press treated this confidential chat between the two most discussed statesmen of Europe.

We have two direct sources of knowledge about this luncheon conversation at Thoiry. One is the very detailed memorandum which Stresemann dictated on September 20 from notes that he had taken just after the talk.[36] The other consists of the much briefer notes which Hesnard jotted down as memory aids for Briand.[37] These two sources differ from each other in that Stresemann ascribes certain suggestions to Briand which, according to Hesnard's notes, originated with the German minister. But apart from this one point the two documents are in such great agreement that one can tell with almost perfect certainty what the subject of their conversation was: namely, the German desire for a speedy end to the occupation of the Rhineland and the consideration that France would receive from Germany in return.

In order to understand the *quid pro quo* which Briand sought to acquire through negotiation, one must bear in mind the financial difficulties that France was suffering at this time. The principal symptom of this crisis was the fall of the franc in the international money market. At the time of Poincaré's return to power in July 1926, the franc had sunk to a tenth of its former value: the pound sterling, worth 25 francs before the war, now bought 264.

Heaviest of all the burdens on the French were the debts which they had been forced to contract with their allies in the course of the war. The illusory hope that these obligations could easily be repaid out of German reparations had long since vanished, leaving the French no choice but to make the best settlements they could with their creditors — principally the United States and Great

Britain. On April 29, 1926, an agreement with the United States was concluded at Washington, according to which France undertook to repay its debt in sixty-two annual installments which would rise gradually from $30,000,000 to $125,000,000. But this agreement had not yet been ratified by the French parliament.

Repeated negotiations had failed to produce a settlement of the French debts to England. And so in July 1926 the French minister of finance, Caillaux, went to London himself in hopes of arriving at an agreement with the British chancellor of the exchequer, Winston Churchill, through direct negotiation. And indeed, on July 12 the two men were able to sign an accord governing the settlement of the French war debt. Here again France undertook to pay sixty-two installments, beginning with £4,000,000 and rising in annual increments to £14,000,000. In these negotiations Caillaux had tried especially hard to have the French payments to England linked to the German reparations payments to France. But he had been unable to achieve anything more in this direction than the reservation, expressed in a letter from him to Churchill, that France would retain the right to renewed negotiations in the event that German payments should fall below one half of the Dawes Plan's stipulations.

But Caillaux never had an opportunity to present this treaty to his parliament. On July 17 Briand's cabinet, and thus Caillaux, was voted out of office. The Wilhelmstrasse seems to have regarded Caillaux as a friend of Germany. One gathers this from an exchange of letters in July of the following year between Stresemann and the German ambassador in Bern, Adolf Müller. Müller reported to his minister that "the well-known problems in Paris" were becoming "acute." "Caillaux's friends in the press have exhausted their bag of tricks. If we wish to help him maintain his influence vis-à-vis Poincaré, we had better act now." Müller then went on to recommend financial aid, which Stresemann went so far as to promise — though within bounds — in his letter from Wildungen of July 23, 1927.[38]

When Briand met with Stresemann at Thoiry in September 1926 to try to find a general solution to the many points at issue between their two countries, all these unsolved financial problems were pressing down on France. It was true that his Premier, Poincaré, left the general handling of foreign affairs up to him, but Briand was aware, nevertheless, that Poincaré had quite different feelings about the Germans than did he, and that the Premier would agree to make concessions only in return for considerations in that area which was dearest to his heart: that of finance.

It sounds almost paradoxical when one records that at this time, in 1926, Germany, which had stood at the edge of economic ruin in 1923, was in a position to help France, her recent conqueror. But the men who were officially concerned with these affairs saw nothing very odd about the fact. The few years since the currency reform and the introduction of the Dawes Plan had marked an extraordinary resurgence of the German economy. Foreign confidence in the permanence of this new strength was demonstrated by the extensive credits which were being made available to Germany from abroad. The Americans in particular enjoyed unlimited optimism in this respect. Agents of American banks were traveling throughout Germany offering loans not only to large industrial enterprises, but to German municipalities as well. Official statistics report the granting of foreign loans worth more than three billion marks to Germany in the two years 1925–1926; of these, some 2.25 billion came from America alone.[39] In 1926 the German national economy profited especially from the great coal strike which paralyzed a considerable portion of the British economy from May until November.

It was therefore quite understandable that Briand should count on the Germans' willingness to make a financial return for the great step with which he intended to grant their most passionate desire: the evacuation of the entire remaining area of occupation. For no matter who first raised the point in the talk at Thoiry, there can be no doubt of Briand's complete willingness to discuss such a "general solution" and, if possible, to carry it out. His mind operated in this way. He hated to concern himself with details. He knew quite well that others, especially his intimate opponent Poincaré, excelled him in the handling of details, particularly when economic or financial matters were concerned. But it was of precisely such financial matters that the *quid pro quo* which Briand had devised — or had picked up from his advisers, perhaps even from Poincaré himself — was to consist.

Under the provisions of the Dawes Plan, the German National Railways had deposited bonds with the par value of eleven billion gold marks with the trustee of the Reparations Commission. These obligations were backed by a first mortgage on the company's entire real estate and thus were thought to be "as good as gold." Briand's idea was to "mobilize" or "commercialize" these debentures, that is, to put them on the money market, using France's share of the proceeds (52 percent) to cover her debts and strengthen her finances. Briand evidently had exaggerated notions of the amounts that might be involved in such transactions. Stresemann did well, therefore, to quiet these hopes with the observation that the world money market — and that meant primarily the United States — would hardly buy more than 1.5 billion marks' worth of the bonds, yielding France 750 million marks as her return.

Stresemann then went on to point out that in Germany the entire project would be opposed by precisely those people who were regarded as financial experts, something neither Stresemann nor Briand could be called. For, in essence, such a transaction meant the drastic weakening of perhaps the most important gain that the Dawes Plan had assured the Germans: the foreign-exchange safeguard. This critical provision had stated that Germany would fulfill her obligations by paying reichsmarks to the reparations agent, and that no more of these marks could be transmitted to her foreign creditors than could be exchanged without injury to the German currency. With this provision the Dawes Plan had given the mark a protection which was extremely significant not only economically, but also politically and psychologically; for there was nothing the German people feared more than inflation. But if a portion of these rail debentures were to pass into private hands, they would naturally no longer be covered by the foreign-exchange safeguard. For the private creditors could not be expected to agree to receive their interest and amortization payments only when the reparations agent had found the payments unobjectionable.

Indeed, even the success of such a commercialization could have unfortunate effects on future German reparation payments, for it would announce the world's great confidence in the German economy, and at subsequent negotiations Germany's creditors would be able to make good use of this flattering faith.[40] One can therefore understand why a man like Bernhard Dernburg, international financier and former minister, said that he would rather go without such political concessions as the ending of the Rhineland occupation than disturb the basic structure of the Dawes Plan's guarantees. This was clearly an economic problem of considerable complexity, one to which neither Briand nor Stresemann felt himself equal. They quickly agreed that they both would have to consult their technical experts before further progress could be made on this problem.

They also considered antedating the return of the Saar District on these same lines. For this would quickly put the repurchase price for the Saar mines — 300,000,000 francs — at France's disposal.

Of greater political significance, however, was their discussion of the abolition of military controls. Stresemann could not deny the fact that Germany had not completely satisfied the prerequisites for the suspension of these controls. But he described the German delinquencies as minor, and Briand showed the greatest inclination to agree. On the other hand, the French foreign minister took another issue much more seriously, namely, that of the paramilitary forces which were so active in Germany at the time. His military advisers had clearly made serious remonstrances to him upon this score. More specifically, they had given him a book of instructions published by the *Stahlhelm* which gave directions for military training, weapon-handling, and the maneuvering of troops.[41] Did that not show, Briand demanded of the German foreign minister, that this *Stahlhelm* regarded itself as a supplement to the regular army? And since almost all its members were former soldiers, this was no light matter to the French.

Stresemann tried, of course, to play down the military significance of the *Stahlhelm*. He quoted Gessler's joking observation that the *Stahlhelm* hoped to replace the imperial army in the eyes of servant girls, offering them military music, uniforms, and kisses. Stresemann pretended that it was a manifestation of man's universal thirst for "color, joy, and movement," a thirst which the Republic "in its dull, black mantle" did not satisfy.[42] The *Reichsbanner Schwarz-Rot-Gold* had sprung up on the Left out of this same need. Stresemann failed, of course, to say that the President of the Republic, Field Marshal General von Hindenburg, was an honorary member of the *Stahlhelm* and cherished his membership dearly.

According to Stresemann's notes of the conversation, Briand replied that he personally did not take these organizations too seriously, but that he would appreciate it if Stresemann would see to it that henceforth French military advisers would have no reason for lodging such complaints with him. Hesnard's notes say that Stresemann was rather embarrassed by Briand's complaints about the paramilitary groups; that Stresemann agreed that the German minister of defense should have concerned himself more vigorously with the issue; and that, indeed, he thought the minister of defense yielded too frequently to his generals — who were not always to be trusted.[43] According to this version of their talk, Stresemann never uttered the name of Seeckt, but that was the general whom Hesnard — and clearly Briand — called to mind.

Without going into all details of a conversation that lasted several hours, one can say that two points became apparent as they talked: the honest intention of both the ministers to find a general solution to their problems, and the obdurate difficulties against which they struck and to which, at the time, they could find no adequate answers. Both men realized — and told the other candidly — that they were not empowered to commit their governments in any way, but rather that the governments would first have to arrive at policy decisions on the strength of their reports. This conclusion was apparent, too, in the communiqué which Briand composed for publication after the conversation: "If the ministers' views are approved by their two governments, they hope to resume their collaboration in order to arrive at desired results." But the communiqué also said that the conversation had concerned a "general solution" (*solution d'ensemble* or *Gesamtlösung*).

It is in the nature of mass psychology that this term made a much greater impression than all the restricting clauses with which Briand had both explicitly and implicitly surrounded it and that the expression vigorously excited men's imaginations, especially in Germany and France. One cannot be astonished that many Germans waxed ecstatic at the thought that perhaps the last French soldier would now be withdrawn across the border, while on the other side of this same boundary many Frenchmen were seized by the fear that their country's safety was being all too lightly risked. Under such circumstances it was clearly the duty of responsible statesmen to take the greatest possible care that their public utterances did not awaken hopes which the statesmen themselves could not expect to see fulfilled.

Stresemann himself was not sufficiently mindful of this obligation when, four days after Thoiry, he addressed the German colony at Geneva in the hall of the Gambrinus brewery. It is true that he avoided making any reference to the talk at Thoiry, but it was only natural that the entire world should relate his address to that luncheon conversation, and that it assumed that the German demands which he proclaimed there in the brewery had been the topic of discussion with Briand. In this address Stresemann said that the occupation of German soil and the exclusion of Germany from her former colonies were not in concord with the new situation which had been created by Germany's admission to the League of Nations and, further, that Germany had every reason to support the right of national self-determination. (The latter observation could be easily taken as a reference to a future Austro-German union.)

Even if one accepts these demands as legitimate goals of German foreign policy, one must also agree that it was politically inappropriate for Stresemann to voice them at this particular moment. Of course domestic considerations were at work once more. For again Stresemann had found it necessary to defend himself against his nationalistic opponents, who were renewing their severe attacks upon him in their press. Of critical importance here is the fact that, in this self-defense, Stresemann let himself to seduced into raising the war-guilt issue once again.

Prior to Germany's admission to the League of Nations, Stresemann had been careful to explain that such a step would not imply a repetition of the confession of war guilt which the Germans had been forced to make at Versailles. He had had to be content with the Allies' reply that they did not understand why he chose that moment to raise a long-dead issue. But since that time delegates to the League had greeted Germany's admission with loud applause. Stresemann was now trying to construe that applause as an acquittal of Germany on the war-guilt question.[44]

This was, of course, his own completely arbitrary interpretation of the scene. It is extremely doubtful that any one of the diplomats and parliamentarians assembled at Geneva that September had felt himself obliged to alter his opinion of Imperial Germany — which they still felt bore the chief guilt for the war — simply because the German Republic had finally found the way to the League of Nations. Rather, it is much more likely that at least the experts among them had regarded this German step as a welcome departure from the policies of William II, who, at the time of the Hague Conferences, had stubbornly and arrogantly opposed every international organization designed to help maintain peace. And perhaps one League delegate or another had read William's offensive * comment on the First Hague Conference which had been published a few years before in a volume of the *Grosse Politik*.[45]

But however that all may be, Stresemann's interpretation was certain to excite that man upon whom Briand's policy of reconciliation was uniquely dependent: Premier Poincaré. At this time Poincaré was the one man who enjoyed the confidence of the French people, and they paid the greatest attention to everything he said. From the Germans' point of view nothing could have been more stupid than to challenge this man to a public debate. Poincaré, as Stresemann certainly should have known, was never at a loss for answers. And he soon began giving them in two speeches, on September 26 in Saint-Germain and on September 27 in his birthplace, Bar-le-Duc. Predictably, in these orations Poincaré pounded his thesis that Imperial Germany was responsible for starting the war and emphasized that rapprochement with Germany was possible only if such a development did not cast any doubts on the Imperial government's historic guilt.

Stresemann chose to reply to Poincaré in a polemical speech be-

* In a dispatch of June 21, 1899, the German Foreign Minister von Bülow reported on the First Hague Conference to his Emperor. William covered the margins of the dispatch with his usual pithy comments and concluded: "Now and in the future I will make it my practice to rely only on God and my sharp sword. And I shit on all their resolutions." (*Die Grosse Politik der Europäischen Kabinette*, Berlin, 1924, vol. XV, p. 306, Doc. no. 4320.) TRANSLATORS.

fore the People's Party convention in Cologne on October 2. The French government, in turn, responded with an official declaration saying that the Premier's statements had been discussed by his cabinet "with respect both to form and content" and that they expressed the government's "unaltered view" (*opinion constante*). Nor was the French government alone on this issue. An editorial in the London *Times* declared that public sentiment in Great Britain, as in the other Allied countries, was in accord with the French opinion. Thus, by raising the war-guilt issue in such an utterly unnecessary way, Stresemann had blundered into a defeat at the very time when every partisan conflict endangered more important issues. "Useless remembering" and "fruitless strife" had once more, to use Goethe's words, proved detrimental to "the living moment."

One must constantly bear in mind that Stresemann kept dragging out this war-guilt question not for reasons of foreign policy — for he saw its unfortunate results there — but out of domestic, partisan motives. This insistence that Germany was not responsible for the war was both a complement and supplement to the myth of the "stab in the back." The proponents of this legend had no interest in an objective investigation of the origins of the war and the relative responsibilities to be attributed to one side or the other. All they wanted was to hammer home to the German people the idea that Germany had been drawn into that fateful war through no guilt of her government and that Germany had lost the war only because "the November criminals" had attacked the unconquered German armies from behind. Of what concern was it to the zealous proponents of this partisan dogma that none of the professional, scientific historians who were sifting the evidence in every land accepted this German claim to innocence, however much they might differ among themselves in dividing the guilt among the governments and general staffs of the great powers?

This same indifference to objective truth was shown by the Reichstag's Investigating Committee, which was still meeting and which was becoming increasingly unable to arrive at a conclusion as the parties on the Right gained strength within the group. Professor Eugen Fischer-Baling, who took official part in all the committee's work, tells us about the proceedings:

It has often been said that the committee should have come to some valid conclusions after ten years' time. And it would have if some of the experts had not deliberately impeded progress. Anybody who actually watched these men operate still explodes with rage at the way they used marked cards in this game of making their own notion of the national interest prevail. It is true that some responsible members sought to present . . . a view of events which emphasized the interrelationship of the power struggles of all countries. Such members concluded that they had to assign joint responsibility for what had ensued; nevertheless they regarded the policies of Russia and Germany as the chief causes of European unrest. Other members of the committee, however, *flatly refused to admit that Germany had made any mistakes whatever or had even caused any provocations.* They were adamant on this point because they thought any admission from Germans would foul their own nest and weaken their front in their battle against the Treaty of Versailles.[46]

This last argument, by the way, proved so seductive than many unbiased Germans succumbed to it, including even so clear-headed a man as the noted historian Hans Delbrück, who fearlessly opposed Ludendorff and the myth of the stab in the back.

All this makes it easier for us to understand Stresemann's behavior, especially since the doctrine of Germany's innocence prevailed in his own party and its acceptance was generally considered essential to any truly patriotic German. Nor can we be astonished to learn that the number of Germans who supported this thesis kept growing at an even greater rate as Rightist tendencies became increasingly preponderant within the nation and as Germans found it easier than ever to believe that all the burdens they had been forced to assume at Versailles would vanish like a bad dream if only this thesis could be made to prevail. It was merely in extension of this earlier development that the National Socialists snuffed out the life of the Investigating Committee as soon as they became the strongest party in the Reichstag and could claim the presidency of the chamber. Their Reichstag President, Hermann Göring, not only put an end to the meetings of the committee, but also forbade any publication of its discussions and of the testimony it had taken.

In view of this development special relevance must be attributed to certain remarks which Poincaré made on April 20, 1928, in a confidential interview with the German journalist Victor Schiff, a correspondent for *Vorwärts.* [47] In the course of this interview, which Léon Blum, leader of the French Socialists, had arranged, Schiff reproached Poincaré with making a practice of continually irritating the German people in his addresses by blaming them for the war. "I have never argued that," Poincaré replied. "I have frequently spoken of the Imperial German government, but I have never accused the German people." He even went on to agree that Article 231, the so-called "war-guilt" clause, was couched in "regrettable" terms. What constantly disturbed him was clearly the strong and totally unnecessary habit of German republican governments to identify themselves with the former Empire no matter how inappropriate the occasion might be.

This interview took place at a time when Poincaré had already made a public declaration in favor of a rapprochement between France and Germany. (See his speech in Carcassonne on April 1, 1928.) Indeed, in this interview with Schiff, Poincaré surprisingly claimed credit for having been the first to propose the conversation at Thoiry. "At that time, just before Briand's departure to Geneva, I directed an official note to him in my double capacity as Premier and as minister of finance. In this note I urged him to discuss with Stresemann the matter of a speedy settlement of the reparations question in connection with a general solution of all remaining problems."

It would seem that even this cool calculator had let himself be carried along for a time by the hope that all the issues dividing France from Germany could be settled with a single blow.

Thus it is all the sadder to report that the meeting at Thoiry led in fact to retrogression rather than to an advance. No real progress was made on any of the important questions discussed there. The great financial offer from Germany, which Briand had desired, did not materialize. For the situation had proved much more complex than Briand had imagined. His most important economic consultant, Seydoux, had clasped his hands to his head when the German ambassador, von Hoesch, told him what Briand had proposed at Thoiry, expressing horror at the way the foreign minister, who knew absolutely nothing of finance, had ventured out upon such slippery ice.[48] German experts were equally critical. Schacht, who had initially found the proposed transaction impossible, assumed a slightly more favorable position later on. But even then he continued to voice grave technical misgivings from his banker's point of view. He was strengthened in these doubts by the critical views of other men, especially those of Montagu Norman, governor of the Bank of England.[49]

The German cabinet had established a special committee, which included the president of the Reichsbank, to consider the fiscal issues raised at Thoiry. But the committee never arrived at a base for further negotiations with the French, for the entire situation became different once it was apparent that Poincaré was going to be able to save France's finances without the help of German rail debentures. Within three months the franc had climbed from its nadir of 264 to the pound up to 124. With this rise French interest in a mobilization of the rail bonds — complicated in any event — disappeared.

With it, understandably, went any interest in the *quid pro quo* that Briand had discussed: the early evacuation of the Rhineland.

There can be no doubt that this was a very great disappointment for Gustav Stresemann, who had his whole heart set on the liberation of the Rhineland. But he was not the sort of man to give up such an important goal simply because his first attempt had failed. This was also a grave disappointment for the German people, who had thought the evacuation closer than it ever in fact had been. And, unfortunately, in the hearts of many Germans this disillusionment turned into a new and greater wrath. They convinced themselves that they were being deprived of something they had been promised. They were deliberately encouraged in this false belief by those politicians who wished Stresemann anything but success. And so that luncheon talk at Thoiry, which was designed to bring Germany and France together, had the reverse effect in many groups where nationalistic resentment and bickering were gaining strength.

Stresemann's international reputation as a sturdy collaborator in the common work for peace received emphatic corroboration when, on December 10, 1926, the Nobel Committee of the Norwegian parliament decided to give the Peace Prize for 1926 to the foreign ministers of France and Germany, Aristide Briand and Gustav Stresemann, while at the same time awarding the Peace Prize for 1924 to Austen Chamberlain and General Dawes. In Germany, of course, Stresemann's prestige was still the subject of violent debate. This discussion came to a head in August 1926, when Stresemann celebrated his fourth anniversary as Germany's foreign minister. But certainly among responsible newspapers recognition — indeed, admiration — for his achievements was preponderant. Among the personal congratulations he received, that from Hjalmar Schacht is particularly noteworthy. Alluding to a much disputed statement of the foreign minister's, Schacht wired: "After three more years of foreign policy under your direction the silver streak * will have become golden morning light." [50]

It seems a symbolic close to a chapter of German diplomatic history that Lord d'Abernon left Berlin that autumn. His German critics had mockingly called him "The Lord Protector" of Germany.

---

* During the dark days of the French occupation of the Ruhr, Stresemann had sought to give hope to the German people by saying that in spite of present difficulties, he could see "a small silver streak on the horizon." For years Rightists and superpatriots taunted him with the phrase. On one occasion in 1928, when Stresemann attempted to speak at Munich's *Bürgerbräukeller* — the scene of Hitler's "Beer Hall Putsch" — some 500 Nazi thugs, bedecked with tinsel streamers, commandeered seats near the speaker's platform and yelled derisively, "Where is that silver streak, Herr Stresemann?" Later that night Gustav Stresemann suffered a new attack of his kidney ailment and from that time never recovered his health. TRANSLATORS.

He, however, preferred to call himself "An Ambassador of Peace." He had gone to Berlin as British ambassador in the summer of 1920 with the firm intention of helping to rebuild European peace and to bridge the gap which still separated Germany from her former foes. There, in Berlin, he had lived through the tragic days of the Ruhr invasion and the happier days of reconstruction that had followed, supporting with his clear wisdom successive German governments along their tedious way. When, in the autumn of 1926, he compared the situation to that of autumn 1923, did he have the right to tell himself that he had sown good seed, seed which had already begun to bear fruit? Would there ever be a full harvest?

Fate did not spare this man who had steadfastly preached faith in the Germans to his own government and to the world. He was to live to see the Wilhelmstrasse, where he had labored with Stresemann and his colleagues on the organization of European peace, ruled by the master of all evil, who systematically tore down Stresemann's work in every piece, and who sent the Horsemen of the Apocalypse out over the fair fields of Europe once again to murder and to plunder and to burn.

III

REICHSWEHR TROUBLES;
MARX'S DISMISSAL AND RETURN

A⊤ the same time that Germany was experiencing such disturbing problems in foreign affairs, she was also confronted by crises on the home front. A veritable sensation was caused by the sudden announcement, in October 1926, that the resignation of Colonel General Hans von Seeckt, chief of the army command, had been accepted by the President of Germany, Field Marshal Paul von Hindenburg.

General von Seeckt himself had dug the pit into which he fell. Clever as he was, he had not escaped the danger of overestimating both his personal and his official powers. By this time he had stood at the head of the German Army for so long, had accomplished so much, and had received such great recognition, that he had come to regard himself as indispensable and his position as unassailable. One can, without hesitation, concede that he had no intention of undermining the republic which he served. But the men who represented this new state — the delegates and ministers in civilian dress — failed to impress him. He regarded most of them with the traditional arrogance of an Imperial German officer. And he stood in sharp political opposition to the most influential member of successive cabinets, Stresemann, transferring, as was Seeckt's way, this official feud into personal enmity, as indiscreet statements by his wife made clear.[1]

Toward his own minister, Gessler, Seeckt had assumed an increasingly abrupt and overweening manner.[2] It may well be that he simply could not adjust to having a mere civilian as his superior, directing him in military affairs; for in old Prussia the minister of war had always been a general. To be sure, he could not ignore the fact that Gessler had used his great talent for political negotiation to defend the Reichswehr from one threatening storm after another. But he probably regarded these successful services as simply "the accursed duty and obligation" of the minister. In any event he never thought of entering the parliamentary battle at Gessler's side. And when the Social Democrats pressed hard for the introduction of special provisions for the punishment of duelists, he left this extremely difficult battle up to Gessler alone, even though he himself had provoked the fight by issuing a decree concerning courts of honor, in which he had sanctioned the reinstitution of dueling.[3]

And now, in June 1926, the former crown prince of Germany approached General Seeckt with the request that his eldest son, Prince William, be granted an opportunity to take part in a military exercise.[4] Through Stresemann's efforts the former crown prince had been permitted to return to his native land from his cheerless exile in Holland. And in the prince's family this minister was known as "Uncle Gustav." Prior to his return, the crown prince had promised not to engage in any kind of political activity. But neither this earlier assurance nor his personal obligations now kept him from making a request with such important political implications that Stresemann would probably be obliged to interfere. Or should one conclude that the crown prince had not comprehended the political significance of his request? The answer must depend on the particular political blindness with which one credits this son of William II.

Seeckt, of course, was much too clever and experienced to fail to see the significance of the occasion. According to dynastic rules the young Prince William was the deposed emperor's heir and thus pretender to the throne in the eyes of all the monarchists loyal to the House of Hohenzollern. The granting of the crown prince's request would, therefore, have been as if a general of the French Republic had smuggled young Louis Napoleon, son of the former Emperor Napoleon III, or some grandson of Louis Philippe's into the republican army.

The Third Republic had had the foresight to bar members of former dynasties from France. The German Republic, on the other hand, had been too magnanimous to pass such a special law; but it received no thanks for this generosity. Nor had it followed the French example of excluding the princes from service in its army. German republicans had assumed that every member of the *Wehrmacht* would have to swear to uphold and obey the Weimar constitution; they had never considered the possibility of a prince's undertaking military service without becoming a formal member of the Army.

Now Seeckt knew full well that many republicans suspected the Reichswehr of nurturing the germs of monarchist reaction. And he must certainly have foreseen that these suspicions would be intensely strengthened as soon as it was known that the Hohenzollern pretender had participated in an army maneuver — no matter what his formal role might have been. And it was equally certain that the affair could not be kept a secret. But Seeckt, in all his massive self-confidence, "didn't give a damn" what the newspapers and politicians might say. He granted the crown prince's request without even notifying Gessler, let alone asking his opinion. Why did they have a civilian minister of defense anyway if he could not, with a little special pleading, extricate a general from such a minor embarrassment? And so the prince was attached to a regiment for the autumn maneuvers in Württemberg.

Everything happened just as could have been foreseen. The affair naturally became known and the democratic press seized upon it with an eager wrath. A brother of the crown prince, Prince Oscar of Prussia, had added his bit, too, that September at the German Day in Nuremberg — a raucous demonstration against the "Weimar Traitors" — by boasting of the "young Hohenzollerns" who were "presently serving in the German Army." So bold had the Hohenzollern eagle already become.

It was only natural that the newspapers directed their attacks primarily at Gessler, whom they intended to hold responsible for the event. But, in fact, Gessler had known nothing of the entire affair.[5] Only after the event did he learn about it at all — and then through purest chance.

At the end of September, when he returned to Berlin after having been away for some time, he found himself confronted by a wave of public indignation, the righteousness of which he could not dispute. He neither knew nor guessed that Seeckt had played this nasty trick on him; he considered the general far too clever and foresighted to commit such a stupidity, one that Bismarck would have called a piece of lieutenant's folly. Only on October 1, when he sought Seeckt out in order to discuss the affair with him, did he learn to his horror that Seeckt was in fact the responsible party.

Gessler's discomfort was in no way relieved by the arrogant tone in which Seeckt chose to carry on the conversation. The general explained that he had ordered that the prince be temporarily attached to the Army for traditional reasons and that he was prepared to assume full responsibility for his decision. But "for traditional reasons" clearly meant to serve the monarchistic tradition. Seeckt's decision had therefore been in deliberate violation of the duties of his office.

And what good did it do Gessler to have the general "assume full responsibility" in a political matter like this? Gessler made it very clear that this was no military matter but rather one of politics, and he made it equally clear that Seeckt had had the duty of discussing the matter with his minister *beforehand*. He then went on to sketch out for Seeckt the effects his irresponsible behavior would have on German foreign affairs.

This conversation — the only one that Gessler and Seeckt ever had on the affair — convinced Gessler that there was no point in hoping to smooth things over or to reach a compromise. And under no circumstances would he assume responsibility for the general's gratuitous affront. In the course of his long service as minister of defense, Gessler had said and done many things for which conscientious republicans censured him. He had been able to justify these lapses to himself on the ground of political necessity. But no such argument could be used in this case, and no member of the Reichstag would have supported such a thesis. However brilliantly Gessler might perform his rhetorical repertoire, he would only have created the impression that he was willing to put up with anything from his generals.

"I have no desire to play puppet for General von Seeckt," Gessler told his colleagues. His position was already difficult enough. The thought of putting an end to all these troubles by resigning had occurred to him more than once, especially after the tragic deaths of his two promising sons had stricken him and even affected his health. In the spring of 1926 he sent the President a very earnest letter of resignation, and Hindenburg, who valued Gessler's political judgment highly and placed great importance upon his continued help, succeeded in convincing Gessler to keep his office only by pleading that Gessler could not abandon an old man. Resignation at this moment would indeed have been tantamount to desertion, and Gessler did not intend to leave to some successor the decision which was properly his own.

Saturday, October 2, the day after his unsettling conversation with Seeckt, Gessler told his closest assistant, Adjutant General Schellbach, and Colonel von Schleicher, without whose assent no political decision concerning the Army could be made, that he would probably have to dismiss Seeckt; that this was a difficult decision, but one which he would have to make alone; that no one could give him counsel on the matter; and that he therefore was going to spend the weekend in some — unspecified — place outside Berlin, where he could ponder the affair in rest and quiet.[6] When he returned on Monday, his decision had been made. He went to the President, explained the nature of the case, and declared that he saw no possibility of satisfying the Reichstag and the Entente unless General von Seeckt were dismissed. He requested the President to discuss the matter with Chancellor Marx, simultaneously, however, making clear his own readiness to resign. Both Hindenburg and Marx approved of Gessler's plan; other ministers do not seem to have been consulted, especially not Stresemann, at whom Seeckt's suspicions were naturally directed and against whom the German Nationalist press now unleashed a new campaign of hate.[7]

On the following day, October 5, Gessler sent an unambiguous letter to the general in which he stated that "under the circumstances" he could "see no other possibility of settling the severe crisis in which both the cabinet and the Wehrmacht [found] themselves than through the resignation of the chief of army command." He refuted Seeckt's argument "that only notorious enemies of the Army were attacking" by pointing out that "it is particularly among the moderate parties that bitterness over this affair is sharp. For these moderates do not wish to be continually disturbed by such demonstrations while they are trying to secure the German state politically both at home and abroad." All this was perfectly apt. Gessler's indignation at the arrogance with which Seeckt had treated — or rather ignored — him was expressed only in his allusion to the parliamentary scene: "I might point out in passing that I have been exposed to the curse of ridicule."

Did Colonel General von Seeckt now finally realize what he had done? Certainly not, if we are to believe his biographer, General von Rabenau. Rabenau, whose account of the crisis is ample — as well as frequently distorted in his hero's favor — states flatly that "on October 5 and 6 Seeckt was still very much considering *employing the instrument of power at his disposal, even if this meant the use of violence*, so long as it remained a crisis in which the President was not immediately implicated, but rather one above which Hindenburg stood or in which he might even come to Seeckt's defense."

Rabenau expressly mentions the then Lieutenant Colonel Freiherr Werner von Fritsch — later the victim of Göring's intrigues and Hitler's brutality — as the man who urged Seeckt "to resist with force." Rabenau is even clearer when he reports that Seeckt was confronted by the question "whether he wished to use the power of what he was and of what he had created to place himself at the head of the German people" and, also, when he tells us that Seeckt's enemies had left him no other road to take "than that of his own dictatorship."[8] In other words, these officers considered the subordination of civilian authority to military power such a natural state

of affairs that they believed themselves quite justified staging a coup
d'état to set things right. One must observe, however, that a note
by Seeckt's adjutant suggests that the plot never really progressed as
far as Rabenau claims. According to this note, the generals concerned, including Fritsch, did play with the idea of resistance but
dropped it because the "time for putsches" was past.[9]

One factor disturbed Seeckt and his friends: the President's attitude. To be sure, if they had given the matter a moment's thought,
they would have had to tell themselves that Gessler hardly would
have taken such a critical and sensational step as telling the chief
of army command to resign without having first arrived at an understanding with the President. But Seeckt, blinded by his feeling
of superiority, either ignored the point completely or else was confident that Hindenburg would yield when confronted face to face.

Relations between the two men had not been very friendly since
the war. One may assume that Seeckt considered himself the old
marshal's intellectual superior. Perhaps, too, he harbored the secret
thought that the position Hindenburg now held belonged by rights
to him. But, whatever the nature of his own feelings toward Hindenburg, Seeckt probably counted on the President's honoring that
sense of solidarity which had always united Prussian generals in the
face of civilian attack.

Hindenburg, however, had his own good reasons for being dissatisfied with Seeckt. The first time he and Gessler had discussed
the chief of army command, Hindenburg had complained: "The
man is ruining the character of the officer corps with all his vanity." [10]
In any event, in his personal conversation with the President on
October 7, Seeckt learned the bitter truth. It is true that Hindenburg
promised to take note of all Seeckt's protests and demurrings, but he
kept full freedom of decision for himself.

The decision came the next day in the form of a communication
from the President saying that he was forced to accept the general's
offer to resign. In his message Hindenburg referred to the facts that
the minister of defense had termed any other solution to the crisis
"intolerable" and that the Chancellor had threatened to resign with
his entire cabinet in the event that Seeckt's resignation were not accepted. Seeckt should have been able to predict this, too, if only
he had not been too haughty to pay proper respect to the parliamentary institutions of the state. He had even once said of himself that
he was "too genteel" to think of appearing in the Reichstag.

And so on October 8, 1926, Seeckt was dismissed. In his wrath
he made the revealing observation: "Herr Gessler is the mighty man
who was able to do what the foreign enemy and the parliamentary

Moloch never achieved." How difficult, indeed, was the task of a democracy that had to work with tools like this! Seeckt's successor was General Heye.

Outside of Germany people were very much impressed to see Gessler make his authority prevail so clearly over a general of such power and importance. They sensed that civilian power in Germany was greater than they had assumed. "The successful vindication of the authority of the civil power has greatly strengthened the German government" were the words of an editorial in the London *Times* on October 12. Thus it helped "preserve the Locarno-Thoiry atmosphere."

But inside Germany those who found this atmosphere unpleasant had become all the more disturbed. They tried to use Seeckt's dismissal as propaganda material against Stresemann, pretending that the general had been forced to go in order that the foreign minister might be aided in his policy of reconciliation with France. Prince Oscar of Prussia became especially prominent in this vilification. But nothing that this son of an emperor did should surprise us, for he had not hesitated to send a personal letter and fifty cigarettes to a young man in jail on the charge of having attempted Stresemann's murder.[11] By way of excuse the prince could say only that he had not realized the prisoner was suspected of having tried to assassinate Stresemann; he had, as he wrote to the minister, merely heard that the lad had been imprisoned "on account of some patriotic excess." How much mischief and how many misdeeds were hidden under that word "patriotic"! And if Stresemann ever thought of the favor he had done for the former crown prince, he could only tell himself: "Such is the gratitude of the House of Hohenzollern!"

Yet, although Seeckt's dismissal had stirred up fresh opposition on the Right, it had not sufficed to restore the Social Democrats' shattered confidence in Gessler. The minister of defense was able to see this for himself when, on October 29, he met in Stresemann's office with the premier of Prussia, Otto Braun, and his state secretary, Robert Weismann. Braun had come armed with voluminous evidence which the Prussian authorities had furnished him concerning the activities of the "Black Army" (*Schwarze Reichswehr*) and the connections between the regular Army and certain Rightist organizations. He explained that he was not interested in what had happened in 1923; * but he did intend to see things cleared up now.

---

* On September 30, 1923, the Black Army under the command of Major Bruno Ernst Buchrucker had staged an abortive coup against the Weimar Republic. Gessler had not supported this so-called "Küstrin putsch"; but he certainly knew about and supported the clandestine and illegal activity of the Black Army. See his testimony to the Reichstag in *Verhandlungen des Reichstags* (Stenographische Berichte),

Gessler excused himself by referring to the difficulties with which Seeckt had always blocked his efforts in this area: he had never received an honest answer from him. Now that Seeckt was gone, everything would be quite different, especially since he and the new chief of army command saw eye to eye upon this point. Gessler's remarks, however, failed to satisfy Braun, who pointed out that Severing had said there was no point in speaking with Gessler, since everything would be denied and nothing would be changed. Braun went on to quote Colonel von Schleicher as having said that the Reichswehr had had enough of the Prussian government's "sniffing around." In his notes Stresemann observed that Braun's tone was "extraordinarily irritated." Yet Stresemann too seems to have found Gessler's arguments not very convincing. [12]

This dissatisfaction on the part of the Social Democrats made the national government quite uneasy, since it was only with their help that it could count on a parliamentary majority. These difficulties were increased still more by the fact that the Social Democrats disagreed with the government's basic program on many points.

An important element in this conflict was the proposed law for the protection of German youth from worthless and obscene literature. Article 118 of the Weimar constitution, which stated the principle of freedom of speech and of the press, forbidding censorship in general, had, however, allowed for legislative action against literary obscenity and trash. One may assume that it was the Centrists who pushed for such a measure at this time. But it was the Democratic minister of interior, Dr. Wilhelm Külz, who was responsible for preparing and presenting the new law.

In his draft Külz proposed to place worthless and obscene works on a special list of books which could not be sold to minors. But what are "worthless and obscene works"? The very phrase is reminiscent of the Heinze Law of 1899 with its notorious and much-disputed definition of such literary works as those which, "without being pornographic, rudely offend the reader's modesty." [13] The controversy which had centered about this law seemed about to break out again when many literary and artistic figures rose in passionate protest against the measure which they regarded as a threat to their freedom of artistic and literary expression. On the other side many people — especially those concerned with the education of children

— pointed to the heaps of trash, devoid of any artistic or literary merit, which were flung upon the market to be sold to the young in a trade which was as lucrative as it was injurious.

Two principles, both equally justified in theory, faced each other squarely here in a problem with which the legislators and courts of all nations have wrestled to this day. The sharpness of division on this point became particularly apparent in the Democratic Party. While a majority of the party and, especially, the party press vigorously attacked the proposed legislation (which had been introduced by a Democratic minister), several prominent delegates whose liberal convictions could not be questioned — such as Theodor Heuss and Gertrud Bäumer — gave it their firm support. The Social Democratic Party, however, opposed it strongly to the very end, not even being swayed by significant modifications in the draft.

On December 3, 1926, the Reichstag passed the measure at third reading by the considerable majority of 250 to 158. To satisfy public protests the law had been amended to include an explicit "partisan clause" (*Tendenzklausel*) which prohibited a work's being placed upon the list "because of its political, social, religious, ethical, or philosophic content." Furthermore, the danger of an excessively bureaucratic and unilateral administration of the law had been foreseen and — one hoped — avoided by the establishment of an "Examining Office" (*Prüfstelle*) which would be responsible for making up the list of works barred to minors.[14]

The Social Democrats were more disturbed by the warped nature of their general position than by differences of opinion vis-à-vis the government on separate legislative issues. Friedrich Stampfer, who was certainly well acquainted with his party comrades' moods in his roles as Reichstag delegate and editor-in-chief of the party organ, *Vorwärts*, observed that "the Social Democrats in the Reichstag were sick and tired of being in such an ambiguous position: they wished either to be represented in the cabinet or else to be free to fight for popular support and thus for power as an opposition party."[15] One can perhaps put this another way by saying that the Social Democrats had finally become aware of the error they had committed on Christmas 1925, when they had preferred to abstain from responsibility. But what one has lost from the passing minute cannot be regained at some later hour by merely pounding one's fist upon the table.

The leaders of the Social Democratic delegation in the Reichstag finally showed they realized this truth when they commenced conversations with Chancellor Marx with a view to the possible revision of the cabinet. Marx was certainly not opposed a priori to the idea of adding a few Social Democratic ministers to his government and, thus, of turning it into a cabinet of the Great Coalition, supported by a secure majority in the Reichstag. And one can also assume that Stresemann — if only in defense of his foreign policies — would certainly have preferred such a combination to a "Bourgeois Bloc" that included the German Nationalists.[16]

Indeed, even the *Reichspräsident* had little use for German Nationalists now. It is with some astonishment that one reads in Stresemann's diary under November 12, 1926, that Hindenburg had had a conversation with the leaders of the German Nationalist delegation in the Reichstag which had ended "on a very sharp note." Hindenburg had protested that what they were engaging in could not be called rational policy; the German Nationalists, however, had replied that they would continue their program and therefore, most particularly, their opposition to Stresemann's foreign policy.[17] It is true that in the Reichstag foreign policy debate of November 25–26, 1926, Professor Hoetzsch had assumed a somewhat milder tone; his colleague Professor von Freytagh-Loringhoven, however, spoke harshly of the "fruitless" Locarno-Thoiry approach. But at least this time the German Nationalists did not join the Racists and Communists in a vote of no confidence against Stresemann; they were content to abstain.

But when Stresemann, the leader of the People's Party, assumed an unprejudiced attitude toward plans for another Great Coalition, many of his party — including the Reichstag leader Dr. Ernst Scholz — deserted him again. While the foreign minister was attending a meeting of the League of Nations Council in Geneva, Dr. Scholz was scurrying about his electoral district, East Prussia, delivering speeches which did nothing to support a Great Coalition. In an address at Insterburg on December 5, he had been particularly explicit in citing reasons why cooperation between the People's Party and the Social Democrats was impossible: they could agree neither on the question of the working day nor on military policy.[18] The *Vorwärts* immediately took this to be a "declaration of war" and reported that the Socialist leaders, Hermann Müller and Rudolf Breitscheid, had personally called the Chancellor's attention to the dangerous situation.

These interparty skirmishings were suddenly interrupted by a bomb of much greater impact. For on December 3, the Manchester *Guardian* published an extensive article on the clandestine connections between the German Army and the Soviet government. There is an interesting background to the article. The Junkers Company, the famous airplane plant in Dessau, had been commissioned by the

Reichswehr to build factories in Russia for the manufacture of military aircraft specifically forbidden to Germany by the Treaty of Versailles.

The project fell through, and Junkers demanded compensation from the Army. Since the confidential nature of the matter meant that he could not press his case in open court, Junkers prepared a detailed memorandum giving a full account of his complaints and claims. He gave copies of this memorandum to several members of the Reichstag in order that they, in turn, might apply pressure on the government in the settlement of his case.[19] Somehow a copy of this document fell into the hands of an English reporter, who worked it up into an article for England's leading liberal publication.

Here at last one could read how Junkers had erected an airplane factory in Russia for the production of military aircraft for both the Russian and the German armies. Furthermore, there had been plans for building chemical plants which were to supply both armies with poison gas. Officers of the Reichswehr had traveled to Russia on false German passports and equally false Russian visas. Seeckt, who had been on excellent terms with the high officers of the Red Army, had known about all this. How much Gessler had known was not yet clear. On December 6 the *Guardian* continued its disclosures, giving details of the agreements between the Reichswehr, Junkers, and the Soviet government.

On December 9, the *Vorwärts* broke the news to Berlin in a translation under the headline: "Soviet Grenades for German Guns." The paper went on to argue that when Stresemann had departed for Geneva he knew he would be asked to account for the Reichswehr's illicit relations with Russia. There was no reason why Germany should not learn of these events which were known to the rest of the world. Then the newspaper turned its attack on the Communists, who, while plotting a German revolution with Russian aid, had simultaneously kept their eyes closed to the way the Russians were arming the counterrevolution.

Pure chance had given the Social Democrats more material for another attack against both the Communists and the Army. In the harbor of Stettin, stevedores had been unloading three German freighters which were bringing artillery shells from Russia for the Reichswehr. The workmen had received extra pay in return for a promise of secrecy, but some Social Democrats among them had contacted a party functionary in Berlin, Reichstag delegate Künstler, thus enabling him to make a private investigation of the facts. Naturally the *Rote Fahne*, the Communists' paper in Berlin, denied everything. But several former Communists — Ruth Fischer among them — who had been expelled from the party for "deviation" spoke out publicly against this strange alliance between the German Army and Russian revolutionaries. Whereupon they were branded as "parlor pinks" and "counterrevolutionaries" by their former comrades.[20]

It was even more embarrassing for the Reichswehr when such a respected Social Democrat as the President of the Reichstag, Paul Löbe, sent Gessler an open letter demanding that a different method be used for army recruitment,[21] Löbe proposed that a committee of the Reichstag be established to supervise recruitment procedures and to see to it that the Army was not giving special preference to the enlistment of Rightists. There was much to be said both for and against this recommendation. But whatever its merits, one certainly has to doubt the ability of such a committee — even if it had functioned properly — to achieve the goal Löbe really had in mind: a meaningful increase in republican-minded recruits.

For under the circumstances of that time such recruits would have had to come from the ranks of young workers. But so long as they enjoyed the prospect of industrial employment, the young workers showed no desire to serve twelve long years in the Army as professional soldiers. Stampfer, the editor of the Vorwärts, expressly admits as much.[22] This being the case, the workers' party had no reason to complain if Army replacements were drawn quite disproportionately from the traditionally conservative rural areas. The chief responsibility for this unfortunate situation must be fixed on the Allies, who had forced a professional army upon Germany without considering the inevitable political consequences of this act. This truth does not, of course, in any way exculpate those regimental commanders who made a practice of clearing would-be officer-candidates' applications for enlistment with the Werewolves,* an extremely Rightist organization.[23]

During all these developments Stresemann was at a meeting of the League of Nations Council in Geneva, where he was negotiating — especially with representatives of France, Great Britain, and their allies — the cessation of military controls in Germany. Naturally these men, too, had read the Manchester Guardian's report of the German Army's collusion with the Reds. But did they let this knowledge affect their decision on the future military control of German

---

* In 1919, at the request of the Republic, the one-armed war hero Lieutenant Peter von Heydebreck had formed a Free Corps which he called the Werewolves. After the Free Corps were theoretically disbanded in 1920, Heydebreck's men fought in Upper Silesia in 1923, then went underground and were affiliated with the Black Army. He continued to enjoy the confidence of the Republic's army even though he despised the Republic. (See his memoirs, Wir Wehrwölfe, Erinnerungen eines Freikorpsführers, Leipzig, 1931.) TRANSLATORS.

disarmament? Not at all! Nor should this fact surprise us, for the same issue of the *Guardian* that had made these sensational disclosures also included an editorial which called for an end to military controls. The more conservative London *Times* took the same position, although it did declare that, in light of the recent disclosures, it was obvious that militaristic tendencies still existed in Germany. The *Times* hoped, however, to counter these forces with the free development of responsible public opinion in Germany — the growth of which was only being hindered by the continuation of military controls.

And so the negotiations at Geneva ended in complete victory for Stresemann. On December 12 an Investigation Protocol was signed, encompassing five points. Of these, however, only one — the third — was of practical importance. It stated: "On January 31, 1927, the Inter-Allied Military Control Commission will be withdrawn from Germany." To be sure, the point went on to say that from that day forth Article 213 of the Versailles treaty would take effect. But nothing will be served by looking up this article in the Treaty of Versailles. (The article provided for investigations by the League of Nations.) For it never was applied, nor did the slightest possibility ever exist that it ever would be employed. It is no exaggeration — but rather the sober statement of a simple fact — that, starting on January 31, 1927, the victors of 1918 had forsworn every means of precluding violations of the disarmament provisions of Versailles. Or in other words, from this day on the Reichswehr was free to expand as much as German finances and public opinion might permit.

What German public opinion on the question of secret rearmament really was became apparent a few days later in the Reichstag session of December 16, when Scheidemann sought to bring the government down by making a vehement attack on conditions in the Reichswehr.

This open attack had been preceded by negotiations between the Social Democratic executive committee and the national government on the subject of broadening the latter's representation, that is, with a view to bringing the Social Democrats into the cabinet. These negotiations were being carried on with the express approval not only of the cabinet, but of the various leaders of the parties as well. But even so, the Social Democratic spokesmen were not satisfied by the assurances which the Chancellor offered them. One may assume that the Reichswehr proved the principal stumbling block, and that the Social Democrats were demanding that Gessler go.[24] But they also lacked confidence in Ernst Scholz, the chairman of the People's Party Reichstag delegation. That Scholz would make it difficult to form a coalition is shown by Hilferding's reaction to word from Stresemann that he planned to take a four or five week vacation at the end of the year: "But while you're gone Scholz will ruin everything!" [25] As late as the afternoon of December 15, Marx and Stresemann were still negotiating with the Social Democrats, who were giving clear vent to the ill will they bore Gessler. Gessler was summoned to the conference, but his explanations failed to satisfy the Social Democrats. When one of them reproached him with the charge that munitions had been unloaded in Stettin just a few days before, Gessler replied — as Stresemann tells us — "in his usual manner, that he did not know anything about it." Stresemann immediately sought out General Heye, who was waiting in the next room. Heye declared that the Social Democrats' accusations were utterly false: no such munitions had been bought or ordered.[26]

These negotiations were clearly being carried on with both sides desiring an agreement. For the ministers got the Social Democratic delegates to agree that, in regard to the Reichswehr, they would publicly demand explanations only on quite specific points, and Stresemann undertook to provide them with the replies that Marx would make. Hermann Müller, chairman of the delegation, went so far as to assure Stresemann, in answer to a direct question, that the Social Democrats had not the slightest intention of connecting the Russian issue with that of the Black Army.

But in the evening after this conversation there was a meeting of the Social Democratic Reichstag delegates, and here the young backbenchers seem to have won out over their more cautious party leaders. For the delegation decided not only to introduce a motion of no confidence the next day, but also to demand that the present cabinet resign *prior to* any discussions of what the next government should be. The cabinet unanimously rejected this demand the following morning, and the Chancellor opened the Reichstag debate that afternoon with the statement that his government was determined not to resign and that it therefore left the Reichstag responsible for subsequent developments.

At this point Scheidemann took the floor to support his party's motion of no confidence. His address consisted of a bitter criticism of the Reichswehr and its responsible minister, Gessler, against whom he voiced his party's special distrust. His attack was primarily directed at "the financing of the Reichswehr by Russia" and the Army's connections with industrial magnates and Rightist groups. He made detailed reference to the Manchester *Guardian's* disclosures and then went on to discuss the Russian shells in the harbor of Stettin. He emphasized the fact that the Communist cell at this port had been fully informed of what was going on, and he found evident pleasure in thus exposing the German Communists' duplicity to all the world.

Philipp Scheidemann was a very effective orator. But the effect he achieved on this occasion — while indeed highly dramatic — was by no means favorable to his cause. The *Vorwärts* gives the following description of the scene:

> Scheidemann's speech exploded like a bomb . . . The Rightists hurled a wave of insults at the speaker and left the chamber. The Communists shrieked and yelled as though possessed. But even in the seats of the Centrists and Democrats there was distress. One can indeed say that all parties to the right or left of the Social Democrats were extremely discomforted by the address . . . And so the Social Democratic delegation — we say this quite calmly — stood alone in the Reichstag.[27]

And even in the Social Democratic delegation there were many, as we know from other sources, who thought Scheidemann had gone too far. The sharply critical reaction of former *Reichskanzler* Joseph Wirth to Scheidemann's speech was particularly disappointing to the Social Democrats. For Wirth firmly declared his approval of collaboration with the Russians, whose resources were necessary for the world's economic recovery. Despite Germany's admission to the League of Nations, Wirth went on, her bonds with Russia should not be slackened, but rather made more tight.

The abusive interruptions from the Right had called Scheidemann a traitor who, blinded by partisanship, was yielding important state secrets up to foreign foes. In truth, of course, this was not the case at all, since the most compromising facts had already been printed for all to see in the Manchester *Guardian*. Yet it was only natural that these revelations should receive a heightened effect by being stated from the rostrum of the Reichstag. And, most important, the further repetition of these facts had thus been freed of criminal liability. (One can assume that this was not the least of Scheidemann's motives for his speech.) For the German courts had developed a principle which barred all such statements: the revelation of violations of the Treaty of Versailles had become high treason, and it was no defense for the accused to argue that he had been trying to uphold a treaty which had been formally signed by the German government.[28] But truthful reports of the Reichstag's proceedings were protected from such prosecution, and so the Socialist press was free to spread Scheidemann's words throughout Germany without fear of being haled into court. The essential truth of Scheidemann's charges is no longer disputed, least of all by those military circles which, at that time, thought they were fulfilling their historic mission by circumventing the disarmament provisions of Versailles.[29]

Can one really accuse Scheidemann of having acted in an unpatriotic fashion by making these revelations? One's answer must depend in part on the extent to which one regards it as a real blessing for Germany that she secretly rearmed. If one considers the endless misery and misfortune to which the path of rearmament finally led the Reich, one will scarcely be able to answer the question with yes. The Reichstag debate of December 16 certainly provided an odd sequel to the Investigation Protocol of December 13. But the former Entente powers did not use it as grounds for the revocation of any of the concessions they had made. They preferred, rather, to take no formal notice of the revelations, a decision not precisely designed to have a frightening effect on those who were carrying out this secret rearmament. There was, instead, better reason to fear an adverse effect on the general disarmament negotiations, in preparation for which the League had already appointed a commission that included — in Count Bernstorff — a German member. For thoughts of such a general disarmament were based on the presumption that Germany had already disarmed. Could one still cling to that position?

But even after one has refuted all the material arguments against Scheidemann's address, one still cannot say that it was wise. The Social Democrats' attack was designed to bring about a coalition government in which they would have a part. Scheidemann's speech was, as Severing puts it neatly in his memoirs, "the most inappropriate of means" to reach this goal.[30] One does not create a coalition by bashing one's potential partners on the head. Entirely apart from the People's Party, many delegates in the Center and in the Democratic Party — including not a few who hoped for a more democratic army and a peaceful, civilized political scene — had been gravely offended by what Scheidemann had done. In the Center, Wirth had always been considered the best republican and the leader of the party's Left; and Wirth had given Scheidemann a curt rebuff. Today, when we know how Wirth had nurtured this connection of the Reichswehr with the Red Army, his attitude is, of course, simpler to explain. And one can also say that even if the Centrists and Democrats had felt inclined to expand their coalition so as to include the Social Democrats, their constituents would probably have refused to follow.[31]

And how did Scheidemann expect the President to react to such a speech? No matter what one's personal or political relations with Hindenburg were, one dared never forget that the constitution charged him with the function of naming the chancellor and the national ministers.[32] Who could expect him to use this power in favor of a party that had attacked — with extraordinary bitterness — that one organ of the state to which everyone knew he was particularly attached. And the Social Democrats should have foreseen that he would be especially indignant at this attack because just a few weeks before he had clearly demonstrated his acceptance of the constitution by dismissing Seeckt.

Furthermore, the Social Democrats should never have forgotten that they were in no position to overthrow a government by themselves; they simply were not strong enough numerically for that. Their motion of no confidence could have been adopted only if other parties — no matter what their reasons — had voted for it; but, then, of course, the Social Democratic Party would no longer have had the situation under control. The Democratic delegate Ludwig Haas was quite right when, in the Reichstag debate, he declared: "Before one requires a cabinet to resign, one should consider what the next government will be. Sooner or later we shall have to adopt the principle that a government can be dismissed only when consensus has been reached on the nature of the next." The Social Democrats had violated this basic parliamentary principle and were to harvest disaster in return.

Actually it was the German Nationalists who helped carry the Social Democratic motion of no confidence. To be sure, the resolution was a blatant blow at the Reichswehr and thus struck all the Nationalists' traditions and sensitivities full in the face.[33] But in their defense the leaders of the German National Party could quote Bismarck's famous observation that similar votes do not always bespeak similar motives. Let the devil take the Reichswehr! What the German Nationalists wanted was to overthrow the moderate government from which they were excluded, and so they did not hesitate to mount the battle horse after their bitterest enemies had been good enough to hold the stirrup. In this maneuver they were joined not only by the Racists, but by the Communists as well, who the day before had wanted to tear Scheidemann to shreds. Thus 249 votes were united in support of the Social Democrats' motion, against which the government could gather only 171. Marx had fallen; the Social Democrats had had their parliamentary victory; and now they were about to suffer severe political defeat. For the ones who really profited from the Social Democrats' success were the German Nationalists.

Thus for the third time the German Republic celebrated Christmas with a governmental crisis, and it immediately became apparent that each crisis *strengthened the position of the President.* Chancellor Marx had firmly expected to be entrusted with the formation of the next cabinet.[34] But Hindenburg had other plans. Especially after the Social Democrats' disruptive scene, he was quite prepared to let people notice that he was steering a bit more to the Right. He would have preferred to ask Scholz to form a cabinet. This former mayor of Charlottenburg made a very good appearance and had all the proper manners. He had served as an officer in the field, and the dueling scars which adorned his face certainly did not prejudice the old field marshal against him. Furthermore, Hindenburg probably regarded Scholz's speech at Insterburg against the Social Democrats as a patriotic deed that deserved some recognition. But Scholz knew that he was unloved among the Centrists, and without the Center no government could be formed. So he had to decline the President's offer.

Hindenburg then turned to another member of Scholz's delegation: not to Stresemann, of course, but rather to the other minister from the People's Party, Julius Curtius. In any event Stresemann would not have been the man to form a cabinet including German Nationalists, and that is exactly what Hindenburg wished to have. According to Curtius, Scholz and Stresemann had agreed between themselves to propose him to the President as a *homo regius*, the loyal servant of his lord. And Curtius explains his reason for accepting the commission with the significant words: "I acted like a political soldier, declaring myself ready to follow his commands." [35] But after a few days he realized that despite his good intentions he could not reach his goal, and so — on January 14 — he had to ask Hindenburg to find somebody else. He, too, had foundered on the Center.

This is not to say that the Centrists were opposed in principle to collaboration with the German Nationalists. On the contrary, some Centrist delegates seem to have been fostering such a plan. It is in this connection that Stresemann first mentions the name of Heinrich Brüning, who had been a member of the Reichstag only since 1924 but whose diligence and knowledge — especially in the fields of welfare and finance — had already won him considerable influence. It was Brüning who suggested that, in order to bring the Center and the German Nationalists together, the foreign minister should declare that he would be able to continue his foreign policy only if German Nationalists joined the cabinet. In his diary Stresemann ironically described the idea as "brilliant." [36] What really united the two parties was their common interest in confessional schools. But the Center did not intend to enter into such a combination only to give up their recent leadership to the People's Party. To old Hindenburg this all seemed a frivolous game, and when Curtius had to report that he could not form a government, the President pathetically exclaimed: "Partisan spirit, I accuse you before God and History!" But the Center had very good reasons for its attitude.

For Hindenburg now had no other choice but to request Marx to form another government. Marx first tried to construct a moderate regime but could not compromise the differences between the People's Party and the Social Democrats. The Social Democrats refused to support such a government if they were not included in it; and the People's Party refused to serve in a cabinet which included Social Democrats. Again this sort of intransigence had the effect of *transferring initiative to the President*. Hindenburg sent a message to Marx in which he pointed out that neither a government of the Middle nor an extension to the Left was possible. Thus the only remaining possibility was a cabinet based upon a majority of the bourgeois parties. But he made it particularly clear that even such a government "would have the special duty of guarding the just interests of the broad working masses along with other necessities of state." Of course this move of Hindenburg's accorded with the wishes of the German Nationalists, but the Social Democrats had no reason to complain. For they had created the problem to which there was no other answer.

Marx was prepared to initiate negotiations with the German Nationalists, but only under the condition that Stresemann would continue to direct foreign policy. Marx had given his minister a free rein in these affairs, and he knew that it was Curtius' intent, in the event that he were made chancellor, to concern himself extensively with foreign affairs. When one recalls the failure with which Curtius later ended his service as Stresemann's successor, one can only rejoice at the fact that Stresemann — and Germany — was spared his leadership at this time.

In a letter of January 14, 1927, Stresemann had expressed himself to Marx at length on the question of whether a continuation of his foreign policy would be possible under a government in which German Nationalists sat. Quite rightly he pointed to the dangers that such a coalition would mean to Franco-German rapprochement:

The French believe that the German Nationalists are a nationalistic party in support of those volunteer armies which are the real nightmare of the French. Their addition to the cabinet will naturally mean that Briand's domestic foes will sharpen their language and say that the re-actionaries have begun to take over in Germany — and that this Rightist development in domestic politics will bring a change in foreign policy as well . . . It is also relevant that this difficulty occurs at a time when Briand's domestic position has already become sensitive *because of the discussions of the evacuation of the Rhineland — which perhaps we pushed too hard.*

In view of all these considerations Stresemann requested that the German Nationalists be required to offer guarantees not only of his unobstructed freedom to continue his foreign policy, but also of their intention *to help strengthen Germany's republican form of government,* "for that too is an element of our foreign policy." In short, "every uncertainty with respect to the political attitude of the German Nationalists will have to be precluded."

The letter had originally included another passage, warning against any German Nationalist deviation from the path of general reconciliation "in favor of a narrow, bilateral rapprochement with Italy" or of a "military alliance with Soviet Russia." [37] These references were omitted from the letter on sound political grounds when it became necessary to show the letter not only to Marx but to others.

The German Nationalists, in order to join the government, actually made the declaration which recognized the legal validity of the Locarno treaties. Instead of an oath of allegiance to the Republic, however, they affirmed, in a weaker version, their "recognition of the legal validity of the Weimar constitution." How little that really meant was made clear by Count Westarp on February 3, in the first Reichstag debate on the acceptance of the new cabinet. Westarp took pains to emphasize that the German Nationalists had not been required to make — nor had they made — a confession of republican faith and a disavowal of their monarchistic convictions. With this said, he then proceeded to skip lightly over another concession which his party had had to make in order to join the cabinet.

For years now the German Nationalists had been obstructing the prosecution of the nation's foreign affairs with their constant, pathetic screams demanding a clear statement from one cabinet or the next on the question of the "war-guilt lie." And even now, in a conference of the German Nationalist party leaders with Stresemann and his closest assistants, on January 25, Count Westarp had demanded that a paragraph on this point be included in the new cabinet's declaration of policy. Stresemann advised strongly against this step, pointing out its probable effects upon Franco-German negotiations: it would only endanger Briand in France and thus make the evacuation of the Rhineland effectively impossible. State Secretary von Schubert was even more explicit; he bluntly told the German Nationalists what results such a protest would have: "We would get ourselves an official box on the ears." [38] At this the Nationalists yielded, contenting themselves with a phrase about "moral equality" that offended — and impressed — no one.*

* Stresemann's attitude to the war-guilt question and its political implications is especially illuminated by an exchange of letters, in August of 1927, with the Prussian minister of culture, Carl Becker. The law faculty of the University of Kiel had recommended the appointment of Professor Hermann U. Kantorowicz to a chair that had recently become vacant. In a letter of August 15 from Norderney, Stresemann expressed his objection to the appointment because Kantorowicz, in his report to the Reichstag committee investigating the war-guilt question, had reached different conclusions on this issue from the official views of the German government. [Kantorowicz — like F. W. Foerster — had been critical of Imperial Germany's prewar foreign policy. TRANSLATORS.]

Stresemann had not read Kantorowicz' statement himself, but rather was basing his objection to the appointment on reports from Johannes Kriege, formerly head of the Legal Division of the Foreign Ministry and now a representative of the People's Party in the Prussian Landtag. According to Kriege this testimony by Kantorowicz had given the struggle against German war guilt "a blow from which we shall hardly ever recover. And if the man who delivered this blow is now called to a prominent post by the Prussian Ministry of Culture, he will thereby be certified as an outstanding scholar and his opinions will become all the more significant." Stresemann found a strange — and false — reason for honoring Kriege's objections: "because in no other race is the compulsive need to search out objectively one's own sins — leaving innocence to others — so strong as among the Germans. It is carried even to the point of masochism. A man like Professor Foerster could not have existed in any other nation." As though, for example, criticism of one's own government were not carried on much more vigorously in England and America than in Germany, and as though neutral judges would lend any weight to German protests against the war-guilt verdict if such protests were simply produced on orders from above rather than the results of free, unbiased scholarly discussion. Stresemann went on to say: "Even as foreign minister I am of the opinion that we shall gain much more if we restrain ourselves and let the others do the talking. But if we do speak, then we should not direct the attack at our own throats on this issue, an issue in which, I am sincerely convinced, justice is clearly and completely on our side."

Becker, himself an adornment to the ranks of German scholars, rebuffed this political attack on German university affairs in a truly superb fashion. On August 22, 1927, in a private letter from Marienbad, he replied: "Kantorowicz is one of those remarkable — one might even say 'genial' — personalities that are to be found among German and English scholars — but among them alone. The strong academic idealism of these men can mean their governments' discomfort now and then." Becker, a famous Orientalist. then proceeded to remind Stresemann of a British Orientalist who had castigated the Oriental policy of the English government "in the most unbelievable way."

Becker went on to point out that Kantorowicz had done eminent work in the field of medieval law, and that the Kiel faculty had decided to stand by his nomination after Kantorowicz' report had been brought to their attention. "I can reject this nomination only if I can see that granting it would injure Germany's prestige. Be.ore the war perhaps no man did more to destroy other nations' faith in Germany's good will (Mr. Obstacle at the Hague conferences) than that very man who now is arguing everywhere — and evidently to you, too — that to call Kantorowicz to Kiel would be to injure Germany's reputation severely. I am prepared to presume the good faith and honest convictions of both these gentlemen and ask myself the simple, sober

In any event the Democrats had good reason to decline to participate in such a government. This refusal meant that Peter Reinhold, the minister of finance, had to leave the cabinet. Both Stresemann and Curtius would gladly have seen him stay, for he enjoyed a popularity that is rarely accorded a finance minister. Gessler, who remained in the Ministry of Defense at Hindenburg's special request, resigned from the Democratic Party.

Thus Marx's fourth government was based upon the Center, the Bavarian People's Party, the German People's Party, and the German Nationalists. This last party was allotted no less than four ministries: Interior, Justice, Food, and Transport. Initially the Nationalists wanted to assign one of these portfolios to Walther Gräf, a Thuringian delegate whose claim to fame was his refusal, as vice president of the Reichstag in 1925, to make the customary call on Ebert, the President of Germany. But this was simply too much for Stresemann, and on January 30 he wrote Marx a letter which can

---

question: whether, under present circumstances, our *failure* to appoint Kantorowicz might not hurt Germany's prestige abroad still more." Becker explained that Professor Radbruch, the former minister of justice, had told him that nothing was in Kantorowicz's report save what was also the firm belief of the entire Social Democratic Party. "Is the Prussian minister of culture to refuse the appointment of such a man because a couple of gentlemen from the German Nationalist and People's parties take objection to a scholarly affidavit? . . . Foreign policy is not my responsibility; that is why I have inquired of you. But I am certainly responsible for *defending the academic freedom of our professors against inroads made out of political considerations.* I find this decision extraordinarily difficult, because I think just as you do about the war-guilt issue . . . But would not the official silencing of a man with Kantorowicz' qualities and prominence be perhaps an even greater error?"

Kantorowicz received the appointment and taught at Kiel until the outbreak of the Hitler regime, which of course drove him into exile. His report has never been published; along with all the other committee documents it was burned in a bombardment of the Reichstag in 1945. (Eugen Fischer-Baling, "Der Untersuchungsausschuss für die Schuldfragen des ersten Weltkrieges," in *Festschrift für L. Bergstraesser,* Düsseldorf, 1954, pp. 126, 127. For a description of Kriege's activities on the investigating committee see p. 134. Kantorowicz' attitude to the question of German war guilt is apparent in his book, *Der Geist der englischen Politik und das Gespenst der Einkreisung Deutschlands,* which was published in 1929. For a treatment of Kantorowicz as a person see Radbruch's memoirs, p. 97.)

Remarkably enough, Stresemann's letter shows how deeply disturbed he had become at the spirit that prevailed in many academic circles: "I am most saddened at the confusions in public opinion that one constantly finds in Germany today. Last evening I was forced to become quite ill-mannered to a gentleman with many degrees — a person truly outstanding in scholarship and art — because he had taken no little pleasure in reporting that the Marburg students had refused to hear the Prussian minister of culture speak . . . I often imagine what would have happened in royal Prussia — which evidently is the political ideal of these people — if students had dared to do something like that . . . Yet I continue to hope that our national recovery from these confusions will stem from German youth. So far as I can judge the nature of academic life today, the politically active students are a good bit cleverer than the so-called Old Gentlemen [that is, the alumni members of the student fraternities]." (Stresemann Papers, 7346H).

be reduced to the simple words: "Either Gräf or me." [39] As a result of this message the German Nationalists finally consented to propose their Reichstag delegate Walter von Keudell instead of Gräf, and von Keudell was duly appointed minister of interior.

Von Keudell was a son of Wilhelm von Keudell, a former ambassador, who in his youth had been an intimate friend of Bismarck.[40] But he was no more suited to be the principal guardian of the Weimar constitution than is the proverbial wolf to guard the sheep. In 1920, for example, he had been dismissed from his post as a Prussian *Landrat* (local magistrate) for having played a major role in the Kapp Putsch. (Otto Landsberg made energetic objection to von Keudell on this ground in the Reichstag debate on the new government.)

Besides von Keudell, the German Nationalist ministers included Oskar Hergt, as vice chancellor and minister of justice; and Martin Schiele, who had stumbled over Locarno in 1925, as minister of food; while an otherwise unknown delegate, Wilhelm Koch, was promoted to minister of transport. The Centrists put the Baden minister of finance, Heinrich Köhler, into the national ministry that had just been vacated by Reinhold. Wirth, too, had been Baden's minister of finance before assuming the national portfolio.

The Center — or, in any event, a large number of the Centrist delegates — did not find it easy to agree to such a coalition with the German Nationalists. This uneasiness found almost grotesque expression in the Reichstag debate of February 3–5, 1927. After Count Westarp had taken full advantage of his opportunity to widen the gap between the new government and the Social Democrats, the Centrist delegate von Guérard — who certainly was not particularly inclined toward the Left — replied with an extended, polemical speech. As the leader of the Democrats, Koch-Weser, remarked with wit, Guérard could have made his message much more brief if he had simply let the Reichstag know those points on which he now suddenly agreed with his new German Nationalist friends.[41] Of course every politician knew what the one point of agreement was: the intended school law. They also knew that this proposal was causing severe headaches in the ranks of the third major member of the coalition: the People's Party. But at this moment the coalition was still holding together. It received the Reichstag's confidence by a vote of 235 to 174. The opposition consisted of Social Democrats, Democrats, Communists, and one Centrist delegate, Joseph Wirth.

Thus after Scheidemann's speech the Social Democrats found themselves pushed into even sharper opposition than before. They had, of course, no reason to let any consideration for this new gov-

ernment keep them from trying to make maximal political profit
from his revelations. But they did nothing of the kind. The Russians
had been extremely worried lest the German government find itself
obliged to make disclosures embarrrassing to the Soviets. Ambassador Krestinski had characteristically suggested to Stresemann that
he deny everything. Stresemann had good reason not to follow this
advice.[42] But he did promise to inform Krestinski in advance of
whatever disclosures he might have to make.

The time for such explanations came in the first days of February 1927, when the new Reichstag Committee on Foreign Relations
met. At this time Stresemann was recuperating at San Remo, so
State Secretary von Schubert had to represent the Foreign Ministry
at the meeting. The Russians and Brockdorff-Rantzau were, to quote
State Secretary Pünder's letter to Stresemann, "frightfully disturbed." But everything went off smoothly: "As a result of the
Chancellor's extensive conversations with all the parties, especially
the Social Democrats, and of the careful preparation of the government's explanation — which was finally delivered by Gessler —
the affair may be regarded as completely concluded. State Secretary von Schubert is radiant." [43]

Does one do the Social Democratic delegates an injustice if one
concludes from this outcome of the affair that they too had begun
to doubt the wisdom of their tactics in December?

IV

SOCIAL, ECONOMIC, AND FINANCIAL PROBLEMS

The German economy achieved a certain degree of stability after the acceptance of the Dawes Plan, the Locarno treaties and Germany's admission to the League of Nations. This therefore seems a suitable place to glance at the problems in social and economic policy which the Weimar Republic faced. I have, of course, no intention to treat these problems extensively and in detail here, but rather to discuss them so far as seems necessary to complete the history we have thus far observed and to add to our comprehension of what follows.

After a revolution which the socialistic laboring class could regard as its own work, it was only natural that the cry should be raised for that special cure which had previously been the principal goal of the movement: *the nationalization of means of production* or, as it was called at this time, socialization. But however comprehensible these expectations were, and however loudly and emphatically the cry for them was raised, those Social Democrats who were in politically responsible positions saw the many difficulties that stood in the way of such a program. And, in fact, the immediate postwar period was singularly inappropriate for such radical changes in the nation's economy. The war was de facto over but peace was not yet concluded; the currency was showing signs of softness; and the economy faced an immeasurable task of reconstruction. Thus the early Social Democratic government could in fact do nothing more than appoint a committee to investigate the problem and make recommendations for carrying out the socialization of Germany.[1]

But little came of this attempt, and there is little sense in trying to determine whether this failure was due to the difficulties inherent in the problem or whether subjective complications had also been at work. But however that may be, it remains obvious that as the German people gradually got a clear idea of the size of their reparations burden, and as their currency sank deeper and deeper into the pit of inflation, only the fanatics among them could still believe that Germany's distress could be alleviated through socialistic experimentation. Moreover, each successive election showed with increasing clarity that the supporters of socialism constituted only a minority of the German people. It is true that Article 156 of the Weimar constitution gave the Reich authority "to effect socialization by transferring appropriate economic enterprises into the public domain" upon payment of proper damages (Article 153, Paragraph 2). But the Social Democrats failed in their attempt to turn this authorization into a governmental duty.

Yet the pressure in favor of introducing the public interest further into areas of the national economy remained so strong that the National Assembly created new and special organizations — under the catchword of "socialization" — for two important industries: coal (the law of March 23, 1919) and potash (April 24, 1919). This legislation sought to reach two different ends: the enforced cartelization of industry and the internal transformation of these cartels through the admission of representatives of workers and consumers to their governing boards. It was hoped that industry would in this way take on a "public economic" (*gemeinwirtschaftlich*) character and thus, in contrast to purely private organizations, pay proper heed to the interests of the entire community.

This hope was not fulfilled. Walter Eucken describes the actual results in the following passage.

When the labor force shares the profits of monopoly, then the workers have as strong an interest in maintaining and enjoying the benefits of the monopoly as does the entrepreneur. The coal miners agreed to the cartel's demands for higher prices so long as their wages were to be increased proportionately. The participation of workers' representatives in the management of the monopolies gave the cartels broader bases. In this way the workers joined the entrepreneurs in a *single* group of monopolists. This union did not protect the common national interest.[2]

But a truly auspicious attempt to unite employers and workers in joint, peaceful collaboration for the common interest had been begun during the last months of hostilities. In the exhilaration of the first months of the war it had been easy to unite both sides in such common endeavors. This mood, however, understandably lapsed as the war drew on and each person began to worry more about his private interests in the future times of peace. Thus there was a real danger that the entrepreneurs would return to their roles of "lords in their own manors" which they had liked so much before and that radical agitators would seduce the broad laboring masses into revolt against their "appeasing" union leaders.

Opposing this danger was a small group of men who realized that the German economy would be able to afford such cannibalistic warfare even less after the war than during its course. Hans von Raumer, who at that time directed the central organization of the electrotechnical industry, may claim the credit for having taken the initiative in this matter. In October 1918 he approached the chairman of the Free Social Democratic Unions, Karl Legien, with a well-considered plan.[3] Legien, a sober-minded, responsible man,[4] agreed completely with the idea of creating an industrial council which would seek compromises between opposing interests and foster peaceful conciliation between management and labor — providing that the workers and their unions were assured full equality in such a council. It was perhaps even more important that Raumer succeeded in ensuring the cooperation of Hugo Stinnes, whose great successes had won him admiration and a willing following among most other entrepreneurs.

Under the direction of these two men the negotiations proceeded so rapidly that even the outbreak of the Revolution did not terminate them. In mid-November 1918 the trade unions and the employers' associations signed the agreement which created a new central committee on a balanced basis. In December 1918 the committee gave way to the Cooperative Association of German Industrial and Commercial Employers and Workers (*Zentral-Arbeitsgemeinschaft der industriellen und gewerblichen Arbeitgeber und Arbeitnehmer Deutschlands*), which was pledged in its charter to "the responsible recognition that the re-establishment of our national economy demands the concentration of all economic and spiritual forces and requires harmonious collaboration on all sides."[5]

The Cooperative Association honored this pledge during the first years of the Republic, contributing greatly to the preservation of Germany from chaos after the Revolution. Karl Legien's early death (December 26, 1920) was a heavy loss. Hugo Stinnes' decision to name one of his new freighters after the late labor leader was one more expression of the spirit of candid collaboration that pervaded the group. But even Legien would probably not have been able to hold it together much longer in the face of the growing conflicts caused by inflation and the ever increasing economic difficulties. Furthermore, the Temporary National Economic Council

(*Vorläufiger Reichswirtschaftsrat*) had assumed many of the association's duties.

From the very beginning the labor unions had had to contend with the opposition of their most radical members, who saw something tantamount to a betrayal of their traditional sense of class warfare in the deliberate attempts at conciliation that the Cooperative Association explicitly announced. These rebellious tendencies naturally grew in strength as the nation's distress increased and political differences grew sharper. The inflation had emptied the unions' treasuries, thus weakening the authority of their central offices vis-à-vis the rank and file and giving those employers who wished to use it a good opportunity to revert to a policy of rugged individualism. To be sure, the most prominent entrepreneurs were not among those who so reverted; they held firmly to the idea of conciliation. But even they could find no satisfactory solution to the very acute problems of wage and hour policy. When the most important unions resigned, during the fall and winter of 1923, the Cooperative Association was virtually killed.

The problem of the working day had confronted the association with difficulties from the very moment of its founding. After their victory in the Revolution the labor unions had insisted that their old cardinal demand for the eight-hour day be included even in the association's charter. The founders had skirted this point successfully by arriving at a supplementary agreement making the institution of the eight-hour day in Germany dependent upon international participation in such a measure. In accordance with this agreement the eight-hour day was presumed and included in regulations for German demobilization. But attempts to achieve international cooperation on this measure failed.[6] It is true that the Washington Agreement on the eight-hour day was achieved in late 1919. But in view of the burdens placed upon Germany by the Treaty of Versailles, the German government had declined to ratify the Washington Agreement before it had been ratified by Germany's economic competitors.[7] When the British government declined to ratify the agreement in 1924 there was no further possibility of favorable German action.

But the severe consequences of a lost war — exacerbated as they were by inflation and the occupation of the Ruhr — turned out to be obstacles to the preservation of the eight-hour day in Germany. A majority of German employers declared it an insufferable burden in their present, hard-pressed position. Their reaction was of the greatest political importance, because the two opposing points of view on this issue were adopted by the two parties which were to be the indispensable supports at either end of the Great Coalition. Thus, while the Social Democrats were forced by their whole past to cling to the demand for an eight-hour day, the German People's Party assumed the advocate's role for the "economy" or, as their opponents preferred to say, for "heavy industry."

But in truth it was not only industrial management that considered the widely prescribed eight-hour day incompatible with the solution of postwar Germany's burgeoning economic problems. The conservative economist Lujo Brentano's outburst against the eight-hour day during the International Congress on Social Welfare, held in Prague in October 1924,[8] was perhaps just the product of a momentary flood of wrath at the Versailles treaty. But Brentano's views on the eight-hour day were shared by social scientists of a distinctly liberal-progressive bent, such as Professor Heinrich Herkner, and even several Social Democratic revisionists concurred. The working-day decree of December 21, 1923 — issued by Marx's first cabinet on the strength of the Enabling Law of December 8, 1923 — had been pointed in the direction of compromise.[9] In it the eight-hour day was maintained in principle, but so many possibilities were opened to its modification, especially through industry-wide collective bargaining, that the principle became more of an exception than a rule.

The recognition of the tariff contracts (*Tarifverträge*), that is, "collective agreements made with the employees' trade groups," [10] had been one of the most important items in the Cooperative Association's charter. It had been in accordance with this provision that on December 23, 1918, the People's Representatives had issued an "Order concerning Tariff Contracts" which increased their importance considerably in two ways: by making them invulnerable to further local bargaining and also by making them universally binding within a trade upon acceptance by the appropriate government authority.[11] The order further established the basis for the settlement of every kind of labor dispute through arbitration. The government hoped that this process of arbitration would limit the number of strikes, which, especially in the first, convulsive, postwar years, threatened to endanger the entire economy. On October 20, 1923, Stresemann's government used its powers under the Enabling Law of October 13, 1923, to issue a further decree concerning arbitration. This act created arbitration committees throughout Germany, each to deal with disputes in its region.[12] These committees combined the principle of labor-management equality with that of government authority by including representatives of labor and management in equal numbers but by being headed by one or more neutral chairmen who were named by the land government.

In addition to this provision, the position of "arbitrator" was created, one to be appointed by the national minister of labor for each major economic region. This arbitrator had special significance. For although the arbitration process aimed in general at arriving at a solution acceptable to both parties, the decree also recognized the possibility that the decision might be rejected by one or both parties to the dispute. In that case the arbitrator had the right to declare his decision binding if he found "it proper after a just consideration of both parties' interests and its execution in the national interest on economic and social grounds" (Paragraph 6). Thus the arbitrator was given a task as difficult as it was important, one which went far beyond the functions of a judge. This system worked satisfactorily for a few years; but in 1928 it was to face its most severe test in the great battle of the western iron industry, of which a more extensive report is made below.

This system of cooperation between a neutral, official chairman and representatives of employees and employers had existed for some time in the trade courts (*Gewerbegerichte*) for the settlement of industrial workers' wage disputes. (See Trade Court Law of 1890.) Later, in 1904, the institution was extended to cover mercantile employees. But even then the jurisdiction of these courts was limited in a way which contradicted the demands of the new age — especially those of the trade unions. For the unions were demanding labor courts which would deal with *all* kinds of labor cases, including those which stemmed from collective tariff contracts. But such an innovation would have made severe inroads into the unity of German administration of justice and was therefore strongly opposed.

This issue was of special, practical importance to attorneys, who were prohibited from appearing before trade and merchant courts and who thus would be excluded from the whole field of labor law if the jurisdiction of the special courts were extended in this way. It therefore took several years before a labor court law was ready to proceed from the drafting stage to that of parliamentary consideration. But the energetic and knowledgeable Heinrich Brauns, a welfare official from the ranks of the People's Union for Catholic Germany (*Volksverein für das katholische Deutschland*) who directed the National Ministry of Labor no less than eight years (1920–1928), was indefatigable. In April 1926, under Luther's second government, Brauns presented the draft of a labor court law to the Reichstag; in December of that year, just before the dismissal of Marx's third government, the much-amended measure was adopted by the Reichstag with the German Nationalists and the Communists in dissent (Labor Court Law of December 23, 1926).[13]

Following the wishes of the trade unions, the labor courts' jurisdiction had been extended as far as possible, especially by abolishing all consideration of the value of the item in dispute and by including all disputes based on tariff contracts. The unity of German administration of justice was maintained by the creation of two higher levels of appeal, land labor courts and a National Labor Court, which were to be attached to their respective regular land and national supreme courts. In these higher courts attorneys could appear, although they had to compete with equally qualified union secretaries. Cumbersome as it may have been, this arrangement did mean that the German bar maintained its interest in labor law and thus was able to take part in its development and interpretation.

In the realm of social security, Bismarck's insurance measures and, later, the National Insurance Law of 1911 had laid the basis upon which the Germans could have continued to build firmly had not inflation intervened, inflation which not only consumed the great reserves of the insurers but often kept them from being able to meet their running expenses. Therefore, once the value of the mark had been restored, the legislators' first task was to reintroduce order to the finances of German insurance. The task was made more difficult by forces that tended constantly to extend the range of required insurance. This extension is only partly attributable to the fact that the inflation required many people, formerly able and willing to care for themselves, to turn to this sort of financial protection.

Health insurance had a particularly significant growth. Between 1924 and 1928, especially because of its increasing importance as a required fringe benefit, the number of health insurance policyholders increased from fourteen to twenty million.[14] This meant, of course, that the range of private medical practice was narrowed considerably. Furthermore, the health insurance authorities tried to restrict the physicians' freedom of residence, partly out of their financial concerns and partly, too, because of the tendency of any vigorous organization to extend its influence and powers. The physicians thus began to fear, to use Roepke's expression,[15] lest they "be turned into supervised health workers on an assembly line," and an antagonism developed which even threatened at times to lead to a doctors' strike.[16] These differences were of political importance, too, because the health insurance companies were generally regarded as Social

Democratic organizations and it was easy to interpret antagonism toward them as antagonism toward the Republic.

But the gravest social security problem in the years following the inflation was a financial one: specifically, the burdening of the national budget. It was inevitable that the national government should step in with financial aid in order to make the insurance companies solvent again after the inflation — for which, after all, the national government had been more or less responsible — had emptied their treasuries. One can, however, question the wisdom of extending such government subventions to cover even the companies' running expenses and of submitting to their ever greater claims for this aid. The national burden for such welfare insurance rose from 129 million marks in 1924–1925 to 259 million the following year, then to 345 million in both 1926–1927 and 1927–1928.[17] These figures do not include the costs of unemployment insurance, which will be treated below in connection with the law of July 16, 1927, on employment offices and unemployment insurance.

After every major war the most urgent social problem is new housing. For during the course of a war — even in those countries where dwellings are not destroyed by enemy action — the construction of new homes necessarily ceases. During the inflation the Germans faced this problem rather helplessly. Indeed, they even exacerbated their situation by depressing rents through artificial means; only slowly, and then only incompletely, were the rents allowed to climb to counteract the falling of the mark.

After German currency had been stabilized, legislation opened the way to a gradual return to prewar rents; these former levels were reached in 1925. Simultaneously, however, the owners of prewar houses were saddled with a burden which was designed to assist the construction of new dwellings. The Third Emergency Tax Decree, of February 14, 1924, increased preinflation mortgages — which had dissolved as the mark lost all value — by 15 percent of their former value (later legislation raised this figure to 25 percent) and imposed on residential property owners a rent tax (*Hauszinssteuer*) which originally amounted to 10 percent of the prewar rent but which gradually grew to 15 to 20 percent. The guiding principle here was that the property owners, having been enriched as their mortgages disappeared, should yield a portion of their gains to the construction of new housing.

The proceeds from this rent tax accrued to the lands and, through them, to the towns. The towns were permitted to keep part of this income for general purposes; the rest, however, was to be used for new — primarily low-rent — housing.[18] Thus housing construction became, to a large measure, a public matter, while private residential construction declined sharply. Much was accomplished in this way. The number of new residential units increased from 205,-000 in 1926 to 309,000 in 1928.[19] Indeed, some demographers even came to the conclusion that the amount of new construction exceeded the nation's predictable needs.[20]

However that may have been, surely the greatest difficulty in the housing market was caused by the fact that the construction costs of new buildings had risen phenomenally with respect to prewar times, while the rents of prewar buildings were forcibly held to a level that no longer had anything to do with relative supply and demand. On the one hand, this meant that in postwar buildings rents had to be subsidized with public funds. On the other hand, with respect to prewar buildings, it created a situation which Professor Waldemar Zimmermann of the University of Hamburg described in the following way to the meeting of the Congress for Social Welfare at Königsberg in September 1930:

Under the planned economy of the housing market and the controlled suppression of rents in prewar housing, a lease on a prewar apartment (or the right to such a lease) has become in essence a monopolistic title of value with which the owner is loath to part because, under this planned economy, he cannot easily regain or replace such a title through his own efforts. And so it is that everyone clings tightly to his old apartment, even if it no longer suits his needs. There are fewer vacancies than a free housing market with higher, prewar rents would yield; indeed, on a national average more residential space is being occupied per person than was the case in 1910. The family sticks fast to the same old apartment even when the children all have left. People are unable or afraid to move . . . The simple offer of such a lease evokes an unnatural, speculative demand . . . The statistical number of people looking for such apartment leases swells far beyond the true demand for housing space.

Zimmermann outlined the effect of such policies on the German economy as follows: "Entirely apart from actual loss in national income, we suffer a diminution in capital value to less than reproduction costs — indeed, to a point far below the original construction costs — a narrowing of the national credit base, and a lessening of disposable capital at a time of need that calls for the creation of capital." [21]

This policy that was so objectionable economically had, of course, motives of welfare. It was designed to help keep as low as possible that part of the employee's pay check which he had to use for rent. This motivation was, understandably enough, especially marked in the larger cities, where the great mass of voters were wage earners.

We are obliged to limit ourselves to this sketchy and necessarily incomplete overview of the social problems and policies of the Weimar Republic. It has shown the Republic's clear tendency to favor the workers as much as possible and to satisfy the wishes of their unions, even in those cases when this meant slighting the interests of other groups. One cannot, therefore, help but ask whether this favoritism strengthened and made firm the bond connecting the workers to the German democratic state. Perhaps one should not overestimate the importance of the signs which Radbruch reports the Social Democratic young workers carried in their parades: "*Republik, das ist nicht viel, Sozialismus ist unser Ziel*" (A republic is nothing grand; for Socialism we take our stand).[22] But these signs did show that the younger workers had very little respect for their fathers' republican ideals, and that they did not know how to make responsible use of a victory that a historical accident — which their party's strategy had not foreseen — had tossed into their laps.

Yet even more important is the fact that in the following years the election results gave no affirmative answer to this question of the workers' loyalties. Or at least one cannot observe as strong a turn of labor sentiment toward the Republic as would have been necessary to outweigh the distaste for the Republic which prevailed in those circles which believed that the new German state had favored the workers at the expense of their own legitimate interests. And these disaffected groups were, if less numerous, still economically and, in part, intellectually of a political importance which could not be ignored.

The condition of German industry and agriculture after the inflation was characterized by a marked lack of operating capital. To be sure, the physical plant was still there and the mortgages had almost disappeared. But bank accounts and other credits had also gone up in smoke.[23] And capital was necessary not only to carry on business, but also to pay the taxes which the national government had to impose on an unprecedented scale if the new currency were to be preserved and the national budget kept in balance.

This capital, which Germany had lost in her inflation, was made available from other lands. Foreign lenders, especially Americans, were attracted by the high rate of interest which was the natural consequence of the lack of German capital. Then, too, there was the great confidence which foreign countries had in the German economy. Despite the gloomy pessimism prevalent in Germany, people abroad considered the German economy — especially German industry — basically sound and had a high regard for German diligence and economic efficiency. This willingness to lend capital to the Germans also expressed the conviction in other countries that German politics had reached a state of calm; that neither domestic revolt nor belligerent adventures were to be feared.

This confidence in German political affairs was demonstrated especially by the readiness of foreign lenders to grant quite considerable credits to German lands and municipalities. According to the reparations agent's report, these loans to German public corporations amounted to 1.25 billion marks in 1925, only to climb to almost 1.7 billion in 1926 and to total 1.5 billion in 1927.

The lessening that is visible in the final figure was partly due to the institution of a certain degree of control by the national government. The Law of March 21, 1925, made these foreign debts incurred by German municipalities and associations of municipalities subject to the approval of the national minister of finance, who established an Examining Office (*Beratungsstelle*) for the consideration of such cases.[24] Prospective foreign loans to lands had also to be presented to this office. In the period from January 1, 1925, to September 30, 1927, some 25 percent of these requested land debentures were denied. The cities were less successful in their quests for loans: they were refused 46 percent of their prospective funds.

The office examined the purposes for which the debts were to be incurred and approved only those which promised immediate returns, that is, public works which would yield direct profits sufficient to cover interest and amortization payments. Many municipal political leaders opposed this policy. In the discussion at the 1928 meeting of the Congress for Social Welfare in Zurich, Ludwig Landmann, the mayor of Frankfurt am Main, argued that there was no essential difference between using foreign capital to build a power plant and using it for a hospital.[25] He went on to explain the basis of his stand: the construction of any kind of new works meant employment for labor; what the municipalities saved on the interest charges of a forbidden foreign loan, they had to spend in the support of their unemployed. To this Julius Bonn, speaking for the other side, replied that this use of foreign loans to fight German unemployment amounted to "semi-inflation." [26]

Schacht in particular took care that these foreign municipal debts were publicly discussed in a lively — indeed, often passionate — fashion. He accused the cities of throwing this money away for superfluous, or at least unnecessary, "swimming pools, parks, libraries, and playgrounds," and these accusations were eagerly echoed by his followers. The amount of strong exaggeration that was involved in these accusations is shown in the letters of protest which men like Mayor Karl Jarres of Duisburg wrote and which now are to be found in the Stresemann papers. No one who knows Schacht will be surprised to learn that he still maintains his objections; while, on the other hand, the German Municipal Congress (*Deutscher Städtetag*), in its *Festschrift* of 1955,[27] resolutely insists "that the cities were made public scapegoats on this issue of their alleged 'luxury projects.'"

Today it seems reasonable to say that this increase in municipal expenditures was an inevitable consequence of the altered political situation. The substitution of equal, universal suffrage for the Prussian three-class franchise was bound to lead to a retreat of the bourgeoisie — formerly in political command of municipalities — before the advance of the large working class which now could achieve its demands. The bourgeoisie, especially residential property owners and proprietors of medium-sized businesses, had for obvious reasons always pushed for government thrift in what the masses frequently felt to be unjustified, or even deliberate, ignorance of the workers' interests. Now, of course, things were quite different, and no municipal government could completely resist these new pressures.

Yet, even apart from this consideration, it is quite doubtful whether Schacht's campaign against the long-term foreign loans made sense unless there were to be a simultaneous restriction on short-term municipal borrowings as well. For, when the world financial crisis broke, its pressure on German municipalities was increased enormously by notices given on these short-term notes.

German industry used its credits from abroad principally for the "rationalization" of its plant, that is, to fill those gaps in equipment which war and inflation had torn and, further, to acquire new, more efficient machines. This sort of increased efficiency means that fewer workers are required for the manufacture of the same product or, expressed in other words, that some of the former workers become superfluous.[28] This fact is of little concern as long as the economic upswing remains so strong that workers displaced from one plant can find appropriate employment somewhere else. It becomes, however, a grave and dangerous problem when the business index levels off and starts to drop; for then unemployment grows faster than would have been the case without the newer, more "efficient" machines.

Rationalization is supposed to reduce production costs. But only in a free market does it lead to lower prices. If, through the formation of cartels or monopolistic mergers among firms, the rationalized industry finds a way to escape competition, then it can keep its prices unchanged, thus depriving the consumers of the benefits of rationalization. In Germany this was frequently the case. To be sure, the Cartel Order of November 1923 represented a legislative attempt to combat monopolistic mispractices. But, however much may have been accomplished here and there by this order, it neither obstructed nor even slowed the further spread of cartels. As early as 1925 there were 2500 such trusts.[29] The policy of protective industrial tariffs, which spared German industry competition from abroad, fostered this development. It also had the psychological effect of letting the German industrialist lose his taste for competition, accustoming him instead to the shelter of his powerful cartel.

German agriculture also attracted a great amount of foreign capital. Its new debts, incurred after the inflation had wiped out former obligations, have been estimated at seven billion marks.[30] Of these, a considerable portion stemmed either directly or indirectly from abroad. These new investments were also supposed to assist in rationalization; but various political circumstances prevented this form of improvement.[31] The most important — at least politically — of these hindrances was the low level of German agricultural prices. The question therefore arose whether the farmers should be afforded the same sort of protective tariff that they had enjoyed before the war.

The great majority of German economic experts were quick to give a firm no to this question. In September 1924 more than one hundred professors of economics at German universities issued a declaration stating that they favored industrial and agricultural tariffs only in so far "as they represent a necessary and promising means of creating a freer form of international trade." The declaration went on to decry as "particularly questionable" any "agricultural-economic measures which would lead to an artificial increase in German cost of living at this time." For, they argued, "a mere continuation of the prewar protective tariff" would not "improve in any important way — but rather worsen — the desperate straits of German agriculture." A large number of the signers of this unambiguous statement had been supporters of blatant protectionism before the war. Indeed, at the September 1924 meeting of the Congress for Social Welfare in Stuttgart, Professor Max Sering, the prewar leader in the fight for high agricultural tariffs, was greeted with enthusiastic applause when he pleaded for a "trade policy essentially free but armed with all the instruments of competitive rivalry."[32]

But practical politicians paid no attention to these academic protests. They continued, instead, ever further on the path of protectionism. Their first step was the so-called Small Tariff Revision of August 12, 1925, which reinstated — although at lower initial levels than those of 1902 — the agricultural tariffs that had been abolished at the outbreak of the war. Furthermore, the Decree of September 3, 1925, reintroduced the system of import licenses, thus ensuring that the new tariffs would mean higher prices for domestic grain as well.[33]

All this legislation was intended to give better protection to German agricultural interests. It was the work of Luther's second cabinet — the one dominated by a Rightist coalition — and had been sharply opposed by the Social Democrats in particular. But one must quickly add that later governments of quite different political compositions continued along this same path, while the academicians, on the other hand, began to waver in their protest. Max Sering's report to the Congress of Social Welfare at Königsberg in 1930 can be said to exemplify this later change. After a study trip to America, where he had observed the influence of mechanization on agriculture, he now defended agricultural protective tariffs — especially on grains — most strongly as a form of aid to infant industries.

The advances which the German economy — except for agriculture — made during these years represent all the greater an achievement since they were accomplished under a tax burden which exceeded anything known before the war. Helfferich had budgeted the national government's regular expenditures for three billion marks in 1923.[34] In 1924 the regular expenses amounted to 6.8 billion, and in the succeeding years they climbed to 7.3 billion. In addition to these mounting national expenses there were also the budgets of the lands and municipalities, and they, too, showed a constant tendency to rise. Indeed, here was one of the most pressing and burning problems of German public finance. For all these government bodies had to be supported by a single economy, and this economy had therefore to be protected lest any one government body claim a source of income which another had already sucked dry. Yet, at the same time, the lands and municipalities were insisting on a large degree of financial independence in order that they might meet the different demands being made upon them.

This problem of "fiscal equilibrium" (*Finanzausgleich*),[35] as it came to be called, is peculiar to a federal state and existed in the days of the Empire, also. But now it had become much more severe and much more critical, for the consequences of the war required the central government not only to invade the realm of direct taxes (formerly reserved to the separate principalities or, now, lands), but also to take over from the lands the responsibility for the collection of tax monies. This had been the essence of Erzberger's national financial reform; it had been much criticized but its inevitable necessity had never been seriously questioned.

It is therefore not astonishing that the solutions which were found to these problems did not prove permanent but rather led, after a year or two, to still further attempts to discover still better solutions. The national administration of finance enjoyed the services of the recognized German authority on these matters: the state secretary of the Ministry of Finance, Professor Johannes Popitz. Not only was he a prominent expert and a lawyer of superior intelligence, but he also had a broad and well-founded background.

Yet, in practice, the determination of this fiscal equilibrium was not made on the basis of any expert's well-considered opinions. Rather the decisions were reached by negotiations among the national government and the various land governments, and these decisions inevitably reflected the complexions of the political parties which happened to be in power in these governments at any given time. This government by "polycracy" — as Popitz disdainfully called it — gave, from the very start, an ephemeral character to the definition of fiscal equilibrium.

Since the Reich had seized for its own purposes those sources of income upon which the federated German principalities had previously depended for most of their budgets, the lands now demanded that a large share of these new national funds be returned to them. After the inflation the Third Emergency Tax Decree of February 14, 1924, gave the lands and municipalities 90 percent of the receipts from income and corporation taxes and 20 percent of the sales tax. But no more than one year later, after the acceptance of the Dawes Plan, the lands and municipalities saw their share of the first group of taxes dropped to 75 percent, although that of the second group was raised to 30 percent by this same Law of August 10, 1925.

Thus in their financial activities the lands and municipalities were largely dependent upon the policies of the national minister of finance. If he found ways to draw vast sums from the economy, the land ministers of finance and local treasurers could count on having large balances. And this was the case when Luther was collecting taxes. For after the ravages of inflation he had intended to set the Reich on such a firm financial base that there could be absolutely no danger of another inflation. From the standpoint of the national minister of finance this meant the careful avoidance of another national debt and deliberate provision for sufficient supplies of even future cash on hand. He achieved this goal, and this accomplishment remains his historic merit.

But to the German economy his achievement was a most painful operation, especially since the strong pressure of Luther's taxes was exerted at that moment when the inflation-flooded economy had not yet returned to dry land. It should not be held against Luther that he erred in the direction of caution, that is, that his estimated income from taxes proved lower than the amounts he actually found. For, given the state of the German economy at that time, overestimation would have been far more dangerous. As Otto von Schlieben, Luther's successor as minister of finance, pointed out in his budget address of April 30, 1925, income from customs and taxes had yielded 7.3 billion marks instead of the estimated 2.5 billion; and of these 7.3 billion, the Reich kept 4.5 billion marks, transferring the rest — some 2.7 billion — to the lands and local governments. It was in this way that the municipalities received that fatal impression of fiscal plenty which characterized their financial policies from that time on. For local governments are peculiarly prone to find projects which can be considered useful — indeed, necessary — and which demand execution when the necessary money is available.

But one cannot hold it against the taxpayers, from whose pockets all these billions had come, if they regarded the surplus simply as so much plunder wrenched from them, especially since they were suffering a lack of capital themselves and had to borrow operating funds for their concerns at high interest rates abroad. The demand for lower taxes therefore became quite loud, and various parties — the People's Party and the Democrats, among others — made it part of their national platforms.

The Democratic delegate Hermann Fischer was one of the sharpest critics of the financial policies of Luther's government and of his finance minister, von Schlieben, in particular. For von Schlieben was not satisfied simply to avoid a deficit today; he felt obliged to take care that there should be no deficit in the future. This was what his opponents called von Schlieben's policy of "thesaurization" or hoarding (*Thesaurierungspolitik*). He wanted to keep the 500 million marks which remained of his surplus — after debts and earlier deficits had been covered — as a form of national working capital. With this fund he wished not only to cover whatever cash shortages should occur at the end of an occasional month, but also to create a reserve against times of economic crisis, a reserve with which the national government could finance extraordinary work projects in order to prime the economy's pump and get money circulating once again.[36] At that time a majority of the Reichstag supported this policy, and Schlieben was permitted to create his 500 million mark reserve.

But then came the Treaty of Locarno and the departure of the German Nationalists from the government. Schlieben, much more the bureaucrat and technical expert than a party politician, had favored Locarno and did not share his party's intransigent attitude. But since he had sat in the cabinet as a German Nationalist, he considered it his duty to maintain party discipline and thus resign. His successor in Luther's second cabinet was the Democrat Peter Reinhold, who previously had directed the financial affairs of Saxony. Reinhold was the direct opposite of von Schlieben. Theirs was a basic difference which constantly reappears in public finance: on the one side stands the treasurer who regards his well-filled vaults as the best guarantees of a prosperous land; while on the other side we see the man who thinks that those monies bear richest fruit which are at work in the general economy, and who considers it a mistake to deprive the economy of even one mark more than the state requires for its immediate purposes.

Reinhold, who had a broad background in business, defended this second point of view with a clear determination and with his extraordinarily persuasive powers of argument. The difference between his policies and Schlieben's hoarding could not be put more sharply than in Reinhold's axiom that the national budget should stick "close to the brink of deficit." To carry out this program he proposed tax reductions, especially a lowering of the sales tax. It is no wonder that he found public approbation for this step. He was, indeed, probably the only German minister of finance who, at the conclusion of a speech to representatives of the business community, was greeted by an enthusiastic ovation.

Reinhold's experiment was successful. According to the testimony of Count Lutz Schwerin-Krosigk, who at that time was budgetary reporter in the Ministry of Finance, an economic revival began which brought even higher tax returns into the Treasury. Only experience could have tested the lasting value of Reinhold's policy. But by the end of 1926 Marx's government collapsed, and Reinhold could not join the new cabinet — which included four German Nationalists — because his fellow Democrats were now in the opposition.

V

MARX'S RIGHTIST CABINET

ONE of the best and most valuable qualities of Chancellor Wilhelm Marx was his utter sincerity. He treated his associates with a candid, unconditional loyalty which frequently evoked their fidelity in return. And so it took him only a relatively short time to create a corporate feeling in his new cabinet. By the end of February Hermann Pünder, state secretary of the Chancellery, was able to send Stresemann, who was still recuperating at San Remo, an almost idyllic picture of the collaboration between the older ministers and their new colleagues: "The settlement of the Keudell case proved difficult but quite successful in the end. The character of the new national minister of justice [Hergt] is doubtlessly above any suspicion. I share your opinion that he will prove an especially strong and valuable link between the old and new members of the cabinet. Herr von Keudell clearly feels himself especially obligated to the Chancellor, who handled this affair in, again, a model manner."[1]

But Keudell did not take long to show the world that his policy would differ sharply from what had gone before: on April 12, 1927, he abruptly placed two of the leading members of his ministry into temporary retirement. One was State Secretary Schulz, a Social Democrat who presumably did not agree with the new minister's plans, especially in the matter of schools; the other was Undersecretary Arnold Brecht, one of the best of all the nation's civil servants, a man who, although strictly nonpartisan, left no room for doubts about his firm democratic beliefs. The Prussian premier, Otto Braun, took care that this valuable resource was not lost by making Brecht director of his own ministry.[2] This appointment, understandably, did not please Keudell very much, especially since Brecht would now represent Prussia in the Reichsrat, over which Keudell presided.

The German Nationalist ministers also tried to exert influence on the personnel policies of their cabinet colleagues. In the spring of 1928, in a general reassignment of German diplomatic posts, Stresemann wanted to offer his seasoned ambassador in Riga, Adolf Köster, the more important post of Belgrade; but Hergt intervened, objecting that Köster was — a Social Democrat. Stresemann energetically rejected this invasion of his prerogatives. "This is the same attitude," he wrote to Pünder, "that the Conservatives had in the old Empire. To all of this I can only say that the gentlemen have learned nothing, but have forgotten all." [3]

From Stresemann's point of view the decisive question was whether or not the German Nationalist members of the cabinet would disrupt the continuation of his foreign policy. As late as the end of March he was still confiding his doubts on this score to Ambassador von Maltzan in Washington. Stresemann did not, however, cast doubts on the ministers' good will. But he did touch a sore point when he quoted Stinnes as saying that the German Nationalists' speeches were meant for home consumption and were not export articles at all.

In truth the addresses of his German Nationalist cabinet colleagues often caused him considerable trouble and embarrassment. While he was trying to arrive at a commercial agreement with Poland, a sharply anti-Polish speech by Hergt disturbed his plans. And, in May of 1927, while Germany was proposing tariff reductions at the World Economic Conference in Geneva, the German Nationalist minister of agriculture, Schiele, publicly demanded higher tariffs on agricultural products. Ernst Trendelenburg, state secretary of the Ministry of Economics and Germany's representative at Geneva, lodged a complaint with Stresemann, warning him that he (Trendelenburg) would have to withdraw from the conference completely if Schiele's speech were to prove the signal for a basic change in German trade policy. [4]

At this, Stresemann found himself obliged to consult with Marx, in order to obtain the Chancellor's explicit agreement to a statement that the German government had no thought of such a change in policy. At this conference Marx uttered the significant complaint that for him it was an impossible situation to have all the German Nationalist ministers always voting with Schiele so that he, as Chancellor, always had to break ties with his vote. But even Marx's own Centrist colleagues failed now and then to exercise prudent self-restraint. On April 28 the British ambassador, Lindsay, complained to the German foreign minister that the finance minister, Heinrich Köhler, had stated publicly that he did not think Germany would be able to carry out the Dawes Plan in the future. [5] Under these cir-

cumstances how was Stresemann to make progress on the evacuation of the Rhineland? Stresemann reported this event to the Chancellor, who also was clearly displeased by Köhler's remarks.[6]

But if the principal problems of foreign policy were brought no
closer to solution in 1927, this was less the fault of the partisan composition of the German government than of the difficulties inherent
in the problems themselves or, to put it another way, of the opposition, especially in France, to further rapprochement. It is quite comprehensible — particularly after the discoveries the Allies had recently made — that the problem of the evacuation of the Rhineland
could not be settled over night. One need only think of the deterioration in France's military position that such a move would have necessarily involved. German public opinion merely displayed its own
impatience for the Rhenish fruit to ripen when it interpreted this
delay as simply another example of French ill will.

It is nevertheless true that as early as November 15, 1925, the
Allied Conference of Ambassadors had solemnly promised Germany
to reduce their occupation forces, and Stresemann was completely
correct in telling the British ambassador that it was time to proceed
from those fine words to deeds. Nor was Stresemann alone in this
stand. At the Geneva Conference of June 1927, in which Chamberlain and Vandervelde, along with Stresemann and Briand, took part,
the British foreign secretary made it abundantly clear to his French
colleague that things could not go on much further in this way: the
situation was intolerable to Great Britain, and the Allies would have
to satisfy the Germans on this point. In a private conversation with
Briand, he even went so far as to say that he would decline to make
any accusations of the Germans "as long as our hands in this matter
are as dirty as they are at present" — and straightaway he shared
this thought with his German colleague also.[7]

To this British caveat the French could only reply weakly that
certain aspects of German disarmament still remained to be settled.[8] This was true enough; but in relation to everything that had
been accomplished in Franco-German relations, this deficiency was
insignificant, and the French generals made a rather poor impression by making so much of the issue. On the other hand, it was
equally lamentable that in all this time the German government had
been unable to put its military house in order. Today one can certainly see that it was not only in France that military circles were
meddling dangerously with politics. In any event, by the summer
of 1927 negotiations had progressed to the point where the problem
of German disarmament could be considered settled, and an Anglo-
French compromise on occupation policy was reached. On August

27 the Allies decided to reduce their occupation forces by 10,000 men. This decision had been reached just before the fall meeting of the League of Nations, at which Stresemann made formal announcement of the impending reduction of troops. German public opinion, of course, regarded this as too slight a step. And in fact an occupation force of almost 60,000 men remained. This was certainly too large a force if things stayed quiet. But could France be sure they would?

Among those Germans who continued to cause the French concern was no less a man than the *Reichspräsident* himself, Field Marshal von Hindenburg. Even while the League of Nations was still in session at Geneva, the Tannenberg National Memorial commemorating the great German victory over the Russians in August 1914 was unveiled in East Prussia. As was only natural, the President, whose name was gloriously connected with this battle, took part. The ceremony was significant in two ways. It widened the gap between Hindenburg and his former quartermaster general; for Ludendorff declined to share a car with Hindenburg to review the troops. And second, the President proceeded to deliver an address in which he again raised the war-guilt issue, proclaiming Germany's complete innocence to the entire world in the most explicit terms.

No one will doubt that Hindenburg, who had scarcely examined the documents of July 1914 at any time, believed in his country's complete innocence; nor will anyone doubt Hindenburg's private, personal right to express such an opinion. But he was speaking as President of Germany, and it was as such that he wished to be heard. This made the matter considerably different. And if there was anything that could have added to the painful impression his words made outside of Germany, it was the telegram which the former Emperor sent to his former field marshal at the unveiling ceremonies. In this unfortunate message William tried once more in his old style to push his worthy personage into the center of events, signing the telegram "William, Emperor and King" as though he were still sitting on the imperial and royal throne in Berlin rather than in Dutch exile. What means could be better calculated to awaken suspicions that the President of the German Republic and the former Emperor were simply two different names for the same character?

This is exactly what people presumed not only in France, but also in the other nations of the Entente. In Geneva, too, there was great excitement — as Stresemann quickly told his Chancellor. The German foreign minister regretted that the President had omitted from his speech a sentence which had been meant to give his original

draft more the flavor of a personal observation than an official statement by the chief of state.[9] Von Hoesch, the German ambassador
in Paris, found himself obliged to wire Stresemann that in the opinion of "leading French personages" the address had been "rather
inopportune. This sort of public discussion of the war-guilt question . . . will lead to no positive results, but only to unpleasant
antagonism." The Allied chiefs of state had intended to send congratulatory messages to Hindenburg on his eightieth birthday. But
after the Tannenberg address the King of England categorically
declared that he would send no good wishes to Hindenburg, and
with this, naturally, the matter was closed.[10]

Yet despite all these intervening difficulties, Germany's international position had improved extraordinarily. This progress became especially apparent in the course of the Anglo-Russian tensions of 1927. In May of 1927, after a police investigation of the
London offices of the Arcos (All-Russian Cooperative Society) and
those — in the same building — of the Russian trade delegation, the
British government had determined that both agencies were cen-
ters of Communist espionage and agitation.[11] Thereupon — on May
26 — England broke off diplomatic relations with Russia. The Soviets
proceeded to depict this move as the first step in a British war of
aggression against Russia.

This British action had also excited some discontent in several
Western European countries, a discontent which grew when, on
June 7, the Russian ambassador to Poland was assassinated in the
Warsaw railroad station by a White Russian student. On this same
day Chicherin sought out Stresemann in Baden-Baden, where the
German foreign minister was on vacation, and had a rather extended
conversation with him. Whatever sympathies had been with Russia
in this quarrel with England quickly gave way to horror at the news
of the mass executions with which the Soviet authorities relieved
themselves of "unreliable persons."

At this point — in June — when Chamberlain, Stresemann, and
Briand gathered in Geneva for a meeting of the League of Nations,
another intimate conference among the so-called Locarno powers
took place. It was only natural that they discussed the situation
created by the Anglo-Russian rift in some detail. After Chamberlain
had reviewed the origins of the quarrel, Stresemann was asked to
present his country's point of view. The German foreign minister
noted that, while he recognized the need, which was also felt in
Germany, to combat Bolshevist agitation, he strongly opposed any
attempt to isolate Russia by common action among the Western
powers, let alone any "crusade" against the Reds. He did not forget

to allude to Germany's economic interests in vigorous commerce with Russia — which were hardly suffering from the Anglo-Russian conflict — and even rose to the exceedingly optimistic prediction that Russia would be led down the road of peaceful evolution by means of such lively economic traffic with the West.

The other statesmen too, especially Briand, had no desire to engage in active conflict with Russia; nor was this Chamberlain's intent. Indeed, Briand appeared quite distressed by the turn Russo-Polish relations had recently taken; and he was especially worried when Stresemann reported that Chicherin had told him Pilsudski was a "pipedreamer and adventurer" who wanted to unite Lithuania, Byelorussia, and the Ukraine with Poland into one federal system and was eager to unleash a war.[12]

Although the assembled statesmen did not endorse this one-sided description of Pilsudski, they all agreed that the international situation was extremely uncomfortable. And at this point Chamberlain turned to Stresemann and asked him to use his good relations with Russia, and with Chicherin in particular, to help ensure the peace of Europe. "Join me," he urged the other statesmen there, "in a request to Herr Stresemann that he employ his relationship to Chicherin in order to preserve Russia and the world from a general conflict over this incident."[13] And this was just nine months after Germany had joined the League of Nations! Stresemann was quite right in writing from Geneva to his Chancellor that everyone who had participated in the conference was convinced of the importance of Germany's membership in the League. And among these he expressly included the German Nationalist member of his delegation, Otto Hoetzsch.[14]

Yet, the majority opinion in Germany was that Stresemann had not achieved very much at Geneva.[15] His German Nationalist colleagues in the cabinet had no interest in emphasizing the successes of his policies; they had always opposed them in the past and intended to fight them again whenever domestic circumstances should permit. Furthermore, Stresemann's natural allies were now in the opposition and hence were more inclined to criticize his efforts than to support them. The Right had kind words for Stresemann only when, as at Geneva, he attacked those German pacifists who were complaining of secret German rearmament.[16]

In the course of one such rebuttal Stresemann went so far as to call Professor Friedrich Wilhelm Foerster, editor of the pacifist magazine *Die Menschheit* in Wiesbaden, a "scoundrel" (*Lump*). This slip won him a letter of protest from Foerster's eighty-year old uncle. Stresemann, who in the meantime had clearly recognized his error, replied to the letter in a way that the professor could take as a veiled apology. Foerster, a man of high moral sensitivity, preferred to regard Stresemann's letter as a retraction of an insult. He set forth his position and unburdened his anxieties in a heated and detailed message to the foreign minister.[17] In his letter he claimed to be "one of the most German of Germans" and pointed with alarm to the dangers of revived Prussian militarism which he saw threatening Germany:

I have not the slightest doubt . . . that the parties in question are being supported in their attempt to regain power for themselves — by inexhaustible material resources, arms, the force of tradition, ideology, and three hundred years of German standing at attention and goose-stepping — to such an extent that their final domestic victory (despite temporary uncertainties and setbacks) appears absolutely certain *unless* people in Germany and abroad recognize the danger in time and do everything in their power to show those parties that they will not be caught napping.

To Stresemann's objection that he was injuring Germany's interests he replied:

I am a German with more intimate and varied relationships abroad — some of them inherited [Foerster's father, Professor Wilhelm Foerster, was the famous astronomer and chairman of the German Society for Ethical Culture] — than any of my compatriots, and I can assure you that, quite without our warning and long before it, numerous parades, manifestoes, and political manipulations in Germany . . . had brought things to such a pass that even in ever widening circles of the Left . . . a distrust in the intentions of the German Right and in the power of the German Left . . . to block completely and in time the realization of those intents has been growing ever stronger . . . My entire aim has been to demonstrate the necessity of such action to the Germany of Locarno and to provide it with the required evidence to show clearly what is going on behind the scenes and how the passivity of peaceful Germans appears to foreign eyes when accompanied by such things. Among them belong, too, most of the treason trials, of which the radical paper *Volonté* recently wrote that it was intolerable to have the German solicitor general, Werner, "contradicting the reassuring words of M. Stresemann before the eyes of the civilized world."

Today who can still accuse Foerster of having painted too black a picture or of having exaggerated? And perhaps what he said about the "intentions of the German Right" and the "power of the German Left" made a lasting impression on Stresemann. He does not appear to have answered Foerster. But the documents show that he at least tried — with the assistance of Minister of Justice Hergt — to get Roettcher, editor of the *Menschheit*, released from his imprisonment on suspicion of treason. The foreign minister was motivated in this effort, as he wrote to the pacifist Helmut von Gerlach, by a desire to keep Roettcher from becoming a martyr and also to avoid creating the impression that someone in Germany might have a reason to hinder him from making his own defense.

Stresemann went on to say that he hoped to oppose in open court "the *Menschheit's* absurd claim that I had any knowledge whatever of Germany's so-called rearmament program." And, he continued, he wanted to determine by sworn public testimony "whether it is the *Menschheit* or the responsible German military authorities who are lying." [18] One should not, of course, take this statement to mean that Stresemann was denying the existence of *any* secret rearmament in excess of the limits set at Versailles. He certainly knew that such things were going on, even though he presumably took care not to learn more about them than was unavoidable. His denial referred only to the rearmament plan which the *Menschheit* claimed existed — and which even von Gerlach considered a mirage.[19]

It may well be that, while reading Foerster's letter and while considering the treason trials against the pacifists, Stresemann thought of the unscrupulous manner in which Rightist agitators — especially the petty ones — hurled the most extreme and insulting accusations of treason at himself and his fellow "fulfillers." It was, for instance, at this time that he learned how, at a *Stahlhelm* meeting, a speaker had accused him of "unabashed falsification" and of "high treason." Seldte, chairman of the *Stahlhelm*, when pressed upon this point, could only offer the excuse that the speaker had been talking not as an officer of the *Stahlhelm* but rather as a private citizen.

Or there was the time that a German Nationalist party secretary grumbled aloud in a public café that Stresemann was "a common blackguard" and "could be bought." It is true that Stresemann's complaint to Hergt had some effect: the party removed the gentleman from his post. But how many such filthy libels circulated unknown and uncensured through the country? Stresemann was determined not to take personal refuge in the courts; he had had bitter experiences in his libel suit against a Racist lawyer in Plauen. Was it wrong, then, to speak of a "crisis in the nation's confidence in the administration of justice" when even those who bore responsibility for the welfare of the state did not have enough faith in German courts to entrust them with their honor?

The political composition of Marx's new cabinet had nothing

to do with the fact that in the spring of 1927 the government was able to present the draft of a new criminal code to the Reichstag. For the reform of the criminal code had been on the agenda ever since the new school of criminal law — which is most particularly linked to the name of Franz von Liszt — had gained influence over general legal thinking and had created its own organization in the International Union of Criminalists. Official German authorities had been engaged in this revision since the beginning of the century, keeping theorists and practitioners of criminal law busy preparing proposals and counterproposals in plenty. In autumn of 1926 the national Ministry of Justice, in which the undersecretary, Erwin Bumke, was especially concerned with this reform, had presented the draft to the Reichsrat. In May of 1927 it reached the Reichstag and had its first reading that June.

This first reading was made memorable by the broad and stimulating address with which the Nestor of German jurisprudence, seventy-eight-year-old Professor William Kahl, a delegate of the People's Party, opened the debate. The various parties, which usually guarded their rights of precedence with jealous zeal, had unanimously agreed to give him the floor first. Immediately after his speech, the spokesman for the largest party delegation, the Social Democrat attorney and former national minister of justice Otto Landsberg, was recognized. He began his speech with the following words: "No matter how much may separate our views here, it is fortunate that there are sentiments, too, in which we all agree; and among these is the honor we bring to the honorable. And so I trust that you will let me serve as your common speaker in expressing to the honored gentleman who has just spoken my honest admiration for his address, in which the wisdom of age was coupled with the fair ardor of youth." These were words which one seldom heard in the German Reichstag, which was so racked with partisan emotions. And it is for this reason that so rare and moving a moment should not be forgotten here.

The draft was referred to a committee from which, unfortunately, it never returned. It is one more part of the German democratic tragedy that the constant government crises kept this committee from being able to bring its deliberations to any positive conclusion.

The most fruitful legislative acts of Marx's government stemmed from his two Centrist ministers, Brauns and Köhler. Heinrich Brauns, national minister of labor since 1920, had, through his various official actions, gained a reputation for being a social progressive. He knew quite well how displeased the worker members of the Center were with their party's allegiance with the Right, and he was therefore especially eager to show them that even in such a combination they could continue to proceed vigorously with welfare legislation. In this, indeed, he found support throughout the cabinet.[20]

One of the most important questions was that of the working day.[21] Brauns succeeded, albeit only after violent quarrels among the government parties, in fashioning a new legal version of the decree that stemmed from December 1923. His version introduced a rule of great practical importance: extra time beyond the normal working day stipulated in the tariff contract or otherwise was to be paid for at a rate above the normal wage (Paragraph 6a of the Law of April 14, 1927).[22] It was rather paradoxical that not only the Communists, but the Social Democrats as well, voted against a law which, on this decisive point, brought such real progress to the workers.[23]

Even greater was the importance of the law of July 16, 1927, concerning employment offices and unemployment insurance. This law, which had been enacted only after long dispute and many changes, basically granted unemployment relief to any German citizen who was willing and able to work, had no job, and met the conditions of the law (Paragraph 87). This was doubtlessly a great step forward in welfare. But in their enthusiasm over this success, the progressives had let themselves be carried away by a financial optimism to which the facts soon presented a tragic contradiction. The insurance fund was to be built up and supported by a 3 percent tax on wages, to be paid in equal shares by the employers and the workers. But only 700,000 workers at best could be cared for by this fund. In addition to this, an "emergency fund" was to be created, by means of which 400,000 more workers could be supported in time of crisis. But this *maximal* total of 1,100,000 workers was far less than the 1,300,000 *minimum* to which the number of German unemployed had sunk in the best months of 1926.

In other words, the lawmakers relied on the hope of a future economic recovery to finance their unemployment insurance scheme. There were good reasons for anticipating such an upswing — indeed this hope was fulfilled for a short time — but the plan meant that whenever self-financing proved temporarily inadequate to meet the demands of the unemployment fund, the Reich was obligated to make up the deficit in the fund through federal loans. Here lay the germs of severe problems and bitter conflict.

Of similar importance was the measure which is to be regarded as the sole work of the national minister of finance, Heinrich Köhler:

the raising of civil servants' salaries. Köhler, who had come from the middle ranks of German bureaucracy himself, had a very strong sympathy for the way government officials had been forced into straitened circumstances by their insufficient pay. In most cases their standard of living was lower than it had been before the war. At that time their salaries, if by no means sumptuous, were at least adequate. Most important, many civil servants had been able to supplement their government salaries with the interest on their private fortunes or those of their wives. Furthermore, the thought of the title or decoration which beckoned to the official after years of loyal service repaid him for the paucity of his material perquisites. The "chancellery counselor" was a person respected by his friends, even if they knew he had to ponder every penny that he spent.

But now their fortunes had been annihilated by the inflation and the Republic had deprived herself of the simplest means to console her servants for the emptiness of their purse: the Weimar constitution had banned titles and decorations. If civil servants were to be helped, the Treasury would have to be resorted to; and Köhler believed that the condition of national finances permitted that. But a natural consequence of raising the salaries of federal civil servants was that land and local officials also demanded an increase. And since the lands and municipalities energetically denied that they could pay this additional sum from their own revenues, at least a part of this further burden fell upon the national government in the form of higher subsidies to lands and towns.

Once the national minister of finance had placed the question of these salary increases on the Reichstag's agenda — and he did so quite quickly — the trend became irresistible. For there was no party that dared to disaffect the administrative bureaucracy. As voters, the civil servants, with their organized, identifiable unity, made up in cohesiveness for whatever they may have lacked in numbers; and as delegates they commanded respect and fear in all the German legislative assemblies.[24] Of the 493 members of the Reichstag, no less than 156 were civil servants, and it was principally from among these administrative legislators that the parties selected their representatives for the committee which was considering the proposed salary change. It was natural that the Social Democrats should be concerned mostly about the lower categories, and the German Nationalists more especially about the higher levels; but on the question as a whole the parties united in a solid front supporting all ranks, from the bottom to the top.

After the finance minister had opened the gates, the flood could not be restrained. Originally he had been considering increases of perhaps 10 percent; but by the time the bill was ready for enactment, they had risen to between 21 and 25 percent. There was no lack of warnings, even from the ranks of the minister's own party. Heinrich Brüning, who already was considered one of his party's financial authorities, feared lest these increases lead to a general rise in wages and hence to a dangerous permanent increase in German production costs.[25] Delegate Stegerwald shared Brüning's fears and was even bold enough to mention the threat of corruption involved in having so many civil servants in the Reichstag.[26] But when the final vote was taken the salary increase was accepted by the great majority of 333 to 53 votes.

Both the cabinet and the delegates, who together had wished this new burden upon the nation's finances, knew that their move had incurred the disapproval of one authority whose opinion carried great weight: the agent general for reparations. A young American banker, Parker Gilbert, had been given this extremely important post. Gilbert did not consider that he was fulfilling his duties simply by making sure that Germany met her reparation payments promptly — and he had nothing to complain of on this score. He was also particularly concerned lest German financial policies endanger the future operations of the Dawes Plan.

This second aspect of his responsibilities required that Gilbert have cordial, sympathetic relationships with authorities in the German Ministry of Finance. Unfortunately, this rapport did not develop.[27] State Secretary Popitz in particular seems to have made no efforts in this direction. All the more intimate, therefore, were Gilbert's relations with the President of the Reichsbank, Hjalmar Schacht, who shared Gilbert's misgivings about those financial policies of the government that he had not suggested himself. In his semiannual report of June 1927, Gilbert had expressed these doubts emphatically. He especially criticized the rising claims on the national treasury — including national subsidies to lands and local governments — and urged the German government to make "normal provisions" for the maintenance of a stable, balanced budget.[28] As a consequence of this report a special cabinet meeting was held, to which the Chancellor invited the *Reichsbankpräsident*.[29]

Here Schacht gave free vent to his criticism. He claimed that for the last two years he had been saying what the reparations agent had just observed, and he insisted that the government's increase of civil servants' salaries and its general financial policy could not go unchanged. Although much of his criticism was well taken, his manner was so arrogant and overweening that the ministers became highly irritated. Stresemann sought to control his temper by sketching all sorts of Roman numerals on his paper, and after the meeting Köhler — who, of course, had been the principal object of Schacht's attack — called Schacht "Germany's opponent, representing the creditors' interests against those of the nation." [30] The ministers' anger grew all the greater when they learned that afterwards, at a party in the home of the German Nationalist delegate Dr. Quaatz, Schacht had boasted of his performance, scornfully recounting how the ministers had suffered his philippic "like drenched poodles."

As early as March 1927 Parker Gilbert had directed a confidential letter to Köhler, in which he expressed his misgivings about the intended alterations in Germany's fiscal equilibrium and especially about the national government's guarantee to transfer 2600 million marks to land and local governments.[31] In October Gilbert took another, greater, step when he sent the minister of finance a comprehensive memorandum which Köhler felt obliged to make public — along with his reply.[32]

In this memorandum Gilbert pointed out to Köhler that in two years' time Germany's government expenditures had risen by 1.7 billion marks; he emphasized that the lands and municipalities were receiving larger national subsidies than ever before; and he warned of the financial consequences which could ensue from the Reich's obligation to assume full responsibility for any future shortage in the unemployment insurance fund. With special emphasis he accused the government of having let itself be pushed along step by step in the matter of raising civil servants' pay, pointing out that the German Treasury now faced additional expenses of between 1.2 and 1.5 billion marks to meet the bill. On the other hand, he argued, there had been no effective attempt at a thorough administrative reform. And the final observation in the memorandum was opened with a quite obvious implication: "If one were to permit the tendencies just described to take their full effect, it is, on the one hand, practically certain that they would lead to observable economic recessions and depressions, and, on the other, highly probable that they would strengthen the impression that Germany was not allowing proper consideration to her reparation obligations."

The publication of this memorandum aroused great excitement in Germany. Most Germans tried to reject it as an unauthorized attempt on the reparation agent's part to interfere with things which were none of his concern. Many Germans lamented the fact that their country had sunk so low that a foreigner dared appoint himself as critic of the Reich's internal affairs; for this showed that Germany was not really a sovereign power. But there were other voices which agreed that Gilbert was right in what he said.

The Democratic delegate Hermann Fischer [33] complained that the German government had given the reparations agent this opportunity "to express such a sharp and all too justified criticism of the principal features of German financial policy at the national, land, and local levels." Professor Adolf Weber of Munich, an academician who stood far from party politics, told the Congress for Social Welfare that it was one "of the gravest errors made since the World War that, in a time of gradual adjustment to a new state and social structure, civil servants' salaries were raised so high that an annual financial burden had been created *which falls little short of the annual reparation payments.* This was an error principally because this salary increase was not simultaneously connected with that rationalization of the government administration which alone could have made this burden — which the national economy suddenly had to bear — in some measure tolerable." [34]

The Ministry of Finance, in its answer to Gilbert's memorandum, tried to demonstrate his exaggerations, although it did accept his arguments on many points. In justification of the new salary schedules Köhler emphasized the political considerations involved: the granted increases were designed "to preserve a very large segment of the German population from most severe distress and to restore their somewhat shattered confidence in the state's concern for their well-being." He argued that Germany could experience "no worse hindrance in the work of reconstruction than to have the German civil service, famous for its loyalty and honesty, sink into a state of unreliability."

This was certainly a relevant argument. But it had force only if one were certain that the national, land, and local governments could maintain this higher salary scale *permanently.* For if they were later to find themselves forced to take back from their officials what they had given them in 1927, the effect would be much worse than if the increases had never been awarded at all. And this later demoralization of the civil service would perforce occur at a time of general crisis, when the state would be encountering many other threats to its existence. Even Otto Braun observes in his memoirs: "This relatively excessive salary increase scarcely won any civil servant to democracy, but the salary cuts which later proved necessary drove countless officials into the National Socialists' camp — where, to be sure, after 1933 they discovered that they had jumped from the frying pan into the fire."

When Parker Gilbert accused the German government of having failed to make any serious attempt to reform its administration, he was by no means the first man in Germany to argue the need for such a step. For some time critical minds had occupied themselves with the question whether the constitutional and administrative structure of the Reich were not much too complicated to meet the demands of the time. In these considerations the discussion centered primarily around the basic German problem: the relationship of the national government to its constituent members, previously called "federal states" (*Bundesstaaten*) and now known as "lands" (*Länder*). Hugo Preuss had recognized this problem clearly — especially the problem of Prussia versus Germany — but had been able to carry out his plans for centralization only in part because of the opposition of the separate state governments and of their supporters in the National Assembly.

The solution with which the framers of the Weimar constitution had had to content themselves, therefore, satisfied neither the centralists nor the federalists. Chief spokesman for the federalists was, of course, the Bavarian government, which presented its proposals in memoranda to the national government first in January 1924 and then, again, in January 1926.[35] Among the proponents of centralization, the chairman of the Democratic Party, Erich Koch-Weser, was particularly prominent. Koch, however, simultaneously supported a far-reaching decentralization of administration and an expansion of home rule.[36] It was even more extraordinary when the premier of Prussia, Otto Braun, used an address he was delivering to Social Democratic students of the Berlin University in February 1927 as an occasion to declare firmly his strong desire for a centralized German state.[37] But even its supporters were not agreed on how this program of centralization was to be carried out.

It was also Braun who, together with Carl Petersen, the mayor of Hamburg, proposed to the national government that a conference be called at which this problem could be discussed by representatives of the national and the separate land governments. The federal government held such a lands conference (*Länderkonferenz*) at Berlin in January 1928; and one would probably not be wrong in assuming — especially in the face of Gilbert's criticisms — that the national government was glad to take this opportunity to show that it was not standing idle before the problem of simplifying its administration. At this conference the premiers of the most important German lands expressed their views, all the way from the Bavarian federalist Heinrich Held to the Prussian centralist Otto Braun.

Since the opinions of these men differed so widely, they could only agree that the present state of affairs was unsatisfactory. No agreement was reached on the proper manner of repair. So they could do nothing better than accept a rather vague resolution and establish committees to study the separate issues and bring them closer to solution. And in fact these committees did do much to illumine the problems involved and to investigate the implications of various plans for reform. The reports of the Prussian representative, ministry director Arnold Brecht, were recognized by experts as being especially valuable. But, given the sharply divergent interests of the parties involved, it was impossible for them to arrive at a practical result in the short time left the Germans for peaceful political progress.

To a certain extent it was understandable that Bavaria should cling to its federalistic traditions throughout these negotiations. For the Bavarian People's Party was still the ruling party in the land. From its ranks had come Premier Held, who held this post for more than eight years, from 1924 to 1933. He had seen the folly of Kahr's ways and knew perfectly well that no political movement ran more contrary to the federalist program of the Bavarian People's Party than did the National Socialists. Conflicts with the national government, such as the shortsighted and stubborn Kahr was always stumbling into, were carefully avoided by Held. But he could not help the fact that in Berlin — and in republican ranks in general — people had a longer recollection of the dangers which Bavarian policies had brought the Republic than the men of Munich would have liked.

Now the federalists' standpoint was essentially fully as legitimate a topic for discussion as the centralists', and the Bavarians could justly point out that of all the non-Prussian lands theirs was the only one large enough in size and population to be able to play the role of a true state. And with equal validity the Bavarian People's Party could point out that a great part of the Bavarian population — especially the small farmers and the urban middle classes — had remained its faithful supporters through good days and bad. At every Reichstag election the party gained its million votes, and until 1933 it remained the strongest party in the Bavarian Landtag, furnishing every premier and a majority of ministers.

Yet, ever since 1922 the party had had to form a coalition with the German Nationalists in order to create a majority in the Landtag. Franz Gürtner ruled in the Bavarian Ministry of Justice as the Nationalists' minister. He alone sufficed to give any supporter of the Republic — indeed, any supporter of an objective administration of justice — earnest misgivings. For he had been responsible for the parody of justice that marked the Hitler trial.[38] And it was he, again, who was responsible for the fact that the Bavarian prosecuting attorney raised no objection when Hitler's imprisonment was eased in a way that made neither political nor penological sense nor when the Austrian was paroled with truly scandalous speed, after serving only six months of a mandatory five-year term.[39]

Some people may have considered it merely a question of relative efficiency whether the administration of justice should be left to land officials as before or whether, in the future, it should be "nationalized" and carried out by agencies of the national government. But when the Bavarians replied to this demand for nationalized justice with the pathetic plea that judicial sovereignty was an essential and immutable property of the separate lands, one was forcibly reminded of the way Bavarians dispensed justice in their so-called "people's courts." A man like Minister of Justice Gürtner certainly was no adequate safeguard against the evils wrought by these courts.

The lighthearted manner in which the Bavarian government — even under the direction of so moderate a man as Heinrich Held — ignored inconvenient provisions of the Weimar constitution was exemplified by the way it granted titles in the face of the express prohibition of Article 109 of the constitution. Thus, for instance, Bavarian jurists were granted the title of privy counselor of justice (*Geheim Justizrat*), and — apart from a few striking exceptions — they accepted the title without a second thought even though the maintenance of constitutional law was a part of their professional duties. Only a Supreme Court decision of December 9, 1929, on an appeal by the national minister of interior, put an end to this mischief.[40]

Vigorous as the debate about constitutional reform may have been among the experts and affected authorities, one can hardly say that it excited much interest among the general population. Only one item of the debate was an exception to this rule: the allocation of tax receipts. Even the most fervent Bavarian particularist realized that the national government, which was carrying the reparation burden, had first claim to tax monies. All he asked was that his land receive special consideration in the collection of these funds.

The law that established German federal fiscal equilibrium had provided that the lands which were relatively poor in tax returns (*steuerschwach*) — that is, those whose tax receipts per capita were less than 80 percent the national average — should have this difference made up, within certain limits, by subvention from Berlin (Paragraph 35). The principal beneficiary of this Poor Land Clause was Bavaria, which, for instance, received such a national subsidy of no less than 3.7 million marks in 1926.[41] The government of Prussia, where per capita tax receipts were close to the national average, opposed this practice sharply. And Otto Braun's indignation at the favoritism Bavaria was enjoying waxed even hotter when the Bavarian premier had to confess to him that in many Bavarian villages the schoolteacher and the postman were the only taxpayers.[42] In other words, the Bavarian peasant, as a rule, did not pay taxes — a fact which, of course, did not keep him from screaming loudly at the way Prussia and Berlin were exploiting him and his land.

At about the same time that Held made this confession to Otto Braun, Adolf Müller, the well-informed German ambassador to Bern and formerly the editor-in-chief of the Social Democratic *Münchener Post*, told Stresemann of a recent visit he had made to Munich, where he had found the mood of the peasants and those economically dependent upon them nothing less than "rabid." [43] Landtag delegate Thimm, the "quite peaceful and easygoing" leader of the Social Democratic delegation, was quoted by Müller as saying significantly that: "The beer tax had exhausted the farmers' patience entirely, and their wrath is being richly exploited by those who have an interest in revolt."

This beer tax was an especially sensitive issue in Bavaria.[44] People there could not forget that this had been a state tax until 1919 and that it had then been transferred to the national government — but only for due compensation. (Württemberg and Baden had done likewise.) These compensation claims had become repeated subjects of legislation and of quarrels. In April 1927 when a national law granted these three South German lands a rather generous compensation, Prussia objected to the act for showing an unjustified preference, especially for Bavaria, at the expense of the other lands. Prussian delegates voiced these objections in the Reichsrat, but they were defeated — with the help of the votes of some Rightist Prussian provinces. Thereupon the Prussian government went all the way and lodged a complaint with the Supreme Court, arguing that such a law required more than a simple majority vote.

Here Prussia found success. In an extremely important decision of November 17, 1928, the Court declared the compensation law unconstitutional and hence invalid. This was the first such decision of the Court.[45] It was clearly this judicial defeat of Bavaria to which Müller was referring when he said that Bavarian opinion had been brought to a full boil.

One item of the national expenses which showed a persistent tendency to climb was the defense budget. Military expenditures rose from 476 million marks in 1925 to 504 million in 1926 and 553 million in 1927. The corresponding naval figures were 156, 200, and 215 million marks. The opposition found such a steady increase inexplicable in view of the unalterable limits to the Army set by the Treaty of Versailles.

Defense Minister Gessler was particularly embarrassed by the fact that it was none other than his own Democratic Party that demanded a 10 percent cut in the defense budget; he had to exert all his powers of rhetoric and debate not only to reply to this demand but also to fight the Left's growing lack of confidence in the Army. "One can make no progress," he argued, "by constantly declaring one's distrust. You will never win the Army's loyalty that way. You can destroy the Army, but you cannot win it to you. It, too, wants a little praise now and then." Gessler went on to say that the Army obeyed its leaders and that he was convinced one could rely upon them absolutely. Antirepublican types, he said, were being barred from enlistment. The military budget was accepted as proposed.

This was Gessler's final budget speech. In January of the next year he was forced to resign.

The causes of his dismissal were the impenetrable and unconstitutional financial activities of the Defense Ministry. In order to be able to make expenditures which would remain hidden from the Entente, the ministry presented false budgets to the Reichstag. The correct figures were shown only to representatives of the Reichstag's Budget Committee, who, "out of patriotic sentiment, collaborated" — as Henry Bernhard, Stresemann's confidant at the time, reports.[46] One of these two gentlemen belonged to the Center; the other to the Social Democratic delegation — clear evidence of the extent to which the opinion had spread that it was every good German's duty to help circumvent the disarmament provisions of Versailles. Yet this collaboration also shows that people regarded the clandestine expenditures only as a means of strengthening Germany's defenses. Neither a Centrist nor a Social Democrat would knowingly have helped in secret preparations for aggressive war.

But the several million marks which could be smuggled into the defense budget in this way did not satisfy the eager men on the Bendlerstrasse.* They thought they could raise many millions more if the ministry were to become silent partner to a number of profitable enterprises. One of the most active members of the ministry in these endeavors was a Captain Lohmann, chief of the Marine Transport Division. Lohmann regarded the film industry — among several other areas — as a particularly fruitful field of operations, and so he invested some ministry funds in the Phoebus Film Corporation. But

* The German defense offices were situated on the Bendlerstrasse in Berlin. TRANSLATORS.

instead of bringing him the millions he expected, Phoebus merely swallowed up his investment and then went bankrupt.

In the bankruptcy proceedings all the corporation's financial transactions were uncovered, and it became apparent that loans of considerable magnitude had been accepted from the government. The first of these loans — in the amount of three million marks — had been made in March 1926 over the signatures of Finance Minister Reinhold, Defense Minister Gessler, and the chief of the Marine Transport Division. The Leftist press naturally made much of this affair, criticizing it as a radically unconstitutional form of financial behavior. There was no evidence of a desire for personal profits on the part of the officials concerned, but the simple facts were bad enough, and Gessler realized that he could not defend them before the Reichstag. And so, on January 14, 1928, he tendered his resignation, basing it on his poor health and the heavy blows that he had suffered from fate. Hindenburg accepted it immediately.

Thus ended not only Gessler's official service, but his political career as well. Since he had previously resigned from the Democratic Party and had joined no other, there was no place for him in parliamentary life. He had been minister of defense for eight years, constantly under attack but almost always victorious. Some of the accusations that were made against him were certainly well founded. Nevertheless one should not forget the real service he rendered Germany, especially in 1923 — the year of worst crisis — when he fought to save the Republic, and in 1926 when he forced Seeckt to resign. It is true that he made many enemies; but his many friends recognized his eminent intelligence and his ability to cope with the most difficult situations, and they honored his selfless patriotism. These friends stuck by him both in good times and in bad. The tragedy of Gessler's life — and perhaps the tragedy of the German people — was his failure to succeed Ebert as President of the Republic. German political life suffered in the loss of so talented a man.

Who was now to take Gessler's place? Article 53 of the Weimar constitution gave the president the right to appoint his ministers, but restricted him to the chancellor's nominations. Thus it was Chancellor Marx's obligation to submit to Hindenburg the name of that man whom he felt fit to fill Gessler's shoes. But, again, it became apparent that the political center of gravity had shifted in a way unforeseen by the constitution. The government coalition had just been severely shaken by events which will be dealt with immediately below. New Reichstag elections were about to be held, and they were generally expected to show a strengthening of the Left.

One could make a good case for the proposition that a minister of defense should have a longer tenure than the national cabinets, up to this time, had enjoyed. In concrete terms this meant that Gessler's successor should not be a man who would have to resign if the Social Democrats gained a decisive voice in the next government. But even more important than these rather sophisticated considerations was the simple fact that the President was a field marshal who regarded the Reichswehr as a personal concern in which he was loath to let a civilian interfere. He had got along well with Gessler, whose intelligence and political talents had impressed him and who knew how to observe the formalities dear to the Old Gentleman's heart. But Hindenburg had no desire to discuss military affairs with whatever professional politician the kaleidoscopic shift of relative party strengths might put in Gessler's place. So the Old Gentleman seized the initiative which properly was the Chancellor's.

The object of his choice was General Wilhelm Gröner.[47] Whether Hindenburg hit upon Gröner independently or whether others — especially General von Schleicher — directed the President's attention to him is unimportant here. The significant fact is that the President made the nomination and that the Chancellor accepted it. The German Nationalist ministers cannot have been especially charmed by this appointment, but they knew full well that their own days were numbered. Their party colleagues who were among Hindenburg's "Old Comrades" probably complained vehemently to him about the choice, but they were unable to suggest a better man and they could not deny the arguments in Gröner's favor.

They certainly had no objection in principle to the appointment of a general as minister of defense. And where was another general to be found with Gröner's extensive experience as a minister? (He had been minister of transport from 1920 to 1923.) Was the President to appoint perhaps General Count von der Schulenburg, the former chief of staff of the Army Group "Crown Prince" and now a German Nationalist member of the Reichstag? In all likelihood neither Marx nor Stresemann would have accepted him, and in any event the new, predictably more liberal Reichstag would have put an end to Schulenburg's ministerial glories. The Old Comrades could make only two objections to Gröner: first, that he was a democrat, and, second, that he had advised William II to abdicate. But under the prevailing political circumstances, the first item argued in Gröner's favor, not against him. And Hindenburg knew the facts behind their second objection better than they ever could themselves.

For here, indeed, was the field marshal's sore point: he knew all too well that on November 9, 1918, in Spa he had not acted as the monarchist myth would have it now, and he also knew that no one was more aware of this than Gröner. But Hindenburg was also convinced that he could trust the general completely. Gröner had given full proof of his devotion when he suffered in silence the bitter attacks unleashed by nationalistic officers — with Hindenburg's tacit acquiescence — on the events of that November ninth. At the time Major von Schleicher had aptly written to his mother that "these vicious attacks constitute a crime committed by the Rightist parties for tactical reasons against their better conscience." [48]

The monarchists accused General Gröner with special emphasis of having told several gentlemen of the imperial retinue that day that in times of revolutionary upheaval the concepts of "military oath" and "Supreme Commander" lose their meaning.[49] The truth of this statement was completely obvious on November 9, 1918; but for this very reason it had to be passionately denied by those who wished to glorify the old regime. At that time, in order to put an end to the attacks, Gröner had voluntarily submitted himself to a court of honor composed of former officers. In autumn 1919 the court — albeit with tongue in cheek — pronounced the accusations against Gröner unjustified.[50] Throughout this trial, which was so critical to his career and reputation, Gröner had taken pains "to avoid in his testimony any statements that might have cast even the slightest doubts on other personalities." Most important among these "other personalities" was, of course, Hindenburg, who had every reason to be grateful to Gröner for what he had done.

And at still another even more important occasion Gröner had again selflessly relieved the field marshal of a dread responsibility. This was in those unnerving days of June 1919 when the crucial decision either to sign or to reject the Versailles treaty had to be reached. President Ebert had just made a personal telephone call to the Supreme Army Command at Kolberg to determine the generals' final recommendation. At that critical moment Hindenburg absented himself from the room. Gröner was thus left to give President Ebert the advice that both the field marshal and Ludendorff knew was inevitable and urgent. Hindenburg undoubtedly knew what he was doing when he covered himself in the mantle of silence and let Gröner do the talking. For as soon as the conversation was over he re-entered the room and told Gröner, "You have assumed a heavy responsibility. Once more you will have to play the scapegoat." Once more! On June 23, 1919, even as on November 9, 1918.

Gröner had his reasons for letting Hindenburg use him as his scapegoat. On March 22, 1935, after he had suffered the full measure of Hindenburg's ingratitude and after Hindenburg was dead, Gröner wrote: "I deliberately sought to glorify Hindenburg's name for political reasons." These political reasons did not lie, of course, in the realm of party politics, for which Gröner had no taste; rather they were grounded in patriotism. For Gröner considered it his patriotic duty to maintain the German people's faith in the man they had chosen as their hero. He did this in full knowledge of the popular idol's shortcomings. He knew just as well as General Hoffmann [51] — who had been prominent in Hindenburg's general staff on the eastern front — that the field marshal had contributed little but his name to the great military events that took place there. In the letter quoted just above Gröner also says: "On my second visit to the supreme commander of the eastern front I received the distinct impression that Hindenburg was nothing but a figurehead . . . But despite his phlegm and inactivity the old fellow was quite ambitious, not just during the war but until he died." These ambitions required Hindenburg to use a scapegoat, and Gröner offered himself for the role, confident that he was serving his country by so doing.

Can one then be astonished that, when he answered the President's invitation to join the cabinet, Gröner believed he would have a thankful friend in Hindenburg; one on whom he could safely rely in all the storms and crises which he knew would lie ahead? We shall see how greatly he was to be deluded in this trust.

Gröner was also bitterly deceived by another man: General Kurt von Schleicher.[52] How often had Schleicher called himself Gröner's "most faithful and devoted admirer"? Or extolled Gröner as his "most honored friend and mentor in all the important things of life"? And, at the end of Gröner's first year as minister of defense, Schleicher — now chief of the minister's office — wrote him an enthusiastic letter which culminated in the following peroration: "The fulfillment of my desires is that I may continue to be honored by having such a superior with whom and for whom I may work and strive onward. Such an association as mine must be a joy and real delight to any reasonable man. It is in this spirit that I hope Your Excellency will accept this testimony of my gratitude for the year just past and of my unalterable fidelity for the year to come." And Gröner, who valued Schleicher's intellect and mental agility and who had expressed his attachment to him by calling him his "adopted son," believed in this "unalterable fidelity."

Chancellor Marx saw no reason to reject the nomination Hindenburg had made and on January 19, 1928, Gröner was named national minister of defense. The public was not unaware of the fact that the new minister had been selected by the President, and that many fervent supporters of the Weimar constitution were concerned about this new, unconstitutional method of appointment — however much they may have agreed with Gröner's being in the post. Indeed, the new minister was greeted much more warmly from the Left than from the Right. And even Scheidemann, the leader of the fight against the Army, devoted a sympathetic column to its new minister.

Gröner had learned from Gessler's bitter experiences that an end had to be put to the veiled, impenetrable financial doings of the ministry. He found it intolerable that these operations should force upon the minister of defense a responsibility which he was neither able nor eager to bear. And so on October 18, 1928 — that is, after the elections had been held and a new government had been formed — a cabinet meeting was called at his request. Here General Heye, for the Army, and Admiral Raeder, for the Navy, were asked to make a clean breast of the secret expenditures which were being made contrary to the provisions of the Versailles treaty. Among those present at this meeting were the new Chancellor, Hermann Müller, and his new minister of interior, Severing. Much later, on May 21, 1946, at the Nuremberg Trials, Severing recollected that the clandestine military payments had totaled between 5.5 and 6 million marks.

At the conclusion of the meeting it was agreed and directed that in the future no military authority would make such extraordinary expenditures without the defense minister's express approval, and that the minister would report all such cases to the cabinet, which would then assume full responsibility for the acts. On May 15, 1946, in the course of his trial at Nuremberg, Admiral Raeder said that Gröner was most sensitive on this point and that he dissolved all the so-called Black Army formations, usually with Severing's help. Gröner held firmly to this policy. Yet Severing was astonished to learn, in the course of the Nuremberg Trials, that the German Navy had had a submarine built at Cadiz between 1929 and 1931.[53]

Wilhelm Gröner had joined a cabinet that was already marked for death. The lack of agreement among the coalition parties on foreign policy became openly apparent on January 30 and February 1, 1928, in the Reichstag debate on the Foreign Ministry's budget. Baron von Freytagh-Loringhoven, a German Nationalist delegate, took this opportunity to attack Stresemann sharply. Freytagh-Loringhoven, a wartime immigrant from Livonia who had

already caused the more conciliatory leaders of his party acute embarrassment, pounced upon Stresemann with such vehemence that
the Centrist Father Ulitzka, leader of the Upper Silesian Germans,
called his address an opposition speech in both substance and form,
one which could only discredit Germany and its government at
home and abroad. While the German Nationalists and the Centrists
were opposing each other this way on foreign policy, the school
issue separated both of them from the German People's Party by
an unbridgeable gulf.

Here was one of the oldest and most intractable problems of
German domestic policy. The division of the rights of the State
from those of the Church in educational matters is a sensitive, complex problem in any country where a powerful church makes claims
which are regarded as ill-founded by a meaningful segment of the
populace. In England these complications made educational legislation the object of passionate political strife for more than a generation. In France "secularization" was the focus of political attention in the 1920's; and even today, when French interests have
turned to more material matters, the issue still can inflame passions
and affect the fate of governments.

In Germany this problem was made all the more intense by the
facts that the nation was divided into two main faiths and that
German liberals hoped to bridge this theological gap with a form
of school in which more than one confession would be represented:
a common or "simultaneous" school (*Simultanschule*). Moreover,
since about 1890 a quite strong movement had been developing in
favor of cutting all ties between churches and public education and
of banning all religious instruction from the public schools. The Social Democrats were the principal political representatives of this
point of view, although it was by no means rooted only in the Left.

These difficulties had become apparent while the constitution
was still being framed. The Catholic Center Patry knew that its
support was necessary if the Republic were to survive, and it used
its political indispensability to further as fully as possible those of
its demands which, by its very nature, the party held most dear. It
was only in the final stages of deliberation that the three parties
to the Weimar Coalition — Centrists, Social Democrats, and Democrats — arrived at the compromise which was stated in Articles 146
and 174 of the constitution.

These articles provided for the establishment of a common
school — one which would permit religious instruction to all de-
nominations — as the *norm*. But deviations from this norm were

made possible by the very significant provision which permitted, upon the petition of the parents of school-age children, those entitled to public education to have separate, local public schools of their own faith or philosophy.

The basic regulations for the implementation of this policy were to be set forth in a national law which would govern subsequent legislation in the individual lands (Article 146, Paragraph 2). Pending the passage of this federal law, the legal situation was to remain unchanged (Article 174). This temporary freezing of the status quo favored those regions, such as Prussia, where conservative rule had fostered reactionary provisions for the schools, but the supporters of the new common school were assured by the next clause of this article. It directed that forthcoming national legislation make special allowance for those regions — that is, Baden, Hesse, and those parts of Prussia which were once Nassau — where common schools, open to more than one denomination, already existed. Thus a distinct element of compromise was explicitly manifested in these two articles of the constitution. And, as is so often the fate of such compromise settlements, these articles became the battlegrounds of opposing interpretations.

While the Center, from the standpoint of the Roman Catholic Church, was demanding separate confessional public schools, the German Nationalists were serving as the Protestants' political advocates of the same cause. Thus the two parties were agreed on their school program, much as the Conservatives and Centrists had agreed on this issue in the prewar Prussian Landtag. The national minister of interior, Walter von Keudell, devoted special efforts to finding a solution to the problem. His final proposal allowed for five possible kinds of public schools: Roman Catholic, Lutheran, and Reformed denominational schools; common schools, each offering instruction in more than one faith; and secular, nondenominational schools. Von Keudell was then prepared to let parents in each locality decide which sort of public school they wished to have.

This compromise solution effectively destroyed the concept of nation-wide common schools which had been incorporated in the Weimar constitution. The national government accepted von Keudell's proposal, although Stresemann and Curtius, the two People's Party ministers, kept voicing their misgivings. Understandably enough these two men regarded themselves as heirs to the traditions of the National Liberal Party, which had continually supported the idea of common schools and of a sharp limitation of ecclesiastical influence on public education. They were prepared, however, to keep their misgivings in abeyance, hoping that subsequent parliamentary negotiations would yield a new compromise with which they could be satisfied.

They were deceived in this hope. On the one hand, objection to von Keudell's plan proved stronger — not only in the Reichstag but also among the general public — than had been anticipated. While on the other hand, the Center in particular let itself be carried away more than was politically wise by its keen desire to make full use of this rare parliamentary situation which appeared to promise fulfillment of its dearest hope. Stresemann was enraged when, in a conversation of December 1927, the influential Centrist delegate von Guérard threatened that the Center would drive him from his ministry if the school issue should lead to Reichstag elections in which the foreign minister would direct his party in fighting Keudell's plan.[54] As Stresemann explained to State Secretary Pünder, this Centrist attitude made it impossible for him to help find an acceptable solution. Along with Guérard, Stresemann blamed another Centrist delegate, the prelate and professor George Schreiber, for having ruined all hope for compromise through his excessive zeal. An attempt on the President's part — by means of a letter to the Chancellor on February 9, 1928 — to bring the government parties to some agreement failed.

The collapse of Marx's fourth cabinet was occasioned by differences over a specific issue: the preservation of common schools in Baden. As a delegate from Baden, Minister Curtius had a special interest in the matter. When it finally became apparent that no compromise could be reached upon this point, the interdelegation Reichstag committee of the coalition parties held a meeting in which not only von Keudell's plan, but also the government coalition, was buried. Significantly enough, at this meeting it was Guérard who was the first to proclaim the end of the coalition and thus the cabinet's fall. Stresemann, who at this time was at Cap-Martin regaining his health, was astonished by the sudden developments. Conversations with Hindenburg and Marx just before his departure had given him the impression that negotiations on the school issue would be suspended for a time in the hope that subsequent discussions might lead to an agreement.

Marx's coalition had collapsed, but his government could not leave office immediately. There was a whole series of pressing legislative proposals to be dealt with, especially the national budget for 1928 and the supplementary budget for 1927. The government therefore agreed to an "Emergency Program," which was also more or less accepted — either actively or passively — by the opposition parties after the cabinet had assured them that it would dissolve the Reichstag and call for new elections once the program had been passed. This Emergency Program was accepted and, on March 31, 1928, the Reichstag was dissolved. The new elections were set for May 20.

In the national budget for 1928 there was an item which was to excite political discussion for a long time: the request for nine million marks as the first installment on the construction of a heavily armed cruiser. The Treaty of Versailles had allowed Germany — under certain conditions which now had been fulfilled — to build armored ships of up to 10,000 tons' displacement as replacements for the six battleships she was permitted to keep (Articles 181 and 190). Allied naval experts had clearly assumed that armored ships of such slight size — "pocket battleships," as they were called — would not be worth their costs, and this had initially been the Germans' opinion, also.

But in the course of the years the Germans had found a way to build ships which stayed within these bounds and yet combined a heavy armament with considerable speed. German military authorities naturally demanded that the German Navy make use of the alternatives granted in the Treaty of Versailles, and it was just as natural that President Hindenburg should warm to the thought. When Gröner became minister of defense he, too, agreed. On March 1, 1928, he presented the Budget Committee of the Reichstag with a request for the first installment on the construction of an armored ship — temporarily known as "Cruiser A" (*Panzerschiff A*). He succeeded in winning the committee's approval despite opposition from the Social Democrats, Democrats, and Communists; and this request served as the core of the speech with which he presented himself to the full Reichstag on March 14.

The general program which Gröner outlined in this address was sure to win him favor on the Left. He made the clear, unambiguous demand that every member of the Reichswehr "be a faithful, loyal servant of the state" and threatened with dismissal anyone who broke this rule. But he was even more effective when he said: "Like most of those who served in the World War, I am a firm believer in a *sound and intelligent pacifism* — though not in one that leads to servile submission." These were quite unusual words in the mouth of a German general, and anyone who knew Gröner well knew that to him this was not an empty platitude. In supporting his request for the armored ship, he argued that a modernized fleet would represent an increase in the strength of the nation's defenses, especially if one was convinced that Germany's land forces were insufficient to cope with real hostilities. But, he went on, if Germany were able "to prevent a fait accompli and to defend her borders until reinforced by the great military powers or international authorities," then her defenses would have served their purpose. He did not have to speak more clearly in order to make his listeners understand that he was thinking primarily of the possibility of a Polish attack.

The Social Democrats and Communists moved that the item be struck from the budget. Speaking for his delegation in one of these debates, Severing pointed out that the acceptance of the item would lead to the construction of four such armored ships at a total cost of over 100 million marks — a sum which could not possibly be raised in the next few years. He argued further that such naval construction would contradict the demands for disarmament which Germany was then making on other powers.[55] A majority of the Reichstag, however, supported the government and refused to strike the item.

But the Reichstag's acceptance of the budget was not enough. It had now to be presented to the Reichsrat, where a majority — led by Prussia — opposed the item. Yet, if the Reichsrat had raised an objection to the budget as passed by the Reichstag, an impossible situation would have existed. For according to Article 74 of the Weimar constitution the budget would then have reverted to the Reichstag for reconsideration. But the Reichstag had already been dissolved, and the national budget could not wait until the new elections. And so, on March 31, the Reichsrat contented itself with a resolution requesting the government to postpone work on the new armored ship — except for the preparation of detailed plans — until after September 1. The government accepted this restriction.

This peculiar situation enabled the Social Democrats to treat the question of the armored ship as an open, debatable issue in their election campaign. They made fullest possible use of this opportunity, hurling at the voting masses the battle cry "Not armored cruisers, but food for children" (*Keine Panzerkreuzer, sondern Kinderspeisung*). The election results showed that their propaganda had been extremely effective. But more thoughtful Social Democrats, like Severing, objected to this oversimplified formulation of the problem as a "concession to the terminology of the party's most radical wing." [56]

VI

THE GREAT COALITION ONCE AGAIN

Wʜɪʟᴇ the election results of May 20, 1928, showed German
Nationalists that participation in the recent government had hurt
their popularity at the polls, the Social Democrats observed that
there were advantages to be gained from being in the opposition.
Votes cast for the German Nationalists decreased from 6.2 million
to less than 4.4, to which the half million cast for the agrarian
Deutsches Landvolk * should be added. The number of Nationalists in the Reichstag dropped from 103 to 73, to whom the ten Agrarian members frequently allied themselves. The Social Democrats
could congratulate themselves on an increase of 1.3 million, from
7.8 to 9.1; they now enjoyed a delegation strength of 153 (in contrast to their earlier 131), which made them almost twice as strong as
the German Nationalists. Less pleasant from the Socialists' point of
view was the fact that the Communists had gained half a million
votes (from 2.7 to 3.2 million) and, with their 54 delegates, were
rather close behind the Centrists' 62.

The moderate parties had done very badly. The Center had lost
400,000 votes and, with them, seven seats. The Democrats had not
only lost what they had gained in 1924; they had dropped even
lower, to one and one-half million votes and 25 delegates, even
though they had most recently been in the opposition. The German
People's Party, which not only had belonged to all recent governments but had, through the person of their leader, Gustav Stresemann, set the tone of most of these regimes, had not fared much
better. Their delegation had shrunk from 51 to 45 and their sup-

---

* Formally entitled the Christian-Nationalist Peasants' and Rural People's Party
(*Christlichnationale Bauern- und Landvolkpartei*), it is not to be confused with the
German Peasants' Party (*Deutsche Bauernpartei*), also known as the *Bayrischer
Bauern- und Mittelstandsbund*. ᴛʀᴀɴsʟᴀᴛᴏʀs.

porters from 3 to 2.67 million. Yet at the same time the Economic Party, which candidly represented bourgeois interests, had gained six seats and almost 400,000 votes, showing that in broad middle class circles economic interests were becoming more important than political principles. Supporters of the Republic could, however, find comfort in the fact that the National Socialists had lapsed from 900,000 to 800,000 votes and would have only twelve representatives in the new Reichstag.

The Prussian Landtag elections, which took place the same day, showed the same results: a considerable strengthening of the Social Democrats, an equally great weakening of the German Nationalists, but also an even greater weakening of the Middle. Braun's government had gained at the polls, and he now had a majority — if a small one of 229 out of 450 seats — in the Landtag.

No matter what general attitude one took to the election results, one thing was immediately clear: time had run out on the Rightist coalition that had been in power; Marx would have to resign. He left office on June 17, 1928, just one day before the newly elected Reichstag convened. But what would be the composition of the next government? The Social Democrats, bolstered by their successes at the polls and by their delegation's strength, claimed the chancellorship, and the other parties yielded to this demand. Even the President bowed to constitutional procedure and after the customary consultation with party leaders declared that he was prepared to appoint a Social Democrat as Chancellor.

At this point it became the party's responsibility to determine which person they wished to propose for this highest office. Two men came into consideration: the Prussian premier, Otto Braun, and the party's Reichstag leader, Hermann Müller, from a Franconian district.[1] If the party had chosen Braun, they would have provided the occasion for an interesting experiment — a return to the imperial system in which the offices of German chancellor and Prussian premier were united in a single person. Both technically and politically this union would have been much more difficult under the Republic than had been the case before. But the experiment was not attempted since there was such strong support in the party for Müller that Braun conceded him the post.[2]

The appointment of a chancellor, however, obviously did not solve the problem of composing a new cabinet. The principal question was that of forming a government which would be supported by a majority of the Reichstag. A mere combination of the so-called socialist parties, that is, the Social Democrats and the Communists, would have been numerically insufficient, quite apart from the fact that these mutually hostile comrades had assumed radically different attitudes to the constitutional, republican state. The only possibility, therefore, was for the Social Democrats to form a coalition with parties to their Right. But for a parliamentary majority, not only the Democrats were necessary, on whose collaboration one could count, but also several other parties which had belonged to the most recent government, in particular, the Center and the People's Party. To bring all these parties into a common cabinet was anything but simple. The German People's Party, for instance, was to prove especially intractable.

During the election campaign Stresemann's health had broken down completely. He had let his Bavarian party friends persuade him to head the party slate in two of their districts. With this he had undertaken too great a load. On April 25, when he was holding a mass meeting in Munich, it became apparent that the National Socialists, who had lost all national significance at the time, were still strong enough in Bavaria to deprive an opponent of his right to speak. With their shrill whistling and loud singing they succeeded in drowning out the voice of the speaker they hated so much, so that after about an hour and a half Stresemann was forced to give up. Once more the Munich police had shown themselves unable to guarantee the right of assembly — even to the foreign minister of Germany.

This battle with the National Socialist rowdies had made greater demands on Stresemann than his already weakened health could endure. When, at the request of his party, he continued to campaign outside Bavaria for two more weeks holding meeting after meeting, he finally collapsed. On May 8 he had to return to Berlin and submit to medical treatment. He was found to have a serious infection of a paratyphoid nature that had affected his kidneys and was ordered to remain inactive for the immediate future. Shortly after the new Reichstag met, he repaired to the Bühlerhöhe health resort near Baden-Baden; thus he was not in Berlin at the time negotiations were proceeding on the composition of the next cabinet.

As a Social Democrat, Hermann Müller understandably placed the greatest importance on retaining Stresemann to direct German foreign affairs. For in all essentials Stresemann's policy had consistently been in agreement with the Social Democrats. Furthermore, one can interpret the election results to mean that a majority of the German people supported a continuation of that conciliatory policy of which Stresemann was the principal symbol. Nor was any objection raised to keeping the other People's Party member of the last cabinet, Julius Curtius, minister of economics.

But the People's Party thought it could use this situation to regain that position in Prussia which it had so thoughtlessly abandoned after the elections of 1924. And so, when Müller invited the party leaders to join his coalition, they said they would accept only if they were simultaneously guaranteed admission to the government of Prussia. But in this demand they met resistance not only from the Prussian Social Democrats — especially Otto Braun — but also from the Prussian Centrists, who refused to yield ministerial posts to the People's Party. Braun refused on principle to admit any connection between the formation of national governments, with their continual crises, and that of the government of Prussia, where parliamentary democracy enjoyed a stability unknown elsewhere in the Reich. Thus Müller's attempt at a Great Coalition had, for the moment, failed.

Good reasons can certainly be adduced for Braun's decision. One can well understand his misgivings at the thought of endangering his government, which was functioning satisfactorily, by admitting to it a party with which he had already had such unhappy experiences. But in retrospect one keeps wondering whether even this sacrifice might not have been worth the price if it had succeeded in uniting the People's Party firmly with the other groups committed to a republican Germany. Of course, whether it would have had these results remains a question.

Since Müller's efforts to form a regular coalition based directly on party participation had failed, he sought to bring into his government leading personalities from various parties. Such men, while not binding their party delegations in any formal way, would ensure, through their influence and importance, that a sufficient majority of the Reichstag would support them on critical votes. Müller felt safe in assuming that once such a government actually got under way, those delegates who did not oppose it in principle would hesitate to conjure up another crisis by causing it to fall.

Stresemann's cooperation would be the most critical prerequisite to such an experiment. Fortunately he, too, had already concluded that such a cabinet was the only hope. To be sure, he refused to join a "Weimar Coalition" (Social Democrats, Centrists, and Democrats) as a so-called "expert" without implicating his party in the government. But from Bühlerhöhe he had been corresponding with Erich Koch, the leader of the Democratic Party, and the two men had agreed that in the present situation there was nothing else to do but form a "cabinet of personalities." In this exchange Koch had observed that on most issues the People's Party was closer to the Democrats than was either the Bavarian People's Party or even the Social Democrats — as, for instance, the school debate had shown.[3]

The decision was finally reached in a telephone conversation between Hermann Müller and Stresemann on June 23. Stresemann immediately confirmed the burden of the conversation in an extensive telegram to the Chancellor-designate. The essence of his message was that "personalities from the parties of the Great Coalition will agree on a program, with which they will go before the Reichstag and with which they, in turn, will stand or fall. The formation of such a cabinet is also in the spirit of the German constitution, which recognizes only the personal responsibility of ministers, not that of party delegations."[4]

Stresemann's party, however, flatly rejected the argument expressed in this last sentence. Their repudiation of his interpretation constituted the root of the conflict which immediately broke out between him and his party delegation. When Curtius published the telegram — with the approval of Stresemann and the delegation's secretary, Kempke — Scholz, the chairman of the delegation, regarded this "shot from Bühlerhöhe" as an insult which required his resignation in reply. Stresemann, on his part, felt hurt by a resolution the delegation passed, which said that "the correct direction of the party and its Reichstag delegation requires all those who participate in political decisions to maintain a constant exchange of opinions and views among themselves and with the delegation's head."

The German press — especially the papers not friendly to the People's Party — naturally seized upon this resolution as a repudiation of Stresemann and of his independent negotiations with Müller. Stresemann, however, was not the sort of man to yield meekly. In addition to a sharp telegram, he sent his party's Reichstag delegation an incisive letter which set forth the problem in detail.[5] Here he argued that the previous mode of partisan negotiation among the several delegations was pernicious to the development of a healthy parliamentary system: Such partisanship "removes us more and more from any true sense of liberalism and subjects us as a party to a purely formal concept of democracy by forcing the government to make critical decisions of lasting importance on the basis of fortuitous majorities in the Reichstag." Whether one accepts or rejects this basic point of view, it remains clear that Stresemann knew he was not only the undisputed leader of his party but also its only member with a strong personal following in the German electorate, thus giving the party much greater benefits from his affiliation than he ever got from it.

When the People's Party organization in Baden expressed to

him their indignation at the resolution their party's Reichstag delegation had just passed, Stresemann replied, on July 2, that he wished to make perfectly clear that he would resign from both the delegation and the party if he did not receive a full apology for the imputations of this resolution, "which makes a public fool out of the chairman of the party." And the senior member of the party, Professor Kahl, was so offended by the delegation's action that he, too, seriously considered resigning his Reichstag seat.[6] In a more positive vein, Stresemann inquired in the letter whether the delegates would refuse to cooperate with the Social Democrats in any way — an attitude "which would stand in sharp opposition to my own views." He went on to insist that Curtius join the cabinet with him, since he had no intention of serving in it alone as an example of token integration.

Stresemann's energetic reaction had its desired effect. The party's Reichstag delegation declared that they had no objection to seeing the two ministers join the cabinet, although they did decline to recognize any party responsibility for the new government. These controversies are also noteworthy because they show that after hopes for a regular party coalition had been dashed, the President had sought some one other than Hermann Müller for the Chancellorship. To be exact, Hindenburg had asked his State Secretary Meissner to inquire of Ernst Scholz, leader of the People's Party delegation, whether he would like to try to form a cabinet.[7] There was, of course, no such possibility once Stresemann and Müller had agreed.

With this agreement Müller's chief problem had been solved. But the way did not yet lie clear before him; for now it was the Center that made difficulties. It is hard to see just what was going on. Even Heinrich Brauns, the former minister of labor, was unable to give Stresemann a satisfactory answer, calling the events "curious."[8] The end result was that only one Centrist, Guérard, entered the new cabinet — as minister of transport. And, at that, he belonged to his party's right wing. In addition to this oddity, the Center had reserved the right to demand more portfolios in the fall.

None of these developments gave any reason for men to be optimistic about the future of the new government, which was formally constituted on June 28, 1928. The cabinet included ministers from no less than five parties: Social Democrats, Centrists, the Bavarian People's Party, the German People's Party, and Democrats. This variety was certainly no advantage, especially since these parties were divided by many issues which were at the moment unresolved and which — like the question of the armored cruisers — would have to be settled rather soon.

But in any event Müller had succeeded in uniting quite a number of good minds and experienced politicians in his cabinet. Most important of all, he had managed to persuade his fellow Social Democrat, Carl Severing, to be minister of interior. (Severing was sufficiently recovered to assume the burdens of a new office.) Hilferding returned to the Ministry of Finance. In spite of his mistakes in 1923 he was still the Social Democrats' expert on government finance. As the fourth Social Democrat, Rudolf Wissell took over the Ministry of Labor, which had been directed by the Centrist Brauns since 1920.

Despite the limited size of their delegation, the Democrats were given two portfolios: Dietrich, that of Food; and Koch-Weser, that of Justice. But these appointments were made with the prior understanding that Koch would probably yield his position to a Centrist in the event that the negotiations scheduled with that party for the fall yielded positive results. Gröner, who considered himself nonpartisan, remained as minister of defense. The Bavarian People's Party was represented by Georg Schätzel, who remained minister of posts. These, together with Stresemann and Curtius — who remained minister of economics — from the People's Party, comprised a list of ministers of which the new government could well be proud.

The new Chancellor, Hermann Müller, enjoyed a Reichstag reputation that extended far beyond the ranks of his own party. He was known as a clever, thoughtful man who did not confuse tenacity with radicalism and who knew how to handle differences of opinion in a realistic way. But quite unlike Stresemann he was deprived of the gift of making an impression on the general public. His phrases were rarely picked up and echoed by other men. Yet, surprisingly enough, Müller succeeded in making a good impression in quite an extraordinary place: old Hindenburg was — initially at least — thoroughly satisfied with him. In intimate company the President once remarked that Müller was the best Chancellor he had ever had; it was only unfortunate, he added, that the man was a Social Democrat.

The weaknesses of the new regime became immediately apparent on June 3, when the ministers presented themselves to the Reichstag. The government's declaration, which Müller read, emphasized a great number of points on which the ministers were agreed and to which a majority of the Reichstag did not object. But the new government did not wish to risk a formal vote of confidence, for that would have unleashed all the quarrels which had accompanied the formation of the cabinet and which had taken so much time and energy to still. So instead of requesting the usual endorsement of the government, they were content to ask for approval of the government's declaration. When this was voted (261 to 134, with 28 abstentions), the Reichstag adjourned for the summer and the ministers could begin their work.

It was not long before they were confronted by a decision which — to the Social Democratic ministers, at least — was extremely hard to make. Gröner, the minister of defense, insisted that the construction of Cruiser A, which had been approved in principle by the previous Reichstag, be undertaken. Until this time, and in accordance with the Reichsrat's resolution, work on the vessel had been restricted to the preparation of plans. But now September 1 was approaching — the terminal date for the investigation of the project's financial feasibility which Prussia had insisted that the Reichsrat demand. That is, the time had come when steps would have to be taken if the ship were to be built. As was to be expected, Gröner declared that the construction costs would be well within Germany's capabilities. And, indeed, it was difficult to argue that the first installment of nine million marks represented an intolerable burden in a budget which already provided for expenditures of between seven and eight billion. That this first installment alone would build no ship and that the first armored cruiser would quite possibly be followed by three more was all very true. But in this respect Gröner expressly guaranteed the cabinet full freedom of later decision. Consequently, at its meeting of August 10, the government approved his request.

This decision excited extraordinary public notice. It accorded, of course, with the customary constitutional doctrine of cabinet responsibility that no public statement was made of how the individual ministers had voted on the question; this remained a cabinet secret. Excitement raged not only among the Social Democrats, but also in a large part of the Democratic press. But this opposition does not seem to have been representative of the mood of the Democratic voters. For at the next Democratic convention, when Koch, without disclosing how he had voted, merely recited the points for and against building the ship, his audience remained calm and unmoved. But when Dietrich candidly declared: "I voted for the armored cruiser," he was answered with most vigorous applause.

With the Social Democrats, of course, the issue was much more serious.[9] They had campaigned under the handy motto urging "Not armored cruisers, but food for children," to which they attributed a large part of their success. Were they to disavow these words now that they had won? And even more significant was the fact that the Prussian premier, Otto Braun, regarded the recent cabinet vote as a personal blow. For he had been the one who put through the Reichsrat the resolution requiring a moratorium until September 1. He had done so in the hope, of course, that the more Leftist government which he expected the new elections to bring would bury the entire naval project. But now this new government — and with a Social Democrat as Chancellor! — had done precisely the opposite.[10]

The embarrassment and concern of the Social Democrats is perfectly understandable. But what follows shows how little the basic principles of parliamentary government were comprehended by those very Germans who were most clearly committed to democracy. In this connection one is forced to recall the worried and warning words that Hugo Preuss directed especially at the parties of the Left in a meeting of the Constitutional Committee in 1919; in all too prophetic phrases he told them that they would have to change their very modes of thought — which were still based upon the assumptions of an authoritarian state — if a German parliamentary government were to survive.

On August 15, that is, just five days after the cabinet had made its decision, the Social Democratic leaders and the party's Reichstag delegation joined in a resolution that criticized the Social Democratic ministers for not having openly opposed the construction of the armored cruiser. The logical consequence of this resolution should have been the ministers' resignations. But the party did not want that to happen either. Instead, its executive committee and its Reichstag delegation proceeded to pass a second resolution which declared that it was of the utmost importance for the party to continue its participation in the government, "out of consideration for the general interests of labor" — certainly a significant reason. The logical consequence of this second resolution should at least have been the total abandonment of the naval issue by the Social Democrats. For further discussion of this point could only make still more difficulties for the Social Democratic ministers and, more important, for the government itself.

But here again Goethe's words proved true: "We take our first steps free; thereafter we are slaves." Having made their opposition to the armored cruiser a central issue of the Reichstag elections, the Social Democrats could not satisfy their constituents with a silent acceptance of the vessel now. Furthermore, the Communists took care that the pot was kept boiling. They initiated a petition for a referendum that would bar armored cruisers. Their maneuver failed completely, of course. Indeed, although they had won 3.25 million votes in the recent elections, their petition found only 1.2 million supporters, quite short of the constitutional requirement of at least 4 million voters. Nevertheless, in view of their constituents' traditional distaste for everything that smacked of militarism, the Social Democrats were acutely embarrassed by this Communist competition. And so they decided to wage yet another Reichstag fight against the armored cruiser.

When the Reichstag reassembled in November, the Social Democratic delegation moved that the construction of Cruiser A be halted. This move naturally evoked strong and angry reactions from the other ministers and their parties. Gröner made it clear that he would resign if the motion were adopted. Such a step could well have had serious consequences for the entire government. All this could have been foreseen. But the dogmatists among the Social Democrats forced a resolution through the delegation, requiring that *all* party members, including the Social Democratic ministers, support the delegation's motion en bloc. Even the President's personal suggestion that the ministers be at least permitted to abstain found no mercy at the hands of the delegation's majority. Thus, on November 17, 1928, the German Reichstag witnessed the grotesque spectacle of Chancellor Hermann Müller voting against a decision which a cabinet he had chosen had passed with him in the chair.

Let us imagine for a moment what would have happened if the Social Democrats' motion had been passed. In that case not only Gröner but many other ministers would have resigned (Wirth threatened a vote of no confidence in the event that the Social Democrats should ever try such a trick again); the entire government would have fallen apart; and the Social Democrats would have been responsible for it all. But to their good fortune they were in the minority on the vote: against the 202 Social Democratic and Communist votes the parties of the Middle and the Right were able to marshal 257, while 8 delegates abstained from voting. Thus the government survived the crisis. But its prestige had suffered severely, and German critics of parliamentary democracy poured torrents of scorn on a system that admitted of such absurdities and which *its own supporters clearly did not know how to operate.*

Among the Social Democrats themselves there were many who were severely critical of the entire maneuver. There was Julius Leber, for instance, at that time a Reichstag delegate from Lübeck and one of Hitler's victims after July 20, 1944, who declared: "I have no idea how many armored cruisers I would vote to have constructed if I could thereby save the Republic and democracy in Germany." And in a private letter he prophesied that future historians would recount with a wistful smile "how in these critical hours the largest German democratic party was racked by debate over the question whether construction on an armored cruiser to replace a World War battleship should commence in 1931 or not until 1932." Such an experienced parliamentarian as Württemberg's Wilhelm Keil had similar feelings.[11]

Yet this entire affair can be regarded from still another point of view. Under the Empire Bismarck had succeeded in freeing the military and naval budget from the annual legislative determination that is customary in parliamentary states and had set it on the longer legal basis of the Septennate. His successors had followed his example, as was especially exemplified by the several provisions for the Battle Fleet. Not until the Weimar Republic had the practice been abandoned. This change made little difference to the Army, for its limits had been set by the Versailles treaty. But it was of real importance to the German Navy, which was bound to suffer if every change in the composition of the Reichstag were to imply a change in defense policy with each new parliament feeling free to ignore its predecessor's acts.

While the Social Democrats were demonstrating that they were not politically mature enough to direct a government coalition, the principal opposition party, the German Nationalists, were proving just as disappointing. It is usual to find defeats engendering criticism of leadership, and it is therefore not astonishing that many members of the party considered its chairman, Count Westarp, responsible for its losses. The basic question was whether the party was wise in entering two of the Republic's cabinets even though it was fundamentally a party of the monarchistic opposition to the Republic. Many party members insisted — at least after the fact — that their party should not have entered these government coalitions. Moreover German Nationalist civil servants were displeased that their party's participation in these governments had not brought them the personal benefits they had expected. But the party leaders were embarrassed even more when a German Nationalist Reichstag delegate wondered out loud whether the party should continue to demand that all its members commit themselves explicitly to a restoration of the monarchy.

Walter Lambach was the man who raised this point. His political significance derived from the fact that he was one of the leaders of the German National Commercial Employees Union, which

boasted some 300,000 members. And as such he had been given
second place on the party's national, supraregional list of candidates
for the Reichstag. When Lambach argued that now, ten years after
the Emperor's fall, the monarchy's splendors and attractions had
paled — especially in the minds of the younger generation — he
was certainly drawing on experiences he had had in his Employees
Union. And he was by no means the only man in the party's councils who held this view. Count Westarp's papers show that the former minister Schiele had wished to announce publicly "that every
national-thinking German — even if he is a convinced antimonarchist
— is welcome in our party; in other words: nationalist republicans,
too."

But Lambach's argument was greeted with indignation by many
German Nationalist organizations. *Landesverband Potsdam II*, the
party unit to which Lambach belonged by virtue of his residence,
made short shrift, dropping him from the party's rolls in July. It is
true that this banishment was revoked by the highest party court
and that a reprimand was issued in its stead. But Count Westarp
evidently considered himself unable to direct the party effectively
on this issue. Consequently during July, when he found himself
in a minority on a vote taken at a meeting of party representatives,
he resigned as chairman. At this, Hugenberg entered all the more
energetically into the fray. In late August his Berlin *Lokalanzeiger*
carried an editorial, the contents of which are adequately described
by its headline: "Men or Mousse" (*"Block oder Brei"*).[12]

On October 20 another meeting of German Nationalist district
party leaders was held in Berlin, this time to fill the chair that
Westarp had vacated. Hugenberg was chosen — and, it seems, unanimously — as the party's new chairman. In his later denazification
proceedings Hugenberg insisted that no other candidate was nominated.[13] But since it is clear that Hugenberg had many opponents in
the party, this seeming unanimity can be explained only on tactical
grounds: the party wished to give the external appearance of solidarity.

It is not a mark of prejudice to say that Hugenberg did not owe
his election to any outstanding personal qualifications. In Reichstag
discussions he had, with exceedingly rare exceptions, stayed in the
background. Nor was he accomplished as either a speaker or a
writer. Indeed, as a person he made very little impression at all.
He looked more like a disgruntled, petty bureaucrat than the powerful, successful industrial magnate that he was. Nevertheless he was
recognized as an able organizer and as a man of tremendous will
power who held with obstinacy to the course that he thought right.

Political figures both within and without the German National People's Party had no doubts about what was to be expected of such a man: the strongest conceivable challenge to the Weimar Republic and, particularly, to the foreign policy of Stresemann, for whom Hugenberg had always nursed a special hate and whom he now, upon entering into his new office, labeled "a hollow man of no convictions" (*den Typus der Halben*). The Centrist's leader, former Chancellor Marx, expressed most clearly the general apprehension felt at Hugenberg's election when he called it "a threat to Germany's domestic peace."

A letter of November 2, 1926, to Stresemann from the German ambassador at The Hague supplies an ironic commentary on the violent battle within the German National People's Party concerning the restoration of the monarchy. The ambassador had just paid a visit to the former Emperor in Doorn. While touching on German politics, William had — as usual — interspersed his conversation with observations that were at times quite intelligent and at others completely silly. But the most interesting part of the letter is its final passage, in which the ambassador condensed and recorded his impressions of William's real intent: "*The Emperor is not seriously contemplating a change in his present circumstances* — which I believe he finds quite pleasant and which in any event are restful and secure. My own conclusions on this point were corroborated most strongly by Herr von Ilsemann, who is probably his closest confidant." But this moment of circumspection quickly passed. When another visitor came to Doorn — the comedy writer Rudolf Presber — William, quite typically, did not hesitate to present him with a personal photograph boastfully inscribed: "I hereby proclaim everything that all of you have done in Germany to be null and void. William." [14] Dramatics had gotten into his blood.

Those tendencies in the German National People's Party which had prevailed at the election of Hugenberg became equally apparent in organizations which, while bearing no party label, were carrying on the same sort of nationalist agitation. The *Stahlhelm* was one conspicuous example. It was clear that its members had lost their last remnant of political sanity at the sight of another Social Democrat at the head of the Reich. At a provincial convention in Fürstenwald, Brandenburg, in September 1928, the nationalists' wrath at having been defeated in the recent Reichstag elections took the form of a resolution which read, in part, as follows: "We hate the present form of the German state with all our hearts because it denies to us the hope of freeing our enslaved Fatherland, of cleansing the German people of the war-guilt lie, [and] of gaining necessary living space [*Lebensraum*] in Eastern Europe . . . We oppose the political system that regulates the present state, and we oppose those who support this system with all their compromises." It is worth noting how this masterpiece of political sagacity manages to combine moral indignation at "the war-guilt lie" with a longing for a new war against the Poles.

Obviously nobody could be better qualified to reform the Weimar constitution than the possessors of such political wisdom! And this is precisely the decision reached by the *Stahlhelm's* executive committee during a meeting in Magdeburg on September 23, immediately after the convention. A referendum was to be initiated, which would amend the constitution so as to increase the power of *Reichspräsident* Field Marshal von Hindenburg, honorary member of the *Stahlhelm*. This blatant invasion of politics by the *Stahlhelm* had at least one result: the People's Party delegations in the national and the Prussian parliaments voted to forbid their members to belong to the organization in the future — a step which many of the delegates clearly found difficult on tactical political grounds. The President of Germany, however, found no reason to separate himself from an organization which had inscribed its banners with hatred for the state over which he presided. Shortly after the Fürstenwald declaration of war, Stresemann had written to a friend that "pronouncements of this kind . . . put the President in an impossible situation."[15]

But Hindenburg did not find his situation at all embarrassing. Even when the *Stahlhelm* declared in its newspaper that its members still felt bound by their oaths to the Emperor — thus making national and land authorities wonder whether a civil servant should be permitted to belong to it — President Hindenburg merely asked the chairmen of the *Stahlhelm*, Messrs. Seldte and Duesterberg, to come to his office and give him an authentic interpretation of this statement (February 23, 1929). The gentlemen explained, of course, that the *Stahlhelm* was restricting itself to legal methods in pursuit of its goals and that it did not mean to question the republican civil servants' oaths of office. Hindenburg declared that he was satisfied with this explanation — and remained an honorary member of the *Stahlhelm*.[16]

While the Right wing of the Reichstag opposition was taking this clear turn toward an extreme position, things did not look much different among the Communists upon the Left. It was, for instance, at about this time that the Comintern — the central, Moscow office directing all the separate, national Communist parties — made a radical reversal of policy.[17] After the total failure of the

German Communists' revolutionary attempts in 1923, the Comintern's official watchword had been a proletarian "united front," that is, cooperation with the Social Democrats against the bourgeois parties of the Middle and the Right. This had meant the expulsion of such radical revolutionaries as Ruth Fischer; but otherwise there had been little sign of real rapprochement between the two parties.

And so, to borrow a phrase from Bismarck, the Social Democrats and Communists plowed the same, disputed field, and this was enough to ensure the eventual failure of any conciliatory attempts. The case of the Russian artillery shells had shown with what speed and passion these brethren of the Left could fall upon each others' throats. But, on the other hand, the recent Reichstag elections had also shown that neither party had been hurt by such fratricide. And so, when the period of the united front was brought to an end in 1928, this was — in the opinion of experts of the Bolshevik movement — due less to German politics than to those of Russia.

This shift in Communist policy became apparent at the Sixth World Congress of the Comintern held in Moscow during the summer of 1928. The congress forbade national Communist parties to engage in any further collaboration with either Social Democrats or unions which were members of the Second International. From this date on the Social Democrats were to be the Communists' principal and most bitter enemy. To make their new hostility especially clear, the German Communists began mocking their Social Democratic competitors for labor votes as "social fascists." The utter falsity of this label must have been obvious to every observer of the political scene whether or not he sympathized with the Social Democrats. At the beginning the Communists surely knew this, too; but in the course of time their uninterrupted use of this abusive term had the same stultifying effect upon them that such misuses of language had had in Thucydides' day: in the end they convinced themselves that the fascist threat was incorporated primarily in the Social Democrats — to the delight and advantage of the real fascists.[18]

One of the results of the Comintern's prohibition against collaborating with Social Democrats and unions was that on May Day, 1929, the Communists refused to continue the practice of joining the others in a united labor parade. They planned instead to hold a separate one themselves. Since processions of this sort had recently led to a series of serious public disturbances, Karl Zörgiebel, the Social Democratic commissioner of the Berlin police, prohibited all parades and open-air assemblies for the forthcoming first of May. Both the unions and the Social Democrats obeyed the order and held their meetings indoors. The Communists, however, considered this a good opportunity to demonstrate their revolutionary determination in the face of the police. They defied the order. The result was sanguinary disturbances in those parts of Berlin — for example, Wedding and Neukölln — where the Communists were strongest. The police found themselves obliged to shoot; seven dead and more than one hundred wounded were the product of this pointless demonstration.

The Communists, of course, proceeded to cover their crime by calling "Stop, thief!" At the next meeting of the Reichstag the spokesman for the Communists accused Zörgiebel and his Berlin police of "slaughtering workers" and called upon the workers of Berlin to protest against the Social Democratic "thugs" by holding a general strike until "Murderer Zörgiebel" was chased from office. The Communist speaker who preached revolt with such violent words was none other than Herr Wilhelm Pieck. At that time there was, of course, no way for him to know that one day he would be the "authority" who would answer the Berliners' thirst for freedom with Russian tanks.

Important as these developments within the opposition were, the government was much more concerned with changes occurring among the Centrists, one of whom was a member of the cabinet. Wilhelm Marx, who four times had been the Chancellor of Germany and head of quite different coalitions, now felt tired and so resigned as leader of the Center. At Cologne in December 1928 the party convention, by a considerable majority, elected the Reichstag delegate, prelate, and professor Monsignor Ludwig Kaas as Marx's successor. His rival candidates had been Joseph Joos and Adam Stegerwald, both of whom were closer to the Roman Catholic labor movement than was Kaas.

It is possible that this choice merely expressed the party's fear of becoming too closely linked to a group with such special economic interests.[19] But the choice did assume a peculiar cast when combined with an address which Kaas had delivered a few weeks earlier — on November 19 — in the Reichstag debate on foreign policy, and which even then had been of special importance because Kaas was a member of the German delegation to the League of Nations. In this speech Kaas had spoken of the "undeniable failure of German foreign policy up to now," although he had also declared, on the other hand, that "at the moment" there was "no reason to change the strategy of German foreign policy." Nevertheless, he concluded that "Germany must adjust its diplomatic posture with changing circumstances while any divergence from the recent course would be a fatal error." Now here was a speech which invited widely different interpretations. But its general tone departed radically from the unconditional endorsement which Marx had given to Stresemann's foreign policy.

Ludwig Kaas was a man of academic reputation, considerable culture, and high intelligence. In non-Catholic circles it caused some surprise when the Center formally entrusted its official leadership to a priest who was, moreover, a papal domestic prelate.* After his election Monsignor Kaas therefore took pains to emphasize the defensive character of Centrist policy, "in order to dispel the fear that the robe he wore was a foreboding of a change to a more aggressive manner." In 1929 — at Kaas' express desire — Heinrich Brüning was made chairman of the Centrist Reichstag delegation, thus taking another step in his extraordinarily rapid parliamentary career.[20]

Was German foreign policy of 1928 really as fruitless as Monsignor Kaas had maintained? It is true that during a great part of the year Stresemann was away from Berlin in ill health. Having stayed at Bühlerhöhe till mid-July, he had gone to Karlsbad and then to Oberhof, near Gotha, for a continuation of his treatments. But here he seems to have concerned himself with political affairs too greatly, for a mild stroke temporarily deprived him of his powers of speech. Although he quickly recovered from this setback, his doctors energetically opposed his plan to go to Paris in late August for the signing of the Kellogg-Briand Pact and to Geneva in September for a meeting of the League of Nations. His doctors finally permitted him to go to Paris, but only under the condition that one of them, Dr. Zondek, accompany him to supervise his activities. And he had to leave the representation of Germany at Geneva up to the Chancellor. From Paris Stresemann went directly to Baden-Baden to recover as best he could. Concerned greetings and wishes for a speedy recovery followed him there from Germans and foreigners. The American ambassador, Jacob Schurman, wrote: "Germany as well as Europe needs you badly."

But the National Socialist *Angriff*, Herr Dr. Goebbels' newspaper, published an editorial on Monday, September 10, 1928, under the headline: "Stresemann's Days Are Numbered." As a document of shame it warrants perusal in some detail:

From a confidential source close to the Jewish — we observe in passing — Professor Zondek we learn that the foreign minister's health is much worse than the public assumes and that it has given cause for some concern . . . There are only two likely sources of this sort of kidney trouble:

* An honorific ecclesiastical title bestowed by the Pope and similar to that of papal chamberlain but, unlike the latter, granted for life. TRANSLATORS.

either a severe inflammation of the throat or the excessive consumption of alcohol and heavy, indigestible foods. To the best of public knowledge the foreign minister has not suffered from an inflammation of the throat in recent years.

There is nothing more to say about this trash. It is frightening that German men and women who considered themselves decent and honorable — and who were so in other areas of their lives — could join or cooperate with a party that used such despicable methods.

In Baden-Baden Stresemann made a satisfactory recovery, even though he was constantly being drawn into the most difficult problems of foreign policy by numerous important visits, for example, that of Chancellor Müller on his way back from Geneva, and messages, such as a letter from Schacht. On November 3 Stresemann found it necessary to return to Berlin.

Aside from the Kellogg-Briand Pact, which will be discussed immediately below, German foreign policy during 1929 centered around two important issues: the evacuation of those parts of the Rhineland that were still occupied and the alteration of the reparations payments prescribed in the Dawes Plan.

According to Article 429 of the Versailles treaty the second (Coblenz) zone of the Rhineland was to be evacuated after ten years — that is, in 1930 — and the remainder of German territory after fifteen years, that is, in 1935. In Germany, however, people insisted on the view that, having accepted the Dawes Plan and the Treaties of Locarno, Germany had not only a moral, but also a *legal* claim to an immediate evacuation of the entire Rhineland. They thought they could base this legal claim on Article 431 of the treaty, which reads as follows in the definitive, French version: "Si, avant l'expiration de la périod de 15 ans, l'Allemagne satisfait à tous les engagements resultant pour elle du présent Traité, les troupes d'occupation seront immédiatement retirés." In other words, the occupying powers were required to evacuate their troops the moment that Germany met all the requirements set at Versailles. This condition had been met, the Germans argued, on August 30, 1924, with the signing of the London Agreement under the terms of the Dawes Plan. With this signature, as Schacht, for instance, said, "Germany had fulfilled all her treaty obligations." [21]

Easy as it is to understand why the German government adopted this favorable interpretation, it is difficult to convince oneself that it is correct or even compelling. To every jurist the distinction between a promise to pay — and the London Agreement was no more than that — and actual payment is elementary and sharp. Security is not returned when the promissory note is signed, but rather when the debt is repaid.

It was, of course, even more bootless to expect the Allies to accept this German interpretation. Along with the most closely affected French, the English law officers declared that there was no legal basis for the argument that Germany had met all the obligations imposed upon her by the peace treaty (Austen Chamberlain in the House of Commons on December 3, 1928).[22] In drafting Article 431 the authors of the Versailles treaty had clearly been thinking of the situation that had come about in France in 1873, when the indemnity of five billion francs was paid *before* it was formally due and, in consequence, the German occupation troops left French territory well before the date set for their evacuation in the Frankfort Treaty of 1871.

One can hardly doubt that Stresemann and his advisers were aware of the legal weakness of their position, nor that they regarded it simply as a suitable base for further negotiations. But what was perhaps to be justified so long as it was limited to diplomats' discussions became dangerous when made a part of public agitation. For it is characteristic of the Germans to consider a favorable reading of the law to be correct, especially when it can be made to appear a matter of national honor. Indeed, Goethe had already described this side of his fellow Germans in one of his *Zahme Xenien*:

> The German people are quite fair;
> Each only claims his fitting share.
> By "fitting," though, he understands
> What fits his and his cronies' hands.
> Everything else is too complex
> For their simple, honest intellects.

This whole matter had now become a campaign issue, and every speaker was forced — if only because of competitive rhetoric — to place the strongest emphasis on Germany's absolute legal right to an immediate evacuation of the Rhineland. Curtius, national minister of economics at the time, later testified:

> The demand for an immediate evacuation of the Rhineland . . . was . . . a universal element of future foreign policy among both "ins and outs," that is, across the entire range of coalition and opposition parties. How these demands were to be effected in the face of international realities was neither asked nor shown . . . Again it was a fatal case of making foreign policy a domestic campaign issue and, thus, *exciting in the Germans' minds expectations which could not be fulfilled.*[23]

It was, indeed, most unfortunate that in Germany the voice of reason was always being drowned out by passionate, nationalistic cries and that the government, in trying to gain a tactical advantage in diplomacy, placed the instruments for undermining the government's own position into its unscrupulous opponents' hands. For the only Germans who could benefit from these demands were the irreconcilable foes of any international understanding. Stresemann was completely right when, in a Reichstag speech of June 24, 1929, he objected to Hugenberg's followers that in this duel "the weapons [were] not equal." The foreign minister could not display his personal doubts about the thesis he was maintaining without losing whatever tactical advantage it afforded him in negotiations with the West; the opposition, however, remained free to accuse him of being too weak to make his point prevail.

Parker Gilbert, the Allies' reparations agent, was the man principally responsible for bringing the reparation problem into sharp focus at this time. The Dawes Plan had deliberately avoided a final solution to the issue, aiming instead at the limited goal of establishing a transitional stage during which the German economy could be rebuilt and confidence in it could be restored. In Parker Gilbert's opinion this mission had been accomplished, and the time had come for a final solution, according to which Germany might meet her definitive obligations "under her own responsibility, without foreign supervision and without transfer protection." [24]

This phrase revealed the reparations agent's central argument. In his report of December 10, 1927, Gilbert had written: "The very existence of transfer protection . . . tends to save the German public authorities *from some of the consequences of their own actions,* while on the other hand the uncertainty as to the total amount of the reparation liabilities inevitably tends everywhere in Germany to diminish the normal incentive to do the things and carry through the reforms that would clearly be in the country's own interests." [25]

When Gilbert chose this precise moment to press for a final solution, he did so certainly not for personal reasons alone — he had just been given a very attractive offer to join the New York banking house of Morgan — but primarily out of objective considerations. His basic axiom seems to have been that there was hope for a final solution only so long as Germany's economy remained in a rather fluctuating condition. For if the economy were to take a clear and significant trend upward, the Allies' demands would climb so high that agreement would become extremely difficult. While on the other hand, if a crisis were to occur, then there would be no possibility whatsoever of arriving at a permanent arrangement. One also has every reason to assume that Gilbert expected this final solution to yield a considerable reduction in the German annual payments which, according to the Dawes Plan, were to be at a level of 2.5 billion marks starting September 1, 1928. Furthermore, the Dawes Plan included the so-called "improvement certificate," according to which Germany's payments would have to climb still higher if the index that had been agreed upon were to show a rise in the German standard of living — and there was scarcely any doubt of this.

Parker Gilbert found a very powerful supporter for his idea in the president of the Reichsbank, Hjalmar Schacht. An important role in the execution of Gilbert's plan would have to devolve upon Schacht in any event, not only by virtue of his official position and his good relationships with the heads of other central banks — especially with Montagu Norman, governor of the Bank of England — but also because in foreign countries no less than at home he was considered one of the leading experts in economic, and especially monetary, matters.[26] Schacht's good relations and frequent collaboration with Gilbert, even when it contradicted the policy of the German government, have already been discussed. Schacht now considered the international situation favorable for implementing Gilbert's proposal: "The *psychological moment has now come to strike for everything*. Almost more important than the sums at stake is the *opportunity to regain our absolute international freedom*. Every remnant of obligations, controls, and unresolved questions must disappear." [27] Thus did Schacht write in a letter of September 20, 1928, to the much more skeptical and hesitant Stresemann. Frequent reference will be made below to this letter.

Schacht was certainly not the only German to share Gilbert's point of view. Minister of Economics Curtius also urged that the reparations agent's proposal be accepted, and in the general public scene many voices were loud in its favor; many, however, were opposed. Meanwhile, Gilbert was busy with representatives of the Entente governments, trying to create a general desire for a permanent solution to the question. The most important creditor nation, France, was particularly interested in the idea because if the exchange protection were abolished, the French could capitalize and commercialize a portion of the German reparations debt and thus, in short, return to the Thoiry plan. Furthermore, the French were faced with the necessity of ratifying the Mellon-Bérenger Agreement (concerning payments on the French war debt to the United States) before August 1, 1929; otherwise they would have to pay $400,000,000 immediately.

The Kellogg-Briand Pact — for the formal signing of which

Stresemann had gone to Paris on August 27 — had evolved from negotiations during 1927 and 1928 between Frank Kellogg, the American secretary of state, and Aristide Briand, the French foreign minister. During these years Briand had originally proposed that war between France and America be forsworn by a treaty signed by the two countries. To counter this proposal Kellogg utilized the popularity of the movement for the "outlawry of war," initiated by Salmon O. Levinson, a Chicago lawyer. Kellogg's reply to Briand was that *all* the great powers should sign a comprehensive treaty renouncing war as an instrument of national policy. Great Britain and the Dominions signed — albeit with certain reservations — and on April 27, 1928, Germany accepted the invitation to join the group.

The critical first article of the pact includes the solemn declaration by the signatory powers "that they condemn recourse to war for the solution of international controversies, and renounce it as an instrument of national policy in their relations with one another." These words did not, however, in any way limit a country's right of self-defense against attack; the American note of June 23 made this explicit. If this fact had not been expressly stipulated, it was because of the "difficulties encountered by any attempt to define what constitutes an *'attack.'*" All countries were free to join the pact. The Soviet Union, which had been invited only after the formal signing, joined on September 6, although not without some grumbling remarks.[28]

When Stresemann arrived in Paris, he was welcomed with an enthusiastic ovation. "Hats were waved and children held on shoulders; French and German voices mingled in a mighty shout of welcome — from which, however, a few mocking whistles (we counted three) were not absent." These were the words of the *Frankfurter Zeitung* Paris correspondent. But in all likelihood it was neither the solemnity of the occasion nor the promise of such a welcome that had induced Stresemann to ignore his physicians' counsel and make this trip to France. For he sought this important opportunity to speak with leading French political figures in Paris in order to bring the two burning issues of the Rhineland and reparations closer to solution. He naturally discussed these matters with Briand, who again expressed his hopes for a "general solution" — that is, the evacuation of the entire Rhineland without any distinction between zones two and three — but avoided making any concrete proposals on this problem or on reparations.[29]

But more important than seeing Briand, whose methods and whose ways of thought Stresemann already knew quite well, was this chance to meet another man, one whom he had never seen face to face and whom he well knew to have even more influence on French policy than did the foreign minister. This was Premier Poincaré.

Five years earlier Poincaré had inflicted a severe defeat on Stresemann. But in the meantime the German foreign minister had become a much-admired statesman of international renown, while Poincaré's foreign policy had been scorned by his fellow Frenchmen. (It was only to their confidence in his financial skills that he owed his return to office.) Nevertheless it was clear to Stresemann that Poincaré could not be considered a political nullity, and that he remained an important element in the shaping of Franco-German relations. In June 1928, probably in preparation for his conversation with Poincaré, Stresemann had asked Victor Schiff, editor of the *Vorwärts*, for a copy of his notes on the interview the French Premier had granted him during the previous April, when Poincaré had boasted of having initiated the Thoiry conference.[30]

In this interview the question of the occupation of the Rhineland had also been discussed. Poincaré had described it as France's sole guarantee for regular reparation payments. And, when Schiff asked whether the occupation could not be abandoned now and resumed later in the event that a German government should deliberately refuse to make its payments, Poincaré had raised his hands in the air, exclaiming: "Never! . . . Once the evacuation is carried out, a second occupation in these times would mean lighting the fuse of the powder keg." In discussing the question of reparations, Poincaré had emphasized their close connection with the Allied war debts to America. Interesting, too, was his statement to the Social Democrat Schiff that a Leftist German government could expect ten times more from him than could a Rightist regime like the one just chased from office. (The interview was held during the election campaign.) "We Frenchmen," Poincaré explained, "are principally concerned about the amount of confidence we can place in Germany's peaceful intentions."

Stresemann's conversation with Poincaré took place on August 27, 1928, under medical supervision.[31] Zondek was waiting in the ante-chamber, and after an hour had passed he felt it his duty to urge his patient to conclude the conversation. After another fifteen minutes, when this suggestion had proved to be in vain, Zondek sent a second note to Stresemann which caused Poincaré to break off their talk before the ailing German minister had been able to say everything he had had on his mind.

At the beginning of the conversation Stresemann had tried to assure Poincaré that the general German attitude was far from thoughts of revenge. To this Poincaré replied by alluding to a report which Wickham Steed, former editor of the London *Times*, had given him of the vengeful mood of the professors in Berlin. Stresemann sought to counter this with reference to the Heidelberg faculty, which had unanimously awarded honorary degrees to the American ambassador, Schurman, and to himself. But Poincaré could not be moved from Steed's statement that the Berlin professors had told him they intended to indoctrinate German youth with the aim of regaining Alsace-Lorraine. And no one who knows Steed and the German academic atmosphere of that time can doubt the validity of his report.

To Poincaré's thesis, that the occupation of the Rhineland was France's sole guarantee for reparation payments, Stresemann responded with his own, namely, that Germany's need to preserve its international credit and good name was an even more effective guarantee. Poincaré stuck fast to the argument that German reparations were closely connected with debts to the United States. America's debtors had been obliged to bind themselves to payments lasting 62 years; they would therefore require an equal period of German reparations. On the other hand, Poincaré explained, he personally considered this period far too long not only for Germany, but also for those countries with debts to America. This clearly meant that a reduction of the German payment period was conceivable only if the United States were to prove equally considerate of its debtors. But this question would remain uncertain until after the American presidential campaign between the Republican Hoover and the Democrat Smith. The conversation subsequently turned to Thoiry and to the question of what had ruined the general solution which then had seemed so close. But at this point the second warning from Stresemann's doctor brought an end to the conversation which had been marked by the utmost politeness on either side.

Although this talk yielded no immediate, tangible results, it certainly had not worked any harm, and Poincaré's assurance to Stresemann that he, too, hoped for reconciliation between France and Germany remained valuable. In any event there was absolutely no reason for the storm of indignation that immediately swept over the German Nationalist press. The real target of this indignation was probably the meeting of the League of Nations that was about to take place and at which Chancellor Hermann Müller was to represent Germany.

Before Müller departed for Geneva, Schacht gave him a report of a conversation he had had with Parker Gilbert. The reparations agent had expressed the hope that in his public address concerning the evacuation of the Rhineland, the Chancellor might include a sentence to the effect that although the German government recognized no connection between the evacuation and reparations, it was nevertheless *ready at all times to discuss the reparations problem.*[32] This advice, which Schacht attributed to French initiative and which he clearly supported, was intended "to prepare the way for an understanding and conciliatory response from Briand." But Müller did not follow the advice — to Schacht's great displeasure, as is apparent in Schacht's letter to Stresemann of September 20, 1928, where he even went so far as to say: "This omission [of the conciliatory remark that Schacht had recommended] and the *naked demand for evacuation* necessarily determined the tone of Briand's reply."

For the French foreign minister had replied to Hermann Müller's address of September 7 to the League of Nations Assembly with a speech, three days later, of astonishing bitterness. That Schacht bases the Chancellor's failure on Müller's refusal to follow his advice is hardly surprising, given Schacht's constant overestimation of himself. But his disapproval of Müller's "naked demand for evacuation" showed that he accepted the necessity — even from the German point of view — of treating the two questions of reparations and evacuation together. Later, in his polemical *The End of Reparations* (1931), Schacht found a way to accuse the German government of failing to prevent a linking of these two issues at Geneva and, thus, of letting "the legal and moral question of the evacuation of the Rhineland become a matter of money and debts."[33] But this only showed that Schacht, and not the German government, had effected a change in course. And his phrasing also shows that this change was motivated by a desire for the approbation of the nationalistic enemies of the Republic.

Yet in his letter of September 1928 Schacht expressed delight at the end results of the Geneva negotiations. For the conversations had led to an agreement between the German representatives and those of the Entente — including Japan (September 16) — on three points: (1) on the inauguration of official negotiations concerning the German requests for an early evacuation of the Rhineland; (2) on the acceptance of the necessity for a final determination of reparations and for the establishment of a commission of financial experts; and (3) in principle, on the establishment of a Control Commission of "Verification and Conciliation." This third point can be summarily dismissed here with the simple observation that Stresemann succeeded in persuading Briand to drop it.

For the rest, this agreement can be regarded as the successful result of the reparations agent's efforts. But it also represented a victory for German foreign policy to have the two issues which plagued Stresemann the most recognized in this official manner as topics of general European interest and of peaceful, international understanding. And it was another German victory, too, to find it assumed and accepted on all sides that Germans would serve as members with full rights on the proposed committee of experts. The Dawes Committee of 1924 had been composed exclusively of representatives from creditor nations. But that practice belonged to an era which men now considered over and done with.

From this point on the most important task of the German government was to help direct the committee of experts, who were to deal with the reparations issue, along the most fruitful path. This involved most particularly the collection of data for the determination of Germany's productive capacities — for the Germans had every reason to focus attention on this matter — and the selection of German financial experts to serve on the committee.

Hjalmar Schacht, of course, was of the modest opinion that the government should seek his advice first. As early as September 20, just a few days after the conclusion of the Geneva conversations, he wrote a letter to Stresemann which has been quoted above and in which he made eight proposals — that he had already cleared with Parker Gilbert. There is no objection to be made to these proposals, but the tone Schacht assumed in making them is more that of a man issuing orders to a government than that of an expert offering his country his advice. No less than four times the phrases "at all costs" and "under no circumstances" occur.

Stresemann invited Schacht to join him at Wiesbaden for a conversation. The talk took place in late October in the presence of Leopold von Hoesch, the German ambassador to France. Von Hoesch was one of the skeptics who considered a final determination of reparations still premature.

In the meantime Parker Gilbert had been traveling from country to country trying to win the Allied governments to his plan, or in plainer words, trying to persuade them to accommodate the Germans' desire for a lightening of their reparations burden. But the fruits of all his travels served only to depress his hopes severely. France and England both took the position that the German payments to them would have to be high enough to permit them in turn to satisfy their creditors — that is, the United States. In other words, if America were to grant a further remission on its loans, the favor might well be passed along to Germany; if America did not relent, the Germans could hope for no relief. The Americans were in the middle of a presidential campaign and could therefore say nothing;

but even during the campaign it became apparent that neither the Democrats nor the Republicans were prepared to grant a diminution of the debts. And Herbert Hoover, who won a decisive victory on November 6, refused to consider such a step.

In late September Poincaré had taken a public position on the issue, announcing to the entire world that, in addition to the equivalent of her own war debts to other nations, France would require a "substantial" supplement to cover the costs of reconstructing her ruined districts.

When Gilbert finally returned to Berlin, Schacht invited him to a conversation (on October 25) with Chancellor Müller, at which Schacht and Finance Minister Hilferding were also present. The reparations agent continued to urge a final determination of reparations but he was obliged — without going into specific figures — to make clear to the Germans that they could count on only slight concessions from the Allies. After Stresemann had returned to Berlin on November 3, Gilbert sought him out (on November 13), and the two had a very detailed, impassioned conversation.

Both participants left notes on this conversation. Stresemann dictated his immediately after the talk. It is not clear from the records just when Parker Gilbert made his report; it was not until May 1, 1929 — at the time of the crisis of the Paris Conference — that he delivered it to the German Foreign Ministry.[34] These notes of Gilbert's are extraordinarily extensive — twenty-six single-spaced typewritten pages — and therefore contain details which Stresemann's more condensed version lacks. But they do not change the general impression given by the German's record.

According to his own notes, Stresemann regarded the idea of a final determination of reparations at this time quite skeptically, especially since one could predict from the official French and British statements that the Entente would demand between 2 and 2.2 billion marks per year. Gilbert insisted that the Allies had not yet hit upon any fixed sums, and he even went so far as to refuse to discuss any figures at this juncture. At the same time, however, he made it quite clear that the Germans had absolutely no reason to expect to be let off lightly. The Germans, he argued, should take the English and French declarations most seriously. And under no circumstances could there be any chance of America's yielding. Stresemann was so little charmed by this dreary prospect that — according to Gilbert's report — he expressed real doubts of his ability to recommend the establishment of the experts' committee to the Reichstag.

Stresemann sent a copy of his notes to the President of the Reichsbank. For the German government had already decided that in any

event Schacht would be one of the German experts and had therefore directed that he be informed of all matters relevant to the reparations question. Schacht was therefore in a position to advise the
government, in the face of the reparations agent's pessimistic fore-
cast, to drop the entire project or to postpone it until a greater inclination toward compromise was evident among Germany's creditors. Schacht did not do this. On the other hand, one cannot say that
Stresemann accepted the figure of between 2 and 2.2 billion marks,
as Schacht later maintained. For in the Reichstag debate of November 19, 1928, Stresemann expressed his rejection of the notion that
the creditors' calculations might be definitive by arguing, instead,
that the productive capacity of the German economy was the critical factor. Only so long as this was not exceeded could there be any
talk of a real solution to the reparations issue.

The Reichstag rejected, by a two-thirds majority, a National Socialist motion of no confidence in Stresemann, and the foreign minister was therefore able to use the meeting of the League of Nations
Council at Lugano (December 9–15, 1928) as an opportunity for
conversations with Briand and Chamberlain. These discussions led
to a final, firm agreement on the establishment of the experts' committee (Poincaré–von Hoesch Protocol of December 22, 1928). It
was of great practical importance that, just as in the case of the
Dawes Plan, American experts were to cooperate in the work.[35] (After initial hesitation the American government finally agreed to
this.) Equally important was the stipulation that the members of
the committee would be independent agents, not bound by instructions from their respective governments. Of course this provision
meant, as its converse, that the governments were not bound by their
experts' conclusions and that, for instance, the French government
would remain perfectly free to reject whatever concessions the
French experts might propose.

Germany was to be represented in the same manner as the other
participating nations: with two experts on the committee. One of
the German seats was reserved for Schacht. The German government had already agreed unanimously on this point, and Schacht
himself showed no hesitation about accepting the post even though
he could hardly have any doubts at this time that the actual results
of the negotiations would fall far short of the high-pitched German
hopes. The government entrusted its second seat to a leading Rhenish industrialist, the chairman of the board of the German and Luxembourg Mining and Refining Corporation, Albert Vögler. The fact
that Chancellor Müller, a Social Democrat, declared his satisfaction
with this choice of an industrial magnate of the far Right, instead of

insisting on the appointment of a labor leader,[36] is worthy of notice. Alternates were selected for each regular representative: for Vögler, Ludwig Kastl, the director of the Federation of German Manufacturers (*Reichsverband der deutschen Industrie*), a man highly regarded in broad circles of the German business world;[37] for Schacht, the Hamburg banker Carl Melchior, who had served on a German delegation once before — at Versailles.

Heavy industry did not approve of Melchior, and both Vögler and another leading industrialist, Paul Silverberg, protested his appointment to Stresemann.[38] But the foreign minister, who from numerous international conferences knew Melchior to be a "cool and considerate" negotiator, found no reason to alter his choice. "Along with Schacht, who perhaps — like myself — possesses a certain excess of temperament," he replied to Vögler, "it seems desirable that we have a cooler personality like Melchior."

Stresemann's correspondence of this period also demonstrates that he was quite aware of the opposition he would have to face. In early January of 1929 he wrote to Silverberg.[39] "I share your opinion that against Hugenberg's predictably vehement opposition we must construct a barricade of personalities strong enough to survive the attacks of the Hugenberg press. It is for this reason that I am counting on the cooperation of Vögler and Kastl." But here, as soon became apparent, Stresemann overestimated Vögler's constancy. Hjalmar Schacht makes it clear that the constancy and loyalty of Vögler was given not to the German government but to Schacht. "Throughout the entire conference," he writes, "the collaboration of the four delegates was loyal and candid." [40]

The Conference of Experts met in Paris on February 9, 1929 — and with American participants.[41] Owen D. Young, who had been a member of the Dawes Committee, was elected chairman. The other American member was J. P. Morgan, son and successor to the famous American financier.

The negotiations took place in secrecy, although all sorts of details leaked through the closed doors — perhaps more than served the purpose at hand. Schacht and his German colleagues gave a detailed exposition of their country's financial and economic position, trying to demonstrate to the conference that there were very narrow limits to Germany's ability to pay. On the other hand, the representatives of the creditor nations sought to prove that there were even narrower bounds to their ability to compromise, since their countries' financial difficulties required them to insist on minimum reparations of quite considerable size. Indeed, if one added their separate demands, one arrived at a figure which even exceeded the regular payments under the Dawes Plan. At the end of March, when the experts parted for the Easter holidays, the creditors' demands and the Germans' offers still stood impossibly far apart. Even the Americans, who were the most sympathetic to the Germans, refused to retreat one step from their basic position that they had already shown enough consideration for their debtors and could not cancel a further dollar of their debts.

After the Easter recess the negotiations entered their critical stage. For now the creditors began to quote specific figures; figures which, if added together, yielded a sum that the Germans declared was completely unacceptable. And even after the chairman had achieved a certain reduction in these demands, annual payments rising from 1.8 to 2.4 billion marks were still involved, and the Germans insisted these far exceeded their country's productive capacity. Thereupon, on April 16, the creditors' representatives told the German experts to submit a counterproposal in writing. This was handed in the following day.

The German memorandum[42] argued that experience had by no means demonstrated the practicality of the Dawes Plan. For the Plan had been based on the presumption that Germany would pay her reparations from profits on exports. But the payments had in fact been drawn from the foreign loans to Germany, which had reached a total of no less than fifteen billion gold marks. In a more positive vein the memorandum then proposed that Germany should pay an annuity of 1.6 billion marks for 37 years.

But even this proposal was tied to special conditions: Germany would have to have colonial sources of raw materials again, and the losses which Germany had suffered through the forced cession of her eastern areas of agricultural surplus would have to be made good.

Schacht later tried to justify the adduction of these conditions by arguing that they were of an exclusively economic nature and by no means political in tone. But this was pure casuistry. The important thing, of course, was the manner in which these demands were taken — and could be expected to be taken — by the creditors. And these countries could only conclude that the Germans were demanding the return of their colonies and of the Polish Corridor. Whether this demand might be justified or not is not the question here. The fact remains beyond doubt that it was not the German experts' task to raise this point.

The experts' behavior was especially reprehensible since the German government had expressly warned them against taking such a step. On March 1 one member of the delegation, Kastl, had made an oral report to the cabinet on the progress of the negotiations. In the course of this report he mentioned that an American observation had encouraged the German party to raise the issues of colonies and the eastern border. Both the Chancellor and Stresemann immediately and firmly expressed their opposition to such a plan, "for it would have been intolerable — and quite harmful to any eventual solution of these political problems — if the experts' conference . . . were finally *to founder* because of the suspicion that *Germany* had ruined it by trying to turn it into *a political* conference." [43] At that time Kastl had expressed his complete agreement with the ministers' point of view. And the correctness of Müller's and Stresemann's argument now became immediately apparent; the conference was in great danger of exploding.

Yet another regrettable episode is connected with the German financial experts' foray into politics, an excursion for which Schacht must be held chiefly responsible. The episode is still relevant today for it casts a light on Schacht and his relations with Stresemann. During the Conference of Experts, Richard Kühlmann, former German state secretary of the Foreign Ministry, also found himself in Paris. He apparently deemed it wise to write a letter to Sir William Tyrrell, the British ambassador to Paris, whom he knew from earlier days. His letter sought to awaken British sympathies for a restoration of Germany as a colonial power. Tyrrell transmitted the letter to the Foreign Office, whereupon Chamberlain instructed the ambassador to Berlin, Sir Ronald Lindsay, to inquire of the Wilhelmstrasse whether Kühlmann had been acting under the direction and with the consent of the German Foreign Ministry.

Stresemann, with a clear conscience, was able to assure Chamberlain to the contrary. And since Kühlmann, in his letter, had spoken of the report the German experts were about to submit, even mentioning Schacht by name, Stresemann gave the event a harmless interpretation, venturing that Kühlmann probably had derived his opinions from the frequent conversations he held with Schacht. Stresemann then informed Schacht of this exchange (April 6). Schacht immediately flew into a frenzied rage and sent a coarse letter to the minister claiming injury.[44] The distinct reproof which he subsequently received from Stresemann was well deserved.[45] But he would not have been Schacht if he had let it go at that. In his later pamphlet, *The End of the Reparations*, he exhumed the event in order to cover Stresemann — who had died in the meantime — with poisonous accusations. Here Schacht gives the impression that throughout his presence and activities in Paris he had had nothing whatever to do with Kühlmann. But this is simply not true. The

documents show that on April 24, 1929, Kühlmann formally assured
State Secretary von Schubert that "before the Paris negotiations had
begun" Schacht "had impressed upon him most emphatically that he
[Kühlmann] was to stand beside him during the conference." [46]
Kühlmann had responded to this emphatic request, but only after
notifying Finance Minister Hilferding — not the Foreign Ministry.
In Paris, his report continues, he saw Schacht almost every day.

An entry in Stresemann's diary for May 1929 shows that the
foreign minister now had serious doubts about Schacht's trustwor-
thiness.[47] It reports how an acquaintance had told him that a very
close relative of Schacht's, whom this acquaintance had met in
Egypt, had said: "If I can warn you of any man, let it be of Hjalmar
Schacht. Nothing about the man is honest. His ambitions are boundless. He walks over anything that blocks his way." We do not know,
of course, whether this acquaintance reported the conversation
truthfully and exactly to Stresemann, and, still less, whether
Schacht's relative had judged him correctly. Every practicing jurist
knows that relatives' testimony is to be regarded with great caution,
even though he might disagree with the old Prussian judge who used
to tell his law clerks: "Relatives and neighbors are the natural enemies of every man." But the fact that Stresemann entered this anec-
dote in his diary, so as to preserve it from oblivion, shows with what
critical eyes he was regarding the president of the Reichsbank at
that time.

In any event, the impression which the Germans' memorandum
of April 17 made on the other experts was as bad as it could possibly have been. A subcommittee of the conference, chaired by the
British delegate Lord Revelstoke, examined it on April 18 to see
whether there were any reason to continue the consultations at all
and arrived at a negative conclusion. The subcommittee agreed,
therefore, to propose that the conference adjourn at the full meeting of the experts on the next day.

The situation was now worse than serious. The collapse of the
conference would have been no less than fatal for Germany — as
was quickly evident. And only a tragic accident saved the meeting
in its final hours. The scheduled plenary session had to be postponed
when Lord Revelstoke died suddenly just a few hours before it was
to gather. The necessary recess led to more peaceful judgment and
to private attempts at reconciliation. The German delegation took
the greatest pains to erase the impression that had prevailed up to
then, namely, that the German memorandum was to be regarded
as their final word. On April 18 the obviously well-informed Paris
correspondent of the London *Times* had reported that Schacht's pro-

posal had been deliberately composed in such a way as to enable him later to say that he had meant it as an ultimatum. In other words, the political demands that Schacht made at Paris stemmed from his concern for his own political future in Germany. The day after the publication of this dispatch the correspondent was able to cable London that, in a personal conversation, Schacht had assured him the proposal had not been intended as an ultimatum after all.[48]

Schacht must have finally realized that Germany was neither financially nor economically able to risk the ruin of the conference, for this would have resulted in the *total collapse* of the German credit structure. The simple news that the conference was in danger led to an almost catastrophic withdrawal of gold and foreign exchange. The Reichsbank lost more than one billion marks in just a few days and found itself obliged, on April 25, to raise its discount rate from 6½ percent to 7½ percent in order to stem this flow. Schacht blamed the French central bank for this development, saying that it had caused other French banks to call their German loans. This may have had a contributing effect, but it fails to explain the drain on German gold and foreign exchange that had already begun. Certainly the basic cause of these withdrawals was the weakening of foreign confidence in Germany at the suspicion that the Germans were prepared to wreck the very conference that had been assembled at their request.

Schacht used the recess in negotiations to travel to Berlin with Vögler in order to consult with the cabinet (April 21). In these conversations Stresemann made it perfectly clear that in his opinion the economic experts had overstepped their mandate by making political demands and that, in a more objective sense, they had acted most unwisely.[49] In the notes that he prepared for his remarks at this meeting he emphasized not only the disadvantages they had occasioned to German foreign policy but also the most undesirable domestic burden which would fall upon the cabinet if, under the pressure of an ensuing crisis, it were forced to raise the experts' reparation offer at some later conference.

Severing described to Schacht the severe social consequences that would be entailed if the German experts caused the conference to fail: the government would be faced with still more unemployment and deep unrest, and its organs for keeping the peace would be most sorely tried. "To all this Schacht could only reply that *then we would simply have to shoot*," Severing reports.[50] Nevertheless, the government assured its delegation — and the general public — "that it wished to continue to give the German experts complete discretion in conducting the negotiations."

Schacht undoubtedly realized now that he had to do everything in his power to help bring the conference to a successful conclusion, even if this meant raising the Germans' reparation offer. It was, however, principally to the credit of the chairman of the conference, Owen Young, that the meeting got off dead center. For he had worked out a compromise which consisted of 37 rising annuities, beginning with one of 1.68 billion marks, to which 21 further payments of 1.7 billion were to be added to correspond to the inter-Allied war debts. On April 27 Schacht and a Mr. Eberstadt, representing Young, arrived at an agreement in principle on this plan.[51]

But Schacht was not at all happy with this result. Although, from the German point of view, the new schedule of reparations represented an improvement over the Dawes Plan, the gain was hardly as great and striking as Schacht had envisioned it when he supported Gilbert's proposal for a final determination of the German debt. For Schacht knew just as well as did Stresemann that nationalists of the Hugenberg persuasion were waiting for an opportunity to attack the outcome of the Paris conference with patriotic fervor; and he feared that the outcome, as he could foresee it now, would not disarm their wrath. Furthermore, he realized that he, Hjalmar Schacht, would stand there as the man who had delivered Germany into the hands of "international capital" — a socialist phrase which the nationalists had adopted as their own.

Haunted by these reflections Schacht immediately laid careful plans to slip out of this front-line position and to transfer the onus of responsibility to the shoulders of others. These "others" were, of course, to be the ministers of Germany. In early May, therefore, Schacht pretended that the German cabinet had assured Gilbert, even before the conference, that they were prepared to settle on an annuity of between 2 and 2.2 billion marks. We have already seen how baseless this statement was and how false Schacht's complaint was that he had not been informed of negotiations which preceded the conference. And in addition to all these maneuvers, Schacht also tried to exert pressures on the government to force it to relieve him of responsibility for accepting Young's proposals.

On Monday, April 29, two days after he had personally accepted the figures involved in Young's plan, Schacht returned to Berlin for a meeting of the Reichsbank board. Naturally he used this occasion to negotiate with the national cabinet. Fortunately, we possess Curtius' detailed and obviously accurate account of these conversations, from which it is clear that *at this time* Schacht failed to tell the ministers that, in fact, he had already accepted Young's proposed schedule of payments. Curtius says that Schacht used these critical discussions "to try to force *sole* responsibility for accepting Young's schedule upon the cabinet first by avoiding the Chancellor's inquiry about his [Schacht's] own opinion and then insisting, with increasing theatrical effect, that the delegation would sign the Young Plan only if the cabinet so directed." [52]

The ministers, however, declined to do Schacht this favor. He had to return to Paris without the cabinet decision that would have relieved him of personal responsibility. Nevertheless, on the next morning (May 2, 1929), he undertook to persuade Kastl and Melchior, who had met him at the Belgian border, to accept the Young proposals — of which they were to receive official notification that afternoon. And only after Schacht had persuaded his colleagues to accept did he receive a letter from the German government communicating its decision of that same day (May 2): that the acceptance of the Young Plan was, as Schacht had argued, "inevitable." [53]

Schacht makes no objection to the material contents of this decision in his pamphlet. He adds only the indignant cry: "This was the independence they gave their financial experts!" Yet this shout is clearly nothing but an attempt to obscure the truth. For, as has been shown, there can be no doubting of the two facts that Schacht accepted the Young Plan *without* being directed to do so by his government and that, therefore, he and his fellow delegates bore the responsibility for having decided, as independent experts, that Germany's burden under the Young Plan would be more tolerable than the consequences of a suspension in negotiations.

This, of course, is not to deny that a strong political element entered into this decision. The question where the limits of a nation's productive capacity not only lie today, but will lie in ten or twenty years, cannot be answered with any real degree of certainty by even the most informed expert. "If 1.65 billion marks did not exceed Germany's productive capacity," Curtius correctly observed, "who could seriously argue that 300 million more would break its back?" [54] And Schacht must already have known quite well how politics and economics lie in an uneasy state of mutual determination when he supported the proposal for an international conference of independent experts and accepted a place on the German delegation. It has been necessary to go so fully into such details because they illustrate Hjalmar Schacht's change of attitude. Schacht had already been expelled from the Democratic Party — which he had helped to found — over the issue of the expropriation of the princes. His increasing gravitation toward the Right was soon to prove of fatal importance to the Republic. People who knew him well have explained this shift by saying that he hoped to become president of Germany when

the gray-haired field marshal's term ran out.[55] The fulfillment of
this ambition required that he find support among those who called
themselves nationalistic, and he would have forfeited all hopes for
such support if, in Germany's name, he accepted a reparations load
which the nationalists found too heavy.

This all became quite apparent a few days later when on May
23 Vögler, heavy industry's representative, announced his resignation from the German delegation. He had first traveled to Berlin
to acquaint the cabinet with his decision. It is true that the strenuous
objections made by the Chancellor and by Finance Minister Hilferding made a strong impression on him. But he went from them
to a meeting of the executive committee of the Federation of German Manufacturers, and here several gentlemen worked on him
with such success that he finally decided to stick by his decision to
resign. Fritz Thyssen, who was soon to become a financial supporter
of Hitler,[56] played an important role at this meeting. When Kastl
took Vögler's place, he did so contrary to Thyssen's express desire.

Several days of the most vigorous discussions then ensued, in
the course of which Schacht requested and received from his government a repeated attestation of his full freedom of action.[57] By
May 31 the basic agreement of all the delegations on all the issues
could be established, and one week later, on June 7, 1929, all the
regular members of the conference — for Germany, Schacht and
Kastl — signed the experts' report which is usually known as the
Young Plan.

The experts' report was an extraordinarily comprehensive document and, though remarkably brief, was involved with numerous
and highly complex problems. Only its most important points can
be treated here.

The annuity which Germany was to pay for the next 37 years —
that is, from September 1, 1929, to March 31, 1966 — amounted to
an average of 1.99 billion marks. But this average rate was not to
be reached until the fiscal year 1937–38, for the schedule of payments was to begin with 1.7 billion and end in 1965–66 with 2.4
billion. A special concession to the Germans was made by postponing
the first payment to September 1, 1929, and by requiring a payment
of only 742 million marks for the remaining seven months of that
first fiscal year (at an annual rate, in other words, of 1.27 billion).
On the other hand, the payments were to extend another twenty-
two years beyond 1966, although in lesser amounts. For the obligations of the inter-Allied war debts were to last until 1987–88, and
the German annuities would have to cover them.

The characteristic elements of the Dawes Plan had been dropped: the protection of foreign exchange and thus the reparation agent. Gone too were the foreign controls of such segments of the German economy as the national railways and the Reichsbank and the guarantees that had formerly rested in the creditors' hands. In short, Germany's sovereignty in these domains was relieved of its former limitations. In this respect the goal which Parker Gilbert had proclaimed and which Schacht had adopted as his own in his letter of September 20, 1928, had been attained: Germany had regained exclusive responsibility for her own finances.

But the experts had also agreed that Germany required some form of protection against unforeseen and unforeseeable difficulties in making the scheduled payments. With this in mind they divided each annuity into two parts: one "unconditional" and one "postponable." Only 660 million marks were unconditional — that is, to be paid without fail every year. They were to be furnished by a direct tax upon the German railways. The "postponable" nature of the other part of each annuity meant that, under certain circumstances, Germany could withhold its transfer to the creditor nations for a period of up to two years. A third part of each annuity was to be delivered in the form of material goods.

For the control and administration of their plan the experts proposed a new international body, the Bank for International Settlements, the nonpolitical character of which was to guarantee the quality of its economic services. The bank's purpose, as the Young Report put it, was "to perform the whole work of external administration such as the receipt and distribution of payments and the commercialization of those parts of the annuities which are susceptible of being commercialized." The bank was to be equipped "with machinery which will provide an elastic element between the payments to be made by Germany and their realization." [58] The bank was also to serve as a tribunal to which the Germans could appeal if they found that the required reparations payments were endangering their currency and economic life. The bank was to have the central banks of the participating countries as its constituent elements, with their directors serving on its governing board. It was only natural that the Reichsbank should play a full role in this international management; and thus the German central bank was able to cooperate responsibly in the supervision of reparations payments.

The Young Plan eliminated other elements of the Dawes Plan: the cost-of-living index and with it the so-called "index of prosperity" — which the Germans had regarded as an ever present danger.* The Young Report was quite right in stating: "the disappearance of this element of uncertainty is wholly to her [Germany's] benefit." [59] Under the Young Plan the annual reparations payments could no longer be increased but only lowered.

This, then, is a rough outline of the plan which was presented to Germany and her creditors in June 1929 for the permanent solution of the reparations problem. But before we describe the reception of the plan in Germany and the conflicts to which it gave birth, we must first review the domestic events of 1928 and early 1929.

In the winter of 1928–29 German economic circles — and, indeed, German public opinion as a whole — were disturbed by a great labor struggle in the Rhenish-Westphalian iron industry.[60] The labor unions had abrogated the wage contract with employers as of November 1, 1928. They now demanded a fifteen pfennig per hour raise, a rather sizable increase. They supported this demand with the argument, among others, that the industrialists had just increased iron prices considerably. To this argument the employers replied that the economic index was slipping and that the industry was far from being able to afford such wage increases.

Since the negotiations between labor and management were leading to no agreement, the dispute came before the Düsseldorf Board of Arbitration (*Schlichterkammer*), which consisted of a neutral chairman and an equal number of representatives of the two parties. When it was apparent that no further progress could be made, the chairman — a provincial superior court counselor — decided on October 26 to issue an arbitration decree drawn up by *himself alone*. In this decree he granted an increase of six pfennigs in hourly wages. The unions accepted the decree, but the employers' association rejected it.

Now, even before the publication of this arbitration decree, the employers' association had announced that all hourly workers would be dismissed on November 1, 1928 — that is, the day on which the former wage contract expired. The labor unions petitioned the national minister of labor to declare the arbitration decree binding. The Social Democrat Rudolf Wissell was then minister of labor. He had been minister of economics in 1919 but had resigned after a few months in office when his proposals for a planned economy were rejected by the cabinet. On October 31 — the last day before the

---

* Under the Dawes Plan Germany would have been obliged to pay increasing annuities whenever the index of prosperity indicated that Germany's capacity to pay had improved. TRANSLATORS.

mass dismissals were to take place — Wissell declared the arbitration decree to be in effect. But the employers did not yield. They stuck to their previous announcement and closed their plants on November 1. More than 200,000 workers were locked out.

The employers' decision amounted to open rebellion against the declaration that the arbitration decree was binding. And the employers could adduce good legal arguments in defense of their position — as they were already doing in a petition to the labor court at Düsseldorf that the arbitration decree be voided. Their most powerful argument was that the decree had not been arrived at by a majority of the arbitration board, but was only the chairman's decision. Such "one-man decrees," however, were not according to the law. For the two basic principles of arbitration are that under the influence of a neutral chairman the two parties to a dispute gradually approach each other and that at least one party should assume responsibility for the decision through having helped compose it. In the case of such a one-man decree, it was argued, these principles had been violated. Even the party that had gained some partial success from the process was still clinging stubbornly to its original demands and showed no inclination to assume responsibility for a decree which had granted only part of what it asked.

Behind this legal argument — the basic validity of which was recognized by the decision of the National (Supreme) Labor Court on January 22, 1929 — lay a most significant effort of the industrial employers: they were fighting off government intervention in wage disputes. They argued that the state was in no sense able — and hence not at all empowered — to determine the wage scale appropriate to the economic situation of business enterprises. Only those parties who bore responsibility for a firm and for its profits could make such decisions. But in fact, their argument continued, governmental agencies did show a tendency to set wages at ever higher levels; for at the expiration of every contract the unions demanded a wage increase, certain that the state would grant at least a part, if not all, of what they asked. But this constant increase in labor costs would prove dangerous — indeed, catastrophic — to German industry if the economic index were to start slipping.

These are, of course, problems which were peculiar neither to this specific time nor to Germany alone; they occur frequently in all industrialized countries, and a completely satisfactory way to treat them has not been found. In Germany, however, at this particular moment the national government faced an extraordinarily difficult situation. It had no power to break the lockout by force. The Reichstag debate of November 12–14 on the conflict in the iron industry showed all the difficulties of the problem and the great divergency of the opposing interests — even if one allows for purely partisan rhetoric.

When the Reichstag finally accepted a compromise resolution, directing the German and Prussian governments to furnish affected communities with funds for the support of locked-out workers, it demonstrated the unions' influence on the parties. The motion can, however, also be taken as a sign of the extent to which the drastic step taken by the employers' associations had embittered public opinion against them. Even Curtius, minister of economics from the conservative People's Party, recalls in his memoirs how he "was repelled by the tactics of the entrepreneurs' associations." [61] On the other hand, it is significant that at the vote on the resolution (which was passed 267 to 59) no less than fifteen members of the People's Party abstained.

Curtius was clearly one of the ministers who wanted the national government to intervene in order to end the conflict before Germany's economy were mortally wounded. And so, in the presence of ministers Curtius and Wissell, Chancellor Müller held conferences with representatives of both parties to the dispute. Müller proposed that the national government appoint a special arbitrator and that the parties announce *in advance* their intention of abiding by his decision.[62] The man on whose shoulders the German government placed this exceedingly difficult burden was a member of its councils: Carl Severing, minister of interior.

Severing had once been a metal worker himself and was completely familiar with the affected area; Hugo Stinnes had once called him an "authority on the region and its people." [63] The fact that the employers accepted this Social Democrat as a neutral arbitrator — faster, indeed, than did the Metal Workers' Union — illustrates how thoroughly Severing had won the confidence of even those who differed most sharply with his political views.

The first consequence of this voluntary submission by both parties to whatever Severing's decision might be was the employers' immediate cessation of the lockout (December 3, 1928). Severing characterized this step as the "one real success of his mission," at the thought of which he felt "unalloyed satisfaction." His decision was announced on December 21. It expressly recognized the unfavorable situation of the industry, and reduced the wage increase that the former arbitrator had granted. Severing included, however, the important provision that the higher wages granted in the decree of October 26 should remain in force through December 31, 1928, as a "pedagogic lesson" against breaking tariff contracts.

With this the great battle was ended. Severing's success was not
diminished by the fact that both parties were dissatisfied by his
decree. He had not expected them to be pleased. Yet, in spite of
all the alarms that the press and industrial organizations sounded,
one can still assume that many a worker — and many an employer
too — privately agreed with the saying: Harmony feeds; discord
breeds needs (*Friede ernährt, Unfriede verzehrt*). Nevertheless,
Severing was completely justified in regretting that his "efforts to
reconcile the warring parties — at least for the immediate future —
had not met with the slightest recognition by either of the opponents." For even those who reject socialism must admit that this
Social Democrat knew better than did either the labor unions or
employers' associations what the German economy needed.

In June 1928, when Hermann Müller's cabinet was being formed,
there was a general understanding that further negotiations would
be held with the Center that autumn to explore the possibility of
binding the party more closely to the national government and thus
replace the provisional Centrist representation of only one minister
(Minister of Transport von Guérard) with a broader and more permanent arrangement. It was not the Chancellor's fault that 1928
came to an end before any progress had been made along this line.
The conflicting claims of the parties were proving all too irreconcilable. This general lack of agreement became quite evident in early
February 1929, when Müller — openly supported by Stresemann —
entered into negotiations with the leaders of the national parties
and of their Reichstag delegations.

The Center demanded three seats in the cabinet. But the People's
Party would agree to this only upon the condition that it be granted
two seats in the Prussian government — to which the Centrists
raised objections of their own.[64] After the negotiations had failed,
the Center assumed the offensive and on February 6, 1929, withdrew von Guérard, its sole minister, from the national cabinet.
This was just three days before the Conference of Experts was to
meet in Paris. At such a moment the government could not resign;
it had no choice but to continue in office and pursue its former program. In any event, this was Müller's and Stresemann's judgment;
and the *Reichspräsident* agreed.

Another pressing argument against provoking a second governmental crisis lay in the extremely serious financial condition of Germany. The economic index had dropped significantly, and agricultural conditions had been poor for quite some time. Unemployment
had risen considerably: in the exceptionally severe winter of 1928–

29 there were 2,600,000 Germans unemployed — a frighteningly high figure. Moreover, this meant increased financial obligations of the Reich, since the National Office for Unemployment Insurance, established in 1927, was incapable of meeting these demands. And, of course, tax receipts were dropping off as business conditions grew worse.

It was only natural that this critical state of the nation's finances should cause both widespread unrest and mounting criticism of the government. The opposition press sought to exploit popular discontent by pointing out that even in such a critical situation the parties close to the government were unable to unite on a common solution, and that each was only looking for some way to put the necessary new financial burden on the shoulders of someone else. There was talk of a crisis in parliamentary government, and those who saw deeper could not help fearing that even more was at stake.

No one sensed this more strongly than Stresemann, who was also getting all sorts of reports about the plans being worked out in Hugenberg's circles. There, Stresemann heard, men hoped that the present conflicts over taxes and the budget would open the way to a Directorate (*Direktorium*), with which they planned to replace the national cabinet. Hugenberg was expected to provide the controlling influence in this Directorate, though, of course, from well behind the scenes. Especially disturbing was the news — reported to Stresemann by a well-informed member of the Foreign Ministry — that certain people in the Defense Ministry were already turning to their old acquaintances in the Black Army with the word to stand ready. And even the oldest generals, it was said, were taking part in maneuvers because they expected a revolt.[65] Nor could Stresemann help but realize that his own party bore a considerable share of responsibility for the sorry state of the Republic. He therefore decided to seize the bull by both horns and use the forthcoming meeting of the party's executive committee (February 26, 1929) for a candid, thorough debate on the issue.

In the main address with which Stresemann, as party chairman, opened the meeting, he characterized the situation as "a crisis for parliamentary government in Germany — much more than a mere cabinet crisis." In Stresemann's opinion the basic weakness of parliamentary democracy in Germany lay in the excessive assumptions of power by the Reichstag party delegations, both in the formation of a government and in the supervision of its activities. It was with special emphasis that he declared: "I take personal objection to the use of the phrase: 'a delegation "withdraws" its ministers' . . . Such a 'withdrawal' of ministers means that in reality they are without any personal political wills, serving instead only as agents of an organization. This attitude is fatal to liberal democracy."

Then, after he had described the financial and economic troubles of the time, Stresemann demanded that the parties' irresponsible competition for transitory popularity be stopped: "Confronted by these displays of partisanship, many of our citizens are lapsing into a kind of passive resignation which is the worst thing that can befall a democratic state . . . Party squabbling over the distribution of political power creates in the people an attitude of indifference — if not disgust." Nor did Stresemann fail to comment on the fact that plans for dictatorship were being whispered about. He warned that those people who liked to think of a dictatorship always expected to be favored with the dictatorship of their choice. And he concluded his speech by saying that the German parliament had to feel the urgency of finding within its ranks a genuine — rather than a merely formal — commitment to the principle of majority rule.

But his words fell upon deaf ears. Parties, like men, do not like to be told: *De te fabula narratur* (people are talking about you); and many speakers rose to differ sharply with this party leader who had dared ask that they subordinate their special interests and desires to the common good. Although at the close of the meeting the usual sort of motion was adopted to smooth over the differences that had come to light, Stresemann knew all too well that he had counseled reason in vain. Deeply distressed, he seriously considered resigning from the party which he had founded. He had no intention, however, of joining another.

His mood is expressed in several bitter letters which he wrote at this time from Geneva, where he was attending a meeting of the League of Nations, and from San Remo, where he went for a brief rest, to personal friends in the People's Party [66] — men like Curtius and Kahl. In these letters he clearly identified the source of the conflict when he characterized the opposition as follows: "They wish to get out of the government; they wish, as they put it, to leave all responsibility to the Social Democrats; and they think of the joys of being in the "nationalistic" opposition, where *they can let fly with all the phrases that they learned from the* Stahlhelm *and Hugenberg* . . . You know me well enough to know that I cannot go along with such a crowd." Sentences like these should suffice to convince those people who still cannot rid themselves of the idea that Stresemann paid only lip service to the ideal of international conciliation while remaining an unreconstructed nationalist at the bottom of his heart.

Stresemann also knew the sources of his intraparty opposition:

"The neighborhood tavern clubs [*Stammtische*], which have such a predominant voice in our party, roar loudest approval to those who repeat the phrases of Herr Seldte or Herr Duesterberg [the two *Stahlhelm* leaders]." But even more dangerous than these neighborhood taverns, where town and village worthies "beat the drums of what they called patriotic enthusiasm," were the great industrial associations which were trying to make the party serve their ends. "We are no longer a party with a philosophic point of view," Stresemann complained to the aged Kahl, who had experienced the grand days of the National Liberal Party. "We are becoming more and more the party of the industrialists. Today our Reichstag delegation simply no longer has the courage to oppose the great employers' and manufacturers' associations."

This was indeed a tragic situation for a party leader who could say of himself that he was perhaps the only German political figure of the time who enjoyed an international reputation. It was all the more tragic because his health was ruined. He was becoming increasingly aware that the tide of his life was ebbing, that soon, in the midst of his most productive years, he would be cut off. The only thing that kept him going was the realization that he alone could save German foreign policy from the "party patriots" and plutocrats of Hugenberg's ilk; only he could achieve the goal for which he so ardently yearned: *the liberation of the Rhineland.*

Stresemann's warning to his party did not go completely unheard. The London *Times* was certainly right when, in an editorial of April 29, it noted, "The remarkable speech of Herr Stresemann just before his departure for Geneva in February undoubtedly made a serious impression on the Deputies and on their constituents." [67] Furthermore, his efforts to effect an agreement among the parties which would permit a reorganization of the coalition finally achieved success — although not until the critical problems of financial policy had been cleared away.

Hilferding had made no attempt to obscure the severity of the financial situation in his budgetary address to the Reichstag on March 14, 1929. He pointed out that the present difficulties stemmed, in the main, from the deficits incurred by the emergency budgets for 1926 and 1927. These deficits meant that the German capital market had been unable to furnish the loans to fill the scheduled need. Thus the Treasury's cash balance had become dangerously low when, along with other demands, it was obliged to extend to the National Office for Unemployment Insurance a massive credit which already amounted to 150 million marks and which would probably grow to 250 million by the end of the fiscal year. Having painted this gloomy picture, Hilferding set forth his proposals for balancing the budget. In addition to the usual appeal for government thrift and a reduction in federal subsidies to the lands and municipalities, he recommended several tax increases on spirits and beer, on inheritances, and on personal property. He estimated that these measures would yield 379 million marks.

His proposals met with resistance not only from the political opposition, but also from those parties represented — if only informally — within the government. The great commercial pressure groups opposed all tax increases, and their allies in the German People's Party blew the same horn. But the pressure for some solution was so strong that the financial experts of the five unofficial coalition parties — including the Center — agreed on steps necessary for balancing the budget.

They lowered many requests for expenditures — cutting the government subsidy of air transport by 20 million marks — and increased the Treasury's income by raising the taxes on both distilled spirits and property. On the other hand, the proposal that the beer tax be increased was rejected, not because the experts thought such a move unnecessary, but rather because the Bavarian People's Party insisted upon this rejection as the price of their cooperation with the national government. As a result of this concession to ruthless particularism, Hilferding's original proposals, which had envisaged tax returns of 379 million marks, were cut to a yield of only 110 million. The cabinet — including Hilferding — finally succumbed to political pressures and accepted the recommendations of the inter-party committee. The melancholy history of German public finance was subsequently to show that the government had made a serious mistake in accepting these tax cuts. But at the time they were made, the burden of taxation weighed so heavily on the German economy that one can well understand why political parties were unwilling to add still further to that load.

With sufficient agreement finally reached on the financial program, the necessary conditions for a return of the Center Party to the coalition seemed assured. But at this junction Kaas, the leader of the Center, raised new difficulties. He revived the issue of the armored cruiser and demanded a promise from the Social Democrats that, in the forthcoming Reichstag vote on the second appropriation for the cruiser, they would not oppose the measure but rather, at most, abstain from voting. A majority of the Social Democratic delegation declined to make this commitment. But in the end even this obstacle was overcome, presumably after the four Social Democratic members of the national cabinet had promised that on this issue they would at least not vote with the opposition.

And so on April 10, 1929, the government was able at last to announce that it accepted the budgetary recommendations of the five Reichstag delegations, and that it consequently expected these parties' support in carrying out its work. More explicitly, the government set forth its expectation that "projects of basic significance would be proposed and carried out only in a spirit of cooperative collaboration." This statement was accepted by all parties concerned. Thus Müller had come as close to the goal of another Great Coalition as the circumstances allowed. The Center received three ministries: von Guérard became minister of justice; Stegerwald, of transport; and Wirth, of occupied areas. The reputation and respect these men enjoyed within their party could be regarded as a guarantee that their colleagues would maintain party discipline.

This reshuffling also meant the resignation of Erich Koch-Weser, who had won admiration and respect on all sides as minister of justice. Yet this was a sacrifice which the Democratic Party was obliged to make in view of its numerical weakness, and to which Koch made not the slightest objection. The People's Party had to suffer a denial of their request to rejoin the Prussian cabinet.

The People's Party would perhaps have been wiser if they had accepted Braun's compromise proposal — seconded by Stresemann — that they furnish one minister and one state secretary. And, as later developments were to show, this would have been better for the Prussian government, too. In early 1930 Braun tried once again to draw the People's Party into his ministry. This attempt failed also — particularly because the People's Party demanded the Ministry of Culture, which the Social Democrats strongly wished to have.

Since 1925 this position had been occupied by Professor Carl Becker, a formal member of no political party but probably closest to the Democrats in his general point of view. A distinguished scholar and an attractive person, his administration of the ministry's cultural responsibilities had won the admiring recognition of men who otherwise had little use for Braun's regime. But now the Social Democrats, making repeated reference to the strength of their Landtag delegation, were insisting that they deserved more than two Prussian portfolios.

Arithmetically their claim made perfect sense; nevertheless, it was a grave political error when, on January 30, 1930, Braun required Becker to resign in order that he might transfer the ministry to Adolf Grimme, a loyal Social Democrat who was in no way ca-

pable of filling his predecessor's shoes. Braun, himself, admits in his
memoirs that he took little comfort from this move. But he certainly
did not fully realize how unfortunate it was for his cabinet — indeed, for the government of Prussia — that even objective observers
now were saying that in this new Prussia the party was more important than the man.

This conflict concerning the composition of the Prussian cabinet
was sharpened — especially between the Center and the People's
Party — by the question of the concordat which had been the object
of negotiation between the Roman curia and Braun's government
since the spring of 1926. There had long been a prejudice against
concordats in German liberal and Protestant circles, because in the
nineteenth century such agreements had almost always led to
Roman Catholic religious hegemony. Furthermore, the concordat
which Bavaria had concluded on March 29, 1924, contained many
provisions which were objectionable from both a general and a
legal point of view.[68]

Yet, on the other hand, the political and social convulsions of
1918 had raised a great number of legitimate church-state problems
which did require solution, especially since the Roman Catholic
Church had just normalized its inner law in accordance with that
magnificent achievement, the *Codex Juris Canonici* of 1917.[69] In
the days of Marx's conservative cabinet the idea of a national concordat — which, of course, the Center supported strongly — had
been much discussed; but it was subsequently buried along with
the proposed school laws.

This national setback, however, had not permanently shattered
the prospects of a Prussian concordat, especially since the papal
nuncio in Berlin, Pacelli (later Pope Pius XII), devoted all his extraordinary stores of diplomatic skill and patience to this end. Minister of Culture Becker and Premier Braun represented Prussia in
the most important negotiations. In these talks the Roman curia
demanded, as was consistent with its basic point of view, that educational matters be included in the concordat. The Prussian ministers,
however, rejected this argument stubbornly and completely, pointing out that their Landtag would never accept a concordat which
related to the Prussian schools.

It was most fortunate that they maintained their stand, for the
treaty, which was concluded on June 14, 1929, contained no word
relating to educational matters.[70] The concordat was duly accepted
by the Landtag on July 9, largely as a result of Braun's ability to
bring the strongly resisting Social Democrats into line. It was, of
course, not astonishing when, shortly thereafter (August 5, 1929),

Pacelli made clear in a message to Braun that the Roman curia had not abandoned its educational claims in Germany by signing the concordat.[71] For, as Georg Jellinek, the distinguished legal philosopher, had observed years before, "the Church will never renounce anything she considers necessary for the completion of her divine mission."[72]

The German Nationalist members of the Prussian Landtag had based their objection to the concordat on the fact that the government was not simultaneously concluding agreements with the Protestant churches. Such agreements had, however, been the government's intention from the start. And so, on May 11, 1931, after long and tedious negotiations, a treaty was written between the Land of Prussia and the Protestant Churches of Prussia — a treaty with which even the German Protestant Union (*Evangelischer Bund*) declared itself content. Thus in Prussia, at least, the relation of State to Church was satisfactorily regulated.

Yet one concordat was still lacking, the one called for by Professor Gustav Deissmann, a Protestant theologian and rector of the University of Berlin, in his speech at the Constitutional Celebration in 1931: "The concordat between Germans and Germans! We Germans have yet to learn . . . that God did not give us hands to clench as fists against each other in bitterness and hate, but rather that . . . we might extend them to our brethren in the handclasp of community."[73]

But such words fell unheard in Germany.

VII

THE FIGHT FOR THE YOUNG PLAN,
STRESEMANN'S DEATH, AND
THE RISE OF HITLER

IT was fortunate for both the cabinet and the Reichstag that the consolidation of the government had been accomplished before the negotiations at the Conference of Experts in Paris had run their course. For the Young Plan had no sooner been announced than the storm of protest that Stresemann had predicted was raised in full strength by the Hugenberg press, the *Stahlhelm*, and all the other Rightist groups and publications. As usual the Communists joined the indignant chorus.

Hugenberg had opened his offensive with an address to the students of Marburg University. He had, of course, offered no hint of how the Germans might fulfill their obligations under the Dawes Plan if they were to reject the Young Plan. Instead, he had declaimed the pompous principle: "It is better for all Germans to live together as proletarians until the hour of freedom strikes, than for some of us to exploit our own people by becoming the agents and beneficiaries of foreign capital." This man, so good at reckoning costs and gains in his own affairs, thought he could solve the difficult problems of international finance with a few empty phrases. When this sentence was quoted by Stresemann in the Reichstag debate of June 24, 1929, it was met with well-deserved "uproarious laughter." But outside the chamber, in all the nationalist taverns and cafés, where people were beating the drums of what they called patriotic enthusiasm, it was precisely such empty formulas that found the greatest praise.

Significantly enough, Hugenberg did not take part in the Reichstag debate. He left that up to Count Westarp and Professor von Freytagh-Loringhoven, neither of whom, as mere party politicians, were any match for the statesman Stresemann, weakened though he was by his disease. The other parties' spokesmen were careful about what they said. Even while they were expressing their preferences for the Young Plan rather than a continuation of former conditions, they explicitly emphasized the heavy burdens which even this new alternative would entail. German Nationalists, Communists, and National Socialists introduced motions of no confidence against Stresemann, all of which were rejected. In any event, the Reichstag raised no objections to a continuation of the previous foreign policy. In particular, it endorsed participation in the prospective political conference among the powers concerned with German reparations, that is, those whose approval was required to implement the Young Plan. Thus the German government could consider itself empowered to take part in the conference which had been called at The Hague for August 6.

In the meantime, however, important changes had been made in both the French and British cabinets. Poincaré, who had been French Premier for three years — an extraordinarily long tenure for first ministers in the Third Republic — was obliged to resign in July 1929 in order to undergo critical surgery. This decision marked the end of a long career which has evoked much criticism, but the historical significance of which remains undisputed.[1] Poincaré's last parliamentary action involved the open support of the Young Plan and the ratification, by his Chamber of Deputies, of the French war-debt agreements with the United States (Berenger-Mellon) and with Great Britain (Caillaux-Churchill). It may be regarded as illustrative of the change in the international atmosphere that this man, who was Germany's severest foe in 1923, closed his political career six years later with a deed which he hoped would keep the way open to Franco-German reconciliation. It seemed almost natural that Briand should succeed him.

In Great Britain the Conservatives were severely defeated in the elections of May 30, 1929. To be sure, the Labour Party had not won a majority in the House of Commons, but it was able to count upon the support of the much-weakened Liberal Party, led by Lloyd George. Ramsay MacDonald was thus able to form his second cabinet, in which he entrusted the office of chancellor of the exchequer to Philip Snowden. Snowden was the man who would represent Britain at the Hague Conference and who, consequently, would step temporarily into the international spotlight.

Philip Snowden, one of the founders of the British Labour Party, was known for the sharpness of both his mind and tongue. Crippled by an accident in his youth, he could walk only with the aid of crutches. In temperament he combined a demagogue's fire with a Yorkshireman's hard head. In the House of Commons he had already taken a position on the Young Plan by declaring, under pressure from Lloyd George, that the experts' proposed allocation of German reparations payments would place Great Britain at an unjustified disadvantage. On the other hand, in a speech of July 25, he had also expressed himself clearly against any increase in German payments over those required in the Young Plan.

The German delegation included no less than four national ministers: Stresemann, Minister of Economics Curtius, Finance Minister Hilferding, and Minister for Occupied Areas Wirth. Stresemann's illness had already progressed to such a point that he was able to take part only in the meetings of the subcommittee on political affairs, where the question of the evacuation of the Rhineland — by far his principal concern — was to be treated. Fortunately, the Dutch government, host to the conference, had housed the German delegation in Scheveningen, where Stresemann could regain some of his strength in the fresh sea air between the wearing meetings of the group. In the subcommittee on finance, where the toughest battles were to be fought, Curtius had to assume the German leadership.

Snowden was primarily to blame for the fact that the Hague Conference did not take the quick and easy course that the Germans had expected.[2] Especially in the finance committee the atmosphere was heavy from the start. At the very first session Snowden voiced the British complaint that the proposed new allocation of German reparations violated the Spa agreements of 1920. And in doing so, Snowden assumed a tone which seemed almost calculated to irritate the other delegations — especially those from France and Italy. For in one of his statements he even went so far as to accuse both these Allies of having broken promises made before the Paris Conference.

The French minister of finance, Chéron, and the Italian delegate, the industrialist Pirelli, offered immediate and energetic rebuttal. Pirelli, who had been a party to the preliminary London negotiations, turned white with anger when Snowden voiced his moralizing objections. The Italian insisted that no word had been uttered at London about maintaining the earlier Spa agreement. Snowden was obliged to retract his accusation. But this hardly lessened his combativeness, especially toward his colleague from France. And the ill feeling he was engendering reached its acme when he called

Chéron's interpretation of the much-cited Balfour note "ridiculous and grotesque." Extended private negotiations and sharp semantic distinctions proved necessary before this stumbling block could be cleared away. Even then the journalists enjoyed reminding each other how Chéron, pointing to Snowden, had muttered to his associates, "There sits the man who burned Joan of Arc!"

Since Snowden had made clear from the beginning that he desired no increase in total German payments, the German delegation was able to take the position that it was up to the creditor nations to resolve their differences. A statement to this effect was soon forthcoming from Stresemann. But this was a position that could not be held for long. Snowden kept rejecting as totally unacceptable all the proposals for compromise that France and the other creditors presented to him. Finally, in the sharpest manner, he threatened to leave the conference if he did not receive satisfactory consideration of his demands forthwith. There had already been serious talk of the danger that the creditors would agree among themselves at Germany's expense. Under these circumstances the German delegates decided it was to their advantage to participate directly in these discussions.[3] By doing so they could not, of course, keep a part of the "sacrifice" which Britain asked of its allies from being passed on to Germany. But the German delegation's tenacious and expert arguments did keep their country's payments within tolerable bounds. Most important, the delegation won agreement that absolutely no new German concessions would be called for before the political goal of the conference, the evacuation of the Rhineland, had been achieved.

It was for the attainment of this end that Stresemann literally spent his remaining strength. In his memoirs Curtius tells how on one of the last days of the conference, after an exciting and exhausting session, Stresemann collapsed, exclaiming, "I cannot go on." Hilferding, who as a physician could read the symptoms, took Stresemann to his hotel, and upon his return told Curtius that "the clock has run down."

Indeed, it had. Gustav Stresemann's life was near its end. But before it was completely over, he experienced the grand moment for which he had been yearning: Briand finally gave him the assurance — which with good reason had been withheld for quite some time — that by June 30, 1930, the last member of the occupation forces would have left the Rhineland. It was on a lovely afternoon, on Stresemann's balcony there on the North Sea, that the French Premier spoke the words for which the German foreign minister had been waiting so fervently and so long. Paul Schmidt, who was present at this conversation as interpreter, recounted this "unforgettable afternoon" with lyric feeling even after many years: "Suddenly the sun shone even more brightly, and the sea reflected the light more fully. The reflections played upon the faces of the two statesmen who had contested so hard with each other and with their respective nations in search of a solution. And now, at this moment, both hoped that a new age had come, one in which France and Germany would truly become good neighbors." [4]

But alas! This new age, which the evacuation of the Rhineland was to usher in, turned out to be quite different. In the proclamation of July 1, 1930, which the government of President Hindenburg and Chancellor Brüning issued on the occasion of this historic event, no mention was made of Stresemann at all. Instead, the President of Germany used the celebrations of the liberation as occasions to extort from the Prussian government a revocation of the ban on the *Stahlhelm* in the Rhineland and Westphalia.[5] Thus the *Stahlhelm* was able to hold a rally in Coblenz which could only serve as provocation to the French. And in the course of the withdrawal of French troops the German population engaged in excesses which made Briand feel obliged to enter earnest protests with the German ambassador to Paris, von Hoesch.[6] Moreover, Stresemann's successor, Curtius, had personally offended Briand by ignoring von Hoesch's suggestion that he express to Briand the gratitude which the Frenchman felt he deserved for having effected the evacuation ahead of schedule in spite of all resistance.[7]

The German nation gave the clearest expression of its real sentiments when, in the first Reichstag election after the evacuation of the Rhineland, it cast six and one-half million votes for the National Socialist candidates. The British ambassador to Berlin, Sir Horace Rumbold, observed at this time that ingratitude was an unpleasant characteristic of the Germans. Rumbold was commenting on Hindenburg's manifesto celebrating the evacuation. But his point is also illustrated by the support given the Nazis, the Germans' failure to appreciate the great services of Stresemann, and their insistence that one concession always required more. In his letter of July 3, 1930, Rumbold wrote to his foreign secretary, Arthur Henderson: "It is an unattractive feature of the German character to display little gratitude for favours received, but when the receipt of favours is followed by fresh demands, there are grounds for feeling impatient. With the exception of the Social-Democratic press and a few Democratic newspapers, the remainder of the political journals put forward a list of demands which have to be granted before Germany can feel that justice is done to her." [8]

After this brief look into the future let us now return to the Hague Conference of August 1929. The position of the German delegation — which, by the very nature of the case, had little hope of scoring a financial victory — was especially weakened by the attitude of Dr. Schacht. Both the other experts, Kastl and Melchior, collaborated loyally with the delegation. But the policy of the Reichsbank president struck his colleagues as being based principally upon consideration of the impression it would make on the excited German public, which was being stirred up by wild agitation.

In July a national committee had been formed to promote a referendum against the Young Plan, and influential economic organizations were already making their opposition known. It is true that Schacht had recommended the acceptance of the plan, under certain political conditions, in an extended report to the executive committee of the National Conference of Industry and Commerce; but he took care to disassociate himself from the government's position. And on August 29, when the German delegates at The Hague found themselves obliged to alter the proposed schedule of unprotected payments, Schacht — in sharp contrast to Melchior and Kastl — declared that he could not join in such a move and that he would therefore have to resign from the delegation.

His statement led to an animated discussion — one which made so great an impression on Schacht that he retracted his former resignation, retaining only the right to make a later decision, which he would then express to Stresemann. But shortly after this delegation meeting it became known that Stresemann had just gained his great victory in the political subcommittee: the evacuation of the Rhineland had been won. At the meeting of the German delegation that followed this turn of events, Schacht assumed a much more cooperative tone, expressly promising to make no more difficulties for his colleagues. Many members of the delegation gained the impression that now, after Stresemann's significant political victory, Schacht no longer felt it necessary to distinguish his position from that of the delegation, preferring instead to keep both ways free for whatever moves future developments should suggest.

By August 31 enough progress had been made so that the conference could be closed with the signing of a protocol by all participants. Snowden had won a great financial victory: Britain's share of reparation payments had been increased significantly over that envisaged in the original plan. This gain had the almost absurd consequence that the socialist chancellor of the exchequer was welcomed home as a national hero, especially by British financial circles, which ordinarily had little use for him. But whether this financial gain was also a political victory is doubtful. Snowden's brusque manner had certainly not helped pave the way toward that reconciliation of national differences and encouragement of peaceful compromise which is surely more important than any number of separate treaties.

The fact that Germany had to provide a considerable portion of the additional payments which Snowden had extracted from his allies was not of overwhelming financial significance. But it did create real political difficulties for the German government — difficulties much greater than the sums involved might seem to have warranted. For the opposition was quick to accuse the government of having yielded once more to the Allies; and very, very few Germans were willing to weigh the burden of financial concessions against the value of the legal gains that had been won. Thus Snowden's intransigence at the conference played into the hands of the German Rightists. Curtius was certainly justified when, at a meeting of his delegation, he declared that Snowden deserved to be made an honorary member of the Hugenberg committee.

Yet, in spite of the financial concession they had granted, the German delegates had good reason to be content with their accomplishments. It is, of course, true that the unprotected portion of annual payments for the next few years was going to be higher than the Young Plan had proposed. (The original schedule had set unprotected payments at 660 million marks; they now had been raised to start at 700 million — 88 million for interest and amortization of the Dawes Loan and 612 million in reparations — and would diminish gradually as the Dawes Loan was retired.) And Germany forswore her share of the 300 million surplus that would be created in the transition from the Dawes Plan to the Young Plan. It is also true that starting September 1, 1929, Germany would have to pay 30 million marks per year as her share of occupation costs. And with respect to the liquidation of German private assets by the Allies the delegation had been able only to win agreement in principle that those assets not yet liquidated would be returned to their former German owners. Nor was much more to be gained in the agreement with Poland that was signed shortly thereafter, on October 31, although it did allow something like 12,000 German farmers to keep the properties they held in what was now Polish territory.

Still, despite all these exacerbations, the Young Plan had as its end result a reduction in Germany's reparation burden.[9] For it meant the release of all securities by the Allies and the removal of all the creditors' financial and economic controls. And most important of all, the financial disadvantages of the Young Plan were more than outweighed by the total evacuation of the Rhineland five years earlier than the Treaty of Versailles had provided. The proponents of German nationalism should have been particularly elated by this result since the French did not press their former insistence on a control commission (*Commission de constatation et de conciliation*).[10]

And this was almost exclusively Stresemann's work. Austen Chamberlain, out of office at the time, recognized this in clear and candid words when, on September 9, he wrote to Stresemann expressing his pleasure at the successful conclusion of the Hague Conference and assuring the German minister that it was to *him* and *his policies* that Germany owed her success.[11]

Even in Germany there were many thoughtful people who recognized this same truth. Theodor Wolff,* in a letter to Stresemann of September 1, congratulated him and likened those who minimized the evacuation of the Rhineland to dogs "howling in vain at the moon." And how would those who had been continually shouting about German grandeur and demanding liberation for Germany react? With what shouts of thanksgiving would these Pan-Germanists greet Stresemann upon his return? The answer came during the Pan-German convention held immediately after the close of the Hague Conference. Their leader, Counselor of Justice Class, who had barely escaped trial for high treason, pronounced the following judgment on the men who had served Germany at The Hague: "Men like Hilferding and Stresemann should be brought to political trial. Stresemann is the essence of all the dangerous tendencies in our nation; his psychic degeneracy is clearly derived from his political decadence." [12] This self-styled patriot and statesman explained away Stresemann's feat of linking the evacuation of the Rhineland to the Young Plan by saying that the foreign minister had wished to cheat the German people out of an opportunity to vote on the Hugenberg referendum. In such ways did the Pan-Germanists — who had done more than any others to make Germany hated throughout the world — rail against the one man who had succeeded in regaining friends for Germany after her defeat. It was indeed a strange sort of pleasure to be directing German foreign policy at this time.

The referendum that Hugenberg wanted to get passed was being

* Theodor Wolff (1868–1943), one of Germany's most distinguished liberal publicists, was the cofounder of the literary periodical *Freie Bühne* and, from 1906 until forced out by Hitler in 1933, the editor of the *Berliner Tageblatt*. He later fled Germany and was tracked down by the Gestapo in southern France. In his seventy-sixth year he was murdered in the Nazi concentration camp of Oranienburg, just outside his native Berlin. TRANSLATORS.

promoted by a national committee which had come into being on July 9, 1929, even before the Hague Conference had convened. It was only natural that Hugenberg should be its chairman. And it was equally natural that Seldte, of the *Stahlhelm*, and Counselor Class were Hugenberg's assistants. Indeed, the only truly surprising thing about the committee was that its membership included Adolf Hitler, leader of the National Socialists. For until this time the German Nationalists had taken care to dissociate themselves from this convicted and sentenced traitor and his demagogic agitation. But Hugenberg had lost even this last bit of political decency — and wisdom.

For now Hugenberg, the proper Prussian official and the confidant of German industrial magnates, a man to whom the mere word "socialism" was like a red flag, allied himself with a man who had claimed the right to engage in revolt and treason and who preached his own peculiar variety of socialism. It never entered the hard head and narrow mind of this overlord of the press and the cinema who controlled the Berlin *Lokalanzeiger* and the Ufa *
that in supporting Hitler he was conjuring up spirits which he could never escape or that the passions he now whipped up would benefit only the man who had the fewest scruples. For Hitler, on the other hand, it was a major triumph to be thus received into proper society.[13]

If Stresemann had had the time and strength, he would have undertaken the defeat of the committee and its referendum. But such was not to be. A few days after the conclusion of the Hague Conference, he went back to the League of Nations meeting at Geneva and there, on September 9, 1929, delivered his last public address. In it he urged the League to settle the issues of the Saar, on which no progress had been made at The Hague. He also supported Briand's hopes for a "reorganization of political relations in Europe," speaking out against those "constitutional pessimists who doom every new idea to sterility if it does not suit prevailing modes of thought." He concluded this last public speech with Schiller's lines in praise of "untiring industry"

> Which only sets one grain of sand
> Upon the next, that aeons may be built;
> Yet as it does just this, its hand
> Strikes minutes, days, and years from ages' guilt.

* Ufa was the abbreviation for Universum-Film-Aktiengesellschaft (Universal Film Corporation), Germany's largest and most influential motion picture company. By the 1930's it controlled the distribution of films to some 120 theaters with a seating capacity of about 126,000. Hitler took over control from Hugenberg in 1936. TRANSLATORS.

One can only wonder whether these final words represented a premonition on Stresemann's part that behind his back an era of German history was approaching which would add to the "ages' guilt" in a most horrible way.

This speech was the last flickering of a dying flame. Antonina Vallentin depicts Stresemann's appearance at Geneva in frightening strokes: "A marked man stood there in the shadow of death. His suit flapped about his shrunken figure . . . His breathing came so hard that his sudden coughing often drowned out his words . . . One could almost hear the fevered beating of his heart." [14] And then Stresemann left Geneva for a short sojourn at Vitznau on Lake Lucerne. But even here the pressing problems of state gave him no peace. The leader of the Democratic Party, Erich Koch-Weser, had been a delegate at Geneva. He now sought out Stresemann in order that they might discuss a matter of common interest and concern: the possibility of uniting "all groups which oppose the misdirection of nationalistic feeling," as Koch put it in a letter of September 11. Stresemann was in complete agreement with this effort. But was it still possible to repair the damage done at the founding of the German Democratic Party? For this project, too, the most necessary element was lacking: time.

On September 25, when Stresemann returned to Berlin, he found the national government in great distress because of the financial necessity for changing the unemployment insurance program. He was also disturbed by the extremely poor health of Chancellor Müller, who had returned to the capital in no sense recovered from a long illness. In spite of these difficulties, however, Stresemann did succeed in getting the executive committee of his party to pass a clear resolution opposing the Hugenberg referendum. Then, on the afternoon of October 2, at a meeting of the People's Party Reichstag delegation, he sought to persuade the delegates not to ruin all hopes for an unemployment insurance reform by clinging too stubbornly to their own demands. It was clear that the lively and strenuous discussion on this point was disturbing Stresemann deeply. One delegate, von Raumer, thought he could already see the coming catastrophe in the foreign minister's features, and he urged Stresemann to leave the room, assuring him that he would bring the matter to a satisfactory close. And, indeed, the delegation decided to abstain unanimously from the vote, thus obviating a crisis on the issue.

Upon returning to his home, Stresemann had to go immediately to bed. Although he did receive Curtius for a conversation that evening, the clock had truly run down. And in the early morning hours of the next day, October 3, 1929, the clock finally stopped. A stroke had put an end to Gustav Stresemann's life after only fifty-nine years.

How short a life! And how untimely a death! One can fully sense the tragic foreshortening of this career only by stopping to realize that the man who today (1963) directs the fortunes of the German Federal Republic with full vigor was born two years before Stresemann. Death reaped a rich and early harvest among the leaders of the Weimar Republic: Ebert and Friedrich Naumann, Walther Rathenau and Erzberger, now Stresemann and shortly Hermann Müller. They all died while still in the prime of life. It is hard to estimate what part these tragic losses played in the history of the Republic. But the fact that Stresemann's death meant a loss to Germany — indeed, to all Europe — was apparent to many people in Germany and elsewhere even then. And many an enemy of the Republic rejoiced in secret to see Germany lose one of her best supports.

Throughout his life Stresemann stood in the middle of battle, and thus it is almost fitting that the evaluation of his career is still under dispute. But the parties to the skirmish have completely changed sides. Alive, Stresemann was accused of sacrificing the legitimate interests of his fatherland to utopian thoughts of universal peace. Dead, he is criticized for not having been sincere in voicing hopes for peace, for having mouthed these idealistic phrases simply as a means of persuading Germany's former enemies to agree to remove the obstacles to Stresemann's real goal: a revitalized Germany, ready and willing for war.

I believe that such critics have gone much too far and have reached completely false conclusions. This is especially true of those who harbor the suspicion that Stresemann ever considered, or even desired, a war of revenge. It is, of course, quite true that he did not have Briand's ecstatic faith in the coming reign of peace. For he had not sprung, as had Briand, from the intellectual soil that nourished the French Revolution and utopian internationalism. Rather, as a youth he had joined his fellow students in drinking the intoxicating wine of triumphant nineteenth-century German nationalism. Stresemann had probably tried hard to blend into this fervent milieu since he was always aware of his petty bourgeois origins and regarded his background as a hindrance in the career his ambition and his talents seemed to promise. Toward the end of the war, when the possibility of introducing members of the Reichstag into the Imperial cabinet was being considered, Stresemann remarked to his party colleague Schiffer that he would decline any such invitation because, as the son of a Berlin beer dealer, he would constantly fear being treated in a condescending manner by the members of the entourage of William II.[15] And even in later years sympathetic observers noted signs of an inferiority complex which they attributed to his petty bourgeois background.

One can well imagine that this sense of personal inadequacy was even stronger in his youth, and that he tried to compensate for it then by emphasizing the nationalistic enthusiasm which was so popular in student circles and so congenial to his extraordinary rhetorical gifts. It is difficult to free oneself in later years from such habits acquired in one's youth, and it is quite understandable that Stresemann frequently relapsed into these unfortunate patterns of thought when addressing student groups. He found it especially difficult to outgrow these former ways after having founded, to the right of the Democrats, a party in which, as he later said himself, "the neighborhood tavern clubs . . . have such a preponderant voice."

But it is precisely for this reason that one should not take Stresemann's mode of speech for more than what it was: a means of gaining the support of those men whom his private thoughts had already outpaced. And his confidential statements, especially toward the end of his life, showed his growing awareness of the depth of the gap which separated him from his reactionary colleagues.

None of this, of course, is meant to dispute the proposition that all of Stresemann's political thought and action revolved around his hopes for German glory — as, indeed, befits any major German statesman. But he sought to achieve this grander German future by taking the paths of peace. He did so not merely because he saw no present prospects for military success, but primarily because he was convinced that international reconciliation offered a better opportunity for realizing the true interests of Germany.

Thus, when he regarded the Treaty of Versailles as an obstacle on the road to a true and lasting peace and tried to alter or annul it bit by bit, he was merely sharing the opinions of many men in other lands. And even when he ignored the secret rearming that was taking place in Germany contrary to the provisions of the Versailles treaty, he found himself in the company of the Western powers, which were abandoning one species of control after another even though they were certainly not persuaded that Germany was totally disarmed. In any event, after Scheidemann's sensational Reichstag speech about the Russian ammunition, the Allies must have been fully aware of what they could expect from German generals.

In February 1930 the British chief of the imperial general staff,

General Milne, made a report on the military situation in Germany. His report demonstrates that people in London were well informed of the numerous German circumventions and violations of the Versailles treaty and that British authorities were fully aware of how the German generals were attempting "to organize the nation as a whole, and industry in particular, so that it may be ready once more to convert itself into a war machine, should the necessity arise, and in the meantime to prevent the military spirit from dying out in Germany." [16] But in the same breath the British general declared that "the present *Reichsheer* [*sic*] is not a menace to the peace of Europe." In consequence of this reassurance, London did absolutely nothing. If British military authorities preferred to disregard the hard evidence of Germany's well-known "secret" rearmament and reassure themselves with the thought that such efforts would not make Germany dangerous for a long time, the German foreign minister had every reason to follow suit.

Regardless of the position one takes on the controversy over Stresemann, no reasonable person can deny that he made great contributions to his country. Thanks to him Germany regained that place among the nations of the earth which she had forfeited in war. She was heard again in the councils of the world because in Stresemann she possessed a man the world would listen to. Gustav Stresemann had won this victory for Germany by first winning a victory over himself in giving up the battle for the Ruhr. The capacity to accept defeat in order, indefatigably, to build anew is the hallmark of the truly great statesman.

After death had robbed Germany of the man who had wished to lead her uphill on the path of peaceful reconciliation, another man stepped ever further into the foreground who was to lead her back down to another war and a second defeat. Adolf Hitler spent the six months' fortress arrest which the Munich People's Court had found a just atonement for high treason in the Bavarian fortress at Landsberg until December 20, 1924. The Bavarian Ministry of Justice had certainly not gone out of its way to make life there miserable for him. He was assigned a sunny, comfortable room, given good food, permitted to enjoy whatever gifts his admirers sent, and allowed unlimited visitors. In short, it is no exaggeration to say that in his fortress Hitler enjoyed a more pleasant life than ever before.[17] All this did not, of course, keep him from regarding himself as a martyr who was suffering the severest tests for his convictions.

Two of his supporters remained at the fortress with him as voluntary secretaries. One of them was Rudolf Hess, whose better education was a help to Hitler's writing. It was to these secretaries here at Landsberg that Hitler dictated the first chapters of a programmatic book to which his publisher, Ammann, gave the title *Mein Kampf*. Hitler, with his highly developed sense for publicity, dated the book from "Fortress Landsberg on the Lech" even though at the completion of the first volume he had long since been set free.

This first volume, more than 400 pages long, appeared in June 1925. It attracted more than 9000 buyers that first year, netting Hitler more than twenty thousand marks. The second volume, which followed a few years later, met with less success. Yet as early as 1930 annual sales of the complete book had risen to fifty thousand copies. And after the so-called "seizure of power" various forceful measures raised sales to 850,000 per year.[18] By 1940 the book had enjoyed a total printing of 5,950,000 copies, and Hitler could boast of having written the world's most widely read book — except the Bible.

Whoever, encouraged by its reputation, takes up the book with the expectation of finding it an original work of real quality — indeed, whoever expects merely a worthwhile, interesting, and readable book — will be bitterly disappointed. The first few pages, perhaps, in which Hitler sketches his wasted youth in false and flattering strokes, can still be considered reasonably readable. But as soon as Hitler starts dwelling on his political ideas, he exhausts the reader with an endless cascade of words and with insufferable repetition. Seldom before has Goethe's aphorism been more applicable: "Getretener Quark wird breit, nicht stark." *

There is scarcely a trace of originality in the entire book. Most of the contents are coarse simplifications of other men's ideas, derived from such German-Austrian fanatics as Schönerer or Wolff, who were coarse enough in their own right. Only in the rarest cases can one speak of arguments at all. In their stead one finds vulgar terms of abuse such as had never before appeared in German political literature. Even a dedicated and determined opponent of socialism and of Marxism must turn away, disgusted, from Hitler's polemics which are as superficial as they are brutal and libelous. His limitless capacity to mock democracy and democrats, parliamentarians and parliaments, is comprehensible only if one realizes that all his exalted praise of the *Führerprinzip* has but one meaning: I, Adolf Hitler, am determined to be that leader beneath whose monstrously powerful will — which is free from every moral scruple — every person and every thing will be inexorably bent. Whoever

---

* A line which Clementine T. Barnett has adroitly translated, "Rancid butter put on bread tastes no better when it's spread." TRANSLATORS.

harbors other thoughts, whoever refuses to accept me as leader, is a Jew or the hireling of a Jew.

Thus Hitler reaches the triumphant conclusion in his tirade against parliaments and democracy: "Only a Jew can praise an establishment that is as filthy and false as himself." And this is the refrain to which the entire book resounds. Jews are responsible for literally everything that Hitler does not like. They are, for instance, working for mastery of the world. Proof: "The Protocols of Zion." The fact that the *Frankfurter Zeitung* insists that they are a forgery is in itself sufficient proof that they are genuine.

Such is Hitler's logic, that makes light of every difficulty. With logic like this, of course, every problem becomes a simple one. Indeed, Hitler is the most frightful of the *terribles simplificateurs* of whom Jacob Burckhardt so emphatically warned. And that distinguished modern German historian, the late Friedrich Meinecke, undoubtedly had his eye on Hitler when, in an academic address of 1948 on Ranke and Burckhardt, he depicted the usurpers that Burckhardt had foreseen: "Supported by militaristic institutions, they . . . would . . . command the masses: Shut up! Forget your private desires. Assemble to the roll of drums every morning, survive your daily share of misery, and be led by drumbeat home again at dusk." [19]

Any German patriot who today, after the awful harvest of the dragon's teeth, could summon the necessary self-control to wade through all the verbal muck of Hitler's book would have to hide his head in shame at the thought that millions of Germans once considered it the source of unique political wisdom and regarded its author as a national prophet. Yet the miserably low intellectual and literary value of the book explains also why Hitler's political opponents failed to pay it much attention. For they simply could not imagine that such shoddy scribbling could make an impression on any reasonable man and thus rob them of their voters. How wrong they were!

At first, of course, it seemed that they were right. While Hitler was sitting in prison his henchmen fell to quarreling among themselves. General Ludendorff became the leader of the Racist bloc in the Reichstag, uniting under his direction the National Socialists with their North German comrades, men like von Graefe, Major Henning, and Count Reventlow. But the great war leader could not hide his political inabilities for long. Mommsen calls Labienus, Caesar's errant subordinate, "one of those people who combine complete inability as statesmen with military usefulness and who are subject to mad fits of dizziness when misfortune requires or impels them to engage in politics." [20] Does that not sound as though it were written expressly to describe Ludendorff? The Reichstag election of December 7, 1924, seemed to indicate that the German people's return to reason had put an end to the National Socialist threat. More than half the people who had supported Hitler's party in May deserted him in winter (leaving 907,000 out of 1,918,000); and of the thirty-two National Socialists in the Reichstag, only fourteen were returned.

During his fortress arrest, the most important question to Hitler was whether he really would be released on parole after six months, thus being set free, and whether the Munich government — quite contrary to law — would permit him to remain in Bavaria. Minister of Justice Gürtner took care of the parole, but even in Bavarian government circles there were people who realized that Hitler's continued residence constituted a constant threat to the domestic peace.

Munich police headquarters, which had responsibility for maintaining the security of the state, requested twice that Hitler be deported: on May 8 and again on September 22.[21] In his report of September 22 to the Bavarian minister of interior, the director of the state police predicted that, as soon as Hitler were released, he would, by dint of his inner energies, immediately become the driving force of the National Socialists; that he would provoke more serious disturbances and pose a continued threat to the state; and that he would not shrink from further criminal acts even if they might endanger his probation. One did not have to be a prophet to foresee that much, but the Bavarian government did absolutely nothing. And so, on December 20, 1924, Hitler regained his freedom and could return to Munich.

His release did not, of course, put an end to all the quarrels among the National Socialists, some of which were directed against Hitler himself. But his demonic energy, which carried all opposition before it, enabled him to reorganize the party and, most important of all to him, to bring the reorganized party completely under his control. In the long run his opponents within the party — men like Gregor Strasser — would have to yield. Besides, the party's newspaper, the *Völkischer Beobachter*, belonged to Hitler.

Hitler gained a special victory at a conference of *Gauleiter* (regional leaders) at Bamberg in February 1926, where he succeeded in winning to his side the young Dr. Joseph Goebbels, who had supported Strasser until then. For Goebbels was by far the party's cleverest head: a successful organizer and a journalist as cunning as he was unscrupulous. Hitler rewarded Goebbels for his new allegiance not only by admitting him to his most intimate circle of confidants, but also by appointing him *Gauleiter* of Berlin with responsibility only to the Führer himself.

These organizational gains were not accompanied by similar political successes. This was in part, perhaps, because Hitler had been prohibited from giving public speeches in Bavaria, Prussia, and several other lands. But certainly the most important reason was the increasing stability in German life. The German people had the feeling that they were working their way out of the nation's massive catastrophe and thus had little use for demagogues who wished to tear down what little still remained and who called every conciliatory policy high treason.

The National Socialists were roundly defeated in the Reichstag elections of 1928. Only in two Bavarian districts did they win the 60,000 votes required for the direct election of a Reichstag delegate. Four more were chosen through district coalitions, and six others from the national list. This total of twelve delegates included Goebbels, the former air ace Captain Hermann Göring, Gregor Strasser, and Gottfried Feder, the party's economic "expert" who had found the panacea for all economic and social ills in the "breaking of interest bondage."

In the eyes of the National Socialists the great advantage of these Reichstag seats lay in the fact that their delegates received railroad passes valid throughout the Reich — thus relieving the party treasury of the costs of transporting demagogues — and legislative immunity, which protected them from prosecution for what they chose to say. They made full use of these liberties, especially in the press. With cynical insolence Goebbels noted: "I am not a member of the Reichstag. I am a PI and a PRP: a Possessor of Immunity and a Possessor of a Railroad Pass." [22] The party was of parliamentary significance only as a constant irritant.

Hitler was rescued from this precarious political position by Alfred Hugenberg. When this mighty leader of the German Nationalists accepted Hitler, the man who had previously been rejected and despised by "decent" people, and made the National Socialist his close ally in the fight against the Young Plan, an issue so important for Germany's future, many Germans felt obliged to take Hitler seriously and to forget his record of misconduct. Furthermore, when the *Stahlhelm* patriots, who could count President Hindenburg among their honorary members, paraded publicly in the company of Hitler's Brown Shirts and their swastikas, peaceful citizens might well conclude that it was safe to forget their earlier suspicions. Indeed, when one regarded the activities of the "National Committee for the German Referendum," it was hard to tell whether its chairman was really Hugenberg or Hitler.

The national constitution (Article 73, Paragraph 3) required that a popular referendum be initiated by the submission of a "detailed legislative proposal" to the national minister of interior. (See also Paragraph 27 of the Referendum Law of June 27, 1921.) [23] And so, on September 28, 1929, just a few days before Stresemann's death, Hugenberg's national committee submitted a draft of its so-called "freedom law." This document illustrates with frightful clarity the way the minds of the self-styled "nationalistic opposition" operated and what these self-appointed saviors thought the German people wanted. The draft consists of only four paragraphs, but each of these paragraphs deserves a special place in any political and constitutional chamber of horrors.

Anyone familiar with the mental processes of Hugenberg and company could predict that they would begin with the "war-guilt lie." It is true, of course, that with their entry into Marx's government the German Nationalists had silently let the issue die. But this simple fact did not deter their new leader from inscribing the motto on their banner again, now that they were back in the opposition. According to the national committee there was a surpassingly simple way for the German people to treat the whole question of responsibility for the war. Their solution, contained in the first paragraph of their proposal, would have had the government of Germany "notify all foreign powers immediately and formally that the confession of war-guilt forced upon Germany in the Versailles treaty is contrary to historical truth, rests upon false assumptions, and has no force in international law." [24]

And then what? Did not the German voter, if he used the slightest bit of logic, then have to ask what was to be achieved through such a unilateral declaration by one party to a contract? Paragraph 2 tried to answer this query with a further directive to the government that it "make every effort to get the declaration of [Germany's] war-guilt in Article 231 [of the Versailles treaty] . . . formally annulled." Just what the petitioners expected their government's "efforts" to be and just what the government was to do if the Western powers declined, were problems significantly left unanswered by the proposed freedom law. Presumably the petitioners expected that their names alone would make such a deep impression on the West that their former enemies would immediately yield to the German "efforts."

And what a doughty defender of German innocence the petitioners had in the person of the Honorable Counselor of Justice

Class, the chieftain of the Pan-Germanists! This was the man who even before 1914 had written: "Whoever loves his countrymen . . . must yearn for war, the awakener of all that is positive, strong, and healthy in any person." Hitler, of course, could offer Class strong competition. For in *Mein Kampf* he complained that the general tone of Austria's ultimatum to Serbia seemed to him "much too considerate and in no way excessive or even brutal." He also recalled that he had greeted the outbreak of war as a "deliverance" and wrote: "Overcome by violent enthusiasm, I fell to my knees and from an overflowing heart thanked heaven that it had blessed me with an opportunity to live in such times." To the minds of the superpatriots, declarations such as these were, apparently, examples of the "false assumptions" upon which the "war-guilt lie of the Versailles treaty was based."

Given this attitude of mind it can cause the reader no astonishment to learn that Paragraph 2 went on to direct the German government to exert further efforts to effect "the formal annulment" of Articles 429 and 430 of the Versailles treaty — which concerned Allied occupation rights in Germany — and thus to have "the occupied areas immediately and unconditionally . . . evacuated without regard to the acceptance or rejection of the Hague Protocol." The third paragraph, however, opposed the Young Plan even more directly by forbidding the national government "to assume, with respect to foreign powers, any new burdens and obligations" which might imply Germany's acceptance of war guilt. The recommendations of the Paris Conference of Experts were expressly included among such assumptions.

The national committee was not even content with this sweeping prohibition. It added a fourth paragraph, according to which "any chancellor, minister, or authorized agent of the state" who might dare "to sign treaties with foreign powers" would be guilty of treason according to Paragraph 92, Section 3, of the Criminal Code, and punished with not less than two years' imprisonment as common felons.

But men write poor laws when thirsting for revenge. Among the "authorized agents of the state" was the President of Germany, Field Marshal von Hindenburg, and the *Stahlhelm* suddenly realized that this man, their chief honorary member, was threatened with imprisonment because he had joined the *Stahlhelm's* president, Seldte, in signing a treaty. Goebbels, of course, took no exception to this, but Seldte and the German Nationalists, now frightened by their own audacity, succeeded in effecting a slight change in the text of their proposal. It now read "chancellor, minister, or their authorized agent" instead of "or authorized agent of the state." Thus Hindenburg was spared the danger of imprisonment. But it remained the unanimous opinion of the national committee that the foreign minister belonged in prison. Such was the nationalistic opposition's farewell to the dying Stresemann.

There were good grounds to question the admissibility of this "proposed legislation" to a popular referendum. For the Weimar constitution had expressly barred such action on budgetary and fiscal measures, and the Young Plan, which the freedom law was designed to bar, clearly involved matters of public finance. But the government did not wish to precipitate a conflict over questions of constitutional law and hence set the machinery for a referendum into operation.

And so in the second half of October 1929 supporters of the referendum were to have an opportunity to show their strength on official petitions. Extraordinarily vigorous agitation was unleashed under Hugenberg's affluent auspices. The national committee was unscrupulous in its techniques, even trying to use Hindenburg's name for its purposes. Indeed, it went so far as to produce a campaign film centered around the President. Finally Hindenburg had no choice but to assure his Chancellor by letter that no one was authorized to "announce his [Hindenburg's] personal opinion on this issue" and that he would adopt a public position on this question only if the constitutional processes of legislation required such a decision of him. Thereupon the national committee withdrew the Hindenburg film.

If the popular petition were to lead to a referendum, it had to be signed by at least one tenth of the national electorate. This meant more than 4.1 million signatures, and they were found. For over 4,135,000 valid signatures, that is, 10.02 percent of all German voters, were counted. Of these, more than three fourths came from those regions east of the Elbe — Mecklenburg, Pomerania, and East Prussia — where the Nationalists were strong enough to exert social and economic pressures on reluctant signers. The results, though not exactly striking, were sufficient, and the national committee celebrated its victory with a menacing proclamation. But at the same time doubts about the wisdom of Hugenberg's ways began to appear even in the Rightist press.

At this point the national government was obliged to present the proposed freedom law — or, as Hugenberg now preferred to call it, "the law against the enslavement of the German nation" — to the Reichstag with a recommendation that the measure be either accepted or rejected (Article 73, Paragraph 3). Naturally, the cabinet recommended that the bill be dropped. At the Reichstag session of November 29 Stresemann's successor in the Foreign Ministery, Curtius, gave the government's reasons for rejecting the measure.

He delivered an impressive and completely candid speech, in which he took sharp issue with Hugenberg, calling the fourth, punitive paragraph an "infamy which is not excused by even the most bitter political differences." His words were greeted with loud applause from a majority of the chamber, and it was now up to Hugenberg to point his lance, loose his reins, prance into the arena, and show the world how a doughty savior of his fatherland fights fearlessly for the common cause. But alas! Once more he lacked the courage to look his opponents squarely in the face, and so one of his henchmen, a schoolteacher named Oberfohren, had to leap into the breach.

On the next day the Reichstag voted. It was, of course, clear from the start that the freedom law would be defeated, but the margin of defeat was even greater than had been expected. The first paragraph was rejected 318 to 82, and the next two by similar majorities. But at Paragraph 4, the penitentiary provision, the German National People's Party fell apart. Of its 78 delegates, only 55 supported Hugenberg; the rest could not bring themselves to support such "infamy."

At this point Hugenberg thought he had strength enough to take sharp disciplinary measures against these deserters. But they responded by resigning from both the delegation and the party. Among them were men who, until this time, had been prominent German Nationalists: Schlange-Schöningen, von Lindeiner-Wildau, von Keudell, the agrarian leader Schiele, and Hoetzsch, the party's expert on foreign affairs. One of the most outspoken of these dissident members was young Gottfried Treviranus, a former naval officer who openly accused Hugenberg of denying German Nationalist members of the Reichstag "that freedom to act according to one's conscience required by our constitutional responsibility to the nation." And it was even more impressive when Count Westarp resigned as chairman of the party's delegation.

The Reichstag's rejection of the freedom law led, by constitutional rule, to a popular referendum on the measure. The national committee had naturally been counting on this step. Indeed, they had probably expected to derive considerable advantage from an exploitation of popular dissatisfaction with the Reichstag. But the defeat in parliament had been so resounding, and its consequences in the German National People's Party so disruptive, that Hugenberg and his helpmates, who had proudly predicted victory when their petition was handed in, now found their hopes considerably dampened. But at this moment they received unexpected support from Schacht.

The president of the Reichsbank had finally decided which of the two routes that he had kept open for himself at The Hague he really wished to follow. Consequently, on December 6, 1929, he submitted a lengthy memorandum to the government expressing his opposition to the freedom law — and to the Young Plan as well. His memorandum accused the government of having accepted unnecessary changes to the plan to Germany's disadvantage. He then went on to attack the cabinet's financial policies vigorously. Most sensational of all, however, was the fact that he gave his memorandum to the press directly, before any consultation with the government. Thus all Germany was able to read Schacht's declaration of war: "For my part I find myself most resolutely obliged to decline responsibility for the execution of the Young Plan so long as its purposes and presumptions continue to be disregarded in the manner made clear by [Western] measures and demands at The Hague."

The publication of this memorandum was an attack which broke even the most elementary rules of political decency. And the German government used the most extreme form of understatement when, in an immediate reply to Schacht, it expressed its astonishment that he should make such a public statement "in the midst of official conversations on the subject." In the Reichstag debate which quickly followed on December 12, Chancellor Müller pointed out to the president of the Reichsbank that the so-called "concessions" which Schacht wished to use as an excuse to desert the government were a simple result of the unfortunate fact that the German experts had not been able to make their point of view prevail on all issues at the Paris conference. The Reichstag accepted this interpretation and expressed its confidence in the cabinet by a vote of 222 to 156. The minority consisted, as usual, of German Nationalists, National Socialists, and Communists.

Naturally it would have been demanding too much to expect the German voters to master the extremely sophisticated issues raised by the Young Plan. The simple fact that the principal German expert at the Paris conference had declared his opposition to the Young Plan could only improve the chances of the freedom law. Under these circumstances it amounted to another resounding defeat for Hugenberg when, on December 22, only 5,825,000 Germans supported the referendum instead of the 21,000,000 required to make it law. By way of comparison the reader may recall that three years earlier the Social Democratic and Communist referendum for the uncompensated expropriation of the princes — which also failed — attracted 15,500,000 votes.

This severe defeat of the nationalistic opposition was all the more apparent since its new ally, Schacht, had forced the Social Democratic minister of finance, Hilferding, to resign from office the day before the vote. But this event must be regarded in connection with the severe financial problems which were pressing down upon the cabinet and the Reichstag.

VIII

THE COLLAPSE OF THE GREAT COALITION

Throughout the violent and inflammatory disputes over the revision of reparations, the German government was almost constantly suffering acute financial distress.[1] We have already seen that the national budget for 1929 had been determined in a manner which accorded less with the financial policies of the responsible minister, Hilferding, than with the unwillingness of the coalition parties to vote new taxes. This solution might have sufficed if the economic index had begun to improve. But exactly the opposite occurred. The economic situation worsened, at first slowly but then with an ever greater and more fatal speed. The worst blow was felt in October 1929, when the New York Stock Exchange suffered an unparalleled collapse, one which marked the beginning of an extended and extremely severe economic crisis for the United States.

Since the war the economic importance of the United States had increased to an extraordinary extent. A debtor until then to many nations, it now had become the principal creditor in the world. Indeed, a large part of the German reparations were designed to flow finally to America in satisfaction of that nation's claims against its recent allies. Up to this time the economic development of the United States had been so brilliant that people spoke of the "American economic miracle" and many people were even convinced that this miracle would last indefinitely. All this misplaced confidence made the new sense of catastrophe all the deeper and men's panic all the greater — and not in America alone.

Even before the American crisis the worsening of the German economic situation had worked two different effects on public finance: a decrease in government income from taxes and an increase in expenditures for unemployment relief. This second effect in particular was proving acutely troublesome to the government. For it was becoming increasingly impossible for the national unemployment service to pay claims out of the funds contributed by workers and their employers. The national government was therefore forced to subsidize the operation with ever mounting grants which, to be sure, were formally designated as loans, but the repayment of which could not really be expected.

In late April 1929 Hilferding was obliged to warn the Reichstag that the sum of these credits would grow to something like 370 million marks by the end of June. Obviously things could not go on like this forever. Some way had to be found to make the unemployment service financially independent once again. This meant that either its expenses would have to be lowered, that is, its payments to the unemployed decreased, or its receipts increased, that is, the contributions from workers and employers raised. And this, in turn, had the effect of summoning interested parties on both sides into the lists.

It is, of course, not at all astonishing that such a novel experiment as this national unemployment insurance should include errors of design or of administration which would have to be ironed out in the light of practical experience. The existence of such shortcomings was denied by neither side; but there was considerable difference of opinion concerning their magnitude and financial significance. And the representatives of labor's interests took it as an unjustified, partisan insult when their parliamentary colleagues to the Right argued that unemployment relief had, through its excesses, sapped the German workingman's morale.

A committee of experts, consisting of employers, workers, legislators, and economists, made some proposals for reform. Since their original plan would have covered only part of the deficit they also recommended a temporary increase in contributions of another ½ percent of wages. But neither management nor labor was satisfied: one side found the improvements insufficient and the increased contributions intolerable, while the other fought the proposed decrease in aid.[2]

It was politically unfortunate that the two parties to this dispute were linked to two opposing political factions. The division here did not distinguish a government party from one in opposition, but rather cut straight through the middle of the coalition. More precisely, the Social Democrats confronted the People's Party over this issue, both in the Reichstag and, more important, in the cabinet itself. And this critical situation was made even worse by pressures of time. The very nature of the trouble demanded quick reform, but all necessary decisions were made more difficult by the fact that some of the most important ministers — Minister of Finance Hilferding and Minister of Economics Curtius — had to be at The Hague that August, negotiating the Young Plan. So Wissell, Minister of Labor, and Severing, Minister of Interior, found it necessary to go to The Hague to meet with their colleagues in order to arrive at a temporary solution.

With the aid of the Prussian government a compromise was finally arrived at and passed by the Reichsrat on September 16 with a margin of one vote. In the minority were the conservative Prussian provinces: East Prussia, Brandenburg, Pomerania, and Lower Silesia. The compromise took the most disputed provisions out of the experts' proposals and united them in a special, temporary law which was to remain in effect only until March 31, 1931. During this interval the employers' and workers' contributions were to be increased by ½ percent to a total of 3½ percent. This proposed compromise evoked an immediate storm of protest from the German Employers' Union and the Federation of German Manufacturers. Both proposals (the experts' and the special compromise) suffered numerous alterations at the hands of the full Reichstag and of its committees. The question of the temporary increase in contributions was never resolved.

It is significant that, in the course of the Reichstag debates, the People's Party on its own initiative offered a long series of amendments — all of which were rejected at their second reading on October 2. This separation of the People's Party from the other members of the government was regarded as a serious threat to the coalition. In the course of the debate the Democratic delegate Haas sharply pointed out the dangerous implications of this move. And the Chancellor made no attempt to conceal his intention to resign if the reforms were rejected, while the Center gave the People's Party to understand that it would regard the coalition as dissolved if at least a considerable number of People's Party delegates did not support the government's proposals at the third reading.

Not even Stresemann could bring this about when, on the day before his death, he chaired his party's caucus for the last time. But he at least obtained his delegation's agreement to abstain en bloc in the coming roll call. This ensured the passage of the proposed reform, which, at its third reading on October 3, was adopted by the 238 votes of the other coalition parties against 155 members of the Economic Party, German Nationalists, National Socialists, and Communists. Once more, if only barely, the concern for the maintenance of parliamentary government had prevailed over special

interests. This was Stresemann's final service to the German Republic.

But this temporary solution of the unemployment relief issue
by no means solved the larger problem of national finances. For this
problem consisted not only of the difficulty — indeed, the impossibility — the government was experiencing in trying to restrict its
outlays to its income, but also of the Treasury's sheer inability to
meet its current obligations. Hilferding had already called express
attention to this threat in his budget address of March 14, 1929. The
state of the German money market was such that the raising of
funds for current expenses through bank loans or bond issues was
extremely difficult. By May the situation had become so desperate
that the government decided to offer a 500 million mark bond issue with extraordinarily favorable conditions: not only an interest
rate of 7 percent, but also exemption from income, property, and
inheritance taxes. On May 15 the Reichstag approved the loan by
a slender majority. The issue was a complete failure: only 177 million marks' worth was subscribed. This clearly indicated that German capital had no faith in either the health or the prospects of
the German economy.

It is true, of course, that these 7 percent bonds were being sold
at a time when the Reichsbank was offering the extraordinary discount of 7½ percent. But such a minor difference in interest rates
does not explain the failure of the government loan; political considerations also took their toll. Not only was the reparations Conference of Experts meeting in Paris at this time, but also the Rightist
opposition had been doing everything in its power to shake the German people's confidence in their government's finances. During the
Reichstag debate on the loan, for example, the spokesman for the
German Nationalists mixed his metaphors to call the measure "the
last, desperate act of a political system which has turned into a run-
away pump" and "the panic loan of a regime that has lost its head."
This calumny was so extended and severe that even the People's
Party spokesman, Carl Cremer, deplored these "extended fantasies
about a coming catastrophe" as a menace to the German economy.

Despite this foreboding failure the German government managed to survive May and the following summer months without too
much embarrassment. It was, however, painfully clear that the coming winter would bring a real crisis. Schacht sought to make full
use of this situation to further his own notions of economic policy
by trying to deprive the Finance Ministry of further credits until it
adopted those fiscal measures which he personally deemed acutely
appropriate. This behavior of the president of the Reichsbank

aroused the wrath of many men, among them Johannes Popitz, state secretary of the Ministry of Finance. For in Schacht's maneuver Popitz saw an attempt to diminish the authority and prestige not only of the national minister of finance, but also of the entire ministry staff, at the head of which he stood.

Popitz was a man of extraordinary ability and peculiar manner.[3] He was an excellent jurist, perhaps the leading German expert on financial law and a master in the art of formulating and rationalizing fiscal legislation. Although in no sense a practical politician, Popitz did have quite definite opinions on certain basic political issues. In particular, he hated what he called the "polycracy," that interlocking web of conflicting forces which were all trying to make the government serve their special interests and which consequently made a unified, consistent policy impossible. It was in this light that he had viewed the reparations agent's criticism of German financial policy and had opposed Gilbert sharply, even when the American's conclusions were based on fact.

And it was in this same light that Popitz now watched the president of the Reichsbank force his will upon the German government instead of trying to help it out of its financial difficulties. He sought to escape Schacht's pressure by finding the necessary credits elsewhere, that is, abroad. Popitz therefore entered into negotiations with the American banking house of Dillon, Read and Company, which was willing to provide temporary, short-term credits until a more permanent agreement could be reached.

At this point Schacht's manifesto of December 6 suddenly appeared, baldly accusing the German government of disorder in its accounts and of general fiscal irresponsibility: "A true balance of the budget has yet to be achieved; no steps have been taken toward an organized settlement of the former deficit; while new, constantly increasing deficits and fresh demands keep appearing, deficits and demands which in the final analysis can only be covered by further taxation, that is, by a still greater financial burden on the nation." At this point the Americans, struck no doubt by such a sensational attack on the government's financial policies, grew more cautious and inquired of the Reichsbank whether it would have any objection if America granted the desired loan to Germany. This inquiry gave the president of the Reichsbank an opening for a sharp attack.

In the words of Schwerin-Krosigk, director of the Ministry of Finance at the time, "Schacht really let fly." [4] Popitz found himself obliged to tender his resignation and had to be let go. But Hilferding refused to let his state secretary bear the sole responsibility for the miscarriage of his plan. He, too, announced his resignation, and the Chancellor had no choice but to accept it. As Defense Minister Gröner was to write to a friend a few years later, "Hilferding is a truly decent fellow, a great financial pundit, stuffy and not particularly ambitious. His bitter opponent was Schacht, a man of consuming ambition and deceptive manners who now is commending himself to the German people as a candidate for president." [5]

And so for the second and final time Hilferding's activities as minister of finance ended in defeat. Just as in 1923, he had been unable to find a way out of extraordinary difficulties by impressing his will upon the cabinet and the Reichstag. He had demonstrated once again that he did not lack clever ideas. What he lacked was effective power. This deficiency is partially attributable to the failure of his party to support him. Noske tells how Hilferding complained of the "truly intolerable situation of having a party behind one which is utterly without leadership or direction . . . [and one in which] policies are determined by people who were ready to let German democracy and the German Republic go to the devil . . . over the question of thirty pfennigs for the unemployed." [6]

But entirely apart from the imperfections of his fellow Socialists, Hilferding faced the truly insuperable problem of being a Socialist minister of finance in a capitalistic state governed by a cabinet coalition and a Reichstag majority of bourgeois parties. Even if blessed with the greatest talents, he could not have carried out a socialistic financial policy. Of course Hugenberg and his men kept screaming about the "Marxist" tendencies of the Social Democratic minister of finance. But that was just demagogic ranting, whether in their mouths or, as proved increasingly frequent, in Schacht's. For not the least trace of Marxism is to be found in Hilferding's policies or proposals. The Social Democrats were simply trying to allocate the extremely heavy financial burden, incurred by a lost war and increased government expenses, in such a way that those elements of the population which the party represented bore as light a load as possible while enjoying as many benefits as could be had from the developing welfare state.

This aim did not differ from what the German Nationalists and the People's Party were seeking under other banners. The Economic and Peasants' parties were even more candid in this respect, while the Bavarian People's Party introduced the special note of territorial particularism to the already richly confused political scene. When, in this conflict of special interests, the Social Democrats claimed that their simple plurality in the Reichstag should give them precedence, they did so in vain. For the parliamentary law of marginal utility increases the importance of even a small, fringe party when its votes are essential for the creation of a majority. Naturally, the individual delegate, mindful only of his voters and his seat, does not see this truth as clearly as does a minister who is responsible to the entire nation and, especially, for a balanced budget.

It was therefore a measure of relief for the Social Democrats that the new minister of finance was not selected from their ranks, although their prestige suffered heavily, of course, from this slight. The new minister was the People's Party delegate Paul Moldenhauer, professor of insurance at the University of Cologne. Shortly before this time he had assumed the national Ministry of Economics when Curtius had succeeded Stresemann as foreign minister. One had every reason to assume that, with his membership in the People's Party and the expertise promised by his academic post, Moldenhauer would meet with less resistance in those economic circles whose confidence and support is particularly important to a minister of finance.

By way of recompense a Social Democrat, the calm and capable Robert Schmidt, received the Ministry of Economics. Fortunately, the government was able to find a first-rate personality, Hans Schäffer, formerly a permanent secretary in the Ministry of Economics, to succeed Popitz as state secretary of finance. In his former post Schäffer had dealt with reparations problems, participating in numerous international conferences on this issue. Since these questions would now become less important, he was available for a new post. Although he was not the expert on tax matters that Popitz was, he kept a correspondingly closer watch on the government's expenditures and, especially, its cash balance than had Popitz, who had preferred to concentrate on policy.

The national government had, of course, to yield to Schacht's demands. Essentially these amounted to the establishment of a sinking fund of 450,000,000 marks. This was a sound proposal; indeed, it had already been included in the government's financial program.[7] But the service that Schacht rendered Germany in this way was more than counterbalanced by the dictatorial methods which he employed to gain his end. For, by threatening to deny the nation his assistance in its quest for the necessary credits, Schacht forced the cabinet and the Reichstag to pass, in only three days, a law that required subsequent national budgets to include provisions for a sinking fund which, by the end of fiscal 1930 at the very latest, was to reach a total of 450 million marks. With this legislation in his pocket, Schacht designated a consortium of German banks which would provide the necessary temporary credits.

At the same session in which the Reichstag passed the "Schacht Law," it accepted two other measures which further illustrate the difficulties encountered by a government which finds itself surrounded by pressing emergencies: a protective tariff designed to help German agriculture, and a ½ percent increase in contributions to the unemployment insurance fund, that is, up to 3½ percent. This latter provision was, however, to be in effect only through June 30, 1930. Thus this question, so critical and embarrassing to the government coalition, was going to have to come before the Reichstag again in spring. In addition to these major measures, the cabinet's request for an increase in taxes on tobacco products was accepted, in order that the Treasury might find some additional income.

From an economic point of view the real burden of the Schacht Law fell upon those groups that had been working unceasingly for a reduction in taxes. For there was no prospect of such a move while the sinking fund was being accumulated. The political consequence of the law, however, was massive discontent on the Left. For the measure seemed like an encroachment by high finance upon the constitutional organs of the state.[8] This general dissatisfaction, on both the Right and Left, served neither to lessen class conflict nor to increase the stability of the Republic. And such a further weakening of the government's position was all the more regrettable at this time, since the second Hague Conference was about to assemble for the final consideration of the Young Plan.

The conference opened on January 3, 1930. The German delegation was led by Stresemann's successor, Curtius, with three other ministers (Moldenhauer, Wirth, and Robert Schmidt) at his side, Snowden was again England's principal representative. And Briand appeared once more for France, this time, however, not as premier but only as foreign minister. For his cabinet had been voted out of office on October 22, 1929. Among the issues which had led to this dismissal, foreign affairs — especially the evacuation of the Rhineland — had been a significant factor. The new French cabinet was therefore inclined further to the Right than Briand's had been; indeed, in Germany its Premier, André Tardieu, was known as one of Clemenceau's assistants at Versailles and as the author of a book which, in 1921, had argued for a rigorous execution of the treaty. Yet on the other hand, Tardieu had shown his intent to continue Briand's policy of reconciliation by leaving the former premier at his ministerial post on the Quai d'Orsay.

However that may have been, the debate in the Chamber of Deputies before and after this change of government showed that recent events in Germany had evoked discomfort and, indeed, distrust in France. On November 7, Franklin-Bouillon, a leader of the more extreme French nationalists, had referred to the Hugenberg petition, asking whether, after its success, one could still have faith in Germany's good will. For, he argued, behind the four million signatures stood the German universities, German heavy industry, and the German Army. To this Briand replied that Hugenberg spoke of the late German foreign minister the way French Hugenbergs talked about their own. And when he called Stresemann a man whose death was already felt as an irreparable loss by the whole world, the entire left side of the Chamber answered with loud applause.

This man, Briand continued, on whom the Hugenberg press heaped such filth, had sat sick and near death before him in The Hague; but he had doggedly refused to die without placing one more stone in his structure of European peace. Then, referring to the murders of Erzberger and Rathenau,° Briand asked a question that was greeted by thunderous applause by a majority of the Chamber: "Does one have to die in order to prove that one truly desires peace?" But the problem still remained: what could France do if a German government controlled by the German Nationalist Party — which had, after all, already declared the Young Plan void — were simply and coolly to say that it could and would make no further payments? And on December 17, in the face of a disturbed electorate, Briand, for all his good intentions, had to inquire of the German ambassador, von Hoesch, what he should tell the Chamber when the question came.[9]

The German delegation to this second Hague Conference was therefore forced into the position of discussing an embarrassing topic which had previously been skirted: possible future sanctions against Germany on the part of her creditors in the event that she failed to make reparation payments. That the German delegation had been placed in this awkward position was entirely a result of Hugenberg's and Hitler's demagoguery and the intrigues of Schacht. The French opened the discussion by referring to Article 430 of

° Erzberger and Rathenau were both murdered by members of the so-called "Organization Consul," a post–Free Corps nationalist organization which was dedicated to killing leaders of the Weimar Republic. Erzberger was killed while walking in the Black Forest near Griesbach on August 26, 1921. His murderers, Heinrich Tillessen and Heinrich Schultz, were given false passports by the Munich police and fled to Hungary. Tillessen was later imprisoned for plotting other murders. But as a result of the intervention of Chancellor Brüning, who considered Tillessen "a decent sort of chap," he was released after serving a few months' sentence. Rathenau was murdered while riding in his car in Berlin on June 24, 1923. His killers were Ernst Werner Techow, Erwin Kern, and Hermann Fischer. The Hugenberg press hailed these and similar murders as "acts of liberation." TRANSLATORS.

the Treaty of Versailles, Tardieu's own work. This article gave the Allies the right to reoccupy the evacuated zones of occupation in the event that the Reparations Commission should decide that Germany was refusing to fulfill her reparation obligations. But one of the provisions of the Young Plan was that the Reparations Commission should cease to exist. Did this mean, the French inquired, that all of Article 430 was to become null and void, and that they therefore would be deprived of every legal means of defense against a willful refusal by Germany to pay?

Tardieu, who led the French delegation, raised this question not in the official negotiations but rather in a confidential talk with Curtius. In this private conference Tardieu asked Curtius to agree formally that Germany would not regard as hostile whatever actions the creditors might take if Germany should later repudiate the Young Plan. In this discussion Tardieu made express reference to the possibility of a German government dominated by Hugenberg, Hitler, or the Communist Thälmann. Curtius immediately and successfully rejected this request as an unacceptable intrusion into German domestic affairs.[10] Such a reply was Curtius' political duty and, indeed, correct in terms of the legal doctrine of nonintervention. But these truths do not alter the fact that, as later developments showed all too well, Tardieu was quite justified in his request.

Without entering into a detailed discussion of the negotiations, one may call it a signal diplomatic victory for Curtius that he succeeded in persuading Tardieu to desist from his request and to defer questions of German payments to the Permanent Court of International Justice at The Hague. According to Curtius' plan, this court would have the power and responsibility to decide whether a German governmnt "had committed acts which demonstrated its intent to repudiate the plan." Tardieu admitted, even in public, that this agreement represented a complete change from his original plan; in the Chamber session of March 29, 1930, he likened himself bitterly to Ugolino, who ate his own children, "en mangeant l'article 430, mon enfant." [11]

Curtius' diplomatic victory did not, of course, keep the German nationalistic opposition from accusing the government of having wounded the nation's dignity through this so-called "sanction clause." Schacht, for instance, devoted an entire chapter of his pamphlet to this point, concluding his discussion with the triumphant cry that the clause "represents the low point of the policy of abasement and castration that the Social Democrats and their camp followers have been pursuing ever since the war." [12] The time-honored adage that the complaining party is generally in the wrong proved true here.

The worst thing about the whole affair, however, was that Schacht, in order to arrive at this damning judgment, interpreted the Hague Agreements in a manner which not only was false but also could have proved extremely dangerous to Germany if the Allies had adopted his view.

For, while on other issues people like Schacht took the position that the interpretation favorable to Germany was the only correct one, an entirely different approach was made here, in order to arouse the German people against their government. The nationalistic opposition clearly thought this the best way to obscure the central fact that probably no one would have raised the question of sanctions in The Hague if that distinguished German patriot Hugenberg and his petitions had not forced upon the French the extremely painful consideration of what they might expect from a German government led by Hugenberg or Hitler.

And it was Schacht who saw to it that the otherwise peaceful conference was not concluded without one sensation. He found his opportunity during the negotiations concerning the establishment of the Bank for International Settlements which had been proposed by the Paris Conference of Experts.[13] The bank's organization and procedures had been considered the preceding October in Baden-Baden at a meeting of delegates from the appropriate central banks, among whom was, of course, the Reichsbank's Schacht. The hotly debated question of the International Bank's location had finally been settled in favor of Basel. And now only the final articles of incorporation remained to be signed.

On January 13, 1930, Schacht appeared in The Hague at a meeting of the Committee on the International Bank. Now Schacht was not a member of the German delegation to this second conference. Chancellor Müller had offered him a place, but Schacht had declined it, evidently fearful of a trap. And on December 28, 1929, in a discussion with the German ministers going to The Hague, Schacht had spoken freely of his opposition to the government's policy, assuring them explicitly "that he would make absolutely no public mention of his differing views until the *conclusion* of the Hague Conference." [14]

Schacht immediately proceeded to break this promise at the meeting of the committee on the bank. Here he had the clerk read his letter of December 31, 1929, directed to the representative of the American banks concerned, in which he expressed the Reichsbank's refusal to participate in the International Bank unless certain political requirements were met. Among these were the nullification of the liquidation agreement that had already been concluded at the first Hague Conference and the final abolition of the Allied powers of sanction as provided in the Treaty of Versailles. Throughout the discussion which followed the reading of his letter, Schacht maintained this negative point of view. Thereupon, all the other delegates, including the Americans, whose attitude Schacht had clearly misjudged completely, declared that under these circumstances further negotiations were useless. The discussion was terminated with no provision for its resumption.

Meanwhile the German ministers were concluding their conversations with the other governments on a few unsettled matters. Not only had Schacht failed to tell them of his plan to reject the bank by making such impossible demands, but that very morning he had even told Finance Minister Moldenhauer that everything would go smoothly at the bank committee meeting.[15] Naturally the ministers' meeting exploded, although not until Curtius had proposed and won a recess of at least two hours. The German ministers used this time for an extended talk with Schacht, in the course of which use was made of such clear terms as "mutiny before the enemy." At this moment something odd occurred. Now that Schacht realized that the German delegates were not going to let him lead them home and that the representatives of the other central banks were firm in their opposition to his letter, he suddenly became the one who was eager to find ways to keep the conference from foundering. But even then, as Curtius puts it, Schacht "refused to draw the only possible conclusion, the one which the rest of us . . . expected on the basis of our conversation: that he would either accept . . . the government's position or else resign forthwith." [16]

The German ministers, seeking some way out of their sudden embarrassment, thought first of asking a consortium of German banks (Reichskreditgesellschaft and Preussische Seehandlung) to replace the Reichsbank in the international negotiations. But then, on January 14, they adopted Moldenhauer's idea that the Reichsbank be required by German law to participate in the International Bank. When Moldenhauer informed Schacht of this plan, the president of the Reichsbank immediately agreed, giving Moldenhauer the distinct impression "that Schacht was happy to be relieved in this way of all responsibility for the decision." [17]

Thus ended, at least for a time, Hjalmar Schacht's attempt to play the hero's role on the international stage. Although he returned to Berlin still president of the Reichsbank, even he finally realized that the curtain had come down on this act. And so, on March 7, 1930, while the Reichstag was debating the Young Plan, he resigned. Curtius reports that Schacht, in first tendering his resignation, had given an explanation which President Hindenburg had rejected as unwarranted. Hindenburg accompanied his rejection with a written request for a better explanation, stating that "it would be both regrettable and destructive if the acceptance of a principle already valid under international law were to be construed as introducing new and expanded possibilities for sanctions." [18] Whatever his personal attitude toward the Young Plan may have been, the old field marshal simply would not tolerate gross breaches of discipline.

On January 30, 1930, the second Hague Conference ended with a joint signing of a protocol that included the accomplishments of both meetings. It now devolved upon the governments concerned to persuade their several parliaments to ratify the decisions. The German Reichsrat accepted the agreements on February 5 by a vote of forty-eight to six. The opposition consisted of the usual Prussian provinces beyond the Elbe — East Prussia, Brandenburg, Pomerania, and Lower Silesia — along with Thuringia, which, since January 14, had been enjoying a Rightist government with the National Socialist Wilhelm Frick as its minister of interior and education. Bavaria and Mecklenburg-Schwerin abstained.

The Young Plan and the Hague Agreements were debated for three days in the Reichstag at first reading, February 11–13. Hugenberg entered the discussion in person with a very bitter speech. He characterized the six million voters who had supported his referendum as the kernel of a new, embryonic Germany and argued against the adoption of the Young Plan because it contained obligations more frightful and more dangerous than those of Versailles. But, as Curtius immediately pointed out, Hugenberg totally neglected to say what he would do if he were in the cabinet's place. And he had to accept the minister's accusing observation that he, Hugenberg, alone was responsible for the fact that the Hague Agreements "included provisions for the event of a willful repudiation of the Young Plan."

The speech by Brüning, leader of the Centrist delegation, was even more significant. For it contained the declaration that the Center could not accept the proposals without first receiving a full and clear report on the financial position of the Reich and the financial consequences of the new plan. The spokesman for the Bavarian People's Party made the same point. These demands were generally understood to indicate the intent of these two government parties to make their support of the Young Plan conditional upon a satisfactory reform of the nation's finances. This interpretation was corroborated by the two parties' behavior in the Reichstag committees where, on February 28, both abstained because, as Brüning had explained before the vote, the measures taken to reorganize the treasury's position at the moment and to insure it for the future had not been satisfactory.

Brüning's concern for the nation's finances was only all too justified. It is true that the transition from the Dawes Plan to the Young Plan promised an immediate saving to Germany of 700 million marks. But the hope of using these millions to reduce taxes had to be permanently abandoned on January 27, 1930, when Moldenhauer explained to the Reichstag that the prospective saving in reparations payments would just suffice to cover the deficit of the current fiscal year. And in order to ensure his treasury's cash position, Moldenhauer had had to take an extraordinary step. Kreuger's Swedish Match Trust had offered the German government a loan of 125 million dollars, that is, some 500 million marks, in return for the grant of a match monopoly in Germany. The cabinet had accepted this offer, as did the Reichstag, on January 28, despite strong opposition.

But the continued decline of tax revenues on the one hand and the steady growth in demands for unemployment benefits on the other soon conspired once again to pose a very severe threat to the government's finances. That both halves of this vise were closing was due to the inexorable pressure of the steadily sharpening economic crisis and not to any partisan policies. But the question of how the deficit, which Moldenhauer estimated at 700 million marks, was to be covered became the subject of a partisan debate which clearly was not going to be settled quickly. Yet to postpone the ratification of the Young Plan until these questions of national financial policy had been solved would have meant leaving the nation's most critical political issue dangling in mid-air for several months.

Brüning realized this quite well. He and his party's delegation therefore voted for the acceptance of the Young Plan at its second reading on March 11. But a sensational episode had preceded this apparent change of course. For on the morning of the day of the vote, Brüning paid a call on President Hindenburg in order to discuss the reform of the nation's finances. Shortly thereafter, the *Germania*, the Centrists' organ in Berlin, announced that Brüning had insisted upon the absolute necessity of such reform to the President, and that Hindenburg had agreed with him completely. In the course of their conversation, according to the *Germania*, Hindenburg had declared that he would "make use of all constitutional means" to execute a prompt reform. To this the *Germania* added the comment that this presidential guarantee was more valuable to the Center than any number of party promises. The newspaper then became even clearer when it went on to say: "If the German parliament cannot accomplish this task, then the President will . . . assume whatever powers are appropriate and necessary . . . The dissolution of the Reichstag, or Article 48, or both, stand ready for service if the parties fail."

This was a remarkably accurate prediction of the events that actually occurred in the course of the next few months. Yet perhaps even more remarkable was the fact that the Centrists' paper expressed its approval of such a development in advance. And Brüning, himself, alluded clearly to his talk with the President when, in the Reichstag, he explained his delegation's change in attitude by referring to the "significant assurances" and "firm guarantee" that the protection of Germany's finances which he had required as a precondition for an acceptance of the Hague Agreements would, indeed, be forthcoming.

Naturally, these events were the subject of vigorous discussion in all political circles. Many people took them to mean that Brüning had already been selected by the President as a so-called *homo regius*, a loyal servant of his lord, who would be charged with the construction of the next cabinet.[19] This much, at any rate, was true: Hindenburg had lost his taste for Müller's government. Curtius, who saw him often during these days, suspects with what is probably good reason that the field marshal's "Old Comrades," a preponderant majority of whom were certainly against the Young Plan and, most especially, the liquidation agreement with Poland, had been exercising their influence on him again.[20] While it is true that they did not win Hindenburg to their side on this issue, it is easy to imagine that they strengthened to a considerable extent the discomfort which the President could not help but feel at the continued bickering among the coalition parties.

Under these circumstances the Young Plan skirted its final difficulties. The Hague Agreements were ratified by a vote of 266 to 193. The German-Polish Liquidation Agreement was accepted by a bare majority, 236 to 217. At this late juncture the opposition tried to draw the President into their fight against the Young Plan. Citing Article 72 of the constitution, they moved that the publication of the new laws be postponed. Since the support of only one third of the Reichstag was required for postponement, their motion passed, 173 to 289. The opposition's purpose was, of course, to evoke a popular referendum on the issue as provided in Section V, Article 73, Paragraph 2. But the government majority countered quickly by calling upon the second sentence in Article 72, which said that the President could promulgate any national law in spite of a demand for a postponement if both the Reichstag and the Reichsrat declared it to be "urgent." And urgent this law certainly was. The Reichsrat joined in making the declaration by a vote of forty-two to five.

This meant that the President could now proceed to sign the laws. It was up to him to decide whether he wished to exercise this right or, by foregoing it, to bring about another referendum. On March 13, the day after the Reichstag vote, Hindenburg signed the Hague Laws with, as he put it, "a heavy but determined heart." He defended his decision in forceful public statement, in which he urged his countrymen "to overcome our divisions and differences and to unite in working toward a future which again shall see a free, sound, and strong German nation."

The nationalists' response to this appeal destroyed any last hope of finding some inclination among them to bury the hatchet. Ludendorff even went so far as to pronounce Hindenburg unfit to wear the field-gray uniform and accused him of destroying now, as President, everything he had fought for as field marshal.[21] A few days later the President also signed the liquidation agreement with Poland, after determining that no constitutional objections could be raised.

Thus, in March 1930, the great reform of the reparations that Parker Gilbert and Hjalmar Schacht had set under way in the summer of 1928 was finally complete. It naturally fell far short of the hopes of those Germans in whose eyes the only acceptable way to reform reparations would have been to abolish them, and who had convinced their henchmen and themselves that the reparations burden was not the consequence of a lost war but rather of the "war-guilt lie" in the Treaty of Versailles. Without doubt, the burden of reparation payments remained severe, even after the reform; and the question whether Germany could carry this burden year after year was fully justified, as later developments were to show. But these considerations did not alter two vital facts: the Young Plan had lessened the burdens of the Dawes Plan in a meaningful manner both for the moment and for the foreseeable future; and the sheer achievement of this amicable agreement opened the way to yet another possible revision of the reparations and, perhaps, their final cancellation.

The principal objection which the opposition voiced, namely, that the Young Plan would visit the reparation costs on the second and third generations for sixty-two years, was essentially sentimental. As a practical matter, as the Democratic delegate Bernhard Dernburg argued in the Reichstag, it is by no means inappropriate

that the heavy burden of a frightful war be borne, in part, by generations other than the one which "had already experienced immeasurable sacrifices of blood and treasure and suffered hunger and dep-
rivation, suppression and inflation." Nor did the Young Plan put future Germans in any worse position than that forced upon coming
French and British generations by the inter-Allied war debts.

Political economists went on to point out the slight present value
of a promise to make payment in some thirty or forty years, even
without regard to the obvious political and economic uncertainties
involved. And subsequent events provide a clear answer to this
question of later uncertainties: the German generation which the
nationalists feared was being menaced with an intolerable financial
burden not only failed to pay these debts, but also waged a new
war which devastated parts of the whole world, Germany in particular, and imposed endless financial obligations on people everywhere.

Quite apart from financial matters, the Young Plan freed Germany from two onerous provisions of the Dawes Plan. Foreign controls were ended and German securities were returned. One might
well have thought that German nationalists would have regarded
both as highly progressive steps. But such was not the case. It is a
measure of the extent to which partisan passion had confused calm
political judgment that the nationalistic opposition heaped scorn on
these obvious gains. The Rightists were even more scornful about
the predating of the evacuation of the Rhineland, a great concession
that was made possible only by Germany's acceptance of the
Young Plan.

If, from the standpoint of the year 1930, these events seemed
to justify the policies of the German government and Reichstag,
they appear quite different if one looks back at them over the thirty
intervening years of German and world history. Today the overriding consideration in evaluating the Young Plan must be this: to
what extent did the reform of the reparations it embodied really
further world peace? For that was the goal and the stated purpose
of the Committee of Experts which drew up the plan. Their report
issued in Paris on June 7, 1929, sought "to banish the atmosphere
of war, to obliterate its animosities . . . and to work together for
a common end in a spirit of mutual interest and good will." The conclusion of the report reiterates this purpose: "We realize . . . how
much depends on the future attitude toward one another of the
peoples which . . . are to become parties to this agreement. For the
solution of the reparation problem is not only a German task but in
the common interest of all the countries concerned and requires the
cooperation of all parties."

One would have thought that the German people would be the first to move toward this goal by welcoming the Young Plan with enthusiasm and relief. But the nationalist opposition made such a response impossible. In this sense the Rightists' success is not to be measured by the six million votes cast in favor of their referendum, but rather by the amount of unrest and excitement that their agitation produced among the entire German people. The opposition succeeded in keeping their fellow citizens from sensing the spirit of compromise that Germany's creditors were manifesting. Thus even the German proponents of the Young Plan were forced into a defensive posture and found themselves unable to admit the existence of any conciliatory spirit in the West. Did not Brüning, for instance, the spokesman for the second strongest coalition party, completely falsify the facts when he explained his acceptance of the reforms with the argument that "the Young Plan is no contract between equal parties; it is a unilateral *Diktat*, and it is to this *Diktat* that we now bow."

It needs to be emphasized that the Young Plan was a settlement between creditors and debtors in which the creditors had yielded less than the debtors had requested. This sort of thing had happened countless times before in the affairs of men, even as it will happen countless times again, and no one would think of calling such settlements *Diktats*. But if even such a reasonable man as Brüning assumed a tone like this, one cannot be surprised to learn that no spirit of reconciliation came over the German people and that the hope for international understanding, far from being strengthened by the plan, was actually shattered.

This, of course, by no means implies that the creditor nations did everything necessary and possible to convince the German people that their justified demands had been satisfied. Politically, the Allies would have been better advised to rest content with somewhat lower figures, perhaps simply the sums that Schacht had offered. In the long run — that is to say, in the reparation payments that were actually made — such a decision would, as we know today, have made no difference at all. But if the Allies had had some inclination in that direction — and it must be admitted that they probably did not — Schacht would certainly have disenchanted them with his memorandum of April 17, in which he introduced political demands into the matter of reparations payments. For the Western powers could take this only to mean that the Germans would make further demands, menacing world peace, if their present arguments concerning reparations payments were permitted to prevail.

And were the Western statesmen wrong in thinking so? Would

the German people have become peaceful and contented if their creditors had shown a greater spirit of compromise? Would concessions on the part of the Allies have made any more impression in Germany than did the relinquishment of controls, the return of securities, and, indeed, the evacuation of the Rhineland? Nothing in world history since 1930 gives one reason to believe that the West made a critical error here. On the contrary, the subsequent course of events leads one only to the melancholy conclusion that world peace would have been better served if the controls had *not* been relinquished, if the securities had *not* been returned, and if the Rhineland had *not* been evacuated — or if, at least, the Control Commission had remained in being, as Briand had proposed and Stresemann had so successfully frustrated. For is it not conceivable that such a policy would have precluded Hitler's remilitarization of the Rhineland in 1936, which made the Second World War unavoidable?

These considerations are not meant in criticism of the men who arrived at the Hague Agreements in the firm hope and intent of thus promoting the spirit of reconciliation on both sides of the Atlantic. Yet their efforts, too, were thwarted by the powers of circumstance that Schiller's Wallenstein depicted in his famous words:

> The hands of fate are full of jealousy . . .
> We simply place the seedling in their care
> And wait to reap good fortune or despair.

No sooner was the Young Plan ratified than the necessity of domestic financial reform forced itself upon the German government. One could even say that matters had become still worse. On March 18, 1930, upon signing the liquidation agreement with Poland, Hindenburg had directed a memorandum to the Chancellor outlining a program of emergency relief for German agriculture, and for the hard-hit eastern provinces in particular. This, too, would cost money, and the memorandum included Hindenburg's candid admission that finding necessary funds would be "difficult in Germany's present financial situation." It is, therefore, all the more remarkable that a cabinet directed by a Social Democrat successfully proposed higher tariffs on agricultural products, and that food minister Hermann Dietrich, who saw the bill through the Reichstag, belonged to the Democratic Party, traditionally supporters of free trade. One can not accuse the German Left of having failed to listen with good faith to agriculture's demands. (This does not, of course, apply to the Communists.)

But in the foreground there still remained the problem of financing unemployment insurance payments. The issue had assumed almost catastrophic proportions in the course of the economic crisis. In December 1929 the number of former workers on relief had exceeded 1,500,000; during January it grew by almost another million.[22] One could therefore scarcely accept as realistic Moldenhauer's assumption of 1,200,000 unemployed on which he had based his scheme for financial reform. Yet even this optimistic assumption would have yielded an unemployment insurance deficit of 321 million marks. There was therefore no hope that the unemployment service would be able to repay its debts to the Treasury in the foreseeable future. On the contrary, it would continue to require further subventions which, although unpredictable, would certainly amount to hundreds of millions of marks. Where was the almost bankrupt government to find such sums?

Thus the Germans stood again before the question they had only postponed the spring before: How could the unemployment deficit be reduced? Either the national service would have to restrict its expenditures, that is, reduce relief payments to the unemployed, or it would have to increase its revenues, that is, not only extend the present level of contributions — already raised to 3½ percent — beyond the provisional limit of June 30, 1930, but even raise it further. The Social Democrats regarded a diminution of relief payments as both an injustice to the unemployed and a dangerous temptation to management to lower the wages of those who still had jobs. On the other hand, German industry maintained through its political spokesmen, principally the People's Party, that under such poor business conditions higher contributions were impossible.

There was every reason to take both objections seriously. And the Social Democrats indulged in an unwarranted simplification of the facts when they pretended that the People's Party was concerned only with the interests of German heavy industry. Most medium-sized and small firms in manufacturing and commerce were facing equally difficult odds and had equally great fears of increased costs, especially when, as the Social Democrats kept making clear, all hopes of tax reduction had to be abandoned. Some sense of the situation can be gained from the fact that Social Democratic circles began entertaining the idea of an emergency tax on assured incomes, a proposal that would have meant at least a partial cancellation of Köhler's increase in officials' salaries. But neither the cabinet nor the opposition parties were prepared to consider such a step.

On March 24, in his scheme for financial reform, Moldenhauer proposed that the directors of the national unemployment service be authorized to raise the contribution rate from 3½ percent to 4 per-

cent, with the proviso, however, that a majority of both the labor
and management representatives on the board agree. Most of the
coalition parties had agreed to this compromise, but the People's
Party had not. There is no reason to believe that the party hoped
to bring about the fall of Müller's government in this way, for its
new chairman, Ernst Scholz, who was regarded with special misgivings on the Left, had just announced at his party's convention
that for the moment, at any rate, a government opposed by — or
even without — the Social Democrats could not possibly stay in office. Be that as it may, the People's Party remained firm in its resistance to this proposed measure, even though Moldenhauer was one
of the party's two representives in the cabinet.

In the interparty discussions which now were being carried on
continuously within the coalition, the Centrists and the Democrats,
the two government parties least attached to one of the affected interests, took the lead in seeking some way out of the impasse. Oscar
Meyer, a Democratic delegate and legal adviser to the Berlin Chamber of Commerce, had expertise but no personal involvement in the
question. He drafted a compromise which he succeeded in persuading Brüning to sign also. Their solution proposed that the national
government grant an annual fixed subsidy to the unemployment service, the sum to be determined in each budget and to be 150 million
marks for the current fiscal year. In the more than likely event that
this subsidy should fail to balance the service's books, the unemployment board not only would be expected to take steps to cut expenses,
but also would be permitted to raise the rate of worker and employer contributions to 3¾ percent — rather as Moldenhauer had
proposed before.

This Brüning-Meyer compromise now became the focus of discussion. For a while it seemed as though an agreement were about
to be reached. For all the government parties accepted it save the
Bavarian People's Party and the Social Democrats. And even three
of the four Socialists in the cabinet — Müller, Severing, and Schmidt
— approved it. But their fourth colleague, Rudolf Wissell, minister
of labor, rejected the proposal and remained firm in his solitary opposition. Wissell's intractability put the issue up to the Social Democratic delegation, which met on March 27 to determine the party
position.

Now it is no simple matter to lead a bloc of one hundred and
fifty men. And it is twice as difficult when these delegates have been
elected on the basis of proportional representation. For this method
favors political mediocrities and the representatives of organized
interests. In the Social Democratic Party the special groups so rep-

resented were, of course, labor unions. Thirty-seven percent of the Social Democratic delegates were union leaders, including five members of the executive committee of the General German Federation of Labor.[23]

The Social Democratic Party owed much to the labor unions. Only with their help had the party been able to bring the revolutionary workers' and soldiers' councils to accept a peaceful, parliamentary regime. But the issue on which the delegation was now obliged to take a stand was more political than social; and, like other affected parties, the unionists saw the immediate disadvantages they would derive from the proposed solution more clearly than they could determine the ultimate political consequences of their failure to accept it. And so the union representatives voted unanimously to support Wissell in his opposition. Their objection to the Brüning-Meyer compromise was that it represented a threat — in the long run, if not at the moment — to unemployment insurance. One spokesman for organized labor at this delegation caucus not only declared the proposal unacceptable, but also threatened to voice labor's objections to it clearly and emphatically in the Reichstag, the press, and the party, should a majority of the delegation accept the plan.

One can well imagine the impression that such a threat made on those delegates whose seats were already menaced by Communist demagogy. Furthermore, there was a tenacious, if not strong, splinter group in the delegation which was eager to desert the government in favor of the green fields of opposition. The Social Democratic Chancellor, Hermann Müller, tired of political battle and weakened by severe illness, was not the man to face this storm. In the words of Friedrich Stampfer, who certainly was there, the delegation voted "almost unanimously" to reject the compromise.[24] Wissell had triumphed. But at what a cost!

The tragedy could no longer be forestalled. At the cabinet meeting which immediately followed the Social Democratic caucus, the Chancellor was forced to report that he and his party colleagues rejected the Brüning-Meyer plan. Müller then tried to persuade Moldenhauer to revive his former proposal, but his minister of finance firmly declined. For how could he be expected to oppose his own party in such a sharp and sudden way? His colleagues in the People's Party had accepted a compromise which had subsequently failed simply because the Chancellor had been deserted by his fellow Socialists. Moldenhauer refused to make his party now appear responsible for a crisis which the Social Democrats had, in fact, provoked.

It was painfully evident to the entire cabinet that there was no way out of the impasse. The play was over; the curtain had to fall. At the Chancellor's suggestion, the cabinet voted to resign en bloc, without appearing before the Reichstag even one more time.[25]

The President accepted this joint resignation and asked the chairman of the Centrist delegation, Heinrich Brüning, to form a new government. The Great Coalition was finished — and forever. It had survived Stresemann by barely half a year.

Today it is apparent to everyone that this change of government was of great and disastrous significance. And even then there were those who said as much. The great Democratic press, in particular, which was still regarded with respect even though the Democratic Party had grown small, was not sparing in its criticism of the Social Democrats, whom it had customarily treated in a rather friendly way. The *Berliner Tageblatt* lamented "a crisis over ¼ percent," and the *Frankfurter Zeitung* inquired accusingly: "Has the Social Democratic Party considered the effects this crisis may have on our entire domestic development and on the prospects of German democracy? Their decision has suddenly made the future dark and unclear. Will we have a dictated budget under Article 48? Or perhaps a nonpartisan cabinet of civil servants with no clear parliamentary support? In any event we are about to experience momentous developments." [26] And even among the Social Democrats, as the Berlin correspondent of the Manchester *Guardian* reported, "the wiser heads have complained about the inordinate pressure of the trade unions which has forced the party into such a fateful decision."

The question here is not whether the rejection of the Brüning-Meyer compromise was well-founded. (In fact, later history proved both the Social Democrats and the People's Party right; for soon both the higher contributions demanded by the former and the tightened payments desired by the latter proved necessary.) The sole significant fact is that the Social Democrats blocked this compromise at a time when it was apparent to any reasonable person that the solution to Germany's critical situation was to be found in compromise alone.

It is a time-honored rule of politics that one should never make that move which one's opponent most ardently desires. For years the opponents of the Socialists had filled the air with the cry that no one could run a government with the Social Democrats. The most elementary feeling for politics should have warned the Socialists against furnishing their opponents with such striking proof that the opposition's claim was justified. They should have remembered the admonition of their own leader, Fritz Ebert, the first President of Germany. Ebert, who was not only a good Social Democrat but also a statesman, had warned his colleagues after they had forced Stresemann from office, "Your reason for unseating the Chancellor will be forgotten in six weeks. But you will still be suffering the consequences of your stupidity after ten years have passed."

This time the Social Democrats had been given an even clearer warning that they would have done well to heed: the report of Brüning's conversation with President Hindenburg. For this report not only made clear that the Centrist leader would be the next chancellor; more important, it showed that Brüning could rely on Hindenburg for the political support which he would not be able to find in a sharply divided Reichstag where no majority would exist. One cannot reasonably accuse the Social Democrats for having failed to foresee the entire catastrophic development which was about to start running its course. Yet they certainly should have realized that Müller's resignation would lead to a fundamental displacement of the political center of gravity in Germany, and that this displacement was all the more to be feared since the national presidency was occupied by a man whose heart was not attached to the Republic, however conscientious his efforts may have been to observe the constitution he had sworn to uphold.

It is certainly safe to assume that Hindenburg had a strong desire to rid the German government of Socialists as soon as the Young Plan laws were safely passed. This desire probably derived both from the President's personal inclinations and from the influences of his social environment. And it may also be true that the matters of agricultural policy which he treated in his letter of March 18 to Müller played a large role in this decision. But however that may be, was it politically wise of the Social Democrats to make things so easy for Hindenburg by throwing the keys to the citadel at his feet over what was certainly a debatable political issue?

The Social Democrats cannot slough off their responsibility for this turn of events by pointing to the regularity with which the People's Party had opposed the government's proposals for reforming the unemployment insurance service. For the critical fact remains that the People's Party did in fact accept the final compromise which the Socialists rejected. Nor should one credit their argument that Brüning had been only halfhearted in joining Meyer in their common proposal. On the contrary, Brüning's insincerity made it all the more advisable for the Social Democrats to attach the Centrists to the plan by accepting it themselves.

In the final analysis, the Socialists' inability to rise to this occasion is to be explained by the class consciousness they had developed as the constant opposition party under the Empire. Now,

under the Republic, they did not wish to lose this class consciousness even though political circumstances had become completely
different once they had been invited to bear their share of responsibility for governing and preserving the entire nation. Undoubtedly
it sounded very good indeed when, at Social Democratic conven-
tions, speaker after speaker assured his audience that "the party and
the unions are as one." But in truth their interests and their tasks
were quite dissimilar.

The labor unions were quite within their rights when they fur-
thered the special interests which they represented as forcefully and,
if necessary, as ruthlessly as possible. But the Social Democratic
Party always had to bear in mind that it could share in the government of Germany only in the company of other parties representing
other interests; and that mutual accommodation was therefore a
basic prerequisite for any government in which the Socialists might
take part. This was the overriding national interest which they
should have guarded. One of their spokesmen showed the immatu-
rity induced by their years of Leftist opposition when he explicitly
refused to put "some imaginary national interest before the proletariat's class interest." [27] Barely three years were to pass before it
became brutally apparent to every German worker that he had a
great deal more to lose than what the party's terminology called
his "proletarian class interest."

Hermann Müller survived his cabinet's fall by only a year. On
March 20, 1931, he finally succumbed to a liver ailment which had
plagued him for a long time, undermining his vitality. Upon receiving word of Müller's death, Hindenburg spoke warmly of his "honest
will and fearless character." Müller's party colleagues honored him
with good reason. But he left only a faint impression on the memory
of the German nation.

Before we pursue the course of national political events further,
mention must be made of an event which properly belongs, it is
true, to the local history of Berlin but which, however, had considerable implications throughout the Reich; namely, the Sklarek
scandal.

A Prussian law of April 27, 1920, had united Berlin with all its
suburbs into one municipal corporation. In the Prussian constitutional convention the Social Democrats had used the majority which
they had gained at the polls in January 1919 to effect this major reorganization of Berlin, designed to bridge and eventually abolish
the economic and social distinctions between the predominantly
middle class municipalities in the western part of the metropolitan
region and the more proletarian communes to the east. Although

much could be said in favor of this measure, from both an economic and a sociological point of view, the question nonetheless does remain whether this total abolition of the political independence of the former municipalities was not harmful to a healthy spirit of local self-government. For the twenty boroughs (*Bezirke*) into which the 339 square miles and four million inhabitants of Greater Berlin were now divided possessed only the shadows of their own administrations, while on the other hand the new metropolitan unit was much too large to allow a citizen to regard its affairs as essentially his own. Moreover, the City Council was constituted in a purely partisan fashion — thanks especially to the introduction here, too, of proportional representation and its attendant party lists. This partisan council had, as its natural consequence, the development of a partisan city government. At the same time, however, the municipal administration had expanded to such a size that its central authorities confronted difficulties of the highest order.

Gustav Böss had been mayor of this new Berlin since 1921. A member of the Democratic Party, Böss was a sincere republican. He possessed great experience and expertise in the art of municipal government and personal energies which often enabled him to work his will upon a politically divided City Council. But it was also Böss who was personally involved in the Sklarek scandal.

The Sklarek brothers operated a clothing factory in Berlin. They had managed to win the city contract for the various types of uniforms required by the metropolis. They were, however, not content with the legitimate returns which this arrangement offered. They aspired to play a major role in Berlin society life and even to own a string of race horses. To achieve these ends the brothers had thought out a method of receiving payments from the city treasury for deliveries which were never made. Naturally, the system and, with it, the entire Sklarek concern finally collapsed. The subsequent investigation showed that the Sklareks had rendered favors to city officials and local political figures that were more than merely similar to bribery. Two of the brothers had joined the Social Democratic Party — clearly not because they had any sympathy with its purposes, but because they could thus establish connections which would further their own ends.

The principal scandal, however, came to light when it was learned that Mayor Böss had let one of the brothers talk him into buying his wife a fur coat for a price which even a rank amateur would have recognized as unrealistically low. For some unaccountable reason Böss, who was on official business in America when the disclosures were made, failed to sense the importance of the news and made no haste to return. When he finally did arrive in Berlin, he was received at the station by a shouting mob that the National Socialists had organized with their customary demagogic skill. Only then did Böss realize that his position had become untenable. He suspended himself from office, even initiating disciplinary proceedings against himself.

The Prussian Ministry of Interior went to work with great energy to investigate the damages and misdeeds that had been exposed. The nationalistic and anti-Semitic press fell with real glee upon the case; for the Sklareks were Jews, and their connection with the Social Democrats made it possible to implicate the latter in the scandal. In order to sustain popular excitement over the affair, the Rightist members of the City Council, aided by their Communist allies, dragged out Böss's request for retirement and the election of a new mayor as long as was possible.

Not until April 1931 was Böss's successor finally elected: Heinrich Sahm, formerly president of the Senate (that is, mayor) of Danzig. As assistants he had two associate mayors: Lange, a Social Democrat and formerly a city syndic; and Elsas, vice-president of the Conference of German Municipalities and one of the best municipal authorities who ever served Berlin. The proceedings against Böss were finally completed on October 1, 1930, with a judgment by the Surpreme Administrative Tribunal, the court of highest appeal, fining him 3000 marks, the equivalent of one month's salary. As soon as Hitler came to power Böss was immediately imprisoned under severe criminal accusations. He was, however, never required to face formal charges. One can, therefore, assume that he had in fact been guilty of no crime.

These improprieties in the Berlin municipal administration induced the Prussian Landtag in March 1931 to pass a special law granting the mayor authority to put into effect even those measures which the City Council had rejected.[28] Sahm had to make repeated use of his new power. This was hardly calculated to increase the city councilmen's sense of responsibility. For it was so simple — and seductive — to reject a necessary but unpopular ordinance if one knew that the mayor would decree it anyway.

IX

FROM PARLIAMENTARY GOVERNMENT TO ARTICLE 48

O F all German chancellors Heinrich Brüning is the most difficult to understand. He was unquestionably a man of superior intelligence. And even his political opponents did not really doubt the decency and honesty of his motives. His foreign policy was motivated by a patriotic desire to improve Germany's international position; and he sincerely wished to achieve this goal through reconciliation with Germany's former enemies. But time and time again Brüning thought it necessary to assume a tone that could only increase international tensions, and his idea of a customs union with Austria provoked an international storm which inflicted severe damages on Germany.

Brüning's domestic policy is equally difficult to analyze. At the bottom of his heart he was a deeply conservative man, without, however, being a reactionary. Although monarchistic impulses were not foreign to his nature, one has every reason to credit him with a sincere desire to uphold the German Republic. But one cannot ignore the fact that he often misused his powers in defending the state, interpreting the constitution in a manner that verged on dangerous casuistry. Conscious of the magnitude of the National Socialist threat, he hesitated all too long before employing the organs of the state energetically against it.

His political attitudes had been strongly determined by two experiences. For years he had been active in the Catholic labor movement, thus acquiring a firsthand knowledge of social conditions in Germany and a personal interest in the workers' lot. After Brüning had worked his way up in the Reichstag to the point of being the Centrists' leading expert on finance, his personal background found expression in such measures as the *Lex Brüning*, which bore not only his imprint, but his name. This law sought to protect wage earners from excessive taxation by setting an upper limit to the government revenues that might be derived from payroll taxes, an attempt which, of course, was thwarted by the increasing financial troubles of the Reich.

Brüning's other formative experience was his service on the front during World War I. He was thirty years old at the time. Having studied in Germany and England, taking a doctorate in political science at Bonn, he had joined the army as a volunteer at the outbreak of the war. Distinguishing himself in battle through both his bravery and his prudence, he advanced to the rank of lieutenant and section leader. From this he had learned "that the great destinies of this world are mastered only through sacrifice, selflessness, and voluntary subjection to discipline." [1] But the experience had also left him with a special respect for the supreme commander of the German Army in this war, Field Marshal von Hindenburg.

In simple human terms one can only credit the former reserve officer Brüning for honoring his old superior in this way. But this relationship assumed a special significance when Hindenburg was President and Brüning his Chancellor. And the special circumstances which led to this political combination could serve only to increase the President's sense of supremacy. It was therefore all the more necessary, even as it was all the more difficult, for the Chancellor to insist that the President respect the limits which the constitution had set upon his powers.

Former ministers had already experienced Hindenburg's inclination to extend his authority beyond these constitutional bars. On November 26, 1928, after the President had tried to make Stresemann give him a binding assurance to which the foreign minister did not think the President was entitled, Stresemann replied: "Having sworn, upon my entry into government service, to uphold our nation's constitution, I feel I owe it to my conscience to explain to you, Herr President, that I do not see how either the sense or the wording of the constitution permits me to accept such a request as a constitutionally justified demand." [2]

One can hardly imagine that in such a case Brüning would have given the *Reichspräsident* and *Generalfeldmarschall* an equally unambiguous reply. On the contrary, it is highly revealing that in a letter to a friend Brüning explained his assumption of what he knew would be the thankless, thorny task of Chancellor with this sentence: "In the end I could not resist the President's appeal to my *soldier's sense of duty*." [3]

Whoever met Brüning gained the impression of a singular, indeed a rather peculiar sort of man. His ascetic, smoothly shaven face with its fine-cut features could have been that of a prince of the Catholic Church. François-Poncet, who came to Berlin in 1931 as French ambassador, remarks that Brüning's appearance evoked a sense of trust and sympathy. He added, however, that "his heavy brows, narrow forehead, thin lips, and unsteady glance from behind his glasses remained less promising signs." [4] This, then, is the way the man looked who was to head the German government for the next two years.

Brüning succeeded in forming a cabinet in an astonishingly short time. On Sunday, March 30, 1930, three days after Hermann Müller and his cabinet had resigned, President Hindenburg was able to sign the new ministers' commissions. Many Social Democrats claimed that this speed showed Brüning had had his list of new ministers ready in his pocket while still negotiating the Brüning-Meyer proposal with Müller's cabinet. Their point was, however, ill-taken, since as late as March 29 Brüning had still faced difficulties which could have blocked his attempt to form a government. And furthermore, even if these suspicions had been correct, they would not have constituted a just accusation of wrongdoing on Brüning's part. The critical position of the coalition cabinet had been apparent to political leaders for weeks, and Müller's presumptive heir was only doing his duty when he tried to make the transition to the next government as quick as possible. Germany had already suffered enough from week-long cabinet crises.

Brüning took most of his ministers from Müller's cabinet. This seemed almost natural in the case of Defense Minister Gröner. For Gröner can be considered one of the authors of the new political combination. It is true that he respected the "distinguished" Social Democratic Chancellor both as a man and as a politician. But he had become increasingly convinced that Müller's government was about to founder on its own internal contradictions. After his experiences with the Social Democrats on the armored cruiser issue, it is understandable that Gröner should now put the principal blame on them for the cabinet's weakness. In a revealing letter which he wrote to his friend Gleich on January 4, 1930, Gröner remarked that "the Social Democratic Party is afraid of losing the mass of its constituents to the Communists if it joins the bourgeois parties in swallowing the financial reform." Gröner once even went so far as to advise Müller to "say goodby" to his party, advice which Müller — unlike Ramsay MacDonald in 1931 — refused to follow.

Since Gröner had considered the fall of Müller's government inevitable, he had thought himself justified in making preparations for a new, non-Socialist cabinet that would be ready to replace Müller's when the proper time had come. In these efforts he received the obviously enthusiastic assistance of his friend, General Kurt von Schleicher, whom he had appointed chief of the Defense Ministry Office (*Chef des Ministeramts im Reichswehrministerium*). It was Schleicher whom Gröner had in mind when, in the letter to Gleich quoted just above, he went on to say: "During my official absences from Berlin my 'cardinal for political affairs' . . . has been doing excellent work behind the scenes. I have the best trumps, and the lead is on my left. And so we shall wait to see what 1930 will bring." [5]

But Gröner did not wait long before sending the Reichswehr an emphatic "pastoral letter" of January 22, 1930, in which he warned the Army of the threat presented to the nation not only by the Communists, but also by the National Socialists, whom he bluntly accused of wishing to incite a civil war.[6] Gröner was therefore not one of those who were duped by the radical Right's use of the term "nationalistic." In general, his views were similar to Brüning's. Before Brüning became Chancellor, he took a long walk in the Grunewald with Gröner, in the course of which they discussed the problems the next government would face and apparently found they agreed on almost all issues.

The Foreign Ministry remained in Curtius' hands; the rest of the world would regard his presence there as a guarantee that Stresemann's policies would be continued. The Finance Ministry would likewise remain under the direction of Curtius' party colleague Moldenhauer. Müller's three other Centrist ministers — Wirth, von Guérard, and Stegerwald — each assumed a new ministry: interior, transport, and labor. Schätzel, who had represented the Bavarian People's Party in Müller's cabinet, retained his Postal Ministry, as did the Democrat Dietrich his Ministry of Economics. Thus all the parties that had participated in Müller's cabinet, excepting, of course, the Social Democrats, were represented in the new regime. But Brüning had also tried to extend his front to the Right. He appointed Professor Bredt, the leader of the Economic Party, minister of justice, and made two former German Nationalists, Treviranus and Schiele, ministers for occupied areas and for agriculture.

A friendly relationship had existed between Treviranus and Brüning since the war. People thought principally of these two men when they said that the "generation of the front" was now coming to power. Treviranus had rejected Hugenberg so completely and had been opposing his desperado tactics with such force that the new Chancellor could trust him absolutely. With Schiele, however, the situation was more complex: he was still a member of the German Nationalists' Reichstag delegation, the chairman of which, Hugenberg, had bluntly refused to have anything to do with the new government.

But Schiele, the president of the Agrarian League (*Reichslandbund*) regarded himself principally as a representative of agricultural interests and demanded an extensive program of farm relief if he were to join the cabinet. Hindenburg had already expressed his support for such a program in his message of March 18. It was Hindenburg, too, who proposed that Schiele be named minister of agriculture and who helped overcome the difficulties that his program later met. With Schiele's appointment the new government moved close to the "green front," which had been formed in 1929 through an amalgamation of all agrarian organizations and which was therefore exerting a constantly growing influence on political developments. In order to avoid a conflict with his former delegation colleagues, Schiele resigned his Reichstag seat upon entering the cabinet.

Only a minority of the Reichstag was represented in the new cabinet. The Social Democrats, now a part of the opposition, together with the former opposition parties on the far Left and far Right, controlled a bloc of some three hundred votes and, therewith, a majority of the house. But even the assumption that the new government could rely on the participating parties was valid to only a very limited extent. None of these parties had assumed any formal, parliamentary responsibility for the regime; and so — particularly in the cases of the Economic Party and the Bavarian People's Party — the degree of their support always depended on the extent to which they felt their special interests were being properly served on the issue at hand.

A minority government like this had no choice but to seek support outside the Reichstag, that is, from the President. This truth was especially emphasized in the comments of the foreign press. In an editorial of March 31 the London *Times* paid homage to President Hindenburg who, without veering one bit from his constitutional proprieties, had employed all his personal influence to consolidate and direct the government of his country. The author of this editorial probably hoped to flatter the old field marshal by hazarding the opinion that his prestige was now as high as Ludendorff's was low. The Manchester *Guardian* was equally quick to praise the German President, although it did point out that government by emergency decree was a confession of parliamentary failure which was especially regrettable in a time of rising fascism.[7]

This opinion was corroborated by the very first sentences of the new government's declaration, which Brüning read to the Reichstag on April 1, 1930. They referred to "the President's explicit request" that the new cabinet "be identified with no party coalition." This meant that it was doubtful from the start whether Brüning's government conformed to Article 54 of the Weimar constitution, which required that the Chancellor and his ministers have the confidence of the Reichstag. Brüning, of course, made it quite clear that he would dissolve the Reichstag if it refused him its support: "This cabinet had been formed for the purpose of solving as quickly as possible those problems which are generally comprehended to be vital to our nation's existence. This will be the *last* attempt to arrive at a solution with *this* Reichstag."

The means which the new government's statement proposed for this solution were essentially those which the previous cabinet had recommended: Moldenhauer's budget and reform plan. New, however, was the program for agricultural relief, in which people saw the influence of Hindenburg and his trusted Schiele. Brüning carefully emphasized that his government "would not shrink from employing even extraordinary measures." He announced a special program of "eastern aid" (*Osthilfe*) that was designed to effect a refinancing and amortization of agricultural debts, a lowering of interest rates and other payments, and a reform of the credit structure for the purpose of strengthening and maintaining existing agricultural enterprises.

The Social Democrats answered this government statement with a motion of no confidence. Breitscheid, who made this motion, stated that his party had considered the consequences of the step and that the Social Democrats had no fear of new elections. Obviously he was obliged to talk like this; it is less certain, however, that he really was so confident. His criticism of Brüning's statement took the form more of warning than of faultfinding. Breitscheid warned especially against too free a use of Article 48, such as might correspond to what he called the "sea cadet's temperament" of the new minister Treviranus. To this Brüning replied that he would make "use of this ultimate constitutional power only if there were no more hope that the German parliament and political parties could fulfill their mission."

The fate of the no-confidence motion, and thus of both the Reichstag and the government, depended on the German Nationalists' decision at this point. They alone had enough votes to enable the government parties to fend off the Socialist-Communist attack. Yet Hugenberg would have been false to his entire political career if he had not strongly opposed this cabinet, in which opponents and defenders of the Young Plan together with Stresemann's former critics and supporters all sat around a common table. For a government like this was, to use his pet expression, "mousse" and not "men," and his press proceeded to make the point emphatically clear. But, on the other hand, this cabinet had just promised valuable aid to German agriculture; and members of the German National Party, heirs to the German Conservative Party, felt themselves called and, indeed, obligated to represent German agricultural interests.

This agrarian tradition among the German Nationalists meant that Hugenberg had to fear lest a great part of his delegation would desert him if he directed them to support the no-confidence motion. In order to avoid a further splintering of his party, he directed the delegation to oppose the motion. But he accompanied his delegation's vote with a speech expressing such sharp criticism and lack of confidence in the regime that his words, which stood in truly absurd contrast to his party's vote, were drowned in laughter from the entire house.[8] Even nonpartisan observers must have found it increasingly difficult to understand why the German Nationalists had selected precisely this paragon of political clumsiness to lead them, and why they stuck to him faithfully through one ridiculous stumble after another.

When the no-confidence motion was defeated, 253 to 187, Brüning was satisfied, as were, in all likelihood, the Social Democrats as well. For Hugenberg had been the real loser, and he knew it.[9] He alone had really desired a dissolution, and he had forestalled one, very much against his will, with his delegation's vote. But the world is round and keeps turning; today's defeat can win high praises in a week. During the course of his denazification proceedings in 1949, when Hugenberg had to defend himself against the accusation of having helped Hitler into power, he argued that on April 3, 1930, he had "rescued Brüning's government"! It is not at all surprising that among the documents attached to this testimony there is no copy of Hugenberg's Reichstag speech of that date.[10]

A few days after that speech, at a meeting of the Centrist national committee, Brüning himself commented on the situation that had been created by the Reichstag vote: "As the parliament becomes increasingly sterile and the parties increasingly divisive, the position of the President grows automatically more powerful." Hindenburg, he went on, could be trusted to observe the constitution. But the constitution gave him "means which could be employed, if the parliament failed, to effect a restoration of parliamentary rule and democracy in Germany." This, Brüning made clear, was his government's goal. And when he took this occasion to warn the Social Democrats not to burn the bridges that linked them to the Center, he was generally understood to be referring to the government of Prussia, which depended on the collaboration of these two parties.

The Rightist parties, of course, would have been just as glad to see the Prussian coalition dissolved as they had been to see Müller fall. Otto Braun, the premier of Prussia, knew this, and he took all the more pains to avoid this danger. As a man in a highly responsible position, he strongly condemned his fellow Social Democrats' short-sighted tactics in the Reichstag both in chasing Müller from office and in proposing such an untimely motion of no confidence in Brüning. He was distressed by the superheated polemics that the Socialist press was hurling at Brüning's cabinet in what Braun called "the euphoria of the opposition's irresponsibility," and in the Prussian Landtag he tried to block such excesses by reminding speakers to address themselves to the subject.[11] Fortunately, neither the Prussian Centrists nor their leader, Hess, had any desire to play the Rightists' game, and so the Prussian government remained untouched.

But the general national tendency toward the Right became quickly apparent in a conflict between Brüning's government and that of Thuringia. And remarkably enough it was Wirth, who of all the Centrists enjoyed the best reputation on the Left, that first showed these signs of turning to the Right.

In 1923 Thuringia had been ruled by a coalition of Communists and Socialists. But in January 1930 it found itself with a Rightist regime in which the politically critical office of minister of interior and education was held by a National Socialist Reichstag delegate, Wilhelm Frick of Munich. The Thuringians, of course, had not sought out this Bavarian to be their minister; but rather, as Hitler boasted in public, Frick had been selected by him "to represent the National Socialist movement in the government of Thuringia."[12]

Frick's behavior in office corroborated Hitler's boast. He ruthlessly used the powers of his position to further National Socialists in the school system and in the land's police. Frick finally went so far as to remove a Weimar school principal from office for having forbidden his pupils to join a National Socialist organization. At word of this, on February 17, 1930, Carl Severing, the national minister of interior and hence protector of the national constitution, directed a letter to the Thuringian ministry, asking whether this National Socialist organization were pursuing unconstitutional ends and what the government of Thuringia intended to do if this were, indeed, the case. The Thuringian ministry, clearly under Frick's firm control, did not reply. And Frick boasted at a public meeting that Severing would have to wait a long time for any answer.

In the face of this outspoken provocation, Severing dispatched a very clear message to the Thuringian ministry on March 18, stating not only that his national Ministry of the Interior would reply to no more letters from the Thuringian government until his letter of February 17 had been answered, but also that, in view of the National Socialists' infiltration of the Thuringian police, he would block further national subsidies to help the land defray its police expenses until the Thuringian ministry had furnished him "convincing proof that it was honoring in every way the required conditions for this federal subsidy." With this, of course, the Thuringians found their tongues again, and, although they at first affected ruffled indignation, it quickly became apparent that they were the ones who would have to retreat.

At this point Müller's government resigned, and Severing handed over the direction of the national Ministry of Interior to his successor, Joseph Wirth. Instead of using the advantage which Severing had gained to repress the National Socialists' agitation, Wirth, on April 17, relaxed the bar on police subsidies to Thuringia, citing a few accommodating statements by the Thuringian cabinet. At this, of course, Frick puffed up again and hastened to show the new national minister of interior the truth of the old saying that if you wish to squeeze hornets, you have to squeeze hard. He responded to Wirth's retreat by directing the Thuringian schools to open daily instruction with something that he called a school prayer but which was, in fact, a venomous piece of anti-Semitism. Furthermore, he proceeded with even greater speed to fill the ranks of his police with National Socialists. Wirth's protests against these steps were without result, and by June 6 the national government was exactly where it had been in mid-April: again the police subsidies to Thuringia had to be suspended.[13]

This time the affair was brought before the Supreme Court, which declared Frick's "school prayer" unconstitutional. An enabling act by means of which the Thuringian government had hoped to rid itself of recalcitrant officials suffered the same fate. It was apparent, therefore, that the national government was not completely devoid of weapons with which to proceed against National Socialist acts of force on the part of a land government. Finally, in December 1930, a settlement was arrived at under the leadership of Chief Justice Bumke, according to which the national government was to resume payment of the subsidies while the Thuringian government promised to mend its ways and assumed *full cabinet responsibility* for the promised reform.

Unimportant as the entire incident appears, it did achieve significance through the fact that it involved the first attempt by the National Socialists to use the powers of a constituted government for their private ends. And this significance was heightened even further by menacing National Socialist activities which were making themselves felt in the Reichswehr at this same time. These machinations will be treated in some detail below.

Another shift in German political attitude also manifested itself when the liberation of the Rhineland was completed with the departure of the last soldier of the occupation army on July 30, 1930. True, there was nothing new in the reaction to this event of the Rightist press. Predictably, it assumed a pious air, accused the French of lacking any shred of magnanimity, and once more warmed up the old legend that the evacuation really should have taken place immediately after Germany signed the Dawes Plan or even after the Treaty of Locarno. All this cant had already been used by the Rightists in their losing battle against the Young Plan.

But there were some new and ominous notes struck in 1930. It was, for instance, significant that the chairman of the Center Party, Monsignor Kaas, sounded very like the Rightists in an article in his party's organ, *Germania*. Here he demanded that Germany renounce the demilitarization of the Rhineland as a first step toward an "equal treatment" for Germany in foreign affairs. What Kaas was really doing here, of course, was renouncing the Treaty of Locarno.

But it was even more significant that the proclamation which President Hindenburg and the entire cabinet issued on this occasion (July 1, 1930) did not devote a single word to the policies that had led to the liberation; indeed, it did not even once refer to Gustav Stresemann, who had worked himself to death to free the Rhineland. The President and the Chancellor share the guilt for this shameful omission. Their responsibility is made all the greater by the fact that the Prussian government, which was supposed to join in signing the proclamation, had taken pains to point out the omission explicitly. When the Prussians were put off with a vacuous excuse, they replied by refusing to sign the joint proclamation and issued a special one of their own.[14] One can explain this odd behavior on the part of Hindenburg and Brüning only by assuming that they did not wish to endanger their efforts to find Rightist support by giving official recognition to Stresemann and the fruits of his policies. And perhaps they thought that their supporters on the Left would be mollified if the Chancellor, in the name of the President, were simply to place a wreath on Stresemann's grave.

The effect Hindenburg's proclamation made on an objective, foreign observer is illustrated by the report of July 3 that the British ambassador, Sir Horace Rumbold, sent to his minister, Arthur Henderson, whose peaceful intentions are no more to be doubted than are those of his ambassador.

The manifesto appears to me to exemplify two of the besetting weaknesses of the German character, ingratitude and tactlessness. The internal affairs of Germany are not our affair, but one might have expected that Dr. Stresemann's name would have appeared in the Government manifesto, and that some mention of the policy which he pursued with such tenacity and at such sacrifice would have been made . . . For reasons of general policy the German Government might have seen fit to insert some recognition of the loyalty of the Powers of occupation and the punctuality with which the French troops executed their programme of withdrawal.

But I am more concerned with the reference in the manifesto to the evacuation of the Saar. It is an unattractive feature of the German character to display little gratitude for favours received, but when the receipt of favours is followed up by fresh demands, there are grounds for feeling impatient.[15]

Worse things were soon to follow. The German President used this celebration of the evacuation of the Rhineland as an opportunity to display himself in public as a member of the *Stahlhelm*, and to do so in such a way as to challenge the government of Prussia. For in October 1929 the Prussian government had banned the *Stahlhelm* in the provinces of Rhineland and Westphalia; citing the federal law of March 1921, the government had pointed out that the *Stahlhelm* was carrying out military exercises and was training its members in the use of military weapons. Now, in mid-1930, when the liberation festivities were drawing near, the leaders of the *Stahlhelm* sought to induce the Prussian government to reverse its position. They tried the long road first, hoping that Hindenburg and Brüning would prove effective advocates for their cause. But when Braun refused to respond to such circuitous endeavors, they condescended to direct a formal petition to him (July 4, 1930), asking that the ban be dropped.

On July 19, when negotiations on this point were still being carried on, and when, in fact, it was only a matter of formulating the declaration that the Prussian government intended to require of the *Stahlhelm* prior to the revocation of the ban, Hindenburg suddenly declared that he would not take part in the Rhineland celebrations unless the ban were revoked. He defended this decision in a letter to Braun, which was published immediately, by arguing that the ban was unjustified and illegal, and that the declaration the government of Prussia was about to require of the *Stahlhelm* was unacceptable.

As Prussian premier, Braun was neither able nor willing to tolerate this sort of treatment. He answered the President immediately with a detailed letter in which he vigorously refuted the argument of an "unjustified" ban by referring to the undisputed evidence at hand, and in which he reaffirmed his insistence on a written declaration by the *Stahlhelm* leaders. The two leaders, Seldte and Duesterburg, did sign the declaration, although in a somewhat weakened form. And so Hindenburg was able to participate in the festivities throughout the Rhineland to the great enthusiasm of the populace.

Braun, however, prevailed upon Hindenburg to receive him in Brüning's presence for a conversation on the entire incident. It is clear that the Prussian premier wasted no words in getting to the point. According to the report that Braun gives of this talk in his memoirs, the President restricted his reply to a few obvious generalities without being able to address any words to the issue at hand. Braun is, of course, not only our reporter but a party to the case, yet his report does not give the impression that he is being unjust to the Old Gentleman." [16]

In any event this episode also showed how Hindenburg was veering to the Right. One might almost say that he now felt free to follow the inclinations of his heart.

It was far more important, of course, for the new government to determine whether — and if so, how — it could cope with the nation's financial distress. Journalistic and academic experts had been making unnumbered proposals for new taxes designed to plug the gap in the national budget. As early as 1929, for instance, Gustav Stolper, the editor of the influential weekly, *Der deutsche Volkswirt*, had proposed a national tobacco monopoly from which he predicted an annual profit of over 1.5 billion marks. He pointed out that tobacco was taxed much less heavily in Germany than in Britain and argued that this was an absurd situation for a country like Germany, which was in dire need of capital, burdened by a heavy tribute, and forced to import capital from abroad.[17]

But such avenues were not open to the government since it had to respect the desires of the parties whose support it hoped to gain. Thus, for instance, the Bavarian People's Party objected to the finance minister's proposal that the beer tax be raised by 75 percent. And even when, at a meeting chaired by the Chancellor on April 10, all the other government parties had agreed to an increase in the tax of only 50 percent, the Bavarians still refused to sign. On the other hand, the middle class Economic Party insisted that the increase in the sales tax be accompanied by a special surtax on the receipts of department stores and consumers' cooperatives. This measure only increased, of course, the opposition of the Social Democrats, who regarded the cooperatives as their special protégés.

At this point the situation became even more complex when the government adopted agriculture minister Schiele's far-reaching program of agrarian reforms. No one disputed the catastrophic condition of German agriculture. Even the Social Democrats agreed to this, as Hilferding made clear in the Reichstag, and in Müller's government they had voted for tariff increases which in former decades their party would have called criminal robbery of the workingman's pocket. But Schiele's program went much further. For rye, for example, he proposed a sliding tariff scale which would keep the German domestic price roughly double the world price. The same would have been true of wheat. His entire program would have given the government extensive powers that it had never had before.

It was common knowledge that Schiele's program enjoyed the President's warm support. The force of this endorsement was considerably weakened, however, by the equally common knowledge that the President was not without a personal interest in the issue now that he had become master of the East Prussian estate of Neudeck. This former possession of the Hindenburg family had been given to him in 1927 on his eightieth birthday. The funds for this purpose had been raised principally among German industrial magnates. The idea, however, had sprung from the mind of the clever and cunning leader of East Prussian landowners, the extremely conservative junker Elard von Oldenburg-Januschau. His aim had clearly been not only to link Hindenburg's personal economic interests with those of East German landowners, but also to bring the President under the more general influence of the eastern landowners among whom he now regularly enjoyed his holidays as a fellow junker.

What people did not know at first — but what Ludendorff, in his boundless hatred for his former commanding officer, quickly made public — was that the President of Germany had let himself be persuaded to undertake an extremely questionable circumvention of taxes. For in the local land court the deed to the estate of

Neudeck had been registered under the name not of Paul von Hindenburg, to whom the estate had been given, but of his son Oskar, clearly in order to evade the inheritance tax which would have fallen due at the President's death.[18]

It required a high degree of self-discipline for the coalition parties, which were all dedicated to the maintenance of a free economy, to accept Schiele's arguments and to join in this new agricultural plan. The Social Democrats, of course, had no reason to support Schiele and the cabinet on this issue. The Rightists were therefore all the more eager to adopt the measure. Included in their ranks were not only those delegates who had followed Treviranus and Schlange-Schöningen out of the German National Party, but also a large number of those who had remained true to Hugenberg.

From the cabinet's point of view there was a danger that, while Hugenberg's Rightists would join in the adoption of this new agricultural program, they would also join the Communists and Social Democrats in rejecting the proposed financial reforms. The government parties sought to avoid this possibility by linking both bills together inextricably by a so-called *Junktim*, that is, they included in the farm bill a paragraph stipulating that the measure would go into force only after all the proposed financial reforms had been accepted. Brüning lent all his authority to this device by declaring that the rejection of this *Junktim* would lead to an immediate dissolution of the Reichstag. On April 12, 1930, the joint measures were passed by the bare majority of 217 to 206.

The German Nationalist delegation had fallen apart on this issue. Only a scant minority of twenty-three delegates had stuck to their leader Hugenberg in opposing the bills, while the majority, under the delegation's former chairman, Count Westarp, voted with the government. But anyone who thought that this division had marked the end of Hugenberg's regrettable domination of the party was sorely disappointed a few days later, on April 25, when the executive committee of the party held a meeting. Here an overwhelming majority of the committee backed Hugenberg's policy, stating that the party's purpose was to oppose Brüning. This was a severe blow to the insurgent delegates, for it made clear that, if the party were to split, its organization and its funds would remain with Hugenberg. It also put an end to whatever hopes the Chancellor and his friend Treviranus had of extending their government to the Right.

Nevertheless, at the moment it was clear that Brüning had won a great political victory. And even those who found much to criticize in the new laws thought they had discovered a quality in the new Chancellor that was especially to be valued at that time: the ability to lead. But unfortunately the new laws in no way solved the nation's financial problems, and the 1930 budget remained to be passed. Although it was possible to balance the budget on paper, more or less, the continuing economic crisis and, in particular, the increasing rate of unemployment defied all attempts to predict the government's accounts.

Early in June 1930 the finance minister and, with him, the entire cabinet concluded that they would have to reckon with an average of 2 million unemployed workers instead of the 1.4 million they had previously estimated. Using this figure, Moldenhauer predicted a total deficit of about 750 million marks. The cabinet wished to devote another 100 million to a program of public works, so a total of 850 million marks remained to be found. To cover this deficit Moldenhauer proposed a program which embroiled him in a conflict with his own German People's Party. Accordingly, on June 18 he tendered his resignation as minister of finance. Brüning had no choice but to accept Moldenhauer's request.

The Chancellor then went to Neudeck to discuss with Hindenburg the choice of a replacement for this post, which had become the most important in the cabinet. Brüning's tentative candidate was his present minister of economics, the Democratic Reichstag delegate Hermann Dietrich, in whom he sensed the necessary knowledge and energy. Hindenburg agreed, and so on June 26 Dietrich's appointment was made public. At the same time Dietrich was also named presiding officer of the cabinet in the Chancellor's absence. The Democratic delegation quickly passed a motion declaring that Dietrich had accepted this new office on his own responsibility and that the party would not regard itself as sharing responsibility for all parts of his financial program.[19] At first no new economics minister was appointed; instead, State Secretary Trendelenburg was entrusted with overseeing the ministry's affairs.

Meanwhile the Reichstag had been considering the budget for the current fiscal year. In the course of these debates partisan differences had become strikingly apparent. But chief interest was reserved for the new financial proposals which Dietrich presented to the Reichstag on July 7. In addition to cuts in expenditures, the new plan included a whole series of increases in both direct and indirect taxes, such as a 5 percent supplementary income tax, a 10 percent supplementary tax on unmarried persons, a more efficient collection of the cigarette tax, and the like. The greatest sensation of all was Dietrich's special tax of 2½ percent on the salaries of government officials; this he euphemistically called "national aid" (*Reichshilfe*). And he proposed two hotly contested methods to rationalize the unemployment insurance program: a limitation on relief payments by which Dietrich hoped to save 100 million marks, and an increase in the contribution rate to 4½ percent from which he expected to realize some 200 million more.

Local units of government were naturally suffering the severe effects of the depression too as their welfare burdens kept rising. Several new sources of municipal revenues were therefore authorized in Dietrich's plan, with the municipalities left free to put the measures into effect as they saw fit. Among these new taxes were one on alcoholic beverages and a poll or "citizen" tax. The poll tax was based on the idea that every member of the community should bear the same sort of share in its burdens that he does in the deliberation of its affairs. One might regard this argument as the converse of the principle with which the American colonies had justified their rebellion against the British mother country in the eighteenth century. The motto then was "No taxation without representation." Now the argument was "No representation without taxation." Originally the poll tax was conceived as a minimal charge against every citizen regardless of his income. This failure to allow for differences in ability to pay provoked the severest sort of opposition among the Social Democrats.

The critical decision occurred at the second reading of Dietrich's program. The Chancellor opened the debate on July 15 with an extended address in which he placed Dietrich's bill in the context of a still broader program of reforms that were to be carried out in the coming months and years and for which the proposed new revenues would be required. With unusual force and emphasis he urged the legislators to be mindful of their responsibilities at this important hour, arguing that by passing this single bill the Reichstag could do more to ensure German democracy and parliamentary government than had been done in many former years. But if, he continued, at this decisive moment the Reichstag were to fail the German nation, then the government would "have to make use of *all* constitutional means necessary to cover the budgetary deficit." This final point was, of course, the most sensational and significant portion of his speech. For it was immediately understood as an announcement of Brüning's intent to employ Article 48 of the Weimar constitution.

Meanwhile, a large number of Social Democrats had come to realize the errors they had committed in wrecking the Great Coalition and, again, in proposing the no-confidence resolution. It was for this reason that their delegation's spokesman, old Wilhelm Keil of Württemberg, made it quite clear that, in spite of his specific criticisms of Dietrich's bill, his party was prepared in principle to offer its support to some such measure if the cabinet were equally prepared to make a few concessions. The Social Democrats even went so far as to invite the Centrists, as the strongest government party, to join them in seeking some mutually acceptable compromise. The Center did not accept this overture. But, to keep the way open for some such future step, the Social Democrats abstained from the vote on the first article of Dietrich's bill, in order that the measure might pass. Once more the German Nationalists, National Socialists, and Communists found themselves together in the opposition.

On the morning after this vote it was learned that the President had given Brüning full power to carry out the financial reforms through emergency decrees under Article 48 in the event that the Reichstag were to reject the bill. This step proved necessary on the next day, July 16, when the Reichstag voted on Article 2 of Dietrich's program, the section that authorized the so-called national aid. The Social Democrats opposed this solidly, as did not only the Communists and National Socialists, but also a large number of German Nationalists as well. As a result, the measure failed by a vote of 256 to 193, and the Chancellor immediately arose to declare that the government thought no purpose could be served by further parliamentary consideration of the matter. With this the attempt to reform the nation's finances through parliamentary procedures was over and done with. The German Republic had arrived at a critical crossroads.

On this same evening the cabinet passed two emergency decrees putting the financial reforms into effect through presidential authority under Article 48. To this the Social Democrats immediately replied with a motion, under Paragraph 3 of Article 48, that the Reichstag nullify the decrees. In the session of July 18 Otto Landsberg defended this motion with keen legal arguments. He pointed out, among other things, that the use of Article 48 required that public peace and order be endangered at the time the emergency decrees are published. A concern lest disorder develop later did not, he argued, constitute legitimate grounds for its employment.

The delegate Oscar Meyer, along with his fellow Democrats, could claim to have made every possible effort to block the cabinet's use of Article 48. Yet he preferred to ignore the question whether the cabinet had observed the constitutional restrictions on its authority to issue such emergency decrees. For, he argued, constitutional authorities of all times held that any such government misstep could be rectified by a parliamentary statement of approval; in this case, therefore, by a rejection of the Social Democrats' motion that the decrees be nullified. Severing's memoirs show that even some of

the Social Democrats had misgivings about Landsberg's legal arguments. For it was apparent that a financial emergency did in fact
exist, and that effective relief had to be found as soon as possible.
As Severing saw it, "Something had to be done immediately. And
given a government which desired under all circumstances to maintain an orderly financial policy, it was quite easy to understand that
it would use Article 48 as its final measure of self-preservation." [20]

Brüning entrusted the political justification of the decrees to
the two members of his cabinet who stood furthest to the Left.
Wirth, minister of interior, warned of the critical threat to German
democracy that would be the inevitable consequence of a nullification of the decrees. And Dietrich made a stirring impression not
only on the Reichstag, but also on a large segment of public opinion,
when he closed his forceful and impassioned speech with the words:
"The same German people who now spend millions of marks for
tobacco and beer are certainly able to fill a gap like this one in the
national budget. Today the only question is whether the German
people are an assortment of special interests or a state." [21]

The answer lay in the hands of the German Nationalists. Ernst
Oberfohren, speaking for the delegation, delivered a confused state-
ment opposing the decrees. Count Westarp, on the other hand, spoke
out strongly in their support. The problem now became whether
Westarp could lead a sufficient number of Rightist votes into the
government's camp. The answer became apparent when the Social
Democrats' motion was passed by a slight majority: 236 to 221. Only
a small number of German Nationalists had opposed their tyrant
Hugenberg in his alliance with Socialists, Communists, and National
Socialists against President Hindenburg's decree.

Brüning replied immediately to this vote by reading another
presidential decree which dissolved the Reichstag. While the great
majority of delegates were leaving the chamber in a serious mood,
the Communists staged a childish demonstration that culminated
in their singing the International. Goethe's Mephistopheles was all
too right:

> Men never know the devil's there,
> Though he may have them by the hair.

This dissolution of the Reichstag elected in 1928 — the last to
have a republican majority — was one of the most fatal events in the
history of the Weimar Republic. For it opened the gates to a disaster
which poured first over Germany and then across all Europe. It is
therefore all the more important to consider whether this step was
really necessary; whether it was Brüning's only move out of what

was certainly a critical and permanently untenable situation. Was no compromise possible that would have avoided a retraction of the government's bill, the publication of the President's emergency decrees, and the dissolution of the Reichstag?

The Social Democrats have always maintained that such a compromise would have been possible, arguing that they would have accepted the decrees if the poll tax had merely been graduated according to income — as, little more than one week later, on July 26, the second emergency decree was to provide.[22] At first glance this sounds like the wisdom of hindsight, trying to slough off responsibility for the dissolution and all its disastrous consequences. Yet such an interpretation would certainly do them an injustice. For, as we have seen, at the last moment the Social Democrats did make a real attempt at compromise.

The crucial question remains whether this attempt was sufficiently clear and strong to give them reason to expect a reciprocal move on the cabinet's part. Oscar Meyer, for instance, who was working hard to effect such an agreement, declared before the entire Reichstag that the language in which the Social Democrats had couched their offer made negotiations on the issue seem fruitless from the start. And Dietrich certainly had the Socialists, among others, in mind when he spoke of the "chaos in the Ways and Means Committee" which had forced him to conclude that "Things can't go on like this; everyone wants to cook his private soup." Yet again, in the account that Keil's memoirs give of the negotiations that filled these hectic days, it appears that Dietrich was prepared to respond to the Social Democrats' invitation, but was restrained from doing so by Brüning.[23]

And Curtius' testimony is even more convincing: "In those decisive hours I implored the Chancellor not to take the fateful step of dissolution."[24] His words were in vain. Why? Curtius' explanation is that Brüning felt himself obligated "to protect the President's authority after it had been threatened by the nullification of the decrees." If this interpretation is correct, Brüning's behavior shows the fatal influence of his romantic — or, if you will, his field-gray — relationship to Field Marshal von Hindenburg.

For the President's right to issue emergency decrees and the Reichstag's authority to nullify them both derived from one and the same article of the constitution. Each of the two powers was at the same time the other's complement and counterweight. One turns the constitution upside down if one sees a personal insult to the President in the Reichstag's use of an undoubted right. The authority of the President extends no further than the constitution says, and it certainly may not be turned into a superiority over the Reichstag in the face of constitutional provisions to the contrary. For such an unjustified interpretation would destroy the trust due the President as upholder of the constitution.

One would, however, be justified in supplementing Curtius' interpretation of Brüning's behavior with thoughts of the Chancellor's political and tactical plans. Both Brüning and Hindenburg wished to replace the shattered Great Coalition with an alliance of the moderate parties with the Right, insofar as members of the Right could be found who were loyal to the Republic and fit to govern. If Brüning had veered from this course he would have been in danger of forfeiting the President's confidence. And if he had reached an agreement with the Social Democrats, he would have left that course, even if he had had no intention of taking them into his government. For the predictable consequence of such a move would have been the defection of even those Rightist delegates who recognized the stupidity of Hugenberg's "opposition at any price."

Brüning, however, still seduced by his success of April 14, had persuaded himself that he needed only to assume a determined and unyielding stance in order to gather a majority around himself. And indeed, he was not so very far from being right; the margin against him totaled only fifteen votes. It is true, of course, that in any event he would have been wise to take to heart the warning implied by the vote of confidence Hugenberg had just received from his party's central committee. For this vote had made it clear that any insurgent German Nationalists would have no party organization to support them and consequently no prospects at the polls. A statesman who had taken notice of this sign would have changed his course at this final moment and accepted the Social Democrats' support if it were to be had at a reasonable price, that is, one that did not jeopardize the financial reform.

No one will ever know whether such a price could have been arrived at. Our judgment of Brüning's tactics must consequently be restricted to the observation that he did not do *everything* to avoid the disaster, the magnitude of which he surely did not foresee. He hoped, as he explained later, "to secure a Reichstag with a democratic majority . . . through new elections." [25] But here, as the new elections were to demonstrate, he had duped himself completely. Other statesmen have proved poor prophets without being blamed for this shortcoming. But one asks in vain what there was in Germany in 1930 that gave Brüning any hope for finding democratic support, even if one extends the meaning of "democratic" further than was really justified in fact.

At the Reichstag session of July 18, Ernst Scholz, leader of the People's Party delegation, argued in defense of Brüning's actions, pointing out that even Müller's cabinet had considered using Article 48 to put the financial reforms into effect. And much later, in a letter of 1947 to Rudolf Pechel, editor of the *Deutsche Rundschau*, Brüning stated that Müller had proposed to Hindenburg that emergency decrees be issued, but that the President had rejected the idea.[26] Another source attributes Hindenburg's opposition to the influence of the Defense Ministry.[27] According to this report, Schleicher could reach Hindenburg at any time through his son Oskar, with whom Schleicher had served in the Third Foot Guards. And at the time of Müller's proposal Schleicher told Hindenburg that Gröner wished the President to understand that, in a cabinet that intended to govern with emergency decrees, he (Gröner) "could accept responsibilities only if Social Democrats were not in charge."

Yet, on the other hand, Carl Severing, who certainly was in a position to know, assures us that neither Hermann Müller nor any of his ministers ever asked the President to employ his emergency power.[28] Severing's testimony on this point carries all the more weight since he concedes that, far from being opposed in principle to the idea of such emergency decrees, he had even suggested their use to Finance Minister Hilferding in the spring of 1929, receiving a prompt if humorous rejection in return. Indeed, one can hardly imagine a time during that critical March of 1930 when Müller could have made successful use of such presidential decrees. In contrast to Brüning, Müller enjoyed the support of a majority in the Reichstag so long as his coalition held together. But if the coalition had been shattered by the desertion of a party on either wing, then even emergency decrees would have been no help, because they would have been nullified by the majority in opposition. Furthermore, Müller must have been aware of Hindenburg's distaste for the idea of keeping the Social Democrats in power through the use of his own extraordinary powers. One must therefore assume that Brüning's letter to Pechel rested on some mistaken recollection, and that Schleicher's reported maneuver took some other form.

The President's emergency decree had been nullified by the Reichstag vote. But on July 26, that is, after the Reichstag had been dissolved, official publication was made of a new emergency decree "for the relief of financial, economic, and social distress." This measure fixed the national budget for 1930 even more rigorously than had the former, nullified decrees. One important difference was the institution of a graduated poll tax, which now ranged from three marks for the lowest income bracket up to a maximum of one thousand marks. The decree also included extreme measures of eastern aid: a moratorium on mortgage foreclosures for the rest of the year and government credits for the transportation and training of farm labor. Opponents of this method of governing by Article 48 pointed out that the new presidential decree represented a circumvention of the Reichstag's earlier act of nullification. But even these people could not dispute the fact that at the moment — and certainly before the next Reichstag could meet — some steps had to be taken to put the nation's finances in order.

The government set the new elections for as late a date as the constitution allowed (Article 25, Paragraph 2): Sunday, September 14. From the very beginning the election campaign was marked by the naked aggression of the National Socialists, who assumed the most violent tones not only in their own meetings, but also in those of their opponents, where they scorned neither verbal nor physical abuse.[29] "The pronounced activity of the National Socialists and the apathy of the general public" were the British ambassador's principal impressions of the campaign.[30] All the "bourgeois" parties of the Middle were being pushed hard into a defensive posture. Resignations from the German National People's Party kept increasing. Count Westarp had tried to carry on his opposition to Hugenberg within the party as long as possible; but now he, too, decided to resign. With his supporters and Treviranus' group he founded a Conservative People's Party. But their hopes of uniting in it all the conservative elements dissatisfied with Hugenberg's leadership were dashed when the Agrarians (*Deutsches Landvolk*) and a Protestant group called the Christian Social People's Service (*Christlich-Sozialer Volksdienst*) proposed candidates of their own.

Moderates sensed that a merging of their forces was necessary if the idea of liberal democracy were to be preserved through such unfavorable times. Scholz, the leader of the People's Party, and Koch-Weser, leader of the Democrats, both worked toward this end. But the results of their negotiations were very scanty, yielding only the amalgamation of the Democratic Party with the "Order of Young Germans." The Young Germans (*Jungdo*) had originally been extremely Rightist in their views and had practiced all sorts of medieval rituals. Gradually, however, they had come to assume a more constructive and constitutional attitude, especially after conflicts with the National Socialists. Koch hoped that a connection with them would afford an entree for democratic and republican thought into circles that had been closed to such ideas in the past.

A majority of the Democratic Party's central committee joined him, if in many cases grudgingly, in this hope. It was even decided to abandon the party's former name and to call their new amalgamation with the *Jungdo* the German State Party (*Deutsche Staatspartei*). Picking up the challenge Dietrich had earlier voiced, they campaigned on a platform that accused the former Reichstag of revealing, at the critical moment, that it was "an assortment of special interests, not the political instrument of a nation-state." But the election campaign quickly showed how difficult it was to establish a working harmony between the two elements of the new party. And the more extensive attempts to connect this German State Party with the German People's Party failed completely, so the two parties waged competing campaigns.

From the very start the election campaign was heavily influenced, of course, by the critical economic conditions which were felt in varying degrees by all portions of the population. The depression was certainly bad enough. But the opposition exerted every effort to make it appear even worse and more hopeless than it really was. Anyone listening to these extremists could not avoid getting the impression that, as a result of the malicious designs of her recent governments, Germany was headed for certain ruin unless her fate were entrusted to the opposition, that is, variously, to Hitler, or Hugenberg, or the Communists.

Yet another characteristic of this campaign was the freedom with which the Germans gave vent to their nationalistic feelings. This feature did not escape the British ambassador. In a report of August 29 to his foreign secretary, Arthur Henderson, Sir Horace Rumbold observed: "The snowball of 'revision' continues to roll down the electoral slopes, and, as it rolls, it is gathering speed and size. It may now indeed be said that the first electoral campaign which has taken place in Germany without the shadow of the Rhineland occupation has brought out into the open, through one party or another, all that Germany hopes for and intends to strive for in the field of external affairs." [31] For here, as in every such campaign, no party wished to appear wanting in "patriotic determination." So when one party, complaining of Germany's mistreatment at the hands of her former foes, made extreme demands for revisions of foreign policy, the other parties felt forced to meet and raise the bid. In a contest like this there was no place for the calm consideration of achievements to date and what further achievements sensible negotiations might yet gain. With Stresemann's death his policies had lost by far their best advocate.

Brüning's government was publicly committed to a continuation of Stresemann's program. The presence in the foreign office of the late minister's long-time party colleague and cabinet associate, Julius Curtius, appeared to guarantee as much. But not all the other members of the cabinet were sincere in this intent. On August 10 the "Patriotic Eastern Leagues" (*Heimattreue Ostverbände*) held a demonstration in celebration of the tenth anniversary of the postwar plebiscites in West and East Prussia. Now all these "patriots" had done their duty from the German point of view without regard to party or religion. But in the course of time their leagues had slipped ever further into the nationalists' wake.

Minister Treviranus had accepted their invitation to deliver the principal address at the celebration, and he demonstrated his ability to fit their mood. In flaming words he demanded "the united mobilization of the entire German nation" in order that "the open wound in Germany's eastern flank" might be healed. He gave the Poles to understand that their future would be secure only "if Germany and Poland are not kept in eternal unrest by unjust boundaries" and went on to speak of "German regions, lost to us today, which will be regained in the future." And how was one to comprehend his closing exclamation: "Away with all idle talk of a catastrophe! What we need is the courage to banish our distress!"?

In Poland, of course, these words were taken as incitement toward a German-Polish war. The Polish foreign minister, Zaleski, lodged an official protest against a German minister's "creating attitudes incompatible with the bases of peaceful collaboration." Reactions in France were the same. Poincaré, whose illness had kept him out of active politics, replied in a caustic speech; and the *Temps* warned the Germans not to expect further concessions, for the Allies had already made too many sacrifices "in a spirit of mutual confidence which Germany has yet to justify in any way." Even the British ambassador wrote: "Herr Treviranus is a young and apparently headstrong ex-naval officer, but his attitude reflects a tendency discernible in Germany today, which I can only hope may be fleeting, to go too fast and too far." [32] But he could also report that Herr von Bülow, Schubert's successor as state secretary of the Foreign Ministry, was clearly disturbed by Treviranus' encroachment on the domain of foreign affairs. [33]

Indeed, Curtius had hastened back to Berlin from a vacation to remonstrate with Brüning that Treviranus' "fanfare" had to be retracted publicly or at least weakened in some way. And in the subsequent cabinet meeting he seems to have made his opinion clear to his younger colleague. For in a second speech, Treviranus modified his earlier statements by explaining that he had not meant to imply the use of force. And the Polish minister had to express his official satisfaction with this reply to his protest.

A Polish newspaper, however, said that Treviranus had only barely stopped short of declaring the Treaty of Locarno "a scrap of paper" of no more importance to Germany than the guarantee of Belgian neutrality once had been. And Brüning himself felt obliged to state in a formal address that his presence and that of Curtius in the cabinet should surely "give assurance that the German government will engage in no adventures." Yet the incident certainly did not strengthen the authority of the cabinet; indeed, within the cabinet, as Curtius makes clear, a good measure of ill will still remained.[34] Sir Horace Rumbold conceded that the German foreign minister maintained a spirit of sanity in his speeches and that, in so doing, he showed "the courage of patience." But, he regretfully concluded about Curtius, "the trouble is that he cannot make himself interesting enough, and at the moment he is being overlooked."[35]

X

THE ELECTIONS OF SEPTEMBER 1930: BRÜNING ON THE DEFENSIVE

"Goats, go there to the left!" the judge will some day direct us,
"And you sheep, now I want you all to stand on my right."
Fair enough. Yet there is still one more order to hope for:
"Reasonable men, will you please take up your posts in between?"

Measured against Goethe's forty-eighth *Venetian Epigram*, the "reasonable men" of Germany had dwindled to a hopeless minority by September 14, 1930. To be sure, the Center had demonstrated its holding power once again, even increasing its votes by 400,000 and its delegates from 62 to 68. But this party was supported and held together by other than political forces: the Roman Catholic Church still exerted an overwhelming influence, especially on women voters. Moreover, the personality of the present Chancellor, formerly leader of the Centrists in the Reichstag, must have provided a certain attraction. Treviranus' and Westarp's Conservative People's Party, on which Brüning had set such great hopes, did not win even 300,000 votes and had to be content with four delegates. In addition to these, however, the new Reichstag also included fourteen members of the Christian Social People's Service and nineteen Agrarians — although the Agrarians could scarcely be considered moderates.

The more liberal parties had experienced disastrous losses at the polls. The German People's Party, which had lost its only popular figure when Stresemann died, lost one million constituents and one third of its seats, returning thirty delegates instead of forty-five. The new State Party did not lose as many votes, receiving 1,300,000 compared to the Democrats' 1,500,000 in 1928, but it was inwardly divided. Of the twenty delegates elected from its list, the six former Young Germans seceded after only a few weeks "because of incompatible philosophies." Thus the intended amalgamation had completely failed, and Koch-Weser, who bore principal responsibility for the attempt, accordingly resigned from both the Reichstag and his post as party leader.

His successor as chairman of the Democratic delegation was August Weber, who had served his parliamentary apprenticeship as a National Liberal delegate from 1907 to 1912. The Young Germans never campaigned for the Reichstag again. One finds it hard to believe that they had brought the State Party many votes, certainly not enough to have warranted the six seats which were allotted them by internal party agreement. With the fourteen delegates left to them, the Democratic delegation in the Reichstag had shrunk to a negligible quantity in spite of the extraordinary amount of talent which even such opponents as Schlange-Schöningen admitted there was in its ranks.[1]

The Social Democratic Party had survived rather well. It had suffered some losses, but these had remained within tolerable bounds: ten seats and some 600,000 votes. And so the Socialists, with their 143 delegates, were still the strongest party in the Reichstag. But the Communist Party had made much progress on their Left. With seventy-seven delegates and 4,600,000 votes the Communists were prepared to stand up to the Social Democrats and dispute with them the role of representing the proletariat. If one were to add all the votes cast for what the Rightist press liked to call the "Marxist" parties, one would find an increase of 700,000 over the 1928 results.

On the Right, Hugenberg, who had been principally responsible for the dissolution of the Reichstag, suffered a severe defeat. The number of German National voters had dropped from 4,300,000 in 1928 to 2,400,000; the Nationalists' Reichstag delegation was accordingly diminished from seventy-three members to only forty-one. If one recalls that in December 1924 more than one hundred German National delegates had been elected, one can almost speak of the political catastrophe to which Hugenberg had led his party. But Alfred Hugenberg was not the sort of man to learn anything from defeat. He stuck to his stubborn opposition even though it was now apparent that its fruits would be gathered not by him, but rather by his allies in the referendum campaign, allies who had already captured a large number of his former voters.

The political significance of all these changes was as nothing compared to the astonishing rise of the National Socialists, which exceeded both their own hopes and their opponents' fears. 6,400,000 votes were cast for Hitler's list. Instead of the small group of 12 delegates, a veritable host of 107 National Socialists were going to enter the new Reichstag, comprising its second largest delegation.

This was a landslide unique in German parliamentary history. In order to understand it one must first recall the mathematics of the situation. Four million more Germans voted in 1930 than in 1928. The number of qualified voters had increased by 1,700,000 during this interval, while voter participation rose from 74½ percent to 82 percent. One can assume that the majority of these new voters had succumbed to the National Socialists' blandishments. But even this assumption does not explain an increase of some 5,500,000 votes.

The greatest influence at work was certainly the pitiful condition of the German economy and the frighteningly high number of unemployed workers (over three million in September 1930), almost all of whom voted for either the National Socialists or the Communists. The discontent and general restlessness which were only natural under these conditions were of special profit to the National Socialists because Hugenberg's "nationalistic opposition" had already succeeded in convincing large numbers of German voters that the Young Plan was the chief reason for their plight. In fact, of course, the Germans were simply suffering their segment of an international crisis that was striking other countries just as badly as their own. But it was only natural that the Germans should be quick to blame the reparations for their troubles, especially since no German politician dared counter this claim. And once they had reached this general conclusion, they found it easy to take the next step and point the finger of guilt directly at the Young Plan, especially since most Germans were incapable of judging what their situation would have been like without the Plan.

The National Socialists found a particularly welcome reception among the rural population. Here the depression had created bitter moods which found expression in bombings and similar acts of violence. It is true, of course, that Brüning's government had just introduced a novel, radical agricultural program designed especially to relieve this distress. But the new measures had not yet had time to take effect, and so did not influence the vote. Schleswig-Holstein, where the rural population had a time-honored, liberal democratic tradition, yielded no less than 240,000 National Socialist votes, more than one fourth of all the votes cast there. On the other hand, the new taxes, with which the cabinet hoped to pay for this rural relief, provoked opposition among many who were especially affected by them. It was particularly unfortunate for the Reich that among the Germans smarting under these new measures was such a strategically important group as government officials.

But over and above these special influences the National Socialist opposition was historically favored by the disintegration which the long war and unexampled inflation had wrought on the German middle class. Distress is sensed particularly severely by those who have known better times or who have grown up expecting something better. This was especially true of young people in Germany; they contrasted the pleasures and glories of an already almost legendary past with their own gray, hopeless present without realizing that they were yearning for a paradise the gates of which had closed forever on August 1, 1914, no matter which German party were put into power.

The radically nationalistic tone of German youth was especially apparent at the universities and technological schools.[2] Such sociological factors as the worsening of career prospects were, of course, not the only causes. The nationalist spirit that was propagated by most of the professors at most of the German universities [3] was a powerful influence, with the result, however, that most of the students turned National Socialist while the professors were content to support Hugenberg's nationalistic opposition. These academic circles regarded the Republic with all the more distaste since it was opposed to the student corporations and their duels. And ever since Treitschke's days anti-Semitism, the National Socialists' most powerful instrument of propaganda, had been flourishing in the German student population. The students therefore thought they were putting their professors' patriotic words into practice when they condemned Stresemann's conciliatory policies as weak and un-German, preferring to worship power and to cherish more or less confused notions of revenge. The low age limit which the Weimar constitution had set for voting (twenty years) gave these youthful tendencies far too great and dangerous a strength.

Indeed, the new provisions for the election of the Reichstag proved to be one of the principal contributing factors to the National Socialists' success. It will be recalled that the constitution provided for official party lists on which the name of the party far outweighed the personality of the individual candidate. Because of the general party ballots the Reichstag was flooded with an army of Nazis who were for the most part untried and unknown and who included such criminals as the Vehmic murderer Edmund Heines. Only the scantest few of them could have found an electoral district prepared to choose them on the strength of personal ability if proportional representation and the attendant party lists had not cut the bond between the voter and his representative. At the same time this procedure had given so much power to the party organizations that a delegate who differed sharply with his party generally had no choice but to resign his seat and choose a new career. It was precisely this pre-eminence of other parties over their own candidates that the National Socialists violently condemned, while forcing it upon their own members with unexampled sharpness and rigor.

Then too, many voters were attracted by Hitler's "leader principle" (*Führerprinzip*) because it promised to relieve them of the burden of personal responsibility. A democratic state requires constant decisions of its citizens, and one cannot assume that every citizen enjoys being confronted by an endless set of problems in this way. How much simpler and more comfortable it was to leave decisions to the *Führer* and content oneself with chanting his praises as a member of the jubilating chorus. One can probably assume that these human weaknesses also brought converts to the Communists; for they, too, had learned to follow orders blindly, in their case, orders issued from Moscow.

Naturally, the National Socialists' exceedingly impassioned, ruthless, and intensive agitation also played a major role in their success. This sort of irresponsible demagogy, that damns all the policies of the immediate past as not merely mistaken but even criminal, is continually attractive to the masses, especially when it is directed by such a fascinating public speaker as Hitler. The untiring intensity alone with which he flew about Germany, appearing here one day and there the next, made a strong impression on the crowd. And the passionate verbal torrents in which he let his hatred flow brought thousands to his meetings, indeed induced them to pay admission fees just to hear him speak. Their tickets did not, of course, suffice to cover the enormous costs of his campaign. Some of the necessary funds came from a number of magnates, like Fritz Thyssen and Emil Kirdorf, who had been backing him for some time. But Hitler must have found other sources, too, sources which have remained secret to this day.

Yet even after one has assembled all these factors to explain Hitler's success, there remains much that defies rational analysis. Again we have to turn to Goethe's words for help. In the twentieth book of his autobiography, *Dichtung und Wahrheit*, the old poet addresses himself to the problem of the "demonic personality," a major concern of his, indeed, throughout his later years. In this passage he tells how in the course of his lifetime he had occasion to observe several people who had become controlled by the demonic:

These are not always especially attractive people, recommending themselves to us by virtue of neither mind, nor talents, nor charity. But a gigantic force flows forth from them, and they exercise an incredible power over all other beings . . . All the combined moral forces of the world are useless against them. The more enlightened member of mankind rail at them in vain, calling them either betrayers or betrayed; but the masses are fatally attracted.

And does it not sound like prophecy when Goethe then goes on to say: "They can be conquered by nothing short of the universe, itself, against which they have taken up the fight."?

The election had a devastating effect abroad. In the West people discovered with alarm that the Germans did not in truth correspond to the picture that proponents of reconciliation had painted of them. The French, of course, were quickest to note this fact, for they were most immediately concerned. In Geneva, where the League of Nations was in session, the mood was one of greatest alarm. Jules Sauerwein, veteran correspondent for the Paris *Matin*, told the German interpreter Paul Schmidt in foreboding words: "If the National Socialists come to power in Germany, another war is certain to come soon." [4] Curtius reports that the "election results set the entire League into a state of consternation," [5] as the president of the Assembly, Titelescu, attested in his closing address. Briand complained, in a speech, of the increasingly radical spirit of the German voters. And if, as Curtius says, he then went on to exclaim "What cries of hatred and what cries of death!" [6] he was only all too right.

In France Briand's nationalistic opponents screamed bitterly that his policies had proved ill-founded, that the French attempt to effect reconciliation with Germany had served only to strengthen the most radical strains of German nationalism. [7] In England, on the other hand, the *Times*, then under the direction of Geoffrey Dawson, sought to play down the National Socialist threat. In an editorial of September 16 it argued: "Though their tactics certainly embody violence and their respect for the ordinary decencies of law and order has been scant, the Nazis have scored their overwhelming success because they have appealed to something more fundamental and more respectable. Like the Italian Fascists they stand for some national ideal, however nebulous and extravagantly expressed, to which personal and class interests shall be subordinate."

It sounded almost comical when the *Times* expressed its astonishment that the bitter distaste of so many German groups for the economic provisions of the Versailles treaty had not been lessened by the

Young Plan, but had rather increased, even though the plan had relieved the German burden considerably. But the British circles whose economic interests depended on the maintenance of peace were clearly unimpressed by the *Times's* soothing phrases. German securities plummeted on the London market. The 5½ percent Young Plan debentures, for instance, which had been issued at 80 percent, fell a total of 5½ points in two business days down to 77.

The same was true in all the money markets of the world. On September 26 the *Kölnische Zeitung* wrote: "A brief glance at the exchange list already shows the effects of the possibility that Germany's domestic peace might be disturbed." For the German government was no longer able to find a market for its treasury bills. The most painful result of this weakness was the heavy withdrawal of gold and foreign exchange from the Reichsbank. In September and October alone these losses amounted to 633,000,000 marks; in all, they totaled something like one billion. The very carefully phrased report of the National Credit Association [8] found that these international gold movements "were the result, either directly or indirectly, of political and psychological conditions." Not only were foreign creditors calling in their loans, but German capitalists were trying to put parts of their fortunes in safekeeping abroad. For these German money-owners had been thoroughly frightened by the National Socialists' threats. One need only recall the Nazis' demagogic demands for the uncompensated expropriation of the "princes of the banks and the exchanges" and their initial demands — so sadly exceeded by later fact — for the robbery of the Jews.

One consequence of the National Socialists' success at the polls was, therefore, a sharpening of the economic crisis. The billion marks it cost Germany in capital withdrawals were far more than half the 1,700,000,000 marks' reparation payment due in the fiscal year 1930–31, quite apart from the fact that the vital flow of capital into Germany from abroad ceased. Even the larger banks were so shaken by the sudden storm of withdrawals which temporarily threatened the banks' liquidity that for months they hesitated to engage in any large-scale credit operations, even with the national government. All this, of course, did not keep the nationalistic opposition from blaming all of Germany's troubles on the Young Plan, while the National Socialists, with their demagogic skill, kept using the misfortunes they had caused as grounds for patriotic railing against "refugee capital."

This feeling of uncertainty was strengthened even further when it became apparent that the destructive influences of National Socialism had even penetrated the Reichswehr. The Army could never have been considered especially republican in spirit; yet it had always seemed determined to follow the precepts of both Seeckt and Gröner and to serve the state. In his so-called "pastoral letter" of January 22, 1930, Gröner had called upon his forces to remain "far from all party politics, saving and preserving the state from both the enormous pressures from abroad and the strife which threatens at home." [9]

From his experiences of 1923 Hitler had learned that a loyal Reichswehr would constitute an insuperable obstacle to any attempt at a National Socialist revolution. He therefore undertook to undermine the Army and win it to his cause. In March 1929 he delivered an address in which he outlined the relationship between National Socialism and the nation's Army. In this speech he sought to convince the officer corps that it was their true duty to help his movement overcome the state that had been established by the "November criminals." The intellectual tone of this speech is conveyed by such central thoughts as "If men wish to live, they are forced to kill others," and "In reality there is no difference between war and peace." After the customary screams against Marxists and Jews he called upon the Reichswehr with these stirring words:

If the German Left gains victory today *thanks to the nonpolitical attitude of the officer corps,* then you can write . . . : The End of the Reichswehr! On the other hand, if our movement wins, we are glad to assure you here and now that we shall exert ourselves by day and night to create those military formations now forbidden us by the Treaty of Versailles.

Hitler considered this speech so effective that he published it in a "Special Reichswehr Edition" of his *Völkischer Beobachter,* which was then pressed into young officers' hands.[10] The Prussian Ministry of Interior was well aware of the dangers presented by this insurgent move. The ministry therefore published a careful analysis of Hitler's speech in an official report which was made available to Solicitor General Werner. It did not, however, stir him to action.[11]

It soon became apparent that this National Socialist agitation in the Army was not without effects when, from September 23 to October 4, 1930, the Supreme Court heard a case of high treason against three lieutenants of the garrison at Ulm. Lieutenants Scheringer and Ludin had been traveling about Germany in order to persuade young officers of other garrisons to join the National Socialist movement as well as to excite them into opposing both the alleged "leftist policies" of the Army command and the attendant weakening of the Reichswehr through ideas of appeasement. The practical purpose of these efforts was, of course, to render the Army incapable of suppressing a National Socialist revolt.

The political sophistication and attitudes of these officers were illumined brilliantly by many of their declarations to the court, for example, "Rightist thinkers, that is, patriotic minds . . . since we as officers are, of course, patriotic and since this patriotic attitude is shared by only a few parties." In short, this was a reappearance of the political amateurism of the old imperial guard officers, in whose eyes anyone who stood left of the Conservatives was an "enemy of the fatherland."

The court sentenced the defendants to eighteen months' fortress arrest for conspiracy to commit an act of high treason. In light of the dangerous nature of their undertaking, this was certainly no severe punishment. Yet the National Socialists staged stormy protest meetings and their *Völkischer Beobachter* spoke of a "politically inspired verdict." After the National Socialists' "seizure of power," the party rewarded Lieutenant Ludin by making him an important Storm Troop leader and finally appointed him ambassador to Slovakia. Scheringer, on the other hand, reaped no such rewards. During his fortress arrest he became converted to Communism, to which he then remained true.

But the greatest sensation of the trial was the statement which the defendants' party leader, Adolf Hitler, made before the Supreme Court. One of the defense attorneys, the National Socialist Reichstag delegate Hans Frank, argued that their party desired to assume the government of Germany only through legal means, and he asked that Hitler be heard as a witness in support of this allegation. Frank, himself, expected his petition to be denied by the court since, as he wrote after the defeat of the Nazis, "the notion that a party leader should bear witness under oath to the legality, that is to say, the constitutionality, of his political activities had never struck anyone in the entire legal history of our nation." [12] But to his astonishment — and to the grave disadvantage of the Reich — the court decided to grant the petition.

And so, on September 25, 1930, Adolf Hitler was given the opportunity to assure the German Supreme Court and the entire German nation in an outpouring as skillful as it was long that he had absolutely no thought of breaking up the Reichswehr; that his Storm Troops were without any military character, serving only to protect his movement against Leftist attacks; that illegal methods were furthest from his mind; indeed, that he had severely forbidden any party undertakings which might have involved conflicts with the law. He admitted that he had talked of revolution, but only in the political sense of a revolution of men's spirits.

The chief justice pointed out to Hitler that he had, however, openly declared that in the coming battles "Heads will roll in the sand, either ours or others'. Let us therefore take care that they are others'." Thereupon Hitler replied with his highest demagogic trump: "When our movement triumphs, then a new Supreme Court will gather, before which the November crime of 1918 will be atoned for. At that time heads will most certainly roll in the sand." The judge could find no words with which to respond to this sanguinary threat. But Hitler's supporters who filled the hall broke into wild applause at what a Nazi journalist called these "wonderful words straight from the hearts of us all." Thus did Hitler use the highest court of the German Republic to tell the world that his party, which purported to be seeking "a revolution only of men's minds" and which had just won the votes of more than six million Germans, thirsted for the blood of fellow citizens.[13]

It was in vain that both the national and Prussian ministries of interior had sent their experts on the case to Leipzig to testify against Hitler. The court admitted only State Secretary Zweigert from the national ministry as a witness.[14] But at least Zweigert was able to provide documentary evidence of the frequency with which Hitler had already broken his word of honor. Yet neither the court nor the German public paid much attention to his testimony, and the court proceeded to find it proper to swear in Hitler as a witness.

This trial of Scheringer and Ludin not only afforded Hitler the opportunity for another demagogic triumph; it also increased the unrest in the German population, particularly in the Reichswehr and the Ministry of Defense. Could one really still trust the Army? Even President Hindenburg was enraged at the way the Rightist parties and their press were trying to drive a wedge between the older and younger elements of the officer corps. Gröner did all he could to settle these misgivings and to preserve the officer corps from Hitler's sabotage. But he met with only slight success.

Another consequence of these Ulm events was the resignation of General Heye as chief of the army command (*Chef der Heeresleitung*). Gröner wrote of Heye: "the good old uncle simply wasn't respected. He let the lieutenants get away with murder." His place was taken by General von Hammerstein-Equord, a man of distinguished military talents who had demonstrated his loyalty to the Republic during the Kapp Putsch. For, although he was the son-in-law of General von Lüttwitz, he had not joined the latter in rebellion, preferring to remain true to the government. It is therefore no cause for wonder that the National Socialists hated him, mocking him in their newspapers as a "desk general." Hammerstein could take energetic action when deeply stirred. But unfortunately it became increasingly apparent that he thought first of his personal ease, preferring to leave the real work up to others.[15]

With the National Socialists setting Germany and the whole world into a state of alarm, the *Stahlhelm* certainly could not remain idle. On October 5, the day after the three lieutenants' sentences were pronounced, the *Stahlhelm* held a convention at Coblenz, in the recently evacuated Rhineland. This meeting was nothing less than a massive military demonstration in which not only some hundred thousand members, but also General von Seeckt and the former crown prince, took part.[16] (Ever since Stresemann's death the crown prince clearly regarded himself as relieved of any obligation to refrain from political activity.)

The *Stahlhelm* leaders had had a motion picture taken of this display of their organization's size and power. The Berlin office of the board of film review — in a decision that was later reversed upon appeal — pronounced this film to be a demonstration of "military readiness for war." Certainly the rally was generally comprehended to be such, particularly in France; nor was the British ambassador reassured by Curtius' empty-sounding phrases.[17] The domestic political program of the *Stahlhelm* was revealed at this assembly by Seldte's passionate attack on the "Marxist" government of Prussia and by a resolution of the national committee which condemned the "sterile Marxist dictatorship in Prussia," threatening it with battle "by all legal means."

To the Chancellor the election results were a severely heavy blow. Not only had they smashed his hopes for a great party on the Right, independent of both Hugenberg and Hitler, but they had even obliterated every prospect of a majority which might offer him support. Before the election he had hoped for a majority which would enable him to govern *against* the Social Democrats; now he could hope to overcome his enemies in the Reichstag only if the Social Democrats voted *for* him. Nevertheless, two days after the elections he announced that he was not thinking of resigning from his post. Clearly he still felt certain of the President's support and thought that with Hindenburg's help he could weather the coming parliamentary storm. But he seems also to have hoped that, by changing the course of his foreign policy, he could catch in his sails part of the new strong nationalistic wind.

Hindenburg and his immediate associates had probably helped

Brüning hit upon this thought. At least Curtius gives the following report in his memoirs:

On the day after the elections Monsignor Kaas . . . , Brüning's confidant, . . . flew [to Geneva]. At first it seemed as though Kaas had brought the news of my imminent political demise. People in Berlin had lost their heads and wanted the German delegation at Geneva to assume the offensive. I was supposed to change course completely, *renouncing all our former foreign policy.* "Yes, and then what?" I inquired of Monsignor Kaas "What sort of policy should I follow instead?" But he gave no answer to my query.[18]

Curtius told Kaas that he (Curtius) would have to leave Geneva if Brüning stuck to these new ideas. He tried to make Kaas understand that this new policy would require Germany's resignation from the League of Nations and that this would mean a defeat for Brüning in both foreign and domestic politics. In any event, he, Curtius, would not join in such a new policy. If one recalls Kaas's behavior in the days of Stresemann, this report seems thoroughly creditable. But in the end Kaas had to agree that Curtius was right. He flew back to Berlin without having altered the attitude of the German delegation in any way.

But what was to happen now? At first even the Social Democrats felt confused. Hermann Müller reported to Otto Braun how, at a meeting of the party's Reichstag delegation, the point was made that "they should let the Rightists have a government, in order that they finally have enough rope to hang themselves — and the National Socialists with them." Fortunately, both Müller and Braun rejected this suicidal thought. Braun describes a conversation he had with Brüning that lasted well into the night, the date of which, however, he does not give. At this meeting, Braun reports, he told Brüning that the present German government had only two alternatives: either to oppose the National Socialists energetically, as the Prussian government was doing, or to admit them to the cabinet "while they are still too weak to carry out their demands for total power." Of these alternatives Braun much preferred the first, seeing considerable danger in the other.

The significant element of Braun's report, however, is his statement that Brüning found himself unable to choose either of these two policies "in consideration of the President and of the reactionary forces with which he [Brüning] would have to reckon in the execution of his general policies." This interpretation was probably correct; ever since the recent elections, the President had been Brüning's only means of political support. But the aims of the "reactionary forces" which were trying to influence the President were illustrated by the resolution, mentioned above, that the *Stahlhelm* had adopted at its convention in Coblenz. And the *Stahlhelm*, from which Hindenburg was in no way estranged, regarded Braun's Prussian government as the principal barrier to a triumph of the nationalists in Germany. It was for this reason that the final sentence of the Coblenz resolution had been directed at the President in person: "In the future, the President of Germany, as chief executive of the Reich [*Reichsverweser*], should also, *ex officio*, hold the office of premier of Prussia."

The article that Braun published in the *Vorwärts* on October 13, the day when the new Reichstag convened, may therefore be regarded as a result of his conversation with Brüning. For it clearly shows a sharp change away from the policy of opposition which the Social Democrats had been pursuing in the Reichstag until then: "In these times, when — unlike 1848 — the number of those members of the German bourgoisie who are ready for real democracy has been steadily shrinking, the German Social Democratic Party has a historical duty of tremendous magnitude, and one that will force us to bear the weight of enormous sacrifices: we must exert all our forces to keep the German Republic from lapsing into a fascist dictatorship." [19] Braun went on to demand of his party policies which, however unpopular, might be informed with a spirit of responsibility. Brüning was able to take this as an offer of support, or at least of toleration, from the Social Democrats so long as he did not make this attitude too difficult for the Socialists to maintain.

The newly elected Reichstag convened on October 13, 1930. The National Socialists made immediate use of the solemn occasion to show the German people what they could expect from Nazi rule. Thousands of party members had gathered in front of the Reichstag building, inside the so-called "neutral zone" (*Bannmeile*), within which political demonstrations were banned. When the police finally forced them to leave the area, they poured down the *Leipzigerstrasse*, breaking the windows of shops owned by people who were Jewish or who the Nazis decided were "Jewish," and attacking pedestrians whose noses they did not like.[20] Dr. Goebbels, who had been inciting this sort of disorder daily in his *Angriff*, had every reason to be content. Hitler, on the other hand, who had just sworn his allegiance to the law, was understandably embarrassed by the excesses. He therefore took pains to explain to foreign correspondents that it was not his worthy supporters who had committed these transgressions, but rather "rowdies, common thieves, and Communist agents." No German with the slightest trace of political com-

mon sense was taken in by this deceit. Yet the editor of *Schulthess'*
Europäisches Geschichtskalender recorded it as the truth.[21]

In the Reichstag itself the National Socialist delegates indulged
themselves with the pleasure of appearing in their brown Storm
Trooper uniforms. Since the wearing of party uniforms was forbidden by Prussian law, the delegates had smuggled their uniforms into
the building and had changed their clothes there. But their attempt
to unseat the "Marxist" Paul Löbe as president of the Reichstag was
less successful. For on the final ballot of October 15, Löbe was re-
elected with 269 votes to Ernst Scholz's 209. Löbe, who directed
the chamber's affairs from 1920 to 1932, was one of the best presidents the German Reichstag ever had: objective and just, calm, self-
assured, and polite.

But all this was obviously just a prelude to the real drama. The
great question was whether the government could prevail against
this divided Reichstag so rent by passions and by cunning agitation.
Only the debate on the government's statement (October 16–18)
would give the answer.

In an effort to provide at least a temporary solution to the nation's
chronic financial problems, the Finance Ministry and the cabinet
had worked out a program which had been published even before
the new Reichstag had convened. In essence, the plan was expected
to cut government expenditures still further while raising revenues
again. This, of course, would mean more burdens for a population
already suffering under heavy taxes, and especially for the civil
servants. Yet at the same time the new program included several
measures for the further protection of German agriculture and a
lowering of taxes on real estate and commercial transactions. Furthermore, in order to preclude a constant drain on the Treasury, the
national unemployment insurance program had to be made financially self-sufficient; contributions from both employers and employees were therefore to be raised a full 2 percent to new totals of
6½ per cent, while cuts were to be made in the insurance benefits.
This was the language of rude facts, and it came just half a year after
the Great Coalition had dissolved over the question of raising the
contributions by one quarter of one percent!

The national Ministry of Finance had already achieved one important success. On October 13 it had received a temporary credit
of 125 million dollars, approximately half a billion marks, from a
consortium of American banks. With these funds the ever threatened
German Treasury would be able to face the December reparation
payment and those of the coming months with some degree of assurance. This expression of confidence on the part of American

capitalists had been especially welcome to the German government because ever since the financial crisis brought about by the elections the German money market had been unable to absorb the short-term notes and bills with which the Treasury ordinarily met its occasional needs. To be sure, the American creditors had required that the law authorizing the government to incur this debt should also allocate 420 million marks in each of the next three years to a redemption fund for the German floating debt. The Finance Ministry was in complete accord with his provision. The only question now was whether the Reichstag would agree.

On October 16, in an extended and well-considered Reichstag speech, Brüning outlined and defended the cabinet's proposed financial and economic program. Again he demonstrated the ability to arrange his significant points in a grand design and to formulate them well. He defended his policies against the accusation that they were intended to effect a permanent decrease in German real wages. On the other hand, however, he did admit that they were meant to bring about a readjustment in the German price structure, which the world depression had made untenable. In this way he brought economic policy and foreign affairs into a causal relationship. For, he argued, only if the German nation fulfilled its "immediate duty of doing everything in its power to create order in its own house," could it also employ those measures "available to Germany by treaty for the protection of its economy and currency." These words expressed the principle upon which all his policies were based, a principle for which he was prepared to suffer whatever unpopularity might be incurred. He then went on to emphasize his government's desire for that general, international disarmament which, he argued, the Versailles treaty had given Germany every reason to expect. In connection with this he promised that his government would keep the German armed forces "firm and obedient, free from the influence of politics and parties."

The ensuing debate was exceptionally violent. A German Nationalist delegate, Schmidt-Hannover, vied with the National Socialists, for whom Gregor Strasser spoke, in his licentious attacks, particularly against the Social Democrats. The Socialists were not slow to make reply. But when the Bavarian Social Democrat Hoegner started reading the National Socialists a list of their sins, they overwhelmed him with interruptions for which the term "unparliamentary" is far too mild. Among those members of the Reichstag who distinguished themselves in this display was the former lieutenant Heines, who had received a prison sentence for his Vehmic crime and still boasted of the fact.

When the presiding officer of the Reichstag, the Centrist Esser, made no move to halt these gross excesses, Carl Severing arose from his seat and called Esser's attention to one of Heines's particularly coarse remarks. At this, Esser properly called Heines to order. But his words only made the Nazi camp explode. The National Socialists threatened Severing with their clenched fists as he calmly strode through their ranks. In his memoirs Severing recalls laconically that "the abusive tongues of the distinguished delegates remained in action and their fists remained raised, but no one dared to touch me." [22] Yet what was to become of the Reichstag if more than one hundred of its members found such pleasure in cultivating the manners of the gutter?

It was not surprising that the parties of the Right fell with delight upon the Ulm officers' trial. Strasser exclaimed that Gröner would continue in the traitorous ways he had exhibited at this trial. When the presiding officer, Strasser's fellow National Socialist, Vice-President Stöhr, let this brazen insult to a minister pass unchallenged, Brüning ostentatiously arose and left the chamber. The Chancellor did, however, decide upon a more active form of riposte on the last day of the debate, when even the German Nationalist delegate von Oldenburg-Januschau used his discussion of the Ulm trial as a springboard for an attack on the absent Gröner. In a speech which won repeated and heavy applause from both the Middle and the Left, Brüning accused the old junker of having "broken the honored tradition of the Prussian army in the most violent way."

The votes which followed the debate showed that at the moment, because of the Social Democrats' support, Brüning could count on a majority in the Reichstag. Following his wishes, this majority proceeded to refer the emergency decree and the various motions pertaining to the Young Plan to the appropriate committees. Then, by a vote of 318 to 236, this same majority rejected several motions of no confidence and went on to the agenda for the day. The three-year amortization that the American banks required was adopted by a similar majority, thus ensuring the needed dollar credits. But on this issue the Economic Party opposed the government and tried to induce its minister of justice, J. V. Bredt, to resign. It was clear that Bredt did not wish to leave the cabinet, but his position there without party support soon became untenable. He therefore resigned in early December.

Brüning's success in imposing his will on this unruly, negative Reichstag made a strong impression both in Germany and abroad. The British ambassador, who had listened to his Reichstag address, praised the calm manner with which Brüning had suffered the continuous and rude interruptions and concluded that "the Chancellor has, in fact, revealed himself as one of the few statesmen to be found in Germany today." But he went on to mention with equal warmth the patriotism of the Social Democrats and the political wisdom of their leader and former Chancellor, Hermann Müller.[23]

Having dealt with these first, necessary measures, the Reichstag then adjourned until December 3, 1931. Brüning's government therefore had a few weeks for undisturbed work. But this self-elimination of the Reichstag from the solution of pressing problems made it only clearer that at the moment there was no hope of eliciting active, productive collaboration from the German parliament.

This dreary truth became even more apparent when the Reichstag reassembled in December. The committee meetings which had been held in the interim had been the scenes of further defeats for the opposition without, however, yielding any commensurate signs of real progress. During this same interval the government had submitted its various proposals, including the budget for 1931, to the Reichsrat, where they were discussed and passed. But on December 1, just before the Reichstag reconvened, Brüning had used Article 48 to publish another emergency decree "for the protection of the nation's economy and finances" over Hindenburg's signature.

This decree put a large part of the October reforms into effect, although with a few modifications which had been agreed upon in negotiations between the cabinet and the major parties. Brüning had learned from his experience with the first emergency decree and the consequent dissolution of the Reichstag that he simply had to respect as much as possible the interests and desires of all parties short of either extreme, and particularly those of the Social Democrats. For he could not ignore the fact that he was requesting a truly great measure of political self-denial on the part of the Socialists in asking, for example, that they support the new policies of price protection and tax relief for German agriculture while the Agrarian Party was reaping the double political profits of opposing the unpopular decree which, however, clearly benefited their rural constituents.

The Social Democrats remained true to the course of mutual compromise, providing a large number of the 293 votes with which the Reichstag confirmed the emergency decree against 253 nays. It is perhaps worthy of note that this decree also lowered ministers' salaries by 20 percent and that the Reichstag had already made a similar cut in delegates' allowances by a unanimous vote in October.

It is also noteworthy that during this session a bit of political sleight of hand, by means of which the National Socialists had hoped to force Brüning's cabinet to resign, failed. On the presumption that

the Social Democrats were prepared to "tolerate" Brüning but that
they would not feel free to express explicit support of his cabinet,
the National Socialists proposed a motion *of positive confidence* in
the government. The National Socialists, of course, planned to vote
against their own motion, but they thought the Social Democrats
would have to join them in such opposition and that, thus, Brüning
would be brought to a fall. They were thwarted, however, by a more
effective, if simpler, parliamentary maneuver: a majority of the
Reichstag found their motion out of order.

Although the National Socialists had been deprived of victories
in parliament, they had been all the busier on the streets. Here the
unscrupulous cunning of Goebbels had succeeded in winning a
triumph of which they could boast in mass meetings for many
months to come. In early December 1930 a Berlin motion-picture
theater showed a film that an American company had based on
Erich Maria Remarque's novel, *All Quiet on the Western Front*.
This book, which depicts the experiences of a simple soldier in the
First World War, was especially repulsive to the National Socialists
because it had been published by the liberal publishing house of
Ullstein and had been bought by hundreds of thousands of Germans.

The National Socialists condemned the book passionately as an
invidious attack on the German Army. Actually it was, as the author's
short preface made clear, "neither a complaint nor a confession."
It gave, however, an extremely forceful and shattering description of
the war. It showed the realities of military life as it had been lived
by millions of Germans, with all its terrors and endless torments,
with all its blood and filth and hunger and painful homesickness.
Such a picture did not at all conform to the one being painted in
brilliant colors by the National Socialists, whose leader would one
day go down in history as the instigator of World War II and who
already were busy glorifying war and screaming about "the German
people's will to resist." Nor did the film conform to the Nazi lie that
the German Army had been "stabbed in the back by the November
criminals." What the film did show with staggering clarity was that
since the summer of 1918 the German soldiers had been fought out,
exhausted, decimated by irreplaceable losses, and that they longed
for only one thing: Armistice. They wanted that armistice which
was finally decided upon by the much lauded German High Command only after it belatedly discovered what every blood-caked
private had known for a long, long time.

The National Socialists' screams had not been able to block the
novel's sales. But when the American film came to Berlin, Goebbels
recognized his opportunity. Not only did he organize his henchmen

in groups that threatened those who wished to see the film; he even sent them into the theater to drive the audience out with stink bombs and — what a stroke of genius! — with mice which they released beneath the seats. Intervention by the police proved in vain. And the fright which the disgusting scene had instilled even in the civil authorities was so great that the chief board of film review, acting on a joint petition of veterans' groups, forbade any further showing of the film "because it would tend to endanger Germany's national prestige."

The original reviewing authority had found nothing objectionable in the film, and in the Reichstag debate of March 1931 both the Democratic delegate Wilhelm Külz (formerly a national minister of interior) and a member of the Economic Party declared that the film had not offended them. General opinion held that the ban represented a capitulation by the government — whose legal advisers had testified before the chief board of film review — to the mob and, especially, to Goebbels.[24] Hindenburg's warm pleasure at this ban can be gathered from his conversation with the Prussian premier, Otto Braun. He had, of course, not seen the film, even as he presumably had not read the book. The "indignation of nationalistic youth" was all he needed to make up his mind. Would one be overrash in assuming that he had spoken this way with Chancellor Brüning, too?

The Prussian police were under the direction of Carl Severing once again. In October 1930, little more than half a year after he had left the national Ministry of Interior at the general resignation of Hermann Müller's cabinet, he was asked by Otto Braun to resume his old office in the Prussian cabinet. For the Prussian minister of interior at that time, Heinrich Waentig, had not proved to be the man for such a demanding post.

One of Severing's first official acts upon rejoining the government of Prussia was the appointment of Albert Grzesinski as Berlin police commissioner. Grzesinski, a politically gifted man who had already been Berlin commissioner of police and Prussian minister of interior, immediately became the object of an especially violent attack from the journalists and demagogues of the Right. And the motion of no confidence which the Rightist parties introduced in the Prussian Landtag even before Severing had taken office simply was one more of those Rightist attacks which had gradually become "local usage."[25] This resolution was, however, defeated by a vote of 228 to 192.

The Prussian coalition was one of the few stable structures re-

maining in German political life. And its very stability seemed only
to excite all the more passionate attacks from the political parties
and other groups of the nationalistic opposition. At one point the
Stahlhelm managed to take the lead in this noble competition by
sponsoring a petition that called for the immediate dissolution of
the Prussian Landtag.

This petition was submitted in the spring of 1931. Close to six
million signatures, far more than were necessary for a referendum,
had been collected. In the ensuing referendum campaign, the Communists joined forces with the National Socialists and German Nationalists. And a majority of the German People's Party joined this
opposition out of spite at having failed to win a place in the Prussian cabinet. In the referendum, on August 9, 1931, this alliance
received 9,700,000 votes and therefore lost. Some 13,700,000 ballots would have been required for success. Nevertheless, the relative strength of this opposition must be made quite clear: the fact
that 37 percent of the Prussian electorate had voted to dissolve their
parliament was a bad omen for the Landtag elections which, at the
latest, would have to be held in the spring of 1932.

On February 3, 1931, the Reichstag met again. This time the
government parties seized the initiative in their battle against the
National Socialists. To foil any other attempt by the Rightists to
misuse the parliamentary vote of confidence for their demagogic
purposes, the cabinet coalition proposed that the Reichstag rules be
made to require all votes of confidence under Article 48 of the constitution to read: "The Reichstag withdraws its confidence from the
Chancellor, etc." * The most important of the cabinet's other proposals concerned the handling of financial matters. In the future, a
motion from the floor to increase expenses or to lower revenues
would be accepted for formal consideration only if accompanied by
another resolution which would provide the necessary funds.[26]

This new legislative rule merely corresponded to the most elementary principles of a sound budgetary policy, especially in such
times of severe economic distress. The proposal also precluded the
innumerable demagogic resolutions with which extremists had hoped
to tease the appetites of first one element of the population and then
another. The furious opposition of the Rightists assumed truly grotesque forms: one speaker for the National Socialists, attorney Hans
Frank, called the national government "merely an agent of our
French and Polish oppressors." And when they finally realized that

* Thus a cabinet could be dismissed only by a majority vote of dissent (in which
the Social Democrats would not join), not because it had merely failed to gain a
majority vote of support. TRANSLATORS.

their cause was lost, the National Socialist delegates left the chamber en masse, heartened at seeing themselves joined not only by the German Nationalists and a portion of the Agrarians, but by the Communists as well.

Within less than twenty-four hours, however, the Communists had second thoughts on the matter. At the next session of the Reichstag they declared that they refused to take part in "the comedy and trickery" of the Rightists, but rather would participate in further legislative considerations. The National Socialists and German Nationalists proclaimed that their walkout was a protest against what they called "virtual violation of the constitution" by a Reichstag which had become "the organizational machinery of international tribute capitalism." The National Socialist delegate who uttered these libels was Franz Stöhr, vice-president of the chamber. His resignation from this office at this time was certainly no loss to Germany. The disingenuous nature of the National Socialists' complaints about the illegality of the Reichstag became apparent when a report of the Rules Committee showed that four hundred different legal charges were pending against the 107 National Socialist delegates.

Naturally, the departure of the Rightist opposition simplified proceedings no little. Not only was the proposed change in rules adopted by a unanimous vote of 303, but now even a proper consideration of the budget was possible. The politically significant aspect of these discussions was the opposition expressed by the Agrarians to Schiele, who certainly had done his utmost to assist the German farmer, and the sharp rebuttal of this opposition by Schlange-Schöningen. Not only the budget, but also the cabinet's proposals for eastern aid and tariff-setting authority, were adopted.

The Communists made one more effort to embarrass the Social Democrats, this time by moving that the funds for Cruiser B be struck from the budget. For with the Rightists boycotting the chamber, the resolution against the cruiser would pass if the Social Democrats supported it, and then the cabinet crisis for which all the extremists were hoping would be at hand. But the Social Democrats, foreseeing this, abstained from voting, and the Communists' motion was defeated. But the Social Democrats were not spared the pain of watching nine of their delegates defy the party caucus to support the Communist proposal.

In general, and under the prevailing conditions, Brüning's government had good reason to be satisfied with this session of the Reichstag.

XI

CUSTOMS UNION AND
BANKING CRISIS

Both Chancellor Brüning and his minister of finance were certainly aware that their financial program was highly unpopular. It asked heavy sacrifices of a nation that was already suffering bad times, and the German farmers, whose aid had been the purpose of much of the program, were by no means inclined to show the slightest gratitude. Naturally, the cabinet could have made itself much more popular if it had authorized a few billion marks for large-scale public works, thus "priming the pump" for prostrate German industry. But such a course was simply impossible, for the nation's Treasury was empty and it had no credit to draw upon. It was already experiencing difficulty enough in placing the usual treasury notes and bills to meet its current monthly expenses. Thus the national government was reduced to playing the role of the man with empty pockets for whom few favors are done. This situation made a balanced budget mandatory. A wealthy country like the United States might afford the luxury of an occasional deficit budget, but not a land as poor in capital and rich in unemployed workers as was Germany at this time.

And all this time the economic crisis was steadily getting worse. In Germany people tended to regard the depression as an exclusively German misfortune, with the nationalists taking delight in attributing it to Germany's reparation burden. But economic experts agreed that this was an international phenomenon which was afflicting other countries, like Great Britain and the United States, as well. For the international price level had sunk, and the consequences of this drop were making themselves felt in a devastating fashion in all nations connected with world trade. Nor was unemployment a peculiarly German affliction; Britain and the United States in particular were suffering it just as severely.

The fact that they were not alone in their distress did not, of course, provide much consolation to the German unemployed, nor to the authorities charged with responsibility for assuring them at least a meager existence. At the end of December 1930 the number of Germans seeking jobs was reported to be 4,400,000; one month later it had climbed to 4,900,000. To be sure, the spring of 1931 witnessed a somewhat greater drop in these figures than had occurred the year before; but, as the report of the National Credit Association pointed out, the difference was "not great enough to indicate anything more than a lessening in the economic index' rate of fall." [1]

Thus the German government could not hope for a quick economic recovery to come to its aid. Realizing this, Brüning directed all the more attention to fashioning a foreign policy that might reap successes abroad which, in turn, might help his cabinet gain greater popularity at home. His principal goal in these endeavors was a reduction in the reparation burden. Were he successful here, he thought he could count on a certain amount of public recognition despite the many other problems still unsolved.

Brüning had no illusions concerning the difficulty of this task. When Curtius suggested to the British ambassador that the German government might find it necessary to request a moratorium, Arthur Henderson, the Labour foreign secretary who was certainly not anti-German, replied on December 2, 1930, with a firm and extensive remonstrance.[2] His ambassador, Sir Horace Rumbold, who transmitted this response to Curtius, made the observation, in his report to London on their conversation, that it was understandable that a government which had to ask its people to make such great sacrifices might wish to sweeten this bitter pill with the hope that decreases would occur in future reparation payments. He went so far as to warn his superior explicitly against taking any steps which might make Brüning's already tenuous situation even more difficult and concluded his dispatch with the following tribute to Brüning: "It is difficult to think of anybody in the Germany of today more capable of directing the affairs of the Reich than the present Chancellor, and it would be a misfortune for the country if he had to go." [3]

Actually, despite Henderson's refusal, Brüning still kept the goal of lower reparations constantly in mind. But he knew that the creditor nations would be prepared to make conciliatory steps only if they were convinced that the Germans had already done everything else possible to put their house in order. For this reason he held firmly to his program of financial reforms and remained undeterred by all the domestic unpopularity that it provoked. Moreover, the Chancellor and his advisers in the Finance Ministry had not forgotten the experiences at the Paris Conference of Experts, where the Germans had been brought to the brink of total ruin, and Brüning was determined to avoid any recurrence of such a situation. Only when Germany had become free of such overwhelming fiscal problems would she be able to defend her interests at international meetings without fear of catastrophe at home.

Brüning's efforts to "reactivate" German foreign policy may be seen as a counterpart to his conservative domestic activities. He instituted, for instance, an energetic drive for that general disarmament which he joined many other Germans in believing had been promised at Versailles. The negotiations of the preliminary international conference at Geneva had been dragging on now for years, and the German representative, Count Bernstorff, had yet to make any real progress in his efforts to have a final conference called.

Another field where German foreign policy became more active was the protection of German minorities in neighboring countries, most particularly in Poland. In those former Prussian territories that had been ceded to Poland — especially in Upper Silesia — incidents had been constantly occurring for which either Germans accused Poles or Poles accused Germans of being instigators. Without entering into a detailed discussion of these events, one can say that the Polish nationalists were no more reasonable and just than were their German counterparts, and since they generally had the civil authorities on their side, their attacks were much more dangerous.

The German nationalistic press replied to such real or imaginary encroachments with passionate outbursts of wrath, designed to bring the traditionally anti-Polish mood of the Germans to the boiling point. The press also accused the Brüning government at every possible opportunity of failing to protect their fellow Germans who now suffered under a foreign yoke. The German government's complaints concerning Polish terrorism in Upper Silesia were to be discussed at the January session of the League of Nations Council. As the time for the meeting drew near, the nationalists increased their furor even more, for they hoped that Foreign Minister Curtius, whom they had long wished to chase from office, would suffer a defeat at Geneva and thus be obliged to leave the cabinet.

But things worked out otherwise. Curtius represented the German point of view at the meetings of the League's Council (January 19–24, 1931) so successfully that the Council unanimously adopted a report which largely corroborated the German complaints. Curtius' triumph was magnified by an address of the Council's president, a man who constantly strove for peace, the British Foreign Secretary. Henderson not only expressed his pleasure at the outcome of the discussions from the British point of view, but also, as president of the Council, congratulated its members for having upheld the League's system for the protection of ethnic minorities in such a determined way.[4] He went on in this vein to urge the two nations concerned to collaborate loyally with each other and the League. But within a few months he was to discover that the policy of collaboration had opponents in Germany who were every bit as ruthless and energetic as the Poles.

Late in May 1931, the *Stahlhelm* held another huge rally. Even as in October 1930, when they had gathered at Coblenz in the recently evacuated Rhineland in order to raise their clenched fists in France's face, so now they assembled in the border town of Breslau in order to be near enough to show the Poles clearly that Poland's western frontier would soon have to be defended again. Despite the economic distress of the times, some hundred thousand members had once more responded to their leaders' call. The guests of honor added not only to the importance of the occasion, but also to the impression that it made abroad. The former crown prince was there, accompanied this time by the crown princess, who, according to informed people, excelled even her consort in ardent hopes of restoration. Seeckt also appeared, along with old Field Marshal von Mackensen and the recently retired General Heye.

In order to make the threatening character of this demonstration unmistakably clear, Chairman Seldte ordered his troops to face the East, the Polish border. He then shouted to them, "Comrades, there is the German East; there lies Germany's future and Germany's destiny." [5] Naturally this threat excited the Poles, and their foreign minister instructed his ambassadors to direct the attention of the great powers to Seldte's remarks. The Polish ambassador to London discussed the matter with Permanent Undersecretary Sir Robert Vansittart, who assured him that he also thoroughly disapproved of such demonstrations. But, Vansittart went on, did the Polish ambassador really believe that the German government could prevent them? To demand such action of Brüning would be to help bring about his fall, and Brüning's government was, after all, by far the best German government that one could hope for. "The alternative government which could take its place filled him — and, he believed, filled everyone — with alarm." [6]

Universal disarmament and the protection of German minorities had also been points in Stresemann's program, and he undoubtedly would have pursued them just as energetically as his successor did. Yet it is clear that both Brüning and Curtius differed from Stresemann's policy on one important point, namely, on German relations with France. Curtius admits this with reasonable candor in his memoirs,[7] although he does try to attribute the initiative and hence the responsibility for this change to France and, in particular, to Tardieu, who was Premier from October 1929 to February 1930 and again from March to December 1930. Specificallly, Curtius quotes a speech Tardieu delivered in October 1930 in which he read a veritable bill of complaints against the Germans: the disorderly demonstrations in the Rhineland after the French troops had withdrawn; the absence of any German expression of gratitude for the predated evacuation; and, especially, the results of the recent Reichstag election with its powerful upsurge of National Socialist votes.

It is quite true that Tardieu made these remonstrances. And today scarcely anybody would deny that all these events — the Reichstag election most of all — were phenomena which could only have disturbed him deeply as a responsible French statesman. Brüning's reply, that the ballot boxes had not contained votes for hatred and threats of war, strikes a rather hollow tone today. And it should be remembered that Tardieu had also said that he rejected all improvised, *ad hoc* solutions and was determined to stick by the principal goal of French foreign policy that Briand had so often proclaimed: the "Organization of Peace."

Curtius and Brüning may well have had their own reasons for choosing to interpret such expressions by Tardieu as signs that French policy was taking a turn away from Germany and hence for concluding that they, too, should diverge from Stresemann's policy of conciliation and strike a "more active" pose in world affairs. Domestic political considerations were obviously important here. It is clear that in this way the Chancellor and his foreign minister hoped to gather the German people more firmly and in greater numbers about the cabinet and thus, perhaps, to cut off the constant flow of despairing republicans into the Nazis' ranks. For the Germans had gradually become accustomed to finding the root of all their evils in the treaties that had ended the war, and most of them were too impatient to be satisfied with a conciliatory foreign policy "which slowly builds, but never breaks." In November 1930, for instance, when the Reichstag delegate Dingeldey accepted the chairmanship of the German People's Party, he first reviewed Stresemann's policies with a condescending eye and then proceeded to announce his party's intention to change that policy: "We no longer have to limit ourselves to the language of restraint and of diplomatic reason. From now on we shall best serve the interests of German foreign policy, and of the responsible minister [his party colleague Curtius], if we once more speak directly from our hearts." This rejection of reason, even if it was embellished with the somewhat inelegant epithet "diplomatic," bespoke unpleasant times to come.

In mid-March 1931 European capitals were rife with rumors that Curtius, while on an official visit to Vienna earlier in the month (March 3-5), had participated in negotiating an Austro-German customs union. Rumor gave way to fact when, on March 21, official announcements in Berlin and Vienna stated that the two governments had agreed on the basic principles and policies of such a customs union. The outline of the proposal was made public on March 23.

From the German side, the spiritual father of the project seems to have been the state secretary of the Foreign Office,[8] Bernhard Wilhelm von Bülow.* In the summer of 1930 Curtius had appointed the then forty-five-year-old ministry counselor to this position when he sent von Schubert, the former state secretary under Stresemann, as ambassador to Rome.[9] Bülow was a man of great ability and extensive education; a master of many languages, he also was considered an authority on international law. Possessing polished manners, a charming personality, and calm objectivity, he was well liked both among his German colleagues and among the foreign ambassadors in Berlin.[10] Although he kept his new office under Hitler, under no circumstances should he be accused of having had National Socialist inclinations or even sympathies.[11] On the contrary, his motive in retaining office was to keep the German Foreign Ministry free of National Socialist influences, having, as his friends assure us, nothing but disgust and disdain for Hitler and his crowd.

The fact that Bülow's ideas on foreign policy differed sharply from those of Stresemann was apparent as early as 1923, when his book, *Versailler Völkerbund* (The Versailles League of Nations), was published. A convinced advocate of the so-called "active" German foreign policy, he thought he had found a promising place to apply it in such political-economic collaboration between the German and Austrian republics.

On the Austrian side the propelling force behind this plan was Johann Schober, foreign minister and vice-chancellor in the coalition cabinet of Chancellor Enders, a Christian Socialist. Schober, leader of the National Economic Bloc, as the former Greater Ger-

---

* Not to be confused with his uncle, Prince Bernhard von Bülow (1849-1929), state secretary of the Foreign Office, 1897-1900, and Imperial Chancellor, 1900-1909. TRANSLATORS.

mans (*Grossdeutschen*) now called themselves, had previously been Vienna police commissioner and, just the year before, Chancellor of Austria himself. It was he who had invited Brüning and Curtius to come to Vienna to discuss plans for a customs union.

Brüning was just as interested as Curtius in the plan. But when it became a matter of accepting Schober's invitation to Vienna, Curtius managed to persuade him to find some excuse to decline, letting his foreign minister go there alone. Curtius argued that in this way the German Chancellor, whose domestic position was already uncertain enough, would not be directly implicated in a possible failure of the project, while he, the foreign minister, would necessarily be involved in any event.[12] It was very good of Curtius to have thought things out so well, but at the same time it shows how unaware the two German statesmen were of the full significance of the project. For, as the immediate future was to show, much more was at stake than German cabinet seats. On such a critically important matter they should have been proceeding carefully, step by step, testing — as Bismarck once put it — the strength of every tussock before setting their full weight upon it.

Stresemann had followed this advice in 1926, for example, when faced with the necessity of concluding a treaty with Russia. He was careful to inform London and Paris of this impending step *before* signing the document. Curtius, however, took quite a different point of view, one which he formulated in his memoirs thus: "Naturally, we were unable to inform the other governments concerned until we had reached agreement on all points." Consequently, announcement of the plan was withheld until both the German and Austrian governments had formally accepted the principles on which Schober and Curtius had agreed. This procedure should not be dismissed as a diplomatic gaucherie. It had perfectly sound reasons in politics — at least in German domestic politics. For the ministers did not wish to be accused from the Right of having sullied the national honor by asking their former enemies' permission before taking such a step.

The principles of agreement had been carefully formulated in such a way as to lend an exclusively commercial character to the treaty and to emphasize "the complete maintenance of the mutual independence" of the two contracting parties. For central to this entire project was the thought that a customs union between Germany and Austria would lead to a political *Anschluss* just as the nineteenth-century German *Zollverein* had been the principal preparatory step toward a united Germany. As early as 1844, for instance, in his *Wintermärchen*, Heinrich Heine had had a passenger in the mail coach say:

The customs union, he opined,
Will found our German nation,
Making a body politic
Out of our loose confederation.

And most Germans thought Heine's passenger correct. In any event,
Prussia had always regarded its primacy in the *Zollverein* a political
asset of prime importance, to be guarded with jealous care. Thus
in the 1850's, when the genial Austrian minister of commerce, Karl
Ludwig Bruck, was promoting his grand design for a comprehensive customs union that would also include Austria,[13] Berlin opposed
his plan with extreme vigor precisely because he was disturbing
Prussia's political plans for the German future. Again in the 1860's
Bismarck exerted all his force to ensure Austria's permanent exclusion from the *Zollverein*.[14]

And now in 1931 most Germans regarded the proposed Austro-
German customs union as the precursor of the political *Anschluss*
that both nations had been demanding as their right of self-determination ever since the Austro-Hungarian Empire had been dissolved. Not many Germans had any clear idea of the economic
benefits that either country would derive from a simple customs
union, but they were enthusiastic about its political future.

The very reasons for the proposal's popularity in Germany made
it highly suspect abroad, particularly in France. Ever since their
hard-fought victory of 1918, "l'Anchluss" had become the same sort
of nightmare to the French that the "cauchemar des coalitions" had
been to Bismarck after his triumph of 1870. That is why the French
had taken care to require in Article 88 of the Treaty of St. Germain
that Austria maintain its independence. And in 1922, when Austria
needed foreign financial aid in order to avoid complete collapse, the
treaty that granted this assistance contained not only a repetition of
this stipulation, but also the further requirement on Austria's part
"to refrain from any actions and any economic or financial obligations which, by their very natures, might tend, directly or indirectly,
either to prejudice Austrian independence or to grant some other
state special advantages which might tend to threaten the economic
independence of Austria."

The German Foreign Ministry had charged its experts on international law to take great care to formulate the terms of the proposed customs union in such a way that they did not conflict with
these treaties. But the French remained convinced that a conflict
did exist, and Briand immediately instructed his ambassador in London to bring this issue to the attention of the British government.

Now the British government was well-disposed toward Brüning and his cabinet. On March 6, just prior to all the complexities introduced by the proposed customs union, Sir Horace Rumbold, the British ambassador to Berlin, had advised Arthur Henderson to give Brüning a friendly gesture of support in his trying domestic struggles. Rumbold recommended that Brüning be invited to make a formal visit to London.[15] Henderson adopted the suggestion eagerly, and on March 11 he informed Briand that he intended to invite both Brüning and Curtius. The formal invitation was issued at the end of March, and the time of the visit finally fixed for early June.

Although the British government was not deterred from this friendly gesture by the announcement of the customs union, it made no effort to conceal its displeasure at the tactics employed by the German and Austrian governments.[16] On March 21 Permanent Undersecretary Vansittart warned the Austrian ambassador, Frankenstein, that the government in Vienna should take care lest it confront other powers with faits accomplis.[17] And the German ambassador, Baron von Neurath, suffered an unpleasant hour on March 23 when he informed Vansittart of the Austro-German principles of agreement.[18] When Neurath reported that the two powers had been working on the project for the past year, Vansittart offered the pointed observation that Germany and Austria had therefore been under all the more obligation to consult with other interested parties.

The British were particularly distressed because the German action had severely shaken Briand's position in France; Rumbold was directed to make this emphatically clear to Brüning. In this conversation the British ambassador cited, among other documents, a recent article by Theodor Wolff in the *Berliner Tageblatt* which had been sharply critical of the German action. Brüning replied rather superciliously that Wolff did not represent German public opinion.[19] This was, of course, quite true, but only because the ordinary German was much more shortsighted politically and much less acquainted with the French people than was Theodor Wolff, who had lived in Paris for several years and had made a thorough study of the politics and national character of the French.

It quickly became obvious that Wolff's warnings had been only all too true. In the first place, it soon became apparent that the governments of Germany and Austria were by no means proceeding at the same pace on this affair. Henderson saw a real question of international law involved here: whether the proposed customs union was in agreement with Austria's international obligations. On March 29 he informed both Berlin and Vienna that he intended to take the matter to the League of Nations Council and, if necessary, to the International Tribunal at The Hague. Brüning replied that in his opinion the League of Nations had no reason to become involved in the affair. Schober, on the other hand, answered that he would have no objection if the legality of the proposed measure were to be examined by the governments which had signed the protocol of 1922. It is significant that Schober gave this answer after Curtius had urged him, by telephone, to pattern the Austrian reply on what the Germans had said; it is also significant that Schober told the British ambassador that he had rejected the German advice. This was no accidental difference in policy, for the Austrians had already begun to doubt their ability to carry out the Austro-German plan.

In the next few weeks Austrian financial and industrial circles had the painful experience of seeing their French creditors call and withdraw short-term loans. The question whether this was done at the instigation of the French government, in order to put pressure on the Austrian cabinet, remains a moot one, since even Curtius is uncertain on this point.[20] But even if this had been the case, it would not have been the first time that finance had been used to serve a national cause. One need only think of Bismarck's ban on the sale of Russian bonds in November 1887, when he was displeased by the policies of the Tsar.[21] Yet neither Berlin nor Vienna seems to have considered such a possibility, although the Wilhelmstrasse in particular should have remembered Bismarck's maneuver. As it was, the desperate plight of Austrian finance was thrown into sharp and sudden light, as though illumined by a flash of lightning when, on May 12, the government announced that it had been obliged to enter into an extremely costly operation in order to save the Österreichische Kreditanstalt of Vienna.

The Österreichische Kreditanstalt, a creation of the Viennese branch of the House of Rothschild, was the largest and by far the most respected Austrian bank. Almost all of Austrian industry was connected with the Anstalt in some way, and hence dependent on its credit. The bank's collapse was not caused by the withdrawal of foreign credits alone; former errors, especially the fatal consequences of taking over the Austrian Land Bank (Bodenkreditanstalt) at the instigation of Schober's government, had occasioned enormous losses. But the withdrawal of foreign funds and the uninterrupted drop in the Austrian market had provided the final blow. In order to avoid a complete catastrophe, the Austrian government found itself obliged to purchase 100 million schillings' worth of Anstalt stock. But only foreign loans could furnish such amounts. And even then, the government experienced severe difficulties in winning parliamentary approval of its plan to finance the operation in this manner.

The collapse of the Kreditanstalt had a devastating effect throughout the whole world. For if such a great and respected institution could not withstand the storms of the time, what could be considered permanent and trustworthy? The general spirit of distrust, which invariably grows in intensity as it travels, now spread throughout Europe. Creditors everywhere — not only the French — called in their loans. This large-scale withdrawal of credit affected German banking in particular.

On May 15, 1931, in this heavily charged atmosphere, the statesmen of Europe gathered at Geneva. Not only the Council of the League of Nations, but also the Europe Committee was to meet. This committee had been appointed in September 1930 to discuss a memorandum Briand had submitted to the League calling for the "organization of a European federation." [22] This was Briand's last grand effort to make war impossible through a union of European states. He therefore could not help but regard the sudden independent action of Curtius and Schober as a threat to his plan. Moreover, as he traveled to Geneva, he could think of excellent personal reasons for being angry with these two.

For on May 13, 1931, the French National Assembly (that is, the Senate and the Chamber of Deputies meeting together) had elected a new President of the Republic. Briand had let himself be persuaded to stand as a candidate; but he had lost to Doumer, and his defeat was a clear sign that the French electorate was dissatisfied with his policy of reconciliation. This dissatisfaction was generally attributed to the recent Austro-German surprise, which the great majority of Frenchmen regarded as the first step toward the dreaded *Anschluss*. Indeed, the representatives of the northeast border districts had been especially prominent in their opposition to Briand. As the London *Times* wrote, they "are always gazing upon Germany with an understandable suspicion." [23] Brüning had been quite wrong when, in response to Rumbold's suggestion that the Germans give some consideration to Briand's position, he had coolly answered that he could not conceive that Briand would really be disturbed by the plan for a simple customs union. [24]

Immediately after his defeat, Briand had resigned as foreign minister. He had, however, yielded to the requests of former President Doumergue, the new President Doumer, and the present Premier, Laval, that he remain at his post for the time being. And so Briand came to Geneva once again, but this time, as Curtius reports, "extremely exhausted and depressed." [25] It was only natural that Briand's ill-humor should find expression in many of the conversations and negotiations. On the whole, however, everything went quite well. Henderson moved that the International Tribunal at The Hague be asked to furnish an opinion on the legal question whether the proposed customs union was consonant with international treaties which Austria had previously concluded, and on May 19 the motion was accepted by the League Council unanimously, with even Germany agreeing.

Still more significantly, Henderson had requested assurance from Schober that no changes would be made in the status quo until the Hague Tribunal had rendered its opinion, and Schober had, albeit with hesitation and only after repeated prodding, agreed. Curtius had declined to make such an unconditional declaration; but, after Schober's assurance had been received, that of Curtius had become superfluous. In Germany people were extremely embittered by this turn of events and accused Henderson of having proceeded unfairly.[26] Yet even at this early point a difference between the two would-be partners became apparent which was to grow increasingly obvious with the course of time. No later than June 17 Schober was prepared to admit to the British ambassador, if only in confidence and unofficially, that the projected customs union had become infeasible, even if the Hague Tribunal should furnish a favorable verdict, and that he had already told the Austrian Chancellor as much.[27]

In Germany, however, the nationalistic opposition tried to make the Geneva discussions serve their own political interest. They accused Curtius — to put it mildly — of having failed to reply sharply enough to Briand and of having yielded to Henderson's "extortion." For a long time now they had been "after Curtius' scalp" — to use von Bülow's expression [28] — since in their eyes he had still remained too firmly in Stresemann's track. Their principal purpose was, of course, to foster dissatisfaction and unrest in Germany, and in this they were highly successful. The fruits of this new agitation were apparent, for instance, in the extraordinary increase in National Socialist votes at the Landtag elections in Oldenburg on May 17. The *Stahlhelm* demonstration at Breslau was certainly another part of this campaign.

And all this time the economic distress was continually growing. Throughout the first six months of 1931 the number of unemployed German workers never fell below 4,000,000, while the number eligible for unemployment benefits dropped only from 3,300,000 in January to 2,500,000 in May. Withdrawals of foreign credits from German banks continued apace; indeed they even increased.[29] And something close to panic was aroused in Germany when, in its first report for June 1931, the Reichsbank was forced to announce that it had suffered withdrawals of more than one billion marks in gold and foreign credits and that its reserves were therefore already dangerously close to the legal minimum of 40 percent of printed currency. The continued depression of the German economy was accompanied, of course, by a constant diminution in government revenues. It quickly became apparent that the budget which had just been balanced with so much difficulty was already severely imperiled.

To meet this threat, the cabinet issued a new Emergency Decree for the Protection of the German Economy and Finance on June 5 over the President's signature. These new provisions required — as the government candidly announced — still more extensive sacrifices from large numbers of the population. The measures consequently encountered vehement opposition once again. To these protests the government could reply only that there was simply no alternative if Germany's financial system were to be preserved from chaos. The Finance Ministry was regarding the approach of every due date with the greatest apprehension, and the credit of the Reich had sunk so low that the ministry was finding even short-term credits extremely hard to raise. Indeed, in announcing this latest emergency decree, Brüning openly declared that "we have reached the limit of the privations we can impose upon our people." And for this reason he felt justified in demanding that the Germans be given "some relief from our intolerable reparation obligations."

This raising of the reparations issue was especially significant since it occurred on the eve of the visit that Brüning and Curtius were about to pay to London upon the invitation of the British government. If Brüning had excited German hopes with what he said, his words had also provoked uneasiness among the creditors abroad. The President of the United States let London know that he was seriously disturbed by Brüning's statement and that he feared lest the conference between British and German ministers lead to the announcement of a moratorium which would be harmful to the entire world.[30]

Now this, of course, had not been the intent of the British government at all. MacDonald and his cabinet held firmly to their original idea that the visit was primarily to be a friendly gesture with which they hoped to strengthen the prestige of Brüning's government in Germany. The British desired "no detailed nor even technical discussions," although they were perfectly willing to engage in a general exchange of views. In order to give as informal a tone as possible to the meeting, the Prime Minister invited the party to his country residence, Chequers, for the talks.

At Cuxhaven, on his way to England, Brüning was greeted by the dockworkers with clenched fists and the Communist war cry "Down with the Hunger Dictator!" And when he returned to Bremerhaven he was received by organized bands of National Socialists complete with their swastika flags and roars of "Germany, wake up! Down with Brüning!" [31] The extremists on both Right and Left chose this way of demonstrating the ideal of their national anthem: "Deutschland über alles, wenn es nur zu Schutz und Trutze brüderlich zusammenhält"! *

How different was their reception in England! Everyone went out of his way to give the German ministers a friendly welcome. Even King George received them. As the *Times* said: this royal reception was "a happy event which, it is to be hoped, will have contributed as much as the homely week-end at Chequers to convince the German people that the British Government looks with equal friendliness upon all foreign countries, desiring nothing more ardently than the obliteration of old dividing lines which have separated us." [32] The fact that the conversations at Chequers did not lead to any concrete conclusions was simply a confirmation of initial expectations, since the British government had emphasized from the start that the discussions would serve as a mutual exchange of views but were not expected to lead to any agreements.

Yet even this simple exchange of views had been completely candid and hence extremely useful, especially because Brüning had succeeded in making a deep impression upon the British ministers through the quiet objectivity with which he thoroughly, but dispassionately, portrayed Germany's economic plight. What interested these ministers particularly was the question whether the German government intended to lay claim to a moratorium in its Young Plan payments. For the British feared that such a step would constitute

---

* Dr. Eyck's version of the anthem might be freely translated: "Germany stands above all other claims, but only when we join fraternally to protect and advance our common aims." Dr. Eyck has indulged in the slight poetic license of substituting *nur* ("only") for *stets* ("constantly") in the original to point up the irony of the extremists' opposition and to stress again one of the theses of this book: responsible patriotism requires compromise and cooperation in the pursuit of worthy national and international goals. The first verse of the German national anthem reads:

> Deutschland, Deutschland über alles
> Ueber alles in der Welt,
> Wenn es stets zum Schutz und Trutze
> Brüderlich zusammenhält.

— TRANSLATORS.

not only a threat to their already precarious budget, but a shock to the credit system of all Europe.

During the course of the conversations at Chequers, three cables arrived from the British ambassador in Washington reporting that Americans were greatly disturbed by the German government's demand, in its announcement of June 5, that the Germans be given "relief from intolerable reparation obligations." The cables were read to the German visitors. The ensuing discussion was enlivened still further by the arrival of Sir Montagu Norman, governor of the Bank of England, who had been in constant telephonic contact with both Vienna and Basel (that is, the Bank for International Settlements) and who now informed the assembled ministers that the crisis of the Österreichische Kreditanstalt was threatening to become a crisis in Austrian government finances as well.[33] All Southeast Europe was endangered. Brüning and Curtius declared that, at the moment, the Germans would not request a moratorium, and that they intended to continue payments as long as possible. But they went on to say in strictest confidence that by November, at the latest, the time would come when they would be forced to request a moratorium. The conference closed with a communiqué that was appropriate to the talks: it restricted itself to friendly generalities.

It is understandable that in Germany this outcome should be regarded as meager and unsatisfactory. But the criticism from the nationalistic Right only demonstrated this wing's lack of any sense of responsibility. Hermann Göring, one of the principal leaders of the National Socialists, declared in a public address that the German government had issued the emergency decree simply in order to make further tribute payments, and that when his party came to power it would not honor any of the present cabinet's promises: "Go ahead and lend them as much as you please; we won't pay a bit of it back!"[34] Now there was an effective way to strengthen international confidence!

What the opposition wanted at this point was an immediate convening of the Reichstag. For the emergency decree and foreign affairs offered promising material for parliamentary debates. But such debate could yield only negative results, since the parties, united only in their opposition to the new burdens, were unable to form a majority agreeing to an alternative policy. Chancellor Brüning, who had returned to Berlin on June 10, made it clear to the Reichstag party leaders that he would resign if they insisted on demanding formally that the Reichstag be reconvened. At this time the economic situation was so desperate that a government crisis would have had catastrophic results. Thus at the meeting of the Reichstag Steering Committee (*Aeltestenrat*) on June 11 only the National Socialists, the German Nationalists, the Economic Party, and the Communists voted in favor of convening the Reichstag. It remained adjourned.

Two days later, on June 13, the Reichsbank raised its discount rate a full two points, from 5 percent to 7 percent. This was a storm signal, and the supporting argument offered by the bank's president, Luther, was quickly corroborated by the bank's mid-June report, which showed a further drop in German gold reserves and foreign credits from 2.7 billion marks to 1.9 billion. In emphasizing the frightful seriousness of the situation, Luther explained that this calling of loans and selling of securities by foreign investors did not reflect changes in the German economic scene but rather were motivated by other happenings, among which the events connected with the Österreichische Kreditanstalt were especially important. In the case of the Kreditanstalt, to be sure, utter chaos had been averted when the Bank of England granted the mortally threatened Austrian National Bank a short-term credit of 150 million schillings. In his memoirs, Curtius claims credit for having persuaded Montagu Norman to make this loan during the course of their conversations at Chequers.[35]

By mid-June, despite the temporary improvement wrought by the increased discount rate, the situation in Germany had become so tense that the cabinet was seriously considering violating the assurance that Chancellor Brüning had made at Chequers and requesting an immediate moratorium on reparation payments. But suddenly the German ministers found themselves relieved of the necessity of making this difficult decision when the President of the United States took a step fully as astonishing as it was magnanimous.

For some time President Hoover had been following European affairs with displeasure and even disapproval. Most recently, he had been irritated by Brüning's declaration of June 5 which he regarded as a warning that the Germans intended to request a moratorium. He feared that such a step might exacerbate the American economic crisis, which was already severe. But, on the other hand, the American ambassador to Berlin, Frederic Sackett, had just returned to Washington with firsthand news from Germany. Sackett was an admirer both of Germany and of Brüning, and the German Chancellor had repaid this esteem by taking the American into his complete confidence. Just before Sackett had left Berlin for Washington, Brüning had poured out his heart to him, explaining the full nature of the Germans' plight and convincing him that even the United States had an interest in supporting German defenders of parliamentary government — among whom Sackett counted Brüning — against the political forces menacing them at home. President Hoover agreed and later wrote in his memoirs, "these democratic governments were the base of any hope for a lasting peace in Europe." [36]

By mid-summer 1931, the situation in Central Europe was becoming increasingly critical, and the American secretary of the treasury, Andrew Mellon, who was in London at the time, urgently advised his government to make some helpful move. President Hoover then decided to cut the knot with one determined stroke. In order to create the proper impression in America, he asked President Hindenburg to send him a forceful plea for aid. The letter finally arrived, but only after Hoover had already announced his own decision. Hindenburg's closing words read as follows: "You, Mr. President, as representative of the great American nation, are in the position to take those steps which could bring about an immediate change in the situation that menaces Germany and the rest of the world today."

And so on June 20, 1931, the world learned that President Hoover had proposed a *one-year postponement* of all international payments of reparation and reconstruction debts. Since America was the final creditor to whom the greatest part of reparation payments was destined to flow, Hoover's statement really meant that the United States was willing to relieve its former allies of their war-debt payments for a year under the condition that they renounce their claims to German reparation payments for the same extent of time. This was an act of magnanimity unique in the history of finance.

In Germany Hoover's pronouncement was greeted as a delivery from certain ruin by both the government and all rational citizens. On June 22 the Berlin Exchange experienced a slight upward trend for the first time in many months. This encouraging sign afforded the prospect of necessary relief from the dangerously depressed prices of negotiable securities.[37] The money market had also become steadier, and the outflow of gold had ceased. The Rightist opposition press acted like a pack of wolves suddenly deprived of their prey. The limits of outraged frustration seemed to have been reached by Goebbel's newspaper, *Angriff*. Its headline over the report of the moratorium screamed: "Germany Again Victim of American Bluff." [38]

Unfortunately, the execution of the Hoover plan encountered difficulties which the American President had certainly not foreseen. While most of the great powers, Great Britain in particular, accepted the proposal and set aside their objections on details,

France was insisting on conditions which appeared to threaten the entire plan. For the French were the principal reparations creditors, and they were particularly interested in the "unprotected" payments which the Young Plan had excluded from any future moratorium.

The French were especially afraid that if even this unprotected payment were not to be paid during the proposed year of grace, then the regular reparation payments would never be resumed. (Later events were to prove this fear completely justified; one can even say that the Germans had hoped the Hoover Moratorium would have precisely this result.) For this reason the Chamber of Deputies emphasized "the indisputability of the unprotected payment" in its resolution of June 27 accepting the Hoover plan. Protracted negotiations, particularly between the Americans and French, proved necessary before agreement was finally reached on July 6. In this final form of the plan, the French *formally* maintained their insistence that Germany had to pay the unprotected sums. But this statement was an empty formalism, since the French also agreed that this payment would be immediately returned to Germany by the Bank for International Settlements. The French were therefore left with nothing more than a paper transaction of only symbolic value.

But there was another side to the negotiations which led to the Hoover plan, and they cast a special light on the German domestic scene. Both the British and American governments were of the opinion that the Germans could and, indeed, should contribute something to the institution of the Hoover Moratorium, which, after all, was designed to save them more than one and one-half billion marks in the current year. One thing they particularly had in mind was the steady increase in German military expenditures, especially the projected second armored cruiser, for which an initial payment of ten million marks had been allotted in the current budget. But when the American ambassador suggested to Brüning that perhaps the construction of this cruiser might be postponed, the Chancellor rejected the proposal out of hand. And one of the three reasons he gave for so doing was that a reduction in the naval budget would lead to President von Hindenburg's resignation.[39]

Naturally, the Americans were furious at this reply and instructed their ambassador to explain forcefully to the German government that the Germans could not expect to reap all the benefits of the Hoover Moratorium if they were unwilling to make even one contribution to the establishment of the plan.[40] Henderson accused the German ministers of having intentionally misconstrued the facts, assuring them that their President's threat to resign could not affect the considerations of the British government.[41] But the very fact that Brüning even made use of this strange argument shows to what a high degree he felt himself dependent on Hindenburg and on the Old Gentleman's moods.

The Old Gentleman clung to every item in the military budget with all the rigidity of his advanced age and the narrowness of his views. And Brüning felt obliged to do the same. The relationship between the Chancellor and the President is illustrated by a discussion which the undersecretary of the Finance Ministry held in November 1931 with representatives of other ministries and of the Reichsbank concerning the future balancing of the national budget. When some of the gentlemen proposed cuts in the military budget, the undersecretary replied: "Nothing can be achieved there. Last time we pressed as hard as we could with the result that if we had stuck to our point a *national crisis* would have ensued. With respect to the budget we are already living under a *military dictatorship* [*Militärdiktatur*]."

The second point on which the American and British governments urged German conciliatory steps was the issue of the Austro-German customs union. Although neither government had strong feelings about the project as such, they understood the political fears of the French and hoped to quite them by removing the specter of the threatened union from the international scene. But when the American ambassador tried to raise the subject, State Secretary von Bülow cut him off short by stating that such a suggestion was "clearly undiscussible." [42] And Curtius assumed the same attitude.

One might have some sympathy for this German point of view if there had been any real chance that the customs union would be realized. But every objective observer of the political scene must have known that the entire project had exploded in mid-air. It was particularly clear that the Austrians had absolutely no further possibility of executing the plan and, indeed, that they had lost all taste for the affair. One can therefore explain the attitude of the German government only by assuming that it wished to avoid any sign of yielding to the West lest it suffer further attacks from its Rightist opposition. For the nationalistic press demonstrated daily that its party leaders regarded the entire complex of international problems purely from the point of view of domestic politics, and sought to advance their own political fortunes by embarrassing their government. Thus, when the discussions between the French and the Americans had resulted in agreement and had thereby ensured the realization of the Hoover Moratorium, B. C. Newton, the British chargé d'affaires, cabled from Berlin: "National Socialist, and to some extent Hugenberg, newspapers show no gratitude for help given Germany, *for obvious reason that it interferes with political campaign against tribute payments.* Remainder of nationalist press is scarcely more reasonable."

Indeed, the same thing happened now that had occurred when the Rhineland had been freed. At that time the nationalistic press had raged against the French all during the time France refused to leave the Rhineland; and then, when the French did leave, the opposition treated their evacuation as the most natural thing in the world, reviled Stresemann, and taunted the French with *Stahlhelm* demonstrations. These same newspapers had been screaming for years now that Germany was being crushed by her reparation burden; but when the load was lifted for a year, they argued that the French had nullified the entire advantage of this move through their hesitation and went on railing in the same impassioned tone. On June 9 a convention of the nationalistic opposition, now jointly led by Hugenberg and Hitler, adopted a motion sharply directed against an alleged "attempt on the part of men presently in power to maintain the policy of fulfillment under new veiled forms despite the visible collapse of the nation and its economy." These patriotic gentlemen clearly considered their own struggle for power more important than the injury which their fatherland was bound to suffer when they shouted of its distress for all to hear.

The German economic scene was certainly depressing enough. On June 23, immediately after the Hoover Moratorium had been announced, the North German Wool Combing and Spinning Mills in Bremen, one of Germany's largest textile concerns, found itself forced to make public its desperate financial situation. It was clear that its total collapse was inevitable. This bankruptcy of "Northern Wool" could be attributed primarily to managerial malfeasance committed by its directors, the heretofore highly respected Lahusen brothers. But of course it was the bad business conditions, especially the depressed textiles prices, that had made their mistakes irreparable. In situations like this the threatening words of the cathedral choir that drove the tormented Gretchen to despair prove all too true: "What is secret will be heard,/ Nothing shall remain obscured."

The enormous attention that this commercial collapse provoked tended to increase public unrest all the more, since the outstanding bank debts of the bankrupt concern amounted to some 100 million marks. These fears were particularly concentrated on the Darmstadt National Bank (Danatbank), one of the four great German banks of deposit that were closely connected with Northern Wool. And in fact the Darmstadt Bank had lost approximately 40 million marks in the textile firm's collapse. The banking public began to withdraw deposits from the Darmstadt Bank, and quotations on its stock began to decline steadily. In order to keep the bottom from falling completely out of their market, the directors of the bank decided upon the questionable step of purchasing their own stock. They tried to borrow the funds necessary for this maneuver from the Reichsbank but were unable to furnish the first-class bills and notes which the Reichsbank required as security on loans.

Thus on July 8 the Darmstadt's directors were forced to inform the national Ministry of Finance and the Reichsbank that they were facing immense difficulties and that in a few days they would no longer be able to honor their depositors' demands for payment. At this point several days of excited and exciting discussions took place among the cabinet, the Chancellor himself, the Reichsbank, and major German banking houses. The president of the Reichsbank, Hans Luther, flew to London and Paris to request the central banks there for the necessary credits; but he returned with his pockets still empty. And so at noon on Saturday, July 11, 1931, the proprietors of the Darmstadt Bank informed the German government and the Reichsbank that, because of the massive withdrawals they had suffered in the last preceding days, they would be unable to open for business on Monday, July 13.

This was a catastrophe unique in the history of European high finance, and there was grave danger that the disaster would spread, engulfing other banking houses. For when people are seized with panic fright, they do not take time to consider the reliability of their debtors but have only one thought: "Every man for himself." To avoid the danger of a total rout, the cabinet decided to guarantee the Darmstadt Bank's deposits as a measure of public safety, and to appoint a public trustee of the bank's affairs.

The necessary decree was immediately published. On Monday the bank's doors remained locked, posted with the government guarantees. But now, of course, the run started on the other banks, and that afternoon their representatives appeared at the Chancellor's office with the message that no German bank could open on the morrow and that at least two "bank holidays" would have to be declared. Brüning had no choice but to announce these holidays despite all his misgivings. For it was easy to see that the matter would not be settled in two days. His doubts were well justified, for not until August 5 could normal payments be resumed. In the meantime it had proved necessary to close the German stock exchanges also. They were not reopened until September 3.

On Wednesday, July 15, the Reichsbank raised its discount rate from 7 to 10 percent. This measure remained in effect until September 1. One emergency decree then followed another, establishing government control of foreign credits, tightening the administration of these controls and of the general tax laws, and even introducing a charge of 100 marks for foreign travel — a charge which was abolished a few weeks later, on August 26, after protest from foreign countries which feared a loss in German tourist trade. Another emergency decree of July 27 authorized the German government to participate in a new Bank of Guarantees and Acceptances (*Akzept-und Garantiebank*) which, in collaboration with major German banks, had been founded with a capital of 200 million marks in order to re-establish the Darmstadt Bank in the German credit structure. During all this time the opposition parties were doing their best to make the situation even more desperate by trying to force a reconvening of the Reichstag. But they did not prevail against Brüning's majority.

Yet all the emergency decrees in the world could not patch the enormous hole that had been ripped in the financial fabric of the German economy by the constant withdrawal of gold and foreign credits. Dietrich declared that, in the course of the credit crisis which had followed the Reichstag elections of September 1930, between three and four billion marks had been exported from Germany. Financial experts estimated that there was still between five and six billion marks' worth of foreign capital in Germany, almost all in the form of short-term loans. Schacht's policies had been directed against the less dangerous long-term foreign credits, while ignoring these vitally important short-term obligations.

The German cabinet could not solve a problem of this magnitude alone; it required the assistance of other governments. Fortunately these other governments realized that a danger of truly international proportions was at hand. For such a severe crisis in one of the largest and most highly developed countries of Europe was bound to spread to other lands through the interwoven strands of international trade if it were not swiftly solved. The British government was quick to call a conference of the major powers, to which Germany was of course invited. The German Chancellor, aware of the special importance these negotiations would have for France, decided to go to London *by way of Paris*.[43]

Brüning personally had not liked to make this choice. He had the strong feeling that the spirit and outlook of Frenchmen were foreign to his own, and he felt much more at home with the English, whose language he had mastered. Moreover, he still regarded France as that hostile power which, even after the conclusion of peace, continued to make things as difficult as possible for Germany and nullified by hesitation and hedging whatever concessions it grudgingly gave. But his advisers had reminded him how important it was that the French not suspect the Germans of intentionally avoiding them in order to arrive at some private agreement with the British and Americans.

And so it was that on the evening of July 17, 1931, Brüning, accompanied by Curtius and Bülow, left Berlin on the Paris Express. Also present in the French capital at this time were not only British Foreign Secretary Henderson, but also two members of President Hoover's cabinet — Secretary of State Stimson and Secretary of the Treasury Mellon — and representatives of Italy, Belgium, and Japan. The head of the French government was Pierre Laval, whom both English and German observers credited with an honest desire to effect a reconciliation with Germany. Laval explicitly admitted the seriousness of Germany's economic situation, which Brüning had depicted in his impressive and objective way, and he mentioned the possibility of helping the Germans with an international loan. But the conditions which he sought to attach to this credit were immediately rejected by Brüning and Curtius.

These conversations in Paris were merely the informal prelude to the London Conference, which took place from Monday, July 20, through Thursday, July 23, 1931, between representatives of Germany and those of her creditors, including America. The ministers of these countries had brought both their financial and economic advisers with them. The published proceedings of the conference show that all the participants demonstrated an honest desire to effect some fruitful agreement, but that they were confronted with some difficulties which were simply insuperable.[44]

Ramsay MacDonald, generally considered no longer at his peak of power, directed the proceedings with his customary calm objectivity in his host's role as British Prime Minister. The French had insisted from the start that the topic of reparations be rigidly excluded from negotiation. The only one to object to this agreement was the British chancellor of the exchequer, Snowden,[45] and MacDonald managed to bring his colleague back into line before Snowden's deviation had done any real harm.[46]

The stated theme of the conference was Germany's present economic plight and the possible means of her assistance. All parties to the conversations emphasized that Germany's economic situation in no way justified the general distrust that had found expression in the massive withdrawals of foreign funds. From this one must conclude that the reasons for the distrust were something other than economic. It was the German political scene which disturbed the other conferees, and they all pointed to the Reichstag elections of September 1930 as the event which had precipitated the withdrawals. What a stroke of political genius it therefore was when, on July 21, Hugenberg and Hitler sent an open telegram to Brüning in London declaring that they would not recognize as binding any agreements of the London Conference which contained French encroachments on German sovereignty.[47]

Brüning, who again was making an excellent impression, wanted only two things from the conference: the assurance that withdrawals of foreign funds would cease and the promise that Germany would receive another loan. On the other hand, he declared himself strongly opposed to a moratorium, since such a step would have the gravest consequences for Germany's credit and for her economy.

Such a new loan would have had to come from France. England was experiencing troubles enough of her own, as the rest of the world was to learn a few weeks later when the Labour government confessed its inability to solve the nation's financial problems and resigned. And England's difficulties became even more manifest when, on September 20, the "National Coalition" government, which had succeeded the Labour cabinet, took the earth-shaking step of leaving the gold standard. Thus the governor of the Bank of England, Montagu Norman, had good reasons for maintaining a guarded attitude at the London Conference and even for explaining, in confidence, that he had no funds with which to help the Germans. Yet on the other hand, the French might have been persuaded to make a further loan, but they were demanding conditions of a distinctly political cast.

This impasse had been apparent even at Paris in the conversations between the French and German ministers; now, in London, the British foreign secretary, Arthur Henderson, tried to learn from Curtius and Bülow just where the difficulties lay. According to Henderson's notes on his conversations with the two Germans,[48] it appears that the French desired some formal assurance that the Germans would not use Article 19 of the League Covenant * to raise the question of their eastern border — and of the so-called Polish Corridor in particular. Curtius explained, in confidence, to Henderson that the present state of German public opinion would not permit his government to make such a formal guarantee, although the

---

* Article 19 provided that "The Assembly may from time to time advise the reconsideration by Members of the League of treaties which have become inapplicable and the consideration of international conditions whose continuance might endanger the peace of the world." TRANSLATORS.

German cabinet had absolutely no intention of raising the issue in the foreseeable future.

Henderson, whose honest desire for peace cannot be doubted, undertook the task of finding some compromise solution. He pointed out to Curtius that it was not a question of asking the Germans to surrender a recognized right; they were merely being requested to leave it in abeyance for a specified length of time. At this point Bülow interrupted to declare sharply that this was a meaningless distinction, that German public opinion would never accept a verbal formula which admitted even the barest possibility that German rights might be left in abeyance. This was too much even for Arthur Henderson. He called Bülow's attitude utterly impossible, likening it to Nero's fiddling while Rome burned.[49] It is therefore no wonder that the entire conference proved fruitless and that the Germans were obliged to leave London as they had left Paris, no richer than they had come.

Yet the London negotiations had not been completely without value to Germany. Even though she had received no new money, the withdrawal of previous loans was finally stopped, and this was a gain of real importance. The conference had recommended to all creditors who still had funds in Germany that they desist from demanding repayment for a specified length of time. The result of this recommendation was the so-called "Standstill Agreement" (*Stillhalte-Abkommen*) which was initially concluded for a six-month period, but which was constantly renewed. In this way a serious menace to Germany was removed.

But there was another side to this matter, one that most members of the conference did not immediately perceive. Carl Melchior, who again was assisting the German delegation with his counsel, saw the point at once, for he not only was familiar with the practical implications of such agreements as an active officer of the Warburg Bank, but he also had a sense of theoretical principles that is rare among such men of affairs. Melchior's observation was given after conversing with important English creditors whom he had helped persuade to postpone their demands for payments legally due them. He remarked to Hans Schäffer, state secretary of the Ministry of Finance:

What we have just experienced is the destruction of the ground-rules of the capitalistic system. Yet the system depends on the strictest observation of these very rules. This is the first time that I have had to refuse to fulfill an obligation to which I had freely committed my name simply because the state required me to refuse. The capitalistic system in Germany will not survive such a deviation from its rules. For the deviations will constantly increase, and the system will accordingly dissolve.

The truth of these words became apparent in the years that followed, when breach of promise became a common tactic.

German interests were also served when the London Conference requested the Basel Bank for International Settlements to appoint a committee of experts to study Germany's immediate need for further credit and to explore the possibility of converting some of Germany's short-term obligations into long-term loans. The members of this committee were to be appointed by the presidents of the several central banks. As German representative on the committee, Melchior served his country once again with skill and knowledge. The governor of the Bank of England had had the brilliant idea of appointing Sir Walter Layton, editor of the *Economist*, as the British member of the committee. It was Layton who composed the group's report, and his summation of the experts' conclusions proved so convincing and apt that it was quickly signed by all the committee members on August 18.[50]

Layton's report made formal recognition of the determined efforts which the German government, operating under trying conditions, had made to set Germany's public finances on a sound basis. And it agreed that if Brüning's policies were executed rigorously they would serve to strengthen German credit. The report then presented a determined argument for making any future loans to Germany exclusively in long-term credits, but it immediately went on to present with equal emphasis the reasons why people were hesitant to subscribe to such loans at the moment. Two principal difficulties were candidly discussed: "The first difficulty is one associated with political risks. As long as the relations between Germany and the other European powers are not established on the basis of friendly cooperation and mutual trust, and as long as the attendant internal difficulties of Germany are not removed, no assurance can be given for a durable peaceful economic development. This political stability is the first and most fundamental prerequisite for establishing credit."

This conclusion was undoubtedly correct, and the admonition to the governments of the world that they take steps to restore international confidence and that they, themselves, establish their international political relationships on a basis of *mutual trust* was wise and justified. The trouble with such prudent counsel is, however, that everyone thinks that it is directed at his neighbors, not himself. Everyone believes the other people responsible for the absence of good faith. Thus the Germans expected the French to take the first step toward a restoration of mutual confidence, while the French replied that Germany had no claim to such confidence so long as the National Socialist movement, which the French regarded as a real threat, continued to grow at the rate indicated by recent provincial elections.

Anyone able to look behind the scenes could not help but observe how Brüning's cabinet, which stood in public opposition to the National Socialists, paid deference to the radical Right in matters of foreign policy. One need only recall Bülow's remark to Arthur Henderson. It is true that Brüning expressed himself more circumspectly in a conversation with Layton on August 23. But Layton nevertheless got the impression that the Chancellor was so impressed with the weakness of his own position that he was afraid to undertake any serious discussions with the French unless certain that the British were on his side.[51]

The second basic difficulty stressed by Layton's report was of a political-economic nature. The system of international payments that had developed since the war involved enormous payments from debtor countries to their creditors. Such payments required the free movement of goods in international trade. But it was precisely this necessary freedom of movement that the governments were constantly restricting with one obstacle after another. Here Layton and the committee were clearly thinking of the steady growth of protectionism in international trade, of which the United States had recently afforded a striking example in the Smoot-Hawley Tariff. Layton discussed this matter, too, with Brüning, and the German Chancellor demonstrated a readiness to conclude a more liberal commercial agreement with Great Britain. But nothing ever came of the idea, in part, perhaps, because of the political changes which took place in England on the following day, August 24, with the resignation of the Labour cabinet.

Further consequences of the July London Conference were the visits which both British (MacDonald and Henderson) and French (Laval and Briand) statesmen paid to Berlin shortly thereafter as demonstrations of their good will and the especially high regard in which their governments held Chancellor Brüning. The most noteworthy event during the French ministers' stay was Briand's visit to Stresemann's grave in the Luisenstadt Cemetery of Berlin. We shall never know what Briand thought and felt at the grave of the man who had been both his opponent and his friend. But we shall probably not be far wrong if we assume that Briand sensed he was also standing at the grave of an entire epoch, whose central figure he had been and which now was quickly coming to an end. A few months later, on January 8, 1932, Briand retired from political life. Fate was kind enough to spare him the necessity of watching his policy of reconciliation be replaced by one which led to a second world war. On March 7, 1932, only two months after his resignation, death overtook the sick and exhausted man for whom Europe had no further use.

These Berlin visits had scarcely any practical results. Although they showed that Brüning enjoyed a signal reputation abroad, they had no effect on his domestic opposition. Indeed, not only did this opposition remain highly critical of his policies, but all signs indicated that it was still growing. To this was added the severe defeat that German foreign policy suffered on the issue of the customs union with Austria.

Curtius had kept pretending as long as possible that there was still some life in the project, even though he was quite aware that the sooner it was buried, the happier Austria would be. But finally, at Geneva on September 3, 1931, Schober stated that the Austrian government had decided to drop the project of a customs union, and Curtius, who undoubtedly had been given prior notification of Schober's intent, had no choice but to voice Germany's agreement. With this, the project was permanently disposed of, and there was only theoretical significance to the declaration by the International Court at The Hague, a few days later, that the proposed customs union conflicted with the commitments Austria had made in 1922 upon receiving the League of Nations loan. But this decision represented the views of a bare majority of the court, nine to eight, and it is therefore not astonishing that it did not receive unanimous approval, particularly among German jurists. Thus it was that, shortly afterwards, a pathetic convention chairman of the German Jurists Society was emboldened to taunt the Hague Tribunal with Schiller's words: "The history of the world is the world court."

But this was not the point. In the first place, the International Court, which by its very nature is a court of both original and final jurisdiction, can — and indeed must — claim the time-honored principle: "Rome has spoken; the case is closed." For this had been the purpose of its founding. Second, and even more important, the legality of the matter was far from being its most important aspect. Any reasonably objective observer had to admit that the Western powers, especially the French, could not help but regard the prospective customs union as the first step toward an *Anschluss*, regardless of how carefully the two governments had tried to formulate the terms of the project so as not to conflict with Austria's treaty obligations.

The intensity of France's feeling is suggested by the following incident. Marcus Wallenberg was a highly esteemed Swedish banker and an outspoken friend of Germany. Indeed, he had often put his valuable services at her disposal. But in June 1931, after an extensive conversation with Tardieu, Wallenberg told a German friend that he could now understand the anger of the French at the prospect of the customs union, even though he thought this wrath should have been directed at Austria alone. For, in making their legal argument that the proposed union did not violate their treaty obligations, the Austrians had tried to utilize a version of the treaty of 1922 which, as they very well knew, had intentionally been kept somewhat obscure lest it bring the Austrian government of that time into domestic disrepute.

Be that as it may; the Germans, from ministers down to school teachers, had always taken pleasure in quoting Bismarck's remark that "Politics is the art of the possible." Yet when it proved necessary for the Germans to cultivate this art, they invariably showed that they had not grasped the wisdom of Bismarck's words at all. Was it really possible for so weak and impoverished a country as Austria to carry out a policy which was certain to bring it into conflict with at least some of the great powers, and especially with those great powers to which it was heavily in debt? And was Germany strong enough to afford to entice Austria into such an escapade and then to join in the adventure herself? Today no one will doubt that the answer to these questions should have been an unmistakable no. And was not Julius Curtius, a former German minister of economics and now minister of foreign affairs, able and indeed obliged to arrive at this same answer? Again one must conclude that his motives and calculations centered on domestic affairs rather than foreign policy. He had wished to steal the nationalistic opposition's thunder by demonstrating that he could show just as much initiative as they in finding ways to advance the "national interest." For naturally he too knew that, as Bülow had told Rumbold, the nationalists were screaming for his scalp.

And so Curtius was not surprised to discover that now, after this defeat, his scalp was as good as lost. As early as September 1931, at the German Nationalist Convention, Hugenberg directed two speeches squarely at Brüning's government, terming the abandonment of the customs union a German defeat and demanding the resignation not only of Curtius, but of the entire cabinet, together with the dissolution of the Reichstag and new elections. The direction of German foreign policy, Hugenberg insisted, had to be entrusted to conservative hands. Would one do Hugenberg an injustice if one were to draw two conclusions from his speeches: first, that he too had interpreted the customs union as a first step toward a political *Anschluss;* and second, that he had inwardly welcomed the project's collapse because Brüning's consequent embarrassment seemed to bring him closer to his goal?

The real tragedy was that the German economy suffered the actual consequences of the ill-fated experiment. This was the year of the Hoover Moratorium; temporarily, at least, Germany was relieved of reparation payments. The consequence of this should have been an upward trend in the German economy, especially if those people were right who regarded the reparations as the most important cause, if not the *sole* cause, of Germany's difficulties. But the withdrawals of foreign credit which had followed upon the attempted customs union exceeded even the amounts of the reparation payments which the Germans had been spared. Naturally the opposition was quick to speak disdainfully of the recent "false spring" that the German economy had experienced on the strength of these foreign loans. But this sort of economic development through foreign loans had occurred frequently throughout the nineteenth and twentieth centuries in countries that lacked capital. By no means the least significant of such economies was that of the United States, which was a debtor nation until the First World War.

Of course such a dependent economic position has its own political consequences, and they can be ignored only at considerable risk. For a debtor nation must try to avoid any step that might disturb international, that is, its creditors', confidence. And yet this is precisely what Germany — and the German electorate even more so than the German government — had been doing ever since Stresemann's death and the collapse of the second Great Coalition. Thus, for instance, Hugenberg had gone out of his way, at the Nationalists' convention, to declare that neither he nor his party considered themselves bound by any agreements which Brüning had already made or might make in the future. Hugenberg had made clear that he was referring to the negotiations the government was then carrying on with the French. Clearly this was not the best possible way to reassure France and to engender Western confidence in the future of Germany and the peace of Europe.

It was obvious now that Curtius had to go. Brüning, however, was able to survive the storm, for the President desired him to stay. The Chancellor did submit his formal resignation, together with those of his entire cabinet, but only to be charged immediately with the responsibility for forming another government. Although most of the ministers were retained, Brüning's second cabinet did reveal a strong shift toward the Right. It would not be wrong to regard this tendency as an accommodation on Brüning's part to the President's desires.

This was certainly true in the case of Joseph Wirth, who was one of the ministers omitted from this second Brüning cabinet. For Wirth had been considered by both his friends and enemies as one of the most vigorous protagonists of republican government in the Center Party, despite all the water he had gradually poured into his democratic wine. But, as the President's undersecretary, Otto Meissner, pointed out,[52] the aged Hindenburg had never forgotten Wirth's address after Rathenau was murdered, in which the then Centrist Chancellor had declared: "The enemy stands on the Right!" And on September 20, 1931, Gröner wrote that "the 'Old Man of the Mountain' wishes all too much to have other men in place of Wirth and Guérard." (Theodor Guérard was also dropped.) Gröner did, however, go on to observe that "Wirth has hardly any more ideas of his own, anyway. His worthy state secretary [Erich Zweigert] runs the ministry while Joseph devotes his time to Pilsen beer." [53]

But Hindenburg's influence was not limited simply to the selection or rejection of specific ministers for the cabinet. His request to Brüning to form a second government contained the provision that, in so doing, the Chancellor should make "no political commitments with any party." In simple truth this meant that the President saw no need to consult the parties, and that the new government was to be even more a "presidential cabinet" than the preceding one had been.

All these efforts were directed primarily against the Social Democrats. Until now it had been their votes which had helped Brüning maintain a majority in the Reichstag, thus keeping the presidential emergency decrees from being nullified there. Hindenburg and Brüning therefore had every reason to be grateful to them. Yet during this same time the relations between the German Chancellor and the Socialist premier of Prussia had cooled considerably. Otto Braun had taken special offense in August, when Brüning had altered an emergency decree, which had been issued in July to cope with a dangerously irresponsible press, in such a way as to point it obviously against the government of Prussia. For in its campaign against the Hugenberg referendum, Braun's cabinet had required the newspapers to carry a statement of correction which had provoked massive indignation on the Right.

On August 20 Braun's state secretary, Robert Weismann, expressed these Prussian misgivings about Brüning in a conversation with the British ambassador, Rumbold.[54] According to Weismann,

even Rudolf Breitscheid, who up to then had been leading the Social Democrats' support for Brüning in the Reichstag, had begun
to wonder whether it was wise for them to continue this policy. One
can well imagine how such a development might have roused the
old field marshal's wrath at the presumptuous Socialists, and there
can be no doubts that Schleicher would waste no opportunity to
drop a hint. It was about this time that Schleicher first made direct
contact with Hitler, certain, of course, that he (Schleicher) would
keep control of the game firmly in his own hands.

Hindenburg, for his part, had probably reverted to that distaste
for Social Democrats which seemed natural to an old Prussian officer. For what else could one expect of a man who, even during the
World War, had told the Imperial Chancellor Bethmann-Hollweg:
"This talk about the German Empire and the Emperor is all well
and good, but [I am] too old for that sort of thing and [see] in him
only the King of Prussia." [55] In any event, Hindenburg's recommendations for the new cabinet clearly demonstrate that he had no intention of deferring to the Social Democrats.

Thus, for instance, Hindenburg suggested that Wirth be succeeded in the Ministry of Interior by Gessler, a man whose unpopularity among the Social Democrats was apparent even to those who
did not differ with his views. Now, to say that Gessler was unacceptable to the Socialists is not to argue that his nomination was ill-
advised; for, because of his parliamentary talents and rhetorical skill,
he undoubtedly would have provided the government considerable
strength in the Reichstag. But Gessler firmly declined to join the
cabinet.

Finally a combination came into being that had probably first
sprung from Schleicher's fruitful mind. It also, however, had the support of Hindenburg and Brüning. In this new arrangement, Gröner,
the minister of defense, also became the national minister of interior.
Brüning defended this dual appointment before the Reichstag with
the argument that because of the endangered state of the nation a
firm concentration of all government power was required. In truth,
however, it was the generals' intention — and to a lesser extent
Gröner's, as well — to bring the Ministry of Interior under their influence in this way. In a personal letter composed shortly after his
new appointment Gröner wrote: "Fortunately, in the Ministry of Interior I have a very intelligent state secretary who is delighted to find
himself backed by a minister who has put an end to all the endless
partisan vacillations. His name is Zweigert, and he is most happy
to work hand in glove with Schleicher. My becoming this sort of
'Double Eagle' is due principally to the Old Gentleman, whose spe-

cial idea it was." [56] Of particular interest here is the attested harmony between Zweigert and Schleicher. For a few months later, when Schleicher forced Gröner to resign, he blamed the authorities in the Ministry of Interior for having led their minister astray.

But Schleicher's double game had begun some time before. On November 4, 1931, almost simultaneously with Gröner's personal letter that is quoted just above, Schleicher wrote a letter to Ernst Röhm, leader of the National Socialists' Storm Troops. In this letter Schleicher shows himself convinced that the National Socialist Party and its leader were employing absolutely legal methods. He also denies having any influence in the Ministry of Interior. This latter assertion is, of course, in direct contradiction to Gröner's letter of approximately this same date. But even more significant is Schleicher's anger at the editors of the *Berliner Tageblatt* and the *Volkszeitung*, which had just reported his conversations with Hitler. He calls them "Mosse Communists" * and inveighs against their "malicious and false reports." [57] Now it is true enough that Schleicher liked to use forceful and informal language. But when he branded these democratic journalists of good repute Communists, he was engaging in the crassest form of libel — unless one is to assume that, in his jocular, dilettantish way, Schleicher simply did not consider it necessary to distinguish among any of the parties left of the Centrists.

Many Leftist journals suspected Schleicher of having been the one who arranged Hitler's audience with Hindenburg on October 10, 1931, that is, during the cabinet crisis. If it had been Schleicher's purpose to make the successful demagogue acceptable to Hindenburg in this way, the general failed completely. Hitler's rhetorical talents were utterly wasted on the old man, and the personal impression made by this "Bohemian corporal," as Hindenburg called him, could not be anything but negative. But if Hindenburg had believed that he could persuade Hitler to assume a more positive attitude toward German political life, he was as fully wrong in his way as Schleicher and Hitler had been in theirs. And so the audience was without immediate results for either party, and Hitler quickly demonstrated that he was not going to be influenced in his demagoguery by any respect for the aged field marshal.

In other respects the results of the rearrangement of Brüning's government were not very impressive. It was characteristic of the Chancellor that he appointed no successor to Curtius; he assumed the Foreign Ministry himself. This disposition naturally increased

* The Rudolph Mosse Verlag, a well-known liberal concern, published, among other journals, the *Berliner Tageblatt*. TRANSLATORS.

the importance of the state secretary for foreign affairs, and here no change was made. Bülow stayed on, and he was the man who, in the opinion of the British ambassador, had been even more responsible for the ill-fated plan of a customs union than was Curtius, who enjoyed considerable respect among the British. Sir Horace wrote of him: "My principal colleagues and I regret Dr. Curtius' departure from the Ministry for Foreign Affairs. Although he had neither the imagination, the wide outlook, nor the political genius of his predecessor [Stresemann], he was a level-headed man, whilst his quiet and courteous manner made him pleasant to deal with." [58] Hindenburg had wished to see the German ambassador to London, Freiherr von Neurath, take Curtius' place, if only because of the sympathy induced in the President by the ambassador's aristocratic lineage. But nothing came of the idea, probably because Neurath thought the time not yet ripe for such a move.[59] The other new appointments to the cabinet were without any great political significance. And the *Vorwärts* consoled itself with the observation that Brüning had at least not included anyone in his cabinet who would have a provoking effect on labor.

On the other side the nationalistic opposition immediately made clear in the strongest conceivable manner that it would continue to oppose the government with all the means at its disposal. On Saturday, October 11, 1931, two days after the appointment of the new cabinet and one day after Hitler's audience with Hindenburg, all the constituent elements of this opposition — Hugenberg's German Nationalists, the *Stahlhelm*, and Hitler's National Socialists — assembled for a massive demonstration at Bad Harzburg. The purpose of this demonstration was expressed in a long-winded declaration that Hugenberg probably composed himself. It is quite sufficient to quote only the first sentence, for it amply illustrates how these men twisted the recent German past into a caricature as irresponsible and, unfortunately, as popular as it was false:

> For years the nationalistic opposition has been remonstrating in vain against the ineffectiveness of German governments and the machinery of the German state in the face of Marxists' terror tactics; against the creeping bolshevization of German culture and the disintegration of our nation through class warfare; against the deliberate exclusion of nationalist forces from the direction of the state; against government policies which go even beyond the *Diktat* of Versailles in the political, economic, and military castration of Germany, etc.

These nationalist brethren, who counted on the Communists' assistance at every Reichstag vote, then went on to boast of their determination "to preserve our country from the chaos of bolshevism." Nothing is to be gained today from a detailed study of the demagogic arguments on which this opposition based its demand that both the German and the Prussian governments be overthrown. Indeed, there is no reason to pay the slightest attention to the addresses delivered at Harzburg since — save for a single exception — they were merely repetitions of well-worn phrases.

The one thing that did lend significance to this Harzburg assembly was the list of participants. Naturally a few Hohenzollern princes were present again, along with the usual number of retired officers, this time led by Herr von Seeckt, who now belonged to the Reichstag as a delegate of the German People's Party. The fact that his party had participated in all the German governments throughout the period characterized by the assembly in such a defamatory way clearly embarrassed Seeckt no more than did the high honorarium which Gröner says Seeckt was receiving from the Foreign Ministry for unnamed and unknown services.[60] The greatest impression made by the Harzburg rally on the general public was that the National Socialists had now apparently united completely with what was usually called the more "honorable" members of the opposition.

In point of fact, however, this firm alliance was a complete mirage. Actually Hitler took great pleasure in ridiculing his "allies" in every possible way. He was especially scornful of the *Stahlhelm*, as was convincingly documented in a brochure directed against Hitler and written by Colonel Duesterberg, the former deputy leader of the *Stahlhelm*. There is only one thing wrong with Duesterberg's pamphlet: he did not write it until 1949. That is, he waited until long after the seed sown at Harzburg had yielded a crop of German horror, after the harvest had been threshed, and after the entire Hitler nightmare was over before publishing his indictment. In the meantime, of course, Duesterberg had learned through personal experience just who was really exercising "terror tactics" in Germany, and in his concentration camp he had seen the brown-shirted guards mistreat their former Harzburg allies, who had since become nothing more than "*Stahlhelm* swine." [61]

The only Harzburg speech with which we should concern ourselves is that of Hjalmar Schacht. The former president of the Reichsbank introduced himself to his audience as a concerned patriot who was a member of no party. He then proceeded to wallow in an unrestrained philippic against the present "system," accusing it of "dishonesty, disorder, and indecision." It was clear that in Hitler, who was listening to this effusion from the speakers' table, Schacht saw Germany's hope and guarantee for a return to "decency and order."

Once more he played the tragic role of the sacrificial lamb that, at the Paris Conference of Experts, had been the victim of a German government "which had enjoyed no national support." This pose could astonish no one who was aware of Schacht's unbridled egoism.

What really evoked astonishment and alarm was the imputation Schacht cast on the truthfulness of the Reichsbank's monthly statements, which, if one were to believe him, were obscuring actual conditions for political reasons. This accusation was not only a thrust at Luther, whom Schacht had not yet forgiven for accepting the post he had been required to resign; it was also — indeed principally — a part of the opposition's campaign to destroy whatever faith might be developing in a German economic recovery. These great patriots who were gathered at Harzburg regarded Germany's economic distress as the battering ram with which they hoped to penetrate and capture the citadel of political power. Nothing would have been less welcome to their eyes than the sight of Brüning's government coping successfully with its problems. Thus, no matter how hard the statesmen and the experts among Germany's former foes tried to convince the world that Germany was, indeed, worthy of faith and credit, these superpatriots kept bellowing for all the world to hear that Germany's plight was not only desperate, but even worse than official German figures would suggest. Since faith and credit are essentially psychological factors, such inflammatory agitation was bound to have a disturbing and depressing effect on the German economy, particularly when it was uttered by a former president of the Reichsbank and a recognized expert in the field.

And so the nationalistic opposition took delight in the depression and in observing that once again they had been correct. It is true that Schacht had been right on several points: German short-term debts had proved to be greater than the Basel experts had estimated on the strength of German figures. But it certainly was not patriotic for Schacht to shout this news out to the entire world without having told, let alone asked, his own government first.

But this time, at least, the German government did not suffer Schacht's outrageous behavior in silence. Dietrich, the minister of finance, declared in his uniquely crisp, effective way that Germany's national interest made statements like Schacht's intolerable; that Schacht's statement that German currency no longer sufficed for normal commercial needs was absolutely false; that, indeed, Schacht's entire argument was based upon untruths and that it was irresponsible and liable to deprive Germany of her last sources of credit. And it was obvious that Brüning had Schacht in mind when, in his speech which opened the Reichstag on Tuesday, October 13, he remarked: "I will not take objection here to specific expressions which were used at Harzburg. But as a responsible politician I must therefore take all the more objection to the fact that expressions were employed which could ruin the German people's faith in their own currency."

The British ambassador found Schacht's address "sensational" and wrote an extensive report on the Harzburg meeting which included the following remarks:

> Prior to the meeting, the democratic *Frankfurter Zeitung* appears to have had wind of Dr. Schacht's intention to make an alarmist pronouncement. At any rate, in its morning issue of the 11th [of October] it asserted that industrialist circles, if they could not win over Dr. Brüning to inflation, were disposed to bring about a fresh banking crisis by a deliberate display of pessimism, and in that way to engineer a collapse of the mark.[62]

It is not justifiable to assume that Schacht had been willing to let himself be used by these circles. Yet one can properly say that such rumors, of which he certainly was aware, should have made him all the more cautious in his public utterances. But one cannot expect a man so blinded by ambition to be governed by those considerations which would be compelling to a professional politician.

Thus the total effect of the raucous meeting at Bad Harzburg was the addition of one more entry to the dictionary of political terminology: "the Harzburg Front." This term was reserved essentially for reference to Hugenberg and his hearties. The National Socialists made little use of it. They were, of course, quite prepared to accept henchmen's service from Hugenberg and the *Stahlhelm*.[63] But not for a moment would Adolf Hitler think of letting Hugenberg and company help determine his strategy and tactics. Only a few weeks later, at a German Nationalist executive committee meeting on December 2, Hugenberg complained that, in spite of the Harzburg meeting, the National Socialist agitation was being directed sharply against the German Nationalists throughout Germany.[64]

In any event the men of Harzburg failed to achieve the real goal of their entire meeting: namely, the fall of Brüning. On Tuesday, October 13, at the session of the Reichstag which followed almost immediately upon the Harzburg weekend, the National Socialist and German National delegations presented a joint resolution that "the Reichstag withdraw its confidence from the government." And their hopes rose high when Eduard Dingeldey, the leader of the German People's Party, declared that although he had a great personal appreciation of Brüning's qualities, his delegation had decided that after their many disillusionments they were unable to support the Chancellor further. Now at last Hugenberg could hope to fell his foe.

But on October 16, when the votes were counted, it became apparent that the Rightists' motion of no confidence had failed again, this time by 295 votes to 270. Several delegates had defected from the German People's Party in order to preserve the inheritance of its founder, Gustav Stresemann. Among these, old Professor Wilhelm Kahl and Siegfried von Kardorff, together with a few friends, voted for Brüning, while two others abstained. And Hans von Eynern, a People's Party delegate in the Prussian Landtag, rebelled against Dingeldey's leadership and resigned his seat. He accompanied this action with a sharply worded declaration in which he stated his adherence to Stresemann's "course of political reason" and called Dingeldey's "option for the National Socialists . . . an irrevocable act" that could never be undone.[65] The Agrarians (*Landvolkpartei*), on whom Brüning had formerly set hope, voted against him with only one exception, Schlange-Schöningen. But the Economic Party backed him solidly, and so both the proposed resolution and the opposition's other motions were rejected.

Brüning could ascribe a large share of the credit for this victory to his own personal efforts. Both the form and content of the addresses with which he had repeatedly joined in the debate had been far above the level of most of the other speakers. With reference to extremists on both the Right and Left, he had emphasized in his concluding address that "the line which must be drawn if Germany is to be saved will always be a line of *compromise and balance* and not one of the *suppression* of one side or the other." However wise those words may have been, and however little they can be debated today, in Germany at that time there were literally millions of people to whom the prospect of suppressing the other side comprised the main attraction of political activity.

Braun had no more reason than did Brüning to bend before the Harzburg bombast. But his Prussian government did suffer a severe loss in the resignation of Hermann Höpker-Aschoff, minister of finance. This resignation had nothing to do with the Harzburg meeting. It was based, rather, on technical differences over certain legislative details. Men can have quite varying opinions on the question whether these differences were so critical that they made Höpker-Aschoff's resignation necessary. Both Otto Braun and Carl Severing reject the minister's argument in the accounts they give of this affair in their memoirs, and many of Höpker's party colleagues who also were unable to see why he felt required to take this step, spoke of his thick

Westphalian head. Braun was not successful in his quest for a worthy replacement. For Otto Klepper, president of the Prussian Central Cooperative Bank, who accepted the post, proved unable to win the respect appropriate to his office in either the Landtag or the Prussian cabinet.[66]

At the end of November 1931, when the so-called "Boxheim Papers" came to light, men were reminded of Brüning's Reichstag speech in which he had recommended the line of compromise in place of that of suppression. On November 15 the National Socialists had won another great victory, this time in the Landtag elections of the Free State of Hesse, where the number of their representatives skyrocketed from one to twenty-seven. But at this same time internal bickering broke out within the party, and one of the newly elected Landtag delegates, a Dr. Schäfer, considered himself obliged to present the Frankfurt commissioner of police with certain records of agreements reached in a meeting of Hessian National Socialist leaders at the *Boxheimer Hof,* an inn near Worms.

These papers included, among other things, a "First Announcement [to be made] by Our Command after the Abolition of the Former State Authorities and the Seizure of the Communes." At that moment all authority was to be vested in National Socialist organizations like the SS.* The documents reveal with frightening clarity just how the National Socialists intended to exercise their power. Resistance against the decrees of any party official "will in principle be punished by death." And after the general order to turn in all weapons, anyone found in possession of a firearm "will be shot on the spot without trial." Similar provisions for capital punishment followed in rapid succession for every conceivable eventuality. All food supplies were to be delivered up to the National Socialist authorities, again under penalty of death. And the party's economic madness celebrated its real triumph in the pregnant provision: "Until other stipulation is made, there will be no more private income." Furthermore, according to the favored methods of every demagogue since Catiline, all demands for the payment of rent and interest were to be annulled. Provisions for forced labor and food rationing were to be so couched that Jews would receive no nourishment and hence were condemned to die of hunger.

The author of these astounding documents was a jurist, *Gerichts-assessor* (that is, a sort of assistant judge) Werner Best, director of the legal division of the party's Hessian branch. In the eyes of Hitler

---

* SS was the German abbreviation for *Schutzstaffel,* the Protective Staff or Black Shirts. SA stood for *Sturmabteilungen,* the Storm Troops or Brown Shirts. Röhm was most notably associated with the SA; Himmler with the SS. TRANSLATORS.

and his henchmen this achievement clearly qualified Best for the highest offices of state, until finally, during the war, he rose to the post of national commissioner of occupied Denmark.

To any juridical mind the plan outlined in these documents constituted a conspiracy to commit high treason in the sense of Paragraphs 81 and 86 of the German Criminal Code. The republican newspapers, which took the event most seriously, called for the initiation of criminal proceedings before the Supreme Court, which had jurisdiction over all cases of high treason. But the German solicitor general, Karl Werner, spread the word through the Telegraph Union, a wire service closely connected with Hugenberg, that he thought otherwise. This was not a case of high treason at all, the solicitor general insisted, because the precondition of the entire plan was the "seizure of the communes' (*die Ueberwindung der Kommune*).[67]

In this fashion the supreme defender of national law and order tried to make serious use of an obsolete political trick that even precinct fledglings had long since worn out along with the soles of their first adult shoes. Even the *Bayerische Kurier*, the organ of the Bavarian People's Party, certainly no Leftist group, refuted Werner's objection with clear logic. The government insisted on the initiation of a preliminary investigation, but, as could be foreseen from the solicitor general's attitude, nothing more was heard of the affair. When Brüning, accepting this denouement, simply let the matter die, François-Poncet, the French ambassador in Berlin, gained the impression that the Chancellor was unable to match the brutality of his enemies and hence was already a beaten man. At least this is what he said later in his memoirs.[68]

But perhaps even more important than the attitude of the authorities was that of the populace. In a nation that still had a strong sense of right and wrong this sort of revelation would have evoked a cry of horror and a determined rejection of these apostles of brutal force. But nothing of the kind occurred. The newspapers that revealed the full menace of the conspirators' activities were preaching in the wilderness, and the National Socialists' triumphant march continued on its way.

Unfortunately, the German government actually helped the Nazis on a matter of very great practical importance. Until this time members of both the National Socialist and Communist parties had been explicitly barred from the Reichswehr because both groups were plotting the forceful overthrow of the Republic. But on January 29, 1932, that is, *after* the revelation of the Boxheim Papers, Gröner issued a new directive on army recruiting policy which included a sharp divergence from this former rule. The euphemistic wording of the new directive meant in actual fact that the only candidates not eligible for enlistment would be those "who had demonstrably participated in efforts to change the [German] constitutional structure through illegal means."

Yet the teeth of even this narrow prohibition were deftly removed by the sentence which immediately followed: "Thus the misdeeds of individual leaders . . . of such organizations do not provide sufficient grounds for the exclusion of all members of the groups." A National Socialist must have been particularly stupid if he could not find a way around this bar, especially since he could count on the friendly assistance of the local commanders who were charged with the responsibility for recruiting. The pernicious influence of these recruiting officers had been well expressed by a distinguished military figure in the Republic: "The local commanders are still unfortunately convinced that a fellow recommended by the big-wigs of a patriotic league is a real find." These had been the words of no one else but Gröner, the author of the directive of January 29, 1932, in a letter to his friend, General Gerold von Gleich, dated April 26, 1931.[69]

Had Gröner forgotten his earlier insights? Or had he yielded to other influences? In the Reichstag debate of February 24, 1932, this directive, along with others, was subjected to the sharp criticism of even so calm and reasonable a man as August Weber, the leader of the State Party delegation. At this time Gröner defended his directive by pointing out the "prior consideration" for this favor that the National Socialists had offered: namely, their promise "to abstain from every sort of seditious activity in the Army; their leader's repeated personal assurance to me that he will ruthlessly expel from his party any man who undertakes such activity; and this same party leader's solemn assurance that he will restrict his party's methods to those regularly sanctioned by law." Anyone who survived the years of Hitler's rule can only shake his head at the naïveté with which Gröner and his associates accepted Hitler's promises on face value, indeed as "prior consideration" for favors in return.

Gröner, who had been negotiating with Hitler at Hindenburg's request, entered his reaction to the National Socialists' leader in the minutes of a military staff meeting of January 11, 1932: "Sympathetic impression; decent, modest chap with good intentions. His air is that of a diligent, self-made man . . . determined to wipe out revolutionary ideas . . . Hitler's purposes and goals are good; but [he is a] fanatic, so full of enthusiasm and volcanic force that he undoubtedly continues to use the wrong means now and then." [70]

Nothing is more understandable than that Gröner's daughter

should wish to clear her father of the charge of having uttered or even approved such nonsense.[71] She points out that the minutes were not signed by Gröner, and she cites one of her father's letters to Gleich, of approximately this same date, in which the general wrote: "Hitler has given me the personal impression of being a slippery politician . . . In our discussions he always avoids practical matters, preferring to ramble with his fantasy through centuries of German history. [I find it] impossible to interrupt in order to bring him back to earth. Just listening to him leaves one exhausted." This letter certainly clears Gröner of any accusation of having always been duped by Hitler as completely as the minutes of the staff meeting would suggest. Nevertheless, his directive of January 29, 1932, which was the subject of the parliament's debate, displayed an unfortunate similarity to the ministry protocol. One certainly cannot argue that this director of two national ministries had a firm and clear opinion at this time about the man who was the most dangerous menace to the German state.

Informed people in the Defense Ministry surmised that Gröner had let his associate, Schleicher, persuade him to issue this otherwise incomprehensible directive. Indeed, the Social Democratic delegate George Schöpflin advanced this charge baldly in an article in the *Vorwärts*.[72] Schöpflin, who was from Baden, was anything but radical and certainly no irresponsible agitator, and as his party's representative in the preparation of the military budget he had been on good terms with Schleicher and the entire Defense Ministry. But now he publicly called General von Schleicher "the responsible editor and original author" of this "capitulation to the Nazis."

When Schleicher replied to Schöpflin in an injured, coquettish tone, the Social Democrat repeated his accusation in an even more concrete and aggressive manner. With special vigor he demolished Schleicher's thesis of the "legality" that Hitler had promised to observe:

Just what is the value of these assurances by Hitler in the face of the fact that all his subordinates, without exception, . . . are daily preaching the use of force and the complete destruction of our present form of government? . . . And now we discover . . . that none other than the Ministry of Defense has found a way to argue that one should not judge a political party by what its individual . . . members say . . . You, Herr General, are responsible for this. The directive was a political act, for military . . . necessity did not require it. And you are the political agent in the Ministry of Defense.

Schöpflin's every word was correct, and one can only ask oneself if so clever a man as Schleicher had really made such a gross miscalculation. How was such an error possible after Schleicher himself had told Carl Severing, upon the disclosures of the Boxheim Papers, "Now one will not be able to touch the Nazis with a ten-foot pole"? [73] The only reasonable explanation is that, in his overestimation of himself, Schleicher was certain he was superior to all these civilian political figures, including Hitler, and supremely confident that in the end he would call the tune to which they would dance. For was he not the "cardinal for political affairs" whose skill was praised by everyone and who enjoyed the special favor of the President? On February 24, when Gröner tried to defend his directive in a Reichstag speech, Theodor Wolff, editor of the *Berliner Tageblatt*, noted: "With the exception of General von Schleicher, who always radiates vigor and good cheer, no one in the chamber seemed to think that what Gröner had done was a stroke of genius." [74]

Brüning realized better than did Schleicher and Gröner how much store could be set by Hitler's talk about "legality." In a radio address of December 8, 1931, the Chancellor told the German people:

Although the leader of the National Socialists has emphasized the legal methods and goals of his political intentions, nevertheless one cannot ignore the sharp contrast to these assurances provided by the violent assertions of no less responsible leaders of this same party who continue to incite Germans to senseless civil war and to diplomatic follies. When one declares that one intends to break down legal barriers once one has come to power in legal ways, then one is no longer observing legality, particularly if clandestine plans are simultaneously being made for revenge.

This final sentence in particular went straight to the mark. But in what way did Brüning act upon his insight? Four weeks later, evidently trusting Hitler's assurances, the Chancellor authorized the enlistment of National Socialists in the Reichswehr. Was his strength of action not equal to his powers of insight, or had he succumbed to pressures from the Presidential Palace?

The radio address that Brüning delivered on the evening of December 8 was principally devoted to an explanation of the new emergency decree which he had issued earlier that day "for the protection of the German economy and finances and the insuring of domestic peace." This decree was extraordinarily radical and far-reaching in its provisions. Its nine sections filled no less than forty-six pages of the National Legal Register (*Reichsgesetzblatt*). In addition to the inevitable financial considerations, the decree was primarily designed to lower prices or, as Brüning put it, "to prevent the sinking of real purchasing power." Not only was a national commissioner of price control appointed for this purpose — Carl-Friede-rich Goerdeler, then mayor of Leipzig and later famous as a leader and casualty of the German resistance movement — but also specific price decreases and maxima were ordered. A few years earlier the German government had helped creditors through legislative re-valuation upwards; now the emergency decree sought to aid debtors by lowering the interest rates on mortgages and similar obligations.[75] And it even tried to lower wages and salaries.

Among the various new imposts, the National Deserters' Tax (*Reichsfluchtsteuer*) is especially remarkable, not because it was in itself very important, but rather because it demonstrates the dangers of such *ad hoc* legislation and illustrates the change in meaning that such laws, once passed, suffer when, as Goethe's Mephisto put it, "wisdom turns to madness." A few instances had been publicized in which wealthy people had liquidated their assets and taken them out of the Reich, in order to escape the burden of German taxes. At a time when every taxpayer was being asked to bear his full share of the nation's load, the government felt it could not tolerate such flight. Thus the cabinet included in the emergency decree this National Deserters' Tax, which confiscated one fourth of such emi-grants' fortunes. But later, when Hitler came to power, the National Socialists did not hesitate to impose this same tax upon the Jews, al-though, far from leaving the Reich in order to escape its taxes, they were being driven from their homeland by all the political and economic pressures of its dictatorial government. Thus the warning in Goethe's *Westöstlicher Divan* proved all too apt:

> Wouldst not be plagued by persecuting thieves,
> Hide gold, your refuge, and what you believe.

The motives behind this emergency decree derived also from considerations of foreign policy, especially with respect to repara-tions. For now, after the Layton Report had strongly urged the par-ticipating governments to make immediate use of measures designed to put an end to both the German and the international crisis, Brüning decided that the time had come for Germany to take the steps provided in the Young Plan for the postponement of the un-protected reparation annuities. Consequently, on November 20, 1931, after extensive diplomatic preparations, in the course of which Great Britain, in particular, had displayed a quite accommodating attitude, the German Chancellor requested the Bank for Inter-national Settlements to call a meeting of its Special Advisory Com-mittee.

Brüning was aware of the high degree of trust and respect that he had gained among the statesmen of Europe, especially through his personal visits to London, Rome, and Paris. He now hoped to use this prestige to win concessions from the Western powers. And so the German message was accompanied by an extensive preamble which not only sought to justify the proposal under the terms of the Young Plan, but went on to request that the special committee examine "the problem in its entirety and with consideration of all its factors." In France — and probably in other parts of the world as well — people took this to mean that Germany was aiming straight at an abolition of reparation payments both for the present and for all time. The French government therefore felt obliged to reply that although it recognized the necessity for far-reaching compromise in the present, critical situation, it did question the proposition that Germany would *always* find itself in such a state of crisis. For this reason, the note went on, France would continue to insist that, in principle, the reparation payments be maintained.

The Bank for International Settlements acted very swiftly. As early as November 25 it was able to announce the appointment of the special committee, many of whose members had served on the previous Committee of Experts. Thus, for instance, Germany was again represented by Melchior and England by Layton. And before the year's end, on December 23, 1931, the special committee submitted its conclusions. Not only did this report treat in considerable detail the German economic crisis and the significant impact of reparation payments on the German economy, but it also referred fully and warmly to all the measures, including the Emergency Decree of December 8, that the German government had employed to alleviate the crisis.

This sympathetic foreign recognition of his efforts consoled Brüning to some extent in the face of the sharp attacks his policies had brought him at home. The committee declared Germany's request for a postponement of payments according to the Young Plan fully justified, and it even went on to state vigorously that this crisis "of unparalleled severity . . . undoubtedly exceeded the relatively short depression" presumed by the provisions of the Young Plan. The report concluded, therefore, that the suspension of all international obligations — reparations as well as other war debts — would constitute the only permanently effective step toward that restoration of confidence "which is the surest basis of economic stability and real peace." The committee closed its report with an earnest recommendation that the governments concerned take appropriate steps along these lines immediately.

The German Chancellor had every reason to be content with this report, for it provided him a favorable basis for further negotiations. But German public opinion accepted the committee's recommendations as reasons for a further stiffening of attitude. On the last day of 1931 the British ambassador observed that Germans of every political persuasion were united in the common belief that the reparations problem had to be permanently settled at this time, and that the only possible solution lay in a complete and final annulment of the debts.[76]

The special committee's report had not considered the question whether Germany would be able to afford further reparation payments after the present crisis had been settled. Yet one could conclude, notably from their comments on the future prospects of the German National Railways, that the experts had been assuming a later resumption of payments. For in this connection they had remarked, "once Germany and the world at large have recovered their balance and return to something like the economic conditions which we are accustomed to regard as normal, the Reichsbahn (fundamentally a sound undertaking) will be able in future years, managed on a commercial basis, to yield a net operating surplus comparable with that earned by other big foreign railway systems." [77] Furthermore, on January 13, 1932, the British member of the special committee, Sir Walter Layton, declared in a public address that Germany would later be in a position to pay something.[78]

The participating governments were quite prepared to accept the special committee's recommendation for swift action. The British and French governments proposed an immediate conference at Lausanne. But it proved quite difficult to arrive at a mutually satisfactory time for the meeting, since all the principal ministers had to take their parliamentary duties into account. Indeed, the French government had just survived a crisis of its own: on January 12, 1932, after Briand's retirement from public life and the death of André Maginot, minister of war, Laval's cabinet had resigned. Laval, however, had quickly formed another government, in which he, like Brüning, assumed the Foreign Ministry himself. And so the several governments were able to announce that the conference would be held in January, after all.

At this point a fateful event occurred. On January 8 the German Chancellor received the British ambassador for a conversation about the forthcoming reparations conference.[79] In the course of this talk, in which von Neurath, the German ambassador to Great Britain, also took part, Brüning declared explicitly that at the conference he intended to state that Germany was in no condition to pay further reparations at the moment nor to resume them at any foreseeable future time. In other words, Brüning had adopted German public opinion as his own.

The German Chancellor could expect the British government to display an understanding of his new position. The foreign secretary of the National Coalition at this time was Sir John Simon, one of the most prominent members of the British bar and a former Liberal who had once been a member of Asquith's government. The fact that Simon had resigned from Asquith's cabinet during the war because he could not bring himself to accept responsibility for universal conscription was a rather clear sign that he suffered an underestimation of the relevance of military power that ill becomes a foreign minister in stormy times.

Simon seems to have regarded the complete annulment of the reparations as the best solution to the difficult problem. His opinion on this matter had probably been influenced by the views of London financial circles, where the same conclusion had been reached on sober, business grounds. For the City was largely interested in defending and pressing those private claims against German debtors that now were frozen under the Standstill Agreement. And the London financiers had good reason to fear that these demands would never be honored so long as they were made to remain subordinate to reparation claims. Indeed, such private creditors throughout the world found themselves forced to become allies of Germany in their common fight against the reparations.

Moreover, Simon had been deeply impressed by the great menace to world peace that had been developing in East Asia ever since September 1931, when the Japanese invaded Manchuria. If it is true that this new threat from the Orient induced Simon to assume a more passive, yielding attitude toward European problems, it remains equally true that this conciliatory posture was consistent with his general conception of British diplomatic purpose at this time. It is, for example, quite significant that a letter Simon wrote on January 18, 1932, contains the term "appeasement" which was later to earn such ill repute.

But Simon was wise enough to realize that he could not make public his willingness to have the reparations completely annulled without provoking a sharp protest from the French. The Chamber of Deputies had expressed itself most strongly on this subject, and any French cabinet that accepted a complete annulment of the German reparations would have been immediately swept out of office. Another, no less serious complication derived from the attitude of the United States. For Britain could consider an abrogation of its

German credits only if, in turn, its debts to America were remitted. But the United States was unwilling to recognize this connection. Indeed, on December 19 and 22, 1931, in voicing its acceptance of the Hoover Moratorium, Congress had expressly stated that under no circumstances would the war debts of America's former allies be reduced. Thus it would have been fatal to Simon's hopes if the question were broached too soon.

And this is exactly what happened. The message Brüning had communicated to the British ambassador on January 8 was reported to London by Reuters that same evening and appeared in all the British newspapers the following morning. An indiscretion had occurred, the facts of which have yet to be disclosed. One can, however, say with certainty that no guilt can be attached to the British embassy in Berlin.[80]

The news release produced tremendous excitement in France. The minister of finance, Flandin, sent the British ambassador, Lord Tyrrell, a note in which, among other things, he argued that such a total surrender to the German demands as the annulment of reparations would not lead to European peace; on the contrary, it would only invite *further German claims* for amendments to the Treaty of Versailles. In support of this prediction Flandin cited the German attitude after the evacuation of the Rhineland in 1930 and went on to state that a public acceptance by the British government of the Germans' claim would rupture the Anglo-French Entente. And that, he argued, was precisely what the Germans hoped to achieve.[81]

Simon made every effort to calm the storm. And on that same day, January 9, Brüning summoned the executive editor of the Wolff Wire Service in order to deliver a declaration which, although it did not contradict the Reuters report, was clearly designed to soften its effect.

It was at this time that François-Poncet, the French ambassador to Berlin, told Lord Tyrrell that he was becoming increasingly distressed by German developments. He pointed out that reparations were no longer simply a financial matter; they had become a burning political issue. Germans were now "mobilized" for the attack on reparations, and political leaders were speaking triumphantly of a "breakthrough" and of "revenge" for the failure of the *Anschluss*. The Germans, François-Poncet continued, demonstrated that Bismarck's ruthless power politics still determined German policy. To be sure, Brüning was a charming, reasonable man, but he was surrounded and supported by the officials, the social structure, and the organs of a state which had threatened Europe for years before the World War. The Chancellor, he concluded, was prey to these influences, however honest his personal hopes and intentions might be.[82]

It soon became apparent that the Lausanne Conference would have to be postponed — probably until June or July. The British government sought to persuade the several countries concerned to agree that, in the interim, the Hoover Moratorium would be extended for another year, that is, until June 1933. The French government was prepared to accept this agreement, but only if the attendant conditions of the Hoover Moratorium were also to be extended. France's point here was that Germany should continue to be required to deposit the unprotected annuity with the Bank for International Settlements, with the continued understanding that the bank would immediately return the payments to Germany or, more exactly, to the German National Railways.

Simon adopted this proposal and urged the German government to accept it, too. He did not neglect to point out that England was assuming a considerable risk in proceeding this way, since it had received no assurance from the United States that the prospective moratorium would be extended to include payments on the British war debts to America.[83] But none of this made any impression on Brüning, who was clearly depending once more on von Bülow for advice. The German Chancellor flatly rejected any attachment of the so-called Hoover Conditions to the new moratorium, even though von Neurath had admitted that the acceptance of these conditions would be a necessary concession on Germany's part.[84]

Simon expressed his disappointment in a cable to Sir Horace Rumbold: "The attitude of the German Government seems most unhelpful. There has hitherto been, as you know, a good deal of sympathy here for the German case. The attitude now foreshadowed will destroy all this and the Germans will simply appear as people who are always asking for something to be done for them and are never willing to do anything in return." [85] Yet despite this sharp criticism, Simon yielded to the Germans once again. And the final consequence of all the extended negotiations was simply that the Lausanne Conference on the permanent settlement of the reparations question was postponed till June.

But when June came, Brüning was out of office and could only watch Herr von Papen gather the crop that other men had sown.

With nothing more to be done about reparations until June, Brüning turned with the same sort of energy to the other international issue of special concern to the German people at that time: disarmament.

In February 1932, after years of preliminary negotiations, the International Disarmament Conference met at Geneva. In the general discussion with which the meeting was begun the German Chancellor delivered a highly significant address outlining his proposed policy to an eagerly attentive world. His prospective program was essentially contained in the following sentences:

> The German government and the German people, having been disarmed themselves, now challenge the whole world to join them in disarmament. Germany has a legal and moral claim to such a general disarmament, one that nobody can dispute . . . I hereby declare that Germany, as a fully empowered and fully obligated member of the League of Nations . . . will press with all her authority for such general disarmament, for that disarmament of a clear and unmistakable nature which the Covenant of the League prescribes for all its members, for that general disarmament which will create an equal measure of security for all nations.

Thus Brüning pronounced the thesis of equal rights for Germany as the principal note of German foreign policy. This position, of course, constituted the antithesis to the international legal situation created by the Treaty of Versailles. It meant that Germany now claimed the right to be freed from all the limitations she had assumed in Part V of the treaty° unless the other nations of the world were prepared to submit to the same limitations.

This thesis of equal rights for Germany had been voiced even before the conference and had become the subject of a long and detailed exchange of notes among the great powers. In Britain the argument was assured a sympathetic reception on the part of a large segment of the population. Universal conscription had been unknown there until the World War, and it had seemed only natural that it be abolished immediately after the cessation of hostilities. Further, British Leftist circles regarded such universal disarmament as an automatic guarantee of universal peace. Moreover, a typically English characteristic was at work. Lord Templewood (formerly Sir Samuel Hoare) describes it in his memoirs:

> We are bad haters. Having been reluctantly drawn into a fight, we wish to forgive our enemies as soon as it is finished, and forget their evil deeds . . . The tendency to forgive and forget was further strengthened by the wish to be freed from the financial burden of armaments . . . So sure, indeed, were we of the virtues of disarmament that we easily be-

---

° Part V of the treaty included military, naval, and air clauses of limitation, provisions for Inter-Allied Commissions of Control, and General Articles requiring Germany "to give every facility for any investigation which the Council of the League of Nations . . . may consider necessary." TRANSLATORS.

came irritated with other countries, and particularly our former allies, the French, when they did not agree with us. The anti-French feeling became very strong. Annoyance with our former allies went very near to becoming affection for our former enemies.[86]

Naturally, the problem presented a quite different aspect to the French.[87] For they were Germany's immediate neighbors and had seen her armies on their soil three times within a century. They pointed out that Article 8 of the League's Covenant, which contained provisions for disarmament and which Brüning had been citing, had expressly limited "the reduction of national armaments to the lowest point consistent with national safety" and that their national safety would be threatened most severely either if the more populous Germans were permitted to rearm or if they were forced to reduce their own powers of defense. For every Frenchman was convinced that the danger of attack existed only from the German side and that his countrymen had no idea of such a step.

The French agreed, of course, that the situation would be quite different if Great Britain and the United States were to assure them the sort of aid in case of attack that they had promised at Versailles but which had faded into thin air once the Americans had reneged. But to this every British government had to reply that the British nation unconditionally rejected any further international obligations. The French government had prepared a draft version of a general disarmament agreement which provided for the establishment of an international army or police force under the auspices of the League of Nations. Whether this idea might ever have enjoyed prospects of acceptance by the other powers we shall never know. For Brüning rejected — and thus killed — the plan in his opening speech at Lausanne.

Thus, as was clear from the start, the conference was not going to be concluded quickly; yet it was impossible for the German Chancellor to spend more than a few days there. He had to return to Berlin as soon as possible in order to devote his attention to German domestic affairs. Most important among these was the matter of electing a national president.

XII

HINDENBURG IS RE-ELECTED
AND STABS BRÜNING IN THE BACK

Article 43 of the Weimar constitution reads, "The President's term of office shall last seven years. He is eligible for re-election." Since Hindenburg had been elected president on April 26, 1925, and had taken office on April 29, his term expired in April 1932. In October 1931, he had become eighty-four years old. Was it possible for so old a man to execute the duties of the highest and, as was becoming increasingly clearer, the most responsible post in the German Reich? And if not, then who should take his place? Brüning regarded this problem as his prime concern, for he not only was the responsible leader of German politics, but he also considered himself Hindenburg's confidential adviser.

Max Weber, who was more responsible than anyone for the direct election of the president under the Weimar constitution, seems to have believed that there would always be several "outstanding leaders with popular support" among whom the Germans might take their choice.[1] But in truth it became apparent that Germany was remarkably deficient in such men. There was Adolf Hitler, of course, who certainly had popular support. He doubtlessly would attract millions of votes as a candidate for president. But Brüning correctly considered it his principal duty to obstruct the election of so extreme a demagogue. Yet, wherever Brüning looked, he found no one who could be expected to beat Hitler in an election except the aged Hindenburg.

It seems quite likely that Brüning had connected another, rather astonishing notion to this plan of renewing and continuing Hindenburg's tenure as president: the idea of restoring the monarchy in a reformed and modernized version. At least Wheeler-Bennett, who based his Hindenburg study on conversations with Brüning, suggests as much.[2] And other people who were in contact with Brüning at this time assume Brüning had concluded that the Republic was untenable under the prevailing conditions and that his only real problem was to find some way back to monarchy without risking either civil war or revolution. According to this analysis, Hindenburg's re-election struck Brüning as just such a route, for at the proper moment the old field marshal could appoint the former crown prince as his successor rather as the French monarchists had once hoped Marshal MacMahon would do.

All these possibilities are too undocumented to warrant serious historical treatment. One should, however, mention the undisputed facts that Rightist circles did consider nominating the former crown prince for president and that he would have been glad to accept had his father not vetoed the idea.

Brüning was quite aware of the many strong arguments against the re-election of the eighty-four-year-old field marshal, especially since he reports that Hindenburg had suffered a temporary mental collapse a few months before. It is true that Otto Meissner, the President's state secretary, completely denies Brüning's report. But whatever the real facts may have been, many people knew that there were only a few hours in every day when the Old Gentleman was really capable of serious activity and conversation, and that the burden of his constantly increasing responsibilities was pressing down upon him hard.

However diligently Hindenburg may have worked to increase his presidential powers at the expense of those of the Reichstag and the political parties, he found it unpleasant to be forced to use his power to publish emergency decrees that were unpopular and, indeed, bitterly opposed. In a revealing conversation with Otto Braun, Hindenburg once observed, "I have a great dislike for all this party politicking and parliamentary bickering. As a professional soldier I was accustomed always either to command or to obey." [3] Now, of course, he could still command through the emergency decrees, but the substance of his commands was not designed to contribute to his popularity. Hindenburg did not shrink from these unpleasant duties, but the man who kept asking him to sign these necessary decrees diminished, with each such request, the store of good will that Hindenburg had once felt for him.

Nevertheless, Brüning strained every nerve to keep Hindenburg in the presidency. At first, the Chancellor thought he saw a solution to the principal difficulties in the form of a parliamentary extension of Hindenburg's term of office. Such a step would have been an amendment to the constitution and hence would have required a two-thirds vote of the Reichstag. (See Article 46 of the Weimar constitution.) No legal objection could be made to this procedure, especially since it had been employed before, in October 1922, for President Ebert. But how was the necessary two-thirds majority to be achieved? Even if all the delegates who had ever supported Brüning could be persuaded to vote for such a measure, their number would have fallen far short of the necessary total. Brüning was therefore obliged to enter into negotiations with the two leaders of the nationalistic opposition, Alfred Hugenberg and Adolf Hitler.

Brüning turned to Hitler first. Gröner invited the Nazi leader to come to Berlin for conversations, receiving him there on the evening of January 6. On the next day Brüning joined in the discussion, to which Schleicher was also invited, while Hitler was accompanied by Ernst Röhm. Schleicher evidently thought that he would be able to induce Röhm to persuade Hitler to join in the Chancellor's plan.

And in fact Hitler did not at first seem strongly opposed to the idea of such a constitutional amendment; he declared his conditions and reserved his judgment. Among these conditions was the government's formal recognition of the legality of the Nazis' aims and methods. Brüning seemed prepared to consider this point. But it is doubtful whether he would have been equally ready to promise the dissolution of the Reichstag and the new elections which Hitler also demanded. For, entirely apart from other considerations, with such a step the Chancellor would have forfeited the Social Democrats' support, which he needed fully as much as Hitler's for the execution of his plan and which he hoped to secure in forthcoming conversations with their leaders, Hilferding and Wels. But Brüning was spared the difficult decision on this point by the insistence of a majority of Hitler's supporters that they not be deprived of the opportunity of another Reichstag campaign. Goebbels noted in his diary at this time that "the important thing now is that we make no commitments." [4]

And then, on January 9, Hugenberg came to Berlin. It quickly became apparent that no agreement could be reached with him. In their conversation on the following day, the German Nationalist leader informed Brüning that his party would not support the proposed amendment. Then Hugenberg had a long conversation with Hitler, at the end of which he still maintained his negative position. [5] The affidavit that Hugenberg submitted to the Detmold denazification court is rather noticeably silent on the reasons for his stubborn opposition. In his subsequent book, however, he felt constrained to say that the re-election of Hindenburg would have deprived Germany, at this most critical time, "of a clear and effective leader in the position that was decisive in determining the course of German history." [6]

But this smacks of the wisdom of hindsight. Actually, not long before he flatly rejected Brüning's plan, Hugenberg himself had been demanding that President Hindenburg be given even greater power. And in the letter of January 12, in which he explained his reasons for refusing to support Brüning's plan, Hugenberg accused the Chancellor of having already secured the Centrists' and Social Democrats' support. Here we seem to have come upon Hugenberg's principal motivation: the exclusion of the Socialists from the government of Germany remained his most important goal.

Hitler naturally made good use of this opportunity for further agitation by immediately publishing a long memorandum which he had just delivered to Brüning. The doubts adduced by Hitler concerning the legality of the proposed plan are not worth consideration here. But in response to Brüning's argument that an election campaign at this time would have unfortunate effects on Germany's diplomatic front, Hitler replied eagerly that he would regard any event that might lead to the defeat of the Weimar system as a diplomatic triumph for Germany. He then went on to call for a "victory over this system which will remain identified in history with the period of the domestic and diplomatic debasement of our nation." It was easy for Brüning to find the proper sort of answer to this selfish partisan cant. Hitler's real motives became apparent when he told the President's deputy, Meissner, that he was ready to make Hindenburg the joint candidate of the National Socialists and German Nationalists if the President would dismiss Brüning, form a Rightist cabinet, and dissolve the Reichstag. All this just ten days before the opening of an international disarmament conference at which Brüning was to represent the German Republic!

Thus all thought of a parliamentary solution to the problem of the presidency had to be abandoned, and the aged field marshal requested his Chancellor to desist from further negotiations in this direction. There was no alternative to an election, and both the government and its opposition were confronted by the necessity of selecting candidates. Among the ranks of the opposition it immediately became clear that agreement on a common candidate could not be reached. Hitler had not the slightest inclination to place his supporters' votes at the disposal of a man acceptable to Hugenberg. And in the affidavit quoted just above, Hugenberg claims that the idea of a joint candidate, which he had had in 1931, had been abandoned by the time night fell on the Harzburg rally.[7] But this argument only makes his subsequent tactics all the more incomprehensible, since he could hardly expect to be able to match the National Socialists' votes with anything like an equal number of his own. Yet he rejects any interpretation that says he wished to further Hitler's prospects, and he does so with firmness and with what one can accept as subjective honesty. Any attempt to grasp Hugenberg's policies rationally is clearly doomed from the start.

There was never any doubt that the National Socialists would present a candidate. But there was some question whether Hitler would accept the nomination. For he originally foresaw that he would probably suffer a defeat that would be injurious to his grander political designs. Goebbels' diary for this period is full of observations describing the Führer's indecision at this time. Goebbels, himself, was unconditionally in favor of Hitler's candidacy, and by February 22, 1932, the Nazis' discussions had progressed to such a point that Goebbels could announce Hitler's nomination at a mass meeting in the Berlin Sports Palace. And since Goebbels was not a man for half-way measures, he presented his pronouncement as a prophecy: "Hitler will be the next President of the German Reich! . . . For when I say that he will be our candidate, then I know that he will be our President."

Yet this man whose election was so easily assumed had to straighten out one little difficulty first. He was still not a German citizen, and the Weimar constitution insisted upon this single qualification of any candidate for president, although it included none of the other requirements customary for such a post. But this presented no great problem to a man like Adolf Hitler. What better purpose was there for the National Socialist government in the little land of Brunswick? The worthy Wilhelm Frick had already attempted, as a minister of Thuringia, to effect Hitler's naturalization through the back door by appointing him director of land police in Hildburghausen. But this had been too blatant a deceit for even Hitler, and so the Nazi leader had declined. The Brunswick minister (and later SS *Gruppenführer*) Dietrich Klagges approached the problem in a more sophisticated way: he appointed Hitler adviser (*Regierungsrat*) to the Brunswick legation in Berlin. And on February 26, that is, *after* his candidacy for the office of president had been announced, Hitler paid his first and only visit to the legation's office in order to swear his allegiance to the Weimar constitution and thus acquire German citizenship.

Should this be considered a victory gained by the legal methods which Hitler had promised to observe? Or was it a triumph of casuistry that Adolf Hitler would have called a "Jewish trick" had it been employed by a political opponent? In any event it was a worthy forerunner of the Law of April 7, 1933, for the "restoration" of the professional civil service, with which the then Chancellor Hitler introduced his formidable legislative career.

By the time Joseph Goebbels was proclaiming Hitler as the next German President in the Berlin Sports Palace, Hindenburg, on February 16, had already publicly stated his willingness to be a candidate for re-election. The decision had not been easy for him to make. For he was an essentially conservative man. All his sympathies lay with the Right. He had a great dislike for the Social Democrats, while the "Cathlists" (*Katholen*) — as he called the Centrists — lived in a world that was foreign, perhaps even frightening, to his mind. But he was going to need their votes if he wished to be elected. And he found real consolation in the fact that at least some conservatives, although not many, like Count Westarp and his friends, spoke up in his behalf. For he considered that the support of men like these lent a respectable appearance to the whole affair.

Hindenburg was invited to accept the candidacy by a nonpartisan committee headed by the mayor of Berlin, Heinrich Sahm.[8] Sahm issued a proclamation celebrating the field marshal as the victor at Tannenberg and the triumphant queller of partisan strife. Sahm even went so far as to apply to Hindenburg the well-known words in praise of George Washington: "First in war, first in peace, first in the hearts of his countrymen." Hindenburg's popularity was demonstrated by the three million names which were quickly entered on the committee's rolls. When Sahm showed him these lists, Hindenburg declared that he was willing to accept the nomination precisely because it had not come from any particular party or special interest group, but rather from representative committees from all the regions of the Reich. And he used his earliest opportunity to emphasize the fact that, in accepting the nomination in this way, he had unconditionally refused to enter into commitments or understandings with any parties.

The nomination of Hindenburg meant that the parties of the Middle and the Left would not present candidates of their own — except, of course, for the Communists, who ran Thälmann once again. The Social Democrats naturally did not look forward with much pleasure to the prospect of voting for the man whom they had opposed so sharply seven years before. Paul Löbe, the president of the Reichstag, correctly termed their plight "a tragedy," but he also added that they really had no choice, since Hindenburg was the only man who, as President, could block Hitler's march to power.[9]

But this choice between Hindenburg or Hitler, for which Hugenberg was largely responsible, forced the German Nationalist leader to put up a candidate of his own. He could hardly urge his supporters to vote for Hitler, for in that event he would lose them irrevocably to the Austrian. Yet, it was equally clear that he had no chance of being elected himself. Later, in his attempt at self-defense, he explains the decision he arrived at by saying that he wished thus to prevent the first round of voting from being the final one "in order to keep open the possibility that some new, nonpartisan candidate might be nominated for the second ballot." But this, again, is undoubtedly the wisdom of hindsight, and not so very wise even at that.

As their candidate, Hugenberg and the *Stahlhelm* hit upon Theodor Duesterberg, deputy chief of the *Stahlhelm*. In making this selection they certainly must have been mindful of the fact that Duesterberg was a lieutenant colonel in the Reserves and that, as such, he would appeal to the militaristic instincts of the Germans. The National Socialists provided this grand tragedy with a bit of comic relief when they sniffed out quite another fact: Duesterberg's grandfather had been born a Jew. It was quite true that this grandfather had returned from the War of Liberation in 1813 with the Iron Cross.[10] But that fact did not keep the noble Goebbels from branding the German Nationalists' "black, white, and red" candidate as "racially inferior." And Duesterberg was not the only man who marched with the German Nationalists only to trip later over a Jewish grandparent.

The Reichstag debates of February 23–26, in which the election dates were determined, gave a reliable foretaste of the sort of campaign that was about to explode. As spokesman for the second largest delegation, Joseph Goebbels opened the debate. His speech was obviously designed to provoke a scandal. Saying that Hindenburg had been elected to serve Germany's nationalistic interests, he accused the President of having done the exact opposite. Among his fellow National Socialists, Goebbels went on, people were saying: "Tell me who praises you, and I shall tell you who you are. Well, Hindenburg is praised by the gutter journals of Berlin and lauded by the party of deserters" — this last gem being accompanied by a gesture toward the Social Democrats.

This was not a matter of being carried away in the heat of the moment; it was cold, calculated malice. Naturally the Social Democrats exploded in a storm of rage, while the National Socialists sounded their enthusiastic delight. Among the Social Democratic delegates there were, of course, many who had served as soldiers in the war, while the crippled Goebbels had naturally been barred from service. Thus it was the Social Democrat Karl Schumacher, who had returned from the front a severely wounded cripple, that gave Goebbels his sharpest and most telling reply. Calling the National Socialists' demagoguery an "unending appeal to the inner beast in man," he complimented them for having succeeded, for the first time in German politics, "in effecting the total mobilization of human stupidity."

Paul Löbe, president of the Reichstag, expelled Goebbels from the chamber for having grossly insulted the President of Germany. Gregor Strasser, speaking for the National Socialists, termed Löbe's act "an unheard of outrage," a protest which did not keep him from learning later, on June 30, 1934, just what "unheard of outrages" his fellow Nazis were capable of committing.* In this parliamentary debate the National Socialists demonstrated the true sophistication of their intellectual powers by either rudely interrupting the proceedings in an organized way or deserting the chamber en bloc. It is interesting that the German Nationalists joined in these walkouts; so little, even at this moment, did Hugenberg and his followers know how to maintain their political independence.

One of Brüning's great speeches warrants mention here. His rhetorical skill and superior knowledge enabled him to refute the objections to German foreign policy which had been raised by the German Nationalist Professor von Freytagh-Loringhoven and the National Socialist theorist Alfred Rosenberg — neither of whom, one might note in passing, was a native German. The substance of Brüning's rebuttal was as unanswerable as it was simple: "I shall never let myself be seduced into pursuing a foreign policy which is designed to win prestige at home among voters misled by agitation but which would endanger the vital interests of the German people in the longer run." In view of the mood prevalent among the Germans at the time, this was a courageous statement, and it should have made a favorable impression abroad.

But opinion outside of Germany failed to realize how weak and unstable Brüning's position really was. (One might, perhaps, also add that the distinction between a "policy which is designed to win prestige at home" and the "more active foreign policy" of which the Wilhelmstrasse had been boasting ever since Stresemann's death was not always clear.) The way the National Socialists behaved during this speech by the Chancellor of Germany reminded the British ambassador, who was present at the debate, of the scenes he had witnessed in the Chinese parliament at Peking nine years

---

* On Hitler's orders, Gregor Strasser was murdered during the "Blood Purge" of June 30, 1934. TRANSLATORS.

before.[11] And Theodor Wolff wrote in the *Berliner Tageblatt*: "Not since the fishwives of Paris took screaming part in the revolutionary Convention has there been such a collection of unmitigated rowdies in a popular assembly." [12]

Among the delegates' speeches, those of the State Party leader, August Weber, warrant mention here. The State Party had become too small to be able, as a rule, to add any significant weight to the scales of parliamentary balance. But now and then a voice that commanded attention and respect was still to be heard from its ranks. On the second day of the debate Weber had accused the National Socialists of having traveled the route of political murder. The Nazis had replied to this charge with such a wild display that the session was immediately adjourned. Weber, however, did not let himself be stopped by such street-brawl tactics. And so on the last day of the debate he arose once more, this time to furnish the evidence behind his earlier accusation. At this point the National Socialists chose to leave the chamber, lest they should be obliged to hear their list of sins.

The list was frightening. But the report of one special case made the biggest impression of all:

In 1920 a poor farm worker, falsely suspected of intending to inform the Prussian police of local illegal traffic in arms, was murdered; the murderer pressed a pistol to the man's face and discharged the weapon twice. At a trial in Stettin in May 1928 the murderer was sentenced to five years' imprisonment. After the Stettin decision, the National Socialist Party . . . expelled the murderer from its ranks. Today, however, the murderer is once more a member of the National Socialist Party — and of its Reichstag delegation.

Edmund Heines was the delegate about whom Weber reported these irrefutable facts on the strength of the legal record.

One should imagine that Weber's report would suffice to make the murderer unacceptable to any decent people. But in fact it seems to have hurt neither Heines' reputation nor that of his party. Indeed, only a few months later, Heines was one of the National Socialist delegates who attacked and severely injured a certain Klotz, a lieutenant in the Naval Reserve who had displeased them in some way in the Reichstag restaurant. Nor did this incident hurt Heines in the eyes of his party any more than the fact that he was subsequently sentenced to three months' imprisonment for assault and battery. The rage of the nationalistic opposition was directed, instead, at Bernhard Weiss, the deputy commissioner of the Berlin police who, at the request of Paul Löbe, had led the police into the

Reichstag chamber and seized the culprits. For Weiss was a Jew, and that was all the "nationalistic" Germans needed to know in order to determine where justice lay.

The presidential elections provided a fitting sequel to this introduction. Astonishingly enough, it proved difficult to find the necessary funds for Hindenburg's campaign. (Severing reports several amazing details in his memoirs.[13]) On the other hand, Hitler's campaign was clearly not hampered in the slightest by any lack of money. At this time it is no longer possible to discover exactly where the funds came from. Nor should one forget that the National Socialists had the habit of incurring debts without worrying about how they would pay them back. One of the sources of the National Socialists' support is, however, of particular interest here, namely, German heavy industry.

These were bad times for German industry, especially since Great Britain had left the gold standard, thus gaining an advantage in its export trade. Among the industrialists of the Rhineland and the Ruhr, Hitler had acquired a devoted supporter in Fritz Thyssen. This young steel magnate furnished Hitler all the funds that he could raise, as he himself later publicly regretted. Another important supporter of the National Socialists was Ludwig Grauert, secretary general of the Northwest Division of the German Employers' Association, the man who had been the employers' principal spokesman in the Ruhr iron crisis of the winter of 1928–29.[14]

Thyssen persuaded the officers of Düsseldorf's highly respected and influential Industry Club to invite Hitler to address its members. Hitler gave his speech on January 7, 1932. It was a smashing success. These industrialists were glad to accept his thesis that private enterprise, which depends upon inequalities of product and reward, cannot be combined with democracy, which assumes an equality among all men. They even listened to Hitler's fairy tales about the Bolshevik menace and derived inspiration from his announcement that the National Socialists were firmly determined to root out Marxism in Germany. And it evidently pleased them, too, to hear Hitler rail at pacificism, praise the totalitarian state, and make it quite clear that he planned rearmament for Germany.

Although Hitler's unbridled verbosity made the speech last more than two hours, the audience broke into enthusiastic applause when he was done. They had not all, of course, become converts to National Socialism on the spot; but in Hitler they at last had found the man who would support them in their struggle not only against the Communists, but also against the labor unions, which many of the magnates regarded as their most dangerous foe. For Hitler, the speech had one great practical result: the money that he needed so badly now started to pour from the industrialists' coffers.[15]

Hitler was quick to make fullest use of his new funds. One cannot deny that the National Socialists, all the way from their Führer down to the simplest precinct worker, plunged into the campaign with energy and self-sacrifice. Their efforts were certainly unique in German political history. But this noteworthy energy was characterized by vicious and ruthless hatred. The Nazis unleashed every passion among their followers, even encouraging physical attacks and bloodshed. But still worse was to be feared. The national Ministry of Interior received reports that the National Socialists' Storm Troops were trying to discover where the Reichswehr stored its weapons, and it was disturbingly true that the most important positions in the SA were occupied by former Army officers, whom one could expect to have especially good relations with the Reichswehr.[16] The Prussian police followed Carl Severing's instructions and simply kept a sharp lookout. This seems to have sufficed.

Among those who campaigned for Hindenburg, one was particularly conspicuous. That was the Chancellor, Heinrich Brüning. He was tireless in his efforts to address assemblies in all parts of Germany; and his calm, wise, well-considered speeches made a great impression upon all those who had preserved some powers of thought amid the general tumult. Hindenburg certainly owed no small share of his victory in this election to the loyal and indefatigable Brüning.

For Hindenburg did win the election, but not without giving his supporters some anxious moments. On March 13 he received seven million more votes than Hitler, approximately 18,650,000 to 11,400,-000, while Thälmann won only some five million and Duesterberg only half as many. The old field marshal was lacking only 0.4 percent of a majority of the votes cast; and so a second election was required, even though there could be no doubt about its results. Although Hitler had been defeated, he had increased the National Socialists' votes by some 85 percent beyond those cast for the party in the Reichstag elections of September 1930 (6,500,000 to 11,400,000) and could now boast of having received 30 percent of all the votes cast. And so even the most dubious of men had to admit that Hindenburg's candidacy had been the only thing that kept Hitler from being elected President of Germany in 1932.

Duesterberg was not a candidate in the second election. His utter failure had demonstrated Hugenberg's helplessness in the face of more radical competition. Duesterberg asked his former supporters to cast their second votes for Hindenburg,[17] while Hugenberg left his German Nationalists free to choose between the field marshal and Adolf Hitler. Hugenberg's was, of course, the counsel of despair. But desperation at this point was the logical consequence of his shortsighted policies in the past. And all the more attention was aroused when Frederick William, the former crown prince, publicly announced that he would vote for Hitler.[18]

This declaration constituted a complete denial of that assurance to abstain from German political life with which Frederick William had purchased his return to Germany in 1923. For could there be any more flagrant intervention in the political activities of the German Republic than this declaration in support of the most bitter and dangerous enemy of the existing state? With this act the eternally juvenile scion of the Hohenzollerns excluded himself from serious consideration by any decent German.[19]

The crown prince's act had been politically stupid in terms of his own ambitions for a restoration of the monarchy. For it was an open declaration that he had no more hopes in Hindenburg. We shall never know to what extent the aged field marshal and his associates might have been willing to help the younger Hohenzollern regain his lost inheritance. Yet it is significant that Schleicher exploded in rage at Frederick William's ill-considered act because, according to Gröner's report, it had ruined Schleicher's plan for a "restoration of the monarchy via the election of the Crown Prince as President."[20] But the Hohenzollern prince evidently thought that Hindenburg was an old man, no longer of much use, and that Hitler was the man of the future who would be properly grateful for such timely testimony on his behalf.

The belief that Hitler would be ready to surrender the rule of Germany, once he had come to power, to someone else was yet another indication that Frederick William had not even the slightest notion of Hitler's true character and goals. And to reckon on the Führer's gratitude was simply absurd. The only mitigating circumstances derive from the fact that wiser men than Frederick William made similar errors.

In any event the young Hohenzollern had bet on the wrong horse again. For at the polls of April 10 Hindenburg was re-elected with 19,390,000 votes, with Hitler receiving only 13,410,000. Yet even this result meant that Hitler had gained over two million more votes, raising his share of ballots to 36.8 percent. From the psychological standpoint this was bad enough. But no one could tell to what extent this growth stemmed from Duesterberg's former supporters or from the Communists, whose candidate had lost some million votes during this second round.[21]

As Robert Weismann, a Prussian state secretary, confided to the British ambassador, neither Hindenburg nor Brüning was completely satisfied with the results of the second election.[22] The statistics told the two leaders of the Republic that the disgruntled and the youthful elements of Germany were still streaming to Hitler's ranks and that his movement was growing steadily. But however pessimistically one might react to the increased number of votes for Hitler, one could still find some consolation in the fact that a considerable majority — one that could be reckoned in millions — of the German people had refused to vote for Hitler, and that Goebbel's arrogant announcement in the Berlin Sports Palace, that Hitler would be Germany's next president, had proved untrue.

On April 24, 1932, the elections for the Prussian Landtag which the Rightists had been demanding for some time took place. They brought the National Socialists an enormous gain, from 9 to 162 representatives. The German Nationalists, on the other hand, had not the slightest reason to be content with the results, for they dropped from 71 delegates to 31. The Social Democrats, who had sent 137 representatives to the former Landtag, could only muster 94 this time; thus they had to yield primacy as the largest delegation to the National Socialists and, with it, the office of speaker.

The Center once more demonstrated its ability to survive crises, although it did lose 4 of its former 71 seats. The more liberal parties came off very badly: the People's Party was cut down to 7 seats; the State Party, all the way to 2. On the other hand, the Communists could boast of having increased their delegation from 48 to 57. Braun's government had clearly lost its majority, and to this extent the Harzburg Front had made its will prevail. But the Front's wish — indeed, its prophecy — that it would have a majority was not fulfilled. A temporary, unstable balance existed, with both sides needing the Communists in order to form a majority. This crisis and its denouement will be treated more extensively below.

On April 13, just before the Prussian elections, a presidential decree was issued which made it seem as though the aged Hindenburg had, at long last, found the necessary courage and determination to take action against the National Socialists' excesses which were severely endangering public order throughout the Reich. This decree dissolved and banned the National Socialists' private army: the SA and the SS.

In itself nothing was more contrary to Prussian and German tradition than a private army, especially one belonging to a single political party. Yet the excessive military restrictions of the Treaty of Versailles had created a vacuum that almost begged to be filled by such paramilitary bands. The *Stahlhelm*, the Rightist veterans' organization, found its counterpart in the republican *Reichsbanner*, which saw its duty in the protection of the Weimar constitution. But the National Socialists' SA and SS went far beyond these more traditional bounds in both aims and methods. Presumably designed to provide protection at their own party's assemblies, they in fact systematically disturbed the meetings of others and maintained, where they could afford to, a regime of terror against their political opponents.

This was not simply the opinion of, say, the Prussian police, which were directed by the Social Democrat Carl Severing, but also the considered view of the governments of all the central and southern German lands, not least of all the government of Bavaria, which in former years had done its best to help foster Hitler and his movement. The premier of Bavaria, Heinrich Held, could certainly not be suspected of flirting with the "Marxists." Yet in the Bavarian Landtag he declared that as a result of the National Socialists' excesses conditions had become unbearable; that the Nazis were trying to exert such pressure upon the populace, especially the civil servants, that no man would dare do his duty any longer in maintaining the common interests of the state.[23]

If things had come to such a pass in Bavaria, where the Roman Catholic clergy still exercised considerable influence and the Bavarian People's Party was still able to stand up to the National Socialists' attacks, one can well imagine the conditions that prevailed in the East German provinces, where a sincere republican was regarded as either a natural wonder or else a traitor.

In the course of the presidential elections the situation had become significantly worse. In all the ministries, including the national Ministry of Interior, reports began to arrive telling of highly suspicious plans of the SA and SS. On March 17, 1932, the Prussian police found it necessary to undertake investigations and confiscations in several Nazi headquarters. In order to prevent the discovery of his party's plans, Hitler petitioned the Supreme Court at Leipzig to grant a temporary injunction requiring the return of all the confiscated documents. The Prussian representative at the conference of March 24, Ministerial Counselor Badt, was able to assure the court that the police were prepared to release all the documents which would not be required for the further prosecution of their action.[24] Thereupon, the chairman of the conference, Chief Justice Bumke, declared that a temporary injunction was out of the question and proposed a compromise agreement instead, to which both sides agreed.

In view of these facts the beginning of a letter from General von Schleicher to Gröner of March 25 is especially interesting: "First of all, many beautiful Easter eggs, but not the sort of cuckoo's eggs that the firm Severing-Badt has just hatched in Leipzig. Seldom have men tried to save such an ill-conceived action in so treacherous a way." [25] Only a man full of prejudice against the Social Democrats and the Prussian police could have written in this way. For the police investigations had demonstrated that the Brown House in Munich, the National Socialists' party headquarters, had declared a general state of armed emergency for the day of the presidential election, and that many Nazi units were preparing for a German civil war.[26] At this juncture the National Socialists and their friends naturally employed the tactics of the wolf that accuses the sheep of having soiled his water: they claimed that they had been merely protecting themselves against possible Communist uprisings. By the end of March the Bavarian police found it necessary to confiscate the weapon stores of the Bavarian Home Guard in the Inn and Chiem districts in order to preserve them from a National Socialist attack.[27]

Part of the uncovered material was of special interest to the Reichswehr. For years it had been fearful — either rightly or wrongly — of a violent attack by Polish forces on eastern German regions. Not only the Reichswehr, but also the so-called Border Guard (*Grenzschutz*), composed of nationalist volunteers, expected to oppose such an invasion. But now, in a campaign address at Lauenburg, a small town in Further Pomerania, close to the Polish Corridor, Hitler declared that he would not sacrifice his fighters for the sake of the "system," that is, the Republic. Rather, he would protect Germany's borders *only after* the supporters of the present "system" had first been annihilated. This was the most blatant example conceivable of the party's being put ahead of the fatherland. And it corresponded exactly to Hitler's attitude of 1923, when he shattered hopes for a German united front against the French occupation of the Ruhr with the declaration that the "November criminals" had to be dealt with first. And now the police investigations showed that the Lauenburg philippic had not been a mere rhetorical arabesque on the Führer's part; on the contrary, it corresponded precisely with the directions which had been sent out to the SA detachments. It is difficult to imagine anything calculated to evoke greater and deeper disgust in a Ministry of Defense. Yet the disclosures do not seem to have made the slightest impression on the chief of the ministry office, General von Schleicher.[28]

His indifference was not shared by the ministers of all the principal lands; they now demanded that energetic steps be taken against these paramilitary bands of Hitler's supporters, which were largely led by former Army officers. Prussia and Bavaria were not alone in this concern. According to a report from Gröner to Brüning of April 10, 1932, Saxony, Württemberg, Baden, and Hesse were of the same opinion. Gröner assumed that the governments of all these lands would outlaw the SA and SS if the national government were to fail once more to take effective steps itself. "The events of the last few weeks make a decision necessary now."

Gröner's letter also shows the obstacles to effective government action presented by the "assurances of loyalty mechanically produced" by the Nazi leaders: "It is not consistent with the sovereignty of the state that a political party be permitted to maintain a private army organized in a military fashion, the leaders of which — generally former Army officers — necessarily bring it into conflict with the policies and the organs of the state through their efforts to develop the military effectiveness of their forces for promoting their special party interests." This argument was irrefutable, but it was to cost Gröner his head.

In his well-known letter of July 1947 to Rudolf Pechel, editor of the *Deutsche Rundschau*, Brüning included the following remarkable sentence: "The dissolution of the SA and SS after Hindenburg's re-election in April 1932 was decided by the Army and the ministries of interior of the several lands *during my absence from Berlin in the presidential campaign. In my opinion this was an unnecessarily hasty step.*" But the facts were not quite like that. For, as we shall presently see, Brüning's statement in 1947 contradicts the documented facts provided especially by Frau Gröner-Geyer in the biography of her father.[29]

According to the evidence, Brüning was indeed absent from the first meetings in which the issue was discussed. He missed the discussion of April 6 because of campaign commitments and was again absent on April 8, a Friday, when Gröner discussed his plan with the chiefs of army and navy command and with General von Schleicher. At this point Schleicher energetically *supported* an emergency decree to ban the Nazi organizations, a draft of which lay before him. Admiral Raeder, chief of naval command, suggested that they could simultaneously outlaw the *Reichsbanner*, but Schleicher opposed him vigorously. The result of this conference was complete agreement between Gröner and the generals. Schleicher went even further: he called up the state secretary in the Chancellory, Hermann Pünder, to tell him that the psychological moment to strike was now at hand.

Schleicher's behavior on this critical Friday was consistent with the observations he had been making in confidential company. In a letter of June 13, 1932, that is, after Brüning's fall, Gröner told his friend Gleich: "At a dinner at the Russian embassy some ten weeks ago, Schleicher remarked to some other German guests (witness: State Secretary Schäffer) that the Reichswehr will never tolerate the Nazis' coming to power." According to Schäffer's extremely accurate diary, this conversation took place on the evening of March 3, 1932. To corroborate his prediction, Schleicher had asked General von Hammerstein, chief of army command, to join the discussion, inquiring whether he did not agree. Hammerstein assured Schleicher and his friends that he was indeed of the same opinion and noted that he had recently summoned his generals to assure himself that they would follow him unconditionally if Hitler were to come to power and he, Hammerstein, were to refuse to obey his orders. For as Hammerstein pointed out, if the German nation were to prove so stupid as to set a fool at its head, then one would have to decide for oneself what to do and what was necessary if tragedy were to be forestalled. If this was the attitude of Schleicher and the generals, they surely must have welcomed the prospective ban of the SA with enthusiasm.

But by the time that Friday had turned to Saturday, the situation had changed considerably. Schleicher came back to Gröner and confessed that he had been wrestling with tormenting doubts throughout a sleepless night. Not, of course, that he opposed the idea of dissolving the SA, but he felt the government should choose another route. He now proposed that Gröner present Hitler with a list of injunctions and that the dissolution be announced by emergency decree only after Hitler had failed to meet the conditions imposed. This was the typical product of a mind that had an antipathy toward the simple, direct approach. His was the manner of the popular motto: "Why keep it simple if it can be made more complicated?" To his report of this conversation Gröner adds: "In Schleicher's proposal I could see only the sort of tactical feint that conformed to his way of thinking. I had frequently been warned about Schleicher . . . But I had brusquely rejected all these attempts to shake my confidence in the fidelity of my old friend."

Gröner had no taste for Schleicher's idea. But he not only sent his state secretary in the Ministry of Interior, Erich Zweigert, back to Schleicher for a more detailed discussion of his plan, he also reported the general's second thoughts to Hindenburg. The President, however, replied immediately that the first thing to do was not to write a letter to Hitler, but rather to announce the ban. Gröner reports all this in his notes, and the state secretary in the Chancellory, Hermann Pünder, substantiates the accuracy of his report.

Up to this time Brüning had not been consulted on the matter since he was still away on his campaign trip, most recently in Königsberg. But on Sunday, April 10, he returned to Berlin. On the afternoon of that same day he held a conference on the question of the SA ban, in which Gröner and Minister of Justice Curt Joël, together with State Secretary Zweigert, Otto Meissner, chief of the President's office, and Hermann Pünder, chief of the Chancellor's office, participated. Schleicher was also present, as chief of the defense minister's office. Thus all the relevant authorities and ministries of the national government were represented at the meeting. Gröner had already outlined Schleicher's proposal in the report that has been mentioned just above. In this report Gröner had objected that, "At the present moment, when domestic tensions are at a peak, the choice of this [Schleicher's] course of action would signify a weakness of will . . . on the part of the national government. In the public mind the impression would be created that the national government had wished to give the NSDAP [*Nationalsozialistische deutsche Arbeiterpartei*, the National Socialist German Workers' Party] enough time to transform its military organizations into harmless groups." [30]

At Gröner's suggestion, Schleicher had brought along a draft of the letter he thought the minister of interior should send to Hitler. Gröner insisted that it sounded too much like a request and that he therefore would not sign it. Joël went on to make several well-founded legal arguments against such a step. A rather long and vigorous discussion then ensued, in the course of which, according to Pünder's notes, Meissner kept trying to find some solution that would keep Hindenburg as distant as possible from the whole affair. Neither Meissner nor any other participant in the meeting was prepared to accept Schleicher's proposal. Pünder explicitly reports that Brüning declared himself in favor of immediate action, that is, for Gröner's plan, substantiating his opinion "with many examples from the recent past and the observations he had made on his extended campaign trips." These words must certainly be taken to mean that Brüning had found the German domestic situation so untenable in the face of the continued excesses by the SA and SS that only the immediate abolition of these groups could save the Reich. And on the strength of this conference Brüning decided that he would request the President's decision the next morning.

Thus at this decisive meeting Schleicher had been completely alone in wishing to temporize with Hitler. Naturally the general took this isolation very badly and, according to one unsubstantiated report, left the conference in a manner which bespoke a real clash.[31] In any event, his old friendship with Gröner was at an end; and the minister, who at first could not believe the breach had come, was soon to learn the truth. What were Schleicher's motives in this shift? I do not accept the commonly offered explanation that he had deliberately let his old friend "run aground." Rather I agree with Gröner's daughter who finds the answer in Schleicher's letter of March 25, the beginning of which was quoted just above. The letter betrays Schleicher's massive prejudice against the Social Democrats: either he was blind to the way they were helping preserve the government at this time, or else he simply preferred to ignore this truth. For when people like Schleicher rail against "partisan spirit," they always mean the partisan spirit of their opponents, not realizing that their own sentiments are equally strong and disrupting.

A few lines from Schleicher's letter will suffice to show his attitude: "After the events of the last few days, I am really quite happy that we have a counterbalance in the form of the Nazis, even though they are ill-behaved and to be used only with greatest care. Indeed, *if the Nazis did not exist, we should have had to invent them*." Whoever could write words like these could clearly not have joined sincerely in a vigorous move against the National Socialists. Furthermore, these lines not only show that Schleicher was incapable of holding to a steady course for two months in a row — compare, for instance, his dinner conversation on March 3 — they also demonstrate that he did not have the slightest sense of the duties he had assumed as a high official of the state, whose constitution he had sworn to uphold.

Later events were also to show that Schleicher was utterly unable to deal effectively with those menaces that even he could see. It is easy enough to hurl abuse at the "Mosse Communists," but it is quite another and much more difficult thing to bring the storm-threatened ship of state safely into port. It seems to be characteristic of generals who dabble in politics that their self-confidence exceeds their actual skill.

Schleicher was not the man to surrender even when soundly defeated. If he could not succeed by direct attack, he could move in from the rear. On Monday morning, immediately after the Sunday conference, Hindenburg granted his assent to the proposed decree. But in the course of that afternoon Meissner reported to Brüning that the Old Gentleman was experiencing second thoughts on the wisdom of issuing the decree before the Prussian elections, scheduled for April 24, the second Sunday from then, and that these second thoughts derived from Schleicher. Clearly, the general had once more gone to his old regimental comrade, the President's son Oskar, and Oskar had voiced his concern that his father would receive abuse from the Right if he were to issue the decree. This reaction was typical of the Hindenburg circle. The Leftists could write and argue as they wished without disturbing anyone in the presidential palace. But if the Rightists, who had been using every available weapon against the field marshal, even wrinkled their brows in public, the President's staff were smitten with fright and kept trying desperately to find some way to thwart the Rightists without opposing them.

Further conversations with Braun and Severing had convinced Brüning and Gröner that neither Prussia nor the other lands concerned were prepared to tolerate further hesitation on the part of the national government and that, if Berlin refused to act, the local governments would proceed with independent measures of their own. They therefore consulted with the President again, and Hindenburg now assured them that he was firmly prepared to issue the decree. The cabinet agreed unanimously, and on Wednesday, April 13, the ban was published.

All true German patriots welcomed this evidence of firm decision on the part of the President and Chancellor. Ah, but how quickly this fair illusion was to disappear!

On Friday, April 15, two days after the President had ordered the dissolution of the SA and SS, a letter from this same President to Gröner appeared in all the newspapers, suggesting that the minister of defense and interior consider a ban on "similar organizations . . . maintained by other political parties." The field marshal went on to say that he had signed the decree at Gröner's request, and only after the minister had assured him that the order was "absolutely necessary" for the preservation of the state. But in the meantime, Hindenburg continued, he had learned that other parties also had such paramilitary organizations. "If I am to fulfill my obligation to carry out my official duties in an objective, nonpartisan manner . . . I must insist that, if my information proves correct, these other organizations receive the same treatment." And with this letter Hindenburg enclosed the "evidence received," which turned out to refer exclusively to the *Reichsbanner*.

The very form of this letter was a political monstrosity. Even if the President were assailed by doubts concerning a decree that he had signed, how could he bring himself to make these misgivings public without first obtaining the agreement of the Chancellor and the relevant minister — indeed, without even notifying them? Article 50 of the Weimar constitution expressly stipulates: "All presidential orders and decrees, including those in military or naval matters, require the countersignature of the Chancellor or of the relevant minister."

To this point, Professor Anschütz remarks in his commentary that this ministerial responsibility is not merely restricted to orders and decrees in the narrow sense of formal government acts, but rather that it also covers those actions and utterances which, although not cloaked in official form, and possibly quite confidential in intent, like letters, speeches, and private conversations, nevertheless have or could have political effects.[32] The members of the Weimar constitutional convention had had very unpleasant memories of such so-called "private" political utterances in high government circles under William II; it was the intent of Article 50 to preclude their recurrence in the Republic.

But this is precisely what was happening when the President published his criticism of a minister in this way before either the minister or the Chancellor had been given an opportunity to reply. As a matter of constitutional law it does not matter, of course, whether the President took this action on his own initiative or at the suggestion of some unauthorized adviser. No less astonishing was the President's statement that only in the last two days, between Wednesday and Friday, had he learned there were "similar organizations maintained by other political parties." Everybody in Germany knew that he was not only an honorary member of the *Stahlhelm* but also a vigorous protector of the organization.

And then there was the matter of the evidence against the *Reichsbanner*. The documents had been furnished by the Ministry of Defense and had been transmitted to the President not on the initiative of Defense Minister Gröner, as one might have expected, but rather by one of his subordinates, probably General von Schleicher or General von Hammerstein. From the standpoint of orderly administration this clearly deliberate circumvention of the minister, the President's subsequent acquiescence in the misdeed, and his protection of its perpetrators comprised what was truly the worst part of the entire affair.

So this is how the much-vaunted presidential system really worked! Having specifically charged the Chancellor on October 7, 1931, with the task of forming a cabinet "with no commitments to any parties," thus making himself the focus and fundament of the entire system, Hindenburg now considered himself justified in whipping up public opinion against ministers whom he had appointed and who depended on his confidence. And this happened only five days after he had been re-elected President of Germany, with the help of these ministers, over none other than the man who, with the help of the SA and SS, was threatening the order and security of the German state. In return for this assistance Hindenburg now recommended — indeed, he demanded — a ban on the *Reichsbanner*, an organization that had the defense of the German Republic as its purpose and which had protected numerous pro-Hindenburg assemblies against disturbance by Hitler's Storm Troopers during the recent campaign. And all this on the strength of what proof? The evidence furnished by the Ministry of Defense proved so inconclusive that Gröner was able to dismiss it with a single stroke of his pen.[33] He explained to the President that he saw no reason to proceed against the *Reichsbanner* nor — significantly — against the *Stahlhelm*.

And so only the Nazi organizations were banned. Goebbels' diary makes it quite clear that the National Socialists had been expecting this decree for several days. When it finally came, Hitler's propaganda chief noted: "This is Gröner's salvo. But perhaps it can be made to be his ruin, too. We understand that Schleicher does not approve of this policy."[34] And when Hindenburg's letter to Gröner appeared, Goebbels made the following comments: "Hindenburg complains about the evidence against the *Reichsbanner* and demands that the treasonable activities of this organization be made the subject of active government concern. This constitutes a severe moral defeat for Brüning's government."

Unfortunately, Goebbels was right. Hindenburg's letter did indeed reveal a gap between himself and his government, one that especially separated the field marshal from his former quartermaster general, Wilhelm Gröner. Had the Old Gentleman already forgotten all the things that Gröner had done for him and for his reputation? In any event a personal incident had come between the two men, one that also played a part in Schleicher's estrangement from Gröner.[35]

Gröner, for many years a widower, had married again in 1930. Not only his bride's social station, but also the strikingly premature birth of a son cast a dubious light on the match. The aged field marshal, rooted in the old Prussian conservative tradition, could only regard all this as a scandal utterly unbecoming a German general. When he nevertheless made this general a "double eagle" by giving him the Ministry of Interior in addition to that of Defense, he certainly did so in order to extend military influence into the Ministry of Interior and not out of any special personal admiration for Gröner.

The letter to Gröner of April 16, 1932, together with its untimely publication, was clearly not the act of a friend or comrade – to refrain from even stronger terms. In any event, it could only destroy Gröner's confidence in the President who had appointed him to office and had approved and signed the decree he had proposed.

In his *Denkwürdigkeiten*, the former Imperial Chancellor Prince von Bülow recalls the warning he received from the old Colonel von Loewenfeld when Bülow, as a younger man, was offered the post of state secretary in the Foreign Ministry: "Each minister who goes into Parliament always reminds me of a lion tamer, who is expected to enter the cage with the beasts . . . If the animals tear him to pieces, our most gracious lord, watching from his box, will not waste too many tears upon his memory." [36] Gröner could be assured that the old field marshal was not going to waste tears on him; and as far as the "beasts" were concerned, the Reichstag had made such progress since 1929 that now every German patriot was sick at heart. Opponents of liberal democracy blamed parliamentary government for this degeneration. But theirs was only a most superficial view. For every representative parliament is more or less an expression of its constituents' feelings and thought. The offensive incidents in the Reichstag were possible only because millions of German men and women took pleasure from them.

On April 25, 1932, General Gröner, minister of interior and defense, wrote to his old friend Gleich: "It is clear that my ruin is being readied with all available means. Hindenburg has bared his old conservative heart and desires a government oriented even further to the Right than that of Brüning . . . If Hindenburg does not become strong and reliable again like Emperor William I, I see evil days ahead." [37]

But now a very different Hohenzollern, great-grandson of William I, saw fit to speak up. On April 14 the former crown prince wrote a letter to Gröner which included the memorable sentence: "I find it incomprehensible that precisely you, as minister of defense, wish to help disperse the *wonderful human resources* which are united in the SA and SS and which are receiving such *valuable training* there." [38] It would be superfluous today to waste any words on these "wonderful human resources" and their "valuable training," and one can understand why the writer of this letter wished to disown it after the catastrophe that ensued. [39] The real misfortune was that Frederick William, as the former heir apparent, enjoyed considerable influence in the officers' corps and sought to use it, as he candidly admits in this letter, in order to bring about "a feeling of mutual trust between the Defense Ministry and the nationalistic paramilitary organizations, including those of the NSDAP."

Gröner now suffered his worst setback: his own ministry, led by Schleicher, his chief subordinate, deserted him. Schleicher had a plan, although certainly not in any final, detailed form, to transform all the paramilitary organizations into a completely nonpolitical athletic association which later, that is, with the Allies' assent, might be turned into a militia to supplement the regular Army. Schleicher probably assumed that these hopes had been dashed by the ban on the SA. In any event, it is certain that he made secret contact with Hitler at this time.[40] After the Third Reich had collapsed, Schleicher's friends argued that he had entered into this clandestine relationship with the Nazi leader in the hope of thwarting the Austrian's hopes for absolute power. But if this was Schleicher's deeper plan, it only shows that he was entangled in his own illusions and that he failed utterly to recognize either Hitler's unbridled lust for absolute power or his complete inability to honor compromise. Nor is there any merit in the argument of Schleicher's friends that he had been thinking most of all about the defense of Germany's eastern border, since it is clear that the Reichswehr was absolutely unable to rely upon the Nazi groups' assistance in this endeavor; or, in any event, the Reichswehr could rely on them much less than on the *Reichsbanner*, against which the distinguished generals continued to harbor such an ineradicable prejudice.

Yet all these excuses for Schleicher's actions do not erase the simple fact that originally he had approved and even welcomed the ban himself and that even later he had not rejected it in principle but rather had suggested another tactical means of reaching the same strategic end. Still less pardonable were his intrigues with the President behind his own superior's back; for he owed his office to Gröner's confidence in him, and thus he owed him full loyalty under every civil and military code of honor. One does not wish to do an injustice to a man who later was a victim of Hitler's treachery. But it is impossible to avoid the conclusion that in April 1932 Schleicher himself set out along the road which was to lead to his frightful death just two years later.*

Regarded from a more general point of view, these intrigues on the part of General von Schleicher and his comrades, together with Field Marshal von Hindenburg, comprised an attempt not merely to make the Reichswehr a state within the German state, but rather to make it an instrument of power superior to the other organs of constituted government. These gamblers in uniform were playing for high stakes, and the true tragedy was their sheer inability to see

* General Schleicher and his wife were murdered during the "Blood Purge" of June 30, 1934. TRANSLATORS.

how they were endangering not only the Republic, but also the Reichswehr and themselves.

Thus Gröner was deserted by all those on whose support and comradeship he had had every reason to reckon most strongly. And on May 10, when he arose in the Reichstag to defend himself and the President's decree against the vehement attack of the National Socialists, he found himself in the predicament described by Schiller's hero, Wallenstein:

> Intelligence alone protects no man,
> For nature so set eyes upon his face
> That noble loyalty must needs stand guard
> To shield his unprotected back from foes.

Gröner knew that his back was unprotected, and this realization robbed him of a part of the strength and flexibility which he needed so desperately at this time.

The National Socialists had entrusted their attack on the SA ban to their delegate Hermann Göring. This was a very clever choice, for Göring was a former military aviator who had won Germany's highest military honor, the Pour le Mérite, in the war and had the sympathy of the militarists with him from the start. Moreover, by means of his studied geniality he had managed to create the impression that he was a better sort of fellow than the rowdies by whom he was surrounded.

Gröner's reply to Göring's attack was not without compelling arguments. He documented his claim that the SA could not be trusted to assist in the defense of the eastern border. He alluded to the menacing influence of Ernst Röhm, whose efforts had made the SA increasingly intolerable ever since the autumn of 1931 until now it was an "absolutely private army" that had grown into a "state against the state." Gröner also showed the speciousness of the attacks against the *Reichsbanner*, an organization which had never assumed police or military functions nor in any way prepared a putsch. And to Göring's argument that without the SA there would be no order in Germany, Gröner replied with his own argument that was apt enough at the time and corroborated by Hitler, himself, on June 30, 1934: "Were it not for the SA, we should already have had peace and order in Germany for many years."

But Gröner's speech remained without effect. In part this was due to the man's personality. For, as a friendly observer remarked, with all his intelligence he still lacked that ability to elicit a sympathetic response which is so essential to any speaker and which, for example, his predecessor Gessler had possessed in such high degree. This weakness was certainly magnified now by Gröner's sense of having been deserted. One can hardly deliver an impressive and moving address when one knows that not only one's declared foes, but also one's ostensible friends, are lying in wait for the kill. As Gröner remarked in his papers: "The fact that I was not especially happy about this double attack, from the Reichstag in front and the generals behind, can scarcely be held against me." [41] But even if Gröner had been a better parliamentarian, he could not have prevailed against the continuous interruptions and insults with which the National Socialist delegates consciously and systematically harried him. It was unfortunate that when he spoke the presiding officer of the Reichstag was not Paul Löbe, but his deputy, Thomas Esser of the Center Party, a man who was no match for the Nazi storm.

Thus the Reichstag debate had the effect of a severe defeat for Gröner, and it was immediately touted as such by his opponents. Worst of all, Generals Schleicher and Hammerstein now came out openly against him. They spread the rumor that Gröner was ill, and two days later Schleicher had the effrontery to advise him to report himself sick and go on leave. Equally menacing was the attack mounted by the four-man delegation of the Conservative People's Party. Count Kuno Westarp, who presumably still held Gröner responsible for the fall of the monarchy on November 11, 1918, and his colleague, Hans von Lindeiner-Wildau, went immediately from this Reichstag debate to Brüning's office in hopes of persuading the Chancellor to ask Gröner to resign. As Westarp himself reports, he explained to the Chancellor how dangerous it would be if the Reichswehr, *which was so strongly infiltrated by the National Socialists*, were to begin to feel that it was directed by a marked and useless man.

Brüning could not bring himself to drop Gröner. He did, however, let the conservative gentlemen persuade him not to intervene in Gröner's defense at the debate to be held that same evening. And indeed it was not until his great speech on the following day, which was primarily devoted to the question of disarmament and reparations, that Brüning defended the SA ban in public. It is true that in this speech he did express himself clearly: "I have been patient for a very long time but I would be declared irresponsible before the bar of history if I did not now finally put an end to certain things." But even this sentence, which seemed to promise resolute action, appears to have slipped Brüning's mind in 1947, when he wrote to Dr. Pechel that in his opinion the ban had been too hasty. In any event, the majority of the Reichstag remained loyal to the

Chancellor on this issue. The motion of no confidence proposed by the National Socialists, German Nationalists, and Communists against the entire cabinet was defeated, 287 to 257.

Meanwhile, the busy burrowing in the presidential palace had been continuing apace. Again we have Westarp's own report of how, on May 13, Meissner made an appointment for him with Hindenburg, to whom Westarp presented the same hopes and arguments that he had employed to such good effect on Brüning just three days before. "When I again insisted that Brüning had to be kept on for the sake of foreign affairs, the President nodded in agreement." But only two weeks later that nod meant something else. Westarp notes that Hindenburg "considered Gröner's resignation absolutely necessary and discussed with Meissner what was to be done. Meissner reported that at this same time Hammerstein and Schleicher, speaking for the Reichswehr, were demanding that their minister resign, and that he, Meissner, expected Gröner to appear at any moment to request that his resignation be accepted." Thus neither Field Marshal von Hindenburg, nor his state secretary, Otto Meissner, nor the old Prussian Conservative Count Kuno Westarp took any offense at the fact that the Reichswehr had presumed to hand its minister his hat. Was this the old Prussian tradition? Or was it, rather, aping the splendid example of South American officers' revolts? To the honor of Elard von Oldenburg-Januschau it must be remarked here that in a letter of May 21 to Freiherr Wilhelm von Gayl the old junker expressed his disapproval of "the conditions in the Defense Ministry, with all those political generals, this time acting against their own chief," although he was "willing to grant Gröner this unenviable end." [42]

At this point it is important to remember how in 1923 Defense Minister Otto Gessler had foiled General von Seeckt's attempt to withhold the Reichswehr's support from Chancellor Stresemann, and how in 1926 Gessler had forced von Seeckt to resign when the general began treating his minister as a negligible quantity. For at that time Germany still had a Reichstag capable of fulfilling its most important duty. Now the country only had a President and his extraconstitutional staff.

On May 13, 1932, Gröner handed in his resignation. In a letter to a friend he traced his failure to the basic contradiction between the ban on the SA and his decision of January 29, 1932, according to which National Socialists had been admitted to the Reichswehr.[43] But Gröner did not resign from both ministerial posts, as his enemies had hoped he would, but only from the Defense Ministry. He was still minister of interior. One can well assume that Brüning had in-

sisted on this, lest the National Socialists' victory be all too striking, even as no change was made in the SA ban itself.[44] For Brüning was still Chancellor. But for how long? On this same evening
the President left Berlin for a spring holiday on his estate Neudeck
in East Prussia. In what frame of mind would he return?

The part of Brüning's Reichstag address of May 11 that dealt
with foreign affairs had had a great effect. Even the National Socialists had listened to it attentively, foregoing their customary attempts to create disturbance. Indeed, they could hardly have asked
for more if one of their own party had held the Chancellor's post.
The double goal Brüning set for himself and Germany in this speech
was, in truth, extraordinarily ambitious. With respect to disarmament, he claimed what he called "equal rights for Germany through
universal disarmament"; with respect to reparations he called for the
annulment of all intergovernmental debts. In other words, he demanded the complete and permanent renunciation of all reparations.
If these conditions were met, Brüning continued, then at last that
peace would be at hand for which the whole world yearned. Brüning certainly believed all this with complete sincerity, even as did
many of his listeners. Unfortunately the actual course of later events
was to show that they had been quite wrong.

Brüning concluded his address with the statement that he wished
to preserve calm, because "one has special need of calm when one
is *within one hundred meters of the goal.*" And a majority of the
Reichstag answered this hopeful trope with heavy applause and
shouts of approbation. Nor did this optimism seem unjustified, for
Brüning could truthfully report that he had presented this same
point of view and these same arguments to the foreign statesmen
with whom he had been negotiating, and that his opinion "had
found extensive support in many lands."

The Chancellor was referring to a significant victory he had already achieved on the issue of disarmament. In mid-April he, the
British Prime Minister, Ramsay MacDonald, and the American secretary of state, Henry Stimson, were all taking part in the International
Disarmament Conference at Geneva. Brüning used the occasion to
approach the representatives of Britain and the United States with
the confidential proposal that they grant Germany the following demands: a reduction of the term of military service from twelve
to six years; an increase in German military forces in such a way that
Germany might train and arm 100,000 more men, either as additions
to the Reichswehr or as auxiliary reserves; a grant to Germany of the
right to acquire the weapons denied her by the Treaty of Versailles;
the abrogation of the treaty's fifth part, that is, all limitations on

German military, air, and naval strength, and its replacement with a new agreement.[45]

On April 26 both MacDonald and Stimson expressed their approval. In doing so, they clearly were influenced by the thought that now, after Hindenburg's victory over Hitler in the presidential election, Brüning's position was secure for the foreseeable future. And they trusted Brüning. The Italian representative, Grandi, was drawn into the negotiations, and he, too, agreed. At this point Tardieu, the French Premier, was urgently invited by the others to come to Geneva as quickly as he could. But Tardieu did not appear, explaining that ill-health precluded travel at the time. It has often been suggested that Tardieu had diplomatic reasons for exaggerating his indisposition. It is certain that he had at least one political motive in addition to medical reasons for staying in France. For he was in the midst of an electoral campaign and thus scarcely able to agree publicly with the idea of abrogating that one part of the Versailles treaty which a significant number of French voters regarded as their most important guarantee of peace.

Without Tardieu, of course, the settlement of the disarmament question had to be postponed, and Brüning had to return to Berlin with no more than British, American, and Italian approval on a matter which, by its very nature, would affect France most directly. Yet even this much constituted considerable progress, and Brüning could have built on this basis if he had remained in power. But two weeks later, on May 30, he was dismissed from office.

It has often been maintained that Brüning would not have been dismissed if Tardieu had come to Geneva and agreed to the disarmament proposals. Yet this argument is without merit. As we shall see, Hindenburg had quite different reasons for withdrawing his confidence from Brüning. It is true that as late as May 11 Hindenburg had agreed with Westarp that Brüning should be kept for diplomatic reasons. And these international considerations were all the more important so long as the disarmament issue was unresolved. International considerations, however, were certainly not the decisive factor in Brüning's fall. This was shown clearly on the day of his dismissal when Chancellor Brüning was told by the American ambassador that the French were ready to agree if he would come immediately to Geneva for consultation. Hindenburg did not even give Brüning time to tell this good news.

In any event, only the politically naïve would argue that such a diplomatic victory would have strengthened Brüning's position in Germany to any meaningful extent. The fact is that German nationalists took each diplomatic victory of their government as a foregone conclusion or at least as a matter of indifference, while the opposition's agitation only grew stronger.

Moreover, Brüning's Reichstag speech of May 11 was by no means received with universal approval by foreign statesmen otherwise well disposed toward the Chancellor. As Sir John Simon told von Neurath on May 14, the British government wished to serve as "honest broker" between Germany and the other nations of the West. This role would be easier if the German Chancellor would refrain from stating his position so publicly and in such a dogmatic way.[46] For, Simon went on, he feared the reaction of the French, whose Premier, Tardieu, had expressed grave doubts at Briand's funeral concerning the German plans for the disarmament of others and the rearmament of themselves.[47]

Brüning's notion of the simple abrogation of all debts naturally found its severest opposition in the United States. In the course of Anglo-American conversations at Geneva on April 23, Henry Stimson had emphatically told the British ministers present that he hoped Brüning had not persuaded himself that America would accept his central proposition, namely, that Germany was utterly and permanently unable to pay any reparations. For, Stimson pointedly observed, Germany had erased her domestic indebtedness (through inflation) and had completely modernized her industrial plant.[48] Stimson made a similar declaration to the French ambassador in Washington: "America desires that Germany should continue to pay reparations. Nothing could please us more or clear up the situation better than a loyal recognition by Germany, though only in principle, of her pecuniary obligations. On this point we support the position taken up by France." [49]

German and British worries about the attitude of the French were relieved considerably by the outcome of the French elections of May 1 and 8, 1932. The results showed an unexpectedly strong swing of French opinion to the Left. The Radicals in particular had made large gains, and it was clear that their leader, Edouard Herriot, would be the next premier of France. Herriot, moreover, was in favor of rapprochement and a man whom one could with certainty expect to regard the German and British point of view with greater sympathy and interest than did Tardieu.

Thus Brüning's statement of May 11 that he was within one hundred meters of his goal seemed fully justified. Then suddenly, on May 30, 1932, the world was astonished by the news that Brüning and his entire cabinet had resigned.

How was it possible? Only seven weeks earlier Hindenburg had been re-elected president primarily through Brüning's efforts! The full story of Brüning's dismissal is highly complicated, and its details are still in dispute. On one point, however, there can be no doubt at all: the aged Hindenburg had no more use for Brüning; he wanted to be rid of him.

Among Hindenburg's motives the efforts of Brüning's government to reorganize the program of eastern aid (*Osthilfe*) played a significant role. The eastern aid was a grand rescue operation undertaken by the national government for the sake of agricultural interests in the eastern German provinces, most particularly in East Prussia, which was suffering special distress in part for natural reasons and in part because of its separation from Germany by the Polish Corridor.

No one denied that German agriculture was in such a plight that the national government had no choice but to render aid. And everybody had to agree that the increasing national emergency and fiscal distress made a good part of this aid illusory. Yet it was equally clear that the East German landed interests were not going to be satisfied with any help given, and that they still followed the advice of the old junker Ruprecht-Ransern who, in 1893, had told them they would have to scream as loud as possible if they wished to persuade other elements of the nation to make sacrifices for them.

There was only a limited number of ways the national government could respond to such demands, but even so dedicated an agrarian as Freiherr Magnus von Braun, minister of agriculture under both Papen and Schleicher, explicitly admitted "that Brüning and his government did everything in the realm of human possibility." [50] One concrete expression of the cabinet's concern was the appointment of Hans Schlange-Schöningen as national commissioner for eastern aid. He was, of course, a conservative agrarian, but at the same time he was wise enough to oppose Hugenberg's stubborn opposition most firmly and to recognize that Hitler was a severe menace to the German Reich.[51] Schlange-Schöningen certainly did everything in his power to assist his fellow agriculturists. But there were many instances when even the best of will and all available resources were not enough.

One of the principal purposes of the eastern aid was the relief or refunding of the debts that were pressing down so heavily on rural estates. An effort was made to replace the existing loans at high interest rates by more favorable national credits at lower rates. Federal guarantees were used to induce the landowners' creditors to come to some agreement. Yet even after everything possible had been done, there were still cases where there was no hope of refunding the debts and the proprietor could not be maintained in ownership. What was to be done in such instances?

Schlange-Schöningen attacked this problem in consultation with the national Ministry of Labor. At this time the ministry was headed by the Centrist delegate Adam Stegerwald who, as a leader of the Christian Labor Unions, was already regarded with distrust by Rightists. The apprehension of East German landowners was especially aroused in November 1931, when Schlange remarked at a press conference that "given such a plenitude of arable land, a domestic migration of Germans will have to be directed toward the underpopulated East. Agricultural enterprises there which can no longer be made to pay their way will be divided and apportioned out as homesteads as quickly as possible."

No real objections could be made to this idea. Ever since the end of the nineteenth century many agrarian leaders, especially the more conservative among them, had been calling for such "domestic colonization," defined by Max Sering as "the deliberate establishment of new settlements in the traditional homeland of the colonizing nation." [52] One could even ask whether the republican parties, the Social Democrats in particular, had not perhaps done too little in this respect while they were still in power. Especially now, when German unemployment was constantly increasing and had already assumed extremely critical proportions, the idea of settling appropriate unemployed workers and their families upon lands which could no longer be made to support the former owners was not only attractive, it was compelling.

But the landed property owners saw the problem otherwise. From their point of view, families that for many decades, perhaps even centuries, had been managing inherited estates were now to be driven from their ancestral acres in order to make room for members of the metropolitan proletariat who were without any real sense of union with the soil. In the later Napoleonic period, at the time of the Stein-Hardenberg reforms, a junker had exclaimed: "Our country homes will become so many hells if free peasants are to be our neighbors." Now, of course, it was no longer possible for them to be so brutally frank. Yet it certainly does not seem unjustified to assume that many of the deeply conservative, Protestant East Elbian landed gentry simply could not accept the idea of being surrounded by a new yeomanry whose whole background had been proletarian and who were most likely Social Democrats or Catholic Centrists. [53]

The obvious avenue for an attack against such dangerous

schemes was, of course, the President, who, as proprietor of the Neudeck estate, belonged to the East Prussian landed gentry, among whom, indeed, he spent his holidays. In fact, Hindenburg was at Neudeck in May 1932. His state secretary, Otto Meissner, visited him there at the time and recounts in his memoirs that East Prussian landowners like Oldenburg-Januschau and others, whom he also names, had made a great impression on the President with their complaints about the government's plans for "an agrarian revolution." Since all these gentlemen have stated that they never discussed these things with Hindenburg, and since Meissner, himself, does not claim to have been present at such conversations, one cannot accept his proposition as proved.

But not all of Meissner's memories of Neudeck are so uncertain. He reports, for instance, that the President, quite distressed, told him that "throughout the province he had met a wave of rural discontent and mistrust concerning the plans of the national government, and that East Prussians from all walks of life were urging him to appoint nationalistic men with agrarian sympathies to government posts." [54] One can reject this piece of evidence only by assuming that Meissner was deliberately lying. But both the situation at the time and the further development of events gives one no reason to make such a supposition.

Furthermore, at least one document exists which casts a direct light on efforts being made then by members of the East Prussian gentry. This is a letter of May 24, 1932, from Freiherr Wilhelm von Gayl to President Hindenburg. Freiherr von Gayl can hardly be likened to the usual narrow rural conservative. He was a man of talent and of thought. Having been trained in the Prussian civil service, he was now the veteran president of the East Prussian Land Settlement Bank, an enterprise of extreme importance to East Prussian agriculture. He represented East Prussia in the national Reichsrat and in the Prussian Staatsrat, playing a predominant, and naturally German Nationalist's, role in both these upper chambers.

The letter refers to a draft of a proposed decree which was designed to encourage new agricultural settlements in the East. The proposal would have given the "East Office" authority to auction off properties which could not be refinanced and to carry out these auctions whether the creditors demanded such sales or not. In this Gayl saw "a further invasion" of private property rights and "another slip into state socialism."

This final phrase, of course, was intentionally chosen with an eye to the President's prejudices and was consonant with the entire vocabulary of the Nationalists. Another trope designed especially for Hindenburg's ear was Gayl's statement that "moral erosion in the East is continuing at a frightening pace. It is gradually wearing away the effective strength of those very groups which until now have *incorporated the national will to resist Poland.*" [55] If an otherwise responsible person could write like this, one can well imagine in what sort of tones the ordinary East Prussian junkers were screaming, and it would have been the purest form of miracle if their cries had not penetrated through the gates of Neudeck to the old field marshal's ears.

The truly remarkable fact, however, is that the ostensible proposal to which Gayl refers was not at all the final draft of the intended measure, but rather only one of the many versions prepared by some ministry official, such as are always drawn up in greater or lesser numbers in the course of this sort of legislative proceeding in order that responsible authorities may choose among the various alternatives presented. Such drafts are, of course, official secrets, meant only for the eyes of properly authorized persons, and the question immediately presents itself: How did this document find its way to Herr von Gayl's desk? Did the ministries harbor spies who were working for the opposition parties?

It is significant that, in his letter of May 24 to the President, von Gayl said many people and groups in East Germany had been deeply disturbed upon learning of this proposed measure. For it was manifestly impossible that the draft was known by any large number of Germans at that time. This last point has been corroborated by Freiherr von Braun, a man who was quite well disposed toward Gayl. Indeed, Gayl's monstrous exaggeration was later substantiated by ministry director Richard Reichard, an associate of Schlange's in the East Office, in a letter of October 17, 1952. [56]

Hindenburg read Gayl's lamentations and directed Meissner to assure the gentleman that he would make these remonstrances the topic of an early conversation with Brüning. [57] But at the same time Meissner called up Schlange-Schöningen; reported the attack by the East Prussian landowners, who were branding him an "agrarian bolshevik"; and urged him to request an appointment with the President immediately after his return to Berlin "in order to set things in order." [58] Schlange evidently saw no point in such a talk, presumably because he no longer credited the Old Gentleman with the ability to follow his necessarily rather complicated explanations.

So instead of talking directly to the President, Schlange simply sent him a letter which was certainly clear enough. In it he expressed his indignation that precisely those groups for whom he had already done so much were now setting obstacles before him in their blind selfishness. Germany must truly have been in desperate straits if a conservative Pomeranian landowner like Schlange turned with sharp words against "the blinded elements" which, like their predecessors at the time of Freiherr vom Stein, opposed a necessary development and sought to subordinate it to their own private interests.[59] Schlange prophesied that one day the stormy waves of history would wash over these stubborn groups; and the accuracy of his vision can best be judged by those East German landowners' descendants, now refugees from their ancestral homes.

At the conclusion of his letter, Schlange offered to resign in the event that the President would not accept the policies outlined in the final version of his decree. Meissner reports that Hindenburg was indignant at what he called "this young minister's rather unusual mode of behavior." [60] If this report is correct — and we have no reason to doubt that it is — it only demonstrates again that, with reference to the ministers of his government, Hindenburg did not regard himself as the president of a republic which in fact he was by virtue of the constitution and his election, but rather as a general whose primary demand is the discipline of his officers. In any event, there can be no doubt of one important fact: despite the wise warning that Schlange's letter contained, Hindenburg was completely incapable of regarding the problem of allocating the hopelessly indebted estates to new farmers from any other viewpoint but that of a member of the landed gentry.

But Hindenburg's excitement at the supposedly threatening prospect of "agrarian bolshevism" was probably only one of the factors which determined his state of mind upon his return to Berlin from Neudeck. Another component can be described with the single word "Schleicher." One day the general had appeared as a visitor to Neudeck. His other statements and activities at this time permit us to deduce with a high degree of certainty just what he told the President and his son. Now that he had brought Gröner to a fall, he wanted to see Brüning go, too. For some time now he had not been completely satisfied with the Chancellor. Well before the most recent crisis, during that dinner on March 3 at the Russian embassy in the course of which Schleicher had spoken so sharply against the Nazis, he had remarked to Severing with his customary nonchalance that it would be impossible to watch "good old Heinrich" try to play chancellor much longer: the man simply could not make decisions, and increasing numbers of unemployed were streaming into the streets.[61]

It is very significant that it was Schleicher who made this observation; for no one made it more difficult for Brüning to come to a decision in the matter of the SA ban than General von Schleicher, himself. Equally revealing is the subsequent report of Carl Severing that, in his presence, just a few days after this disloyal remark about Brüning, Schleicher treated the Chancellor in the warmest and most engaging manner possible. On one day, a drop of poison; on the next, a winning smile: this sort of game was no trouble at all for a man like Schleicher.

But if in early March Schleicher was still uncertain whether he should keep his dagger hidden in his cloak or strike it home, by May he was definitely determined to make his move. His decision became apparent when he declined Brüning's offer that he succeed Gröner in the Ministry of Defense, especially since he rejected the post in a manner calculated to offend the Chancellor. According to Wheeler-Bennett's version of this affair, which probably is derived from the former Chancellor's account, Brüning concluded the long and bitter conversation with the prophecy that Schleicher would finally get caught in a web of his own making.[62] Obviously this observation did nothing to discourage the general from continuing his intrigues; and his visit to Neudeck, which was clearly a part of these schemes, can have had no other purpose than the destruction of Hindenburg's last bit of confidence in Brüning.

Schleicher cannot have found this a difficult task. The Old Gentleman was already annoyed at his Chancellor, and for a reason which would have made ordinary mortals feel grateful instead: namely, his re-election as President of Germany. For this election had been achieved with the aid of the Social Democrats and of the "Cathlists," as the decidedly Protestant Hindenburg liked to call the Centrists, and against the opposition of many who had supported him in 1925. Hindenburg's Old Comrades took pains to point this out at every opportunity, while Oskar Hindenburg was shuddering at the thought that his father might suffer a social boycott at any time.

The field marshal placed the blame for this undesirable state of affairs squarely upon the shoulders of his Chancellor, who had arranged the victorious alliance and led it to triumph. François-Poncet calls Brüning naïve for not having foreseen that this strange constellation would bring about his ruin.[63] But this charge is completely unjust, for if Hindenburg had not wished to be re-elected with Social Democratic assistance, he should have said so as soon as it became apparent that his election was possible *only* with their aid. In short, Hindenburg should have declined to run for re-election after Hugenberg's blind opposition had destroyed Brüning's hope of obtaining a parliamentary extension of Hindenburg's term of office. But Hindenburg had not declined to run, precisely because he

wanted to remain President. With this decision he forfeited every
right to complain about the way his re-election was accomplished,
especially since all the major campaign decisions were made with
his full knowledge and approval. Anyone with the most elementary
sense for moral values could — indeed, had to — regard the matter
in this light. The odd constellation of political forces had not been
uncomfortable for the field marshal alone, but also for the millions
of republican voters who were in no way captivated by his modes
of thought but who had found consolation in their conviction that
he would defend the constitution and maintain the state against the
National Socialist rebellion. The old proverb is applicable here:
you cannot have your cake and eat it, too. But that is precisely what
Hindenburg wished to do.

It was in this frame of mind that Hindenburg returned in late
May to Berlin. At eleven o'clock on the morning of May 29 the
Chancellor had an opportunity to make a report to his President.
But Hindenburg did not grant him many words. Brüning had had
only sufficient time to speak of the further emergency decrees —
including a national works program — that the cabinet was preparing when Hindenburg interrupted him brusquely with the statement that he would sign no more emergency decrees, and that he
expected all future legislation to pass through the regular three read-
ings in the Reichstag. Then Hindenburg went on to make clear just
what sort of future legislation he had in mind. He read these demands from a prepared sheet of paper. Friedrich Meinecke has reported them as follows on the strength of "a reliable source": [64]
(1) future government policy must be conservative in tone; (2) government by labor union officials would have to stop; (3) an end
must be put to "agrarian bolshevism."

This third point requires no further discussion after what has
just been said above. It demonstrates clearly how well the landed
gentry had succeeded in seducing the old field marshal, either in
Neudeck or at some other place. For, when Brüning tried to explain
the true purpose of the intended changes in the eastern aid, Hindenburg cut him off sharply.

The first point was Hindenburg's way of saying that all remaining national ministers who might be called democratic or republican, such as Dietrich, Stegerwald, and particularly Gröner, would
be dismissed; [65] they were to be replaced by men of German Nationalist opinions, although not necessarily of that party's Reichstag
delegation. Brüning could not avoid the realization that this first
point also meant his own dismissal, for even Hindenburg must have
known that Brüning could not remain at the head of a cabinet that

included his political opponents. Indeed, by refusing to sign any more emergency decrees Hindenburg had already made it sufficiently clear that he did not want to keep Brüning as Chancellor.

Just what the President meant by "government by labor union officials," at which the second point was aimed, remains unclear. He certainly did not intend to include Brüning in this category. There was only one former union leader in the cabinet at the time: Adam Stegerwald, already a *persona non grata* in Hindenburg's eyes as an "agrarian bolshevist." One must agree with Meinecke's interpretation of Hindenburg's three demands: he wanted a "complete break with the Social Democratic working population, that is, precisely with those elements in Germany who were fighting with the greatest determination against Hitler and in defense of the Weimar constitution." Presumably, however, the wording of the second point is also an echo of the industrial magnates' complaint; they were forever lamenting to the President that the German economy could not recover until the labor unions were either suppressed or at least rendered impotent.

The President's consciously cool attitude and language made it clear to Brüning that he was no longer wanted. Indeed, at the end he asked Hindenburg directly if he wished him to resign. The President replied with neither yes nor no. He did, however, say that his conscience forbade him to keep a cabinet as unpopular as the recent elections had shown this one to be — even the old field marshal had mastered this much of the republican vocabulary — but that he wanted Brüning to stay on as foreign minister. As a precedent for this astonishing suggestion, he referred to the example of Stresemann in 1923; but this argument only demonstrated that Hindenburg comprehended neither the completely different circumstances of the earlier cabinet shift nor the magnitude of the change he was proposing now. In any event, Brüning rejected the offer forthwith and told the President that he, too, had a reputation and a sense of honor, which could not be bought with a minister's portfolio.

Brüning immediately called a meeting of his cabinet, at which he reported his interview with Hindenburg and proposed that the entire government resign. All the ministers agreed. Gröner exploded. He had experienced too many examples of his former military superior's infidelity, and now he intended to tell the truth to the entire world. Brüning unhesitatingly opposed this idea with an argument that was typical of him but which in no way corresponded with the latest facts: despite everything, Brüning insisted, the field marshal remained "the only rallying point left to the German nation." This was sheer nonsense from any realistic point of

view. Millions of Germans had voted for Hindenburg only because
of their confidence in Brüning; the moment they learned that the
old field marshal had dismissed his Chancellor, these millions could
only regard the President as a traitor.

Brüning immediately requested an appointment with Hindenburg in order that he might transmit his cabinet's joint resignation.
The appointment was set for 10:30 A.M. on the following day, May
30, 1932. But at 9:00 that morning, before Brüning went to the
presidential palace, he received Frederic Sackett, the American
ambassador, who had insisted on the appointment in order that
he might deliver an important message. His message was certainly
important enough. What Sackett reported was nothing less than
that the new Premier of France, Edouard Herriot, was interested
in accepting the proposals Brüning had made at Geneva two weeks
before and from which Tardieu had carefully kept his distance. An
American negotiator, Hugh Gibson, had been in personal conversations with Herriot and had just telegraphed Sackett, saying that he
should urge Brüning to return to Geneva as quickly as possible, for
now there were real prospects of success. Sackett was deeply shocked
to learn that his message had come too late, that Brüning was just
about to tender his resignation.

In spite of everything that had transpired between them, Brüning's sentimental attachment to the old field marshal, which we have
noted before, had not completely disappeared. The Chancellor seems
to have had some faint hope that Hindenburg's attitude would
change upon receipt of so highly significant a message. At this point
word came from the presidential palace that the Chancellor's appointment had been postponed from 10:30 to 11:55. This change
meant that their conversation would be very short and that Brüning
would have time to do little more than submit his cabinet's resignation. For at twelve o'clock the Skagerrak Watch would parade, and
to the old field marshal reviewing the guard was more important
than changing a cabinet.

The question whether this postponement was a consequence of
Sackett's call upon Brüning need not concern us here. It is certain
that the Chancellor's enemies learned immediately of the visit
through their spies, and it is highly likely that they let some form
of their information reach the President. Yet one can also explain
the postponement by considering the old man's desire to keep the
confrontation with Brüning, which could only be unpleasant and
for which he probably felt in no sense prepared, as brief as possible.
In any event this postponement and shortening of their scheduled
conversation was an unexampled display of rudeness toward the

Chancellor and one more proof of the almost monarchic image which Hindenburg had of his position.

And so, to the blare of military music, the curtain fell and the Brüning era was over.

Heinrich Brüning was deeply shaken by the way he had been treated. "Although I am really not without some internal power of resistance, I have found these past weeks very trying," he remarked to a friend in early June. "I still haven't been able to get over it." He had of course known for some time that his enemies were working assiduously to bring about his fall. But even to the end he had considered himself more than a match for such clandestine foes. Yet Brüning had learned that he could no longer reckon fully on Hindenburg's support as early as mid-April when, after Hindenburg's re-election, he had tendered his cabinet's formal resignation. At that time Hindenburg wished to restrict his charge to the new government by stating that it should remain in office "temporarily," and it took Brüning some time to persuade the President to strike this "temporarily" from the document. But Brüning had learned that by skillfully presenting problems to the old man in the light of his prejudices, it was possible to coax him into proper paths, and Brüning could not now believe that he would not succeed once more. He simply had not considered it possible that the field marshal would cut him off, denying him any opportunity for a reasoned explanation of the facts.

Least of all had Brüning considered the possibility of his dismissal at this juncture. He thought he was securely in office for the foreseeable future, not only because the Old Gentleman was obviously greatly in his debt, but also because the Lausanne Conference on Reparations was just about to begin. For it was clear that Brüning was the best possible representative Germany could send to the meeting. Statesmen of all nations had continually been expressing the special personal confidence they had in him, and those Germans whose brains had not become befogged by the propaganda of the nationalistic opposition shared this feeling. Even Hindenburg would have liked to keep Brüning on as foreign minister. But the old field marshal, with his monarchistic-military mode of thought, did not realize that a statesman of Brüning's caliber could not let himself become a tool in his superior's hand, that such a man would be obliged to consider his own political reputation and the name he would make for himself in history.

By now it was clear to every perceptive person that the so-called "presidential system" had demonstrated its own inability to survive. Indeed, it was only through crude political barter and coups d'état that the system was able to drag out its existence for a few more months. It had become fashionable for conservative Germans to complain about petty party bickering. But could it really be regarded as an improvement when the political parties were replaced by cliques of people who could not see beyond the nearest lamp post and who, too, fell to quarrelling with each other whenever some positive step had to be taken? Hindenburg had once indicted partisan political spirit "before God and history." But was not such a spirit at work when he now demanded that "future government policy be conservative in tone" and, to attain this end, dismissed a cabinet that had finally won the support of a majority of the Reichstag just two weeks before?

It is much more difficult to determine how much blame Brüning himself must bear for the birth of this unviable presidential system. In any event one has no reason to spare him the accusation of having destroyed the last chance for parliamentary government in Germany by dissolving the Reichstag in July 1930. Reference to this aspect of Brüning's recourse to government by presidential decree has already been made in Chapter X. But a brief review of the facts, with special reference to this later development, might be proper here.

The Reichstag that was elected on May 20, 1928, need not have been dissolved before May 1932, that is, before the end of Hindenburg's initial term of office, if Brüning had found a way to establish some modus vivendi with it. But even at that early time the Chancellor had begun to demonstrate his almost mystic faith that with the old field marshal's support he could master all enemies singlehanded. This confidence, especially in the face of the extraordinarily intractable Reichstag of 1930, had consequently led him to the easy but fatal practice of ignoring the traditional and constitutional forms of the legislative process. Thus, while issuing new laws as emergency decrees over the President's signature, Brüning had left the Reichstag, in its brief, sporadic sessions, nothing more than the rubber-stamping function of defeating motions against these decrees.

To a certain extent this development was no doubt necessary. All the unpopular new taxes which the government found itself simply forced to impose would have been trampled to death in the Reichstag's wild disorder. But did every piece of legislation have to be issued as a decree? Was there not one constructive measure which might first have been brought before the Reichstag, where the parties would have had to assume public, formal positions either for or against it, and which, if the negative attitudes prevailed, could have been subsequently issued as a decree? Brüning's method actually helped the radical opposition, especially the National Socialists, maintain an irresponsible, rabble-rousing pose in a very significant way. For if these extremists had been forced to take a public stand on positive proposals, the deep divisions in their own ranks would have become evident and the weakness of their arguments, which sounded good only so long as they were not put to test, would have been made clear.

This became apparent, for instance, in the last Reichstag debate of May 1932, when Gregor Strasser tried to propound a National Socialist economic program. His efforts gave Theodor Heuss an opportunity to demonstrate the dangers that lurked in Strasser's plans and to show that the national economic self-sufficiency which the National Socialists were preaching really meant the deliberate organization of hunger in Germany, that it would drive the best Germans abroad and bring on a new inflation. If there had been more illuminating debates of this sort, the criers on the streets, of course, would not have become quiet, but those who had prospects and property would have become more critical and sober in their thought.

Thus Brüning's way of treating parliamentary problems was not designed to work to the effective disadvantage of the National Socialists; nor did he possess either the necessary firmness of decision or the requisite independence vis-à-vis the President to proceed against them directly. He did not suffer any lack of insight into the dangers at hand, but he could not bring himself to take active steps against them. August Weber, for example, the leader of the State Party delegation, urged Brüning in an extended private conversation to employ the organs of the government against the Nazi enemy. But Weber's entreaties were in vain, and he departed with the conviction that it was only a question of time before Hitler would seize the powers of the state for himself.

Yet even under so critical a light Brüning remains the last significant statesman that the Weimar Republic produced. He was impressive by virtue of his great intellectual gifts, the purity of his motives, and the selflessness of his patriotism. And truly he accomplished enough to secure a place for himself in the history of the German people.

Hitler always referred with venomous hatred to the years of the Republic as the "Years of Shame." The phrase was simple, as was the answering roar of approval from his listeners, who thought they could condemn the painful memory of a lost war to oblivion by blaming its consequences on a parliamentary system. Yet in truth the statesmen of the Weimar Republic wrought mightily in freeing Germany gradually but steadily from the burdens and restraints which had been the inevitable results of her defeat in battle. Stresemann, for instance, not only liberated German soil from every soldier of occupation, but also brought about the abolition of the Inter-Allied Military Control Commission and found a way to keep the other Allied control organs from remaining in the newly evacuated areas.

Stresemann also effected a reduction in the reparations burden set by the Treaty of Versailles, and Brüning brought complete abrogation so close to fruition that at Lausanne it fell, ripe, into the lap of his successor. On the question of disarmament Brüning made the former foes so accustomed to the notion of equal rights for Germany that, again, his successors were able to reap the harvest he had sown. Through the Standstill Agreements (*Stillhalte Abkommen*) he protected the German economy from further loss of blood, and through the careful regulation of foreign credits he assured the German state a decisive — and, as later events were to show, dangerously great — power over the movement of its citizens' fortunes. Brüning and Dietrich together, with ruthless energy and the courage to be unpopular, cut the national government's expenditures from twelve billion marks in 1928 to eight billion in 1932, with, of course, the reparations bill of close to two billion marks the principal saving effected.[66] And they largely overcame the fiscal difficulties which the economic crisis had induced.

Not Brüning, but Hitler, benefited from all these achievements. The Austrian would never have been able to establish his rule of terror nor to have armed Germany for another war if his predecessors had not fully loosened the chains of Versailles and so successfully reformed the finances of the German state. This was an instance of Virgil's ancient warning, "Sic vos non vobis," in its most fatal and frightful application:

Thus you build nests, o birds, though not for your own habitation.
Thus, o you oxen, you draw plows although not for yourselves.

The guilt for this disaster must be placed primarily upon Hindenburg. The dagger thrust with which he felled Brüning on May 30, 1932, in an unexampled display of infidelity, murdered not only the German Republic, but also the peace of all Europe.

XIII

MAJOR PAPEN TAKES COMMAND

F$_{RANZ}$ Z$_{IEGLER}$, the old Prussian liberal (1803–1876), once urged his fellow Progressives to arm themselves with the self-confidence of the junkers. He used to say that if the King of Prussia were to order one of his high-born officers of the guard to direct the Berlin Opera Orchestra, the officer would immediately obey, even if he had never held a director's baton in his hand before. In 1932 there was, of course, no longer a King of Prussia. But there was a former Royal Prussian field marshal, and he found a nobleman who had been a major in the Royal Prussian Cavalry Reserves. To him he could give the order to direct, not the Berlin Opera Orchestra, but rather the political fortunes of the German Reich even though it had never occurred to anyone else that the major possessed talents necessary for such a post.

This cavalry major was Franz von Papen. In social circles he was well known as a horseman, and he played an important role in the *Herrenklub*,* a place where his extraordinary social gifts were fully appreciated. His intellectual powers, on the other hand, were considered to be slight. André François-Poncet, the perceptive French ambassador who had many contacts in Berlin, reports that neither von Papen's friends nor his enemies took him very seriously and considered him a superficial, confused, and untrustworthy thinker and a vain, ambitious, and scheming intriguer.[1] Wheeler-Bennett calls this description "not unfair," and classifies him as, at best, a "fifth-rate" man.[2] And after von Papen's fall, Sir Horace Rum-

---

* There is no adequate translation of the word. "Herr" in this connection means gentleman with distinct overtones of "lord" or "master." Papen had helped organize this club whose members considered themselves to be the international elite. The president of the *Herrenklub* in 1932 was Count Bodo von Alvensleben. Other members included von Papen's close friends, Oskar von Hindenburg, Kurt von Schleicher, and the future premier of France, the unfortunate Paul Reynaud. TRANSLATORS.

bold, with all the restraint of a professional diplomat, wrote that he was a man of "second-rate ability."

This Herr von Papen had once been military attaché to the German embassy in Washington. But during the early years of the war he had been expelled by the United States on the charge, the validity of which has never been determined, of having organized and financed acts of sabotage. He later served on the Turkish front, where his military conduct and, indeed, his courage are a matter of unquestionable record.

Von Papen, a member of the deeply Catholic nobility of Westphalia, was married to a daughter of the owner of the great Villeroy and Boch earthenware concern at Mettlach in the Saar. This connection with a very wealthy and half-French family not only afforded him an opportunity to become well acquainted with the thoughts of those people who looked forward to better relations between Germany and France; it also assured him a financial independence which allowed him to participate in political life. The Catholic peasants and landowners in Westphalia had sent him to the Prussian Landtag, where, in accordance with his constituents' desires, he had joined the Center Party.

But his heart was really not in the Middle with the Centrists; it was far out on the Right wing. Indeed, the only political act worthy of report from his days in the Landtag occurred in 1925, when he blocked the election of the Centrist leader, Wilhelm Marx, as premier of Prussia. Since parliamentary honors seemed denied him, he used his ample means to purchase a controlling interest in the *Germania*, the leading Centrist journal. Yet even then he still did not succeed in finding a way into the Reichstag or the German diplomatic service.[3]

And so unfulfilled ambition burned within him. If it is true that those who denied him political advancement did so because they doubted his political capabilities and expertise, von Papen can be said to have gone out of his way in his memoirs to show how right these people were. Seldom has political ignorance and superficiality been displayed with such self-satisfaction as in this autobiography, while the author forfeited any claim to gentle treatment by his critics when he gave the German edition of the book the arrogant title *Der Wahrheit eine Gasse!* (Make Way For Truth!). In point of fact, Herr von Papen's memoirs do not have much more claim to this title than do the tales of that other noble narrator, the notorious Baron Munchausen.

If by this time the political leaders of Germany had acquired skeptical opinions of Herr von Papen, the generals, on the other hand, had discovered real virtues in him. The honor of having recommended Franz von Papen to Hindenburg as a chancellor belongs to General Kurt von Schleicher. "Fränzchen" and "Kürtchen" were very good friends. Schleicher had no illusions about von Papen's abilities, but he knew von Papen's ambitions and believed he could make them serve his own ends. And Schleicher was convinced that von Papen's supple social talents would commend him to the President.

Von Papen certainly stood far enough out on the Right to satisfy the first point on Hindenburg's program. The fact that he also, and almost paradoxically, was a member of the Center Party was a further advantage in Schleicher's eyes. For the general was still clinging firmly to the foggy notion of giving the National Socialists a share of political responsibility in order to teach them moderation and satisfaction with something less than absolute power. The Center, with its long political experience and the steady support which it enjoyed among a considerable part of the German people, would have been quite helpful to Schleicher in the attainment of his goal.[4] And such an alliance would have led immediately to that dissolution of the Prussian coalition of Socialists and Centrists for which all German Rightists so fervently prayed.

But this part of Schleicher's program failed completely. In all his speculations the general had overlooked the fact that even in parliamentary politics there is something that one can call *esprit de corps*. The Center supported Brüning solidly not simply because it favored his policies, but also because it had personal faith in him. His dismissal, and especially the sly trickery to which he had fallen prey, had enraged the entire party, particularly its leader, Monsignor Kaas. It was for this reason that the Centrist delegation in the Reichstag immediately published a resolution, the sharp language of which differed markedly from the careful, compromising tone for which the Catholic Center had long been famous. The reason for this "unanimous and sharply critical condemnation" of recent events was expressed especially well in just one sentence: "Immediately before international negotiations which were almost certain to yield benefits to Germany, irresponsible intrigues on the part of persons with no constitutional authority have violently disrupted lines of promising development in a general reconstruction program which was already under way."

Nor was the Centrist delegation in any sense alone in this opinion. On June 4 the British ambassador cabled his superior: "Great confusion prevails here and it is evident that the President was very badly advised when he subordinated foreign to purely internal and indeed parochial interests." [5] Rumbold also made it clear to State Secretary von Bülow, who had been complaining about the highly critical attitude of the British press, that the resignation of Brüning, coming immediately before the Lausanne Conference and under the circumstances which attended it, had been a severe shock to public opinion in England.[6]

In the face of his own party's evident anger, von Papen's situation was by no means a simple one when the President offered him the surprising invitation to be Chancellor. Before he could make any formal reply he was obliged — at the very least — to notify the official leader of the Center. Kaas told the Chancellor-Designate in no uncertain terms that the Center would regard it as an unpardonable breach of discipline if a member of the party were to try to put himself into the place from which Brüning had just been thrust. Von Papen, who did not even approach Kaas in intelligence, dialectical skills, or political experience, could find no other response than the solemn declaration that he would *not* accept the office which the President had offered him. The fact that this was the simple substance of his statement is quite clear from Kaas's letter to Papen of June 2:

If words have any meaning and declarations value, I had no choice but to assume with certainty . . . from our recent conversation, that you would have pressing reasons for not accepting the office of Chancellor. On the strength of this assumption, I personally guaranteed the loyalty of your ultimate decision at a meeting of the party's executive committee. Immediately thereafter I received the news that your final decision was contrary to the promise you had given me.

For as soon as von Papen had found himself before the President again, he reversed his reversal and said yes. He later accounted for this astonishing inconstancy in his memoirs by explaining that Hindenburg had told him he "couldn't desert an old man" and that, as a soldier, he had to answer his country's call. Thus, the memoirs argue, he accepted the appointment for patriotic reasons. Yet even if the interview did in fact take this course, Hindenburg's blandishments provide no excuse for von Papen's betrayal of his party. And so even the cavalry major realized that there was no other way out of the blind alley into which he had maneuvered himself than to resign from the Center.

Within less than twenty-four hours the new Chancellor had managed not only to incur the opposition of his party, but also to assume the shame of having broken his word. This latter charge was regarded with special severity by the Catholic Centrists since the broken promise had been made to a priest. One can therefore well imagine with what sort of feelings von Papen's former party colleagues received the announcement that his program would consist of the "vigorous and thorough realization of the immutable principles of our Christian belief."

Yet, despite this severe political and personal defeat, von Papen was able to form a government in an astonishingly short time. This speed, however, demonstrated neither his personal skill nor the strength of the political currents which he represented, but rather the careful preparations of Schleicher and the other kingmakers. The attitude with which von Papen went about the business of forming his cabinet is illustrated by a remark which his food minister, Freiherr Magnus von Braun, reports.[7] "My dear Braun," von Papen inquired in their initial conversation on the subject, "would you like to help me form a cabinet of gentlemen?" * A "cabinet of gentlemen," that is, a government of men who, by virtue of family background and social position, enjoyed the qualifications for membership in an exclusive club; in other words, a government from which workers, union officials, and other people who could not be considered "gentlemen" would be barred.

It is true that Baron von Braun took von Papen's remark quite differently. Yet his private interpretation of Papen's meaning was probably no more accurate than was his general estimate of the man, whom he considered not only a "gentleman" but also "an idealist of the purest form."[8] Von Braun came much closer to the truth in another part of his memoirs, where he wrote: "One really could not deny that most of us ministers came from quite similar milieus. Papen, Gayl, Eltz, and I all belonged to Potsdam guard regiments. Schleicher had served in the same regiment as the Hindenburgs, father and son. Gürtner was from the Bavarian artillery; Neurath, from the Württemberg dragoons; and Krosigk, from the Pomeranian cavalry."[9]

These few words spoke volumes. An attempt was being made to resurrect the reserve officers as the ruling class of Germany. Perhaps this was the right company for a field marshal who also happened to be the President of Germany and whom von Braun reports to have "felt comfortable and content in the company of his new government." Another remark of von Braun's is illuminating here. After noting that von Papen was as much a monarchist as Hindenburg had been throughout his life, von Braun then goes on to re-

---

* The English word "gentlemen" is used in the German text. There is no equivalent word in the German language, although "Herr" had much the same connotation in these circles. TRANSLATORS.

port: "I thought it significant when, in the course of a conversation, the 'Old Gentleman' remarked, 'Yes, but you see, that was back in the time of the republican ministers.' When I involuntarily smiled a bit at this expression, he added, in his beautiful, deep, kindly bass voice: 'O, you know what I mean.'" [10] Thus the German Republic had already been written off by its chief of state, although Hindenburg continued to assure the nation that he would defend its constitution.

The creation of a cabinet of reserve officers was probably also a concession to the generals on the Bendlerstrasse. Indeed their leader, Schleicher, now sat in the cabinet as minister of defense. But precisely what elements of the German nation could be expected to rally around this "cabinet of barons," as it was universally called, was obscure from the very beginning. The premier of Bavaria, Heinrich Held, could scarcely be called a Marxist or, in the words of William II, a "rootless rascal" (vaterlandsloser Geselle); yet on July 27 in a speech at Cologne he characterized the cabinet's most likely supporters in the following way: "The composition of the new government makes it seem as though the German nation were comprised of landed gentry, industrial magnates, and half-baked intellectuals." [11]

There would be little point in a detailed description of the members of von Papen's cabinet. Most of them disappeared from the public scene as swiftly as they had come. "The wind passeth over them, and it is as if they had never been." The most important thing that one can say about them in general is that five of them, with von Papen at their head, became ministers under Hitler. One of these was Franz Gürtner, national minister of justice, who until this time had been minister of justice in Bavaria, where, as we have seen, he had kept his protecting hand over Hitler. Gürtner will go down in history as the justice minister who found "legal" Hitler's murders during the so-called "Blood Purge" of June 30, 1934. The everlasting shame which clings to his name cannot be erased by the fact that, as von Braun insists, by that time Gürtner was a morally shattered man who desired nothing more than release from the reign of terror that he had done so much to help establish. [12]

It is more difficult to understand how another of these ministers brought himself to go along with Hitler. This was the national minister of finance, Count Lutz Schwerin-Krosigk. His book, Es geschah in Deutschland (It Happened in Germany), would seem to have been written by an objective, reasonable man. Until his appointment as minister in 1932, he had been a division head and budgetary representative in the national Ministry of Finance, where he had been respected as an able associate. The British ambassador reported that Krosigk was "blackmailed into taking office much against his will by the threat of dismissal from his post." [13] He remained minister of finance until 1945.

Another member of this "cabinet of barons" worthy of mention is Freiherr Wilhelm von Gayl, the new national minister of interior. Intellectually, Gayl stood head and shoulders above von Papen. He concerned himself with serious plans for reform, none of which, of course, was ever carried out — unless one is to put the successful coup d'état against Prussia in this category. But all Gayl's plans, whether dangerous or wise, suffered a common fault: he never had a clear notion of the means and forces necessary for their execution.

Freiherr Konstantin von Neurath was brought back from the German embassy in London, at Hindenburg's express desire, to become foreign minister. He had made quite a good impression in England, and his new appointment seemed to assure the British that even under Papen German foreign policy would remain reasonably sane.

The Americans in particular had little use for Papen. An American visitor assured Treviranus that public opinion in the United States was still enraged at the memory of the wartime events in which the new Chancellor had been involved. After talking with the American, Treviranus concluded, "They are closing the door on us over there. If we Germans continue to think that we can live alone, all by ourselves, ignoring the public opinion of the rest of the world, then nothing can possibly help us." [14] Even the American secretary of state, Henry Stimson, told the British ambassador in Washington that Hindenburg had appointed as Chancellor a man who "if proposed as ambassador here would unhesitatingly be refused." Stimson also added, however, that the American government would not let its diplomacy be influenced by its opinion of von Papen.[15]

Naturally the new defense minister, General Kurt von Schleicher, enjoyed a special position in the new cabinet, for he had been its principal creator, and he intended to direct it as he pleased. Indeed, it would not be an overstatement to say that Schleicher regarded von Papen as a puppet, whose every movement he could control at will. This meant that conflicts were bound to arise as soon as Papen developed a greater thirst for independence than Schleicher thought he possessed; and the high and prestigious office of Chancellor was almost perfectly designed to evoke such thirst for personal power.

One is not at all surprised to read the following appraisal in the British ambassador's dispatch to London dated June 14, 1932:

"the present Cabinet is a Cabinet of mutual deception. Herr von Papen thinks that he has scored off General von Schleicher and Hitler, General Schleicher thinks he has scored off Hitler, and Hitler, for his part, believes that he has scored off both." [16] Sir Horace Rumbold goes on to make a similar remark about Erwin Planck, who had succeeded Hermann Pünder as state secretary to the Chancellor. Sir Horace writes: "I have it on indisputable authority that Dr. Planck . . . had for a long time past been spying on the late Chancellor on behalf of General von Schleicher and that Dr. Brüning's telephone was regularly tapped by the Reichswehr ministry." Since he was a victim of Hitler's lust for revenge over July 20, 1944,* one learns with satisfaction that after he had realized what sort of creatures he had helped to power, Planck begged Brüning's forgiveness in writing.[17] Planck was the son of the distinguished physicist Max Planck. Another son of a famous man, a Major Marck, whose father was the historian Erich Marck, was also promoted at this time; he became head of the new government's press office. Both men were absolutely loyal supporters of Schleicher.

The new government had been assembled with great speed, but it still faced the difficult problem of finding sources of political support. The President alone would not suffice. Even now he was not an absolute ruler; he could govern only in more or less direct collaboration with the Reichstag. This simple truth could not be changed even by the enthusiastic pronouncements of a few political journalists who greeted Papen's cabinet as the inauguration of a "new state" which would be free of democratic restraints.

After Papen had been dismissed by the Center and rejected not only by the Social Democrats, but also by all the moderate parties that still had any sense of democratic government, he was obliged to seek support on the Right. But here Hugenberg's German Nationalists were not enough. And so von Papen had to make sure that Hitler would at worst tolerate his government. (Schleicher had certainly assured himself of this already.)

At this point Hindenburg and Papen entered into personal negotiations with Hitler. We do not know just what Hitler promised in the form of the desired "toleration"; but we do know that he later broke whatever promises he made. We also know what he demanded and what Hindenburg and Papen promised him: the SA ban was to be rescinded and the Reichstag dissolved. Goebbels properly called this latter concession "the most important one of all."

It was clear enough that Papen could not govern with the exist-

---

* The date of the von Stauffenberg attempt to assassinate Hitler at his headquarters in Rastenburg, East Prussia. TRANSLATORS.

ing Reichstag. So much was certain. But what could he expect from new elections? Was there any reasonable prospect of a Reichstag which would grant him even negative, "tolerant" support? Von Papen evidently wasted no time on thoughts like these. The dissolution of the Reichstag would give him several weeks' grace to exercise his gifts of government without having to take the Reichstag into consideration. The new elections were set for July 31. In any event, von Papen was not the sort of man to think beyond the moment.

On June 16 a new presidential decree rescinded the SA ban as Hitler had demanded and Hindenburg had agreed. The old field marshal accompanied the decree with a public letter in which he expressed the hope that "the conflict of political opinion will henceforth assume more orderly form, and that acts of violence will cease." Everyone who had any connection with German politics and, especially, who was familiar with the National Socialists knew that there was not the slightest basis for Hindenburg's expectation. In any event, the decree constituted an odd beginning for a government that supposedly wished to strengthen the authority of the state. The measure immediately provoked a sharp reaction in Baden and Bavaria, the governments of which swiftly intervened by outlawing party uniforms and reviving other prohibitions. With these steps, of course, the uniformity of law within the Reich, which had just been achieved, was lost again.

But what were the new government's positive aims? Its declaration of June 4 was expected to yield some information on this score. (Since the government dissolved the Reichstag at this same time, the declaration could not be read to the parliament; it had to be broadcast by radio.) The government's statement was singularly uninformative. The first part constituted an attack on Brüning's government and was quickly refuted by its members in a sharp counterstatement based on facts. For the rest, von Papen's declaration offered an anthology of the political catchwords circulating in reactionary quarters at that time. The new government was opposed to the "welfare state," which had "sapped the moral fiber of the nation." It decried not only "class warfare which is inimical to national unity" but also "cultural bolshevism, which threatens to infect our nation's firmest moral bases with its corrosive poison."

On the whole, the declaration seemed more like the editorial of an extreme Rightist sheet than the program of a responsible government. Hermann Dietrich, until recently Brüning's finance minister, emphasized the critical point in an "Open Declaration to Friends": "It really does not matter whether von Papen's new

government intends to exercise political power in Germany according to its own reactionary desires or plans to abdicate its authority
to the National Socialists after the coming elections. In either event
this government is a tool of Hitler's. It has summoned forth *dangers
to the German nation and the Reich* which we all thought had been
banished by our *recent choice of President.*" [18]

Papen, however, was able to escape this flood of displeasure
quite swiftly, since on June 16, 1932, the International Reparations
Conference assembled at Lausanne, and he was naturally expected
to represent Germany there. A few days earlier MacDonald and
Simon had gone to Paris in order to arrive at a common conference
plan with Herriot, the new French Premier. The British led off by
proposing that the reparations be totally abolished for the sake of
world economic recovery. Herriot quickly agreed that at the moment and for the immediate future Germany was unable to make
her reparation payments. But, he added, the Western powers should
not let themselves be fooled by the Germans into turning the situation completely around to the utter disadvantage of the present creditors.

The French Premier recounted how the German ambassador,
von Hoesch, had told him just two days before that the German
reparations debt amounted to 1,500,000,000 marks each year, while
the German export surplus came only to 1,200,000,000 marks. To
this, Herriot had replied that the figures showed at least that Germany could pay "something." For he had the impression that the
Germans intended first to wring every possible concession from their
creditors and then to push the West against the wall. When the
British, nevertheless, persisted in proposing that an abolition of all
reparations be linked to a fifteen-year political truce, Herriot replied
that such an assurance would only be one more piece of paper, and
that paper did not have the same value to the Germans as it did to
other people; one need only ask the Belgians.[19]

Both parties agreed that the reparation payments due on July 1
would not be demanded. A statement to this effect was included in
a declaration of the creditor powers read at the opening of the conference, according to which no payments would be expected until
the conference was over.

Aside from Papen, Germany was represented at Lausanne by
Foreign Minister von Neurath (who was accompanied by State
Secretary von Bülow), Schwerin-Krosigk, and Economic Minister
Hermann Warmbold. The conference began in the usual way with
extended expositions of basic positions by the principal ministers.
Papen's prepared address pleased the creditors because it failed to

repeat Brüning's earlier declaration that even in the future Germany would remain unable to make reparation payments. Moreover, von Papen's flawless French made a favorable impression.

After these first, official plenary sessions, the conference broke up into separate discussions among the delegations of the principal great powers, especially Great Britain, France, and Germany. We have a record of those parts of the conversations in which the British took part. These records show how seriously the British took their self-assumed role of "honest broker." Ramsay MacDonald, the British Prime Minister, had been elected chairman of the conference. He utilized this position not only to push the negotiations along with untiring zeal, but also to assume a more objective attitude than would otherwise have been possible. For his position as chairman permitted him to speak of "our German friends" in the same fashion as of "our French friends" and thus to create an atmosphere which temporarily made Lausanne seem like a peaceful island in a storm-tossed world. We owe our knowledge of the private conversations between Papen and Herriot to the reports which both made to the British ministers as well as to the indiscretions which Papen committed with the press.

From these sources it is clear that the German Chancellor offered the Premier of France a bilateral military alliance, with a constant exchange of information between their general staffs, in return for the abrogation of the reparations.[20] In itself this was a generous — one might almost say a magnanimous — idea. The centuries-old quarrel between these two great nations had been a constant threat to European peace. To replace it now with an alliance which would bring the nations on either side of the Rhine into peaceful reconciliation certainly did sound nice. But such magnanimous ideas are not meant for irresponsible use in a desperate battle for one's domestic political position. Was von Papen's offer not one of those maneuvers which Bismarck had said always made him wonder: *Qui trompe-t-on ici*? Who is trying to fool whom here?

However magnanimous this proposal might have been if it had come from a truly legitimate representative of a truly trusting nation, it was highly questionable when it came from someone who enjoyed absolutely no support among the German people and who, indeed, could keep himself in office only through repeated dissolutions of the Reichstag. For the superannuated President and the wavering, uncertain tactics of a few generals surely did not provide sufficient base for a fundamental change in German policy.

Von Papen discovered that his offer was dangling in thin air when, on June 25, he returned to Berlin for several days in order to consult with those members of his cabinet who had remained at home. From this time on, his tongue, which had been prating so generously to the French, was still, and he spoke no more of a military alliance. On June 27 Herriot told MacDonald: "Today, when I talked with Papen after his return from Berlin, I found him in an entirely different mood, and he said nothing except that Germany could not pay any further reparations." [21] Even more illuminating was Papen's reply to MacDonald's query about the course of his negotiations with the French. Papen said it was true that he had asked whether the French would regard a Franco-German military alliance as "security," but, he quickly added, "the idea was, of course, preposterous whether in France or in Germany." [22]

It is extremely characteristic of Franz von Papen that he simply omitted this important sentence when he cited the British Documents' report in his memoirs.[23] Presumably he did so in order to justify the book's German title, *Der Wahrheit eine Gasse!* ("Make Way for Truth!"). In the face of his actual statement to MacDonald, one has the choice between two interpretations: either Papen wished to trick Herriot by offering him an alliance, or he was tricking MacDonald by calling the idea of such a pact "preposterous." *Qui trompe-t-on-ici?*

No matter which interpretation one prefers, there remained one technical difficulty which Papen never really comprehended at the time and which he evidently never came to understand in later years: his "preposterous" proposal could only strike both the British and the French as an attempt to weaken their own alliance. The fact that Papen undertook such a move without the slightest prior consultation, rather in the fashion of a sudden cavalry dash, shows clearly enough how ill-equipped he was for the post he had assumed. Lord Simon recounts in his memoirs how Herriot whispered to him one day at Lausanne, as he looked across the conference table at von Papen: "The more I study the face of a German cavalry officer, the more I admire – his horse." [24]

In the course of their negotiations with the French, the British finally became convinced that a complete and permanent cancellation of the reparations could not be achieved. The attitude of the French was all the less vulnerable since they could point to the fact that the Americans also had reservations about the idea of total abrogation. The United States was not, of course, a participant in the conference, for it was not a recipient of reparation payments. But it was a creditor of these creditors and hence very much concerned lest the Entente's settlement with Germany be at its expense. (See the State Department's declaration of June 9, 1932.)

President Hoover did not wish to admit the existence of this inherent connection between the German reparations and the Allied war debts, but his secretary of state, Henry Stimson, thought in more realistic terms.[25]

Hoover believed that the abrogation of the Allied war debts could be avoided if the reparation creditors, that is, Great Britain, France, Italy, and Belgium, reduced their military expenditures in order to compensate for the gaps in their budgets which would be caused by the absence of reparation payments. The American President even sent a message to this effect to Geneva on June 27. It does not seem to have occurred to him that this line of thought might lead to another conclusion: in Germany's case the abrogation of the reparations would make it all the easier to prepare for conquest by increasing her armament. And this is precisely what did happen — not immediately, to be sure, but only a few years later.

The German delegation at Lausanne gradually came to realize that a simple abrogation of all future reparation payments was not to be achieved, and that, at least during the time of its economic recovery, Germany would have to make continued payments, which, however, would fall far short of those formerly required by the Young Plan. The German delegates arrived at this conclusion well before their colleagues in Berlin. In early July, Neurath told MacDonald that the ministers in Berlin, at a cabinet meeting on July 1, had unanimously decided that, in the face of current public opinion in Germany, their delegation should reject any obligation to resume reparation payments. But, Neurath continued, the German delegation had refused to accept this point of view.[26]

At this juncture von Papen tried to give the Germans' unavoidable retreat the appearance of a victory by linking it to political concessions on the part of the Entente. Dragging out the old red herring of war guilt, he demanded the abrogation of Article 231 of the Treaty of Versailles. He also insisted that the Entente powers adopt Germany's position on the issue of disarmament, as he chose to call Germany's demands for equal rights.[27]

Herriot firmly rejected these demands, telling the British that he would not let any political conditions be attached to reparation payments. Disarmament, he said, was one matter; responsibility for the war, another; and reparations, a third.[28] If he were to accept the proposed German conditions, the Germans would exultantly shout *Sieg* on all three counts.[29] He desired reconciliation with the Germans, he explained; but he could not accept these German conditions, which smelled so of bad faith. With this, von Papen's proposal was rejected, and he had no choice but to let his conditions be ignored and to recognize Germany's obligation to resume reparation payments without them.

Negotiations on the size of the remaining reparation debt continued for some time, until the delegates finally agreed on the figure of three billion marks. More important than this sum, however, were the means of payment. For the Bank for International Settlements at Basel was linked tightly to these transfers. The German government was to deposit 5 percent debentures with the bank to the agreed sum of three billion marks. But the bank was not to be permitted to sell these bonds before three years had passed, and then only if they could be marketed at no less than 90 percent par. This guaranteed price was supposed to offer assurance that Germany's credit would be restored to its normal strength. With the ratification of these Lausanne Agreements, the Hague Agreements of 1930, that is, the Young Plan, were to be superseded.

This new agreement, which was signed on July 9, 1932, in Lausanne by all delegates to the conference, had one more, initially secret, appendix. For the governments of the creditor nations naturally had to consider how they were to arrange affairs with their own common creditor, the United States. In order to ensure community of action on this point, Great Britain, France, Italy, and Belgium concluded a so-called "gentlemen's agreement." In this private protocol they promised each other that they would undertake the ratification provided in the Lausanne Agreements only after they had arrived at satisfactory agreements with their own creditors. Should these attempts fail, then the legal situation would revert to that which had existed just before the Hoover Moratorium. This separate agreement was communicated to the German Chancellor with the assurance, in response to his immediate question, that a new conference would be called if the Lausanne Agreements were not ratified [30] With this, the conference was concluded.

If we are to bring our account of reparations to a close, we must anticipate a bit of history at this point. The Entente's negotiations with the United States came to naught; the Lausanne Agreements were never ratified; and Germany never paid a single pfennig of the three billion marks that were stipulated. At the end of the three years during which the agreement had relieved Germany of all reparation payments men were writing June 1935. By that time, Hitler had been in power for two years and German universal military service had been in effect for three months.

Anyone who looks back at the Lausanne Conference today has to admit that the governments of the victors in World War I, France as well as England, showed a generous disposition to understand Germany's precarious financial situation. For if the Lausanne Agreements had been carried out, the Western powers would have been renouncing approximately 90 percent of their former reparation claims. Similarly, no matter what one may think of von Papen and his methods, one must admit that he achieved a significant victory at the conference. But if the new German Chancellor had hoped to be welcomed as a returning hero in Berlin, he was sadly disillusioned.

A highly instructive note of July 13 from the British ambassador gives a graphic picture of the contemporary German journalistic scene.[31] Its first sentence strikes to the heart of the domestic situation by showing that the Lausanne Agreements were not being judged on their actual merits, but rather by the uses to which the various parties could put them in the coming Reichstag elections of July 31. Of course, von Papen had no one to blame for this but himself. He was the one who had dissolved the Reichstag just before the conference, thus subjecting its conclusions to this sort of partisan plundering. And, as in the past, whenever issues of foreign policy were introduced into political campaigns, the most extreme views prevailed. For if one party declares: "We will not pay one more pfennig," it would be politically fatal for the others to admit that perhaps, after a few years, under more favorable circumstance, Germany might be able to pay at least a bit.

Sir Horace Rumbold also reported how the National Socialist newspapers were pointing with triumph to the fact that only the "Jewish press" supported the government. By this they meant journals like the *Vossische Zeitung*, the *Berliner Tageblatt*, and the *Frankfurter Zeitung*, all of which tried to judge von Papen fairly in spite of their misgivings. It is therefore not astonishing to discover that Hitler's *Völkischer Beobachter* treated Papen as a weakling who had yielded to Herriot's pressures out of nervous anxiety and who had to be replaced as soon as possible by a stronger man with better nerves. There was no need to ask just who this man might be.

The Centrists' attitude was strongly determined by their personal dislike for von Papen. The Chancellor retaliated by demanding the suspension of the *Kölnische Volkszeitung*, the party's principal Rhenish organ. In an address at Breslau Brüning declared the Center would insist that the Rightist parties assume political responsibility for the Lausanne Agreements by ratifying them. This was also the position of the Social Democrats. But the Rightists were never put to this test. For the rest, the newspapers of the Left pointed out that these latest agreements also fell into the category of "a policy

of fulfillment" and reminded the new Chancellor how much he owed
to his predecessors, those much-vilified proponents of rapprochement with the West.

There is no reason to believe that the Germans would have
shown much more gratitude for the concessions their former enemies had granted at Lausanne even if an electoral campaign had not
been scheduled. Paul Schmidt, the interpreter whom we have cited
more than once, observed "how little notice this abrogation of the
reparation payments . . . received in Germany." [32] For the Germans had decided that they did not intend to pay any more reparations, and they had accordingly talked themselves into believing
that they were under no obligation to bear any of the costs which
the German armies had inflicted on the West. Not so very much
later the time did come when the Germans might well have been
able to pay a few billion marks in measured installments. But then
they preferred to spend them on cannons and submarines, with results that are familiar to us all.

If it is true that von Papen had put himself in a disadvantageous
situation by dissolving the Reichstag at Hitler's bidding, it is even
truer that his repeal of the SA ban quickly resulted in catastrophe.
Napoleon I, who had been a true ruler, knew what he was saying
when he phrased the famous formula: *Ordre, contre-ordre, désordre.*
General von Schleicher and Chancellor von Papen felt themselves
far above such observations of the "Corsican upstart," but the German nation was just about to learn how right the little Corsican had
been and how frightful the disorder was which the barons' cabinet
had conjured into being.

Naturally, the self-confidence of the SA and SS, which Hitler
quickly revived, had been strengthened enormously by the experience of seeing the national government yield to their leader's demands. And they proceeded to demonstrate this confidence in a
manner calculated to excite and enrage the passions of their foes.
Sanguinary street fights were deliberately provoked by both National Socialists and Communists, and it is neither possible nor useful
to try to determine which party was more frequently the aggressor
in these disputes. One can get some impression of the moral level
of these rowdies from reading the triumphant entry which Goebbels
made in his diary for May 28, 1932, after a particularly disgusting
row in the Prussian Landtag: "In three minutes we were the masters
of the hall . . . Our group sang the Horst Wessel song. Eight badly
wounded from various political parties. This was a warning example.
It is the only possible way you can create respect. The assembly hall
was one great shambles. We stood as victors in the ruins." [33]

Within one month the street fights, which were becoming more like skirmishes in a civil war, had yielded a total of 99 dead and 1125 wounded.[34] But the number of victims in this partisan strife did not keep the von Papen government from issuing a decree, on June 28, that even annulled those bans on party uniforms which the governments of individual lands had issued in the interests of good order within their borders.[35] This internecine warfare reached a climax on Sunday, July 17, just two weeks before the Reichstag election, in a veritable battle between parading National Socialists on the streets and Communist snipers on the roofs. The National Socialists were making a political parade through the Communist precincts of Altona, the western part of Hamburg. The Communists regarded this display as a deliberate provocation, which they proceeded to answer with "self-help," that is, gunfire from the houses and the rooftops. This bloody Sunday yielded seventeen dead.

Altona had a Social Democratic commissioner of police. He had granted both the National Socialists and the Communists permission to hold some meetings on this Sunday, and he had refused them permission to hold some others. He had, however, shrunk from prohibiting the National Socialists' parade, probably because the national government's recent attitude led him to conclude that any local prohibition would be countermanded by a federal authority upon appeal by the National Socialists.[36] One may well dispute the commissioner's reasoning on this point. But in any event it provided one more reason for the Communists' "self-help"; for they wished to show the Social Democratic commissioner of police that they could stop the Nazis, even if he was too timid to try.

The Social Democratic Party had been making real efforts to help restore order. On July 13 its leaders, Rudolf Breitscheid and Otto Wels, had had a conference with the national minister of interior, Freiherr von Gayl, to whom they supplied evidence of the gravity of the situation and tried to explain the necessity of reinstituting the ban on party uniforms.[37] But von Gayl had declined to renew the ban, offering the almost cynical comment that maintenance of law and order was the responsibility of the land governments. This was the same man that had just voided these governments' prohibitions of party uniforms with the rather patronizing observation that "the misgivings which are frequently expressed about the renewed exercise of this right [that is, the wearing of party uniforms] are exaggerated."

But Carl Severing, the Prussian minister of interior, had found it necessary to direct another open plea for order to the populace.[38] And on July 18, the day after the bloody Sunday in Altona, von Gayl

found himself forced to take at least a half step backwards by issuing a national prohibition of political parades. Yet when a Socialist
member of the Prussian Staatsrat demanded the renewal of the ban
on party uniforms, the national minister of interior left the chamber.
For von Gayl, von Papen, and von Schleicher had different plans.
To them the sanguinary incident at Altona seemed to offer a convenient excuse to take that action against the Prussian government
which they had been planning for a long time.

Otto Braun's government had responded to the Prussian elections of April 24, which had deprived them of their former majority,
by resigning shortly before the new Landtag met on May 24. Thus
the newly elected delegates were obliged to choose a new premier.
For this, an absolute majority of the Landtag was required under a
change in the chamber's rules which the former Landtag had voted
upon motion by the Democratic delegate Otto Nuschke. But this
absolute majority could not be found. The National Socialists and
German Nationalists controlled some two hundred votes; the Social Democrats and Centrists, some hundred and sixty more. In addition there were the fifty-seven Communists, who were always available for motions of no confidence and other negative purposes, but
whose votes could not be had for the election of either a Rightist or
a Leftist premier.

And so the former cabinet had to go on tending Prussian affairs
for the time being. Indeed, at this time there were such interim,
caretaking governments in most of the German lands, including Bavaria, Württemberg, and Baden. They all suffered a conditional,
lame-duck legitimacy, but even this was certainly no worse than the
plight of Papen's national cabinet, which dangled completely in the
air and, as was to become apparent quickly, enjoyed practically no
parliamentary support whatsoever.

Otto Braun, however, drew his own personal conclusions from
the situation. After the Prussian election returns were in, he regarded himself as a "finished man" and probably felt that he could
no longer rely on his subordinates. After almost fourteen years as a
minister, he had no desire "to expose [himself] to gutter cries of
parliamentary rowdies, in a legislative chamber that had become
no better than a den of thieves, just because the Landtag was unable to appoint . . . a successor." [39]

It is easy to sympathize with Braun; but so much was at stake
that one nevertheless is forced to wonder whether he really did the
right thing when, on June 6, just a week after Brüning had been dismissed, he requested a leave of absence "for reasons of health." Both
his friends and enemies regarded this leave as his resignation from

office. And indeed it was just that. For Braun made no attempt to obscure his "firm intent never to return to the office." The responsibilities of premier were transmitted to the senior member of the government, Welfare Minister Heinrich Hirtsiefer of the Center.

Very soon after Papen's assumption of power, rumors had begun to spread that he planned to appoint a "national commissioner" for Prussia. The land governments, however, had protested so vigorously against this idea that the new Chancellor quickly denied the reports. But he stuck to the plan in secret and was merely waiting for a favorable opportunity to put it into effect. There is even good reason to believe that in this he was bound by a commitment to Hitler, who regarded the Prussian security police as a critical instrument of political power which he wished to wrest from the hands of Carl Severing, the Prussian Social Democratic minister of interior.[40] In any event, von Papen made repeated attempts to interfere in Prussian political affairs. His collaborator in this campaign was the new National Socialist president of the Prussian Landtag, Hans Kerrl, an attorney who later became Prussian minister of justice under Hitler. But their efforts were in vain.

Even if von Papen had no formal obligations to Hitler on this score, he was motivated by the same basic consideration. He too wanted to eject the Social Democrats from their last position of political power and to take control of the Prussian police himself. In his memoirs, von Papen makes it appear as though his purpose had been to keep the National Socialists from gaining control of the police. The careful reader will discover this to be just one more of the many clever afterthoughts with which Herr von Papen fills his remarkable book.

On July 14 von Papen, accompanied by General von Schleicher and Minister von Gayl, traveled to Neudeck to visit Field Marshal von Hindenburg, ostensibly to make a report on the conference at Lausanne, but in fact to get the President's signature on a new decree with which they could really attack the government of Prussia.

It seems worthwhile to repeat here the account which Papen gives of the earlier history of this decree in his memoirs. In doing so, I quote from the English edition, which was published first; in the later German edition several all too obvious errors were omitted, evidently upon some expert's advice.

I had resisted the idea of drastic measures as long as I could, but when I got back from Lausanne, Schleicher told me of a report he had received from a senior official in the Prussian Ministry of Interior. It seemed that negotiations had been going on between Abegg, the Social Democrat State Secretary, and Caspar, a Communist member of the

Prussian State Parliament . . . An alliance between the two Marxist parties was by no means so unlikely, and if it came about, would present a most menacing situation.[41]

From this, the credulous reader is supposed to get the stirring impression of a farsighted statesman who spied a monstrous danger threatening the state and who swiftly thwarted the menacing alliance of the two Marxist parties at the first sign of trouble, as a result of the excellent undercover work of his good friend von Schleicher.

Now it is true that Abegg and Caspar had had a conversation on June 4. But this in itself provided no basis for von Papen's fairy tale, if only because Abegg had never been a Social Democrat in all his life. He considered himself a member of the German Democratic Party and belonged to the Democratic Club. It is, of course, quite true that his superior, Carl Severing, was a Social Democrat; but Severing knew nothing about the conversation, and Papen was careful not to allude to it when, with the newest decree in his pocket, he confronted Severing in an interview we shall consider immediately below.

The "senior official" whose report General von Schleicher had transmitted to Herr von Papen was Government Counselor Rudolf Diels,* one of Abegg's trusted assistants. Indeed, Abegg had asked him to join in the conversation with Caspar. It is uncertain whether Diels served as an informer to Schleicher on his own initiative or was persuaded to do so by close friends who were directly in the general's pay. Until this time, Diels had passed as a Democrat and, like his superior, was a member of the Democratic Club. According to Diels's report — which Abegg vigorously denied — Abegg had explained to the Landtag delegate Caspar and his friend, Ernst Torgler, a Communist member of the Reichstag, how necessary it was that they re-establish a republican government in Prussia, perhaps under new leadership, and that the Communists in the Landtag could be of critical assistance in this endeavor if, for instance, they were to support some respected Centrist delegate as a compromise candidate for premier.

If this is what Abegg said, he was merely stating what every responsible republican already thought; the only thing wrong with his suggestion was the simple fact that the Communists had their minds on something quite different. They had become totally convinced that the Social Democrats were their real foes. Consequently, the Communists believed that the mythical "revolutionary prole-

---

* Diels was also a confidant of Hermann Göring, who appointed him first head of the Gestapo. In April 1934 he was replaced by Heinrich Himmler. TRANSLATORS.

tariat" had not the slightest interest in preserving the Republic — or any organized government in Germany — and there was not the slightest hope of persuading them otherwise.

Carl Severing's memoirs also show that neither the Social Democrats nor the Centrists had any desire to form an alliance with the Communists. And it is a fact that from the day of the reported conversation, June 4, until von Papen's trip to Neudeck on July 14 absolutely nothing had occurred which might have been taken as a change in the Communists' attitude of opposition. This alone should have been enough to assure even someone like Herr von Papen that, whatever its topic may have been, Abegg's conversation with Casper had been totally without effects. That von Papen not only cited the incident in persuading the President to sign the decree, but even served it up to his readers some twenty years later as a fact of direct import, shows how much love of truth and political sagacity this "statesman" really possessed.

Yet even this informer's tale provided a rather weak basis for forceful proceedings against Prussia. And so von Papen kept the emergency decree in his pocket for a few days. When the report arrived of the bloody Sunday in Altona, he thought the time to strike had finally come. On the morning of Wednesday, July 20, he requested Prussian ministers Severing, Hirtsiefer (public welfare), and Klepper (finance) to come to his office in the Chancellery, ostensibly to discuss matters of agriculture and finance. When these gentlemen arrived, Herr von Papen, with Herr von Gayl at his side, informed them that the President had issued a new decree, under Paragraphs 1 and 2 of Article 48, appointing him, Franz von Papen, national commissioner for Prussia and authorizing him to dismiss the Prussian government from office.

Von Papen then went on to declare that Braun and Severing would be the first to feel the impact of his new powers, for he would, of course, assume the functions of premier and had just entrusted the direction of the Prussian Ministry of Interior to Franz Bracht, until now the mayor of Essen. The Prussian ministers, taken completely by surprise, protested violently against this act which was based on neither necessity nor law. To all of Severing's objections von Papen replied that he was operating in the best interests of the country and inquired whether Severing intended to transfer his office voluntarily to Bracht. Severing responded that he would yield only to force.[42]

The national government was fully prepared to use force. Another decree, declaring a state of emergency in Greater Berlin and the surrounding province of Brandenburg, followed immediately upon the first, and Schleicher entrusted the necessary military powers to General von Rundstedt, commander of the Third Army District. Then, with the Army's support, National Commissioner von Papen and his helpmate, Bracht, removed the Prussian ministers from their posts. Indeed, Bracht had only to appear at Severing's office with the newly appointed police commissioner and two officers in order to persuade the minister to "yield to force."

In order to make the political purpose of this operation perfectly clear, the national commissioner immediately proceeded to remove all officials who were unacceptable to the Rightists. Thus the Berlin commissioner of police, Albert Grzesinski, his deputy, Bernhard Weiss, and the chief of police, Heimannsberg, together with state secretaries Abegg, Staudinger, and Krüger, were all forced to leave. Then the provincial governments were quickly purged: practically all the Social Democrats — indeed, all men of generally republican inclinations — were removed from the district and provincial administrations. Whoever was using his eyes could see that von Papen wished not only to kill the German Social Democratic Party, but also to render powerless any man who supported the constitutional German Republic that was still supposed to exist.

All this happened with a speed and simplicity that could only evoke the greatest astonishment, and today we are forced to wonder whether the ministers had no alternative. Was it truly impossible for the Prussian ministers to meet von Papen's force with forces of their own? Could they not depend upon the 90,000 members of the Prussian police? Could not the Social Democratic workers have dispersed von Papen's noisome crew as speedily as they had Kapp's in 1920? At this critical moment the Prussian ministers said they had no choice. And in their memoirs both Otto Braun and Carl Severing continued to hold firmly to the view that their reaction was the only possible one and that any active resistance would have been in vain.[43] Many historians have taken issue with this conclusion, and the world's memory of these ministers who yielded without a struggle has certainly been severely sullied by the passivity they showed at this decisive hour.

In my opinion the reasons which Severing, in particular, adduces can scarcely be ignored. Yet even they leave the final, real problem still unsolved. Severing was certainly quite right in saying that a general strike would not have proved an effective reply to Papen's coup. For how could the trade unions call the workers from their posts when they knew that millions of unemployed were waiting for the moment when these places might become vacant? And there was no reason whatsoever to expect these unemployed workers to refuse the vacant posts out of a sense of labor solidarity. Not only had they suffered hunger and despair too severely and too long, but also a significant number of them never had accepted the proposition of labor solidarity. The German proletariat had in no sense demonstrated that degree of political unity which Socialist leaders had always thought they could assume. Hundreds of thousands of German workers had turned either Left to the Communists or Right to the National Socialists, and both these parties would have been only too happy to show that the unions were too weak to execute a general strike.

Nor did the situation within the unions themselves satisfy the Socialists' former hopes. A letter from Alexander Schlicke, an old and tested leader of the Metal Workers' Union, makes this point quite clear. In this letter, of April 1938, to the Württemberg Socialist Wilhelm Keil, Schlicke displays more resignation than wrath while recounting the unfortunate experiences he had suffered in his union:

I had lost confidence in the masses. The rank and file let themselves be misled first by one man then the next. Stumbling from one extreme to another, they accepted as truth any charge against their own elected leaders which the bourgeois or more radically Leftist journals made . . . If it had been only the new members of the union who acted in this fashion, one might have understood. But even old men who had been members of the union since their youth not only joined in these defections, but even often led them.[44]

Although this description does not refer precisely to the time of von Papen's putsch, one can certainly adduce it here to help explain the unions' passive reception of this blow.

Any comparison of the Socialists' failure to call a general strike at this time with their successful response to the Kapp Putsch is false from the start if only because on the earlier occasion the strikers had public opinion on their side. The attitude of the civil authorities, in particular, had had much to do with their success. But there could be no hope of such aid now. Public opinion was at best divided on the question of such resistance to von Papen. Large numbers of Germans, many of them quite influential, were jubilant at the prospect of getting rid of the Socialists and, if possible, of the unions as well. Nor was this situation altered in any meaningful way when the Communists suddenly called for a general strike. For previously they had joined the National Socialists and the German Nationalists in doing everything possible to unseat what they called the "fascist" Prussian government of Braun and Severing and had applauded when the Socialist cabinet finally fell. No one who had observed all these events could count on the Communists now.

But what about the possibility of armed resistance by the Prussian police? After the publication of the President's emergency decree and of von Rundstedt's orders for its execution, any such resistance would have been a revolutionary act, and nobody can say whether the policemen's loyalty to the constitutional government of Prussia would have sufficed to support them in such an open resistance to the national government and its army. Nevertheless, one might think that Severing, who saw the trouble coming, could have concentrated enough reliable, armed Prussian police in the government area of Berlin to enable him to meet von Rundstedt's force with forces of his own. To be sure, this would have meant the start of civil war, but optimists still think that Hindenburg, though not von Papen, might have stopped short of that.

Perhaps. Or perhaps not. One can discuss such hypothetical cases ad infinitum. The fact, however, is that Carl Severing was not the sort of man to burden his conscience with the responsibility for civil war. Nor were the members of the executive committee of the Social Democratic Party such men. (Long before World War I, Maximilian Harden * had chided the Socialists, who called themselves a "revolutionary" party while boasting of their law-abiding ways: "Revolutions are not fought in the court room!") On July 16, stirred by a premonition of the impending disaster, Severing had consulted with the party's executive committee to determine whether the police could be deployed against the Reichswehr. In the course of this discussion Friedrich Stampfer, editor-in-chief of the *Vorwärts*, told Severing: "You have no right to be brave *at your policemen's expense.*" And Severing accepted this remark as an expression of his own opinion.[45]

But this was a civilian's attitude. The soldier finds it quite comprehensible that the infantry die in battle and that the generals return home in triumph. Indeed, in the Germany of universal military service, during the Empire and the Third Reich, civilians as well as soldiers held this point of view. But Severing and his colleagues were of the old Social Democratic school. They strove for domestic and international peace; to them a statesman who caused bloodshed was guilty of the worst political crime. They can scarcely be censured for this conviction. Yet it certainly cannot be denied that

---

* Maximilian Harden (1861–1927) was born Maximilian Witkowski. He took the name of Harden as an actor and retained it throughout his distinguished journalist's career. In 1892 he founded the political and literary weekly *Die Zukunft*, which he edited until 1922. In addition to his brilliant literary reviews, he was noted for his scathing criticism of German policy both preceding and during World War I. A Socialist, he urged a negotiated peace. His major political works include *Krieg und Friede* (2 vols., 1918) and *Deutschland, Frankreich, England* (1923). TRANSLATORS.

this same civilized point of view made them easy prey for enemies on both the Right and Left who stopped at nothing and fought as ruthlessly in the streets as in the offices of the Ministry of Defense.

However many good reasons may be adduced for the passive manner in which the Prussian ministers and their constituents accepted the Papen-Schleicher-Gayl coup d'état, their failure to resist remains a blot upon their names. Whoever surrenders without a struggle forfeits the sympathy of contemporary and later opinion. The ease with which the reactionary operators disposed of the last real obstacle to their victory, this last republican redoubt that had taken so many years to build, assured these men — and their even more dangerous successors — that they had nothing to fear from the German Republic nor from republican Germans. Nobody knows whether the downfall of the Republic might have been postponed in any way. But the fact that no one moved a hand to stay its fall makes this denouement not only tragic, but deeply depressing.

The Prussian ministers, of course, consoled themselves with the comforting thought that they had legal means of redress against the national government's show of force. For Article 19 of the Weimar constitution had established a Supreme Court with unique jurisdiction over constitutional disputes between the Reich and a land. (See also the Law of July 9, 1921, especially Paragraphs 16 and 31.) [46] Such a dispute lay strikingly at hand. Was there then an orderly way to re-establish the German rule of law which had been disrupted by von Papen's coup? The Weimar constitution seemed to give this assurance in the clearest possible terms. And so the Prussian ministers turned to the German Supreme Court, which, especially under the leadership of Erwin Bumke, chief justice since 1929, had won a reputation of being able to perform its difficult tasks with proper caution, but also with clarity and determination.

Initially, the Prussian government requested the issuance of a temporary injunction ordering the national commissioner to refrain from any execution of his office for the time being. On July 25, after extended and heated arguments, the court declined to issue the injunction, explaining that the grant of such a decree would anticipate the final decision of the case and that such anticipation was contrary to the standard procedures of the court. Thus the battle had to be fought out in the form of a regular trial, and it lasted into October 1932. It was politically significant that by this time the Prussian ministers no longer stood alone. For they enjoyed a certain degree of association with Bavaria and Baden, both of which were represented in the case by their "caretaking" governments.

Papen had taken great pains to forestall such intervention by the

South German lands. On July 20, the day of his coup d'état, he had sent Kurt von Lersner, his representative with both these governments, to the Bavarian premier, Held, to give him a prejudiced and distorted account of what was going on and to quiet any worries that the presidential decree might be the first step in a general action against the federal structure of the German Reich. Von Lersner explained that the Prussian incident was merely a temporary measure, for the Chancellor was a sincere federalist at heart and had no idea of proceeding in this way against any other lands.

Held had good reasons for trusting neither von Lersner nor von Papen, and he declared clearly and firmly that the national government's actions were illegal and unconstitutional, quite apart from the fact that they were also political mistakes. For, as Held emphasized, all the lands had an obvious common interest in opposing this display of force which, if not blocked now, might strike any one of them tomorrow or the day after.[47] The chairman of the Bavarian People's Party, Fritz Schäffer, used even simpler words with von Lersner, accusing the national government of having yielded to the dictates of the National Socialists.[48]

On July 24, having failed in his attempt to pacify Held, von Papen invited the premiers of the German lands, except Prussia, of course, to a conference at Stuttgart, at which he employed all his powers of persuasion in an effort to assure them that his motives were the best. The Bavarian historian Schwend reports: "His rhetorical protestations that he was really a devout federalist at heart were laid on as thickly as possible according to the old Prussian rule that when you go into Southern Germany, you need only lard your conversation with federal terms in order to accomplish whatever you wish. Thus he assured us that ever since Bismarck there had been no German Chancellor so unconditionally a federalist as he."

Von Papen seems rather to have fancied this sort of reference to Bismarck, for they appear recurrently in his memoirs. But however fluently he may 'have spoken, and however diligently he may have tried to strike an honest tone, he remained unable to gain the others' confidence and to convince them of his good faith. The Bavarian cabinet certainly had no great sympathy for the ousted Social Democratic ministers in Prussia, but it did realize quite clearly that, by yielding to Hitler, von Papen and his associates had brought about those very disturbances which they were trying to blame on Severing.

A whole series of events, which continued up to the arguments before the Supreme Court, offered further sanguinary proof of this sad truth. For if Herren von Papen, von Gayl, and von Schleicher had been correct in their analysis of the Prussian situation, the appointment of the national commissioner and the removal of Carl Severing should have been enough to bring the internecine Prussian warfare to an end. But on the evening of July 31, while the ballots in the Reichstag election were still being counted, Königsberg experienced what, in the charming terminology of the National Socialists, came to be known as "the Night of the Long Knives." This bloodbath consisted of bombings and shootings executed by the National Socialists against their political opponents. Among others, they wounded the former police commissioner, von Bahrfeld, who had just been removed from office by the national commissioner although not even his most vicious opponents considered him a "Red." On the contrary, he was close to the German People's Party. A Communist alderman was murdered in his bed by a band of National Socialists. This time, certainly, the customary argument of "defense against Communist attacks" could not be used.

The Königsberg murders were only the worst of many such frightful events which were occurring throughout Germany. The national government could not ignore the necessity for taking some action. For three days in early August (August 4–6) von Papen's cabinet, in consultation with his deputy commissioner for Prussia, Franz Bracht, discussed the situation without being able to decide on any move. *Schulthess' Geschichtskalender* for 1932, which appeared in 1933, that is, after Hitler had come to power, reports: "While the acts of terror, the plots, the armed raids, and the bombings took their course, the national government seems to have hesitated to take any of its threatened steps." On August 5, to be sure, the *Geschichtskalender* reports that the cabinet did go so far as to speak of a "general pacification" which had set in, and quotes Bracht, who attributed the terror to "the deliberate campaign by the leaders and the press of the Communist Party . . . which increased political tensions to such a point that they led to acts of violence."

What a masterpiece of pettifogging casuistry! One indeed which can only disgust even the most ardent foe of Communism and of Communists. It was not until August 9, after von Papen had returned to Berlin from his holidays, that the cabinet decided to meet the Nazis' terror with a new emergency decree. But Hindenburg was still in Neudeck. So his consent to the new measure had to be sought and granted by telephone. Evidently the President had finally concluded that the confidence he had expressed when rescinding the ban on the SA and SS — that the conflict of political opinions in Germany will henceforth assume a more orderly form, and that acts of violence will cease — had been misplaced.

This emergency decree of August 9, 1932, against political terrorism provided the death penalty for anyone who, "enraged by partisan passion, kills a political opponent out of hatred or anger." The death sentence was thus expanded to include cases which did not constitute murder under the regular criminal code, that is, killing with malice aforethought. The decree also established special courts to hear such political cases. This emergency measure was no sooner issued than an especially frightful crime took place; one which, although technically not murder, clearly fell within the provisions of the new measure.

In Potempa, an Upper Silesian village, five uniformed members of the SA forced their way into the home of one Pietzruch, a Communist laborer, whom they proceeded to beat and stamp to death before his mother's eyes. They also severely injured Pietzruch's brother through similar mistreatment. On August 22 these assassins were given death sentences by the special court in Beuthen, sentences which certainly were as just as they were necessary at the time. But the court room was packed with Nazis under the direction of an SA leader in full uniform, Edmund Heines, that same Heines whose Vehmic murders had been recited in the Reichstag on February 26, 1932, by August Weber. When the sentence for the Potempa murders was announced, Heines' rowdies broke out in pandemonium, and he made shouted threats of the vengeance which National Socialist courts would wreak when their turn came.[49] The Beuthen court seems to have taken no action against this disturbance even though it clearly verged on a breach of public peace. It was left for Hitler to have Heines killed on June 30, 1934.

Bad as was this incident in the Beuthen court, it was surpassed as a threat to the public peace by the telegram which Hitler immediately sent to the convicted assassins: "My comrades, in the face of this most monstrous sentence of death I regard myself bound to you in limitless fidelity. From this day on your release is a matter of our common honor; and the fight against the government under which the sentence was possible, our common duty." This telegram was then followed by a proclamation, in Hitler's turgid prose, which adorned the *Völkischer Beobachter*:

Herr von Papen, I now recognize the true, bloodthirsty nature of your objectivity . . . We will free the concept of German nationalism from all those restraints which reveal their true nature in the "objectivity" with which the Beuthen sentence was flung in the face of the German national spirit. With this verdict Herr von Papen has used the blood of national heroes to inscribe his name in the book of German history. He has sown the dragon's teeth. And the growth which rises from them will not be restrained through fear of punishment. The battle for the lives of our five comrades has begun!

If this gibberish makes any sense at all, it can be taken only as a declaration of war against the most fundamental principles of a government based on law. This, then, was what Hitler's repeated assurances of "legality" really meant. This rebellious outcry by the leader of a party that numbered millions provided the clearest possible argument for the immediate execution of the Beuthen sentences. But Papen, who had just assumed the role of strong man vis-à-vis the government of Prussia, could not summon up the courage to stand up to Hitler's wrath. And so the same national cabinet that had established a national commissioner of Prussia, ostensibly to preserve public peace and order, broke down in the face of the Nazis' threats and, on September 2, commuted the Potempa assassins' sentences to life imprisonment, thus assuring them their freedom as soon as Hitler might come to power. Never before had a German government bowed so openly to political terror. Even Franz von Papen, who remains charmed by the memory of everything else that he did, cannot avoid admitting in his memoirs that "in this case mercy was a grave political error." [50]

Thus the threadbare nature of Papen's case for his coup d'état against Prussia had become apparent in less than two months. His representatives nevertheless continued to make the same old arguments before the Supreme Court. The proceedings there lasted six days, with German professors of constitutional law assisting legal counsel on both sides. On October 25 the decision was announced. [51] With its "On the one hand . . . yet on the other" it failed to satisfy the hope that a severe political dispute might be settled through processes of law.

The verdict has been found "worthy of Solomon." [52] Yet such a comparison would have been valid only if the wise monarch had really let the executioner hack the disputed child in half. In fact, however, his knowledge of the female mind assured him that the real mother would not let the child die. What the Supreme Court actually did was divide the authority of the Prussian state in such a way that the illegally ousted Prussian ministers received a theoretical recognition of the merit of their case — but no practical support.

The presidential decree which overthrew the Prussian government had been based upon both the first and second paragraphs of Article 48 of the Weimar constitution. Von Papen's reference to the first paragraph, which presumes a dereliction of duties on the part of the land, was explicitly rejected by the court. After a careful examination of the national government's arguments on this point, the judges determined that no such dereliction of duties had been proved. This part of their decision constituted a severe blow to von Papen, for he had made this claim the fundamental argument for the decree.

But the court assumed an entirely different attitude toward Paragraph 2, which authorized the President to take necessary steps for the maintenance of peace and order "if the public peace should be disturbed or endangered to any great extent within the German Reich." The court found that this required precondition had existed, arguing that it was a matter of common knowledge that the decree had been issued at a time when large political parties faced each other as bitter enemies, prepared for violence at any time. But the judges circumvented the critical question, namely whether the repression of such interparty conflicts required this particular type of decree against Prussia or, indeed, whether the national commissioner's appointment had been an appropriate way to help maintain the peace. On this point the court observed: "In this situation it was possible for the President, after due and proper consideration, to conclude that it had become necessary not only to transfer the critical organs of the Prussian state to the national government, but also to unite all the instruments of power available to the governments of either Prussia or the Reich under a single hand and to direct the policies of these two governments along common lines."

The court did not stop with these dangerous and unconvincing words. It went on to observe: "In this respect it would make no difference even if the charge were true that the menacing situation could be attributed, at least in part, to domestic measures taken by this same national government." Whatever one's legal opinion of this part of the decision may be, it is clear that this observation amounted, politically, to an open invitation to engage in the most daring, Machiavellian maneuvers.

The Supreme Court rejected as unproved the charge that the emergency decree had been issued as a result of agreements between von Papen and Hitler. Indeed, the court felt justified in going on to declare that, even if this collusion had existed, it would not have provided reason to conclude "that the provisions of the decree had been designed for any purpose other than that of restoring public peace and order." Having based its decision on this extraordinarily broad interpretation of the President's discretionary powers, the court proceeded to find nothing constitutionally objectionable in the fact that the President's decree had also granted the national commissioner full authority to seize control of even those divisions of the Prussian ministries "which were not immediately responsible for establishing public policy or maintaining public order."

With the core of Prussian political power thus placed securely in the hands of the President, the Supreme Court was prepared to leave peripheral powers to the ousted ministers according to the following logic: The decree was unconstitutional insofar as it violated those provisions of the Weimar constitution which were binding even upon the dictatorial powers of the President. Specifically, Article 17 guaranteed every land its own independent government. And only this independent government had the right to represent the land in the Reichsrat. Thus the Supreme Court found the decree invalid to the extent that it "deprived the Prussian cabinet and its members of their right to represent the Land of Prussia in the Reichstag, the Reichsrat, or other national organs, in the Prussian Landtag, the Staatsrat, or in relations with other lands."

One can hardly blame the German people for being unable to follow the intricate paths of each convoluted thought and for expressing the essence of the decision in a simpler way: The Prussian ministers kept on being ministers, but they no longer had any power. Franz von Papen, who was officially obliged to comprehend the language of the court, has clearly never really mastered it even now. For he still considers himself free to assure his English readers that the Supreme Court declared his and Hindenburg's measures "to have been completely constitutional." [53] If he had truly understood the decision while writing his memoirs, this statement would have violated his own promise to "make way for truth" in a most irresponsible fashion. Presumably he simply never noticed that the Supreme Court was careful to avoid saying that the President had made proper use of his discretionary powers.

One is obliged, therefore, to tell the former German Chancellor quite clearly that, even under the ruling of October 25, 1932, his coup d'état remained a coup d'état into which an irresponsible adventurer had lured a tired, weak old man. No less an authority than Gröner likened von Papen's action against the government of Prussia to a horsewhipping (*Reitpeitschmanieren*). This expression is to be found in his letter to Schleicher, of November 29, 1932, with which he was replying in a candid, yet friendly tone to his former "adopted son's" attempt at reconciliation. He wrote: "This move to solve the problem of Reich-Prussian dualism through brute force is stupid . . . These horsewhipping manners must cease. Hitler can do this sort of thing too. We do not need you for this." [54]

From a purely juridical point of view the court's decision will no more impress the reader of today, some thirty years after the fact, than it convinced most critics at the time. For it had never been the intent of the Weimar constitution to grant the president such extremely far-reaching emergency powers. One wishes, of course, to avoid being unfair to the judges who arrived at this decision, and to their accomplished chief justice in particular. But it is impossible to avoid the suspicion that they were influenced, if only unconsciously, by their considerations for Hindenburg. They did not wish to offend the old man by finding his entire action against Prussia unconstitutional, thus perhaps unleashing a crisis of unpredictable consequences. Today it is simple to see that nothing could have proved worse than what actually happened three months later.

This decision has been called an example of the "tragedy of the juridical review of constitutional questions" which, by its very nature, is unable to settle "a major political struggle for power between two governments whose basic philosophies are irreconcilably opposed." [55] I consider this conclusion of despair to be in error. A judge must be able to interpret the constitution exactly as every other law, without looking for approval anxiously to Left or Right. It may well be, however, that such an attitude requires the tradition of centuries, the tradition that is embodied in the lord chief justice in Shakespeare's *Henry IV*. This English judge tells the young king that he would not shrink from imprisoning the lawful successor to the throne again if he should dare

> To pluck down justice from your awful bench
> To trip the course of law, and blunt the sword
> That guards the peace and safety of your person.

The epilogue to this decision is quickly told. The Prussian ministers demonstrated their respect for the court by trying once more to regain their lost positions. To this end Otto Braun had a conversation with Hindenburg, at which von Papen was present in his role of Chancellor. But nothing came of the talk. All attempts by the Prussian premier to explain to Hindenburg the implications of the Supreme Court's decision were thwarted by von Papen's supple interjections. As Otto Braun reports: "The President, who probably did not at all comprehend what was at stake, seemed quite distressed by all this arguing. He was of the firm opinion that Prussia and the Reich should be administratively united. Indeed, this was most likely the slogan with which they had won his support . . . for the coup d'état." [56] Of course the Supreme Court had just said that this union could not be effected by emergency decree. But Hindenburg had been deaf to the judges' words.

Braun then adds the following observations to his report of this conversation: "I had not seen the President for quite some time. In the course of our discussion . . . Hindenburg seemed so terribly senile that my anger at his decree was outweighed by my sympathy for this old man who, out of a sense of duty, had accepted the burdens of the presidency once again and who was now being misused by unscrupulous men in such an infamous way." And yet this old man, whose very weakness could excite the sympathy of men he wronged, was the only remaining political authority in Germany whose legitimacy was based on a clear public mandate. For Franz von Papen's authority still rested on the most stunning vote of no confidence ever registered by the German Reichstag. This will be discussed below.

Von Papen did not let the Supreme Court's decision halt him, even momentarily, in his ruthless operation against Prussia. On October 31 he used his authority as national commissioner to appoint so-called "deputies" for all the Prussian ministries. In reality, of course, these deputies were exactly what the court had just said they could not be, namely, ministers. The gentlemen who had received these appointments, including the former state secretary in the national Ministry of Finance, Professor Popitz, persuaded themselves to accept the proffered posts. Then subordinate Prussian officials unacceptable to these new masters began to be removed. Presumably, Herr von Papen considered this the best way to improve the German people's respect for law and order and to demonstrate his own devotion to "the immutable principles of Christian belief."

Let us now return to the Reichstag elections of July 31, 1932. No matter what other things one might say about them, one fact was immediately apparent: the elections represented a total defeat for von Papen's government. A cabinet generally dissolves one parliament in order to obtain another, more tractable to its will. This is what Bismarck, to whom Franz von Papen so frequently refers, did in 1878 and 1887. Yet if Papen had taken the trouble to compare his new Reichstag with the one he had so rashly dissolved in July, even he could not have avoided the conclusion that his prospects had only become worse.

The most obvious result of this election was the fact that the National Socialists had more than doubled both their supporters and their delegates. Some 13,700,000 National Socialist voters were sending 230 representatives to a parliament which consisted of 608 members. Thus the plan of Schleicher and von Papen to educate the National Socialists into political responsibility by including them in a cabinet directed by a presidential confidant had been shattered by the polls. For now it was clear to anyone able to count that Hitler would no longer be satisfied with a subordinate role in any government. Who could imagine that the Austrian would accept a German Nationalist as Chancellor now that Hugenberg's delegation had shrunk to thirty-seven? And if von Papen had persuaded himself that this election would mean the destruction of the Social Democratic Party, which he had been so ruthlessly attacking, this hope had been equally in vain. For the Socialist delegation returned to the Reichstag only three men weaker. The Chancellor's slight joy over this microscopic victory was outweighed by the fact that the Communists had increased from 78 to 89 seats. Nor had the Centrists been visibly hurt by the defection of their former colleague; they had won not only votes, but also seats (going from 69 to 75), as had their close allies, the Bavarian People's Party (from 19 to 22).

On the other hand, the parties of the Middle had lost everything, including hope. Of the liberal moderates, only 7 from the German People's Party and 4 from the State Party (among them, Theodor Heuss) were left. People with liberal, democratic views had become rare in Germany. Similarly, the Economic Party on the moderate Right had shrunk from 21 delegates to only 2. The parties which had ceased to wield effective political power had therewith lost their attraction. Millions of their former constituents had let themselves be caught up and swept away by the Nazi flood.

What then had become of Papen's "New Germany" which eager pens had been busily praising before its birth? Just what had the President achieved by freeing his cabinet from its former party ties? Minister von Gayl was free to celebrate the thirteenth anniversary of the Weimar constitution, on August 11, by listing the "reforms" which he considered necessary. But where were the forces ready to help bring them into being? All that Papen had achieved through his ill-considered favors to Hitler was the necessity of negotiating with him once again. But this time the negotiations had to be held under much worse conditions than those which had prevailed before the Reichstag was dissolved.

These conversations with Hitler took place August 10 through 12 and were concluded by a conversation between Hitler and the President on the afternoon of August 13. Papen and company made all sorts of attempts to square the circle, that is, to treat a totalitarian party as if it were not totalitarian. Even the Center joined in the game, although only under the condition that it be accepted by the National Socialists as a full partner in a coalition cabinet.

All this led to nothing — because it could not possibly lead to anything. Hitler stuck to the only position consonant with his personality and his party: he insisted on leading the new government, indeed, on personally assuming final authority in the new regime. The old field marshal, however, was not prepared to yield so much, and one can safely assume that Franz von Papen, who hardly wished to leave his Chancellor's seat, supported Hindenburg firmly in this refusal. These differences became perfectly clear in the final conversation between Hindenburg and Hitler, and the official statement reporting their talk was clearly intended to emphasize the glaring difference between the President, as representative of the entire German nation, and Hitler, the representative of one political movement. The statement read as follows:

The President inquired of Hitler whether he, either alone or in the company of other appropriate members of the NSDAP, were prepared to join a government under the direction of Chancellor Papen. Hitler said he was not prepared to join in such a government, demanding of the President, instead, that he [Hitler] be granted direction of the new government, with full government powers in his hands. President von Hindenburg refused this demand most emphatically, arguing that neither his private conscience nor his public obligations would permit him to transfer full government powers to the National Socialist movement, which intended to use these powers to further its private ends.

This communiqué was later expanded to include the statement that Hitler had "demanded the same sort of position for himself as Mussolini had possessed after the March on Rome."

The National Socialist press took strong exception to this report that Hitler had demanded "he be granted full government powers." Yet today, after we have seen what a Hitler government looked like in reality, it appears irrelevant whether he actually asked for this specific authority or not. Unofficially, the German public was further informed that the President had told Hitler he was ready and willing to put down any violent attempt to alter the political situation. And reporters circulated the tale of how the field marshal had addressed the "Bohemian corporal" with the unambiguous words: "Herr Hitler, I shall do the shooting."

Millions of Germans sighed with relief. They saw that the old President still possessed enough energy to force the power-hungry demagogue to stay within due bounds. They had no reason to suspect that within a few months the old field marshal would surrender. On the other hand, it is quite comprehensible that Hitler raged at his dismissal and, even more, at the way it had been announced to the German people. But when he remembered the army of voters that he led and the battalion of delegates they had sent to the Reichstag, he had every reason to be certain of his prospects.

For the day of reckoning was drawing near. The Reichstag would be reconvened on August 30 according to Article 23, Paragraph 2, of the Weimar constitution, which required that a new parliament assemble no later than the thirtieth day after its election.

At first the new Reichstag seemed to be developing as Hitler had hoped. To be sure, the National Socialists could not keep the aged Communist Clara Zetkin from presiding over the opening exercises.* Nor could they stop her from expressing, in a frail voice, her hopes for a Soviet Germany. Indeed, the exemplary order which the National Socialist delegates maintained during this traditional address gave a clear indication that they were under orders to avoid all disturbances, lest the government find an excuse to dissolve the Reichstag once again. As soon as Clara Zetkin had finished, the delegates proceeded to the election of their president.

Since a long-standing tradition of the Reichstag required that its president be selected from the largest delegation, it had been clear from the start that a National Socialist would be chosen. Thus Hermann Göring became president of the Reichstag, with 367 votes, while Paul Löbe, who had been president since 1920, received only 135 votes, and the Communist Ernst Torgler, 80. But when the delegates turned to the election of a vice-president, it became apparent that the former tradition of choosing this officer from the opposition had suddenly disappeared. Walther Gräf, a German Nationalist, was re-elected to this post.

In the address with which he accepted his new office, Göring hastened to assure von Papen's government that there was no reason to dissolve this new Reichstag nor to circumvent it with more emergency decrees: "I assert to the entire German nation that my election as president of the Reichstag has clearly demonstrated that the . . . Reichstag enjoys a large, workable majority and that therefore absolutely no legal state of emergency can be said to exist."

Although Göring had aimed his opening address primarily at Hindenburg, he used the President's traditional reception of the Reichstag officers, on October 8, to repeat the message directly. Hindenburg, who was accompanied by Meissner at this occasion, replied that the officers of the Reichstag did not constitute a political authority. Indeed, the officers were not even united among themselves, as became apparent when Vice-President Gräf, the German Nationalist, spoke up. He not only assured President Hindenburg

---

* According to rules of Reichstag procedure, the oldest member, regardless of party affiliation, presided over the organizational meeting during which the official Reichstag president was elected. Miss Zetkin, the remarkable little seventy-five-year-old revolutionary, was given the honor on this occasion. TRANSLATORS.

that the officers of the Reichstag did not intend to offer him any political advice; he even went so far as to characterize Göring's demands as symptoms of a relapse into parliamentarianism and accused the National Socialists, along with the Centrists, of trying to play the old "coalition game" again, which "would signify political retrogression." Gräf then went on to express emphatically his support of Papen's cabinet — the government which Hitler, ever since August 13, had been more determined than ever to overthrow. The difference between the German Nationalists and the National Socialists could not have been made more clear. It was obvious that the Harzburg Front now lay in ruins.

By the time the Reichstag officers presented themselves formally to the President, Hindenburg had already issued a new emergency decree which demonstrated his determination not to heed Göring's warning. On September 4 a voluminous presidential order "for the revival of the economy" had been published, shortly after von Papen had outlined it at a meeting of the Westphalian Farmers' Union in Münster. The new program was based on the general belief, corroborated by many facts, that the bottom of the depression had been reached, and that it was therefore reasonable to start thinking about a gradual reconstruction. The principal means proposed to help speed this revival of the economy were "tax vouchers" (*Steuergutscheine*) which taxpayers were to receive in an amount equal to 40 percent of their sales and land taxes and business license fees for the fiscal year 1932–33. From 1934 to 1939 these vouchers were to be acceptable for the payment of federal taxes; in the meantime, however, they could also serve as "basic credit for new business" and would be negotiable on the open market.

In order that the industrialists might be encouraged to hire new workers, they were given the right to lower wages to the extent that they increased their labor force.[57] This meant, of course, that they were being permitted to cut wages below the tariff contracts. This provision satisfied the wishes of the employers, who had been constantly complaining that the tariff contracts had been ruinous to the private economy. But naturally it only angered the workers, the unions, and the Socialist parties, all of whom regarded any infringement of the tariff contracts as an unexampled, dangerous retreat. Their reaction was to become evident at the next session of the Reichstag, which Göring had set for September 12.

Chancellor Papen had intended to use this session for a general exposition of his intended program. But before the Reichstag proceeded to the agenda — announced by Göring on August 30 — the Communist delegate Ernst Torgler moved that the agenda be altered and that first, without any discussion, a vote be taken on his resolutions repealing the emergency decree of September 4 and expressing lack of confidence in the government.

Such a motion to alter the agenda was admissible only if no delegate objected. At an earlier meeting of the steering committee, the leader of the German Nationalist delegation, Ernst Oberfohren, had stated his objection. But now, in the chamber, when Göring asked if there were any objection to Torgler's motions, his query was met with silence. And so he was able to announce with satisfaction that no objection had been raised, and that therefore the proposed alteration in the agenda would be allowed.

At this astonishing turn of events the Communists shouted: "That was Hugenberg's big gun!" And they were right. The chief of the German Nationalists had obviously learned that the government intended to dissolve the Reichstag immediately, before the delegates could pass a vote of no confidence. Since such a dissolution would have served his interests, Hugenberg had instructed his followers to make no objection to Torgler's motion. But something which he could not possibly have foreseen went wrong with his little scheme. Franz von Papen had neglected to bring the presidential order with him. Just why he had left behind this critical document is not quite clear. In any event, the simple fact that this misfortune overtook him illustrates the cavalry officer's political sophistication. Further disaster was averted for the moment when Wilhelm Frick, of the National Socialists, who evidently had not yet been told how to vote on these issues, arose to move a thirty-minute recess. With the help of the Centrists his motion carried.

During this half-hour respite, von Papen was able to put himself in possession of the presidential order of dissolution. The order had been prepared at Neudeck, where Hindenburg had stayed until September 7. "Neudeck" was simply crossed out and "Berlin" put in its place. Thus, when the session was called to order once again, the smiling, triumphant Chancellor was able to display the famous red dispatch case from which dissolution orders had been produced since Bismarck's time. But having taken the first barrier with so much exertion, the horseman stumbled shamefully at the second. For now the battle for political power in Germany had become a race between Franz von Papen and Hermann Göring. The one wished to announce the chamber's dissolution before a vote could be taken on the motion censuring his government; the other wished to fell the government with the vote of censure — which was certain to pass — and thus keep the Reichstag from being dissolved. It soon became apparent that the former captain in the Air Force excelled the former cavalry major in unscrupulousness, if not in skill.

As Chancellor, von Papen had the right to address the Reichstag at any time. (See Article 33, Paragraph 3, of the Weimar constitution.) This right was valid even when an undebatable motion was before the chamber. Von Papen, of course, intended to exercise that right at this time. But in the very moment Göring brought the meeting to order, he declared: "We shall now proceed to vote." In saying this, he looked steadily to the left. He did so deliberately because he knew that on his right the Chancellor was motioning to be recognized. Papen immediately arose and asked to speak. But Göring rejected his request by explaining, to the jubilant applause of the Communists and his fellow Nazis: "We are already engaged in a vote." Through the great tumult which pervaded the chamber, the Chancellor now proceeded to the rostrum. He laid the dissolution order before Göring, but Göring declined to accept it, thrusting the document aside with a brush of his hand. A second attempt to hold the order before his very face — this time by State Secretary Planck — proved equally unsuccessful, and so the Chancellor had no choice but to protest against the behavior of the Reichstag President by leaving the chamber with his entire cabinet.

In the meantime, however, the vote had been proceeding, and Göring was soon able to announce with satisfaction that the combined motions to repeal the emergency decree and to censure the government had been passed, 512 to 42, with 5 abstentions. Now, at last, he deigned to take formal notice of the dissolution order, but only to declare immediately that it was invalid. For of course it had been countersigned by Chancellor von Papen and Minister of Interior von Gayl, both of whom "were to be considered as dismissed by the vote of censure that had just been passed." Göring then went on to voice a further threat: "I am firmly resolved to maintain both the prestige of the Reichstag and, most especially, the rights of Germany's popular representatives to continue to exercise their proper constitutional functions."

However grotesque it may have been for Göring to play the loyal defender of the Weimar constitution, von Papen's role was equally absurd. He will go down in history as the first German chancellor that never addressed the Reichstag and, indeed, as the one who tried in vain to be recognized by the chair. After all, by this time he should have known what sort of men he had as opponents and should have adopted appropriate tactics. There is little to be said about the legal controversy which ensued between the two — principally in the form of correspondence – in which each accused the other of having violated the constitution. Göring's thesis, that the vote of censure had voided the subsequent dissolution, was, of course, untenable; he even admitted as much in the end, both orally and in writing. Thus the Reichstag remained dissolved, and new elections were set for November 6, 1932. The Social Democrats had favored this solution from the start.

Both the Chancellor and the President completely ignored the Reichstag's resolutions of September 12. The emergency decree of September 4, which the Reichstag had just repealed, remained in effect. Not until December 14 and 17, under Schleicher's cabinet and after debates in the new Reichstag (on December 8 and 9), were the decree's sociopolitical provisions rescinded. And von Papen's government went right on "governing" despite the motion of censure.

But even though the motion of no confidence had been deprived of any legal or practical consequences, it could not be erased from people's minds. The 512 votes which had been registered against Franz von Papen and his colleagues were every bit as much a part of the formal record as was the scant handful which had given them support. In other words, it had now become perfectly clear that this cabinet of barons and reserve officers suffered a degree of political isolation unique in German history. Yet not a single one of these "gentlemen" drew any sharp conclusions from this fact. Could they really hope to be backed by a majority of the new Reichstag? No one in Germany thought such an outcome possible.

Von Papen's cabinet operated on the theory that the opinions of the Reichstag were irrelevant so long as the government enjoyed the President's support. This attitude was particularly apparent in the wording of the presidential dissolution order, which both the Chancellor and von Gayl had countersigned. It stated that dissolution was necessary "because of the danger that the Reichstag will demand the repeal of the Emergency Decree of September 4." In the first place, it is difficult to accept the argument that the "danger" of a future Reichstag resolution provided sufficient reason for the chamber to be dissolved. Second – and even more important – one must recall that the emergency powers of the President under Article 48 were meant to be only *temporary* encroachments on the legislative domain, encroachments which the same article stated "could be repealed by the Reichstag." Thus, to dissolve the Reichstag lest it vote such a repeal meant that the President intended to use his own authority to make temporary measures permanent. In other words, the President wished to change his role from that of the

limited legislator envisioned by the constitution to one of unre-
stricted power. But how could he do this and still claim to be loyal
to the constitution?

Yet when all this has been said, it does remain true that even the
Republic's most loyal supporters welcomed the dissolution, however weak its legal justification may have been. For the Reichstag
which had been elected on July 31, 1932, had proved so incapable
of any positive action that reasonable men throughout Germany
were content to see a quick end put to its existence. Even though
the National Socialists had not enjoyed in it that majority position
they had hoped for, they had gained such overwhelming strength
that people had good reason to fear that, given reasonable time in
this Reichstag, they would seize those full government powers
which Hindenburg had denied Hitler on August 13. What this
danger specifically meant was, of course, clearly apparent to relatively few Germans at the time. But the general populace had already seen enough to come to regard the mere possibility of Nazi
rule with horror and dismay.

In the days immediately preceding the new elections, an incident
occurred that illustrated the National Socialists' lethal unscrupulousness particularly well. The municipally-owned Berlin Transit
Corporation, which naturally was suffering severely from the depression, had commenced negotiations with the workers' unions in
hopes of setting lower hourly wages in the next tariff contract. A
large number of operating and office personnel wanted to call a
strike in answer to this threat. But the vote required for such a
step failed to yield the necessary three-fourths majority. Undaunted
by these results, the Communist "Revolutionary Trade Union Opposition" decided to strike anyway. The regular unions declined to
follow, especially after the arbiter had declared his decision of
November 3 binding.

Now something quite unexpected happened: the National Socialist transport workers' group joined in pressing for a strike and
even assisted the Communists in directing it. Indeed, the composition of its leadership reflects the brutality with which the strike was
carried out. Provisions for emergency transportation had been
organized by Fritz Elsas, associate mayor of Berlin, and a sufficient
number of workers had volunteered their help. But these plans were
thwarted by the brutal force of the Communists and Nazis, who
did not shrink from shedding blood. Goebbels' triumphant entry in
his diary at this time discloses the nihilistic basis of his entire political thought:

Not a single streetcar or subway train is operating in Berlin. The general public is observing an admirable solidarity with the workers. The Red press has been deprived of all its tools of propaganda against us . . .[58] The unions are desperately trying to throttle the strike by means of sabotage. We find ourselves in a scarcely enviable position. Many bourgeois groups are being scared off by our participation in the strike. This is not a decisive development, for we can win them back to us very easily. But if we once lose the worker, he will be lost to us forever . . . The strikers have started exercising active terror against the strikebreakers. In the city streetcar tracks are being torn up, and single streetcars are being inundated with bombardments of stones. A small army of injured and wounded has already been reported . . .[59] The unions have stabbed the strikers in the back. If the strike fails, it will be due to the unions and their fat big-wigs . . . In Wedding and Neukölln [workers' sections of Berlin] violent streetfighting has already broken out. Traffic has been brought to a complete halt. Berlin offers the picture of a dead city. Naturally, our people have seized the direction of the strike in all parts of the city. That's the only way: if you're going to hit them, hit them hard! [60]

So much for the observation made by the publicity director of the National Socialists, a party which, as soon as it seized power, made it impossible for Germans to strike. And in considering the quotation above, one must recall that we have every reason to believe that Goebbels had revised his diaries — for the reading public of his New Germany — before publishing them in 1934.

Naturally the strike failed. When the elections of November 6, 1932, had passed, bringing defeat to Hitler and gains to the Communists, the National Socialists lost all interest in continuing the strike; indeed, the demonstration was called off on the very next day. But the sworn enemies on both political extremes had experienced great pleasure in uniting to deprive the Berliners of public transportation on an election day.

The big news in this election of November 6 was the two million drop in National Socialist votes, from 13,700,000 to 11,700,000. It is true that with their 196 delegates they still remained the largest delegation in the Reichstag. But the legend of their irresistible progress and invulnerability had been shown false. Indeed, one got the impression that the National Socialist movement had passed its peak and was starting to decline.

Since this drop-off in National Socialist votes could be observed in all electoral districts, although, of course, in varying degrees,[61] it undoubtedly was to be attributed to general, national factors rather than to separate, local causes. Had German voters begun to come to their senses? If this were the case, certainly the rude rebuff that Hitler had received from Hindenburg on August 13, along with the President's public accusation that the Nazi leader had demanded full government powers for himself, had played a considerable part. And one can assume that many voters, especially on the Right, had been offended by the way National Socialist Reichstag President Göring had violated all the old traditions in his treatment of Chancellor von Papen at the session of September 12. Grounds for this assumption can be found in the fact that German Nationalists' votes increased from 2,100,000 to 3,000,000 although they had been the only party to support the Chancellor on that day. Thus Hugenberg was able to lead 51 delegates into the new Reichstag, instead of his former 37.

It is also possible to conclude that many voters with economic interests had found von Papen's program, with its tax vouchers and substandard wages, more attractive than that of the National Socialists, who, to be sure, had promised the Rhenish industrialists relief from the unions, but who in Berlin had joined in an irresponsible strike against a public corporation. To this extent one can certainly speak of a victory for von Papen and record that the defeat he inflicted on Hitler was greater than anyone had expected.

But the Communists' increase of 700,000 voters — which raised their delegation to an even hundred — was no gain for von Papen. Could he, for instance, derive any consolation from the fact that the Social Democrats' losses matched the Communists' gains, and that the Social Democrats now had to be content with only 121 seats? The Center and the Bavarian People's Party had also suffered defeat at the polls, losing 300,000 and 100,000 voters respectively. In sharp — if only relative — contrast to such losses, the German People's Party had increased its July strength by more than one half (659,000 instead of 434,000), while on the other hand the State Party had lost a tenth of its former 371,000.

The most important task of any parliament is to form a majority upon which an active government can find support, and the November Reichstag was no more capable of supplying this support than the July Reichstag had been. The fact that Papen's cabinet could find no majority was clear as day. For Franz von Papen's unparalleled virtuosity in offending one political party after another, so that their dislike for him came to outweigh even their enmity toward their natural foes, had ruined his prospects once again. The German Nationalists and the People's Party were the only remaining parties on which he could rely, and their combined delegations of 62 amounted to little more than one tenth of the 584 Reichstag seats.

Although the remaining nine tenths were engaged in the most violent forms of internecine war, they still shared a common desire to chase von Papen and his barons out of office.

The government admitted as much when it declared that the new elections had made no essential change in the political situation. But when the declaration went on to state that the government saw no reason either to change its former policies or to abandon them, it only demonstrated that the cabinet had learned nothing from two Reichstag elections and an overwhelming vote of censure. Von Papen still clung to his idea of a presidential cabinet suspended in thin air even though it had proved to be as fantastic as Baron Munchausen's tale of lifting himself out of the swamp by his own pigtail.

Yet there was simply no workable majority to be found in this new Reichstag. The only combination which might have yielded any slight majority at all would have been an alliance between the National Socialists and Communists, who between them had 296 seats. Such an alliance had been strong enough to push through a vote of censure, but obviously it was utterly incapable of supporting a coalition cabinet. Neither of these two larger parties could form a majority if united with a third; even a coalition of the National Socialists with the Center and the Bavarian People's Party would have fallen a few votes short of a majority. This was still truer of the old Harzburg Front. And all attempts by the Centrists to form coalitions with their former political allies naturally yielded nothing approaching majorities. The German electorate had succeeded in choosing a Reichstag that could do nothing but say no.

Even before the new elections von Papen and von Gayl had tried to present themselves to the German nation as agents of reform who wished to correct the deficiencies of the Weimar constitution and to introduce more order into German affairs. Thus Minister von Gayl had used the occasion of a banquet of the Berlin Press Club on October 28, 1932, to expound his personal program for reform. In doing so, he gave the impression that he was wrestling seriously with the problems, but that he had got bogged down in preliminary details. He offered not the slighest hint of how his ideas might be transformed into practical action. Neither von Papen nor von Gayl were men who could call that sort of broad, popular movement into life which might have brought them closer to the realization of their hopes. Quite the contrary: if ever there was a man who could provoke vigorous opposition even to his good ideas, that man was Franz von Papen.

By this time even the aged Hindenburg realized that the present cabinet would have to be dropped. But he still clung to his loyal Fränzchen, charging him, on November 10, to engage in conversations with the several party leaders in order to determine whether and to what extent they were prepared to support the government in the execution of its stated program. It immediately became apparent that von Papen himself was the principal obstacle to any such cooperation. He found either that he was knocking on firmly fastened doors or else that the doors were opened only long enough to permit words of thundered anger to escape. On November 15, for instance, the executive committee of the Social Democratic delegation voted to refuse the Chancellor's invitation that they join him in discussions about supporting his government.

One can well comprehend the feelings which lay behind this decision. One is nevertheless obliged to call it a mistake. The old axiom that "those who were not there are always wrong" is especially true in this case. Wilhelm Keil, who unfortunately had not been on his party's list in the November election, has called this resolution "all the more politically stupid since it broke off the party's relations not only with the Chancellery, but with the President as well." [62] Keil has pointed out quite rightly that, however little love his colleagues wasted on von Papen, he was a formidable bar in Hitler's way if only because the vain Chancellor was clinging to his office with all the strength of his ambition. But unfortunately neither at that time nor during the next few weeks did the Social Democrats realize that the most important task of all responsible Germans was to keep Hitler from coming to power, and that all political feuds — however justified they may have been — had to be subordinated to this common goal.

The reception that von Papen was given by the Centrists was no warmer than the one he had received from the Social Democrats. Kaas and Joos handed him a memorandum which bluntly demanded his resignation. The leaders of the Center did express their opinion that "a union of political forces to work for the common good" was "completely possible from a technical point of view." But they added emphatically that "under the present political leadership and with the present composition of the cabinet" such an idea was "out of the question." In other words: "Down with von Papen!" And one can well imagine that Monsignor Kaas took particular pleasure in presenting the Chancellor with this bill for his breach of promise on June 2.

In the face of these rejections, what help was it to Papen when Hugenberg and Dingeldey offered him the support of their German Nationalists and the German People's Party? And so von Papen had to write a personal letter to Hitler, who still controlled the strongest battalion in the Reichstag even after his electoral defeat. But the Austrian feared a repetition of August 13 and therefore refused to enter into oral negotiations. Offering an explanation that seemed to express doubts about Papen's honor, Hitler said he would accept only written communications on the subject.[63]

Thus Papen was unable to carry out the mission Hindenburg had set him. Worse yet, his own government was no longer united behind their Chancellor. At the cabinet meeting of November 17 Schleicher proposed that the entire government resign, in order that Hindenburg might engage in direct, personal negotiations with possible chancellors. This was completely contrary to Papen's wishes; he wanted to remain Chancellor at all costs. Yet even he could realize that his program, which was appearing more and more to require the use of force, would need the Army's aid in execution, and that at the moment Defense Minister General von Schleicher and the Army were still one. It also seems that at least some of the ministers supported Schleicher's stand. And so von Papen yielded, accepting Schleicher's motion that they all resign. Personal differences undoubtedly played their part in this dispute, for the Chancellor had become too independent for the general's taste. Schleicher probably also realized that von Papen had maneuvered himself into a blind alley, and that the personal animosities he provoked on every side were going to keep the Chancellor from being able to make use of the victory he had scored over the National Socialists in the recent elections.

Hindenburg did not find it easy to accept the resignation of his faithful Franz, but he had no choice. And so he had to be content with requesting Papen and his ministers to stay on as a temporary, caretaking government until another cabinet could be formed. With this, Papen's government had sunk to that same low state in which they had found Otto Braun's Prussian cabinet — and from which they had expelled it. But we have every reason to assume that not only Papen, but also Hindenburg, hoped that the new negotiations would lead to the former Chancellor's return.

The Social Democrats were excluded from these presidential negotiations "because of the tone and content of their reply" to von Papen. They had no grounds for complaining of Hindenburg's decision on this point, and one or another of their leaders may have begun to realize that the counsel of wrath is seldom wise.

Naturally Hindenburg had to carry on his most important conversations with Adolf Hitler. The first of these took place on November 19, 1932. At Hitler's special request, no witnesses were present. The Nazi leader then consulted with his associates (who now included Hjalmar Schacht), and exchanged letters with Hindenburg, who invited him to a second conversation on November 21. The President then delegated further correspondence to his state secretary, Otto Meissner. The negotiations closed on November 24 with a letter from Meissner to Hitler, expressing Hindenburg's conclusion that the talks had been in vain. Thereupon all the letters were swiftly published by the Nazis, who wished to make sure that the President would not be able to lay his side of the case before the German public first, as he had done in mid-August.

Neither side found it difficult to find gaps and contradictions in the argument of the other. Both made repeated reference to the constitution, but today no one will take this for more than empty words on Hitler's part. As for Hindenburg, he had already distorted the constitution to such an extent — and wished to distort it still further — that the founding fathers would not have recognized their child. Under all this camouflage the struggle centered about the fact that Hindenburg wished to keep the full range of personal powers which he had accumulated in the course of the last two years, while Hitler was seeking a dictatorship of his own in the form of a presidential cabinet.

The very conditions that Hindenburg set from the start are significant. In addition to the establishment of an economic recovery program, he required that the administrative unity of Prussia and the Reich be maintained, in other words, that the emergency measures he had taken under Article 48 — which both the constitution and Supreme Court decision declared temporary — be considered permanent. When he demanded, further, that "no limitation be placed on Article 48," he meant this in the broader meaning of the article which he himself had given it. Furthermore, he insisted on retaining "the final approval of cabinet appointments," that is, he wanted to be free to strike any names he did not like. Beyond all this, he also wished to have the right to appoint two ministers himself: those of foreign affairs and of defense. However important such a proviso may have been when one was considering offering the Chancellery to Hitler, still it undoubtedly constituted a further expansion of the presidential powers beyond their former constitutional bounds. Hitler emphasized this point in his memorandum of November 23, while at the same time he tried to smooth things over by promising, if made Chancellor, to nominate Hindenburg's choices (Neurath and Schleicher) for these two posts himself.

Hitler guaranteed Hindenburg the unlimited exercise of his presidential rights under Article 48 — so long as the President signed only such decrees as Hitler might place before him. At any rate that is the only meaning one can place upon his demand that Hindenburg grant him "at least that degree of authority and prestige which has been enjoyed by other chancellors, even by men who could not add as much to the glory and honor of the name [of Hindenburg] as I shall" (November 21).

In fact, of course, Hitler had much more than that in mind. Thus in point five of Meissner's letter of November 22 we learn that Hitler had demanded the passage of an "Enabling Act" which would authorize him to rule alone and subject his actions neither to the approval of the Reichstag nor — and this was the real point here — to the approval of the President. Hindenburg's advisers recognized the threat to his position which was embodied in this demand, and they persuaded the President to insist that Hitler try to form a "parliamentary" cabinet instead. Meissner expanded upon the point in this same letter of November 22: "A parliamentary government is regularly formed by the leader of one of the majority coalition parties together with representatives of all these parties, and it normally pursues programs upon which the President has minimal or indirect effect." [64]

Now of course Hindenburg had no intention of assuming such a passive role. Therefore, when he demanded that Hitler form a parliamentary cabinet, he must have had one of two ends in mind. Either he expected that in such a coalition government the other parties would constitute an effective block to Hitler's grasp for power; or else he thought that the formation of such a coalition cabinet would prove impossible. The second alternative proved to be the case. With a barrage of verbiage Hitler refused to try to form a parliamentary government, demanding instead that he be placed at the head of a presidential cabinet.

The President denied this last demand, using an argument reminiscent of August 13. In their final letter, of November 24, he had Meissner tell Hitler that the President's oath and sense of duty prohibited him from "entrusting his presidential powers to the leader of a party which has so consistently emphasized its private aims and which has been so strongly opposed both to him and to those measures . . . which he has considered necessary." Hindenburg then went on, through Meissner, to voice his fear that a presidential cabinet under Hitler would "employ forceful means to turn itself into a party dictatorship, thus sharpening the differences among Germans even further." These words expressed not only what millions of other Germans also feared, but also what actually happened two months later. But by then Hindenburg had forgotten what he had told Hitler on November 24, 1932.

It is clear from the pose that Hitler struck through all these negotiations that his recent losses at the polls had not diminished his demands in any way. Despite all the difficulties which the November elections had brought his party and himself, he still acted like the man who held the fate of Germany in his hand. And although much of this seeming certainty was sheer bravado, there was absolutely no reason for the optimism of those who thought that now, after its check at the polls, National Socialism could be regarded as safely dead.

This sort of optimism was felt not only by many Germans but especially by those Leftist English groups which did not wish to be shaken out of their comfortable pacificism and eagerness to disarm by the rude fact that very many Germans were by no means so pacifically inclined. Harold Laski, that shining light of British socialist intellectuals, was quick to trumpet his joy in an article in the principal organ of the British Labour Party. His winged words in the November 19, 1932, issue of the *Daily Herald* read:

> The day when they [the Nazis] were a vital threat is gone . . . Accident apart, it is not unlikely that Hitler will end his career as an old man in some Bavarian village who, in the Tiergarten in the evening, tells his intimates how he nearly overturned the German Reich. Strange battle cries will struggle to his lips; and he will mention names that trembled at his name. But his neighbours will have heard the tale so often that they will shrug their shoulders and bury their faces deeper in their mugs of Pilsener to hide their smiles. The old man, they will think, is entitled to his pipe-dreams.[65]

Such was Laski's prediction, and he was a truly intelligent man who possessed astonishingly comprehensive knowledge.

In late November there was a brief interlude. The Centrist leader, Monsignor Kaas, was charged by the President to determine whether a cabinet could be formed on the strength of a parliamentary coalition. Since not only Hitler, but also Hugenberg, refused to enter into conversations on the matter, Kaas promptly resigned his commission.

At this juncture everything seemed ready for Papen's cabinet to return to full power. This is certainly what Hindenburg had been hoping all along. But now the pressing practical problems that Papen would have to face became apparent. Formerly Papen had extemporized his political career, proceeding from one day to the next and prolonging his life as chancellor artificially by dissolving one Reichstag after another. But now, after two parliamentary elections had demonstrated his steady political isolation — despite his relative victory in the November voting — even Franz von Papen had to concede that he required some new form of support. The most liberal interpretation of the constitution could not offer any help. If one is to credit von Papen, this was naturally not his fault at all, but rather that of the Weimar constitution. As he puts it in his extended apology, "Circumstances had risen for which the Weimar constitution found no provision." [66]

He then goes on to tell us about the cure he recommended to the President:

> I therefore suggested that my Government should remain in office for the time being. We would get our economic programme working and negotiate urgently with the State Parliaments on the subject of the reform of the Constitution. There seemed no reason to suppose that the newly elected Reichstag should not behave in exactly the same way as the previous one. If the Government was not going to be permitted to function [that is, by the new Reichstag], then *it must do without the Reichstag altogether* for a short period. Our proposed amendments to the Constitution would then be made the subject of a referendum or submitted for approval to a new National Assembly. (Italics added.)

In other words, von Papen was prepared to answer a second vote of censure not only with another dissolution of the Reichstag, but also with an indefinite postponement of new elections.

He realized, of course, that such a policy would violate the constitution. He even says as much in his memoirs when he admits that "this procedure . . . would involve a breach of the present constitution by the President." But he fails to mention the fact that he, too, would have violated the constitution which he had sworn to preserve. Indeed, he clearly does not think the point worth discussing. Instead, he immediately makes reference to Bismarck's attitude during the Prussian constitutional conflict in the 1860's. However odd such a comparison of von Papen with Bismarck may appear, it does demonstrate the consequences of traditional, one-sided German historiography.

This, then, is von Papen's report of his conversation with the President on December 1, 1932, when they discussed the possibility of his resuming the chancellorship. According to another source, however, his proposed program included the dissolution not only of the SA and, indeed, both the National Socialist and Communist parties, but of all parties and political organizations whatsoever.[67] In any event, it is reasonably certain that he would have been driven to such measures in carrying out his program, whether he discussed this proposal with Hindenburg or not.

The old President must have found it hard to be asked to violate the oath he had pledged on the constitution. And yet the situation in which he now found himself was nothing more than the logical consequence of his own deeds, of the stab in the back, to be precise, which he had given Brüning and Gröner just six months before. At that time he had dismissed the last German chancellor who still could summon a majority of the Reichstag to his side; and in his place he had put a man who never, under any circumstances, could have mustered such support. In doing so, Hindenburg had taken a path that could lead only to open conflict with the Reichstag.

General von Schleicher, who had accompanied von Papen to this critical conference, seemed able to provide a solution to this desperate plight. Schleicher was the real creator of Chancellor von Papen, but for some time now he had not been on the Chancellor's side in every case. To some extent this falling out may have been the result of jealousy on Schleicher's part, for the great influence and warm favor which Papen enjoyed in the presidential palace may have seemed to threaten Schleicher's own position. But the general certainly had his practical reasons as well. It is difficult to define Schleicher's actual political beliefs, but they certainly cannot have been as reactionary as those of Papen and Hindenburg. As early as July, in a radio address, he had vigorously insisted that the Reichswehr did not exist simply to protect "obsolete economic forms or untenable property arrangements." These words cannot have sounded pleasant to the people and organizations that had already denounced Brüning and Schlange-Schöningen as "agrarian bolshevists" because of their plans to resettle the East.

Schleicher made a point of being thought socialistically inclined, whatever that may have meant. He saw clearly how unpopular von Papen had made himself with all the parties — except, of course, the German Nationalists. And he certainly had some reason for considering himself a good bit cleverer than Papen. But Schleicher was even less able than von Papen to hold a steady course, and he remained stronger in negative criticism than in constructive action. His chief delight lay in confidential conversations with no witnesses — or at least behind closed doors — where one could make veiled allusions that could not be reconstituted concretely later, and where one could promise more than one was really prepared to give. Schleicher had already started such negotiations on several sides: on the one hand, with various union leaders, to whom he showed surprising sympathy; on the other, with National Socialists, whom he tried to convince of the advantages to be found in positive collaboration. The discussions with the Nazis had foundered on Hitler. But

Schleicher still had hopes in Gregor Strasser, who had shown himself much more receptive to his arguments.

At the joint interview with the President on December 1, Schleicher had felt sufficiently sure of himself to counter Papen's arguments and present his own. His purpose, he said, was to split the Nazi Party. He spoke not only of drawing Gregor Strasser into the government, but also of winning the support of a good number of National Socialists in the Reichstag — Papen speaks of "about sixty" in his memoirs. Beyond this, Schleicher went on to develop the idea of a "labor axis." By bringing union leaders of various shades of opinion to his support, he hoped to persuade the political parties to which they were connected, that is, primarily the Social Democrats and Centrists, at least to tolerate a government so well disposed toward labor. In this way, Schleicher argued, there was a possibility of finding parliamentary support and thus of avoiding an open violation of the constitution.

According to von Papen's report, the President listened silently to his ministers' debate; then he decided in favor of von Papen — and of a clear breach of the constitution. Papen tells us that Hindenburg turned to him and said: "Herr Reichskanzler, I desire you to undertake immediately the necessary discussions to form a government, to which I shall entrust the carrying out of your plan." If this report is true, it means that the President was prepared to continue further along the route which he had started, even though he had already discovered that it could lead only to a violation of the constitution. One can hardly doubt that his personal affection for von Papen played a critical part in his choice.

Schleicher may well have lost a battle, but he was far from ready to surrender. Von Papen could speak as glibly as he wished about violating the constitution; the general knew that such actions would require an army that one could trust. It was Schleicher who controlled the Army at this time, and he was just the man to tell his colleagues in the caretaker government exactly what was at stake.

Von Papen's plan, he explained to his fellow ministers, entailed the enormous danger that the two radical parties against which it was aimed — the National Socialists and Communists — would resort to violence. What this would mean, the general went on, was apparent from the Berlin transport strike. What would happen if the dock workers in Hamburg, Stettin, and the Rhine ports were all to strike, and brown and red rowdies joined in defying law and order in the streets? Who could hope to suppress such a revolt? Only the Reichswehr, reinforced perhaps by the Prussian police, which the coup d'état of July 20 had brought under federal control. But would the Army be up to this trial? Would its inner discipline survive such a rigorous test? Doubts like these could not help but take root in the other ministers' minds, and Schleicher knew how to make these misgivings appear to be probabilities bordering on fact. He had already instructed his ministry to organize so-called war games, and the problem this time was to be a civil war.

The execution of these exercises was entrusted to a Lieutenant Colonel Ott, a close confidant of Schleicher's. The two gentlemen even hit upon the ingenious thought of including the possibility that Poland would use this occasion of German domestic disorder for an attack from the East. In the judgment of all the military authorities participating in this "game" there was no hope; the Reichswehr could not be expected to cope with such a situation.[68]

On December 2, 1932, the day after his victorious interview with the President, von Papen called a meeting of his cabinet. He obviously wished to use this occasion to reassert his leadership and control. But Schleicher had brought Ott along and persuaded the cabinet to listen to his report. Ott then retraced the course of his experiment, showing that the double task of protecting the eastern border against the Poles and preserving domestic peace against the National Socialists and Communists exceeded the powers of the Army and the police; from a military point of view he therefore had to recommend that no "state of emergency" (that is, breach of the constitution) be declared. A majority of the ministers joined him — and Schleicher — in this opinion. A violation of the constitution was bad enough; but a violation that was likely to end in defeat had to be avoided at all costs. Von Papen realized that a preponderant majority of the cabinet was against him, and so he terminated the meeting in order that he might report these latest developments to the President.

Were these war games a maneuver on Schleicher's part to check von Papen and force him to retreat? One has no reason to question the professional qualifications and intellectual honesty of the participating officers; they arrived at their conclusions from the problem that was set. But were the hypotheses of the problem valid? Was the government really going to have to cope with invasion and a general strike? The answer to these questions is far from clear. On the one hand the passive behavior of the victims at the time of Papen's coup d'état against Prussia suggests that the Germans would have suffered yet another breach of their constitution in relative peace; yet on the other, responsible government is always obliged to consider the worst possibility. And it is certain that neither the National

Socialists nor the Communists would have felt the same compunctions that had kept Severing and his colleagues from actively resisting von Papen's coup.

It is equally certain that Schleicher was deeply repelled by the thought of embroiling the Reichswehr in a German civil war. Although neither he nor a great majority of the Army officers were truly neutral — or even unprejudiced — with respect to domestic matters, still it was a big step from such antipathy to an open conflict in which soldiers would have to fire on civilians. The Army had no desire to be called "bloodhounds" again, as had happened to Noske's men in 1919. But this time there was still a further complication. At a meeting of military leaders in February 1932, General von Hammerstein had made the undisputable observation: "Fundamentally we all stand on the Right." [69] This naturally meant that the officers would be much slower to aim their weapons at the Right than at the Left. And in their eyes a battle against the National Socialists was a battle against the Right.

This dilemma had become all the sharper once the National Socialists had begun to penetrate the Army. Their infiltration had maintained critical proportions ever since the decree of January 29, 1932, which had declared ordinary members of Rightist organizations admissible to the Army and for which Schleicher had surely been more responsible than his minister at that time, Wilhelm Gröner. Since that date, not only had National Socialists been able to join the Reichswehr, but also many active officers who previously had had to cloak their secret Nazi leanings were able to cast aside their masks and urge their fellow officers openly to join the party's ranks. The repeal of the ban on the SA — which Schleicher had personally achieved — had had much the same effect. Could the common soldier be expected to understand if these organizations, which just a few months ago had been officially declared harmless and even "patriotic," were now called rebellious elements, upon whom he was expected to fire? General von Schleicher therefore had good reason to complain of the deficient reliability of his troops; but he was principally responsible for their present state.

It is rather paradoxical that these war games, which had demonstrated the weakness of the Reichswehr, resulted in the defense minister's assuming the Chancellor's post. For when von Papen told Hindenburg that his colleagues had declined to support him at that cabinet meeting on December 2, thus requiring the President to choose between Schleicher or von Papen, it became apparent even to the aged Hindenburg that he would have to let his faithful Fränzchen go. It was bad enough — though tolerable — that all the parties had rejected Papen; but when even his own cabinet opposed him, the hour for his departure had clearly come. Now the President had no choice but to try Schleicher and his program.

Hindenburg must have found it hard to tell von Papen he was through. We shall never know the truth of Papen's report of this scene in his memoirs — that "two great tears were rolling down his cheeks as I shook his hand and turned to go." But it is certain that the field marshal did pay von Papen the highest tribute of which he could conceive: He inscribed the portrait that he gave him as a parting present with a line from Uhland's song, so popular in the German Army: "Ich hatt' einen Kameraden" (I had a loyal comrade).

XIV

FROM SCHLEICHER TO HITLER

THE German public greeted the news of Papen's resignation with feelings quite different from those the President had expressed. As early as November 19, when Papen had tendered his formal resignation but was still staying on at the head of a caretaking government, Sir Horace Rumbold, the British ambassador to Berlin, reported to his superior, Sir John Simon, that all the German political parties had learned of Papen's resignation with satisfaction and relief and that this general feeling of content was disturbed only by the thought that Papen might find some way to return to power. Even the German Nationalists, Rumbold went on, regretted the resignation of the cabinet, but not that of the Chancellor himself. The ambassador called von Papen's methods "irresponsible" and characterized him with the following words:

> The Chancellor's confidence in himself is unlimited, and he still claims to possess the confidence of the country. A light-weight gentleman rider in his youth, he displayed the characteristics which might have been expected from him when he took office. Not only did he take every political fence at a gallop, but he seemed to go out of his way to find fences which were not in his course. A man of second-rate ability, his record is one of incessant challenge to the political parties, the Federal States and all shades of opinion which did not coincide with his own.[1]

A few months later, on January 25, 1933, Sir Horace expressed his thoughts even more sharply. After a conversation with von Papen, in which the former German Chancellor had let his mind rove freely, the ambassador wrote: "There is, perhaps, nothing very new in this, but his statements and outlook can only confirm the wonder of an observer that the destinies of this great country should have been, even for a short time, in charge of such a light weight." [2]

Against such a dreary background, even Schleicher must have

made a rather bright appearance. Although no party had reason to have confidence in him, he had at least not gone out of his way to offend anyone. Indeed, it was part of the general's technique to suggest to whatever people he happened to be dealing with at the time — quite regardless of their actual opinions on an issue — that he sympathized with their position on the matter. Professional party men regarded him, of course, as another dilettante without political experience. Yet even this scornful opinion gave them grounds for hope that Schleicher would not prove as stiff and inflexible a reactionary as his predecessor had been.

It remained true, however, that he had borne a large share of the responsibility for von Papen's basest deed: the coup d'état against Prussia. This breach of the constitution would not have been possible if General von Schleicher had not put the Reichswehr at the Chancellor's complete disposal. Thus he had no reason to be astonished when the Social Democrats registered their objection to his appointment as Chancellor, although Sir Horace Rumbold was probably correct in surmising that this resolution was contrary to the party leaders' real wishes.[3] Yet the general had stood in the wings while the coup was carried out, and therefore he had not reaped as much personal enmity as had Chancellor von Papen. For this reason, as he confided to Sir Horace, he hoped to find a way to negotiate with the Social Democrats despite their resolution.[4]

But now Schleicher was thrust into the full glare of the spotlight. Most observers thought he found this sudden notoriety rather unpleasant. Indeed, he told the British ambassador as much when he said he would prefer to be back in the Ministry of Defense. Rumbold comments: "I believe this to be true. General Schleicher is an ambitious man, who no doubt hoped some day to be Chancellor, but he did not wish that day to come too soon. Nevertheless, he seems to be accepted, even by papers standing to the Left, such as the *Berliner Tageblatt*, as the only man in present circumstances who could have eased the situation." [5] Rumbold refused to consider Schleicher a Machiavellian intriguer. He found the general a man possessed of keen political instincts who had learned that personal animosities have no place in politics and that, instead, it is wise to be on good terms with all political leaders.[6]

Few conclusions can be drawn from the composition of the cabinet which Schleicher announced on December 3, 1932, since he clearly regarded it as only a temporary government. He kept all save two of Papen's ministers, one of whom was Freiherr von Gayl. On December 2, when von Papen's cabinet deserted him, Gayl had been the only minister to support the Chancellor.[7] And now he joined him again, this time in leaving the government. In his place appeared the deputy national commissioner for Prussia, Franz Bracht, who had demonstrated his calling as a legislator — while providing general amusement, as well — in a decree requiring stricter standards of dress on public beaches. Some clue to the direction of the new Chancellor's thoughts could be found in his appointment of a special "National Commissioner for Public Works." This post was given to Günther Gereke, president of the Congress of Rural Communes. Gereke had already come forward with plans for a make-work program which, of course, had been attacked as "inflationary" by industry while receiving considerable labor support.[8]

Schleicher's grand design — indeed, one might even say the only idea he had in assuming the direction of the German state — was to overcome his opposition by first dividing it on both the Left and the Right. He planned to render the National Socialist movement harmless by bringing part of it into his regime; and he expected to pacify the Social Democrats by keeping the unions content.

Schleicher, both personally and through intermediaries, had had more contact with the National Socialists than any other minister. As early as November 30 he had opened negotiations with Hitler through his confidant, Lieutenant Colonel Ott. In these conversations Schleicher, who clearly was convinced that he would soon be chancellor, had offered Hitler the post of vice-chancellor and several ministries. Hitler took counsel with Goebbels, Göring, Frick, and Strasser — and declined. Goebbels has given us the following report of their reaction to the general's move: "Strasser recommends that we tolerate a Schleicher government. To support this view, he paints the party's situation in black on black. In doing so he exposes a degree of pessimism we would never have credited him with." [9] The report, of course, makes the Führer — and his loyal servant, Joseph Goebbels — appear all the more confident of victory. Remarkable too are the conditions which Goebbels says the party leaders set, presumably for their simple toleration of a Schleicher regime: "Adjournment of the Reichstag until January, political amnesty, *freedom of political assembly*, and *full guarantees of rights to self-defense*" (italics added). Just what these last two conditions really meant is painfully clear to anyone who survived the National Socialists' rule of terror.

Thus Gregor Strasser was Schleicher's only point of contact with any significant number of National Socialists. We can therefore well credit Goebbels' report that Strasser "had a conversation with General Schleicher the following Saturday." We have, however, less reason to believe him when he goes on to add that Schleicher offered Strasser the post of vice-chancellor and that Strasser, in return, promised to head a splinter group of Nazis in the next elections. By now Goebbels was fighting his former patron Strasser with all the weapons at his disposal, and so in this instance his report is even less reliable than usual. In any event, one can safely assume that this report by Goebbels was one of the principal weapons used against Strasser in the intraparty struggle then taking place.

But it quickly became apparent that Strasser was not the man to press a fight against Hitler. He was the leader of the party's bureaucracy and consequently could make a strong case for his proposed policy of compromise with Schleicher by pointing to the party's desperate plight, especially its overwhelming indebtedness and its decline in public favor. On December 6 Goebbels himself observed: "Throughout all Germany our situation is catastrophic. In Thuringia [at the local elections of December 4] we have suffered almost 40 percent losses since July 31." But what help were such arguments against the manic rhetoric of Hitler, who not only promised his followers a speedy victory for the movement, but also threatened to commit suicide if they should desert him now? Gregor Strasser possessed neither the magic powers of speech to match Hitler in debate nor the iron determination required for such a struggle. So on December 8 he resigned all his party posts.

From his own point of view, this was the worst thing Strasser could have done. For by yielding in this way he set his enemies free to make whatever accusations they desired while leaving his own supporters suddenly deserted. People who had formerly been backing Strasser now had no choice but to make quick peace with Hitler and his stone-hearted henchmen. By December 9 Goebbels was able to note in triumph: "Strasser is losing ground with every hour." Hitler, of course, used this opportunity to bind the party membership still closer to himself, even assuming Strasser's former office of party secretary in person.

Within a few days Strasser's intraparty revolt had been completely quelled. But Hitler never forgave him for having dared question his supreme authority. On June 30, 1934, the Nazi leader had Gregor Strasser killed, along with General von Schleicher. And the members of the National Socialist Party accommodated themselves to the murder of their former party secretary just as easily as did the Reichswehr to the murder of its former minister and leader,[10] and as did the German judges to the justice minister's declaration that these murders had been "lawful." One can only wonder what had happened to those other times when Jakob Grimm could state with the simple pride of a German patriot: "There are still some men of conscience even in the face of force."

Schleicher's negotiations with the unions seemed to offer better prospects for success. Theodor Leipart, chairman of the General German Labor Federation, appeared quite interested when the new Chancellor invited him to collaborate on the government's program of public works. In a New Year's Greeting to the federation's members, Leipart defended his attitude against the attacks of those who accused him of abandoning his Socialist ideals to work with reactionaries. He answered these people by saying that he realized quite well that Schleicher's government did not intend to institute Socialism but wished, rather, to strengthen the capitalistic economy. But, he argued, as the regularly constituted representatives of German labor, the unions could not escape their responsibility to help the government provide more jobs. Naturally the unions did not offer to engage in such collaboration without insisting on conditions of their own, such as the repeal of those provisions of the emergency decree of September 5 that had destroyed the validity of tariff contracts. And their demand was accepted. But if Schleicher thought that he could capture the Social Democratic Party by pleasing the unions, he was about to be disillusioned. For we shall shortly see how the party succeeded in cutting the strands Schleicher had woven between the unions and himself.

Nevertheless all these negotiations did achieve the limited success of calming German nerves to some extent. This relative calm became apparent at the short Reichstag session of December 6 through 9, which was conducted without any significant disturbance. In September the honor of making the opening address had gone to the Communist Clara Zetkin as the senior delegate. But this time an even older National Socialist was present, the eighty-two-year-old General Karl Litzmann, and the honor became his. In 1914 Litzmann had won high military fame by achieving a breakthrough at Brzenny on the eastern front and still boasted that Hindenburg owed his field marshal's baton to Litzmann's brigade.

Litzmann, who was by no means an ordinary German general, found sufficient arrogance to threaten the President with an "eternal curse" for "driving the German nation to desperation and abandoning it to Bolshevism even though the people's savior stood at hand." The simple fact that a man with the education and experience of a Prussian general could grind out phrases like these illustrates the atmosphere in Germany at the time. Göring's re-election as president of the Reichstag astonished no one; but the scant majority of votes he attracted — 279 out of 545 — was not without elements of surprise.

The new, more conciliatory mood that pervaded German politics was further exemplified by the Communists' failure to have a motion of censure put on the agenda. The National Socialists, in particular, wished to avoid the dissolution and new elections which they regarded as the certain consequence of a vote of no confidence. Schleicher therefore took pains to spread the report that he had been assured a presidential decree of dissolution. (Whether in fact he actually had such assurance is difficult to say.) The National Socialists made a motion, which was discussed and passed, designating the chief justice of the Supreme Court as acting president of Germany in the event of the President's disability or of "an untimely vacancy in the presidency."

The most interesting aspect of this technically justifiable law was the story of its genesis. Finance Minister Schwerin-Krosigk told the British ambassador that no less a figure than Chancellor von Schleicher himself had suggested such a measure to the National Socialists, pointing out that it would serve their party's interests by relieving Hindenburg of his basic misgivings about Hitler. He had argued that the old field marshal hesitated to appoint Hitler chancellor because he feared that, if he died, the "Bohemian corporal" would become dictator of Germany in everything but name.[11] For according to the governing provision of the constitution (Article 51), the functions of the president would devolve upon the chancellor in such an event. At the time of Ebert's death the problem had been solved by the passage of a special federal law that temporarily transferred the functions of the president to Walter Simons, who was then chief justice of the Supreme Court.

Even more ominous than this law of succession was the extensive amnesty that this Reichstag, like its predecessor, granted. These recurring amnesties, which followed every attempt by the national government to preserve peace and order, constituted a severe threat to public safety and weakened still further the Germans' wavering respect for law. It was significant that the National Socialists and Communists joined forces in the Reichstag once again in order to effect the passage of this latest amnesty law. Their temporary alliance reminded one of an exchange of war prisoners under an armistice, except that in this case both parties to the agreement were determined to resume the fighting as quickly as possible. The further votes required to pass the law were furnished by the Social Democrats, while all the other parties voted against the bill.

On the other hand, it was characteristic of the new, post-Papen scene that Schleicher's cabinet made no move to oppose a resolution of the Centrists, Social Democrats, and National Socialists rescinding the socio-economic provisions of the emergency decree of September 4. The motion sought principally to repeal the employers' right to pay substandard wages under certain circumstances. Schleicher's immediate compliance with this resolution could only increase his support in union ranks.

Indeed, Schleicher had every reason to be grateful to the Reichstag for the way he was being treated. The delegates permitted the Chancellor to remain distant from their deliberations and did not create a situation where he would have to speak. For it was common knowledge that the general had been denied the gift of public speaking, however skillful he might be in small groups and intimate conversations. His interests were also served when the Reichstag adjourned sine die, for this action seemed to afford him the possibility of carrying on those further negotiations on both the Left and Right which he hoped would lead to a stabilization of his new government.

Furthermore, at this same time a diplomatic victory providentially fell into his lap. On December 10 at Geneva, the five principal powers, Great Britain, Germany, France, Italy, and the United States, issued a joint statement recognizing the validity of German claims to equal military rights "in a system which would provide security for all nations." [12] There had been a significant history to this declaration.

On September 14, 1932, the German foreign minister, Baron von Neurath, had addressed a note to Arthur Henderson, formerly the British foreign secretary and now the chairman of the League's Disarmament Commission. In this note Neurath stated that Germany *would not take part* in further deliberations of the commission until its claim to equal rights had been recognized in principle.[13] Neurath, who was rather devoid of personal initiative, was presumably acting under the influence of his state secretary, Bernhard von Bülow, who hoped to find compensation for the defeat he had suffered when the customs union with Austria came to naught.[14] But the foreign minister had also been encouraged in this move by his colleague, the minister of defense; for General von Schleicher seized every public opportunity to raise this demand in the bluntest manner possible.[15]

The French, of course, had greeted the German note with astonishment and fear. They considered themselves deserted by Great Britain and hence — as well as for other reasons — felt unable to offer effective resistance to the Germans' systematic demolition of the Treaty of Versailles. An alarmed Premier Herriot had confided to the British chargé d'affaires that he found the present situation more serious than any since 1919. And where, he asked, would it lead to? If Germany is permitted to rid herself — whenever and however she pleases — from one provision of the treaty after another, Europe will never know peace again. Perhaps the next step will be a violation of the demilitarized zone along the Rhine. Then it will be the Polish Corridor; then Upper Silesia; and finally the former German colonies. After all, Herriot noted, von Hoesch, the German ambassador in Paris, had already said as much — and in ways that one could only call intentionally insulting.

Herriot was convinced that all of Germany's grievances could eventually be satisfied in a just and amicable manner at the appropriate time and in the appropriate ways. But if the Germans were going to persist in forcing this peaceful process, then it was time to call a halt to the entire procedure. Herriot assured the British official of the French desire, and especially that of his government, to proceed as far as possible with a general disarmament; but, he insisted, his cabinet was neither willing nor able to participate in any program that would constitute "an entering wedge" for German rearmament. If this is what the Germans really wanted, the French would prefer to see them violate their treaty clauses in a spirit of open defiance. For then one could at least recognize the problem and take suitable steps.[16] In short, Herriot was in a desperate state of mind; and if one considers the actual moves which the Germans subsequently made, one cannot accuse him of the slightest exaggeration.

This German demand for equal rights was just the sort of request calculated to evoke sympathy in England. For all of British public life is based upon the principle of equal rights for every individual. Only a very few Englishmen recognized the ulterior motives which lurked behind Germany's use of the phrase. No more than a scant few of them realized that Germany was the only European nation bent on war, while the French — especially the French peasants, who had voted for Herriot — were absolutely dedicated to peace. Winston Churchill was one of these few perceptive Britons. He pointed out that an unconditional grant of equal rights would necessarily put the Germans, with their much greater numbers, at a distinct advantage vis-à-vis the French.

To those who persisted in favoring military equality between Germany and France Churchill posed the blunt question: "Do you want another war?" And in the House of Commons he made a remarkably prophetic speech:

For my part, I earnestly hope that no such approximation [of armament] will take place during my lifetime or that of my children. To say that is not in the least to imply any want of regard or admiration for the great qualities of the German people, but I am sure that the thesis that they should be placed in an equal military position with France is one which, if it ever emerged in fact, would bring us within practical distance of almost measureless calamity.

But Churchill found himself in hopeless opposition not only to the British government, but also to British public opinion. Under no circumstances did the public want to be shaken out of their peaceful illusions, though Japan's unimpeded invasion of China should have convinced the dreamiest idealist that "collective security" was still an empty term.

In spite of this general willingness on the part of the British to accommodate German demands on the disarmament issue as much as possible, Sir John Simon had no choice but to criticize sharply the Germans' manner of making their point. In an official statement which he issued on September 15, 1932, he first referred to the generous attitude the creditors had demonstrated at the Lausanne Conference and then went on to observe: "In view of Germany's economic difficulties, the initiation of acute controversy in the political field at this moment must be accounted unwise. And in view of the concessions so recently granted to Germany by her creditors, it must be accounted particularly untimely." [17] Sir John then proceeded to give the British interpretation of the Versailles treaty, rejecting the Germans' claim that they were entitled to permission to rearm. He argued that the provisions for German disarmament were still binding and that they could be rescinded only through mutual agreement among all the signatory powers. Thus, he said, the Germans' only hope lay in further negotiations.

German newspapers were almost unanimous in their rejection of this note. They called it an unfriendly maneuver on Britain's part and started speaking once again of "perfidious Albion" and of British hypocrisy.[18] The German government preferred to make no reply at all.

Sir John Simon, having taken so strong an official position in this manner, was now ready to assume a milder tone. On November 10 in the House of Commons he delivered a speech which expressed the government's willingness to accept the Germans' claim to "the principle of equality" if the Germans were prepared, in turn, to state formally that *under no circumstances* would they seek to gain whatever further demands they might make *through force of arms*.[19] Of course they had already promised as much in the Kellogg-Briand Pact; but Sir John apparently thought it would be wise to have the assurance repeated.

Two days later, when Sir Horace Rumbold presented himself to State Secretary von Bülow in hopes of receiving such a declaration from the German government, he was greeted with so many remonstrances that the ambassador, ordinarily an exceptionally self-controlled man, gave unmistakable expression to his disappointment. He knew that a representative of the Defense Ministry visited Bülow's office daily, and he assumed that this messenger had encouraged Bülow to display such open intransigence. Von Neurath's manner, on the other hand, was considerably more friendly; yet he was equally unwilling to discuss the desired German statement.[20] At this same time the British military attachés, who enjoyed exceptionally good relations with officers in the German Defense Ministry, reported that the Reichswehr was becoming increasingly insistent in its demands.[21]

In early December, after much backing and filling, negotiations were finally commenced at Geneva among representatives of France, Great Britain, Italy, Germany, and the United States. Von Neurath, Herriot, MacDonald, Simon, and Norman Davis, the American delegate, all took part. The Italians had adopted Germany's position from the start; the other three Western powers hoped to use the conversations to persuade the Germans to rejoin the general Disarmament Conference. Even Herriot was willing to work toward this end, so long as French security requirements were not impaired. The solution to these differing interests and desires was found in a joint declaration by England, France, and Italy stating that one of the guiding principles at the Disarmament Conference should be *"the grant of equal rights to Germany* in a system which provides security for all nations."

Germany then joined these three powers in a statement of their common willingness to unite with all European countries in a solemn declaration "that *under no circumstances* would they seek solutions to any present or future differences *through the use of force.*" Germany's signatory to this declaration of December 11, 1932, was Freiherr Konstantin von Neurath. His signature did nothing to keep him from continuing to direct the Foreign Ministry under Adolf Hitler, nor from tearing up the Treaty of Locarno when German troops marched into the demilitarized left bank of the Rhine.[22]

Whatever one may think of the joint declaration of December 11, 1932, as a step on Europe's way to lasting peace, it certainly represented a major victory for the German government. Brüning's demand of ten months before that Germany be granted equal military rights had now been officially accepted by all the principal powers — including France. One therefore had every reason to expect the Germans to greet this news with general jubilation. But on the next day a quite different cry resounded from the German press. To be sure, the *Frankfurter Zeitung* granted clear recognition of what the government had accomplished and carefully emphasized the important parts MacDonald and Simon had played in this achievement. But in the eyes of any "patriotic" German, the *Frankfurter* was a "Jewish sheet" and therefore to be ignored. Hugenberg's press, on the other hand, was much more virile: it bemoaned Germany's return to the Disarmament Conference and even declared forthrightly that what Germany needed was the security afforded by *its own weapons* — that is, German rearmament rather than general disarmament. Goebbels' *Angriff* simply called the joint declaration "a trap for Germany."

This was the tone of the entire "patriotic" press. Hugenberg's German National People's Party criticized the declaration in an especially odious manner, inquiring maliciously just how this governing principle of equal German rights would work out in practice if European disarmament were to proceed only gradually while *Germany's right to rearm* remained unrecognized.[23] One surely cannot err greatly if one takes such expressions to show that the true goal of these newspapers, and of the parties for which they spoke, was a *German rearmament* that would put their country in a position to carry out General von Seeckt's declaration during the negotiations which preceded the Treaty of Locarno: "We must *acquire power*, and as soon as we have power, we will naturally retake all that we have lost."

But what of the general public that was not committed to any particular political persuasion? An interesting answer is given by the interpreter Paul Schmidt, who recalls his shock upon returning from the Geneva negotiations to discover "how little recognition . . . the grant of military equality was given in Germany." And he sounds equally convincing when he goes on to remark "that the public, the press, and the parties all seem utterly unaware of what we accomplished — or to wish to be unaware of it." [24] Again it had become apparent — just as Briand had complained to Stresemann some seven years before — that the Germans were interested in possible concessions from their conquerors only so long as the concessions had not been made. They promptly lost all interest in each issue as soon as their victors had yielded.

This point should be considered by all those people who still believe that Hitler and the Second World War could have been avoided if the Allies had softened the provisions of the Treaty of Versailles even more swiftly. One might also ask whether the

Germans would have been quicker to effect reconciliation if they had won the war. In this connection one is reminded of the response Friedrich Meinecke recalls receiving from his friend the Danish historian Aage Friis to the suggestion that "the disturbed mentality of the German people could be explained by the mistreatment they had suffered under the Treaty of Versailles." Friis answered with the simple question: "If Germany had won, would she have dictated a more moderate peace?" Meinecke passes the query along without comment. Later, however, he does speak of a "frightfully degenerate twist to the political ambitions of those elements of the German nation which formerly had been its culture-bearers." [25] It is also worth remembering that the man who in 1918, in the moment of deepest defeat, had demanded that the German foreign minister "ensure the annexation of Longwy and Briey while making peace," was now President of the German Republic.

Schleicher acknowledged the progress that Germany had made on the disarmament issue in an extended radio address to the nation on December 15. To be sure, he did not thank the British statesmen who had worked so diligently to effect the compromise, nor did he express the slightest gratitude to Edouard Herriot, who had yielded so much to accommodate the Germans. Instead, Schleicher thanked Mussolini for having supported the German point of view. Under these circumstances it was really rather touching when he mentioned how much the nation owed to Heinrich Brüning — whose dismissal he had brought about just seven months before — for having awakened sympathy throughout the world for the German position. For reasons that remain obscure, he also saw fit to thank von Papen for a similar contribution.

The principal purpose behind this radio speech was to make a general announcement of Schleicher's program. Formerly a new chancellor would have addressed the Reichstag to accomplish this end. But a radio talk was simpler: it could not be interrupted from the floor, nor could it be followed by critical speeches from the opposition.

Little exception could be taken to most of what the new Chancellor said. He presented himself as the "nonpartisan trustee of the interests of *all* segments of the German nation for what everyone hopes will be only a short emergency," and he did his best to avoid offending anyone. Perhaps the only novelty in his entire program was his announcement of large-scale rural settlements in the East. He informed his listeners that he intended to devote some 500,000 acres in East Prussia, some 175,000 in Pomerania, and approximately 75,000 in Mecklenburg to this sort of agrarian reform. He called this proposed program "the most extensive utilization of our thinly populated East for the domestic colonization envisaged by Frederick the Great" and an attempt to create a "loosening up and ventilation of our metropolises and an opportunity for even a large number of urban workers to have their own homes and gardens as is so frequently the case in Southwestern Germany."

In order to make his nonpartisan spirit as clear as possible, Schleicher carefully dissociated himself from all the economic systems heretofore known to man. He explained that he was neither a capitalist nor a socialist, and that concepts like "private enterprise or state control" held no terror for him. All this made the new Chancellor sound like a reasonable, conciliatory man even though experts could not help suspecting that a fuzzy amateurism lay behind the genial smile.

In any event, Schleicher could boast that he had provoked no new disorders and that, as even Hindenburg acknowledged, the German Christmas holidays of 1932 were considerably more peaceful than those of recent years. On December 21, when he received the British ambassador, Schleicher was still able to put on an air of confidence and speak — despite Gregor Strasser's recent defeat — of the possibility of winning a number of National Socialists over to his cause. But in this same conversation he also demonstrated that he still had not been able to free himself from his old illusions; for not only did he deny any opposition on his part to the National Socialist Party, he even said that he would regret a collapse of Hitler's movement. He also mentioned the Social Democrats in this connection, voicing the hope that he would be able to enter into negotiations with them; and in all fairness it must be recorded that he really undertook earnest efforts in this direction.

That these negotiations failed completely was the fault of the Social Democrats, not Schleicher.[26] The Socialists, even at this late hour, seemed incapable of realizing that Hitler stood immediately before the gates, and that compared to him a conservative Prussian general — even one suspected of intrigue — was some one to be cherished. And is one not also obliged to ask: Just what did the Social Democrats hope to achieve by opposing Schleicher? Indeed, were not Schleicher's plans for rural resettlement, however uncertain and obscure they may have been, a program on which the Socialists could have offered enthusiastic collaboration?

Gustav Noske, who understood politics and recognized the dangers that were menacing Germany at this time, spoke bitterly of the "people who thought they were leaders" and who, by rejecting Schleicher's offer, "rejected the last opportunity to preserve them-

selves and all their gains from the disaster that threatened." Noske
also describes how Leipart told him that Schleicher had invited him
to discuss the possibility of collaboration between the government
and representatives of organized labor, but that the Social Democratic executive committee had ordered him (Leipart) to report
to the party headquarters first. "There [on January 6, 1933] Breitscheid informed him that the party leaders opposed any form of collaboration with Schleicher, and that they expected the same attitude from him." Leipart acquiesced, and therewith all the strands
between the Chancellor and organized labor were cut.

During these days Noske had a personal conversation with Schleicher; and he has reported, on the strength of this interview, that the
general's determination to block the National Socialists lay beyond
any doubt.[27] Of course one can say that Noske had been one more
victim of Schleicher's conversational skills; but one can also argue
that had the Social Democrats been a bit more accommodating,
Schleicher could have kept his post and held to a moderate course.
In this sense the leaders of the German Social Democratic Party
failed to meet the challenge history set them, and their failure helped
make Hitler's regime inevitable. Whoever laments the fate of German Social Democracy for both political and humane reasons is all
the more obliged to record the melancholy fact that the movement's
own errors helped bring about its end.

While the Social Democrats obdurately maintained this useless
and sterile opposition, their sworn foes on the agrarian Right were
bustling about in full activity. Schleicher's resettlement program
had provided the signal for attack. After all, they had not chased
such "agrarian bolshevists" as Brüning and Schlange-Schöningen
from office in order that a "socialist" general might become chancellor and distribute 750,000 acres of landowners' ancestral soil to the
dregs of the urban proletariat. However glibly these Rightists may
have damned partisan spirit and party rule, they were fully prepared
to deploy their own political strength as soon as the presidential cabinet began to threaten the sacred interests of the landed gentry. The
only difference was that it was easier to make these pressures felt
now than had been the case under parliamentary governments. For
one no longer had to rise in the Reichstag and debate the point in
public; one had only to slip into the presidential palace and gain
the ear of the Old Gentleman, who was always so considerate of
his friends.

On January 11, 1933, a deputation of the National Agrarian
League (*Reichslandbund*) appeared at the President's office in order
to lodge a complaint about the alleged inactivity of Schleicher's

cabinet. According to our reports of the confrontation, the leaders of the group made a special point of attacking the government's tariff and financial policies, while taking care not to oppose the re-settlement plan in particular.[28] Hindenburg had asked the Chancellor, together with Ministers von Braun (Agriculture) and Warmbold (Economics), to be present at this discussion. Their explanations of the points in question satisfied neither the representatives of the Agrarian League nor the President himself. According to one report, Hindenburg terminated the conversation by striking his fist upon the table and berating the Chancellor with these words: "Herr Reichskanzler von Schleicher, I request — and as an old soldier, you realize, of course, that a request is simply the polite form of a command — I request that your cabinet assemble this evening, prepare laws of the kind we have just discussed, and present them for my signature tomorrow morning."

The report from which these words have been taken is a letter from the economic policy director of the Agrarian League, Baron Heinrich von Sybel, of February 2, 1951. Thus the report was written many years after the conference in question, and its reliability is consequently subject to some doubt. Indeed, there has been a debate whether the letter can be admitted as historical evidence.[29] It is, of course, easy to assume that after almost twenty years von Sybel would not be able to recall every individual word that Hindenburg uttered. But, on the other hand, there is no reason to doubt his ability to remember the general sense of such a striking statement by the President.

Nor is any motive for deliberate falsification to be found. Von Sybel had belonged to the Reichstag since 1928, first as a delegate of the Agrarians, and after July 1932 as a National Socialist. In my opinion the dictatorial utterance which von Sybel has reported corresponds perfectly with the picture one is forced to derive from Hindenburg's undisputed words and deeds. Ever since 1930 he had been harboring an increasingly unlimited sense of his presidential powers, especially in the field of legislation; and there is certainly nothing astonishing in the thought that he might have used military terms and manners when expressing his sense of these powers, especially to a chancellor who was also a Prussian general. In this respect, Hindenburg had been rather spoiled by his two chancellors after Brüning.

No matter how difficult the old field marshal found the task of mastering intricate problems in constitutional law or foreign affairs, he always found it easy to arrive at a firm position on questions like this one, which affected his personal interests and everything his education had taught him to hold dear. Nor should one be surprised that he turned on his own ministers in this fashion even, one might say, in the face of the enemy; for one need only recall his unexampled public repudiation of Gröner and the ban on the SA.

After this conference of January 11, the national government learned that, even before the interview with Hindenburg, the executive committee of the Agrarian League had approved a resolution which was a masterpiece of demagoguery and deception. Thus, for instance, it claimed that the "exploitation of the German farmer by the omnipotent money-bag interests of internationally-minded export industries and their vassals" was still going on and accused the cabinet of having allowed the deterioration of German agriculture to assume "proportions considered impossible even under a purely Marxist regime." [30] This resolution prompted the German government to break off negotiations with the league; it also provoked the Federation of German Manufacturers (*Reichsverband der deutschen Industrie*) to take a public stand against the agrarians' "unexampled" attacks "which severely impugned . . . the honor . . . of German industry." The whole incident shows that German agrarians had not changed very much since the days of Caprivi,* whom they had never forgiven for saying he expected Germany to develop into an industrial state.

The special political significance of this incident is to be found in the fact that, although the Agrarian League had been infiltrated heavily by National Socialists, it still exercised a considerable amount of influence in German Nationalist councils. Evidently Schleicher had discussed with Hugenberg the possibility of the latter's entering his cabinet — but not as minister of economics, which was the post that Hugenberg had wanted. Schleicher preferred to remain in full personal command of his government's economic policies. And so Hugenberg and his German Nationalists reverted more and more to their familiar role of opposition.

Yet despite all this, Schleicher could probably have held out some time longer if only his predecessor had come to realize that, having been allowed to call himself Chancellor of Germany for five whole months, a man of his modest gifts had been given all he could rightly ask of life. But Franz von Papen was miles from any

* General Count Georg Leo von Caprivi de Caprara de Montecuccoli, the last German chancellor before Schleicher to have been a general, was Bismarck's immediate successor in the office. His support of German industry, his social legislation in behalf of workers, and his commercial treaties which substantially lowered the price of foodstuffs infuriated trans-Elbian agrarian interests. They organized the pre-war Agrarian League (*Bund der Landwirte*) which was instrumental in forcing Caprivi's dismissal in 1894. TRANSLATORS.

such thought. Indeed, during those months in office Papen's over-estimation of himself had somehow managed to increase, and he still possessed an invaluable political asset: the President's favor. To be sure, the practical difficulties that had proved his undoing still existed unchanged in any way. But, Papen must have asked himself: "How would it be if I were to regain the reins of government with the help of that same man whom I barred from power earlier last fall?" At that time Hitler had dared demand von Papen's post and, of course, had been refused. But now they might find mutual profit in collaboration.

And so on January 5, 1933, the political world was astonished by the news that the former Chancellor von Papen had had a conversation with Adolf Hitler at the home of the Cologne banker Baron Kurt von Schröder just the day before. Anyone in Germany with any degree of political sophistication immediately assumed that Papen was organizing a dangerous intrigue against Schleicher, even at the risk of helping Hitler come to power in Schleicher's place. As is to be expected, Papen devotes several pages of his memoirs in an effort to refute this assumption, an assumption which historical events subsequently proved justified. Papen of course presents himself as the loyal servant whom only an evil master could possibly accuse of nefarious schemes. The great majority of responsible historians have lent no credence to his labored and apologetic defense.[31]

Even the very beginning of his explanation is significant. He tells of an address which he delivered at the Berlin Herrenklub on December 16, 1932, and how, after he was finished, a member of the audience, apparently in an offhand way, asked Papen whether it might not be possible for him to speak personally with Hitler sometime. Fortunately we have an absolutely reliable eyewitness of this event in the person of the historian Theodor Eschenburg. Since the episode is of such critical importance to our evaluation of both the characters and the plot, Eschenburg's account merits direct quotation at some length:[32]

The real purpose of Papen's address . . . was not as he has given in his memoirs, namely, to "see Schleicher's government off to a good start" and to emphasize the necessity for domestic reforms and Franco-German rapprochement. On the contrary, von Papen again demanded that the National Socialists be taken into a coalition cabinet. I heard this speech in person. It evoked great distress on the part of many listeners, including myself. My neighbor . . . whispered to me: "Little bird, I hear you singing!" I, in turn, told our host that evening, Baron von Gleichen: "But you cannot tolerate a speech like this at such a critical time. Why, this amounts to a stab in Schleicher's back. For this offer to form a cabinet with the National Socialists will only give them new encouragement. After all, they know that Papen is still Hindenburg's confidant." I expressed similar misgivings to State Secretary Planck, the director of the Chancellor's office. He merely answered: "Let him talk, let him talk; completely unimportant. No one takes him [Papen] seriously any more." "Except the Old Gentleman," I interjected. "Beside the point," Planck replied. "Herr von Papen takes himself much too seriously. This address is the swan song of a poor loser."

We shall ignore Planck's political blindness in this narrative. He evidently had not yet learned how little statesmanship is required for successful intrigue. We can satisfy ourselves, instead, with the simple observation that in this speech Papen clearly took the initiative in suggesting that the National Socialists be drawn into the German government. Evidently interested by this idea, one member of his audience, the Cologne banker Kurt von Schröder, proposed that von Papen meet with Hitler. The former Chancellor immediately agreed, and the conversation took place on January 4, 1933, at Schröder's house in Cologne. However clear the connections between these events may appear to the modern reader, Franz von Papen does not tire in trying to assure us in his memoirs that his motives were as pure as an angel's: "I had not the slightest intention of causing Schleicher difficulties . . . I thought there was still a possibility of persuading Hitler to join the Schleicher government." [33]

Does this mean that von Papen had already notified Chancellor von Schleicher of his plans to persuade such an important — and embarrassing — figure to join the cabinet? Papen himself must admit that he had not breathed so much as a word of this to Schleicher. The excuse he offers for this oversight is not much better than the schoolboy's chestnut that his tardiness was due to an unexpected interruption in the streetcar service. Indeed, von Papen confesses that he was "somewhat surprised" at having his photograph taken as he left the taxi in front of Schröder's house. [34] For it evidently was not until this moment that he realized his attempt to operate behind Schleicher's back had been discovered and thwarted by the Chancellor's excellent private intelligence service. It was at this moment, and for this reason, that Papen suddenly decided to write a long letter to Schleicher immediately after the meeting. He thought that in this letter he could make the conversation appear as he desired.

Hitler's reasons for accepting Schröder's invitation to this conversation are obvious. He had just fought his way to a personal victory over Strasser, but his party was experiencing severe troubles. Indeed, it was almost bankrupt. Goebbels' diaries for this period speak of the Nazis' financial plight on every page. Of course, one cannot be astonished to learn that their treasury was empty and that their debts were high; in one election after another they had been handing out money lavishly — whether it was theirs or not. And Hitler had his private financial problems, too. He owed more than 400,000 marks in back income taxes alone.[35]

It seems that it was possible for this passionate patriot to course throughout the land, speaking of the grandeur and the sorrows of the German people, and yet completely neglect the simplest duty of any German citizen — the payment of his taxes. If the revenue authorities in Munich had stopped regarding him as a special case and treated him instead like any other delinquent taxpayer, the luxurious establishment at the Kaiserhof Hotel in Berlin would have come to a sudden end. But once Hitler had the powers of the German state within his hands, then he had no more fear of the tax authorities than of the solicitor general, who proved ready to close his eyes to any murder that showed the trace of the Führer's hand.[36] Apart from all this, did not such a conversation with von Papen offer the long sought avenue to power? Everyone knew that Hindenburg had deeply regretted having to let von Papen go. Would not the President therefore regard even the "Bohemian corporal" with more friendly eyes if he were to appear before him arm in arm with Franz von Papen?

For this conversation in Cologne on January 4, 1933, was directed to such an end. We base our account of this meeting on the sworn testimony which the only witness to the conversation, Schröder himself, made at von Papen's Nuremberg trial.[37] Papen, of course, has impugned the truth of Schröder's testimony; but it is impossible to imagine why the banker would have deliberately lied to injure Papen. In any event, according to Schröder's testimony the former Chancellor told the National Socialist leader that it seemed best to him "to unite the Conservatives and Nationalists who had supported him in a coalition government with the Nazis. He then proposed that this new government — if it proved possible — be directed by *Hitler and Papen sharing equal powers.*"

Here the essential difference between the present situation and those of August 13 and November 24, 1932, becomes sharply apparent. On those earlier occasions von Papen had been chancellor and did not at all wish to leave the post. Now he, like Hitler, stood outside and wanted to get in. To accomplish this he needed Hitler's help, and since their earlier negotiations had convinced him that the National Socialist leader would never accept a position under him, von Papen proposed a compromise solution that illustrated his flexibility as well as his total lack of responsibility. For, entirely apart from its impossibility under constitutional law, what could be more grotesque than a government with two coequal heads?

Naturally Hitler rejected the idea. It was easy for him to see from this proposal how much von Papen desired to return to power. Hitler therefore preferred to repeat his old demand that he be named chancellor. Schröder reports: "Then Hitler delivered a long speech in which he said that, if he were made chancellor, it would be necessary for him to be at the head of the government, but that Papen's supporters would be able to join his [Hitler's] cabinet if they were willing to join in his policies."

Schröder's testimony agrees completely with what Goebbels noted in his diary. Goebbels is, of course, hardly a completely reliable source. But one asks in vain what interest he would possibly have had in falsifying his record of these particular events. On the very next day, January 5, 1933, Goebbels noted in his diary that the Nazis had hoped to keep the conversation secret, but that through some indiscretion it had become open knowledge and that Schleicher was having it trumpeted loudly in the public press.[38] And then come the significant sentences: "People seem to sense what is really going on here . . . At least there is one thing that the present government knows, namely, that we are earnestly working *toward its fall*. If this coup succeeds, then *we shall not be far from total power*." On the next day he observed that "the organization's bad financial situation will be irrelevant" if "our coup succeeds this time." A few days later, on January 9, Goebbels met Hitler in Bielefeld and entrusted to his diary what the Führer told him there: "Things are looking up. If nothing extraordinary occurs, we shall probably succeed this time. Naturally, our old demand that the Führer be appointed chancellor remains unchanged."[39] Then comes a detail that throws a special light on the Papen-Hitler negotiations: "In any event, *the present government does not possess a presidential order dissolving the Reichstag*." Only Papen can have betrayed this fact to Hitler, who now knew that he had no reason to fear Schleicher any longer.

Hitler was even clearer with a remark in his so-called "Table Conversations."[40] There, in the entry under May 21, 1942, one can read: "In the face of the increasingly tense political situation, the Old Gentleman had made contact with him [Hitler] through Papen, letting the former Chancellor explore the terrain, so to speak, in their well-known conversation at Cologne. At this meeting he, Hitler, had gained the impression that his prospects were excellent. He had therefore made it absolutely clear that under no circum-

stances would he be party to any compromise solutions." This report, of course, implies that Hindenburg had been involved in
Papen's intrigues from the beginning, and one certainly should not
make this assumption on the strength of a statement by Hitler,
especially since in this case he was trying hard to depict Hindenburg's interest in him as warmer than it really was.

On the other hand, one has absolutely no reason to question
Schröder's final judgment that Papen and Hitler had arrived at "an
agreement in principle." And this conclusion exposes the essential
course of the entire conversation at Cologne. Furthermore, it has
been corroborated by Otto Meissner. This state secretary to German presidents from 1923 to 1945 reported how one of Hitler's com-
panions informed him that the principal subject of the conversation
at Cologne had been the formation of a Rightist government in
which Papen had offered Hitler a sort of "duumvirate." [41] Still more
conclusive is Meissner's testimony that Papen then told Hindenburg
that the question of forming a new cabinet — and of its political
composition — had been discussed in the conversation at Cologne.

From all this it is quite clear that Papen went to Cologne with
the intention of bringing about Schleicher's fall and of putting himself, with Hitler's help, back in Schleicher's place. This was the
opinion of all German political circles, whether they sympathized
with Chancellor Schleicher or did not. The fact that Schleicher issued
a mollifying statement after conferring with von Papen proves absolutely nothing at all. What else was the man supposed to do? He
knew very well how much favor von Papen enjoyed in Hindenburg's eyes, and it was Hindenburg upon whom Schleicher's own
political existence depended. It is, for instance, quite illuminating
that Schleicher tried to persuade Hindenburg to receive von Papen
only in his (Schleicher's) presence — and that his request was refused. For Papen had taken up residence as close as possible to the
President's own quarters — the presidential palace was being re-
modeled at this time — so that he was able to reach Hindenburg
directly through the gardens behind the Wilhelmstrasse without
being observed by Schleicher's agents on the streets.

Von Papen made good use of these opportunities. Thanks to
his powers of persuasion, he succeeded in convincing the senile
President that the Adolf Hitler with whom he was now negotiating
was a much more modest man than the Hitler that had so disturbed
the President in August and November with his demand for full
government powers. Meissner tells us that, after Papen's conversation with the National Socialist leader, Hindenburg told him (Meissner) that Hitler had abandoned his demand for total authority and

was now prepared in principle to participate in a coalition government with other Rightist parties. Meissner also reports that Hindenburg told him he had "given his agreement to von Papen's remaining in personal and strictly confidential contact with Hitler on this basis." [42] In his testimony at the Nuremberg Trials Meissner added a piquant detail: Hindenburg had requested him to make no mention of Papen's mission — *even to Schleicher*.[43]

If Meissner's report is true, one is obliged to conclude that Papen had severely exaggerated Hitler's readiness to compromise and had failed, in particular, to tell Hindenburg that Hitler was still insisting on his unconditional demand to be appointed chancellor. For this was the one point on which Hindenburg had been completely unwilling to yield until now. And Meissner tells us how even at this time the President was still speaking of Papen as the man whom he would like to see as Germany's next chancellor.

The report also tells us that the field marshal had decided to betray Chancellor von Schleicher even as he had betrayed Chancellor Brüning just seven months before. The fact that Hindenburg not only was negotiating with a presumptive successor behind the Chancellor's back, but had even ordered that the Chancellor remain uninformed of this development, is particularly repugnant to any feeling for decent constitutional practice. Hindenburg had clearly reverted so completely to his old military habits of thought that he regarded the head of "his" presidential cabinet as a subordinate officer whom he was free to detach from his staff when he pleased. Certainly his dictatorial behavior on January 11, at the interview with the representatives of the National Agrarian League, is completely consonant with this interpretation.

For a time Schleicher thought of extending his government in various directions. But he very swiftly learned that upon the Right — especially in Hugenberg's circles — he was already reckoned among the dead.[44] On January 21 he received a resolution of the German Nationalist Party that not only demanded a complete reconstitution of the cabinet — which would, of course, have meant Schleicher's resignation as well — but also vented sharp criticism against his regime, using all the old reactionary phrases and concentrating carefully on Hindenburg's hopes and fears. The Nationalists complained that the program of Schleicher's government displayed a clear tendency toward socialistic, internationalist ideas and entailed the danger that urban bolshevism would penetrate the rural countryside. If this thought alone were not enough to send cold shivers through the old President, his attention must certainly have been caught by their complaint that Schleicher's government represented *the liquidation of the authoritarian principle* which the President had established when he appointed von Papen's cabinet.

Hugenberg issued this declaration of war against Schleicher just a few days after the National Socialists had given him another demonstration of their ability to capture Nationalist votes. On January 15 a Landtag election had been held in the tiny land of Lippe-Detmold. Of the land's 165,000 inhabitants, perhaps some 100,000 were qualified voters. Hitler had decided to make an example of this campaign in order to show that his party's prospects were improving again. He had therefore concentrated his own energies and those of his most experienced agitators upon this small land, less than half the size of Luxembourg or Rhode Island. Of course his party's finances were by no means sufficient for such a display of strength; but the predictable victory was won, although in no especially overwhelming way.[45] For, although the 38,000 votes that the National Socialists received did exceed their November figures by 5,000, they did not equal the highwater mark set in July. And the principal losers were not the parties on the Left, but rather the German Nationalists. Indeed, the Social Democrats had gained at the Communists' expense. Thus, even if one had taken this small electoral district as a sample of the entire nation, the returns would not have revealed very much. But the National Socialists, with all their demagogic skill, blared forth the election results as though they constituted a major Nazi triumph. The party regained its self-confidence, and Hitler's position as Führer was firmer than before.

Even Schleicher's optimism seems to have collapsed under the pressure of these events. The Chancellor now realized that men were working toward his fall and that the President was taking part in these designs. It was at this time that Schleicher told the Hungarian ambassador he would resign if the President were to deny him an order dissolving the Reichstag.[46] His hopes of receiving this critical document appear to have sunk low by this time. And since the Reichstag was scheduled to reconvene on January 31, 1933, Schleicher could reckon his government's life expectancy by days.

As though these troubles were not enough, the Centrists and Social Democrats now united in an attack which was aimed at the Rightist agrarians but which could well involve the President and his family. At a meeting of the Reichstag budget committee, the Centrist delegate Josef Ersing mentioned the rumors that were being circulated concerning improprieties in the allocation of "eastern aid." [47] Not only the Social Democrats, but even the National

Socialists, joined him firmly in this thrust at the conservative Right.[48] They charged that millions of marks of eastern aid had found their way to the owners of large estates, particularly in East Prussia, and that many of these recipients either had had no legal claim to such subvention or else had used the funds for purposes other than those for which the program was designed.

The explanations which Agriculture Minister von Braun offered the committee did not satisfy the delegates at all, and on January 25 a majority of the commission resolved to recommend that the Reichstag appoint a special committee to investigate the matter. This investigation was never held, for the Reichstag was dissolved before the committee ever met. One therefore cannot tell to what extent the accusations were deserved; and today, after both guilty and innocent have been struck down by the same terrible fate, the question has lost all practical importance.

What gave the issue special significance at the time was the connection many people made between this threatened investigation of eastern aid and the family of the President. In particular, there were those who said that the National Socialists wished to use this occasion to exert political pressure on Hindenburg. Now in point of fact, Hindenburg had never claimed any eastern aid; he could therefore not be linked with any misuse of funds. But there was the embarrassing fact that Hindenburg had registered the Neudeck estate under the name of his son, Oskar, in order that the inheritance tax might be avoided. Of course for years now this had no longer been any secret. But even so, it would have distressed the Hindenburgs no little to see this matter become the subject of public investigation and testimony under oath. One can, for instance, well imagine that Oskar von Hindenburg did not look forward to such an experience. And if this affair casts a certain shadow on the character of his father, this shadow is made still darker by the fact that in August 1933 the President let Hitler and Göring give him a neighboring estate of some 3000 acres and a great forest — the so-called *Preussenwald* near Allenstein — from the property of the Prussian state. Although Magnus Freiherr von Braun finds this all quite in order,[49] some people may think otherwise.

During January 1933 Papen was still busily at work, without however, making any significant progress. After the elections in Lippe he did succeed in establishing connections between Hitler and the President's entourage. To accomplish this, Papen made use of the good offices of Joachim von Ribbentrop, wine merchant and National Socialist, whom Hitler later appointed not only ambassador to London but also German foreign minister. On January 18 von Papen met Hitler again, this time in Ribbentrop's house. Hitler once more demanded that he be chancellor in any joint regime. Papen tried to parry this insistent attack by explaining that he could not persuade the Old Gentleman to accept such an arrangement. When Hitler seemed to ignore von Papen's words and repeated his demand, someone — apparently von Ribbentrop — suggested that Hitler talk things over with the President's son.

Hitler accepted this proposal, and the conversation took place on January 22, again in von Ribbentrop's house. Franz von Papen, Hermann Göring, and other leading National Socialists were also present. Oskar von Hindenburg had arrived in the company of Otto Meissner. Hitler, however, took the President's son aside, and the two engaged in an extended private conversation. One has every reason to assume that Hitler again persisted in his demand to be appointed chancellor; and this assumption is strengthened by Oskar's remark to Meissner on their return, that he saw no other possibility, especially now that Papen had said he would be satisfied with the post of vice-chancellor. Meissner may well be correct in reporting that in this conversation Hitler had assured Hindenburg's son he would exercise the powers of chancellor "according to the constitution and the laws." [50] Not only does every modern reader know how little this assurance really meant; it is also difficult to comprehend how anyone with the slightest bit of political experience could have taken Hitler's words at face value at the time.

Having won Oskar von Hindenburg to his side, Hitler was now almost certain of success. The aged President had become even more dependent than before on his entourage for help in making up his mind. Even though he rejected Papen's present recommendation that Hitler be made chancellor, it was clearly going to be a simple matter of waiting until he would yield to the combined entreaties of Oskar, Meissner, and von Papen.

In any event, Schleicher had already lost his cause when he presented himself to Hindenburg on January 23, 1933, with a request for an order dissolving the Reichstag. During this conversation Schleicher had, of course, to admit that all his plans to form a majority in the Reichstag had come to naught, and that he too saw no alternative to a dissolution of the Reichstag and an indefinite postponement of new elections. But this would have constituted that same breach of the constitution which Papen had proposed — and which Schleicher had resisted — at his final cabinet meeting on December 2. Hindenburg naturally reminded him of this and reminded him also of his statement at the time that the

Reichswehr could not be expected to cope with such a situation.

Schleicher tried to argue that because of his good relations with the unions the situation was much better now than it had been two months before, and that he — unlike von Papen — ran no risk of facing a general strike. Of course all this might well have been one more of Schleicher's optimistic self-delusions; certainly the strong protests voiced by all the republican parties when they learned of Schleicher's plans fail completely to suggest any basis for his hopes. In any event, under these circumstances one can hardly reproach Hindenburg for rejecting Schleicher's proposition after consulting with Meissner. It is true that on December 1 Hindenburg had told Papen that he was prepared to join him in the very policy he now refused to accept from Schleicher as unconstitutional. But the President simply had much more personal confidence in Papen than in the rather independent Schleicher — even though this confidence in Papen was not shared by many other Germans.

Although the President had good reason to refuse a dissolution of the Reichstag that was to be linked with an unconstitutional postponement of the prescribed new elections, he could well have given his approval to a dissolution that remained within the requirements of the constitution, that is, one that would be followed by new elections within the prescribed period of sixty days. For at this juncture both the President and Chancellor had good reason to assume that the National Socialists feared the prospect of a dissolution and that, therefore, there was no better way for the President to strengthen Nazi intransigence than to deny his Chancellor the order of dissolution. For as soon as it was certain that Schleicher had been denied his request, his cabinet was doomed to fall. Conversely, so experienced a parliamentarian as Siegfried von Kardorff, a former vice-president of the Reichstag, assured the British ambassador that "the mere knowledge that Schleicher had in his pocket the decree of dissolution would have brought both Hitler and Hugenberg to heel," so much did both fear new elections.[51]

We do not know whether this aspect of the matter, apart from the Chancellor's proposed breach of the constitution, was discussed between Hindenburg and Schleicher at the time. But if it is true that as early as their Cologne conversation Papen had assured Hitler that Schleicher would not be permitted to dissolve the Reichstag, then one is forced to conclude that Hindenburg would have denied him the dissolution order now even if no violation of the constitution were involved.

This conflict between the President and his Chancellor shows that the system of so-called presidential cabinets had been overtaken by its natural, inevitable fate. It had fallen prey to its own inner contradictions. Regardless of whether such a government were directed by a belligerent chancellor like von Papen or by an accommodating one like Schleicher, sooner or later the moment of conflict with the Reichstag was bound to come. The President could, of course, postpone the confrontation through his power to dissolve the parliament, but in the longer run the problem had to be faced.

A German government which was responsible only to the President and which rejected any form of party ties would have been conceivable only if a large number of German voters had been ready to support this President with complete loyalty and with no consideration either of the parties to which they had formerly belonged or to the interests which they had been promoting through these parties. But such, of course, was not the case at all. The first requirement for such a situation would have been the nation's confidence in the President's nonpartisan objectivity; yet Hindenburg had destroyed his claim to such trust when he deserted Brüning. In the wider sense, the nation showed absolutely no inclination to approve of a cabinet merely because the President had seen fit to appoint it. And this feeling was strongest on the Right, where Hindenburg thought he was most certain of support.

Of all the German political parties, the Nationalists had been keenest in their praise of presidential cabinets. But now, on January 21, 1933, their declaration of war against Schleicher demonstrated clearly that they were just as prepared to oppose sharply a presidential cabinet that did not satisfy their wishes or their interests as was any other party, and that, even in this critical respect, the Nationalists intended to make no distinction between a presidential cabinet and a parliamentary government. The fact that they cloaked their declaration of war in the form of an appeal "de papa male informato ad papam melius informandum" * changed nothing of its substance. On the contrary, it only shows that these anachronistic sons of Prussian junkers were still clinging to the same old rhyme:

---

* The reference seems to be to Luther's appeal "From the badly informed Pope . . . to inform Pope Leo X better" (a . . . Papa non bene informato . . . ad sanctissimum . . . nostrum dominum Leonem . . . Papam x. melius informandum), written from Augsburg on October 16, 1518, after Cardinal Cajetan, the papal legate, had refused to let Luther defend his suspect views at length, bluntly demanding instead that he recant. See D. Martin Luthers Werke (Weimar, 1884), II, 27–33. This appeal from Cajetan to the Pope, like that of the German Nationalists from Schleicher to Hindenburg, presumed that objectionable policy was not the will of the ruler but rather of his counselors, who were keeping him misinformed. We are indebted to our colleague F. C. Oakley for this reference. TRANSLATORS.

Und der König absolut,
Wenn er uns den Willen tut.†

The impossibility of this so-called "system" was heightened even further by the fact that it was supposed to be directed by an eighty-five-year-old man whose intellectual powers were now even less able than before to grasp the difficult political and economic problems which his successive governments had to face.

Indeed, von Papen had basically abandoned the idea of a presidential cabinet when he decided to ask Hitler for support. For if the National Socialists were going to be included in the next government, they would certainly bring along a set of partisan loyalties and interests quite incompatible with Hindenburg's — and hence von Papen's — former views. The only part of Papen's plan that could have appealed to the old field marshal must have been the thought that the next cabinet would be composed primarily of Rightists. For ever since Brüning's dismissal Hindenburg's program had consisted of "making the government conservative in tone." It can be assumed that von Papen took special pains to assure the President that this desired conservative course would be guaranteed by the fact that a majority of the new ministers would come from the non-Nazi Right.

It was for this reason, for instance, that Papen was so eager to persuade the leaders of the President's beloved *Stahlhelm* to accept portfolios in the new cabinet. He tried his luck first with Duesterberg, who brushed him off, and then with Seldte, who proved unable to resist the temptation of becoming a minister. But Hugenberg was even bigger game. He alone, among all the candidates being considered, possessed a party organization and the requisite political experience. Papen commenced his negotiations with Hugenberg on January 26, that is, two days before Hindenburg told Schleicher he was through.

Duesterberg was also present at Papen's conversation with Hugenberg on January 26. The *Stahlhelm* leader reports that Papen began by stating that the new government would necessarily be headed by Hitler and that, indeed, the *Stahlhelm* also would have to accept his leadership. Duesterberg says that he opposed this idea with vigor and determination, while Seldte, who was also there, was prepared to accept it.[52] Hugenberg's, however, was the critical response.

The German Nationalist leader had no objection to Hitler's be-

† And the King shall have free sway
So long as he does what we say.

coming chancellor. With his peculiar overestimation of himself, he said that there was no danger at all: Hindenburg would still be President and commander-in-chief of the armed forces; Papen would be vice-chancellor; and he, Hugenberg, would take over the whole economy, including agriculture, while Seldte would run the Ministry of Labor. "In this way we will box Hitler in." This was the same man who had tried to make common front with Hitler at the Harzburg Assembly of 1931, and who since then had watched the Nazi leader break through every barrier set against him, making every hope to "box him in" futile. Clearly, one of Alfred Hugenberg's special characteristics was his ability to avoid learning from experience.

Later, in the denazification trial which has been mentioned at several places in this book, Hugenberg declared that Hitler's appointment as chancellor had occurred "without any collaboration" on his part.[53] The facts do not support that statement. On January 26, when Hugenberg was so quick to accept Hitler as chancellor, Hindenburg was still completely opposed to the idea. The old President must therefore have been impressed when Papen told him that even the autocratic leader of the German National Party had declared his willingness to serve under Hitler. Hindenburg might well have told himself that Hugenberg would be a minister around whom a majority of the cabinet could gather and who — along with the loyal "comrade" Franz von Papen, who would again become national commissioner for Prussia — would thwart any attempt by Hitler to misuse his chancellor's powers.

They were still lacking a man for what at the moment was the most important position in the new cabinet: the Ministry of Defense. Schleicher thought that he could always retire from his post of chancellor to his former role as minister.[54] But this was neither Papen's nor Hindenburg's intent. Papen wished to take full revenge on this former patron who had betrayed him in a crisis. And he shuddered at the thought of having Schleicher remain minister of defense, thus in possession of truly significant power. Hindenburg, for his part, did not want Schleicher in the cabinet, where he would only remind the President how he had once leaned upon Schleicher's counsel and then had let him fall.

Yet was there any other German general ready to take Schleicher's place? It seems that indeed there was. They hit upon the former chief of the East Prussian area command, Werner von Blomberg, now Germany's military representative at the disarmament conference in Geneva. In Königsberg, Blomberg had come under the influence of both Ludwig Müller, his area chaplain and later the National Socialist *Reichsbischof*, and Colonel Walter von Reichenau, a fervent Nazi and his chief of staff. President von Hindenburg had already established relations with Blomberg which were to have astonishing consequences once Schleicher's cabinet had been officially dismissed.

Officials in the Ministry of Defense had become deeply concerned at the direction of developments. General von Hammerstein, who formerly had expressed such vigorous opposition to Hitler's being permitted to come to power, now sought the opportunity for a private conversation with the President. He found his chance in the personal report which General von der Bussche-Ippenburg gave the President every month on matters of military personnel. According to Bussche's definite statement, Hammerstein accompanied him, quite spontaneously, when he went to make his report to Hindenburg on January 27, the day before Schleicher resigned.[55]

At this point we are confronted by an issue on which opinion is still divided today. Just what were the generals so concerned about: a Hitler government or one under Papen and Hugenberg? Even the reports which the two generals made of their interview with Hindenburg differ in this respect. General von Hammerstein maintains that he warned the President against a Papen-Hugenberg regime, because such a government could well embroil the Reichswehr in a struggle against both the National Socialists and the entire Left.[56] Bussche, on the other hand, says that Hammerstein spoke darkly of Hitler and his insatiable demands, expressing earnest misgivings about National Socialist infiltration in the Reichswehr. Bussche's version is corroborated by the statement with which, both reports agree, Hindenburg terminated the conversation. Having rebuked them sternly for this attempt to introduce the Army into politics, the President then concluded with the assuring remark: "Gentlemen, surely you do not think that I would appoint this Austrian corporal Chancellor of Germany." If the generals' reports, which agree on this point, are to be credited, Hammerstein's opposition can only have been directed against Hitler.

Yet it is probably going too far to say that Hammerstein must have spoken against *either* Papen and Hugenberg *or* Hitler. It needs to be noted that Hammerstein was a very close friend of Schleicher and that Schleicher, in all probability, told him that he was sure Papen was planning a joint government with Hitler. Schleicher had also learned that Oskar von Hindenburg had been conferring with the Nazi leader. And although it was not yet by any means certain that Hindenburg was prepared to appoint Hitler chancellor, still it was clear that Papen could return to power only with Hitler's help and that any idea of a Papen-Hugenberg government without Hitler was sheer fantasy. Hammerstein must have known all this just as well as did his good friend Schleicher. Therefore, if his later testimony of January 28, 1935, gives another impression, it must not be forgotten that he gave that testimony after Hitler had come to power, indeed shortly after Hitler had had Schleicher murdered. At such a time even a German general had good reason not to proclaim that he had once opposed the Führer.

In any event, Hindenburg's closing comment shows that on January 27, 1933, his refusal to consider Hitler for chancellor was still vigorous and firm. But, as we have seen, Papen had already strayed from the terms Hindenburg had prescribed for his secret negotiations; for he had persuaded Hugenberg and Seldte to serve as ministers under the Austrian.

On Saturday, January 28, the day after Hammerstein's abortive counterthrust, Schleicher tendered his resignation, along with that of his entire cabinet. This denouement seems to have been played in quite a hurried fashion. Minister Freiherr von Braun, for instance, complained to the British ambassador, whom he met that same evening at the Press Ball, that Schleicher's resignation had taken him completely by surprise; that, in fact, he had learned of it just as he was about to go to his office that morning. Sir Horace Rumbold reports that von Braun was unable to conceal his disappointment at the turn events had taken, and that he expressed the greatest admiration for the way the Chancellor had managed the government's affairs: "He said, among other things, that Schleicher had conducted his Cabinet meetings with exemplary efficiency and had shown a remarkable grasp of every detail of the administration." [57]

Thus General Kurt von Schleicher's career as chancellor ended after just fifty-four days. With this, his political effectiveness was also over. In contemplating his career, one is seized by two quite different feelings. On the one hand, Schleicher only reaped what he had sowed when he offered his assistance in overthrowing Brüning and encouraged Hindenburg in his unrealistic thoughts of a presidential cabinet that would hover high above all the separate political parties. The man who in the spring of 1932 had spoken so deprecatingly of "good old Heinrich's" indecision was now accused by all his opponents of an indecision on which the purely negative results of all his efforts could be blamed.

The general who had always slipped so deftly through secret, hidden doors; whose clever maneuvers had let Seeckt balk the threatened dissolution of the Reichstag; whom Gröner had celebrated as his "cardinal for political affairs" — this general had now

been checkmated by other secret intriguers, and he had no grounds
for complaint when he was reproached for having fallen in the trap
that he had dug for others. Did not his conscience assail him now,
when he thought of the fall of Gröner, his so generous friend? And
did he not realize at last that the political problems which confronted German ministers at that time were infinitely more difficult
than the Prussian general had imagined when he had criticized the
civilian politicians with easy scorn from the safe refuge of the Bendlerstrasse? And had he finally come to the realization that a general
who had grown up in the narrow world of the Prussian military caste
was doomed to remain a political dilettante no matter how brilliantly
he could impress a simple member of the Reichstag with his biting
cynicism and his nonpartisan airs?

Yet one must admit that toward the end, at any rate, Schleicher
had grasped at least the basic elements of an idea which might have
led him, and with him Germany, out of their desperate plight. For
he wished to bring together representatives of various parties in order to find common solutions to practical problems. This would have
required, of course, that each side make some concessions, but at
least the structure of the state would have been preserved. Certainly
Schleicher's approach was considerably more statesmanlike than
Papen's method of affronting one party after another and then finally, after he had failed, delivering the apparatus of the German state
to the sworn enemy of them all simply in order that he might return
to personal power and bask again in the President's favor. It is quite
true that Schleicher's plan was tenuous and disjoint, partly because
he lacked the basic prerequisite for any such success: the confidence
and trust that only those men enjoy who have already shown that
they put their cause above their person. Schleicher, like Schiller's
Wallenstein, found himself faced by "a wall of his own works" which,
when he wished to return to the sane ways of realistic, constructive
policies, "hemmed him in."

Along with the news of Schleicher's resignation the German
people were also told that President Hindenburg had requested von
Papen "to seek a clarification of the political situation." This was
popularly understood to mean that, in the vocabulary of the former
Hapsburg monarchy, Papen had been appointed *homo regius*, the
king's man. Papen immediately utilized his new, publicly acknowledged station to importune the President anew to appoint Hitler
chancellor. In this effort he was supported by Oskar von Hindenburg and Otto Meissner. The three of them assured the Old Gentleman that nothing was to be feared from such a course since the
Austrian would be surrounded by such a powerful majority of Ger-

man Nationalist ministers under Hugenberg that no risk would be involved. Hitler, on the other hand, would have only two fellow National Socialists in the cabinet: Göring and Frick.

But Hitler had observed that his prospects were improving and had raised his demands accordingly. Whereas formerly he had asked only that Göring be given a new ministry for civil aviation, he now demanded that his lieutenant also be named national commissioner for Prussia. Papen, however, who wished to keep this post for himself, had finally talked Hitler out of this idea, and the two had hit upon a compromise according to which Göring would be made the Prussian minister of interior. With this appointment Hitler had attained his essential goal. For the only thing he wanted was control of the Prussian police, and this control was certain if Göring became minister of interior. Papen, of course, persuaded himself that, as national commissioner, he would keep final Prussian decisions securely in his hands. But this was just one more of his illusions, even though the argument did serve to make this distribution of cabinet posts more acceptable to Hindenburg. In point of fact, neither Papen's position nor his personality enabled him to offer any opposition to the National Socialists' absolute control of the Prussian police and civil administration.

In any event, these three loyal sons of Germany finally succeeded in persuading Hindenburg to do, on January 29, what he had told General von Hammerstein on January 27 was inconceivable: he found that he was ready to appoint the Austrian corporal Chancellor of Germany.

The list of ministers that Papen presented to the President that same Sunday, January 29, 1933, could have assured only a man as removed from political reality as Field Marshal von Hindenburg. Today there is no longer any need to discuss the political force of von Papen, who was to become vice-chancellor and national commissioner for Prussia. And Hitler's promise to consult the President only in Papen's presence was merely a paper guarantee. Freiherr von Neurath, who was supposed to keep the Foreign Ministry, was a useful bit of window dressing with which to persuade other governments that German foreign policy would remain peaceful under Hitler; but neither his person nor his past suggested that his political judgment would prove useful. None of the other ministers that were to be retained, like Schwerin-Krosigk, Eltz von Rübenach, and Gürtner, could constitute the slightest obstacle to Hitler. The fact that Seldte, of the *Stahlhelm*, was going to assume direction of the Labor Ministry was especially designed to please Hindenburg; in truth, however, Seldte was not cut out to play a political role in a government like this. Thus Hugenberg was the only one whom the German Nationalists could expect to stand up against Hitler and fight.

On the other side stood Hitler as Chancellor, Frick as national minister of interior, and Göring as his Prussian counterpart. Thus in each case the offices with instruments of real power were in National Socialist hands. Frick had already demonstrated in Thuringia how a National Socialist could use his authority as minister to terrorize his colleagues. It sounds therefore almost comic when Meissner praises him in his memoirs for having gained the necessary practical experience as a former Thuringian minister of interior.[58] General von Blomberg, who was to become minister of defense, could certainly not be regarded as a counterbalance to the National Socialists. He had been summoned from Geneva but had not yet arrived in Berlin.

No member of either the Center Party or the Bavarian People's Party appeared on the list of ministers, although both parties had shown a certain inclination to participate in the government. But that sort of arrangement would have served the interests of neither Hitler nor von Papen. For Hitler had no desire to strengthen the opposition in his cabinet by adding men wise enough to see the political significance of his actions and perhaps inclined to support the governments of the lands, with which they had such close relations, against a centralizing Reich. And Papen, who in all likelihood had his personal reasons for declining such company, had convinced himself that the non-Nazi cabinet majority would be more homogeneous if it consisted solely of his political friends.

Hindenburg expressed his approval of the proposed cabinet and asked Hitler and his future colleagues to come to his office the following morning at eleven to receive their commissions. Thus the ceremony was to take place on Monday, January 30, 1933.

But before these formalities could be carried out, other disturbing events occurred.

Schleicher's fall from power was a severe disappointment to officials on the Bendlerstrasse, whose grandest dreams of political success must have been fulfilled when a Prussian general and national minister of defense had, at the same time, become Chancellor of Germany. It was only natural that the question should immediately arise whether this ministry, the most powerful single authority in the German government, would accept so major a defeat in good grace. After all, Schleicher would still be a caretaking chancellor and minister of defense until his successor had been formally appointed. And in fact, during the days that followed Schleicher's resignation, Berlin — indeed, all Germany — was full of rumors about a counterthrust that the Bendlerstrasse was organizing.

As always happens in such uncertain times, everybody who heard and spread these rumors added something to them from his own imagination until they began to assume ever more frightening proportions. In this respect a certain Herr von Alvensleben, a major figure in the Herrenklub who was closely linked to the National Socialists, seems to have played the role which the Norse saga ascribes to Ratatøskr, the squirrel that hops about ceaselessly on Yggdrasil, the world-tree, supplying everybody from the eagle at the top to the dragon underneath with the latest news. In Berlin the rumors penetrated to the ministers-designate, who were impatiently waiting to be sworn in, and to the President's entourage — as the Ratatøskrs had especially hoped. According to these reports, the Potsdam garrison was either mobilized or, worse yet, already on the march toward the Wilhelmstrasse, where it intended to seize the President, his advisers, and the future ministers.

Now just how much of all this talk was really true? The question still remains unanswered today. General Kurt von Hammerstein quite correctly remarked that Schleicher could not possibly have carried out a putsch without his cooperation; and in his statement of January 28, 1935, which we have already noted above, he insisted that there had been no plans for any putsch, calling the rumors to that effect "insane and false." Karl Dietrich Bracher, who has appended Hammerstein's exact statement to his book *Die Auflösung der Weimarer Republik*, argues: "Today there cannot be any doubt but that the rumors of a threatened putsch by Schleicher or Hammerstein had no basis in fact." [59] On the other hand an absolutely reliable witness has told me that on the morning of Sunday, January 29, his good friend Erwin Planck, Schleicher's state secretary, called him by telephone to say that the Potsdam garrison was ready to march "to protect the Old Gentleman from his advisers" in the event that his son Oskar or Papen should succeed in persuading him to appoint Hitler chancellor." Since there is not the slightest reason why Planck should have wished to deceive his friend on this matter, one is obliged to conclude that Planck did make this call and that he did believe the contents of his message.

Does this mean that one should regard General von Hammerstein's statement as false? As was pointed out above, it was made in the period of Hitler's rule, and that was hardly a time conducive to a candid exposition of the truth. Even so, it is difficult to ignore the general's words. For if one also considers how fantastic and foolhardy such a coup d'état by the Army would have been — precisely because it would necessarily have been directed against the person of Field Marshal von Hindenburg — one cannot help concluding that Hammerstein was telling the truth. Of course, this conclusion forces one to assume that State Secretary Planck based his call not upon attested, official knowledge, but rather on some rumors he had heard. That sort of thing can easily happen in days of extreme tension and excitement.

If we refuse to believe that there were plans for any putsch, then the whole question of its political goals dissolves into thin air. Kunrath von Hammerstein, the general's son, composed a memorandum, "Schleicher, Hammerstein und die Machtergreifung Hitlers," for Wheeler-Bennett, in which he argues that the generals had not been opposed to Hitler, but rather to the threat of a Papen-Hugenberg regime.[60] The father, Kurt von Hammerstein, made the same point in his statement of January 28, 1935. And I have already explained why reports which completely contradict Hammerstein's earlier remarks can safely be ignored.

We can therefore file the supposed military putsch among the legends of the past. But there are times when legends are just as effective as firm, attested fact. The rumors of this threatened Army coup achieved an effect which naturally accrued to the advantage of the men against whom the coup was said to be directed. For if the devil Schleicher was planning a revolt against Hindenburg, then Papen took on the appearance of the archangel Gabriel, with his flaming sword drawn in the President's defense.

"If a new government is not formed by eleven o'clock, the Reichswehr will march! We are threatened by a military dictatorship under Schleicher and Hammerstein!" These are the words with which Franz von Papen greeted the *Stahlhelm* leaders, Duesterberg and Seldte, who, with Hugenberg, had been summoned to his house early in the morning of Monday, January 30.[61] Duesterberg reports that as early as seven that morning he had been told by telephone to report immediately to Papen. "When I asked Papen, who kept running about the room, where he had picked up what I could only regard as this incredible rumor of an Army threat, he shouted: 'From Hindenburg's son!'" Thereupon Duesterberg hastened to Oskar von Hindenburg, at whose door a Reichswehr sergeant stood. Duesterberg goes on to report: "I found even Hindenburg's phlegmatic son in an extremely excited state. [In response to my same question he said:] 'I cannot tell you any more details. I have to go to the Anhalt Station now to meet Blomberg. But I intend to make the *traitor Schleicher* pay for this.'"

The man who had been German Chancellor just two days before

was now considered a traitor. And he was the reason for Oskar von Hindenburg's hurried trip to the Anhalt Station. General von Blomberg's return to Berlin had been kept secret by the Papen forces, but Schleicher had found out about it anyway. Schleicher therefore wanted to influence Blomberg before he reported to the President; and so he had sent one of his adjutants to meet Blomberg at the Anhalt Station with an order to report to Schleicher first. But the President's son arrived at the station in time to give Blomberg his father's personal command to proceed directly to the presidential palace and to avoid the Bendlerstrasse on his way.

At this point Blomberg was confronted by the choice between Hindenburg and Schleicher. Since Hindenburg alone could offer him a ministry, he obeyed his President's command. Schleicher's adjutant had to return to the Bendlerstrasse with empty hands, and his report must have convinced Schleicher not only that he had lost another battle, but also that he would never taste victory again. Blomberg, on the other hand, was immediately handed his commission as minister of defense, and thus the first member of the new government received his formal appointment even before the Chancellor had been given his. Of course this was quite unconstitutional. (See Article 53.) But who was still worrying about that?

Now Blomberg hastened to von Papen, who congratulated him on his decision to ignore Schleicher and — according to Duesterberg's report — repeated the earlier charge that "Schleicher and Hammerstein had hoped to establish a military dictatorship today." But the new minister had scarcely finished introducing himself to his future cabinet colleagues when he discovered that their intended ship of state had one more sharp cliff to round before it could sail safely into port.

Again I prefer to let Duesterberg speak, remarking only — by way of introduction — that all the ministers-designate were now assembled in the office of State Secretary Meissner.

Papen greeted . . . Hitler as the new chancellor. Hitler thanked him and stated, to the evident astonishment of everyone there, particularly Hugenberg, that now the German people would have to ratify the new cabinet's composition through a general *election*. It was clear that Hitler recognized the distinct advantages he and his party would derive from another election. Hugenberg, on the other hand, argued firmly to the contrary, pointing out that the November election results had shown relative party strengths and that their new government was the obligatory democratic consequence of those results. Therefore, he said, new elections were not needed at this time.

Of course the democratic arguments proposed by either side

were mere window dressing. Hitler knew this just as well as Hugenberg, for both men were thinking only of their parties. After all his
former experience with Hitler, Hugenberg could well imagine what
another campaign would be like and what the election results would
be if, to his strong appeal to the masses, Hitler were able to add the
splendor of his chancellor's office and the voters' realization that
from now on Hitler's smile or frown would determine a person's fortune. Would not many rush to climb aboard his train? What could
the poor old German Nationalists offer in competition? The balance
of forces in the Reichstag, now slightly in their favor, was bound
to change radically to their disadvantage if new elections were
held. Then what would become of their plan to "box Hitler in"
of which Hugenberg had been speaking so confidently just a few
days before?

Even Franz von Papen should have been able to foresee this
much. To be sure, a farsighted statesman would also have been able
to predict that such new elections could only lead to the President's
total political defeat. But Hindenburg's *homo regius* was not blessed
with such vision. Let us return to Duesterberg's report.

An increasingly violent debate . . . ensued. Hugenberg stuck firmly
to his no. He stood at the pinnacle of his career, and now his dreams of
this new cabinet were being ruined. Realizing what was at stake, Hitler,
who had been visibly confounded by Hugenberg's opposition, stepped
up to him and said something to this effect: "*Herr Geheimrat*, I give you
my solemn word of honor that, no matter how the elections may come out,
I shall never separate myself from any of those here present." But Hugenberg still stuck by his no . . . Papen, however, extremely desirous of
the goal he thought so near, exclaimed: "But *Herr Geheimrat!* Do you
wish to endanger the alliance that took so much work to form? Certainly
you cannot question a German gentleman's solemn word of honor."

But this was a "German gentleman" whose perjury was already
a matter of legal record and who, as Papen knew best of all, had
pledged his "limitless fidelity" to the sentenced criminals in the
Potempa case simply because they were fellow Nazis. Despite the
worthy von Papen's sentimental, patriotic appeal, Hugenberg did
not abandon his objections.

Even as Greek tragedies had their satyr-dramas, this act of the
German tragedy also ended in a comic vein.

"Suddenly," to quote Duesterberg again, "Meissner rushed into
the room with his watch in hand. 'Gentlemen, you were scheduled
to take your oaths of office with the President at eleven o'clock. It
is now eleven fifteen. You certainly cannot keep the President wait-

ing any longer.' At this . . . Hugenberg yielded, and Hitler had won."

To keep the President waiting was evidently worse than delivering the German people into the hands of a public menace. Hugenberg had been able to withstand the entreaties of Hitler, Papen, Göring, and von Neurath. But the Field Marshal President's schedule of appointments? No, he could not bring himself to disrupt Hindenburg's day. For years Hugenberg's stubbornness had embarrassed every German government, had ruined every hopeful turn for the better, and had decimated his own party's ranks. Yet at the one moment when his obstinacy might conceivably have saved the German people from their supreme tragedy, Hugenberg proved as soft as wax. The *Herr Geheimrat* could not keep the Field Marshal President waiting.

Everything was now in proper order, and the aged Hindenburg could install this new government of "national unity" — the government which would divide Germans as they had never been divided before into the suppressors and the suppressed.

On the evening of this Monday, January 30, 1933, as the news of Hitler's appointment spread throughout the city, an endless line of his triumphant supporters, waving torches and singing the Horst Wessel song, paraded through the Wilhelmstrasse. Field Marshal von Hindenburg, half mystified, half astonished, and utterly confused, gazed down at the crowds that waved at him politely, crowds which he had never really known. Only the military marches stirred an echo in his weary old brain.

Hitler, on the other hand, stood in the window of his Chancellery greeting his "brown battalions marching": the SA, the SS, the Hitler Youth, and the thousands of his other supporters who were ecstatically celebrating his victory. The Austrian gazed down at them with the beaming smile of a man who, having accomplished the impossible, had achieved the goal of his demonic ambition.

The attempt by the German people to rule themselves had failed. A time now came when Germany ceased to be a state based on law. This was the time when German judges allowed their courtrooms to be overrun by the mob who drove out the people whose noses they did not like; when the judges saw their independence and security abolished and their professional advancement become dependent on the way their decisions pleased the ruling party; when the judges let the leader of that party declare as law whatever served the interests of the *Volk* — as he determined those interests.

It was the time when Themis, goddess of Justice, had the blindfold ripped from her eyes in order that she might determine the precise ethnic origin and political opinion of every party in the disputes over which she presided; the time when a German minister of justice found it "lawful" that the Chancellor of Germany should have his political opponents slaughtered by the hundreds without the slightest semblance of a trial and should use this convenient opportunity to have some of his earlier adversaries murdered.

It was the time when Germany became the most frightful example of Augustine's admonition, "Without justice, what are states if not great bands of thieves?"; when Germans demonstrated the meaning of Bismarck's statement that they liked so well to quote, "We Germans fear God and nothing else in the whole world," by setting fire to the houses of God and by quivering before every Nazi clerk; when freedom of thought was replaced by "coordination," and personal liberty, by concentration camps to which thousands upon thousands were arbitrarily dragged and where they were exposed to all the torments which a laughing brutality could devise, while their fellow Germans — who, at the theater, were always so deeply moved by the Prisoners' Chorus in *Fidelio* — did not lose a night's sleep over the tortures and injustice which these real prisoners suffered daily.

It was the time when this nation, whose greatest poet had written a German *Iphigenie* memorializing *Gastrecht*, the honored rights of the harbored guest, now observed the customs of hospitality by expelling thousands of German Jews from their own fatherland, people whose fathers and fathers' fathers had lived and worked on German soil for generations but who were now called strangers, *Gastvolk*, by their German rulers because the brutish hate of an alien tyrant demanded this persecution; the time when Germans watched without concern as those who had not found foreign refuge soon enough were carted away into slavery to be murdered in gas chambers or in "experiments"; the time when little children were torn from their weeping mothers and sent to die in some unknown corner of the East.

It was the time when the word "German" became a symbol of everything humanity condemns as brutal, outrageous, and base.

All this started on Monday, January 30, 1933. And young Germans waved their torches in delight.

SUMMARY OF THE REICH GOVERNMENTS
1926—1931

1. *Luther*: Second cabinet, January 20, 1926, to May 17, 1926.
   Center: Marx, Brauns, Haslinde.
   People's Party: Stresemann, Curtius, Krohne.
   Democrats: Külz, Reinhold, Gessler.
   Bavarian People's Party: Stingl.

2. *Marx* (Center): Third cabinet, to January 29, 1927.
   Center: Marx, Brauns, Bell, Haslinde.
   People's Party: Stresemann, Curtius, Krohne.
   Democrats: Külz, Reinhold, Gessler.
   Bavarian People's Party: Stingl.

3. *Marx* (Center): Fourth cabinet, to June 29, 1928.
   Center: Marx, Köhler, Brauns.
   German Nationalists: Hergt, Keudell, Schiele, Koch.
   People's Party: Stresemann, Curtius.
   Bavarian People's Party: Schätzel.
   In addition: Gessler to January 29, 1928, then Gröner.

4. *Hermann Müller* (Social Democrat): Second cabinet, to March 30, 1930.
   Social Democrats: Müller, Severing, Wissell, Hilferding (to December 21, 1929), Robert Schmidt (from December 23, 1929).
   Democrats: Dietrich, Koch-Weser (to April 13, 1929).
   People's Party: Stresemann (to October 3, 1929), Curtius, Moldenhauer (from November 8, 1929).
   Center: Guérard, and, from April 13, 1929, Wirth and Stegerwald.
   Bavarian People's Party: Schätzel.
   In addition: Gröner.

5. *Brüning* (Center): First cabinet, to May 30, 1932.
   Center: Brüning, Stegerwald, and, to October 1931, Wirth and Guérard.
   People's Party: Curtius (to October 1931), Moldenhauer (to June 1930).
   Democrats: Dietrich.
   Economic Party: Bredt (to December 1930).
   Bavarian People's Party: Schätzel.
   Conservatives: Schiele, Treviranus.
   In addition: Gröner, Warmbold (from October 1931).

Bibliographical Note

The best survey of the literature for this period is given in the catalogue of the Wiener Library in London, 4, Devonshire Street: "From Weimar to Hitler, Germany 1918–1933." Later editions are published in the literature surveys in the quarterly bulletin of the library. In the preparation of this second volume the Wiener Library was again of great use to me, and I wish to express my gratitude to Dr. Alfred Wiener and his colleagues, especially Mrs. Wolff and Dr. Reichmann, for their unfailing assistance. Of general accounts of the period I cite the following:

Ferdinand Friedensburg, *Die Weimarer Republik* (Berlin, 1946).

Arthur Rosenberg, *Geschichte der Deutschen Republik* (Karlsbad, 1935). English translation: *A History of the German Republic* (London, 1936).

Friedrich Stampfer, *Die vierzehn Jahre der ersten deutschen Republik* (Karlsbad, 1936).

Paul Merker, *Deutschland — Sein oder Nicht Sein?* (Mexico, 1944).

S. William Halperin, *Germany Tried Democracy* (New York, 1946).

Godfrey Scheele, *The Weimar Republic, Overture to the Third Reich* (London, 1946).

Carl Misch, *Deutsche Geschichte im Zeitalter der Massen von der Französischen Revolution bis zur Gegenwart* (Stuttgart, 1952), chapters vi through viii.

Abundant material is also offered in Cuno Horkenbach, ed., *Das Deutsche Reich von 1918 bis Heute* (Berlin, 1930), with supplements for 1931 and 1932.

NOTES

Chapter I. Locarno

1. Georges Suarez, *Briand, L'Artisan de la Paix, 1923–1932* (Paris, 1952), p. 61. (Vol. 6 of his *Briand, Sa Vie — Son Oeuvre*, 6 vols., Paris, 1938–1952); Francis P. Walters, *History of the League of Nations* (2 vols., London, 1952), I, 275.

2. Sir Charles Petrie, *The Life and Letters of the Right Hon. Sir Austen Chamberlain* (2 vols., London, 1939–1940), II, 227.

3. Walters, *League of Nations*, I, 288.

4. Petrie, *Austen Chamberlain*, II, 259.

5. Viscount Edgar V. d'Abernon, *An Ambassador of Peace* (3 vols., Garden City, N. Y., and London, 1929–1930), III, 115.

6. Great Britain, Public Record Office. *Der schriftliche Nachlass von Gustav Stresemann* (F.O. 520), 7135H. Hereafter cited as Stresemann Papers. (Also available at the United States National Archives, under Germany, Auswärtiges Amt, Politisches Archiv.) See Hans W. Gatzke, "The Stresemann Papers," *The Journal of Modern History*, March 1954, p. 49.

7. Stresemann Papers, 7415H.

8. Gustav Stresemann, *Vermächtnis. Der Nachlass*, edited by Henry Bernhard, Wolfgang Goetz, and Paul Wiegler (3 vols., Berlin, 1932), II, 85 (March 16, 1925). English translation: *Diaries, Letters and Papers* (3 vols., New York, 1935–1940).

9. Petrie, *Austen Chamberlain*, II, 258.

10. *Survey of International Affairs, 1925*, edited by Arnold J. Toynbee (2 vols., Royal Institute on International Affairs, London), II, 27.

11. Petrie, *Austen Chamberlain*, II, 271.

12. *Ibid.*, p. 275.

13. Suarez, *Briand, L'Artisan de la Paix*, p. 162 (February 25, 1926).

14. *Ibid.*, p. 91.

15. Stresemann, *Vermächtnis*, II, 115.

16. Walters, *League of Nations*, I, 286.

17. Stresemann, *Vermächtnis*, II, 109.

18. Stresemann Papers, 7129H; cf. Stresemann, *Vermächtnis*, II, 110.

19. Cf. Friedrich von Rabenau, ed., *Seeckt. Aus seinem Leben, 1918–1936* (Leipzig, 1940), p. 417 (June 26, 1925). Josef Paul-Boncour, *Entre deux guerres. Souvenirs sur la IIIe Republique* (3 vols., Paris, 1945–1946), II, 102.

20. Stresemann, *Vermächtnis*, II, 134, 185.

21. Ruth Fischer, *Stalin und der deutsche Kommunismus* (Frankfurt, 1948). Originally in English: *Stalin and German Communism. A Study in the Origins of the State Party* (Cambridge, Mass., 1948).

22. Jane Degras, ed., *Soviet Documents on Foreign Policy* (3 vols., London, 1951–1953), II, 39, 42, 53. Lionel Kochan, *Russia and the Weimar Republic* (Cambridge, 1954), p. 99.

23. Moritz J. Bonn, *Wandering Scholar* (New York, 1948, and London, 1949), p. 231.

24. Edgar Stern-Rubarth, *Graf Brockdorff-Rantzau, Wanderer zwischen zwei Welten* (Berlin, 1929), p. 145.

25. d'Abernon, *Ambassador of Peace*, III, 165.

26. Stresemann, *Vermächtnis*, II, 513, 516.

27. d'Abernon, *Ambassador of Peace*, III, 169.

28. Stresemann Papers, 7129H; cf. Stresemann, *Vermächtnis*, II, 516.

29. Stresemann, *Vermächtnis*, II, 517.

30. Stresemann Papers, 7129H.

31. d'Abernon, *Ambassador of Peace*, III, 169.

32. Stresemann, *Vermächtnis*, II, 109.

33. Stresemann Papers, 7129H; cf. Stresemann, *Vermächtnis*, II, 151.

34. Stresemann, *Vermächtnis*, II, 310.

35. Alfred Hugenberg, *Streiflichter aus Vergangenheit und Gegenwart* (Berlin, 1927). Borchmeyer, ed., *Hugenbergs Ringen in deutschen Schicksalsstunden* (Detmold, Germany, 1951). Cf. Stresemann, *Vermächtnis*, II, 395.

36. Friedrich Wilhelm Foerster, *Erlebte Weltgeschichte 1869–1953* (Nuremberg, 1953), p. 266.

37. Stresemann, *Vermächtnis*, II, 163, 176.

38. *Ibid.*, p. 153.

39. Rabenau, *Seeckt*, p. 418.

40. *Survey of International Affairs, 1925*, II, 42.

41. Petrie, *Austen Chamberlain*, II, 281.

42. Stresemann Papers, vol. 275 (September 2, 1925).

43. Stresemann, *Vermächtnis*, II, 178.

44. *Deutsche Allgemeine Zeitung* (Berlin), September 19, 1925, evening.

45. *Ibid.*, September 24, 1925, morning.

46. Stresemann, *Vermächtnis*, II, 180.

47. Petrie, *Austen Chamberlain*, II, 235.

48. *Survey of International Affairs, 1925*, II, 48. Suarez, *Briand, L'Artisan de la Paix*, p. 104.

49. Degras, *Soviet Documents*, II, 55f.

50. See Erich Eyck, "Neues Licht auf Stresemanns Politik," *Deutsche Rundschau*, February 1955, p. 111.

51. Stresemann, *Vermächtnis*, II, 516, supplemented by Stresemann Papers, 7129H.

52. Stresemann, *Vermächtnis*, II, 251.

53. Stresemann Papers, 7129H.

54. Stresemann's notes, printed in an appendix to Karl Dietrich Erdmann, "Das Problem der Ost- oder Westorientierung in der Locarno-Politik Stresemanns," in *Geschichte in Wissenschaft und Unterricht* (Stuttgart), March 1955.

55. Stresemann Papers, 7415H.

56. Stresemann, *Vermächtnis*, II, 553. With reference to this, see Robert Vansittart, *Lessons of My Life* (London, New York, 1943), p. 69; Rohan Butler, *The Roots of National Socialism* (London, 1941), p. 267; Leopold Schwarzschild, *World in Trance* (London, 1943), p. 168; Robert Dell, *The Geneva Racket, 1920–1939* (London, 1941), p. 60; Felix Hirsch, "Stresemann in Historical Perspective," *Review of Politics*, July 1953, p. 367; Carl Misch, *Deutsche Geschichte im Zeitalter der Massen von der Französischen Revolution bis zur Gegenwart* (Stuttgart, 1956), p. 351; Sir Austen Chamberlain, *Down the Years* (London, 1935), p. 188; and, especially detailed, Annelise

Thimme, "Gustav Stresemann: Legende und Wirklichkeit," *Historische Zeitschrift*, April 1956, pp. 287f., and particularly pp. 320 f.

57. Henry L. Bretton, *Stresemann and the Revision of Versailles* (Stanford, Calif., 1953), pp. 72, 175; Paul-Boncour, *Entre deux guerres*, II, 204.

58. Cf. Thimme, "Gustav Stresemann," p. 333, n. 1. I am grateful to Professor Ludwig Dehio for the reference to Srbik.

59. Stresemann Papers, 7414H.

60. Hirsch, "Stresemann in Historical Perspective," p. 374.

61. Suarez, *Briand, L'Artisan de la Paix*, p. 119; *Survey of International Affairs, 1925*, II, 60; Hans Luther, "Zur Erinnerung an Aristide Briand," *Schweizer Monatshefte* (Zurich), April 1952, p. 3; Paul-Boncour, *Entre deux guerres*, II, 184.

62. Stresemann, *Vermächtnis*, II, 239.

63. *Ibid.*, p. 191.

64. *Survey of International Affairs, 1925*, II, 51; Walters, *League of Nations*, I, 293.

65. Max von Stockhausen, *Sechs Jahre Reichskanzlei. Von Rapallo bis Locarno*, edited by Walter Görlitz (Bonn, 1954), pp. 182f.

66. Stresemann, *Vermächtnis*, II, 200.

67. Petrie, *Austen Chamberlain*, II, 287.

68. Suarez, *Briand, L'Artisan de la Paix*, p. 129.

69. Paul Schmidt, *Statist auf diplomatischer Bühne, 1923–1945* (Bonn, 1953), p. 92. English translation: *Hitler's Interpreter* (New York, London, 1951).

70. Paul Fechter, *An der Wende der Zeit* (Gütersloh, Germany, 1949), p. 94.

71. Stresemann Papers, 7342H (September 26, 1927).

72. Stresemann, *Diaries, Letters and Papers*, II, 192, 233.

73. *Ibid.*, II, 193.

74. *Ibid.*, II, 193.

75. Carl Severing, *Mein Lebensweg* (2 vols., Cologne, 1950), II, 106.

76. London *Times*, March 12, 1936.

77. Schwarzschild, *World in Trance*, p. 236.

78. Rabenau, *Seeckt*, p. 420 (October 4, 1925).

79. *Ibid.*, p. 423.

80. Stresemann, *Diaries, Letters and Papers*, II, 234.

81. Rabenau, *Seeckt*, pp. 401, 404, 421, 453.

82. London *Times*, November 4, 1933, italics added.

83. Schwarzschild, *World in Trance*, pp. 256–257.

84. Decree of the Reich President, January 28, 1926, Article III. Cf. Fritz Marschall von Bieberstein, *Verfassungsrechtliche Reichsgesetze und wichtige Verordnungen* (Mannheim, 1929), p. 737.

85. Rabenau, *Seeckt*, p. 422.

86. Hans W. Gatzke, *Stresemann and the Rearmament of Germany* (Baltimore, 1954), pp. 46f.

CHAPTER II. Admission to the League of Nations, the Treaty with Russia, and a Conversation at Thoiry

1. Severing, *Mein Lebensweg*, II, 78.

2. *Statistisches Jahrbuch für das Deutsche Reich 1926* (Berlin, published by Statistisches Reichsamt).

3. Severing, *Mein Lebensweg*, II, 80.

4. Stresemann, *Vermächtnis*, II, 321.

5. Hugenberg, *Streiflichter*, p. 83.

6. Stresemann, *Vermächtnis*, II, 437.

7. *Ibid.*, p. 484.

8. Axel Freiherr von Freytag-Loringhoven, ed., *Die Satzung des Völkerbundes* (Berlin, 1926), commentary to Articles 4 and 5.

9. Walters, *League of Nations*, I, 317.

10. *Survey of International Affairs, 1926*, pp. 34f.

11. d'Abernon, *Ambassador of Peace*, III, 228.

12. Schmidt, *Statist*, p. 99.

13. Wolf von Dewall, *Der Kampf um den Frieden* (Frankfurt, 1929), p. 158.

14. *Survey of International Affairs, 1926*, p. 46.

15. Walters, *League of Nations*, I, 321.

16. Suarez, *Briand, L'Artisan de la Paix*, p. 180.

17. Stresemann, *Vermächtnis*, II, 356.

18. Kochan, *Russia and the Weimar Republic*, p. 113.

19. Degras, *Soviet Documents*, II, 103.

20. d'Abernon, *Ambassador of Peace*, III, 246.

21. Kochan, *Russia and the Weimar Republic*, p. 115.

22. Degras, *Soviet Documents*, II, 106.

23. Otto Braun, *Von Weimar zu Hitler* (New York, 1940), p. 214. Friedrich Stampfer, *Die vierzehn Jahre der ersten deutschen Republik* (Karlsbad, 1936), p. 445.

24. *Schulthess' Europäischer Geschichtskalender, 1926*, edited by Ulrich Thürauf (Munich), p. 114.

25. *Ibid.*, p. 116.

26. Braun, *Von Weimar zu Hitler*, p. 218.

27. Marschall von Bieberstein, *Verfassungsrechtliche Reichgesetze*, p. 561.

28. Gerhard Anschütz, ed., *Die Verfassung des Deutschen Reichs vom 11. August, 1919* (2nd ed., Berlin, 1921). Commentary to Article 3, note 4.

29. Braun, *Von Weimar zu Hitler*, p. 190.

30. Paul Weymar, *Konrad Adenauer* (Munich, 1955), p. 135. English translation: *Adenauer: His Authorized Biography* (New York, 1957).

31. *Ibid.*, p. 130.

32. Braun, *Von Weimar zu Hitler*, p. 197.

33. Robert M. W. Kempner, "Blueprint of the Nazi Underground," *Research Studies of the State College of Washington*, June 1945, p. 133.

34. d'Abernon, *Ambassador of Peace*, III, 257.

35. Walters, *League of Nations*, I, 326.

36. Stresemann, *Vermächtnis*, III, 15.

37. Suarez, *Briand, L'Artisan de la Paix*, p. 218.

38. Stresemann Papers, 7414H.

39. Reichskreditgesellschaft, *Deutschlands wirtschaftliche Lage an der Jahreswende 1929–1930.* (Author's note: the Reichskreditgesellschaft circulated its printed releases concerning the economic situation among its clients, but these have not been collected in book form.)

40. Schäffer, notes of August 20 and November 4, 1928 (unpublished).

41. Stresemann, *Vermächtnis*, III, 18.

42. Stresemann Papers, 7332H.

43. Suarez, *Briand, L'Artisan de la Paix*, pp. 224f.

44. Stresemann, *Vermächtnis*, III, 28.

45. Erich Eyck, *Das persönliche Regiment Wilhelms II* (Erlenbach-Zurich, 1948), p. 250.

46. Eugen Fischer-Baling, "Der Untersuchungsausschuss für die Schuldfrage des ersten Weltkrieges," in Alfred Herrmann, ed., *Aus Geschichte und Politik. Festschrift zum 70. Geburtstag von Ludwig Bergsträsser* (Düsseldorf, 1954), p. 136.

47. Stresemann Papers, 7376H (June 5, 1928).

48. Von Hoesch to von Schubert, November 8, in Stresemann Papers, 7335H.

49. *Ibid.*, 7334H (Thoiry-Ausschuss, October 14).

50. *Ibid.*, 7330H (August 13, 1926).

CHAPTER III. Reichswehr Troubles; Marx's Dismissal and Return

1. Rabenau, *Seeckt*, p. 430; Stresemann Papers (Norderney, July 26, 1925).

2. Stockhausen, *Sechs Jahre Reichskanzlei*, p. 232.

3. Otto Ernst Schüddekopf, *Das Heer und die Republik* (Hanover-Frankfurt, 1955), p. 216.

4. Seeckt's description in Rabenau, *Seeckt*, p. 542.

5. Gessler's memoirs (unpublished), p. 16.

6. Letter from General Schellbach to Gessler, March 1944 (unpublished).

7. Stresemann, *Vermächtnis*, III, 84.

8. Rabenau, *Seeckt*, pp. 536f.

9. Reginald Phelps, "Aus den Seeckt-Dokumenten," *Deutsche Rundschau*, September 1952, p. 885.

10. Gessler's memoirs (unpublished).

11. Stresemann Papers, 7334H and 7335H (von Raumer to Stresemann, October 13; Stresemann to von Piersdorff, October 27; Prince Oscar to Stresemann, November 3).

12. *Ibid.*, 7334H. Similarly in Schüddekopf, *Heer und Republik*, p. 214, Document 93 (discussion of December 1, 1926).

13. Eyck, *Wilhelm II*, p. 183.

14. Kurt Häntzschel, "Das Recht der freien Meinungsäusserung" in Gerhard Anschütz and Richard Thoma, eds., *Handbuch des Deutschen Staatsrechts* (2 vols., Tübingen, 1930–1932), II, 669.

15. Stampfer, *Vierzehn Jahre*, p. 453.

16. Stresemann, *Vermächtnis*, III, 95.

17. *Ibid.*, p. 90.

18. Stockhausen, *Sechs Jahre Reichskanzlei*, p. 236 (December 6, 1926).

19. Fischer, *Stalin*, p. 643.

20. *Ibid.*, p. 644.

21. Schüddekopf, *Heer und Republik*, p. 217.

22. Stampfer, *Vierzehn Jahre*, p. 464.

23. Stresemann Papers, 7334H (October 29, 1926).

24. With reference to this, see Schüddekopf, *Heer und Republik*, p. 214, Document 93.

25. Stresemann, *Vermächtnis*, III, 91.

26. Stresemann Papers, 7336H.

27. *Vorwärts* (Berlin), December 17, 1926, morning.

28. Germany, Official Documents. *Entscheidungen des Reichsgerichts in Strafsachen* (Leipzig, 1880–), LXII, 65.

29. Cf. Helm Speidel, "Reichswehr und Rote Armee," *Vierteljahrshefte für Zeitgeschichte* (Stuttgart), 1(1953):9, as well as the introduction by Hans Rothfels, p. 11.

30. Severing, *Lebensweg*, II, 104.

31. Foerster, *Erlebte Weltgeschichte*, p. 406; Stockhausen, *Sechs Jahre Reichkanzlei*, p. 230.

32. Heinrich Pohl, "Die Zuständigkeiten des Reichspräsidenten" in *Handbuch des Deutschen Staatsrechts*, I, 488.

33. Stockhausen, *Sechs Jahre Reichskanzlei*, p. 238.

34. Stresemann, *Vermächtnis*, III, 92; Julius Curtius, *Sechs Jahre Minister der deutschen Republik* (Heidelberg, 1948), p. 47.

35. Curtius, *Sechs Jahre Minister*, p. 47.

36. Stresemann Papers, 7337H. *Vermächtnis*, III, 92.

37. Stresemann Papers, 7338H. *Vermächtnis*, III, 94.

38. Stresemann Papers, 7338H.

39. Stresemann, *Vermächtnis*, III, 103.

40. Erich Eyck, *Bismarck: Leben und Werk* (3 vols., Zurich, 1941–1944), I, 573. Abridged English translation, *Bismarck and the German Empire* (London, 1950).

41. Curtius, *Sechs Jahre Minister*, p. 51.

42. Stresemann Papers, 7337H (January 5, 1927).

43. *Ibid.*, 7340H (February 24, 1927).

CHAPTER IV. Social, Economic, and Financial Problems

1. Ludwig Preller, *Sozialpolitik in der Weimarer Republik* (Stuttgart, 1949), p. 239.

2. Walter Eucken, *Unser Zeitalter der Misserfolge. Fünf Vorträge zur Wirtschaftspolitik* (Tübingen, 1951), p. 8. English translation, *The Unsuccessful Age: or, the Pains of Economic Progress* (Edinburgh, 1951).

3. Hans von Raumer, "Unternehmer und Gewerkschaften in der Weimarer Zeit," *Deutsche Rundschau*, May 1954.

4. Concerning Legien see Severing, *Lebensweg*, I, 317.

5. Preller, *Sozialpolitik*, p. 53.

6. *Ibid.*, p. 244.

7. *Ibid.*, p. 309.

8. *Ibid.*, p. 210. Lujo Brentano, *Mein Leben im Kampf um die soziale Entwicklung Deutschlands* (Jena, 1931), p. 396.

9. Preller, *Sozialpolitik*, p. 275.

10. *Ibid.*, p. 55.

11. *Ibid.*, p. 231.

12. Heinrich Hoeniger, *Arbeitsrecht. Vorschriften über das Arbeitsverhältnis nebst den Bestimmungen über das Bergarbeitsrecht* (rev. ed., Mannheim, 1933), p. 204.

13. *Ibid.*, p. 219.

14. Bernhard Pfister, review in *Zeitschrift für die gesamte Staatswissenschaft* (Tübingen), 107(1951):564.

15. Wilhelm Röpke, *Die Gesellschaftskrisis der Gegenwart* (Erlenbach-Zurich, 1942), p. 351. English translation: *The Social Crisis of Our Time* (London, 1950).

16. Preller, *Sozialpolitik*, p. 329.

17. Allied Powers, Reparation Commission. *Bericht des Generalagenten für Reparationszahlungen* (Berlin, May 21, 1930), I: *Hauptbericht*, p. 148. English edition, *Report of the Agent General for Reparation Payments* (Berlin, May 21, 1930).

18. Moritz J. Bonn, *Der neue Plan als Grundlage der deutschen Wirtschaftspolitik* (Munich and Leipzig, 1930), pp. 179, 183.

19. Preller, *Sozialpolitik*, p. 386.

20. Curt Nawratzki, *Bevölkerungsaufbau, Wohnungspolitik und Wirtschaft* (Berlin, 1931).

21. Waldemar Zimmermann, "Die Grenzen der Wohnungszwangswirtschaft," *Schriften des Vereins für Sozialpolitik* (Munich and Leipzig), September 1930, pp. 235, 237.

22. Gustav Radbruch, *Der innere Weg: Aufriss meines Lebens* (Stuttgart, 1951), p. 178.

23. Eulenburg, "Die sozialen Wirkungen der Währungsverhältnisse," *Schriften des Vereins für Sozialpolitik*, September 1924, p. 87.

24. Arthur Nussbaum, ed., *Bank- und Börsenrecht* (Berlin and Leipzig, 1927), p. 154.

25. Ludwig Landmann, in discussion in *Schriften des Vereins für Sozialpolitik*, September 1928, p. 229.

26. *Ibid.*, p. 269. Compare Bonn, *Wandering Scholar*, p. 304.

27. Otto Ziebill, *Geschichte des deutschen Städtetags. Fünfzig Jahre deutsche Kommunalpolitik* (Stuttgart and Cologne, 1955), p. 257.

28. Bonn, *Neuer Plan*, p. 130.

29. Eucken, *Zeitalter der Misserfolge*, p. 8.

30. Moritz J. Bonn, concluding remarks in *Schriften des Vereins für Sozialpolitik*, September 1928, p. 269; Bonn, *Neuer Plan*, p. 197.

31. Kurt Ritter, "Rationalisierung in der Landwirtschaft" in Ludwig Elster and Adolf Weber, eds., *Handwörterbuch der Staatswissenschaften*, supplementary volume (4th rev. ed., Jena, 1929), p. 787.

32. Max Sering, "Künftige deutsche Handelspolitik," *Schriften des Vereins für Sozialpolitik*, September 1924, pp. 140, 241.

33. Oscar Meyer, "Die deutsche Aussenhandelspolitik" in Hartmann von Richthofen, ed., *Jahrbuch für auswärtige Politik, 1929* (Berlin), p. 108.

34. Karl Helfferich, *Deutschlands Volkswohlstand, 1888–1913* (Berlin, 1915), p. 115.

35. Johannes Popitz, "Finanzausgleich" in Ludwig Elster, Adolf Weber, and Friedrich Wieser, eds., *Handwörterbuch der Staatswissenschaften* (8 vols., 4th rev. ed., Jena, 1926), III, 1017.

36. Lutz von Schwerin-Krosigk, *Es geschah in Deutschland; Menschenbilder unseres Jahrhunderts* (Tübingen, 1951), p. 85.

CHAPTER V. Marx's Rightist Cabinet

1. Stresemann Papers, 7340H (February 25, 1927).

2. Braun, *Von Weimar zu Hitler*, p. 224.

3. Stresemann Papers, 7374H (February 12, 1928).

4. Stresemann, *Vermächtnis*, III, 137.

5. *Ibid.*, p. 134.

6. *Ibid.*, p. 137.

7. Stresemann Papers, 7347H (January 18, 1927).

8. Dewall, *Kampf um den Frieden*, p. 185.

9. Stresemann, *Vermächtnis*, III, 197.

10. Stresemann Papers, 7369H (September 22, 1927).

11. *Survey of International Affairs, 1927*, pp. 256f, 546f.

12. Stresemann Papers, 7344H.

13. Stresemann, *Vermächtnis*, III, 152.

14. *Ibid.*, p. 195 (September 21, 1927).

15. Stockhausen, *Sechs Jahre Reichskanzlei*, p. 248 (June 20 and 21, 1927).

16. Stresemann, *Vermächtnis*, III, 190.

17. Stresemann Papers, 7372H (Paris, December 8, 1927).

18. *Ibid.*, 7374H (February 2, 1928; Gerlach's answer, February 16).

19. For a different opinion, see Hans Gatzke, *Stresemann and the Rearmament of Germany* (Baltimore, 1954), p. 99.

20. Stresemann Papers, 7340H (Pünder to Stresemann, February 24, 1927).

21. Stockhausen, *Sechs Jahre Reichskanzlei*, pp. 243, 245.

22. Hoeniger, *Arbeitsrecht*, p. 341.

23. *Schulthess' Europäischer Geschichtskalender, 1927*, p. 85.

24. Stampfer, *Vierzehn Jahre*, p. 461; Braun, *Von Weimar zu Hitler*, p. 233.

25. Rüdiger R. Beer, *Heinrich Brüning* (Berlin, 1931), p. 48.

26. Stampfer, *Vierzehn Jahre*, p. 461.

27. Stresemann Papers, 7371H (Kastl to Stresemann, November 1, 1927).

28. *Schulthess' Europäischer Geschichtskalender, 1927*, p. 489.

29. Stresemann, *Vermächtnis*, III, 257.

30. Stresemann Papers, 7344H.

31. *Bericht des Generalagenten für Reparationszahlungen*, May 21, 1930, I: *Hauptbericht*, Appendix I.

32. *Ibid.*, Appendix I.

33. Anton Erkelenz, ed., *Zehn Jahre Deutscher Republik* (Berlin, 1928), p. 445.

34. Adolf Weber, "Grundlagen und Grenzen der Sozialpolitik," *Schriften des Vereins für Sozialpolitik*, September 1930, p. 39.

35. Karl Schwend, *Bayern zwischen Monarchie und Diktatur. Beiträge zur bayerischen Frage in der Zeit von 1918 bis 1933* (Munich, 1954), pp. 315, 336.

36. Erich Koch-Weser, *Einheitsstaat und Selbstverwaltung* (Berlin, 1928).

37. Otto Braun, *Deutscher Einheitsstaat oder Föderativsystem* (Berlin, 1927).

38. Schwend, *Bayern zwischen Monarchie und Diktatur*, p. 256.

39. *Ibid.*, p. 292.

40. Germany, Official Documents. *Entscheidungen des Reichsgerichts in Zivilsachen* (Leipzig, 1880 —), vol. CXXVII, appendix 25.

41. Ottmar Bühler, "Die Zuständigkeitsverteilung auf dem Gebiete des Finanzwesens" in *Handbuch des Deutschen Staatsrechts*, I, 337.

42. Braun, *Von Weimar zu Hitler*, p. 261.

43. Stresemann Papers, 7383H (January 26, 1929).

44. Bühler, "Die Zuständigkeitsverteilung auf dem Gebiete des Finanzwesens," pp. 329, 374; Braun, *Von Weimar zu Hitler*, p. 260.

45. *Reichsgericht in Zivilsachen*, vol. CXXII, appendix 17. Bühler, "Die Zuständigkeitsverteilung auf dem Gebiete des Finanzwesens," p. 324.

46. Henry Bernhard, "Seeckt und Stresemann," *Deutsche Rundschau*, May 1953, p. 471; Speidel, "Reichswehr und Rote Armee," p. 22, n. 1.

47. Dorothea Groener-Geyer, *General Groener* (Frankfurt, 1955); Gordon A. Craig, *The Politics of the Prussian Army, 1640–1945* (Oxford, 1955), chap. 11; Schüddekopf, *Heer und Republik*, p. 235.

48. Groener-Geyer, *General Groener*, p. 189.

49. *Ibid.*, p. 390.

50. *Ibid.*, p. 392.

51. *Ibid.*, p. 339.

52. *Ibid.*, p. 250.

53. The International Military Tribunal, *Trial of the Major War Criminals before the International Military Tribunal, Nuremberg, 14 November 1945– 1 October 1946* (42 vols., Nuremberg, 1947–1949), XIV, 81, 255; Severing, *Lebensweg*, II, 494; Schüddekopf, *Heer und Republik*, p. 239, n. 608.

54. Stresemann, *Vermächtnis*, III, 272.

55. Severing, *Lebensweg*, II, 144.

56. *Ibid.;* Braun, *Von Weimar zu Hitler*, p. 250; Stampfer, *Vierzehn Jahre*, p. 481.

CHAPTER VI. The Great Coalition Once Again

1. Stresemann Papers, 7375H (Curtius, March 1928).

2. Braun, *Von Weimar zu Hitler*, p. 245.

3. Stresemann Papers, 7377H.

4. Stresemann, *Vermächtnis*, III, 298.

5. *Ibid.*, pp. 303, 299.

6. Stresemann Papers, 7408H.

7. *Ibid.*, especially Morath to Stresemann, January 29, 1928.

8. *Ibid.*, 7377H.

9. Stampfer, *Vierzehn Jahre*, p. 482.

10. Braun, *Von Weimar zu Hitler*, p. 252.

11. Julius Leber, *Ein Mann geht seinen Weg* (Berlin, 1952), pp. 274, 275; Wilhelm Keil, *Erlebnisse eines Sozialdemokraten* (2 vols., Stuttgart, 1948), II, 344.

12. Karl Dietrich Bracher, *Die Auflösung der Weimarer Republik. Eine Studie zum Problem des Machtverfalls in der Demokratie* (Stuttgart and Düsseldorf, 1955), p. 315, n. 113; Walter H. Kaufmann, *Monarchism in the Weimar Republic* (New York, 1953), p. 185.

13. Borchmeyer, *Hugenbergs Ringen*, no. 1, p. 2.

14. Stresemann Papers, 7335H (November 2, 1926), 7383H (January 18, 1929).

15. Stresemann, *Vermächtnis*, III, 320.

16. Cuno Horkenbach, ed., *Das Deutsche Reich von 1918 bis heute* (3 vols., Berlin, 1930–1932), I, 269; Severing, *Lebensweg*, II, 187.

17. Alan Bullock, "The German Communists and the Rise of Hitler," in *The Third Reich*, edited by Maurice Baumont, John H. E. Fried, and Edmond Vermeil (New York, 1955), pp. 504, 506; Franz Borkenau, *Communist International* (London, 1938), p. 340; Franz Borkenau, *European Communism* (London, 1953), p. 340; Ossip K. Flechtheim, *Die Kommunistische Partei Deutschlands in der Weimarer Republik* (Offenbach, 1948), p. 151; Arthur Rosenberg, *A History of Bolshevism. From Marx to the First Five Years' Plan* (London, 1934), p. 224.

18. Similarly, Flechtheim, *Kommunistische Partei Deutschlands*, p. 172.

19. For a different opinion, see Bracher, *Auflösung der Weimarer Republik*, p. 297, n. 40; see also Max Miller, *Eugen Bolz* (Stuttgart, 1951), p. 337.

20. Beer, *Heinrich Brüning*, p. 51.

21. Hjalmar Schacht, *Das Ende der Reparationen* (Oldenburg, 1931), p. 50.

22. *Survey of International Affairs, 1929*, p. 178.

23. Julius Curtius, *Der Young-Plan. Entstellung und Wahrheit* (Stuttgart, 1950), p. 21.

24. *Ibid.*, p. 24.

25. *Survey of International Affairs, 1929*, p. 127 (italics added).

26. Bonn, *Wandering Scholar*, p. 307.

27. Stresemann Papers, 7349H; Curtius, *Young-Plan*, p. 29.

28. Hartmann von Richthofen, "Die Weltpolitik des Jahres 1928" in Richthofen, ed. *Jahrbuch für auswärtige Politik, 1929* (Berlin), p. 20; Degras, *Soviet Documents*, II, 335, 345; exchange of notes in *Schulthess' Europäischer Geschichtskalender, 1928*, pp. 487–505.

29. Stresemann, *Vermächtnis*, III, 354.

30. Stresemann Papers, 7376H (June 5, 1928).

31. Stresemann, *Vermächtnis*, III, 357.

32. Stresemann Papers, 7349H (September 20, 1928).

33. Schacht, *Ende der Reparationen*, p. 51.

34. Stresemann Papers, 7387H (Schubert, May 13, 1929).

35. *Survey of International Affairs, 1929*, p. 138.

36. Stampfer, *Vierzehn Jahre*, p. 497.

37. Concerning Kastl, see George W. Hallgarten, *Hitler, Reichswehr und Industrie* (Frankfurt, 1955), pp. 87, 121.

38. Stresemann Papers, 7382H (December 23, 28, and 31, 1928).

39. *Ibid.*, 7383H (January 4, 1929).

40. Schacht, *Ende der Reparationen*, p. 57.

41. Bonn, *Neuer Plan;* J. W. Reichert, *Young-Plan. Finanzen und Wirtschaft* (Berlin, 1930); Adolf Weber, *Reparationen, Young-Plan, Volkswirtschaft* (Berlin, 1929).

42. Schacht, *Ende der Reparationen*, pp. 67–75.

43. Stresemann Papers, 7384H (March 1, 1929).

44. *Ibid.*, 7385H.

45. Stresemann, *Vermächtnis*, III, 395–400.

46. Stresemann Papers, 7386H.

47. *Ibid.*, 7387H.

48. London *Times*, April 19 and 20, 1929.

49. Stresemann Papers, 7386H (April 20).

50. Severing, *Lebensweg*, II, 185.

51. Curtius, *Young-Plan*, p. 41.

52. *Ibid.*, p. 44.

53. Schacht, *Ende der Reparationen*, p. 81.

54. Curtius, *Young-Plan*, p. 43.

55. André François-Poncet, *Souvenirs d'une ambassade à Berlin. Septembre 1931–Octobre 1938* (Paris, 1946), p. 281. English translation: *The Fateful Years. Memoirs of a French Ambassador in Berlin, 1931–1938* (London, 1949). Bonn, *Wandering Scholar*, p. 308; Gröner to Gleich, January 4, 1930, in Groener-Geyer, *General Groener*, p. 262.

56. Stresemann Papers, 7387H (Schubert, May 16, 1929); Hallgarten, *Hitler, Reichswehr und Industrie*, p. 127.

57. Stresemann Papers, 7387H (May 24).

58. *Bank for International Settlements: Documents*, ed. by Melvin A. Traylor (Chicago, 1930), p. 62.

59. *Ibid.*, p. 90.

60. Stampfer, *Vierzehn Jahre*, p. 490.

61. Curtius, *Sechs Jahre Minister*, p. 72.

62. Preller, *Sozialpolitik*, p. 405. Helga Timm, *Die deutsche Sozialpolitik und der Bruch der Grossen Koalition im März 1930* (Düsseldorf, 1952), p. 103.

63. Severing, *Lebensweg*, II, 172.

64. Braun, *Von Weimar zu Hitler*, p. 272.

65. Stresemann Papers, 7383H (January 1929).

66. Stresemann, *Vermächtnis*, III, 434f.

67. London *Times*, April 12, 1929.

68. Walter Landé, "Die staatsrechtlichen Grundlagen des deutschen Unterrichtswesens," *Handbuch des Deutschen Staatsrechts*, II, 714; Anschütz, *Verfassung des Deutschen Reichs*, commentary to Article 78.

69. Hans von Schubert, *Der Kampf des geistlichen und des weltlichen Rechts* (Heidelberg, 1927), p. 72.

70. Godehard J. Ebers, ed., *Deutsches (Reichs-) und preussisches Staatskirchenrecht* (Munich, 1932), p. 443.

71. *Ibid.*, p. 468.

72. Georg Jellinek, *Ausgewählte Schriften und Reden* (2 vols., Berlin, 1911), I, 402.

73. A. Deissmann, *Reichsverfassung und Kirchenverfassung* (Berlin, 1931), p. 25.

CHAPTER VII. The Fight for the Young Plan, Stresemann's Death, and the Rise of Hitler

1. Carlo Sforza, *Gestalten und Gestalter des heutigen Europa* (Berlin, 1931), p. 222. English translation: *Makers of Modern Europe: Portraits and Personal Impressions and Recollections* (London, 1930).

2. Henry R. Winkler, "Arthur Henderson" in Gordon A. Craig and Felix Gilbert, eds., *The Diplomats* (Princeton, 1953), p. 326.

3. Curtius, *Young-Plan*, p. 52.

4. Schmidt, *Statist*, p. 183.

5. Braun, *Von Weimar zu Hitler*, pp. 298f.

6. *Schulthess' Europäischer Geschichtskalender, 1930*, p. 311 (July 4, 1930).

7. Curtius, *Sechs Jahre Minister*, p. 137.

8. Great Britain, Official Documents. *Documents on British Foreign Policy, 1919–1939*. Second series, edited by E. L. Woodward and Rohan Butler (London, 1946 —), I, 486. Cf. Franklin L. Ford, "Three Observers in Berlin: Rumbold, Dodd, François-Poncet," in Craig and Gilbert, *Diplomats*, p. 440.

9. Stresemann, *Vermächtnis*, III, 565.

10. *Survey of International Affairs, 1929*, p. 176.

11. Stresemann Papers, 7392H.

12. *Schulthess' Europäischer Geschichtskalender, 1929*, p. 164.

13. Stresemann, *Vermächtnis*, III, 577.

14. Antonina Vallentin, *Stresemann; vom Werden einer Staatsidee* (Leipzig, 1930), p. 278 in 1948 edition; English translation: *Stresemann* (London, New York, 1931).

15. Eugen Schiffer, *Ein Leben für den Liberalismus* (Berlin-Grunewald, 1951), p. 112.

16. *Documents on British Foreign Policy*, I, 603.

17. Konrad Heiden, *Der Führer, Hitler's Rise to Power* (London and Boston, 1944), p. 202.

18. Oron J. Hale, "Adolf Hitler: Taxpayer," *American Historical Review*, July 1955, p. 837.

19. Friedrich Meinecke, "Ranke und Burckhardt" in his *Aphorismen zur Geschichte* (2nd enl. ed., Stuttgart, 1953), p. 150.

20. Theodor Mommsen, *Römische Geschichte* (3rd ed., Berlin, 1861), vol. III, chap. 10.

21. Kempner, "Blueprint of the Nazi Underground," p. 54.

22. Bracher, *Auflösung der Weimarer Republik*, p. 375, n. 30.

23. Georg Kaisenberg, "Die formelle Ordnung des Volksbegehrens und des Volksentscheids in Reich und Ländern," *Handbuch des Deutschen Staatsrechts*, II, 204.

24. Stampfer, *Vierzehn Jahre*, p. 502.

Chapter VIII. The Collapse of the Great Coalition

1. Gustav Stolper, *Ein Finanzplan. Vorschläge zur deutschen Finanzreform* (Berlin, 1929); Stolper, *Die wirtschaftliche und soziale Weltanschauung der Demokratie* (address at the Mannheim party congress of the German Democratic Party, October 5, 1929 (Berlin, 1929)).

2. Preller, *Sozialpolitik*, p. 42.

3. Concerning Popitz, see the editorial in the *Vossische Zeitung* of October 31, 1932, and the memoirs of von Grabower in *Finanz-Rundschau* (Cologne) of December 15, 1954, p. 516.

4. Schwerin-Krosigk, *Es geschah in Deutschland*, p. 92; Schacht, *Ende der Reparationen*, p. 154.

5. Groener-Geyer, *General Groener*, p. 262.

6. Gustav Noske, *Aufstieg und Niedergang der deutschen Sozialdemokratie. Erlebtes aus Aufstieg und Niedergang einer Demokratie* (Zurich and Offenbach, 1947), p. 309; Timm, *Die deutsche Sozialpolitik und der Bruch der Grossen Koalition*, p. 160.

7. Keil, *Erlebnisse eines Sozialdemokraten*, II, 362.

8. Severing, *Lebensweg*, II, 227.

9. Curtius, *Young-Plan*, p. 91.

10. *Ibid.*, p. 93.

11. *Ibid,.* p. 99.

12. Schacht, *Ende der Reparationen*, p. 131.

13. *Survey of International Affairs, 1930*, pp. 511f.

14. Curtius, *Young-Plan*, p. 79.

15. *Ibid.*, p. 81.

16. *Ibid.*, p. 85.

17. *Ibid.*, p. 87.

18. *Ibid.*, p. 106.

19. *Ibid.*, p. 109.

20. *Ibid.*, p. 110.

21. John W. Wheeler-Bennett, *Hindenburg, the Wooden Titan* (London, 1936), p. 335.

22. Reichskreditgesellschaft, *Berichte, Jahreswende 1929–30*, and *Erstes Halbjahr 1930*.

23. Timm, *Die deutsche Sozialpolitik und der Bruch der Grossen Koalition*, pp. 184, 46.

24. Stampfer, *Vierzehn Jahre*, p. 516.

25. Severing, *Lebensweg*, II, 239.

26. Stampfer, *Vierzehn Jahre*, p. 516; Timm, *Die deutsche Sozialpolitik und der Bruch der Grossen Koalition*, p. 191.

27. Petrich's conversational remark of May 1930, cited in Timm, *Die deutsche Sozialpolitik und der Bruch der Grossen Koalition*, p. 186.

28. Ziebill, *Geschichte des deutschen Städtetags*, p. 101.

CHAPTER IX. From Parliamentary Government to Article 48

For this and the following chapter I have constantly consulted the very substantial and thorough work of Bracher, *Die Auflösung der Weimarer Republik*.

1. Alphons Nobel, *Brüning* (Leipzig, 1932), p. 16; Beer, *Heinrich Brüning*, p. 27.

2. Stresemann Papers, 7381H.

3. Beer, *Heinrich Brüning*, p. 54.

4. François-Poncet, *Souvenirs*, p. 17.

5. Groener-Geyer, *General Groener*, p. 262; Craig, *Politics of the Prussian Army*, p. 436; Bracher, *Auflösung der Weimarer Republik*, p. 309, n. 86.

6. Groener-Geyer, *General Groener*, p. 266.

7. Manchester *Guardian*, March 28 and April 7, 1930.

8. Keil, *Erlebnisse eines Sozialdemokraten*, II, 386.

9. Bracher, *Auflösung der Weimarer Republik*, p. 331, n. 3.

10. Borchmeyer, *Hugenbergs Ringen*, no. 1, p. 11.

11. Braun, *Von Weimar zu Hitler*, pp. 297f.

12. Severing, *Lebensweg*, II, 230.

13. Reichstag, June 17, 1930; *Schulthess' Europäischer Geschichtskalender, 1930*, p. 139.

14. Braun, *Von Weimar zu Hitler*, p. 298.

15. *Documents on British Foreign Policy*, I, 486.

16. Braun, *Von Weimar zu Hitler*, pp. 300 f.

17. Stolper, *Ein Finanzplan*, p. 47.

18. Braun, *Von Weimar zu Hitler*, p. 296.

19. Horkenbach, *Das Deutsche Reich*, I, 311.

20. Severing, *Lebensweg*, II, 246.

21. Completely distorted in Magnus von Braun, *Von Ostpreussen bis Texas* (Stollhamm-Oldenburg, 1955), p. 209.

22. Keil, *Erlebnisse eines Sozialdemokraten*, II, 393.

23. *Ibid.*, p. 388; compare also Secretary of State Weismann in *Documents on British Foreign Policy*, I, 510.

24. Curtius, *Sechs Jahre Minister*, p. 165.

25. Heinrich Brüning, letter in *Deutsche Rundschau*, July 1947, p. 12.

26. *Ibid.*, p. 11.

27. Bracher, *Auflösung der Weimarer Republik*, p. 305, n. 71.

28. Severing, *Lebensweg*, II, 247.

29. Curtius, *Sechs Jahre Minister*, p. 165; Keil, *Erlebnisse eines Sozial-demokraten*, II, 395.

30. *Documents on British Foreign Policy*, I, 504 (September 5, 1930).

31. *Ibid.*, p. 502.

32. *Ibid.*, p. 493.

33. *Ibid.*, p. 500.

34. Curtius, *Sechs Jahre Minister*, p. 166.

35. *Documents on British Foreign Policy*, I, 504.

CHAPTER X. The Elections of September 1930: Brüning on the Defensive

1. Hans Schlange-Schöningen, *Am Tage danach* (Hamburg, 1946), p. 25; English translation: *The Morning After* (London, 1948).

2. Bracher, *Auflösung der Weimarer Republik*, p. 146.

3. Theodor Litt, "The National-Socialist Use of Moral Tendencies in Germany," in Baumont, *et al.*, eds., *The Third Reich*, p. 438.

4. Schmidt, *Statist*, p. 201.

5. Curtius, *Sechs Jahre Minister*, p. 170.

6. *Ibid.*, p. 171.

7. *Documents on British Foreign Policy*, I, 509, no. 322.

8. Reichskreditgesellschaft, *Bericht Jahreswende 1930–31*, pp. 43, 28.

9. Groener-Geyer, *General Groener*, p. 267.

10. Schüddekopf, *Heer und Republik*, pp. 281–287.

11. Kempner, "Blueprint of the Nazi Underground," pp. 98–105.

12. Hans Frank, *Im Angesicht des Galgens* (Munich-Gräfelfing, 1953), p. 84 (cited in Schüddekopf, *Heer und Republik*, p. 279, n. 735).

13. Alan Bullock, *Hitler. A Study in Tyranny* (London and New York, 1952), p. 149; Heiden, *Der Führer*, p. 321; Stampfer, *Vierzehn Jahre*, p. 535; John W. Wheeler-Bennett, *The Nemesis of Power: The German Army in Politics* (New York and London, 1953), p. 219; Craig, *Politics of the Prussian Army*, p. 435; Schüddekopf, *Heer und Republik*, pp. 268f; Groener-Geyer, *General Groener*, p. 397 (speech of Major Theisen); London *Times* editorial, September 26, 1930.

14. Severing, *Lebensweg*, II, p. 257.

15. Schüddekopf, *Heer und Republik*, p. 272, n. 703, and p. 295; Wheeler-Bennett, *Nemesis*, p. 199, n. 2; Craig, *Politics of the Prussian Army*, p. 431.

16. Bracher, *Auflösung der Weimarer Republik*, p. 381.

17. *Documents on British Foreign Policy*, I, 524, no. 331 (October 27, 1930).

18. Curtius, *Sechs Jahre Minister*, p. 171.

19. Braun, *Von Weimar bis Hitler*, p. 308.

20. Severing, *Lebensweg*, II, 258; Stampfer, *Vierzehn Jahre*, p. 532.

21. *Schulthess' Europäischer Geschichtskalender, 1930*, p. 203 (October 13).

22. Severing, *Lebensweg*, II, 259.

23. *Documents on British Foreign Policy*, I, 519, no. 329 (October 23, 1930).

24. Severing, *Lebensweg*, II, 266; Braun, *Von Weimar bis Hitler*, p. 315.

25. Severing, *Lebensweg*, II, 260.

26. Johannes Heckel, "Die Budgetverabschiedung, insbesondere die Rechte und Pflichten des Reichstags," in *Handbuch des Deutschen Staatsrechts*, II, 409.

CHAPTER XI. Customs Union and Banking Crisis

1. Reichskreditgesellschaft, *Bericht Erstes Halbjahr 1931*, p. 20.
2. *Documents on British Foreign Policy*, I, 542, no. 338; Winkler, "Henderson," in Craig and Gilbert, *Diplomats*, p. 337.
3. *Documents on British Foreign Policy*, I, 540, no. 340 (December 10, 1930).
4. Curtius, *Sechs Jahre Minister*, p. 173.
5. *Documents on British Foreign Policy*, II, 66, no. 46; *Survey of International Affairs, 1931*, p. 68.
6. *Documents on British Foreign Policy*, II, 68 (enclosure in no. 48).
7. Curtius, *Sechs Jahre Minister*, p. 176.
8. *Documents on British Foreign Policy*, II, 47, no. 34 (Rumbold, May 6, 1931).
9. Curtius, *Sechs Jahre Minister*, p. 146.
10. François-Poncet, *Souvenirs*, p. 240.
11. Compare, however, Friedrich von Prittwitz und Gaffron, *Zwischen Petersburg und Washington* (Munich, 1952), p. 121.
12. Curtius, *Sechs Jahre Minister*, p. 191.
13. Heinrich Friedjung, *Österreich von 1848 bis 1860* (2 vols., Stuttgart and Berlin, 1908–1912), I, 303.
14. Eyck, *Bismarck*, I, 438f.
15. *Documents on British Foreign Policy*, I, 579.
16. Winkler, in Craig and Gilbert, *Diplomats*, p. 338.
17. *Documents on British Foreign Policy*, II, 3.
18. *Ibid.*, p. 6, no. 3.
19. *Ibid.*, p. 14.
20. Curtius, *Sechs Jahre Minister*, p. 198.
21. Eyck, *Bismarck*, III, 488.
22. Walter Hagemann, "Die Europa-Idee bei Briand und Coudenhove-Kalergi. Ein Vergleich," in Herrmann, ed., *Geschichte und Politik*, p. 153.
23. London *Times* editorial, May 14, 1931.
24. *Documents on British Foreign Policy*, II, 15, no. 8 (March 25, 1931).
25. Curtius, *Sechs Jahre Minister*, p. 197.
26. London *Times*, Berlin correspondent, May 20, 1931.
27. *Documents on British Foreign Policy*, II, 85 (May 17, 1931).
28. *Ibid.*, p. 78.
29. Reichskreditgesellschaft, *Bericht Erstes Halbjahr 1931*, p. 20.
30. *Documents on British Foreign Policy*, II, 70, nos. 49 and 50.
31. Schmidt, *Statist*, pp. 204, 207.
32. London *Times* editorial, June 10, 1931.
33. *Documents on British Foreign Policy*, II, 71–77; Schmidt, *Statist*, p. 208.
34. London *Times*, Berlin correspondent, June 10, 1931.
35. Curtius, *Sechs Jahre Minister*, p. 199.
36. Herbert Clark Hoover, *The Memoirs of Herbert Hoover* (3 vols., London–New York, 1951–52), III, 65.
37. *Documents on British Foreign Policy*, II, 92, no. 71.
38. London *Times*, Berlin correspondent, June 23, 1931.
39. *Documents on British Foreign Policy*, II, 116, no. 106 (July 1, 1931).
40. *Ibid.*, p. 150, no. 155.
41. *Ibid.*, p. 119, no. 113.

42. *Ibid.*, p. 129, no. 124 (July 3).
43. *Ibid.*, p. 191, no. 193.
44. *Ibid.*, pp. 435–484.
45. *Ibid.*, p. 460.
46. *Ibid.*, p. 463.
47. *Survey of International Affairs, 1931*, p. 89.
48. *Documents on British Foreign Policy*, II, 220.
49. *Ibid.*, p. 221.
50. *Das Basler Gutachten über die deutsche Wirtschaftskrise. Der Layton Bericht* . . . , translated and edited by Franz Wolf (Frankfurt, 1931).
51. *Documents on British Foreign Policy*, II, 255.
52. Otto Meissner, *Staatssekretär unter Ebert-Hindenburg-Hitler* (Hamburg, 1950), p. 207.
53. Groener-Geyer, *General Groener*, p. 280.
54. *Documents on British Foreign Policy*, II, 252.
55. Friedrich Meinecke, *Strassburg–Freiburg–Berlin, 1901–1919: Erinnerungen* (Stuttgart, 1949), p. 248.
56. Groener-Geyer, *General Groener*, p. 283.
57. Severing, *Lebensweg*, II, 322.
58. *Documents on British Foreign Policy*, II, 278.
59. *Ibid.*, p. 293.
60. Groener-Geyer, *General Groener*, p. 278.
61. Theodor Duesterberg, *Der Stahlhelm und Hitler* (Wolfenbüttel and Hanover, 1949).
62. *Documents on British Foreign Policy*, II, 298.
63. Meissner, *Staatssekretär*, p. 211.
64. *Documents on British Foreign Policy*, II, 360.
65. Severing, *Lebensweg*, II, 308.
66. *Ibid.*; Braun, *Von Weimar zu Hitler*, p. 351.
67. *Vossische Zeitung*, November 28, 1931.
68. François-Poncet, *Souvenirs*, p. 39.
69. Groener-Geyer, *General Groener*, p. 280.
70. Schüddekopf, *Heer und Republik*, p. 329.
71. Groener-Geyer, *General Groener*, p. 285.
72. Schüddekopf, *Heer und Republik*, p. 334.
73. Severing, *Lebensweg*, II, 322.
74. *Berliner Tageblatt*, February 28, 1932.
75. *Survey of International Affairs, 1931*, p. 238.
76. *Documents on British Foreign Policy*, III, 5.
77. *Ibid.*, p. 12 (Rumbold, January 8, 1932).
78. *Survey of International Affairs, 1931*, p. 141, note.
79. *Documents on British Foreign Policy*, III, 12 (January 8, 1932).
80. *Ibid.*, see especially pp. 13, 16, 17, 19.
81. *Ibid.*, p. 15 (Tyrrell, January 10, 1932); François-Poncet, *Souvenirs*, p. 33.
82. *Documents on British Foreign Policy*, III, 23 (Tyrrell, January 10, 1932).
83. *Ibid.*, p. 41 (January 18, 1932).
84. *Ibid.*, p. 45.
85. *Ibid.*, p. 46, n. 2.
86. Viscount Templewood (Sir Samuel Hoare), *Nine Troubled Years* (London, 1954), pp. 111f.

87. *Documents on British Foreign Policy*, III, 46 (memorandum, July 15, 1932).

CHAPTER XII. Hindenburg Is Re-elected and Stabs Brüning in the Back

1. Max Weber, *Gesammelte Politische Schriften* (Munich, 1921), p. 363.
2. Wheeler-Bennett, *Hindenburg*, p. 367.
3. Braun, *Von Weimar zu Hitler*, p. 368.
4. Joseph Goebbels, *Vom Kaiserhof zur Reichskanzlei* (Munich, 1934), p. 18; English translation: *My Part in Germany's Fight* (London, 1935). Bracher, *Auflösung der Weimarer Republik*, p. 448, n. 14.
5. *Documents on British Foreign Policy*, III, 99.
6. Borchmeyer, *Hugenbergs Ringen*, p. 19.
7. *Ibid.*
8. *Documents on British Foreign Policy*, III, 100.
9. Keil, *Erlebnisse eines Sozialdemokraten*, II, 435.
10. Duesterberg, *Stahlhelm und Hitler*, p. 35.
11. *Documents on British Foreign Policy*, III, 101.
12. *Berliner Tageblatt*, February 28, 1932.
13. Severing, *Lebensweg*, II, 323.
14. Hallgarten, *Hitler, Reichswehr und Industrie*, p. 103.
15. *Ibid.*, p. 104; Bullock, *Hitler*, p. 177.
16. Severing, *Lebensweg*, II, 328.
17. Duesterberg, *Stahlhelm und Hitler*, p. 34.
18. Paul Herre, *Kronprinz Friedrich Wilhelm* (Munich, 1954), p. 209.
19. *Documents on British Foreign Policy*, III, 110 (April 13).
20. Groener-Geyer, *General Groener*, p. 327.
21. *Documents on British Foreign Policy*, III, 111. Bracher, *Auflösung der Weimarer Republik*, p. 478.
22. *Documents on British Foreign Policy*, III, 112 (April 13).
23. Cf. *ibid.*, p. 124 (no. 104).
24. Hans-Heinrich Lammers and Walter Simons, eds., *Die Rechtsprechung des Staatsgerichtshofs für das Deutsche Reich und des Reichsgerichts auf Grund Artikel 13 Absatz 2 der Reichsverfassung* (5 vols., Berlin, 1929–1933), V, 149.
25. Groener-Geyer, *General Groener*, p. 304.
26. Severing, *Lebensweg*, II, 328.
27. *Ibid.*, p. 329.
28. Cf. Braun, *Von Weimar zu Hitler*, pp. 380 f.
29. Groener-Geyer, *General Groener*, pp. 296f.
30. *Ibid.*, p. 403.
31. Kurt Caro and Walter Oehme, *Schleichers Aufstieg* (Berlin, 1933), p. 227.
32. Anschütz, *Verfassung des Deutschen Reichs*, note 3 to Article 50.
33. *Documents on British Foreign Policy*, III, 141.
34. Goebbels, *Vom Kaiserhof zur Reichskanzlei*, p. 80 (April 14).
35. Adolf von Carlowitz, cited in "Dokumentation: Zum Sturz Brünings," *Vierteljahrshefte für Zeitgeschichte*, I (1953): 271.
36. Bernhard von Bülow, *Denkwürdigkeiten* (4 vols., Berlin, 1930–1931), I, 15. English translation: *Memoirs* (4 vols., London and New York, 1931–1932).
37. Groener-Geyer, *General Groener*, p. 311.
38. *Ibid.*

39. Bracher, *Auflösung der Weimarer Republik*, p. 492, n. 41.

40. Groener-Geyer, *General Groener*, p. 314; Meissner, *Staatssekretär*, p. 212; Goebbels, *Vom Kaiserhof zur Reichskanzlei*, p. 93; von Noeldechen, cited in "Dokumentation: Zum Sturz Brüning," p. 273.

41. Groener-Geyer, *General Groener*, p. 316.

42. "Dokumentation: Zum Sturz Brünings," p. 277.

43. *Documents on British Foreign Policy*, III, 141.

44. *Ibid.*, p. 143.

45. Walters, *League of Nations*, II, 506; Wheeler-Bennett, *Hindenburg*, p. 382; Schwarzschild, *World in Trance*, p. 205.

46. *Documents on British Foreign Policy*, III, 139.

47. *Ibid.*, p. 510.

48. *Ibid.*, p. 123, no. 103.

49. *Ibid.*, p. 158, no. 125.

50. Magnus von Braun, *Von Ostpreussen bis Texas*, p. 217.

51. Braun, *Von Weimar zu Hitler*, p. 389.

52. *Wörterbuch der Volkswirtschaft*, ed. Ludwig Elster (4th rev. ed., 3 vols., Jena, 1930), II, 81.

53. *Documents on British Foreign Policy*, III, 185, no. 136, paragraph 2 (June 14).

54. Meissner, *Staatssekretär*, p. 220.

55. "Dokumentation: Zum Sturz Brünings," p. 276; Magnus von Braun, *Von Ostpreussen bis Texas*, p. 218.

56. "Dokumentation: Zum Sturz Brünings," p. 281.

57. *Ibid.*, p. 277.

58. Meissner, *Staatssekretär*, p. 226.

59. Schlange-Schöningen, *Am Tage danach*, pp. 5, 70 f.

60. Meissner, *Staatssekretär*, p. 226.

61. Severing, *Lebensweg*, II, 336.

62. Wheeler-Bennett, *Hindenburg*, p. 385.

63. François-Poncet, *Souvenirs*, p. 38.

64. Friedrich Meinecke, *Die deutsche Katastrophe* (Wiesbaden and Zurich, 1946), p. 103. English translation by S. B. Fay: *The German Catastrophe: Reflections and Recollections* (Cambridge, Mass., 1950).

65. *Documents on British Foreign Policy*, III, 165, no. 129 (June 9, 1932).

66. (Anonymous), *Die Sanierung des Reichshaushalts im Kabinett Brüning-Dietrich* (privately printed).

CHAPTER XIII. Major Papen Takes Command

1. François-Poncet, *Souvenirs*, p. 42.

2. Wheeler-Bennett, *Nemesis*, p. 246.

3. Wheeler-Bennett, *Hindenburg*, p. 396. Bracher, *Auflösung der Weimarer Republik*, p. 530, n. 5.

4. *Documents on British Foreign Policy*, III, 167.

5. *Ibid.*, p. 151, no. 122.

6. *Ibid.*, p. 160 (June 7, 1932).

7. Magnus von Braun, *Von Ostpreussen bis Texas*, p. 208.

8. *Ibid.*, p. 230.

9. *Ibid.*, p. 228.

10. *Ibid.*, p. 257.

11. *Schulthess' Europäischer Geschichtskalender, 1932*, p. 132.

12. Braun, *Von Ostpreussen bis Texas*, p. 239.
13. *Documents on British Foreign Policy*, III, 186, no. 136 (June 14).
14. "Dokumentation: Zum Sturz Brünings," p. 288.
15. *Documents on British Foreign Policy*, III, 148.
16. *Ibid.*, p. 186.
17. Bracher, *Auflösung der Weimarer Republik*, p. 534, n. 25.
18. *Ibid.*, p. 535, n. 28.
19. *Documents on British Foreign Policy*, III, 176.
20. *Ibid.*, pp. 271, 387.
21. *Ibid.*, p. 271.
22. *Ibid.*, p. 274.
23. Cf. Erich Eyck, "Papen als Historiker," *Deutsche Rundschau*, December 1952, p. 1226.
24. Sir John Simon, *Retrospect* (London, 1952), p. 188.
25. Henry L. Stimson and McGeorge Bundy, *On Active Service in Peace and War* (New York, 1947), p. 63.
26. *Documents on British Foreign Policy*, III, 332.
27. *Ibid.*, p. 379.
28. *Ibid.*, p. 383.
29. *Ibid.*, p. 385.
30. *Ibid.*, p. 425.
31. *Ibid.*, p. 491, no. 192.
32. Schmidt, *Statist*, p. 255.
33. Goebbels, *Vom Kaiserhof zur Reichskanzlei*, p. 101.
34. Braun, *Von Weimar zu Hitler*, p. 404.
35. Schwend, *Bayern zwischen Monarchie und Diktatur*, pp. 444f.
36. Severing, *Lebensweg*, II, 345.
37. Horkenbach, *Das Deutsche Reich*, I, 240.
38. Severing, *Lebensweg*, II, 344.
39. Braun, *Von Weimar zu Hitler*, p. 395.
40. Schwend, *Bayern zwischen Monarchie und Diktatur*, p. 452.
41. Franz von Papen, *Memoirs* (London, 1952).
42. Severing, *Lebensweg*, II, 349.
43. Braun, *Von Weimar zu Hitler*, p. 409; Severing, *Lebensweg*, II, 352; Arnold Brecht, *Prelude to Silence* (New York, 1944), p. 66.
44. Keil, *Erlebnisse eines Sozialdemokraten*, II, 637.
45. Severing, *Lebensweg*, II, 347.
46. Ernst Friesenhahn, "Die Staatsgerichtbarkeit," in *Handbuch des Deutschen Staatsrechts*, II, 523.
47. Schwend, *Bayern zwischen Monarchie und Diktatur*, p. 456.
48. *Ibid.*, p. 457.
49. Bracher, *Auflösung der Weimarer Republik*, p. 619.
50. Papen, *Memoirs*, p. 201.
51. Lammers and Simons, *Rechtsprechung des Staatsgerichtshofs*, V, 30–66.
52. Braun, *Von Weimar zu Hitler*, p. 415; Misch, *Deutsche Geschichte*, p. 379.
53. Papen, *Memoirs*, p. 192.
54. Groener-Geyer, *General Groener*, p. 332.
55. Willibalt Apelt, *Geschichte der Weimarer Verfassung* (Munich, 1946), p. 285.
56. Braun, *Von Weimar zu Hitler*, p. 417.
57. Preller, *Sozialpolitik*, p. 416.

58. Goebbels, *Von Kaiserhof zur Reichskanzlei*, p. 191.
59. *Ibid.*, p. 192.
60. *Ibid.*, p. 193.
61. Bracher, *Auflösung der Weimarer Republik*, p. 647.
62. Keil, *Erlebnisse eines Sozialdemokraten*, II, 469.
63. Papen, *Memoirs*, p. 213; Bullock, *Hitler*, p. 210; Bracher, *Auflösung der Weimarer Republik*, p. 660.
64. Meissner, *Staatssekretär*, p. 248.
65. Templewood, *Nine Troubled Years*, p. 121.
66. Papen, *Memoirs*, p. 216.
67. Bracher, *Auflösung der Weimarer Republik*, p. 672; Brüning, letter in *Deutsche Rundschau*, July 1947, p. 4; Meissner, *Staatssekretär*, p. 245.
68. Papen, *Memoirs*, p. 253. Wheeler-Bennett, *Nemesis*, p. 264; Schüddekopf, *Heer und Republik*, p. 374, Document 151; Thilo Vogelsang, ed., "Neue Dokumente zur Geschichte der Reichswehr, 1930–1933," *Vierteljahrshefte für Zeitgeschichte*, II (1954): 427; Bracher, *Auflösung der Weimarer Republik*, p. 674; Georges Castellan, "Schleicher, Papen, et l'avenement de Hitler," *Cahiers d'Histoire de la Guerre* (Paris), January 1949, p. 23.
69. Vogelsang, "Neue Dokumente zur Geschichte der Reichswehr," p. 421.

CHAPTER XIV. From Schleicher to Hitler

1. *Documents on British Foreign Policy*, IV, 79.
2. *Ibid.*, p. 390.
3. *Ibid.*, p. 96 (December 7, 1932).
4. *Ibid.*, p. 384 (December 21, 1932).
5. *Ibid.*, p. 384.
6. *Ibid.*, p. 99 (December 7, 1932).
7. *Ibid.*, p. 96.
8. Bracher, *Auflösung der Weimarer Republik*, p. 625, n. 108.
9. Goebbels, *Vom Kaiserhof zur Reichskanzlei*, p. 212 (December 1).
10. Cf. "Dokumentation: Zur Ermordung des Generals Schleicher," *Vierteljahrshefte für Zeitgeschichte*, I (1953): 71, particularly the wretched explanation of Field Marshal von Mackensen, p. 73, n. 8.
11. *Documents on British Foreign Policy*, IV, 91.
12. *Ibid.*, p. 372; Walters, *League of Nations*, II, 515.
13. *Documents on British Foreign Policy*, IV, 163.
14. *Ibid.*, p. 196 (September 23), and p. 201 (September 28).
15. *Ibid.*, pp. 166, 178, 196, 201.
16. *Ibid.*, p. 167 (September 14).
17. *Ibid.*, p. 172.
18. *Ibid.*, pp. 188–190.
19. *Ibid.*, p. 263.
20. *Ibid.*, pp. 271, 273, 284.
21. *Ibid.*, p. 254.
22. Bullock, *Hitler*, p. 313; François-Poncet, *Souvenirs*, p. 251.
23. *Documents on British Foreign Policy*, IV, 378 (Rumbold, December 14, 1932).
24. Schmidt, *Statist*, p. 255.
25. Meinecke, *Strassburg–Freiburg–Berlin*, p. 194.
26. Stampfer, *Vierzehn Jahre*, p. 600.
27. Noske, *Aufstieg und Niedergang*, p. 311; cf. Pechel, *Deutscher Wider-*

stand, p. 20; Bracher, *Auflösung der Weimarer Republik*, p. 690, particu
nn. 56–60.

28. Bracher, *Auflösung der Weimarer Republik*, p. 697.

29. Pro: Bracher, *Auflösung der Weimarer Republik*, p. 698. Con: Wa
Görlitz, *Hindenburg* (Bonn, 1953).

30. *Schulthess' Europäischer Geschichtskalender, 1933*, p. 11.

31. For a different opinion, see Görlitz, *Hindenburg*, p. 397.

32. Theodor Eschenburg, "Franz von Papen," *Vierteljahrshefte für Zeit
geschichte*, I (1953): 163.

33. Papen, *Memoirs*, p. 227.

34. *Ibid.*

35. Hale, "Adolf Hitler: Taxpayer," p. 830.

36. Cf. Grützner, "Dokumentation: Zur Ermordung des Generals Schleicher," p. 91.

37. Erwin Wickert, *Dramatische Tage in Hitlers Reich* (Stuttgart, 1952),
p. 22.

38. Goebbels, *Vom Kaiserhof zur Reichskanzlei*, p. 235.

39. *Ibid.*, p. 238.

40. Henry Picker and Gerhard Ritter, eds., *Hitlers Tischgespräche im
Führerhauptquartier, 1941–1942* (Bonn, 1951), p. 428. (Translators' note:
Picker's text comprises slightly more than one half of the matter contained in
the *Bormann-Vermerke* translated in full in *Hitler's Secret Conversations,
1941–1944*, New York, 1953.)

41. Meissner, *Staatssekretär*, p. 261.

42. *Ibid.*

43. Bracher, *Auflösung der Weimarer Republik*, p. 696 and n. 44.

44. *Documents on British Foreign Policy*, IV, 389.

45. Bracher, *Auflösung der Weimarer Republik*, p. 702.

46. *Documents on British Foreign Policy*, IV, 391.

47. Magnus von Braun, *Von Ostpreussen bis Texas*, p. 226.

48. Braun, *Von Weimar zu Hitler*, p. 439.

49. Magnus von Braun, *Von Ostpreussen bis Texas*, p. 264.

50. Meissner, *Staatssekretär*, p. 263.

51. *Documents on British Foreign Policy*, IV, 397f.

52. Duesterberg, *Stahlhelm und Hitler*, pp. 38f.

53. Borchmeyer, *Hugenbergs Ringen*, p. 25.

54. Hermann Foertsch, *Schuld und Verhängnis* (Stuttgart, 1951), p. 26.

55. Bracher, *Auflösung der Weimarer Republik*, p. 717, n. 137.

56. Notes of General Kurt von Hammerstein of January 28, 1935, printed
in Bracher, *Auflösung der Weimarer Republik*, p. 733.

57. *Documents on British Foreign Policy*, IV, 397.

58. Meissner, *Staatssekretär*, p. 268.

59. Bracher, *Auflösung der Weimarer Republik*, p. 721; also Foertsch,
Schuld und Verhängnis, p. 27; Rudolf Diels, *Lucifer ante portas. Zwischen
Severing und Heydrich* (Zürich, 1949), p. 279.

60. Wheeler-Bennett, *Nemesis*, p. 246, n. 2.

61. Duesterberg, *Stahlhelm und Hitler*, p. 39.

513

arly

ter

INDEX

Abegg, Wilhelm (1876–1951), state secretary in the Prussian Ministry of the Interior (1926–1932), 411–414

Adenauer, Konrad (b. 1876), 68, 213

Agrarian League, 257, 461–463, 469

Agrarian Party, 155, 274, 278, 294, 298, 336

Agriculture: and German Nationalists, 16; foreign investment in, 121; protectionism, 244, 249, 257; eastern aid, 258, 259, 459–460; Schiele's agrarian reforms, 265–266; and September 1930 election, 280–281, 291, 294; in *1931*, 299; and fall of Brüning, 380–384; and Schleicher, 459–460, 461–463

Allied Conference of Ambassadors, 41, 47, 48, 128

All Quiet on the Western Front ban, 295–296

All-Russian Cooperative Society (Arcos), 130

Alsace-Lorraine: and German Nationalists, 11–12; and Stresemann, 28; professors and, 178

Altona incident, 408–410, 413

Alvensleben, Count Bodo von, 393, 482

Angriff, see Goebbels, Joseph

Anschluss, 28, 78, 305–306, 309, 326, 328, 346

Anschütz, Gerhard (1867–1948), 370

Anti-Semitism, 285, 487; Goebbels and, 171, 290, 356; in *Mein Kampf*, 217; and Sklarek scandal, 252; in Thuringian schools, 261; and students, 281; in Boxheim Papers, 337; and National Deserters' Tax, 342; and April 1932 election, 356, 359; and reaction to Lausanne Agreements, 407

Armament, *see* Disarmament

Army: Seeckt's resignation, 85–92; its connection with Soviet government, 94–101; defense budget, 143–145; and Gröner, 256, 375, 376; Nazi influence in, 262, 284–288; and *All Quiet on the Western Front* ban, 295–296; Nazis admitted to, 338–341, 376, 446, 477; and April 1932 election, 360; and ban on SA and SS, 364–365, 366, 373–374;

and Prussian coup d'état, 414, 416, 449; and Papen, 438; and Schleicher, 443, 444–446, 449, 481–483

Asquith, H. H. (1852–1928), 345

Austrian Land Bank, 308

Baden: and school issue, 151, 152; and ban on SA and SS, 365, 401; interim government, 410, 417

Bahrfeld, von, 419

Baldwin, Stanley, 2

Balfour note, 206

Bank for International Settlements, 191, 236–237, 313, 316, 324, 342–343, 347, 406

Bank of England: and German aid to France, 82; and 1931 economic crisis, 313, 314, 322, 324

Bank of Guarantees and Acceptances, 320

Bäumer, Gertrud (1873–1954), Democratic Reichstag delegate, 93

Bavaria: and Austria, 28; and federalization, 104–143; Stresemann in, 157; and Hitler, 215, 218, 219; and SA and SS, 363, 364–365, 401; interim government, 410; and Prussian coup d'état, 417–418

Bavarian People's Party: and formation of Luther's second government, 51–52; and Marx's fourth government, 106; and federalization, 141; and Müller's cabinet, 158, 160, 161, 199; and Young Plan, 238; against Brüning-Meyer compromise, 246; in Brüning's government, 256, 257; against beer tax, 264–265; and Boxheim Papers, 338; and SA and SS, 363; and July 31, 1932, Reichstag election, 426; and November 6, 1932, Reichstag election, 435–436; and Hitler's proposed cabinet, 481

Becker, Carl (1876–1933), minister of culture (1921, 1925–1930): and war-guilt question, 105–106; in Prussian cabinet, 200–201

Belgium: at Locarno, 31; and League of Nations, 55, 58; at London Conference

Atheneum Paperbacks

HISTORY

HISTORY—ASIA